AF352485

CANADIAN URBAN GOVERNANCE IN COMPARATIVE PERSPECTIVE

Canadian Urban Governance in Comparative Perspective

EDITED BY KRISTIN R. GOOD AND JEN NELLES

UNIVERSITY OF TORONTO PRESS
Toronto Buffalo London

© University of Toronto Press 2024
Toronto Buffalo London
utorontopress.com
Printed in the USA

ISBN 978-1-4426-3496-1 (cloth)   ISBN 978-1-4426-3497-8 (EPUB)
ISBN 978-1-4426-3495-4 (paper)   ISBN 978-1-4426-3498-5 (PDF)

Library and Archives Canada Cataloguing in Publication

Title: Canadian urban governance in comparative perspective / edited by Kristin R. Good and Jen Nelles.
Names: Good, Kristin, editor | Nelles, Jen, 1979–, editor
Description: Includes bibliographical references and index.
Identifiers: Canadiana (print) 20240445724 | Canadiana (ebook) 20240445759 | ISBN 9781442634954 (paper) | ISBN 9781442634961 (cloth) | ISBN 9781442634978 (EPUB) | ISBN 9781442634985 (PDF)
Subjects: LCSH: Municipal government – Canada.
Classification: LCC JS1710 .C36 2024 | DDC 320.8/50971 – dc23

Cover design: Heng Wee Tan
Cover images: Maxger/Shutterstock.com; Stepan Petrov/Shutterstock.com; phoelixDE/Shutterstock.com

We welcome comments and suggestions regarding any aspect of our publications – please feel free to contact us at news@utorontopress.com or visit us at utorontopress.com.

Every effort has been made to contact copyright holders; in the event of an error or omission, please notify the publisher.

We wish to acknowledge the land on which the University of Toronto Press operates. This land is the traditional territory of the Wendat, the Anishnaabeg, the Haudenosaunee, the Métis, and the Mississaugas of the Credit First Nation.

University of Toronto Press acknowledges the financial support of the Government of Canada and the Ontario Arts Council, an agency of the Government of Ontario, for its publishing activities.

Funded by the Government of Canada   Financé par le gouvernement du Canada

ONTARIO ARTS COUNCIL
CONSEIL DES ARTS DE L'ONTARIO
an Ontario government agency
un organisme du gouvernement de l'Ontario

For my mentor Prof. Richard Stren and my students of municipal law and urban governance – past, present, and future – who inspired this work.

– Kristin R. Good

For my mentors David Wolfe, David Miller, and Neil Bradford and for Maria Tippett, who would have approved of this return to my roots.

– Jen Nelles

Contents

Part Five – Conclusion: Exploring the Tensions

Figures

Tables

Preface

This book situates Canadian urban governance and policies in an international comparative perspective. While there are several excellent volumes and compilations that tackle a variety of Canadian urban issues with some reference to international contexts (Lightbody 2006; McAllister 2004; Sancton 2021; Tindal et al. 2017; Spicer, Lyons, and Graham 2019), the content in these textbooks deals almost entirely with Canadian cases. It was high time for a collection that showcases the wealth of comparative research on urban governance in Canada, shines a light on a selection of talented researchers and their work, and embeds the Canadian urban experience in international theoretical and political debates on urban governance in a multilevel democratic polity.

This collection covers the material discussed in other Canadian urban politics texts, positioning it in relation to international typologies, theories, and studies of urban politics, but it additionally adopts an explicitly comparative approach by engaging with both intra-national (sub-national) and international comparisons. Furthermore, it balances the traditional Canadian focus on institutions with societal and political economy perspectives on urban governance. It is also unique insofar as it covers municipal policy in a multilevel governance context. It includes both traditional areas of policy such as basic urban services and transit, the municipal role in planning and economic development policy, as well as newer roles that some Canadian municipalities have adopted since the 1990s, such as in immigration policies and policies to respond to urban Indigenous populations and, more generally, a greater role in "social" policy. Through sub-national and international comparisons, these chapters highlight how globalization, country-level institutional contexts, and local actors shape the limits and possibilities of local policy-making.

We assembled and edited the contributions in this book to ensure that it delivers a strong foundation to understand comparative methods, their role in Canadian urban research, and how they can be applied to explore and comprehend the tensions and debates inherent in this context and field. Its engagement with critical themes offers a comprehensive introduction. Throughout the life of the book, we hope to engage with the contributors and other urban scholars to produce additional content to add depth to the debates introduced in these chapters and to explore topics, comparisons, and developments that we could not cover within the space and time limits of the publication process. We welcome your feedback on the material as well as suggestions regarding supplementary material that would usefully add to your teaching resources.

We originally conceptualized this collection as a main textbook for an upper-year course on municipal or urban politics or to supplement another textbook, but as it evolved, it became clear that this book would be of interest to a broader range of readers, both inside and outside of Canada. We see it as a unique, hybrid model of book that is at the intersection of a textbook and an edited volume. We hope that this book informs and inspires a new generation of scholars and urbanists to tackle the challenges facing Canadian cities and understand these as manifestations of global forces and trends that are playing out in urban arenas. We see understanding and empowering local government as crucial to a robust Canadian federal democracy. In adopting the comparative lens, we hope you will agree that local politics is globally significant, and local action, even though it can seem small, is part of a broader tapestry that can be immensely influential in improving urban lives and driving change.

Acknowledgements

This project began close to a decade ago and was interrupted by multiple pregnancies, parental leaves on the part of both editors, and then a global pandemic.

We would like to thank our contributors for agreeing to contribute to this volume and for their patience with the project deadlines which, as an edited volume, were challenging, especially in a time of deep uncertainty and with various professional and personal pressures associated with the COVID-19 pandemic.

We are proud of the quality of the contributions and of the diverse group of scholars we assembled.

We benefited from the support of multiple editors as this project progressed and evolved, including Marilyn McCormick, Stephen Jones, and Rebecca Duce. Thank you as well to Perrin Lindelauf, our book's copy editor, as well as Mary Lui, who oversaw the managing editorial process. We would like to thank the University of Toronto Press for its support and, in particular, Rebecca Duce, whose able support ushered this project to completion.

We would also like to thank our anonymous reviewers, whose detailed, constructive feedback at both the proposal and manuscript stages assisted us in making significant improvements to the book.

Kristin

For me, this project reflects an appreciation of comparison as a method of understanding urban politics that developed at the University of Toronto during my PhD years when debates about a "comparative turn" in the field of Canadian politics were taking place. This engagement with comparative urban politics and thinking about urban governance as a global phenomenon developed further as I wrote my PhD dissertation under the supervision of Professor Richard Stren, a leading expert on comparative urban politics, whose work focuses on countries in the

Global South. I have greatly appreciated his mentorship and friendship over the years. The field of urban politics and comparative urban politics has exploded since the early to mid-2000s, when I wrote my dissertation and developed my passion for the study of urban politics. I would also like to thank my students at Dalhousie University, where I have been privileged to teach courses about municipal politics since my appointment in 2005, even in a time when municipal affairs and urban governance were not always given the scholarly attention that they deserved in political science departments in Canada. My engagement with students over the last couple of decades has made it clear that there is an appetite for understanding municipal and urban politics in comparative perspective and in relation to global trends of urbanization, as well as how municipal government has responded to this phenomenon in a variety of contexts. I dedicate this book to my mentor, Prof. Richard Stren, and to my students (past, present, and future) at Dalhousie University with interests in municipal and urban politics.

I would also like to thank Jen Nelles for agreeing to work on this book project with me. It began as a co-authored book and evolved into an edited volume as we reconceptualized the work as one that would cover not only institutional foundations but also a variety of urban governance and policy challenges. I couldn't imagine working with a more supportive, generous, and insightful colleague. Her editorial comments on all of the chapters were always on the mark and constructive. From a more personal perspective, her feedback was extremely helpful to me as I wrote and edited my own chapters in the face of personal challenges and interruptions in my writing process. She is direct, incisive, and constructive in her approach to feedback, and I benefited from it enormously. Despite the fact that she has always had multiple important books and other projects in the works as this volume progressed, she always made time for it. I am deeply grateful.

I would also like to thank Martin Horak, whose excellent chapter on multilevel governance became one of our book's foundational chapters. He also provided invaluable constructive feedback on chapter 2 of this volume.

Finally, I would like to thank my family, including my husband, Erick Garand, and my children – Jacob, Isabelle, and Wilhelmina – for their support and understanding when I needed to take time away from them to complete this work. I would also like to thank my parents, Chris and Lenore Good, for their ongoing encouragement and my mom (Lenore) for reading early chapters of the book and making a very useful suggestion about chapter order.

Jen

This project was an opportunity to connect my research on international urban and regional governance to my origins in Canadian political science. As a comparativist from the get-go, I've conducted wide-ranging scholarship, both geographically and thematically, touching on topics such as Indigenous-municipal governance, regional intergovernmental relations, planning, urban and regional infrastructure, and place-based innovation policy. Despite working outside of Canada for more than fifteen years, I have maintained strong connections with my

Canadian urban governance colleagues and am constantly impressed at the calibre of scholarship in the people I am lucky enough to consider peers. This book was a particularly important project to showcase Canadian insights and situate them in important global debates. As Canadians, we are often open to what we can learn from others in the world but rarely as vocal about what we have to offer.

For me, this was a kind of extended homecoming and family reunion, and I feel incredibly privileged to have been able to work with such a talented, insightful, and patient (!) group of contributors. There were so many others that could have been included and that I hope I will get to work with in the future. I am also very lucky to work with a great team of colleagues who support my Canadian projects even when they occasionally get in the way of my "real work." I'd like to thank Tim Vorley in particular for constantly putting himself on the line to protect my ability to do what I love. In this increasingly harsh academic world of output and impact measures, there is no greater gift than the freedom, space, and support to pursue intellectually interesting projects. For this, and the added bonus of being friends and collaborators, I am indescribably grateful. I also owe debts to my parents, who taught me lots about writing (and editing books) and still read what I've written (so they say…). Finally, I dedicate this book to three scholars who have and continue to support, inspire, mentor, and more or less tolerate me: David Wolfe, Neil Bradford, and David Miller. The work that I do today is only possible because of their partnership, feedback, encouragement, and friendship.

Bringing a book together is always complicated and challenging but doing it with a brilliant and ambitious collaborator makes it fun as well! I want to thank Kristin Good for bringing me onto this project and navigating its ups and downs with me. Kristin had a clear vision of what this book should be, and it took as long as it did, in part, so that we could, quite rightly, produce something that fulfilled her high expectations. The turbulence of life with a young family in a complicated world, increasing work responsibilities, and an ever-changing urban political landscape required dexterity, perseverance, and a commitment to excellence that Kristin has in ample supply. I value her partnership and friendship and am excited to continue working with her to keep this book "alive" with novel content and (hopefully) new editions in the future.

REFERENCES

Lightbody, James. 2006. *City Politics, Canada*. Peterborough, ON: Broadview Press.

McAllister, Mary Louise. 2004. *Governing Ourselves? The Politics of Canadian Communities*. Vancouver: UBC Press.

Sancton, Andrew. 2021. *Canadian Local Government: An Urban Perspective*. 3rd ed. Don Mills, ON: Oxford University Press.

Spicer, Zachary, Joseph Lyons, and Kate Graham. 2019. *Local Government in Practice: Cases in Governance, Planning and Policy*. Toronto: Emond Publishing.

Tindal, C. Richard, Susan Nobes Tindal, Kennedy Stewart, and Patrick Smith. 2017. *Local Government in Canada*. 9th ed. Toronto: Nelson Education.

PART ONE

Introduction: A Global Perspective on the Canadian City

CHAPTER ONE

Positioning the Canadian City in the Global Context and Debates

Kristin R. Good and Jen Nelles

INTRODUCTION

There has been an explosion of interest in cities and urban governance in recent decades in Canada. Canadian scholars increasingly recognize the unique contribution of systems of local government and multilevel governance to a country's democratic life and to effective and responsive public policy-making. This interest coincides with a global shift in the world's population toward urban places. The world became more than 50 per cent urban in 2010, a trend that is projected to continue and reach 62.5 per cent of the world's population in 2035 (United Nations Habitat 2020, 12). Urbanization, which is in turn driven by changes in the global economy and migration, is a central factor causing change in the place of local government worldwide. Urbanization represents a profound shift in how Canadians live. In 1921, there were only six urban areas in Canada with a population over 100,000, and no metropolitan area had more than one million residents (Bradford 2002, 4). Today, nearly three-quarters (73.7 per cent) of Canada's population lives in urban centres with populations of 100,000 or more (Statistics Canada 2022a). Furthermore, Canadian cities have become increasingly diverse as global migration is driving much of urbanization in Canada.

Globally, there is recognition that cities grapple with many similar issues – such as fostering economic growth and innovation, climate change, the integration of migrants, housing affordability, and poverty and inequality – but in different institutional and societal contexts and, therefore, different ways. What is clear, though, is that city governance is crucial for effective, responsive, and just public policy. For instance, as the World Bank notes, even though just over 50 per cent of the world's people live in cities, more than 80 per cent of global GDP is generated by urban economies (World Bank, n.d.). The importance of cities and city planning to addressing sprawl and its effect on climate change is also increasingly recognized internationally (World Bank, n.d.). For instance, as the World Bank (n.d., para. 4) points out, decisions about infrastructure in cities "can be locked in for generations, leading to unsustainable sprawl." Furthermore, cities are the places where social polarization and poverty are most visible and diversity is most complex; migration flows intersect in major cities in an increasingly global world. As a result, many of the largest cities in countries across the globe have become "superdiverse" – a term that captures the multi-faceted nature of the differences in immigrant populations in major cities around the globe (Vertovec 2007).

Although it has received less recognition, global attention to the urbanization of Indigenous Peoples has also increased. In settler colonial states such as Canada (and other countries that have adopted the Westminster system, such as Australia and New Zealand), cities exist on historic and sometimes unceded Indigenous lands, adding further complexity and significance to urban governance practices. In Canada, more than half of the country's Indigenous population lives in cities, and many more live in communities adjacent to them, with particularly high concentrations of Indigenous people in Prairie cities like Regina, Saskatoon, and Winnipeg. These demographic trends all suggest that a major contemporary urban challenge is to build inclusive and socially sustainable cities and, in settler colonial states, including Canada, to contribute to processes of "decolonization." The complex nature of the challenges facing Canadian cities raises debates about the suitability of its current municipal systems. Although they have evolved, including through the introduction of more permissive and empowering municipal legislation, Canada's municipal systems also continue to reflect deeply entrenched Westminster norms of constitutionalism, which concentrate power in a "sovereign" parliament. In this book, we explore the institutions, processes, and global challenges of municipal government in comparative perspective both in Canada and internationally to shed light on what is similar and different about Canadian urban democracy and governance.

In the chapters that follow, we explore a series of framing questions that we believe are essential for understanding the pressures on cities, the suitability of the tools they have to address them, the role of cities in Canadian political life, and Canadian urban futures. What implications do evolving patterns of urbanization have for municipal government and urban governance? What are the fundamental challenges and debates in urban politics, and how do they manifest and inform policy approaches in Canadian cities and cities around the world? Why are city politics and urban governance important, and what is unique about municipal government in Canada and abroad? What contribution do municipal governments make to developing effective responses to global problems and to equity in cities? What does a comparative approach add to our understanding of urban issues, and what insights can it offer us about how to navigate them in the Canadian context? What are the key tensions – external and internal – that local governments must navigate and the trade-offs inherent within municipal systems?

MUNICIPALITIES ARE FOUNDATIONS OF DEMOCRACY YET LACK SECURE CONSTITUTIONAL STATUS

Studying cities and local government/governance in Canada is crucial because municipalities are a key foundation of local government and of Canada's democratic system. In Canada, municipal systems are created under the authority of provincial governments because "municipal institutions" are an area of provincial jurisdiction in the Constitution Act, 1867 (s. 92(8)) that divides power between the federal government and the provinces. All Canadian provinces have established municipal systems that include laws that delegate legislative powers and taxation powers to municipalities as well as establish rules about the functioning of their democratic systems – including their political institutions and electoral rules. Unlike federal and provincial governments, municipalities do not have an independent constitutional status but rather are "incorporated" under the authority of provincial law. As Tindal and Tindal describe in their foundational textbook on municipal government in Canada, a municipality is a unique democratic institution – it is a "corporation … a legal device that allows residents of a specific geographic area to provide services that are of common interest" (2009, 2). Municipalities are also democratic institutions that enable citizens to identify and tackle communal concerns. As corporations rather than Westminster-inspired parliaments, municipalities are a unique type of democratic institution in Canada, one that is poorly understood and underappreciated by some. In addition to their corporate nature, they are a form of democratic institution governed by elected councils; furthermore, all municipalities raise taxes (with the property tax as their primary source of revenue in Canada) and are territorial in nature (they govern a bounded geographic space) (Tindal et al. 2017). Municipalities serve local interests by making policies and enacting bylaws to shape and regulate urban life. However, what constitutes a "local issue" is, of course, a subject of debate and has evolved through time.

Municipalities, in turn, are part of *local government*, which as Tindal and Tindal note is a "broad term" that also includes "various local special purpose bodies that operate at the local level and defy easy classification" (2009, 2); they are often referred to as agencies, boards, and commissions or "ABCs" for short. ABCs are public agencies of limited purposes that may share municipal boundaries but can equally operate at other urban scales, functioning separately from the council committee structure (Lucas 2013). School boards, library boards, police boards, and transit authorities are only a few common examples of local ABCs. Jack Lucas (2013) describes them as "hidden in plain view" because citizens typically lack an understanding of either their decision-making or financial significance even though they administer around one-third of municipal budgets in some municipalities. The significance of these mainly appointed bodies at arms-length from local councils in Canadian urban life raises significant questions of democratic accountability and reflects a suspicion of democracy, preferring to place decision-making in the hands of "experts" or businesspeople who can be trusted to make decisions "efficiently" (3).

More generally, municipalities' democratic importance and constitutional significance have been minimized by a prevailing constitutional doctrine portraying them as nothing more than "creatures of the provinces" (which they are in only the simplest legal sense) because they lack formal recognition as a distinct order of government in Canada's Constitution (Good 2019). Some argue that municipalities have become more important as democratic governments and policy-makers in what is now a primarily urban country and propose constitutional reform. This book is premised on the idea that evaluating global systems of local government generates important insights to evaluate and understand the place of municipalities in Canada's constitutional system.

MUNICIPAL INSTITUTIONS IN CANADA: DEFICIENT OR SIMPLY DIFFERENT?

Municipalities lack secure constitutional status in Canada's federal constitution, although one could argue that constitutional questions are at the heart of designing municipal systems. Municipal systems are ways of dividing power *within* provinces by creating various types of municipalities, designing their political institutions and dividing authority. As such, they are best conceived as elements of provincial constitutions (Cameron 1980; Good 2019). Since municipalities and municipal systems are created by provincial laws, municipal systems have experienced periods of reform and have been the subject of debates concerning how best to design local political institutions, making them a particularly interesting subject of democratic inquiry. There is a great deal of variation in municipal political institutions, both across Canada and globally, providing a rich laboratory for exploring the democratic potential of various institutional configurations.

In Canada, municipalities are unique in many respects that warrant serious study to understand their implications for democracy. First, power is much more dispersed in many local councils than in legislatures at other levels, and executive authority is often weak (in stark contrast with the political executive at the provincial and federal levels, and particularly the prime minister and provincial premiers, in whom much power is concentrated). Furthermore, municipal elections are generally non-partisan in Canada although parties compete in two of Canada's three largest metropolitan areas – Montreal and Vancouver. In April 2024, Alberta's United Conservative Party government, led by Premier Danielle Smith, introduced Bill 20, which proposes to introduce partisan ballots in municipal elections in Alberta.[1] This development has spurred a province-wide and even national debate about the desirability of partisan politics at the municipal level. The debate has underscored the strength of the non-partisan tradition in many places in Canada, including Alberta. Nevertheless, urban scholars agree that these municipal parties are of a different kind than at other levels – less cohesive and "disciplined" in part because some of the incentives to vote together (like the potential fall of a government and requirement to hold another election) do not exist at the municipal level, but it is perhaps also due to the strength of local non-partisan traditions (see Good 2016 on the debate about non-partisan elections in Canada).

Another distinguishing element of municipal government is that the division of power between provinces and municipalities is much more flexible than federal and provincial authority since it is established in provincial statutes; although they are arguably of constitutional *significance* to Canada's democracy, they are not constitutionally entrenched laws. The legal implications of this *statutory* instead of *constitutionally entrenched* status mean that the division of power (what areas of responsibility are delegated to municipalities) can be changed through the passage of a statute in a provincial legislature (requiring only a majority vote) instead of through a constitutional amending formula that requires a supermajority or the consent of multiple legislatures to change, such as changes to the federal-provincial division of power. This raises ongoing debates about the proper division of power and even whether some municipalities ought to be granted more authority than others in a municipal system. Indeed, provincial statutes govern municipalities' political institutions (including the powers of mayors and council) and electoral rules, including the electoral system itself and whether candidates can appear on municipal ballots as members of parties.

This legal fact presents both challenges for municipalities (and citizens) if they are not consulted on such changes but also significant opportunities for adaptation and reform should provinces be willing to grant municipalities more or different authority. In the 1990s and 2000s, controversial amalgamations of major cities (e.g., Halifax and Toronto) were enacted this way. More recently, in 2018, the Conservative government of Doug Ford imposed (through legislation) a major reduction of Toronto's council in the middle of an election campaign, igniting a heated debate about municipal democracy and autonomy in the city as well as court challenges that made their way to the Supreme Court of Canada (SCC). Ultimately, the SCC decided in favour of the province; however, municipalities' importance was significantly recognized in the minority opinion in the decision (Toronto (City) v. Ontario (Attorney General) 2021). In yet another example, in 2022 the same Ontario government passed legislation strengthening the powers of mayors in Toronto and Ottawa and extended these powers to twenty-six other large municipalities soon after. These "strong-mayor" powers include the power to shape the administration, prepare the budget, and veto council decisions, somewhat akin to strong mayors in American mayor-council forms of government that exist in many municipalities in the United States, including New York City. These unprecedented mayoral powers in Canada are discussed more in chapter 7 and placed in comparative perspective. Arguably, the most controversial aspects of the reforms are the various elements of the mayor's veto power, which include the power to veto council decisions *if they conflict with provincial priorities*, to veto amendments to the budget, and to introduce and pass a bylaw with only one-third of council's support (see Taylor 2023 for an overview of what a strong mayor is and of these changes). Although such reforms could certainly speed up the decision-making process and may empower strong leaders at the municipal level, somewhat paradoxically, they also potentially compromise municipal autonomy and local democracy because of the vague references in the legislation to "provincial priorities." They also limit the deliberative potential of municipal councils, which could be subject to a veto or threatened veto if their position does not align with the mayor's. Alberta's Bill 20 has also raised significant questions about provincial intervention in municipal democratic processes (including the process governing the removal/recall of councillors) as well as in bylaw making (Government of Alberta, n.d.).

These realities provoke us to drill down from our framing questions to engage with debates about what kinds of political institutions are best suited to enable robust local democratic practices while also facilitating effective governance and public policy-making. They also raise questions about what kind of process should be required to make fundamental changes to municipal systems – including political institutions, the division of power, and elections. For instance, is it legitimate for provinces to impose change on municipalities and local communities in the twenty-first century, and if so why? These questions are not only crucial to understanding the Canadian urban journey to now but are also current hot-button issues in several parts of the country.

MUNICIPALITIES IN A MULTILEVEL SYSTEM OF GOVERNANCE: A CHANGING MUNICIPAL ROLE?

Although municipalities are sometimes dismissed as only providing "services to property," the provincial interest in municipal affairs only underscores the extent to which municipalities' importance is growing. Municipalities now provide or contribute to a wide range of vital and politically relevant services. From urban planning to recreation and policing – to name only a few – these fields have profound implications for climate change, housing affordability, equity, and other defining challenges of the era. As we will discover in this volume, municipalities are also taking up new responsibilities directly, sometimes in reaction to the lack of adequate leadership from other orders of government and sometimes simply as a pragmatic reaction to urban challenges and the changing preferences of their constituents. We discuss examples including the emerging role of municipalities in local immigration policy-making and governance, Indigenous-municipal relations, climate change, and steps to tackle structural racism.

Municipal governments are governments of proximity. Peter John, a British urban scholar, argues that "propinquity" is a unique element of the local level of government and that decision-making at this level is shaped by the fact that "actors are close to what they administer" (John 2009, 21). This leads to a tendency to engage in *governance* with other local actors (discussed below) and an arguably more *pragmatic* approach to policy-making. As we discuss in chapter 12 on local immigration policy-making, such pragmatism and practice of collaborating with local non-governmental organizations can be seen globally in the rise of municipalities as important policy actors in global migration.

Canadian urban scholars continue to approach the study of urban politics through an institutional lens; however, attention to *governance* and *governance arrangements* has become more common. Whereas *municipal government* is a term that refers to formal decision-making processes, *municipal governance* highlights that local decision-making and policy capacity are also influenced by the interaction with local business and community organizations. Policies are "co-produced" by municipalities in collaboration (or at least with input from) actors other than members of council and city staff. Some scholars see the shift toward governance as a normative shift reflecting the changing role of urban municipalities in Canada and as a strategy for effecting such changes. As Caroline Andrew, Katherine Graham, and Susan Phillips describe, the shift from a focus on "government" to "governance" draws one's attention to the interdependence between public, private, and voluntary sectors, between orders of government, and across departments within the same order of government (2002, 11). In a governance model of urban politics, "the ability to accomplish policy goals is often dependent upon collaboration among multiple players whose interests and responsibilities intersect in a fluid and contingent way" and urban policy challenges are conceived as "agendas" that include or bring together multiple programs and policies rather than through the lens of policy silos (11). They maintain that the focus on governance is also normative and implies a changing role for Canadian municipalities, one that focuses more on democratic engagement and equity rather than service efficiency alone (12).

Canadian urban scholars who study governance tend to acknowledge its "multilevel" dimensions by, as stated above, acknowledging the importance of intergovernmental collaboration. Such a perspective is also advanced by American scholar Jefferey Sellers (2005), who conceives urban politics as a form of politics that has significant degrees of freedom but is also shaped by national institutions, policy infrastructures, and other national influences on municipal systems. More recently, models of multilevel democracy have been elaborated by Sellers, Lidström, and Bae (2020), discussed more below and in chapter 4.

However, one might challenge the hierarchical elements of the notion of multiple "levels" and counter that the notion of "multi-*order*" democracy is more accurate. More than twenty years ago, Andrew, Graham, and Phillips observed that "hierarchy has given way to horizontality" (2002, 11), wherein urban politics and municipal governance might be conceived of as *different* rather than constitutionally inferior – a form that is able to engage with cities' complexity and diversity. For instance, as local government scholar Caroline Andrew notes: "urban governance must be recognized as important because this is the way that cities work and the way city governments work" (2001, 109). Furthermore, she sees city government as a way to bring ethnocultural and gender issues and the concerns of marginalized peoples to policy discussions; she conceptualizes municipalities as an order of government uniquely positioned to address diversity, with strong progressive potential (Andrew 2001).

Other scholars are more critical of the potential of municipalities to be a force of progressive policy-making and engagement at the local level. Some see the municipal level of government, particularly in North America, as systematically biased toward business interests and property owners. Although municipalities have played a variety of roles historically (including in social services in early colonial times), they are strongly connected to property as a form of government that raises taxes mainly through the property tax. Furthermore, although governments across the Western world progressively eliminated property as a qualification for voting, a non-resident property franchise continues to exist in five provinces in Canada. Some argue that a neo-liberal vision of globalization has led to an increased influence of business communities as cities compete for growth and investment on a global rather than merely national scale.

Neo-liberalism is a broad term that captures a variety of changes apparent in contemporary cities across the globe. It encapsulates assumptions that Christina Gabriel and Yasmeen Abu-Laban note are "frequently presented as common-sense truths" (2002, 21) and that Jason Hackworth (2014) observes to be accompanied by a "discourse of inevitability" that leads actors to perceive their choices as highly constrained (chapter 10, loc. 2657). Neo-liberalism envisions a limited, laissez-faire role for the state and focuses on individual self-sufficiency, seeing free markets as the most efficient and best way to allocate goods and services (Abu-Laban and Gabriel 2002, 21). Jason Hackworth (2014, loc. 317) argues that neo-liberalism is best conceived of as a process that both dismantles policies of the Keynesian era, which saw a role for the state in intervening in the market to support equality (such as public housing), and the introduction of market-driven policies. Neo-liberalism privileges competitiveness, efficiency, choice, and consumerism as values that ought to guide policy-making (Abu-Laban and Gabriel 2002, 21). Hackworth (2014, loc. 308) argues that at the city level, neo-liberal governance (in collaboration with the business community) has become normalized in American cities. As we explore in chapter 3, the norm of the "limited" city that competes with other cities for businesses and residents (Peterson 1981), or in which the business community sets the local agenda privileging growth (Logan and Molotch [1987] 2007), is pervasive in American political theory.

Thus, there is disagreement about how much room for local agency exists. In other words, how much choice do local leaders really have in their decision-making given their institutional (and often strict constitutional) constraints, the power of influential corporate actors in local communities, and ideas that make their interests appear to be the natural and only choice? Exploring the constraints and degrees of freedom in cities is crucial to understanding power. Investigating governance dynamics in cities is a manageable way of studying and understanding power, which is the most foundational concept underlying politics and the study of political science. Urban scholars ask questions such as who (really) governs, how policy capacity develops in institutionally weak environments with governments that are particularly sensitive to their external environments, how urban governance arrangements emerge and are maintained, and who is in, who is out, and why.

We situate debates about the appropriate division of power between "upper" levels of government and municipalities in comparative perspective by asking how multilevel relations and governance are conducted in Canada and internationally. Indeed, although municipalities may become more significant in an urban age, this does not necessarily imply a decrease in significance of other levels of government. Rather, although they have long been conceived as junior partners in the Canadian federation, municipalities might also be seen as the embodiment of important constitutional principles, including the principle of *subsidiarity* within a system of collaborative multilevel relationships. This principle of subsidiarity first emerged in a European Union context and was articulated by the SCC in an important decision for the legal autonomy of municipalities. In upholding a municipal bylaw that regulated pesticide use in the Town of Hudson, Quebec, when it was challenged by a pesticide company, the SCC affirmed the principle that "that law-making and implementation are often best achieved at a level of government that is not only effective, but also closest to the citizens affected and thus most responsive to their needs, to local distinctiveness, and to population diversity" (114957 Canada Ltée [Spraytech, Société d'arrosage] v. Hudson [Town], 2001). Comparative constitutional law scholar Ran Hirschl argues that, by doing so, the SCC "endorsed a collaborative tri-level regime for the regulation of pesticides" in Canada (Hirschl 2020, 80). However, although the courts have recognized degrees of legal freedom for municipalities in this important area of environmental policy-making, the extent to which multilevel governance practices that respect municipal democracy and contribute to effective co-production of policy are becoming the norm is an open question.

In addition to being governed by multiple orders of government, urban agglomerations and metropolitan areas are rarely governed by a single local government but are instead made up of a patchwork of municipal governments that may or may not work together in the interest of the region. We dig into the political consequences of these configurations in chapter 5. Metropolitan areas that contain higher numbers of municipalities or their equivalents (such as communes in France) are considered more fragmented than those that are more consolidated. Different states have different municipal systems or ways in which municipalities (or units with other names) are established in law, including the kinds of local government, the types of municipalities (cities, towns, or others), the geographic scope of municipal units, whether there are multiple layers or a single layer, and so on.

One way to understand approaches to municipal systems is to think about how "fragmented" or "complex" they are in relation to other cities both in the same country and internationally and why. For instance, one central question addressed in seminal works discussed more in chapter 3 has been why Canadian municipal systems are less fragmented than in the United States (Goldberg and Mercer 1986; Taylor 2019) and what the consequences of this difference are. As we discuss in chapter 5, formal urban political spaces (municipalities) and the geographies of urban life rarely coincide. As a result, in the study of urban government and politics (in Canada and abroad), we need to recognize that policy and *governance* occur at multiple scales and that the city is not a hermetically sealed policy space. A large part of our job as comparative students of local government is understanding how it differs from place to place and what governments at different scales can (and ought to) exert control over in different policy contexts. Thus, the challenge of governing cities effectively is both a question of collaboration across multiple orders or "levels" of government as well as of intermunicipal collaboration across city-regions. Indeed, collaboration also happens at the international scale through a variety of city networks and participation in international forums. The term "scale" captures differences in the scope of collaborative activity and the interaction of governments with different boundaries as well as without formal governments in place (like city-regions in places without formal institutions at that scale). The boundaries of communities can be "imagined" and vary across places. For instance, Jen Nelles (2012) employs the concept of civic capital to capture the extent to which leadership and networks in urban places are regional in scale or scope.

Other governmental authorities that are distinct but worth mentioning here are Indigenous governments, which are governments at a more local scale that share similarities with municipalities but are, of course, fundamentally different from a constitutional perspective. These governmental authorities are, however, increasingly part of a complex terrain of intergovernmental relations and multilevel governance at the local level as collaboration between municipalities and Indigenous governments has increased significantly in recent decades in Canada, a development that has significant implications for city governance (Alcantara and Nelles 2016). Although Indigenous governments may have particular territorial boundaries in Canadian law, the fact that many municipalities exist on historical and unceded Indigenous territories underscores the complexity of the governing authorities that exist in any one place.

SITUATING CANADIAN URBANIZATION GLOBALLY: MIGRATION AND THE CHALLENGE OF SOCIAL CHANGE

Although many conceptualizations of globalization argue that territorial boundaries have become irrelevant, an important body of urban scholarship underscores that it has instead involved a reconfiguration of territoriality or "rescaling." These changes are in turn tied to a reorganization of capitalism whereby the important infrastructures associated with economic activity and accumulation have shifted scales from the national to both the global and local (urban) simultaneously. Cities and their physical infrastructures (e.g., transportation and communication) and human capital are enabling globalization and driving national economies within economic markets that transcend national boundaries (Brenner 1999; Courchene 2007). In an influential book conceptualizing "global cities," Saskia Sassen (1991) argues that such cities are at the top of a hierarchy of cities that are connected globally and that command and control the global economy. She also raises questions of equity in cities that have been transformed by globalization, their economies reterritorialized as urban and service based, their social structures significantly altered. These changes have led to greater economic and social polarization in global cities as migration (both internal and international) diversifies cities within a service-based economy characterized by much larger discrepancies in wages than a manufacturing-based economy (Sassen 1991).

However, the impacts of urbanization are highly uneven across countries. Globally, countries have not only become increasingly urban rather than rural but there has also been an increase in cities with large populations, what some call "megacities" of five or ten million people or more (Hirschl 2020, 6). As Hirschl (2020, 6) notes, in 1900 only twelve cities in the world had populations of one million or more, and today there are more than 550 of that size. Most megacities are in countries in the Global South.[2] These countries have both the highest shares of rural populations but are also home to massive megacities. According to the United Nations (2018), the populations of the five largest cities in the world were estimated to be the following: Tokyo (37,468,000), Delhi (28,514,000), Shanghai (25,582,000), São Paulo (21,650,000), and Mexico City (21,581,000). London, with a population estimated at 8,799,800 (ONS 2021), and New York City, with a 2022 population of 8,335,897 (US Census Bureau 2022), have populations that are significantly smaller than these top five even though they are the other two Western "global cities" discussed in Saskia Sassen's (1991) seminal work on the emergence of the "global city." This suggests that population figures alone do not tell the entire story of changing urbanization and global power dynamics.

Toronto, which is Canada's largest city and municipality, has a city (municipal) population of 2,794,356 and a census metropolitan area (CMA) population of 6,202,225 (Statistics Canada 2021). Thus, although Canada is a highly urban country, its scale/intensity is much less than forms of urban settlement globally, and patterns of urbanization vary significantly across the country. Indeed, Toronto is the only city in Canada to pass the population threshold for a megacity (if defined as a city of five million or more). The only other CMAs with populations over one million are Montreal (4,291,732), Vancouver (2,642,825), Calgary (1,481,806), Edmonton (1,418,118), and Ottawa-Gatineau (1,488,307), which is Canada's only CMA to cross provincial boundaries (Statistics Canada 2022b, table 2). Halifax, the largest CMA east of Montreal, had a population of only 465,703 in 2021, although it is currently among the fastest-growing Canadian cities (2022b). These variations mean that municipal governance challenges could be very different across the country and that the extent to which urban affairs are on provincial and federal agendas could also vary. More broadly, this could also lead to increased conflict as various cities compete for the provincial and federal government's attention in policy-making. Indeed, as economic and social relations are "rescaled" to cities, the federal government has an increased stake in their governance regardless of constitutional jurisdiction.

With large populations, density is another foundational aspect of the urban experience and a measure of urbanization that is often incorporated into national statistical agencies' definition of "urban." Urban scholarship shows that density matters a great deal to cities' sustainability, including both their social and environmental sustainability. Broadly speaking, megacities in the Global South have much higher densities than cities in the Global North, with some places characterized by extreme densities presenting significant governance challenges in terms of providing basic infrastructure, including waste management and sanitation systems. For instance, Dhaka, the most densely populated city in the world with a density of 44,000 persons per square kilometre has a "chronically dysfunctional" sewage system (Hirschl 2020, 200). Hirschl (2020, 200–1) also notes that Jakarta, another megacity, is sinking at a significant rate, presenting risks for flooding, and São Paulo has faced challenges with its water supply. Hirschl (2020) highlights the connection between density and "extreme inequality in living conditions" in some megacities, raising significant challenges of economic and social rights (197–206). Furthermore, the densities in cities in the Global South illustrated above miss the full picture of how cities are organized spatially since densities increase even further in poor neighbourhoods in megacities. According to Hirschl, these "extreme density" places have different (and highly pejorative) names in different contexts, including "slums" in Nairobi, "squatters" in Mumbai, or "favelas" in Rio de Janeiro (206). Hirschl notes staggering densities in these places, including Rochinha ($50,000/km^2$), a favela in Rio de Janeiro; the Karachi Central neighbourhood ($70,000/km^2$) in Karachi; Kibera in Nairobi; and Tondo in Manila (200). In Dhaka there are neighbourhoods with densities as high as $100,000/km^2$ as well as a "slum neighbourhood" in Mumbai where 700,000 people live in an area of just over two square kilometres (200)!

Compared with other major cities, even those in other high-income countries, Canadian cities are less dense. For instance, as a report by the Fraser Institute observes:

> The coastal cities of San Francisco [7,171/km] and Barcelona [15,873] manage to balance high incomes with higher densities than Vancouver [5,493], at 1.31 and 2.89 times Vancouver's population density, respectively. The financial hubs of Chicago [4,594], New York [10,935], and London [11,054] are 1.03, 2.45, and 2.48 times as dense as Canada's financial and media centre, Toronto [4,457]. Paris [21,067] is 4.29 times as dense as Montreal [4,916], and even the Toronto suburb of Mississauga [2,468] is 1.17 times as dense as Calgary [2,112], Canada's third most populous municipality. (Filipowicz 2018)[3]

These variations in densities undoubtedly shape the nature of their urban governance challenges. Hirschl argues that people living in extreme density contexts are impacted differently by decisions in a variety of public services, including the density-sensitive areas of public transit, sanitation, health care, education, and housing and should be given greater voice in decisions that affect them differently or disproportionately (Hirschl 2020, 206). Lack of density in cities in the Global North presents other governance challenges, such as addressing car dependence and its impact on climate change. Migration of various forms, both internal and international, is shaping the demographic context of international cities and Canadian cities in different ways, making them the sites where communities must come together to navigate, negotiate, and contest these differences. Two important "flows" that are diversifying Canadian cities are international migration and the migration of Indigenous Peoples, both of which have had highly uneven impacts in cities across the country. With respect to the former, most immigrants to Canada choose to settle in large population centres in Canada, with 90 per cent choosing to settle in census metropolitan areas (cities with populations of 100,000 or larger) between 2015 and 2019 (Statistics Canada 2022a). In this regard, Canada's major immigrant-receiving destinations – especially Toronto, Vancouver, and Montreal, where a disproportionate number of immigrants settle – share more in common with other "global cities" than less diverse and less globally connected cities in Canada. Many international migrants prefer to settle in "megacities." Indeed, a central point of global city scholarship, discussed more in chapter 3, is that population flows into Canadian cities mean that they can be influenced by global developments and that they are connected to communities of cities outside national contexts. Although somewhat dated, the International Organization for Migration (2015) presents comparative global data on multiple global cities that are more diverse than other cities in terms of the percentage of foreign-born residents in their populations. In 2011, the cities with the largest foreign-born populations were Dubai (83 per cent) and Brussels (62 per cent). Toronto was third, with a foreign-born population of 46 per cent in 2011 (IOM 2015, 39). Major American cities, including New York (37 per cent) and Los Angeles (39 per cent), were also identified as among the most diverse global cities in terms of foreign-born populations. Auckland's (39 per cent) and Sydney's (39 per cent) populations were comparable and similarly highly diverse. In general, migrants concentrated to a lesser degree in cities in Europe's most important international migrant destinations, including Amsterdam (28 per cent), Frankfurt (27 per cent), and Paris (25 per cent) (IOM 2015).

Steven Vertovec argues that cities such as London have become "superdiverse" due to international migration insofar as countries of origin, language, religion, migration paths (and, relatedly, legal statuses) have become more diverse. Vertovec (2007, 1043) also notes that the extent to which immigrants (in London) have maintained transnational connections with their home countries is "unprecedented," introducing further complexity to the local politics and governance of immigration. There is a concentration of the settlement of foreign-born populations in other major cities that adopt an "Anglo model" of municipal government (discussed more in chapter 2), such as Auckland, Toronto, Los Angeles, New York, and Sydney. Mohammad Qadeer (2016) documents a common multicultural ethos evident in both formal institutions and governance norms in Toronto, New York, and LA, suggesting that there are variations in the political cultures of cities depending on their diversity. As we see in chapter 12, some of these cities have begun to innovate in local immigration policy-making, challenging their formal exclusion from jurisdiction in this area and, in some cases, in violation of immigration laws with respect to undocumented migrants at other levels through "sanctuary city" policies. Such initiatives in global cities in "Anglo" systems that receive high numbers of immigrants, such as Canada, the United States, and Australia, could become forces of constitutional change in these countries.

However, these high-immigration places in Anglo countries are situated on historical Indigenous lands. Acknowledging this raises fundamental questions about the inclusion of Indigenous representation in local immigration policy-making to decolonize settlement processes, as discussed more by Kristin R. Good in chapter 12.

Indigenous Migration to Cities

More broadly, Indigenous migration or "travelling"[4] to cities is also reshaping their politics and governance in ways that vary significantly across the country. Importantly, Evelyn Peters has pointed out that the language of "migration" is problematic when applied to Indigenous movement within the country, noting that "Indigenous travellers … do not arrive in cities like other migrants," whether national or international. Rather, many are "travelling within their traditional territories" (Peters 2004, 2–3; see discussion in Tomiak et al. 2019, loc. 212–31). Seen this way, the urban and rural/reserve distinction falls apart since Indigenous Peoples maintain relationships to the city, reserve, and larger traditional territory (loc. 212–31). Such a spatial conceptualization also situates Canadian cities as "settler cities," nodes in a system of colonialism and economic relations that seek to forcibly assimilate Indigenous Peoples to assume power over land and resources both within and beyond the city (Tomiak et al. 2019, loc. 284–427). Nevertheless, cities may also become places where colonialism is challenged and concepts such as "reconciliation" and "decolonization" take root in local practices. In Canada's Prairie cities, urban political culture is shaped not only by state violence but also by a strong Indigenous presence and resurgence of Indigenous culture (Tomiak et al. 2019, 222–84). Furthermore, as we see in chapter 13, some Canadian municipalities are engaged in efforts to create new relationships with Indigenous populations living within their municipal boundaries, establishing institutions such as Indigenous affairs offices to create the capacity to engage in this way. We also see local engagement with international rights movements and declarations such as the United Nations Declaration of the Rights of Indigenous Peoples (UNDRIP). Furthermore, as Alcantara and Nelles's (2016) work (discussed further in chapter 3) highlights, municipalities have been "quietly" building mutually beneficial and even decolonizing relationships with surrounding Indigenous communities, although the "decolonizing" variety was still rare when their study took place. In some cases, municipalities and adjacent Indigenous communities develop a "shared civic identity" which Alcantara and Nelles (2016) define as an "understanding that, despite differences, the two (or more) communities are part of a shared region" (table 2.1, loc. 856). This notion of shared civic identity becomes productive, embodying a form of capital that they call "community capital." This example draws our attention once more to the politically constructed nature of the boundaries of urban communities and the potentially transformative potential of local collaboration. How the boundaries are "imagined" by diverse urban populations influences politics and the possibilities for collective action that transcend formal, municipal, or other boundaries.

The Right to the City

Urbanization driven by both internal and international migration is a global trend that is engendering responses at the local level that have become fundamental aspects of countries' "diversity infrastructures" and capacity to manage social change. In many ways, cities are the places where human rights are enforced and made meaningful and tangible. Writing in the Canadian context, Caroline Andrew (2001) argues that social diversity and the importance of local governance arrangements to achieving equitable and effective policy-making for governing cities are crucial reasons why we must not ignore cities and their place-specific contexts. Similarly, and for this reason, Kristin R. Good (2009) argues that empowering municipalities in Canada may be seen as a type of "multiculturalism policy."

Globally, we see evidence of the progressive potential of cities in the global diffusion of a variety of concepts related to Henri Lefebvre's notion of "right to the city," which, simply put, reflects "ideals of the city as a collective space of belonging to all who live in it" (Oomen 2016, 6). One such concept is that of "human rights cities," which captures the variety of ways that municipalities are engaging in human rights definition and implementation at multiple scales. Sometimes this involves cities committing to a particular treaty or cause as we see with municipal endorsement of UNDRIP in large municipalities in Canada. Other examples include European cities joining the European Coalition of Cities against Racism, which is focused on implementing the UN Convention on the Elimination of All Forms of Racial Discrimination (CERD). In yet another example, San Francisco passed an ordinance endorsing the Convention on the Elimination of all Forms of Discrimination against Women (CEDAW) (Oomen 2016, 7).[5] In working to define and implement human rights in cities in a context-sensitive way, "municipalities test the real value of human rights locally" and then may "feed their experiences back into international discussions and contribute to the global strengthening of the human rights regime" (Oomen 2016, 11). Oomen emphasizes the benefits of municipal pragmatism, the ability to create governance arrangements or "stakeholder alliances … that transgress the classic divide between rights holders and duty bearers and move away from a legalistic approach to human rights" (3–4). However, "most important, they ensure that those authorities best placed to actually deliver upon human rights promises bear the brunt of doing so" (3–4). There is evidence of human rights related to 2SLGBTQIA+[6] communities, disability, and aging in the city being addressed at the local level as well. In a ground-breaking work on the role of cities in addressing aging, Megan Joy assesses Toronto's efforts to become more "age-friendly," a concept that is informed by an international Age-Friendly Cities (AFC) policy movement and international program developed by the World Health Organization in 2006–7 (Joy 2020, 5). She finds support for the notion that municipalities and the non-profit sector are best positioned to develop and implement responsive and innovative policy but that they are *significantly hampered by a lack of resources*. Thus, her work also offers an important caution since a paradox emerges in her view whereby AFC programs, which purport to expand the role of municipalities in enacting rights to the city, lead them to narrowing their roles and stressing their jurisdictional limitations due to lack of resources (176). There is a lack of a right *of* the city, in other words, a right of the municipality to resources, which in turn influences its creative potential (176).

In *The Social Sustainability of Cities*, Mario Polèse and Richard Stren note that *density* "has been a source of social stress and social innovation," arguing that "the latter is the chief strength of the city" and "the former its greatest challenge" (Stren and Polèse 2000, 8). They argue that "social sustainability" ought to be a focus of city governance – which they define "as *development (and/or growth) that is compatible with the harmonious evolution of civil society, fostering an environment conducive to the compatible cohabitation of culturally and socially diverse groups while at the same time encouraging social integration, with improvements in the quality of life for all segments of the population*" (15–16). Similarly, in *Segmented Cities? How Urban Contexts Shape Ethnic and Nationalist Politics*, Kristin R. Good, Luc Turgeon, and Triadafilos Triadafilopoulos (2014) argue that dense city contexts and governance practices shape ethnic and multinational relations in complex ways, pointing to the significance of the political economy of cities (including the rise of a global network of cities driven by migration – discussed above), the impact of their ethnolinguistic configurations on nationalist and ethnic conflicts, and the role of urban institutions and multilevel urban interventions in social sustainability. A twin focus on both *social innovation* and *stress* is a necessary corrective since cities are places of both harmony and conflict among diverse groups including as sites of the peaceful coexistence of ethnic and multinational groups and of intense conflict (Good, Turgeon, and Triadafilopoulos 2014). There is evidence of progressive action at the municipal level in cities across the globe and that urban institutions and policies matter to responding to change in cities (Good, Turgeon, and Triadafilopoulos 2014; Polèse and Stren 2000). However, some progressive urban interventions are responses to the ongoing and urgent nature of rights deprivation. To follow through on the example of Indigenous rights in Canada, cities are both places of rights deprivation (fundamental Treaty Rights and rights to land) but also the right to safe and affordable housing and employment free of discrimination. They are also places (in part because of density) of *local social innovation, which we define as authentic, creative, and organically generated collective responses to local, socio-cultural, and political realities that improve city life and enrich local democracy.* Cities are also places of the resurgence of Indigenous culture and hopefully the decolonization of governance practices – which are arguably specific forms of social innovation.

The limited global literature on Indigenous urbanization suggests that the tension between social stress and innovation is widespread for Indigenous Peoples (Stephens 2015, 60; Tomiak et al. 2019). Informed by a global perspective, the 2015 *State of the World's Minorities and Indigenous Peoples* report notes that Indigenous well-being in cities is enabled through "initiatives to support and sustain their identity" which "is most successful when indigenous communities come together and organize themselves" (Stephens 2015, 60). However, the opportunities for Indigenous organizations to thrive and to meet the needs of Indigenous residents are context dependent, with many Indigenous Peoples from Latin America, Asia, and Africa ending up in the high-density and low-income informal settlements discussed above where access to basics such as safe housing, sanitation, and personal security are absent (Stephens 2015, 56).

What does this reterritorialization of human settlement and economic and social relations mean for the sovereign, national state? In his thought-provoking *Urban Nation* (2008), Alan Broadbent, a philanthropist and advocate for urban empowerment in Canada, argues that urbanization has fundamental implications for the place of municipalities in Canada's constitutional order. He proposes radical amendments to Canada's Constitution, including the creation of three city-states (with provincial status) to govern Canada's three largest cities: Toronto,

Montreal, and Vancouver. Ran Hirschl (2020) argues that urbanization is indeed an important (but not the only) driver of the empowerment of municipal governments in constitutional orders across the globe. Western countries are presented as laggards in part because their constitutional and democratic foundations were established when these countries were primarily rural.

Hirschl (2020) argues that the significance of urbanization in the Global South, including the existence of megacities with high densities, along with the later development of democratic constitutions in these places, explains why constitutions in the Global South tend to recognize cities. In fact, countries of the Global South have become the chief innovators in this area of constitutional law. In the absence of extreme densities and megacities in Canada, is constitutional recognition of municipal government in the country's future? Does the political will exist to adapt Canada's systems of municipal government and processes of multilevel governance to urbanization? Which global models are the most promising examples? Hirschl (2020) contends that democratic institutions and, ultimately, constitutions must adapt to the reality of urban agglomeration if we are to address the policy challenges of the era effectively and *equitably*. We would add that institutional innovations to enable municipalities to engage citizens, to actively address human rights abuses and marginalization, and to scale up grassroots challenges to other orders of government when necessary – in other words, robust norms of multilevel co-operation and governance – may also be a crucial aspect of addressing contemporary policy challenges.

TOWARD A COMPARATIVE APPROACH

A fundamental characteristic of local government is their numerosity (John 2009, 20). As a form of government and governance at a smaller scale than the national or, in federations, state or provincial levels, local government provides a rich laboratory of governance processes to be studied. Importantly, *by comparing local governments and urban governance processes both sub-nationally and internationally we can explore the degrees of freedom that cities have to act within their national and international contexts from multiple vantage points.* We can also evaluate the costs and benefits of different institutional configurations for the quality of democratic processes and local decision-making. Importantly, we see enormous value in placing urban politics and local government systems in their national contexts and asking what is similar and different about city governance in cities in the same country, how they differ from international cities, and why. In this way we can also explore what is unique about a particular city in relation to its national and international counterparts and begin to explore reasons and lessons.

Although we may see national patterns in city governance, the complexity of cities presents significant challenges and places limitations on our ability to generalize, a point made in chapter 7 on the nature of local leadership and the variety of municipal institutions even within Canada alone. As alluded to above, cities also contain multiple political authorities and possible governance partners creating even more complexity.

More radical conceptions of urban politics take us beyond the notion of the "sovereign state" and embrace a much more bottom-up, non-hierarchical, and organic view of urban politics and local governance (see various works by Warren Magnusson including 2011 and 2015). Nonetheless, there is still a tendency to think about units of government as "levels" (implying hierarchy) and political authority as "sovereign" and top-down, fundamental ideas about political authority that research on urban politics challenges to various degrees. The notion of the sovereign territorial state as establishing a *single* authority on a defined territory that has generally been continuous and contiguous is the foundational idea underpinning the sovereign states system (Elkins 1995). Such a conception not only misses the richness and interconnected nature of cities but also erases the presence of Indigenous Peoples as well as competing histories of cities and claims to cities and the lands upon which they are situated. It does not capture the "quiet evolution" of municipal-Indigenous government engagement (Alcantara and Nelles 2016), instances of Indigenous resurgence, or the interdependent nature of city and reserve life for some Indigenous Peoples. Wimmer and Schiller (2002) label the naturalization of the sovereign territorial state as the only form of relevant political authority in social research as "methodological nationalism" (Wimmer and Schiller 2002). We agree that we must problematize approaches that see sovereignty as absolute and ignore that there are "overlapping" and "competing" sources of political authority (Enright 2020, 30). According to Warren Magnusson, this involves exploring how cities are ordered and constituted beyond sovereign containers and in a more dynamic way: "To see like a city … is to recognize that the static order we so often associate with the state is an illusion … We have to attune ourselves to deep uncertainty just as we do in a strange city whose ways are unknown to us" (Magnusson 2011, 10, 29).

We also agree that cities are connected to broader processes like the global economy, global networks, and various dimensions of imperialism and colonialism that are international in scope. This only underscores the value of the comparative enterprise, which includes exploring potential similarities in politics and power dynamics internationally. However, in our view, the organization of the states system into "sovereign" containers and constitutions is still a powerful and lasting idea that shapes power relations and city governance in significant ways. We need to first understand how national infrastructures and local political institutions enable and constrain local politics and governance before problematizing it. As Hirschl notes:

> Though we live in the century of the city, we are still captives of constitutional structures, doctrines, perceptions, and expectations that were conceived along with the modern nation-state and germinated through the age of revolution, a historical process that saw the subjugation of the sovereign city. Any attempt to put urban government at the center of the constitutional order will therefore require against-the-grain constitutional thought combined with strong political will, a combination that has generally not yet emerged in politics or scholarship. (2020, 9)

However, we hope that a thorough understanding of the existing local government systems in global perspective can generate new ideas in your classroom.

CANADIAN CITIES IN COMPARATIVE PERSPECTIVE: THE CONTRIBUTIONS

Urbanization is a global phenomenon that is raising profound questions for democratic governance. It is increasingly recognized that many of the most important global policy challenges, including climate change, integrating migrants, and social equality, are urban policy questions. What implications do evolving patterns of urbanization have for municipal government and urban governance? What are the fundamental challenges and debates in urban politics and how do they manifest and inform policy approaches in Canadian cities and cities around the world? Why are city politics and urban governance important and what is unique about municipal government in Canada and around the world? What contribution do municipal governments make to developing effective responses to global problems and to equity in cities? What does a comparative approach add to our understanding of urban issues and what insights can it offer us about navigating these in the Canadian context? What are the key tensions – external and internal – that local governments must navigate and the trade-offs inherent within municipal systems?

The first section of this book explores the foundations of Canadian municipal governance as well as dominant ideas and approaches to the study of urban and municipal politics in Canada. National approaches to the design of municipal governance systems vary significantly around the world. In the Global North, there are at least three national models – the Anglo, Franco, and Northern European models discussed in chapter 2. Canada's municipal systems fall into the Anglo category, one which is dominated by the unitary and top-down notions of sovereignty discussed above. In Anglo systems such as Canada's, municipal institutions are created in statutes passed by provincial (and territorial) legislatures instead of being recognized in the federal constitution (Constitution Act, 1867). Parliamentary sovereignty and supremacy are absolute in relation to law-making in such Anglo systems (with some limitations in federal constitutions such as Canada's and, where they exist, constitutionally entrenched charters of rights and freedoms). Placing Canadian cities in comparative perspective opens potentially new lines of thought about the costs and benefits of organizing political authority in the way that we do in Canada. Although each model has underlying constitutional logics, the way in which political actors practice and adapt each model has varied across countries and history in ways that shed light on the range of possible approaches to municipal government in Canada. A simple lesson from comparison of Canada's municipal systems is that municipal institutions are highly constrained in their autonomy even compared to other Western countries, and particularly in relation to innovations in countries in the Global South, including South Africa.

After rooting readers in the constitutional-institutional framework of municipal and urban governance in Canada, in chapter 3, Kristin R. Good introduces the comparative method and debates surrounding it as well as dominant approaches to the study of urban politics in Canada. She describes and analyzes the contributions of seminal works in the field to illustrate how comparison has contributed to understanding the nature of Canadian municipal systems and urban politics. In this chapter, we see that Canadian municipal scholars have made significant contributions to urban politics through institutionalist and multilevel governance approaches and have offered critical approaches to city development.

However, to understand the place of municipalities within Canada's democratic order, we must also explore the informal processes and state-society linkage mechanisms that shape relationships between municipalities and other orders of government. In this vein, as Martin Horak notes in chapter 4, municipalities/local interests also lack integration into the "national" sphere of policy-making because of the absence of robust linking mechanisms such as common political parties across orders of government and a class of similarly trained civil servants staffing the three orders of government in Canada. He draws on Sellers, Lidström, and Bae (2020), who emphasize the virtues of the "nationalized" and integrated infrastructure supporting local government through linkage mechanisms such as parties and a common civil service. This type of multilevel democracy exists in small Northern European countries. Seen through the lens of this typology, Canadian municipalities are "dis-integrated" from a common national infrastructure of multilevel democracy. Chapter 4 reminds the student of urban politics of the necessity of striking a balance between "unity" and "diversity," which is the essence of the federal principle. What balance ought to be struck between building out – building our municipalities and supporting their autonomy – and building them into provincial and national institutions and policy processes?[7] We hope that this volume will provide you with the tools to navigate these important debates about the future of Canadian municipal and multilevel democracy.

Together, chapters 2 and 4 provide a macro picture of the way in which *institutions* and *governance practices* might shape urban politics and policy-making in Canada and position these trends internationally.

The volume then turns to an exploration of local institutions. It begins with Jen Nelles's discussion of metropolitan governance in chapter 5, comparing Canada's experience with metropolitan governance in major cities (Montreal, Toronto, Vancouver, and Winnipeg) with approaches to metropolitan regionalism in cities in the United States, France, and the United Kingdom. The sub-national comparisons highlight the extent to which provinces have been interventionist in governing metropolitan areas. Nelles finds that the international comparisons highlight that the "Canadian experiment falls somewhere between the relatively hands-off American experience and the more centralized and interventionist French and British approaches" (174).

In chapter 6, we discuss another foundational element of urban and local politics – municipal finance. The chapter lays out a fundamental idea in the municipal finance literature called the Wicksellian Connection, which stresses the need to connect expenditure and taxation decisions.

Enid Slack summarizes: "The best way to design a local revenue system is first to decide what services should be delivered locally and then to put into place the local revenue system (a combination of user fees, taxes, and transfers) that will best induce local decision-makers to finance precisely that package of expenditures that their residents want" (180). Through comparative analysis, she shows that Canadian cities have a higher level of autonomy than international comparator cities but also access to a smaller range of own-source revenues. In her view, this could be a problem for effective city governance in the future, one that could require multilevel financial solutions.

In chapter 7, Kristin R. Good, Kate Graham, and Jesse Helmer explore the nature of local leadership, placing mayoral leadership and council forms in international, comparative perspective. They contextualize the common contention that Canadian mayors are generally "weak" (214), arguing that although the American council-manager form of organizing authority at the municipal level has been influential in Canada, there is significant variation and hybridity in local political institutions in Canada and globally. Furthermore, they stress that although institutions shape the possibilities for local leadership, they do not determine them. Canadian mayors are leading in a variety of important policy areas such as the resettlement of Syrian refugees, drug decriminalization, the environment, and public health in ways that defy their institutional limitations. They argue that a "major part of a mayor's ability to lead is determined by their abilities to mobilize a diverse range of actors around an urban agenda [and] may involve multiple levels of government, sometimes with competing or even conflicting policy goals" (240).

Chapter 8 tackles the important subject of municipal elections and political incorporation. Anne Mévellec, Brandon Bolduc, Guy Chiasson, and Veika Donatien begin by outlining a traditional Canadian "municipal model" of democracy (see also Chiasson and Mévellec 2014) that, compared to other cities internationally, resisted a political conception of the municipality consistent with, for instance, the largely (at least formally) non-partisan nature of Canadian municipal politics. However, they argue that this conception is being challenged in major urban centres where municipal democracy is experiencing a professionalization, diversification and, ultimately, politicization. One cause of these changes may be municipal mergers – in other words, an unintended consequence of top-down provincial decision-making in municipal affairs.

Then, in chapter 9, we introduce a discussion of municipal services and citizen engagement at the local level. John B. Sutcliffe and Sarah Cipkar argue that the variety of municipal systems globally reflects debates about the appropriate scale to deliver particular services, including whether municipalities are mainly service delivery agents or whether they serve important representative roles and how services ought to be delivered at the local level (e.g., by multi-purpose municipal institutions or agencies, boards and commissions, or through public-private partnership). However, they argue for the usefulness of the Anglo category of local government, discussed more in chapter 2, in understanding the Canadian experience of constraints imposed by provinces in the delivery of municipal services. The authors also raise debates about who governs cities in Canada and in other Anglo contexts, noting that some scholarship in these countries points to the disproportionate influence of developers and other business interests. In sum, they discuss what services are provided and how, as well as who influences service delivery, raising important debates about Canadian municipal democracy.

In chapter 10, Zachary Spicer discusses the politics of growth and development using the cases of the political dynamics surrounding stadium construction as well as the push for recognition as a "smart city," a term that the author notes has become synonymous with "technology-infused urbanism" (328). He notes that "few local decisions highlight the dynamics around the growth mentality and boosterism better than stadium construction" (316). However, smart cities may be seen as a more modern iteration of such "growth machine" politics – see the discussion of Logan and Molotch's ([1987] 2007) work in chapter 3 – that "has taken on a new imperative in recent years … in Canada where Google-affiliated Sidewalk Labs pushed [unsuccessfully] to create a new smart city along Toronto's eastern waterfront" (326). Through comparison, Spicer concludes that although a common growth mentality exists in cities in Canada and the United States, institutions matter since Canadian cities are more limited in the inducements that they can offer to businesses to either remain or relocate to their cities.

In chapter 11, Tristan Cleveland and Elizabeth Schwartz explore the role of municipalities in addressing climate change, noting that local governments have significant authority over two areas that are crucial in reducing carbon emissions – transportation and building standards. They examine cities in different national contexts, from Toronto and Vancouver in Canada to New York City in the United States and Stockholm in Sweden, finding that these cities have made substantial progress in policy to reduce carbon emissions. Their chapter shows how municipal creativity is required in this process since they lack the authority and resources in many instances to address challenges directly (e.g., sometimes lacking the authority to change building codes). Although these urban centres have made substantial progress, the authors conclude that a major limitation is that core municipalities only represent a small part of the city-region in these places, which are also governed by suburban municipalities. A truly effective response to climate change will require not only multilevel but multi-scalar governance arrangements in metropolitan areas.

In chapter 12, Kristin R. Good examines the global rise in local immigration policy-making. She notes innovation in municipal immigration policies that are designed for inclusivity or anti-immigration measures, showing that the latter are very rare in Canada and rare even in the United States, contrary to portrayals in the media. She concludes that "whether it is through efforts to address gaps in settlement services, to culturally adapt municipal services to migrants, or to challenge upper levels of governments' monopoly on determining who can legitimately claim the right to live and work on their soil, municipalities in Canada and abroad have taken some bold steps in an area of public policy that is fundamentally implicated in the spatial and economic restructuring of the globe" (392).

Chapter 13 addresses the fundamental question of Indigenous-municipal relations, which take several forms, such as "meaningful consultation" (399), agreements between municipalities and Indigenous communities located adjacent to municipal boundaries, representation of Indigenous

Peoples on local governance bodies, and the resurgence of Indigenous cultural practices and laws. Doug Anderson and Alexandra Flynn note that Canadian municipalities have implemented changes in their governance practices and policies to improve Indigenous-municipal relations particularly since 2010 by establishing Indigenous advisory bodies and Indigenous affairs offices and by endorsing the recommendations of the Truth and Reconciliation Commission's calls to action as well as UNDRIP. They discuss cases of policy innovation in Australia, New Zealand, and Mexico that suggest a more global engagement of municipalities in building stronger Indigenous-municipal relationships. They conclude that a truly transformative relationship would require "the active presence of Indigenous Peoples freely practicing their cultures and responsibilities under their own Indigenous laws and cultural frameworks in urban centres, without interference under municipal bylaws or other forms of Canadian legislation" (424).

In chapter 14, Tari Ajadi and Kristin R. Good address the question of systemic racism in cities with a particular focus on anti-Black racism in policing and planning policy. They show that the racial profiling of Black residents is common in cities on both sides of the Atlantic – including cases in the United States, the UK, and Canada. They also discuss how places in cities become "racialized" through neglect and the location of noxious or undesirable land uses in their proximity and then targeted for "renewal" and displacement (430). However, they also note the importance of resistance in communities through movements such as Black Lives Matter, which have, in turn, influenced municipal governance leading to innovations in those institutions to address racism in Canadian cities.

Chapter 15 explores the local governance of poverty and social polarization in cities. Mara Sidney and Adam Straub discuss two policy areas that cities can employ to address poverty: housing and education policy. With respect to the former, they note that "housing's 'use value' and 'exchange value' often exist in tension with one another" (467) to use Marxian language and the language used in growth machine theory (see Logan and Molotch's [1987] 2007 ideas discussed further in chapter 3). They note that Canadian cities compare favourably with American and Latin American cities with respect to poverty rates and appear to be less influenced by neoliberal ideas in education policy. In addition, they observe that government seems to be more of a driver of policy change in these areas in Canada than in cities in the United States and Brazil, where grassroots movements play a greater role. The authors conclude with a discussion of the impact of the COVID-19 pandemic on inequalities and the variation in policy responses in Canada, the United States, and Latin America. The pandemic has only highlighted the ways in which housing and education policy are crucial to addressing poverty and inequality in cities across the globe.

Finally, in chapter 16, the textbook's conclusion, Jen Nelles and Kristin R. Good provide a summary of the lessons to be drawn from the comparisons in the various chapters as well as the debates that the book raises. It particularly focuses on the perceived weakness of Canadian cities, both in their constitutional and institutional contexts, and it reflects on how the various authors in this volume characterize and grapple with these limitations. The chapter presents some perspectives on pathways for reform but also outlines ways that cities can govern creatively within these boundaries.

We conclude with a challenge to readers, students of Canadian urbanism, and policy makers to use the principles, debates, and insights presented here to shape the future of our cities. Our urban system is a dynamic one. One that has experienced both path dependence *and* disruption in its evolution. Like all political arenas, the urban is one that permits creativity and innovation. As our greatest civilizational challenges will continue to play out at the local level, it is important that we see it as a place that can also provide solutions. Cities matter, and we are all capable of shaping them.

NOTES

1 Specifically, Bill 20 aims to conduct a pilot project on partisan elections in Calgary and Edmonton in October 2025, which could then be expanded to other municipalities in Alberta (Government of Alberta, n.d.).

2 The term "Global South" emerged in the 1970s lexicon of international relations to describe two groups of countries in the world based on level of development. The world's more industrialized countries tend to lie north of less developed countries. Major exceptions are, of course, Australia and New Zealand (United Nations Development Programme 2004).

3 We have added the precise density figures that the same source provides in its table 1 in brackets (Filipowicz 2018, 5).

4 Relatedly, multiple scholars argue that the urban and rural/reserve distinction is part of "a colonial spatial imaginary" that sees the "city" as a fundamentally "settler space," erasing its Indigenous histories (see Tomiak et al. 2019, loc. 229).

5 Further examples of international networks that reflect groups of cities coming together to define and implement a specific human rights agenda include the Cities of Refuge Network (ICORN), nuclear-free cities, and child-friendly cities coalitions.

6 2SLGBTQIA+: Two-Spirit, Lesbian, Gay, Bisexual, Transgender, Queer and/or Questioning, Intersex, Asexual. The + recognizes that there are other ways that people can choose to identify.

7 The distinction between "building out" (support for provincial autonomy) and "building in" (integration into national institutions) is inspired by Richard Simeon's (2002) lessons concerning what has made Canada work as a multinational federation and has helped to manage the threat of secession of Quebec.

REFERENCES

114957 Canada Ltée (Spraytech, Société d'arrosage) v. Hudson (Town), 2001 SCC 40.

Abu-Laban, Yasmeen and Christine Gabriel. 2002. *Selling Diversity: Immigration, Multiculturalism, Employment Equity, and Globalization.* Peterborough, ON: Broadview.

Alcantara, Christopher, and Jen Nelles. 2016. *A Quiet Evolution: The Emergence of Indigenous-Local Intergovernmental Partnerships in Canada.* Toronto: University of Toronto Press. https://doi.org /10.3138/9781442625884.

Andrew, Caroline. 2001. "The Shame of (Ignoring) the Cities." *Journal of Canadian Studies* 35, no. 4 (Winter): 100–10. https://doi.org/10.3138/jcs.35.4.100.

Andrew, Caroline, Katherine A. Graham, and Susan D. Phillips. 2002. "Introduction: Urban Affairs in Canada: Changing Roles and Changing Perspectives." In *Urban Affairs: Back on the Policy Agenda*, edited by Caroline Andrew, Katherine A. Graham, and Susan D. Phillips, 3–20. Kingston: McGill-Queen's University Press. https://doi.org/10.1515/9780773570146-001.

Brenner, Neil. 1999. "Globalisation as Reterritorialisation: The Re-scaling of Urban Governance in the European Union." *Urban Studies* 36, no. 3 (March): 431–51. https://doi.org/10.1080/0042098993466.

Cameron, David M. 1980. "Provincial Responsibility for Municipal Institutions." *Canadian Public Administration* 23, no. 2 (June): 222–35. https://doi.org/10.1111/j.1754-7121.1980.tb00054.x.

Bradford, Neil. 2002. "Why Cities Matter: Policy Research Perspectives for Canada." CPRN Discussion Paper No. F│23, Ottawa, June 2002. Canadian Policy Research Networks.

Broadbent, Alan. 2008. *Urban Nation: Why We Need to Give Power back to the Cities to Make Canada Strong.* Toronto: HarperCollins Canada.

Chiasson, Guy, and Anne Mévellec. 2014. "The 2013 Quebec Municipal Election." *Canadian Journal of Urban Research* 23, no. 2 (Winter): 1–8. https://www.jstor.org/stable/26189248.

Courchene, Thomas J. 2007. "Global Futures for Canada's Global Cities." *IRPP Policy Matters* 8, no. 2 (June): 1–36.

Elkins, David. 1995. *Beyond Sovereignty: Territory and Political Economy in the Twenty-First Century.* Toronto: University of Toronto Press.

Enright, Theresa. 2020. "Beyond Comparison in Urban Politics and Policy Analysis." In "Symposium, Toward an Urban Policy Analysis," special issue, *PS: Political Science & Politics* 53, no. 1 (January): 29–32. https://doi.org/10.1017/S1049096519001367.

Filipowicz, Josef. 2018. "Room to Grow: Comparing Urban Density in Canada and Abroad." Fraser Research Bulletin, Fraser Institute, January 2018. https://www.fraserinstitute.org/sites/default/files/room-to-grow-comparing-urban-density-in-canada-and-abroad.pdf.

Garber, Judith A., and David L. Imbroscio. 1996. "'The Myth of the North American City' Reconsidered: Local Constitutional Regimes in Canada and the United States." *Urban Affairs Review* 31, no. 5 (May): 595–624. https://doi.org/10.1177/107808749603100502.

Goldberg, Michael A., and John Mercer. 1986. *The Myth of the North American City: Continentalism Challenged.* Vancouver: UBC Press. https://doi.org/10.59962/9780774857031.

Good, Kristin R. 2009. *Municipalities and Multiculturalism: The Politics of Immigration in Toronto and Vancouver.* Toronto: University of Toronto Press. https://doi.org/10.3138/9781442690417.

———. 2016. "Municipal Political Parties: An Answer to Urbanization or an Affront to Traditions of Local Democracy?" In *Canadian Political Parties in Transition*, edited by Alain-G. Gagnon and Brian Tanguay, 432–64. Toronto: University of Toronto Press.

———. 2019. "The Fallacy of the 'Creatures of the Provinces' Doctrine: Recognizing and Protecting Municipalities' Constitutional Status." In *IMFG Papers on Municipal Finance and Governance*, no. 46. Toronto: Institute on Municipal Finance and Governance.

Good, Kristin R., Luc Turgeon, and Triadafilos Triadafilopoulos. 2014. *Segmented Cities? How Urban Contexts Shape Ethnic and Nationalist Politics.* Vancouver: UBC Press. https://doi.org/10.59962/9780774825856.

Government of Alberta. n.d. "Strengthening Local Elections and Councils." Accessed June 12, 2024. https://www.alberta.ca/strengthening-local-elections-and-councils.

Hackworth, Jason. 2014. *The Neoliberal City: Governance, Ideology, and Development in American Urbanism.* Ithaca: Cornell University Press. Kindle.

Hirschl, Ran. 2020. *City, State: Constitutionalism and the Megacity.* New York: Oxford University Press. https://doi.org/10.1093/oso/9780190922771.001.0001.

International Organization for Migration (IOM). 2015. *World Migration Report 2015. Migration and Cities: New Partnerships to Manage Mobility*. Switzerland: International Organization for Migration. https://publications.iom.int/books/world-migration-report-2015-migrants-and-cities-new-partnerships-manage-mobility.

John, Peter. 2009. "Why Study Urban Politics?" In *Theories of Urban Politics*, edited by Jonathan S. Davies and David L. Imbroscio, 2nd ed., 518–678. London: SAGE Publications.

Joy, Meghan. 2020. *The Right to an Age-Friendly City: Redistribution, Recognition, and Senior Citizen Rights in Urban Spaces*. Montreal: McGill-Queen's University Press.

Logan, John R., and Harvey L. Molotch. (1987) 2007. *Urban Fortunes: The Political Economy of Place*. 20th Anniversary Edition. Berkeley: University of California Press. https://doi.org/10.1525/9780520934573.

Lucas, Jack. 2013. "Hidden in Plain View: Local Agencies, Boards, and Commissions in Canada." In *IMFG Perspectives*, no. 4. Toronto: Institute on Municipal Finance and Governance.

Magnusson, Warren. 2011. *Politics of Urbanism: Seeing like a City*. New York: Routledge.

———. 2015. *Local Self-Government and the Right to the City*. Montreal: McGill-Queen's University Press. https://doi.org/10.1515/9780773597280.

Nelles, Jen. 2012. *Comparative Metropolitan Policy: Governing beyond the Local Boundaries in the Imagined Metropolis*. Oxon: Routledge.

Oomen, Barbara M. 2016. "Introduction." In *Global Urban Justice: The Rise of Human Rights Cities*, edited by Barbara Oomen, Martha F. Davis, and Michele Grigolo, 1–19. Cambridge: Cambridge University Press. https://doi.org/10.1017/CBO9781316544792.

Office for National Statistics (ONS). 2021. "Population and Household Estimates, England and Wales: Census 2021." June 28, 2022. https://www.ons.gov.uk/peoplepopulationandcommunity/populationandmigration/populationestimates/bulletins/populationandhouseholdestimatesenglandandwales/census2021.

Peters, Evelyn. 2004. "Three Myths about Aboriginals in Cities." Breakfast on the Hill Presentation, Canadian Federation for the Humanities and Social Sciences, Ottawa.

Peterson, Paul E. 1981. *City Limits*. Chicago: University of Chicago Press.

Qadeer, Mohammad Abdul. 2016. *Multicultural Cities: Toronto, New York, Los Angeles*. Toronto: University of Toronto Press.

Sassen, Saskia. 1991. *The Global City: New York, London, Tokyo*. Princeton, NJ: Princeton University Press.

Sellers, Jefferey M. 2005. "Re-placing the Nation: An Agenda for Comparative Urban Politics." *Urban Affairs Review* 40, no. 4 (March): 419–45. https://doi.org/10.1177/1078087404272673.

Sellers, Jefferey M., Anders Lidström, and Yooil Bae. 2020. *Multilevel Democracy: How Local Institutions and Civil Society Shape the Modern State*. Cambridge: Cambridge University Press. https://doi.org/10.1017/9781108672337.

Simeon, Richard. 2002. "Federalism and Decentralization in Canada." Paper presented at the 2nd International Conference on Decentralization, Forum of Federations, Manila, Philippines, July 25–27, 2002. https://www.forumfed.org/libdocs/Misc/20031213-ca-RichardSimeon.pdf.

Statistics Canada. 2021. "Population Counts, for Census Metropolitan Areas, Census Agglomerations, Population Centres and Rural Areas." Released February 9, 2022, accessed February 22, 2024. https://www150.statcan.gc.ca/t1/tbl1/en/tv.action?pid=9810000601.

———. 2022a. "Canada's Large Urban Centres Continue to Grow and Spread." *The Daily*, February 9, 2022. https://www150.statcan.gc.ca/n1/daily-quotidien/220209/dq220209b-eng.htm.

———. 2022b. "Canada Tops G7 Growth Despite COVID." *The Daily*, February 9, 2022. https://www150.statcan.gc.ca/n1/daily-quotidien/220209/dq220209a-eng.htm.

Stephens, Carolyn. 2015. "The Indigenous Experience of Urbanization." In *State of the World's Minorities and Indigenous Peoples 2015: Focus on Cities*, edited by Peter Grant, 54–61. London: Minority Rights Watch International.

Stren, Richard, and Mario Polèse. 2000. "Understanding the New Sociocultural Dynamics in Cities: Comparative Urban Policy in a Global Context." In *The Social Sustainability of Cities: Diversity and the Management of Change*, edited by Mario Polèse and Richard Stren, 3–38. Toronto: University of Toronto Press. https://doi.org/10.3138/9781442682399-004.

Taylor, Zack. 2019. *Shaping the Metropolis: Institutions and Urbanization in the United States and Canada.* Montreal: McGill-Queen's University Press. https://doi.org/10.1515/9780773558427.

———. 2023. "Introduction." In "Strong(er) Mayors in Ontario – What Difference Will They Make?" edited by Zack Taylor, 1–4. In *IMFG Forum*, no. 13. Toronto: Institute on Municipal Finance and Governance.

Toronto (City) v. Ontario (Attorney General), 2021 SCC 34.

Tindal, C. Richard, and Susan Nobes Tindal. 2009. *Local Government in Canada.* 7th ed. Toronto: Nelson.

Tindal, C. Richard, Susan Nobes Tindal, Kennedy Stewart, and Patrick Smith. 2017. *Local Government in Canada.* 9th ed. Toronto: Nelson.

Tomiak, Julie, Tyler McCreary, David Hugill, Robert Henry, and Heather Dorries. 2019. "Settler City Limits." In *Settler City Limits: Indigenous Resurgence and Colonial Violence in the Urban Prairie West*, edited by Heather Dorries, Robert Henry, David Hugill, Tyler McCreary, and Julie Tomiak, loc. 107–638 of 10694. Winnipeg: University of Manitoba Press. https://doi.org/10.1515/9780887555893-002.

United Nations. 2018. *The World's Cities in 2018: Data Booklet.* https://www.un.org/en/development/desa/population/publications/pdf/urbanization/the_worlds_cities_in_2018_data_booklet.pdf.

United Nations Development Programme. 2004. "Forging a Global South United Nations Day for South Cooperation." December 19, 2004. https://www.undp.org/sites/g/files/zskgke326/files/migration/cn/UNDP-CH-PR-Publications-UNDay-for-South-South-Cooperation.pdf.

United Nations Habitat. 2020. "World Cities Report 2020: The Value of Sustainable Urbanization. United Nations Human Settlements Program." Nairobi, Kenya: UN-Habitat. https://unhabitat.org/World%20Cities%20Report%202020.

United States Census Bureau. 2022. "QuickFacts. New York City." https://www.census.gov/quickfacts/fact/table/newyorkcitynewyork/PST045222#PST045222.

Vertovec, Steven. 2007. "Super-diversity and Its Implications." *Ethnic and Racial Studies* 30, no. 6 (November): 1024–54. https://doi.org/10.1080/01419870701599465.

Wimmer, Andreas, and Nina Glick Schiller. 2002. "Methodological Nationalism and Beyond: Nation-State Building, Migration and the Social Sciences." *Global Networks* 2, no. 4 (October): 301–34. https://doi.org/10.1111/1471-0374.00043.

World Bank. n.d. "Urban Development: Overview." https://www.worldbank.org/en/topic/urbandevelopment/overview#1.

Conceptual Foundations: Comparative Methods, Theory, and Rooting the Canadian Case

Situating the Constitutional, Legal, and Historical Foundations of Canadian Municipal Government

Kristin R. Good

INTRODUCTION

Where do Canadian municipalities fit within the global terrain of constitutional-legal arrangements that shape urban governance? A global perspective highlights that municipalities in the Global North lack firm constitutional standing even though urban agglomeration is widespread. Noted scholar of constitutional law Ran Hirschl (2020a, 2020b) observes that many of these countries' constitutions were designed when their patterns of settlement were largely rural. He underscores the "datedness" of the lack of constitutional status of cities in Canada's federal constitution (Hirschl 2020a, 6).

The resistance to constitutional change in response to urban agglomeration is particularly acute in the Anglo model of local government, a model that takes its inspiration from Britain and the Westminster Parliament. The democratic tradition in Anglo countries considers concentrating power in a central parliament to be crucial to "maximizing accountability and responsibility" in a representative democracy, and therefore it considers municipal government to be entirely subordinate to the parliament that enacted municipal legislation (Hesse and Sharpe 1991, 620). The principle of "parliamentary supremacy" or "parliamentary sovereignty" is fundamental to Anglo systems.

In contrast, both the "Franco" and "Northern and Middle European" models of local government discussed in this chapter and common in European countries other than the United Kingdom grant some form of constitutional recognition to municipalities and many have experienced significant decentralization in recent decades. However, as a group, local government systems in Anglo countries, such as Canada, the United Kingdom, Ireland, Australia, and New Zealand (and to a lesser extent the United States), share the tendency to conceptualize local government in a particularly limited way. Strictly speaking, the parliament responsible for passing municipal legislation and incorporating municipalities could choose to eliminate municipal government entirely.

Thus, Anglo countries such as Canada do not afford constitutional status to municipalities and instead perceive sovereignty as residing in a central parliament (Hesse and Sharpe 1991). Even within the context of largely disempowered municipalities across urban agglomerations worldwide, Canadian municipalities stand out as lacking autonomy (Smith and Spicer 2018; Hirschl 2020b). Most fundamentally, this is rooted in their lack of independent constitutional status in Canada's federal Constitution (the Constitution Act, 1867) and in the judicial and political doctrines that emerged in the late nineteenth century that have remained influential (Magnusson 2005). It has also been influenced by "province-building" and the "provincial rights" movement that began in the late nineteenth century and transformed provinces' place in the Constitution (Vipond 1985). Municipalities' inferior position in the governmental system is supported by a political culture that has internalized and accepted the constitutional doctrine that municipalities are only "creatures of the provinces" and lack not only independent constitutional status but also *constitutional significance* (Good 2019). Many Canadians do not seem to consider themselves to have a right to local self-government, which is fundamental to robust democracies (Magnusson 2015).

This political landscape has allowed provinces to impose top-down change in local political institutions unilaterally in ways that violate basic democratic norms of consent and trust in the decision-making systems. A political culture that downplays the political and constitutional significance of municipalities was institutionalized during a reform movement at the turn of the twentieth century, which resulted in changes that were designed to take the "politics" out of municipal decision-making. This type of thinking is reflected in Canada's largely non-partisan elections and, for some, a technocratic, apolitical understanding of Canadian municipal decision-making. However, Canadian municipalities' legal status and institutions vary. For instance, a unique tradition of independent party politics has emerged in some municipalities in British Columbia and Quebec although the non-partisan tradition remains strong even there. Thus, as you progress through this volume, you will notice that although Canadian municipalities may be situated within broader comparative urban politics (and largely national) typologies, they only fit in qualified ways, given the sub-national (i.e., in provincial jurisdiction across the country) and even sub-provincial variation that exists in Canada.

Still, such international comparisons on the country scale are useful as a starting point for understanding what is unique and different about Canadian municipalities, including the fundamental ideas informing the constitutional order and how these differences could affect the quality of local democracy and service delivery in cities. Significant variation exists even among countries in the Anglo category. For instance, states in the United States that have enacted "home rule" measures for municipalities in state constitutions provide valuable comparative insights into what may be possible in Canada.

This chapter situates Canadian municipalities within a typology of municipal systems, highlighting commonalities with other Anglo municipal systems and raising questions about their future. It first presents a typology of local government systems, then it describes the institutional basics of the place of municipalities in the Canadian regime and provides an overview of how this has evolved over the course of Canada's short history. It then compares Canadian municipal systems with systems in other Anglo countries before offering some concluding observations. Ultimately, this chapter lays the foundation for a critical examination of municipalities' place in the Canadian constitutional order, arguing that fresh constitutional thinking is needed to realize Canadian municipalities' purpose as local service delivery and democratic agents.

CHARACTERIZING SYSTEMS OF LOCAL GOVERNMENT: AN INSTITUTIONAL APPROACH

Although there are many ways of classifying local governments, in this section we describe country systems of local governments, situating Canada within them. One of the most influential typologies is Hesse and Sharpe's (1991), which focuses on the intergovernmental dimension of local government's distinct nature in Western countries.[1] The three categories are Anglo, Franco, and North and Middle European (Hesse and Sharpe 1991, 606–7). Some European scholars argue for including European Anglo countries in the North European model (John 2001). However, since municipal and urban politics in Canada is our concern here, we discuss Anglo as a separate category that includes Britain, Ireland, Australia, New Zealand, and the United States, which are typically placed in this category. Among the reasons for grouping Anglo cases together are as follows: They are all long-standing democracies; although their precise historical paths vary, they share a history of municipal government that dates back centuries to Britain; and there has been cross-fertilization in terms of jurisprudence and academic thinking among the countries in this category (see also Dollery, Garcea, and LeSage 2008, 5). Canada also shares a Westminster-style parliamentary system of government, including the Crown in common with all Anglo countries but the United States. The United States and Australia share federal systems of government (and the latter, the combination of federalism with Westminster-style parliamentary government). Anglo countries such as Canada, the United States, Australia, and New Zealand share a common experience of settler colonialism (discussed in chapter 3), wherein cities were a central part of colonial strategies of "displacement and replacement" of Indigenous Peoples with white, British "bodies" celebrated as the civilization of "space" (Edmonds 2010, 7).

The Anglo category offers a more specific way of comparing, allowing us to make observations about the distinctions even within this category either among countries or subunits of federations. However, the popularity of the simpler Northern and Southern European categories should alert us to possible similarities between Canada and other Western European systems of local government (at least in relation to the Franco cases in Southern Europe). Furthermore, there is a great deal to learn by comparing different cases. For instance, much of the constitutional innovation that has taken place in relation to making space for cities in national constitutions has occurred in the Global South with South Africa as a leading example (Hirschl 2020a). We outline the three European-inspired categories before turning out attention to South Africa, an example of constitutional innovation in municipal empowerment.

Anglo Model

The Anglo model is based on the British model of local government. Canada, Australia, New Zealand, Ireland, and the United States fall into this category. In this model, local government and municipal institutions do not have constitutional status (at the national level or in federal constitutions). Instead, local governments (including municipalities) are formed by statute. In the Anglo model, the municipal corporation is the foundation of local government (Magnusson 1986, 2). Warren Magnusson argues that when municipalities became central to local government in Anglo-American systems (beginning in 1835 in England), a conception of municipalities as business corporations was adopted: "Under the new regime, every local government would be a public corporation, owned by the people in the area concerned – or at least by everyone who had property there – and organized to provide a range of necessary services, as efficiently as possible, in accordance with Parliamentary statutes" (1986, 3). In Britain, municipalities are incorporated by the Westminster Parliament. In federations such as Canada, Australia, and the United States, local governments are incorporated under and granted authority by a statute of a sub-national (provincial or state) government.

Although the United States is somewhat different in this respect given that it is a republic and the divided nature of its legislatures, the concept of parliamentary supremacy (or parliamentary sovereignty) generally shapes municipalities' place in the Anglo model. This concept, which originates in the British constitutional tradition, means that the law and the constitution are whatever the parliament of the day legislates (and the Crown assents to). Since municipal governments are created through statutes of "sovereign" parliaments in these countries, they are ultimately subject to unilateral change at the parliament and government of the day's (in the case of a majority government) will. As Wollmann puts it in the English context, "Parliament is the master of all other institutions in the land, with the power to 'make and break' as it wishes" (2000, 34).

According to some, including Hesse and Sharpe, in the Anglo model, responsibilities are clearly divided to "form two separate layers" (1991, 607). They are not as entangled as in other models, and the centre does not supervise localities directly. In England, the concept of "dual polity" (Bulpitt 1983) refers to a constitutional bargain to divide power and respect local autonomy with an understanding that "high politics" would be left to the Parliament

(Wollmann 2000, 34). Wollmann considers the "dual polity" aspect of the British foundations of local government to be an important democratic check on the highly centralized power of the Westminster Parliament (34).

Although it is true that central governments do not serve as overseers of local governments in the way that prefects might in the Franco model (discussed below), in practice they do oversee municipal government, at least in the contemporary era. In Hesse and Sharpe's (1991, 607) words, "The centre ... does not exercise tutelary functions, nor are its own local field services systematically interwoven with local government." The concept of a tutelary function, which implies the role of guardian, protector, or patron of local government, is foreign to Anglo understandings of local government. However, in Canada, ministries and departments of municipal affairs have been established in all provinces to play this role, and tight controls are common in the Anglo world. Nevertheless, unlike the traditional French model, the "degree of hierarchy" and extent of oversight varies *through time* and *by service area* (Hesse and Sharpe 1991, 607). Also, in the Anglo model, local leaders are not represented at higher levels of government through rules and traditions such as the *cumul de mandats* (discussed below).

The role of local government is more functional in this system, involving a self-government role in service delivery. Although variation exists within Anglo countries and through time,[2] in its purest form, local government is conceived as less political, and mayors are less visible. This is reflected in the weak role of mayors as well as in the role of councillors, chief administrative officers, and city managers in overseeing/governing service provision, such as in the council-manager models of government prevalent in Canada.

In the mid-2000s, Anglo countries fell in the mid-range of measures of responsibility for social policy and services, financial autonomy, and spending in relation to GDP (Bäck, Heinelt, and Magnier 2006). However, the guiding principle of municipal government in Anglo countries has meant that the delegation of service responsibility and financial power has varied significantly over time. As Warren Magnusson (1986) argues, the origin of Anglo municipal government as a public corporation has privileged the *principle of efficiency* as a governance value as well as "economic welfare," a logic that devalues local government as a fundamental form of democratic practice. Throughout history, the logic of efficiency has at times supported local autonomy (at least in a limited range of functions), but at others centralization was considered to produce greater efficiencies (Magnusson 1986). In Magnusson's words:

> This obsession with efficiency or economic welfare must inevitably lead to a devaluation of the local polity. Whether the local authority is conceived as a business corporation or a consumers' cooperative or an agency of the state that is itself both of these, it acquires a restricted, essentially instrumental purpose. Moreover, it becomes subject to re-constitution whenever it fails that purpose, and some other mode of organization seems superior. (1986, 17)

This corporate, service-oriented perspective on local government that values efficiency above all else is a common vision of local government in the Anglo model.

Franco Model

The Franco group follows the French Napoleonic model (Hesse and Sharpe 1991). Countries such as Italy, Belgium, Spain, Portugal, and to a certain extent, Greece fall into this category (607). As Hesse and Sharpe describe, in this model, "in its purest form, local government enjoys constitutional status, but, for service delivery, it is usually dependent on the assistance and direction of deconcentrated central field agencies" (1991, 606). Essentially, in the traditional form of this model, local governments have few functions and serve a primarily political role as an expression of community identity rather than a functional role of independent service provision and self-government (Hesse and Sharpe 1991, 606). Power is centralized in this model – local governments are equal (regardless of size) but are functionally and constitutionally subservient to a *prefect*, a civil servant appointed by the central state to supervise the legal, technical, and financial decisions of local authorities (Wollmann 2000, 41). Thus, an elite group of civil servants govern localities/local regions, and politically strong mayors represent cities (and communities) to these administrative agents. Local governments' mandates are limited, and they tend to have few responsibilities for social services.

In France, there are three elected tiers of local government or constitutionally defined "collectivités territoriales" – the régions, départements, and communes. The island of Corsica and large cities such as Paris, Lyon, and Marseille are recognized as "collectivités territoriales à statut particulier" (they have "special status"). In France, the system is highly fragmented with 35,000 mainly small communes (under 1,000 residents) in existence, whose boundaries are deeply entrenched in history, mostly dating to medieval times (Wollmann 2000, 42), coexisting with the other layers of "collectivités territoriales." Although the French system is known for its centralized nature, the strong sense of local identity coupled with the political strength of mayors in a system of "notables locaux" (a concept elaborated further in chapter 8) has meant that few amalgamations have occurred (42). The challenges that this fragmentation and the political strength of localities introduce for metropolitan collaboration are discussed further in chapter 4.

Local governments' functional responsibilities remained limited until the 1980s. However, significant decentralization has occurred. Since 1982, the administrative infrastructure of the central state has been subject to democratic election, including the départements and the régions (created in the 1950s for regional planning in towns and rural areas). These reforms were a "decisive step towards full-blown local self-government" (Wollmann 2000, 51). The regions are governed by councils that are elected and, in turn, empowered to elect an executive (Swift and Kervella 2003). Similarly, the departmental "prefects" who held executive power from 1800 to 1982 are still the *representative* of the state but no longer have executive authority. Rather, executive authority (authority to make decisions and execute them with respect to local services) now resides in an elected general council, which in turn elects a chairperson. The term for all local bodies is six years (Swift and Kervella 2003).

There is no equivalent of prefects in the Anglo system. These civil servants are appointed by the central government, represent the prime minister and government, and oversee the administrative supervision of the department's local authorities (Swift and Kervella 2003). There is a direct link between the central state and the local commune through mayors, who fulfill two roles: one as the elected executive for the communes and the other as the central state's representative in the commune. For instance, in the former role, the mayor controls the budget and other local matters including management of the natural environment and built heritage, the issuance of building permits, and other powers (Swift and Kervella 2003). As the state representative, the mayor serves as the registrar of births and deaths, registrar and officiant of marriages, and is an officer of the police judiciare who is entitled to exercise special powers in connection with controlling crime (Swift and Kervella 2003). Thus, in contrast to the dual state nature of the Anglo model, the French model is characterized by a fusion of the central and local state with the mayor as a sort of linchpin. The mayor's actions as representative of the central state are subject to review by the prefect, to whom the mayor is subordinate, as well as to review by the court (Swift and Kervella 2003).

Although decentralization has occurred in France, comparative data suggests that even in the mid-2000s local governments in France and other Franco countries had less responsibility for social services, less financial autonomy, and tended to spend less than municipalities in other European countries as a percentage of their country's GPD (Bäck, Heinfelt, and Magnier 2006, 28–9).

In addition to French local governments' distinctive role of representing local communities to the centre in the form of the prefect (who continues to represent the central state in the departments), the practice of *cumul des mandate*, which involves holding multiple elected offices at multiple levels of government simultaneously, has been a widespread practice in France. In 1991, Hesse and Sharpe noted that the control of the central state over local government is only formal because, in practice, local governments exert a great deal of influence via either multiple office holding (*cumul des mandats*) or party linkages (Hesse and Sharpe 1991, 606). Indeed, "in 1988 almost half the members of the National Assembly were also local mayors" (Mabileau 1994, 131, as quoted in Wollmann 2000, 42). This practice was limited by legal changes in 1985 and in the early 2000s (Dewoghélaëre, Berton, and Navarro 2006, 313). However, for our purposes, it is noteworthy that it is still possible to hold the office of MP and either an executive authority in a regional government or a mayoralty simultaneously (314).

North and Middle European Model

Scandinavian countries including Norway, Sweden, and Denmark have adopted a slightly different model. However, Hesse and Sharpe (1991) note that other countries share a great deal in common with the Scandinavian model and fit in this category more than the other two. In this group are Austria, Switzerland, Germany, the Netherlands, and Japan (due to its legal system, which is rooted in the Prussian tradition). This is the largest group in Hesse and Sharpe's typology of models of Western local government.

This model of local government is the most decentralized of the categories, combining a strong political and democratic role for municipalities with significant functional responsibilities for service delivery (Hesse and Sharpe 1991, 607). Local government possesses a "strong constitutional status" and "high degrees of policy-making autonomy and financial independence" (607). Municipalities in this category are granted general spheres of authority in addition to specifically enumerated statutory powers (607). In terms of functions, North European municipalities have taken on a greater role in social policy and the delivery of welfare state functions than municipalities in the Anglo and Franco categories (607). Hesse and Sharpe also note an "importance attached to strict procedural rules governing intergovernmental relations" in these countries (607). Bäck, Heinelt, and Magnier (2006) confirm that Northern European countries tend to have greater responsibility for social service provision and greater financial autonomy, and tend to spend more as a percentage of their country's GDP than other models (Bäck, Heinelt, and Magnier 2006, 28–9).

Summarizing and Evaluating the Three Models

How one evaluates the strengths and weaknesses of these models (whose key elements are shown in table 2.1) depends most fundamentally on one's conception of the purpose and potential of local government. As discussed above, the Anglo model is underpinned by a conception of the municipality as a public corporation whose mission is to provide services "efficiently" (Magnusson 1986). Historically, this conception has downplayed the democratic elements of local government in some Anglo countries and limited their role and autonomy when ideas about the scale at which services are most efficiently delivered changed. For instance, as we will see below, in the late nineteenth and early twentieth centuries the local state was seen as the primary arena of government activity. However, as the welfare state developed, ideas about the efficiency of service provision changed, leading either to centralization to the provincial level or to a reconceptualization of municipalities as service delivery "corporations" on behalf of the central (provincial) state (Magnusson 1986). We also see this logic in the imposition of amalgamations upon municipalities even when they went against the democratic will of local communities. The dominant rationale underlying this model informs their constitutional status as "creatures of statutes" that can be changed by a sovereign parliament. Functional and financial autonomy would logically vary through time as well, depending on what is considered the most efficient way of delivering services. The dual polity model characterizes Anglo arrangements, meaning that levels of formal multilevel coordination are low. This model of each level of government pursuing its own areas of responsibility may create clear lines of accountability, but as policy-making has become increasingly complex in a global and urban world, institutional mechanisms that encourage collaboration and the emergence of "multilevel governance" or even a gentler form of "metagovernance" (discussed further in chapter 4) have become more common. Patterns of multilevel politics and collaboration vary through time taking different forms and embodying different types of power relations.

Table 2.1. The Main Features of Three Models of Western Local Government

Model	Anglo	Franco	Northern European
Primary purpose	Service efficiency	Political representation	Self-government
Constitutional status	Creatures of a statute	Exists	Strong
Functional responsibilities/decentralization	Medium	Low	High
Financial autonomy	Medium	Low	High
Intergovernmental integration (administrative and political)	Low	High	High

The French local government model offers strong and integrated political representation and administration. However, the model is typically highly centralized, potentially undermining true local self-government. Historically, formal power was very top-down, concentrated in an unelected civil servant, the prefect. In such a system, local influence likely depended on the size of the commune and the mayor's leadership and ability to convey local service needs to the central state (as represented by the prefect) instead of being subject to direct local decision-making. To the extent that one values centralization and common service standards, this model might be the most conducive to such ends. One might also consider strong local representation in the National Assembly as a strength of this model since it could mean that all state decisions consider local, place-based concerns to a greater extent.

Finally, the Northern and Middle European model stands out as ideal if one values strong local democratic institutions and decentralization. As Hesse and Sharpe (1991) suggest, European countries appeared to be moving in that direction in 1991 – toward more decentralized forms of local government that value local democracies and the principle of local self-government. Specifically, they mention changes in the Franco group "where tutelage [i.e., top-down supervision of local government from the centre] seems to be in slow retreat and where the functional capacities of local government appear to be gaining prominence" (608). With decentralization of responsibility for services, and a historically strong political role for local representatives, especially mayors, there are signs of convergence with municipalities in the North and Middle European category. However, they notably describe municipalities in the Anglo category as the only ones that do not experience a "golden age" of municipal government characterized by decentralization and intergovernmental partnership (619–20).

THE GLOBAL SOUTH AND THE SOUTH AFRICAN CASE

However, Ran Hirschl's (2020b) *City, State* casts doubt on the extent to which any Western country's constitution truly enable local self-government for cities and, therefore, questions the ultimate significance of the distinctions made above. His central thesis is that the constitutions of Western countries (or so-called Global North countries) are characterized by constitutional "stagnation" in the face of massive urbanization and that it is countries in the Global South that have become the innovators in this area. He argues that constitutions that were enacted between the late eighteenth century and the 1970s do not recognize cities as "a fully-fledged order of government" but rather "their *constitutional* statuses range from secondary to non-existent" (Hirschl 2020a, 5). This relationship is true in federal, unitary countries as well as those that have experienced devolution (Hirschl 2020a). Although attempts have been made to reform Western laws and constitutions in recent decades, he notes that they have either failed or simply have not been transformative. In Anglo countries for instance, reforms have been attempted and have either failed entirely (in Australia in 1974, 1988, and 2013) or failed to change the status of local governments in cities in fundamental ways. In another example, Hirschl describes the Greater London Authority Act (1999) and the UK Cities and Local Government Devolution Act (2016) as "more of an administrative and fiscal devolution trend than a constitutional transformation" (Hirschl 2020a, 8). The influence of the centralization of authority in a parliament that informs this constitutional tradition appears to continue to reign in Anglo countries.

Although there are many examples of innovation in countries in the Global South, according to Hirschl (2020a, 2020b), South Africa's Constitution is the most successful example of the constitutional empowerment of cities. Article 40 of the South African Constitution establishes three orders of government, stating that "government is constituted as national, provincial, and local spheres of government which are distinctive, interdependent and interrelated." Then, in chapter 7 (s. 151–64), municipalities' constitutional status and municipal systems are elaborated. Their status in s. 151 is described as follows:

1   The local sphere of government consists of municipalities, which must be established for the whole of the territory of the Republic.
2   The executive and legislative authority of a municipality is vested in its Municipal Council.
3   A municipality has the right to govern, on its own initiatives, the local government affairs of its community subject to national and provincial legislation, as provided for in the Constitution.
4   The national or a provincial government may not compromise or impede a municipality's ability or right to exercise its powers or perform its functions. (South Africa 1996)

Although national and provincial legislatures continue to play a role in defining the types of municipalities within the country and in provinces (within three constitutionally entrenched categories), parliaments (both national and sub-national) are no longer supreme in relation to municipalities since they are protected in constitutional law that is supreme and only alterable through a constitutional amending process. This transformation was confirmed by court interpretation (Hirschl 2020b, 130). As discussed in the next section, in Canada, the supremacy of provincial parliaments continues to govern the provincial-municipal relationship, a constitutional situation that relies on convention and politics rather than law to uphold the principle of local democracy.

CANADIAN MUNICIPAL SYSTEMS: THE CONSTITUTIONAL BASICS

Canada is a federation. In federal systems, a central government (the federal government in Canada) and subunits (the provinces in Canada) rule jointly through institutions and a division of power that provides for local self-rule and for shared rule; the autonomy of subunits is protected constitutionally in a written constitution that establishes the division of powers, and courts are tasked with settling disputes between governments; provision is made for the representation of the subunits in the central institutions of government (usually in a Senate), and an amending formula (or formulas in the case of Canada) protects subunits from unilateral constitutional change by the federal government to either the division of power or the structure of central (federal) political institutions (Smith 2004, 15).[3] Federations are also generally territorial in nature (the political units are land-based, geographic units with territorial boundaries) (15).

As democratically elected, multi-purpose governmental bodies that pass laws (called by-laws), raise taxes, and offer a wide range of services, municipalities share a great deal in common with provinces. However, like municipalities in other Anglo democracies, municipalities' status as an independent order of government is not recognized in the federal Constitution. Instead, municipal institutions are a legislative responsibility assigned exclusively to provinces in the Constitution Act, 1867, which establishes Canada as a federal system of government with a constitutionally protected division of legislative power. Although the Constitution is more complex, this act, along with the Constitution Act, 1982, is widely considered to be the "Constitution" in Canada. These acts are *entrenched*, meaning that they cannot be changed through ordinary legislative process (a majority vote in a legislature) but rather are subject to more onerous constitutional amending formulas. They are higher laws that trump regular statutes in the event of a conflict. The crucial point here though is that, although three orders of government are mentioned in the Constitution, only two orders of government possess autonomous, entrenched (subject to a constitutional amendment process rather than the ordinary legislative process) powers – the federal government and the provinces. Municipal institutions are mentioned, but not as a separate order of government (as they are, for instance, in the South African case discussed above). Instead, they appear as a "head of power," in other words, a legislative responsibility of provinces. More specifically, in s. 92 (8) provinces are given exclusive jurisdiction over municipal institutions, and therefore only provinces (not the federal government) may "create" municipal systems and have exclusive authority over municipalities.

The incorporation of municipalities (recall that municipalities are public corporations) and the design of municipal systems (including the division of power and service responsibilities as well as taxation power) are left to the provinces to establish through legislation. Another way of putting this is that municipal responsibilities are *delegated and statutory* rather than constitutionally entrenched or protected. Thus, from a constitutional-legal perspective, municipalities are completely subordinate to provincial legislatures and subject to the principle of parliamentary supremacy that limits municipal authority in all Anglo countries.

In Hesse and Sharpe's (1991) typology, Anglo systems are described as providing significant autonomy to municipalities in their areas of service responsibility, which reflects the dual state or dual polity principle. Currently, municipal systems are overseen by a minister in provincial governments as well as a department tasked with overseeing municipal affairs in each province. However, according to Stéfan Dupré, municipalities are not entirely subordinate to provinces. He coined the term "hyper-fractionalized quasi-subordination" to describe provincial-municipal power relations in Canada (Dupré 1967). According to him, municipal systems are hyper-fractionalized given the high number of municipalities but only quasi-subordinate to provinces despite their lack of constitutional status because provincial ministries cannot (or are not institutionally equipped) to supervise them all in detail (unlike the historic prefects in France whose job it was to supervise local governments in a specific region). However, the extent to which the parliament and local government's relationship is characterized by hierarchy varies through time (history), place (geographic location), and service area. One could argue that Canadian municipalities do indeed possess significant degrees of autonomy because significant powers are delegated to them. Furthermore, the fact that urban municipalities have begun to act and innovate in areas outside of their formal areas of responsibility (to address immigrant integration, climate change and the decolonization of cities for instance) shows the degrees of freedom they have in Canada's government system. As we discover in the following sections, the levels of provincial control and subordination of municipalities to provinces have varied through time and, indeed, vary across provinces.

THE ROOTS AND BROAD EVOLUTION OF CANADA'S MUNICIPAL SYSTEMS

Although the constitutional-legal system reflects underlying values and shapes the evolution of municipal systems in important ways, these structures are dynamic and have changed considerably over time in reaction to social, economic, and political changes. This section demonstrates that Canadian municipalities possessed significant autonomy in the mid-nineteenth century, when municipal systems were first enacted, and into the early twentieth century. Canadian municipalities' legal basis in provincial statutes has meant that provinces have sometimes intervened in municipal affairs in reaction to municipal financial crises and, at others, have devised reforms proactively with specific policy preferences and political motivations.

The Contested Place of Municipalities in Late Nineteenth-Century Canada and the Baldwin Act Precedent

In the eighteenth and early nineteenth centuries, Canadian colonial authorities initially discouraged the establishment of local governments, taking the lesson from the United States Revolution that "local self-government" was the "seedbed of disloyalty"[4] (Taylor 2019, 48). Indeed, the fear of local government led Nova Scotia to pass a resolution in 1770 making all town meetings illegal (Bourinot 1887; Isin 1992). Engin Isin (1992, 101) also notes an early antagonism toward towns due to their potential to create "different and undesirable loyalties and de facto citizenship practices among the settlers." This fear of the revolutionary potential of cities was in tension with a desire for orderly and compact (rather than dispersed) settlement to ensure obedience to the state. Isin (1992, 141) describes the contradictory goals animating the early establishment of municipal government as a desire for "cities without citizens."

Thus, opposition to local government changed in the 1830s and 1840s as the British began to recognize the importance of municipalities to the effective settlement and governance of the British colonies and to instilling British political principles (Isin 1992; Taylor 2019, 48). Reformers in Upper Canada (now Ontario) had tried to pass municipal legislation in the early nineteenth century but were resisted by a network of influential Tories who governed the colony called the Family Compact (Côte and Fenn 2014, 5). A key turning point came when Lord Durham was commissioned to report on the state of affairs in the colonies within the context of the Rebellions of 1837–8 in Upper and Lower Canada against the oligarchic government. Although Lord Durham is perhaps best known in Canada for recommending a Union Government and introducing responsible government – a government (cabinet) that is responsible to and drawn from a democratically elected legislature and that could be removed by it if it lost its confidence – he was also a proponent of municipal government, a more controversial issue at the time. Lord Durham believed that opposition became polarized in a centralized system. Municipal institutions were thought to provide an outlet for a diversity of views and an incentive to settle in communities rather than in unorganized, scattered ways (Isin 1992). Ultimately, the rebellions resulted in significant democratic reform, including the introduction of responsible government, guarantees of freedom of the press, and "quasi-democratic" local government because the franchise was limited to property owners (Higgins 1991, 51).

After a failed attempt to include municipal government in the Union Act itself, the newly established Union Government considered municipal legislation soon after its inception (Isin 1992, 163–4). The first general-purpose municipal act, the Baldwin Act, was enacted in 1849 (Taylor 2019, 49). In the past, the incorporation of and delegation of power to municipalities had been done through special rather than general legislation (or other legal mechanisms such as royal charters),[5] in other words, through legislation that applied to a single municipality rather than all municipalities (Taylor 2019, 49).

The Baldwin Act consolidated municipal legislation into one general act. It created a system of counties as upper-tier municipalities and distinguished between urban (villages, towns, and cities were considered urban units of municipal government) and rural municipalities (called townships) (Tindal and Tindal 2000, 34). The Pre-Confederation Baldwin Act, which would be emulated across Canada, also established the "dual state" model that some argue characterizes local government in the Anglo model, whereby municipalities are granted autonomy in their own spheres of jurisdiction and are not subject to central control. K.G. Crawford describes the nature of municipal autonomy after the enactment of the Baldwin Act: "Within the scope allowed, and the scope was extensive, the municipalities had gained the right to local self-government with a minimum of parliamentary or executive control, the elected representatives being answerable in matters of policy to their electors and in matters of law to the courts" (Crawford 1954, 32). Similarly, as Zack Taylor puts it, with the passage of the Baldwin Act, of 1849, "Ontario municipalities, large and small, urban and rural, largely went their own way within the strictures of the general law, and the principle of local autonomy became well accepted" (2019, 49).

From Local Autonomy to Provincial Engagement in Municipal Affairs

Nevertheless, the history of provincial-municipal relations in Canada since the Baldwin Act might be summarized as "a pattern of increasing supervision, influence and control" (Tindal and Tindal 2000, 209). Manitoba (1886), Saskatchewan (1908), and Alberta (1911) established departments of municipal affairs to oversee municipalities at the turn of the century. These departments were designed "to give leadership and guidance in municipal development and to provide for the continuous study of the problems of municipalities" (Crawford 1954). British Columbia (1934), Ontario (1935), Nova Scotia (1935), and New Brunswick (1936) established such departments in the 1930s after incremental steps in that direction.

The Depression of the 1930s was a major turning point in provincial-municipal relations, reflecting a period when municipalities lost their financial independence and their historical place in the area of social services (Tindal and Tindal 2000). Municipalities had borrowed irresponsibly in the 1920s and a significant proportion of municipal debt was in default by the early to mid-1930s (Hillhouse 1936, as cited in Côté and Fenn 2014, 7). This led Ontario to establish a minister of Municipal Affairs and an associated department in 1935 (Crawford 1954, loc. 6418). Thus, one of the central functions of these departments was to control municipal finances. Others took on roles in zoning and assessment (Tindal and Tindal 2000, 210). In Nova Scotia, all bylaws were made subject to the minister of Municipal Affairs, and in Quebec, the Lieutenant-Governor-in-Council was authorized to disallow any bylaw (210). Across the provinces, a variety of bylaws were made subject to the approval of a provincial authority of some type and control grew to include staff and employment standards (210). Quasi-judicial boards were created to supervise municipalities, such as the Ontario Municipal Board in 1932. These boards were empowered to govern a variety of matters, from financial decisions (to approve the issuing of debt or to investigate a municipality's financial affairs) to zoning bylaws, and others (Crawford 1954, loc. 6580). By the mid-1930s, provinces' administrative control and supervision were far-reaching (loc. 6580).

Municipalities and the Rise of the Welfare State

In the late nineteenth and early twentieth centuries, municipalities were the main actors in social policy – they were the "primordial home of the welfare state in Canada" (Haddow 2002, 91). Although, at that time, the concept of social policy or the "welfare state" was limited. Still, municipalities in many provinces were either the main providers of "relief" (limited, means-tested, and last-resort benefits) to the poor or did so in combination with charities as in Ontario and in the Western provinces, where charities played a more limited role (Haddow 2002, 91). When social security became conceived more broadly and not only as a temporary measure (but as a social entitlement as part of a "welfare state"), municipalities were poorly equipped to lead in the area because standards were necessary (only possible at larger scales), and they were reliant on property taxes.

Power was highly centralized during the Second World War (1939–45), at which point Ottawa took on powers similar to a unitary state under the emergency powers of the War Measures Act (Simeon and Robinson 2004, 110). In 1941, the provinces signed "tax rental" agreements with the federal government, surrendering their (and by extension, municipalities') ability to raise income taxes. Indeed, municipalities were not always excluded from the income tax – at the end of the 1930s all provinces had some form of municipal income tax in place and poll taxes (or head taxes) were also allowed in every province (Tindal et al. 2017, 204). The federation was centralized as the federal government used its "spending power" (a name for its controversial, constitutional power to spend money in areas outside of its legislative jurisdiction) to fund postwar recovery and to build the welfare state through cost-shared programs with the provinces by providing fifty cents of every dollar spent in exchange for meeting federal standards.

In this period, provinces took over services that municipalities had "outgrown" (based on their own-source revenues – mainly property taxes). According to Tindal and Tindal (2000, 211): "This pattern of responsibilities shifting upward to more senior levels occurred with respect to such matters as roads, assessment, the administration of justice, education, public health, and social services." Municipalities' reliance on property taxes made them particularly ill-equipped to take on responsibilities related to social policy. Haddow summarizes the declining municipal role in social policy in this period: "The municipal share of health and social expenditures by all levels of government, which had been 54 per cent in 1913, fell to 20 per cent in 1930, and to 15 per cent in 1940" (Guest 1980, as cited in Haddow 2002, 93). This trend continued into the 1950s and 1960s (Tindal and Tindal 2000; Haddow 2002). The cumulative impact of processes of provincial "takeover" of services and supervision of municipalities resulted in a great deal of overlap between governments or "entanglement." Beginning in the 1960s (with New Brunswick's Bryne Commission in 1963 and its result – the Program for Equal Opportunity), debates began about how to "disentangle" provincial-municipal responsibilities and which services were most appropriately governed at the local level (Tindal and Tindal 2000, 212–13). This led to service reorganizations and exchanges in several provinces. By the mid-1990s, the municipal share of income assistance and related social services had declined further – it fell to 5 per cent (Haddow 2002, 96). However, the bulk of income assistance spending at the municipal level was happening in two provinces at that time – Ontario (12 per cent) and Nova Scotia (11 per cent). Municipalities in other provinces spent less than 1 per cent of total spending among the three levels of government (96).

Municipal Exclusion from Major Constitutional Negotiations and Accords

The 1960s ushered in an era of intense constitutional debate prompted in part by Quebec's Quiet Revolution and Quebec nationalism. However, other fundamental changes were also taking place, including increasing urbanization. Within this context, municipalities' need for money for increasing service responsibilities led to a greater recognition of a need for a federal-local relationship. A minister of state for Urban Affairs and a Ministry of Urban Affairs were established for a brief period in the 1970s. The Federation of Canadian Municipalities advocated for constitutional recognition of municipalities in the 1970s and 1980s leading up to Patriation[6] without success (Tindal and Tindal 2000). Quebec's refusal to consent to Patriation led to two more major rounds of negotiations that ultimately failed, ushering in an era of decentralization and purported "collaborative federalism." Municipal constitutional recognition was not considered seriously in these rounds. The general thrust of proposed constitutional reforms was highly decentralist after Patriation; nevertheless, decentralization stopped at the provinces. In fact, the Charlottetown Accord, which was rejected by the public in a referendum in 1992, would have strengthened provinces' exclusivity in municipal affairs by clarifying that *urban affairs* (arguably distinct from "municipal institutions") were provincial rather than federal jurisdiction.

Neo-liberalism and Decentralization in the "Collaborative" Period of the Canadian Federation

After the period of federalism focused on large-scale constitutional change, decentralization was enacted politically with the emergence of rules-based intergovernmental relations dubbed collaborative federalism by federalism scholars (Cameron and Simeon 2002). This form of federalism was in part a response to Quebec nationalism, such as in the virtual tie of the "Yes" and "No" sides in the sovereignty-partnership referendum held in Quebec in 1995. One thrust of collaborative federalism was to attempt to show Quebec that the Constitution could be made workable through "non-constitutional" and pragmatic responses to its fundamental constitutional concerns.

Nevertheless, decentralization was also influenced by neo-liberal ideas. Writing in 2002, Yasmeen Abu-Laban and Christina Gabriel (2002, 21) describe "neo-liberal" as "a catch-all" term "signalling a set of assumptions – frequently presented as common-sense truths" including "a more limited role for the state and, consequently, an emphasis on cutting back state policies and programs; a greater stress on individual self-sufficiency; and a belief that free markets are efficient allocators of goods and services." Neo-liberalism privileges "competitiveness, efficiency, choice and consumerism" as values that ought to guide policy-making (21). This ideational environment contributed to a significant reduction of federal transfers to provinces and then from provinces to municipalities in what Graham, Phillips, and Maslove (1998) characterize as a process of tri-level "downloading" (Graham, Phillips, and Maslove 1998, 174). Specifically, downloading involved increased municipal financial responsibility for service delivery and the need to address the impacts of cutbacks in services offered by other levels of government, which were increasingly apparent in cities (174). As discussed further in chapter 12, municipalities in Canada's largest cities, where most immigrants settled, also began taking on new roles in areas such as immigrant integration as these places experienced dramatic social and cultural transformations (Good 2009). The 1995 federal budget that combined federal transfers in health and various areas of social policy into a single transfer (The Canada Health and Social Policy transfer) and reduced it dramatically constituted a critical juncture in that decade. Provincial and federal transfers to municipalities declined "from 45.7 percent of municipal government revenues in 1990 to 25.4 percent in 1994, to only 17.9 percent in 2000" (Tindal et al. 2017, 182). It was within this post-constitutional and neo-liberal context that provinces began to delegate more permissive legislation to municipalities, beginning in the mid-1990s with Alberta's Municipal Act (discussed further below). Although municipal acts became more permissive legally and emphasized the democratic significance of municipalities to a greater degree, significant financial tools are strikingly absent from these laws. Thus, legal efforts to strengthen local democracy by empowering municipalities were limited by the rise of neo-liberal ideas that would limit public spending.

The 1990s and 2000s also witnessed a new wave of reforms in the form of municipal amalgamations, often forced. The stated rationales for these reforms varied but frequently included cost-savings and service efficiency considerations reflecting contemporary neo-liberal policy ideas as well as illustrating Warren Magnusson's (1996) point (discussed above) about the centrality of efficiency considerations in Anglo systems and the damaging effects of this principle on local democracy. Although ideas concerning what amalgamations might achieve varied, Andrew Sancton (2006) argues that a commonality among three controversial amalgamations in major cities in Canada in this period (Halifax, Montreal, and Toronto) is that the province acted autonomously (in other words, in the absence of pressure from organized interests). Indeed, in the case of Metro Toronto, the province imposed the amalgamation of this two-tiered structure in 1998 in the face of sustained resistance among citizens who organized as the C4LD – Citizens for Local Democracy (Horak 1998). The amalgamation was also subject to a court challenge by affected municipalities and citizens. This case confirmed the continued relevance of the constitutional doctrine of municipalities as "creatures of the provinces" to the state of local democracy in Canada. The Ontario Superior Court Decision articulated this doctrine in a simple, direct way:

> (i) municipal institutions lack constitutional status; (ii) municipal institutions are creatures of the legislature and exist only if provincial legislation so provides; (iii) municipal institutions have no independent autonomy and their powers are subject to abolition or repeal by provincial legislation; (iv) municipal institutions may exercise only those powers which are conferred upon them by statute. (East York [Borough] v. Ontario [Attorney General] 1997)

More recently, this constitutional doctrine was upheld by the Supreme Court of Canada when the province's decision to reduce the City of Toronto's wards by almost half in the middle of the 2018 election campaign was challenged all the way to Canada's highest court. The Supreme Court found in favour of the province. However, in what could signify a possible shift in jurisprudence, a substantial minority (four out of nine justices) dissented and, indeed, endorsed the notion that municipalities are more than "creatures of the provinces" (Toronto [city] v. Ontario [Attorney General], 2021, para. 116).

Thus, the provincial-municipal relationship has changed through time with an initial, though short-lived, period of municipal autonomy in the post-Baldwin Act period, followed by increased supervision and financial control through provincial administration, uploading, and conditional grants in the post–Second World War recovery period and as the welfare state emerged. Then, in the 1990s, the pendulum swung to decentralization informed by ideas about collaborative federalism and neo-liberalism leading to tensions in trends in intergovernmental relations, including legal decentralization (with few financial tools), downloading, as well as fundamental reforms to municipal institutions that were sometimes justified as cost-saving measures.

COMPARISONS WITH MUNICIPALITIES' CONSTITUTIONAL-LEGAL STATUS IN ANGLO DEMOCRACIES

Municipalities' subordinate legal status as "creatures" or creations of statutes enacted by a constitutionally recognized and legally "superior" government is common to municipalities in Anglo countries. As we will see in the next section, although the extent of legal autonomy these governments delegate to municipalities and how that authority is granted to municipalities *vary in arguably significant ways*, ultimately they are all vulnerable to intervention by the central government (national, provincial, or state).

Unlike in Canada, local government is not mentioned in Australia's 1901 Constitution. Nevertheless, local governments are recognized in *state constitutions* but are not *entrenched* because they can be changed through a state statute rather than a referendum, which is required for changes to the federal constitution (Sansom 2009). Sub-national constitutional recognition is weak in Australia – states do not recognize specific local powers and one state's constitution (New South Wales) does not even guarantee elected local government (Sansom 2009, 12). Furthermore, like Canada, the principle of parliamentary supremacy is central to Australia's constitutional tradition. An attempt to entrench what Sansom calls "symbolic recognition" of local government in Australia's federal constitution failed in 1988.[7] The proposed statement was as follows: "Each state shall provide for the establishment and continuance of a system of local government, with local government bodies elected in accordance with the laws of the State and empowered to administer, and to make by-laws for, their respective areas in accordance with the laws of the state" (Sansom 2009, 13). Although modest, this statement arguably would have ensured that states could not simply chose not to provide for democratically elected local governmental bodies which, according to many, is not guaranteed in Anglo systems, even in large urban centres.

In some ways, municipalities' status in the United States is distinct because of its divided authority model and reliance on distinct, consolidated written constitutions at both the federal and state levels. Like Australia, the responsibility for local government/municipalities is not written into the American Constitution; it is part of states' residual authority (the authority leftover from what is contained in the federal government's list of heads of power).

In the United States, states are strong and municipalities are fundamentally "creatures of the states." However, American states have pursued various ways of organizing governing authority for local government that fall into two broad categories: home rule and "Dillon's Rule" (Russell and Bostrom 2016). The former grants local governments broad authority to legislate in areas not addressed by state governments, whereas in states following Dillon's Rule, local governments (municipalities) can only legislate in areas of authority that have been explicitly granted to them in state legislation. Dillon's Rule has been influential in Canada although less so in recent decades. As discussed below, the rule has even been cited by the Supreme Court of Canada (R. v. Greenbaum [1993]).

What is Dillon's Rule? The rule stems from the Iowa Supreme Court and decisions made by Judge Dillon in the late nineteenth century (1869–79). The rule is laid out clearly in the court's opinion in *City of Clinton v. Cedar Rapids*:

> A municipal corporation possesses and can exercise the following powers and no others; first, those granted in express words; second, those necessarily implied or necessarily incident to the power expressly granted; third, those absolutely essential to the declared objects and purposes of the corporation – not simply convenient but indispensable; and fourth, any fair doubt as to the existence of the power is resolved by the courts against the corporation. (City of Clinton v. Cedar Rapids and the Missouri River Rail Company 1884)

For Judge Dillon, local governments were not "equal or separate from state government" – they were subordinate "political subdivisions of the state" (Russell and Bostrom 2016, 2). The United

States Supreme Court endorsed this rule in a decision in the early twentieth century, stating that "municipal Corporations owe their origin to, and derive their powers and rights wholly from, the legislature. It breathes into them the breath of life, without which it cannot exist" (Hunter v. Pittsburgh 1907). Almost one hundred years later, the *East York* (1997) decision discussed above echoes this early twentieth-century depiction of municipalities' place in the American governmental system.

In the United States, local governments' rightful place in the governmental system is contested, and another rule is also employed – home rule. Advocates of home rule view local government as a separate order of government (instead of a subordinate political subdivision of states). The notion of home rule finds support in an alternative doctrine, the Cooley Doctrine, after Judge Thomas McIntyre Cooley, a justice in the Michigan Supreme Court. Judge Cooley articulated a view of local governments as possessing an inherent right to self-government in an important case in 1871. The case in question involves a decision on the part of the State of Michigan to appoint a permanent board to govern public works in the City of Detroit. In the decision, Cooley agreed that it was in the authority of the state to create the local government machinery or "provide for and put into motion" but not to run it (People ex rel. Leroy v. Hurlbut 1871). According to Cooley, the issue arising in this case was as follows:

> The question broadly and nakedly stated can be nothing short of this: Whether local self-government in this state is or is not a mere privilege, conceded by the legislature in its discretion, and which may be withdrawn at any time at pleasure? (People ex rel. Leroy v. Hurlbut 1871)

His answer was the following:

> The state may mould local institutions according to its views of policy and expediency: but local government is a matter of absolute right; and the state cannot take it away. It would be the boldest mockery to speak of a city as possessing municipal liberty where the state not only shaped its government, but at discretion sent its own agents to administer it; or to call that system one of constitutional freedom under which it should be equally admissible to allow the people full control in their local affairs, or no control at all. (People ex rel. Leroy v. Hurlbut 1871)

Thus, two very different rules have influenced how grants of authority are made to local governments in the United States. Most fundamentally, home rule establishes a right for local government to exist – it is a "matter of absolute right" as articulated by Cooley above.

Beyond this basic right, what is home rule in practice? Home rule has two primary components – first, it affects the security of municipal boundaries and the structure of their political institutions by, for instance, requiring the consent of affected municipalities for changes to their boundaries and structures (Sancton 2015, 336); second, it influences the way in which authority is delegated to municipalities by American states. Rather than looking for express authority in state legislation (an exhaustive and detailed list of permissible areas of action and legislation), municipalities in home rule states can act more broadly in any area not prohibited by state law (Tindal and Tindal 2009, 178).

Dillon's Rule versus Home Rule in the Canadian Context

How should we think about the scope of political action in Canadian cities in comparative perspective? One way to conceptualize the scope for municipal action is along a continuum with Dillon's Rule at one end and home rule at the other, noting that there is also a "mushy middle" between these two poles as a long-standing and popular textbook does (Tindal et al. 2017). Tindal and Tindal place all municipal grants of authority in Canada in the Dillon's Rule category or in the "mushy middle" in which the scope for municipal action is greater than Dillon's Rule would suggest and less than home rule would imply (Tindal and Tindal 2009, 178). We will first examine the influence of Dillon's Rule on Canadian (provincial) municipal legislation and then discuss the significance of recent legal changes, particularly whether they constitute a move toward home rule.

Most fundamentally, home rule involves an inherent right for local government to exist, a fundamental notion that is not accepted by dominant accounts of the legal status of Canadian municipalities. According to this line of thought, provinces could choose to abolish municipal systems entirely and offer services through a decentralized provincial administration instead. This option is not theoretical when it comes to some forms of elected local government (which, as discussed in chapter 1, is a broader term that includes municipalities, agencies, boards, and commissions that are local, some of which are elected). Some provinces have histories of either dismissing school boards and appointing an administrator in their place or abolishing them entirely (both have occurred in Nova Scotia, where English-language school boards were eliminated in 2018 with little public debate). Section 574 of Alberta's Municipal Government Act states that the province may declare "an order dismissing the council or any member of it or the chief administrative officer," if an inspection, report, or inquiry finds that the municipality has been mismanaged (Municipal Government Act, 2000). A *Calgary Herald* journalist suggested that this little known section should be used to dismiss the City of Calgary council for over-taxing businesses in 2019 (Braid 2019). The current Alberta government has introduced legislation that would strengthen its ability to remove councillors by ordering a vote on the matter (Government of Alberta, n.d.). Indeed, in Canada, some places do not have elected local government at all. They are referred to as "unincorporated" communities. Such communities tend to be sparsely populated and are perceived to lack the financial capacity to offer local services comparable to other communities.[8] All Canadian provinces have systems of elected municipal government (with exceptions made for unincorporated areas in some provinces). The precarious legal status of municipalities is common in commonwealth countries following the "Anglo" model of local government. For instance, as mentioned above, New South Wales in Australia does not guarantee elected municipal government in its state constitution, and a country-wide effort to recognize that states must establish democratically elected local governments failed in 1988. In his work challenging the doctrine of municipalities as "creatures of the provinces," Warren Magnusson (2005) argues that this doctrine implies that provinces could abolish municipal government in Canada.

Dillon's Rule has also influenced Canadian municipalities' legal status in more subtle ways. Provincial municipal acts contain rules concerning the functioning of municipal institutions and also grants of authority that delegate particular areas of service and legal authority to municipalities. However, there are a variety of ways that power can be delegated from a constitutionally recognized government (provinces in the Canadian case) to a legally subordinate one such as municipalities. Historically, the way in which provinces have tended to grant or delegate authority to municipalities has been in a highly constraining and controlling way, although this has changed in recent decades (since the mid-1990s in particular). Even though Dillon's Rule was first articulated and then reaffirmed in American court decisions, it has been influential in the way in which legal authority has been delegated to municipalities in Canada. Indeed, as late as 1993, a court ruling that invalidated a Toronto bylaw regulating vending permits for street vendors cites Dillon's Rule and equates the legal status of grants of authority to municipalities by provinces through this lens (R. v. Greenbaum [1993]).

Dillon's Rule reflects the concept of municipalities as "creatures of the provinces" rather than as an order of government. This rule has also influenced how authority is granted to municipalities through detailed lists in municipal legislation with the implication that anything beyond the list is impermissible. This is called a prescriptive approach, based on the "prescribed powers" doctrine, which can be contrasted with grants of authority to delegate broad spheres of jurisdiction to municipalities (similar to the broad areas of authority granted to governments in federal systems) (Levi and Valverde 2006, 427).

Theoretically, provinces could delegate any of their constitutional powers that are entrenched in the Constitution Act, 1867 to municipalities. They, of course, cannot delegate powers to municipalities that belong to the federal government. This implies that, since municipalities are created in provincial municipal legislation, each province could delegate very different powers to municipalities (and in different ways – following either a prescriptive approach or by granting broad "spheres of authority"). Nevertheless, although there is some variation, provinces across Canada have historically tended to delegate similar areas of authority to municipalities. Andrew Sancton (2009, 6) notes that with a couple of exceptions in Prince Edward Island, all municipalities (urban and rural) have at least some legal authority for the following areas: fire protection, animal control, roads, traffic control, solid-waste management and disposal, land-use planning and regulation, building regulation, economic development, tourism promotion, public libraries, parks and recreation, cultural facilities, licensing of businesses, emergency planning and preparedness, cemeteries, weed control and regulation of cosmetic pesticides, and others. Urban municipalities in Canadian municipal systems have been delegated additional functions for public transit, taxis, water purification and distribution, sewage collection and treatment, downtown revitalization, and regulation of noise as well as functions for policing (with the exception of Newfoundland and Labrador) (Sancton 2009, 6). A more recent study of the policy issues that municipal mayors and councillors consider the most important finds that planning and land use, water supply, roads, highways and bridges as well as economic development are the most important, "bread and butter issues"; emergency planning, parks and recreation, public health, solid waste, and policing are the next most important issues (Lucas and Smith 2019, 11). They also identify policy areas of particular importance to big cities, including immigrant settlement and poverty reduction – noting homelessness, arts and culture, housing, public transit, and climate change as growing issues (11). Interestingly, several of the areas of particular interest to urban municipalities are not specifically listed or necessarily implied by what is stated in provincial laws (e.g., immigrant settlement).

Although the above list of responsibilities is broad, Dillon's Rule has led provinces to list the details of the boundaries of each area of responsibility in significant detail in municipal legislation until recent changes to municipal legislation meant to empower municipalities were passed. The influence of Dillon's Rule persists, though, even in large cities. Take, for instance, municipalities' role in governing trees as defined in the Halifax Regional Municipality Charter (2008), a rather mundane task in some ways that one might think is straightforward. Nevertheless, even for such a responsibility, the power is not just given as a broad area of authority but rather is delegated precisely in s. 77, which includes twelve subsections with the following as examples. The general area of authority is called "Municipal powers respecting trees," itself a function that could have been collapsed under a broader area such as "management of the natural environment": The prescriptive list of powers continues as follows:

> 77 (1) The Municipality may (a) remove dead, dying or diseased trees on public and private property; (b) recommend and encourage (i) the proper pruning, protection and repair of privately owned trees in the Municipality, (ii) the planting of trees of suitable species at desirable sites within the Municipality. (2) The Municipality may not remove trees." (Halifax Regional Municipality Charter 2008, s. 77)

The fact that everything is listed implies that anything not on the list is impermissible. It reflects Dillon's Rule, which says that municipal grants of authority must be in "express words" or either "necessarily implied" or "absolutely essential" to the "declared objects and purposes of the corporation." A detailed list of powers has the advantage of making municipal authority clear, providing municipalities with confidence that their actions would not be found ultra vires (outside their legislative scope) by the courts if challenged. However, such lists set a general tone of constraint on municipal action. Under a Dillon's Rule regime, if municipalities want to enter a new field of authority, they must petition the legislature to enact amendments to the municipal legislation. According to Taylor (2019, 57–9), the legislative overload that this created was a contributing factor to the development of municipal boards and provincial ministries in the early twentieth century.

In contrast, consider the broad areas of jurisdiction granted to the federal and provincial governments in the Constitution Act, 1867, including the federal government's power to legislate in the area of "The Regulation of Trade and Commerce" (s. 91 (2)) or the provinces' jurisdiction in "Property and Civil Rights in the Province" (s. 92 (13)) as well as their broad jurisdiction to raise taxes.

Changing Municipal Legislation in Canada

Although this prescriptive approach was the norm, beginning with Alberta's Municipal Government Act in 1994, provinces began experimenting with legal ways to empower municipalities. A few broad trends can be observed in municipal delegation of authority, including a tendency toward more permissive rather than prescriptive ways to delegate authority to them. One fundamental approach that has been adopted is a move to delegate broad spheres of authority that are similar in breadth to "heads of power" in a federal constitution. These areas of authority are then supplemented with more limited lists of express (Dillon's Rule style) authority (Taylor and Dobson 2020, 16–17). Spheres of power were first adopted in Alberta and now exist in eight provinces, excluding Nova Scotia and Newfoundland and Labrador (17–19).

British Columbia's Community Charter (2003), which is its general municipal legislation, is arguably the most progressive in the country.[9] It establishes spheres of jurisdiction called "fundamental powers" in the legislation instead of listing express powers. Subsection 8 (3) empowers a council to enact bylaws to "regulate, prohibit and impose requirements in relation to" a variety of important areas including, notably "(i) public health" and the "(j) protection of the natural environment" (Community Charter 2003, s. 8). To use the example of trees again, the power appears simply as "trees" (s. 8 (3)c). These spheres of jurisdiction are broad like the federal and provincial heads of power.

Another legal concept that is associated with greater municipal permissiveness is "natural persons powers," which allows corporations to do what an individual person can do. This includes making staffing decisions, entering into contracts with other corporations for services, as well as purchasing and selling land, buildings, and other assets (Tindal et al. 2017, 145). As Tindal and others note, this power is not new, but without the power of a "natural person," municipalities had to find *express authority* in legislation to do them (i.e., these powers had to be explicitly stated or implied in legislation following Dillon's Rule). This power is included in legislation in eight provinces (but does not necessarily apply to all municipalities in these provinces), excluding Nova Scotia and Newfoundland and Labrador (Taylor and Dobson 2020, 20).

Finally, all provinces except Newfoundland and Labrador have granted municipalities a "general welfare power," granting municipalities the power to act to further the well-being and safety of their residents (Taylor and Dobson 2020, 14) as well as the power to expropriate private land either as a sphere of jurisdiction or an expressed power and with different levels of supervision (22–3). Theoretically, general powers could confer a great deal of power on municipalities if the courts interpreted them broadly. The courts, however, tend to take the entire tone of legislation into account and have begun to interpret legislation more permissively as provinces have loosened their legal grip on municipalities.

There is further evidence of incremental shifts toward home rule in some provincial legislation. For instance, some provinces have legislated commitments to consult municipalities on changes to their enabling legislation. Examples of such legislation include the City of Toronto Act (2006) and British Columbia's Community Charter (2003). However, this legislation existed when the Ford government imposed restructuring of ward boundaries on the City of Toronto during its 2018 municipal election, arguing that the city council had become "dysfunctional" and "gridlocked" because of its size and incapable of making decisions about infrastructure and other important matters (Ford 2018). This example shows the limits of such commitments if provinces are committed to imposing their legislative will and flexing their constitutional muscles.

Although rare, there are also examples of provinces providing municipalities legal autonomy concerning their political institutions, including their electoral systems and boundaries. For instance, until recently, Ontario's Municipal Elections Act, s. 41.1 allowed municipalities to experiment with alternative electoral systems (including the ranked ballots which were implemented in the City of London, Ontario). This constituted an incremental move toward the "home rule" principle. The Ontario provincial government under Doug Ford recently rescinded that section of the legislation, forcing even those cities that had already moved to ranked ballots (such as the City of London) to return to the "first past the post" or "single member plurality" model.

British Columbia's Community Charter (2003) goes beyond Dillon's Rule in important respects. For instance, it limits the province's ability to impose amalgamations on municipalities in British Columbia:

No forced amalgamations

279 If a new municipality would include 2 or more existing municipalities, letters patent incorporating the new municipality may not be issued unless

(a) a vote has been taken in accordance with section 4 of the *Local Government Act* separately in each of the existing municipalities, and

b) for each of those municipalities, more than 50% of the votes counted as valid favour the proposed incorporation. (Community Charter 2003, s. 279)

This legislation is exceptional though. This is the only act to require municipal (and public) approval of amalgamation. In all other cases, amalgamation can be imposed by the minister. This limitation on provincial authority to impose amalgamations on municipalities is a "manner and form" limitation on the British Columbia legislature's ability to impose amalgamation.

This is a self-imposed limitation on a legislature's ability to legislate in the future, in this case a requirement that referendums be held and receive the support of at least 50 per cent of the population of affected municipalities before legislation implementing an amalgamation could be introduced into its Legislative Assembly. Although the legal status of such restrictions is uncertain given the importance of parliamentary supremacy to Canada's constitutional tradition, recent constitutional thought suggests that they could act as a form of limited constitutional entrenchment in parliamentary systems. Kristin Good (2019) argues that they could be a key to recognizing and securing municipalities' place within provincial constitutions. The enactment of such restrictions would constitute a form of home rule.

Thus, although standard accounts place all Canadian municipalities in the category of Dillon's Rule, there is also evidence of movement toward home rule insofar as many provinces are introducing empowering legal concepts into municipal legislation – for instance, the introduction of permissive legal concepts such as spheres of jurisdiction and natural persons powers. As such, many provinces are moving into a legal "mushy middle" between the two poles of Dillon's Rule and home rule (Tindal et al. 2017). However, with respect to control over boundary changes and political institutions, they generally remain firmly situated at the Dillon's Rule end of the spectrum, with British Columbia's Community Charter as an exception that proves the rule.

Indeed, a case could be made that British Columbia's Community Charter (2003) constitutes the first case of home rule in Canada (see table 2.2). Its way of delegating authority is permissive, with broad "fundamental powers" delegated to municipalities; it legislates consultation with municipalities on changes to the act, and it has provided a limited form of "entrenchment" of protection against changes to municipal boundaries. Importantly, it also grounds municipalities' constitutional basis in the *will of local communities*. Although it is difficult to gauge when legal empowerment passes a threshold to be considered home rule, the Community Charter (2003) appears to have met that standard.

Thus, British Columbia's general municipal act, the Community Charter (2003), acknowledges municipalities as an autonomous order of government, and it legislates the concept that they are not simply "creatures of the province" but instead that their *authority emanates from the people*. Indeed, they are not only "continued by" the people, they are also "established by" them. In other words, they do not exist at the pleasure of the province; their authority derives from the people. Changes to municipalities' boundaries are also subject to democratic approval by the people through referendums. Finally, municipalities' roles go beyond "pipes and pavement," extending into social, environmental, and economic elements of the community.

In addition, it is worth pointing out that the legal landscape is also murky in the United States. As Taylor and Dobson point out, "Canadian observers tend to overestimate the scope of American home rule" (2020, 31). First, some states fall exclusively into one category, and others apply both rules to different classes of local government. Second, the legal landscape is further complicated by the fact that some states grant home rule through their *state constitutions*

Table 2.2. Home Rule for Municipalities in British Columbia?

Home Rule Principle	British Columbia's Community Charter (2003)
Right to exist	Recognizes municipalities as "an order of government within their jurisdiction" (s. 1) Municipalities are "established and continued by the will of their communities" (s. 1 (b)).
More than a political subdivision of state/province?	Municipalities are an order of government that is "democratically elected, autonomous, accountable and responsible" (s. 1 (a)) and "provides for the municipal purposes of the communities" (s. 1 (b)). Again, municipalities are "established and continued by the will of their communities" (s. 1 (b))."
Control over political institutions and boundaries	S. 279 provides that amalgamations will not occur without the consent of the communities in question (see above).
Ability to act and legislate broadly	Municipal purposes (s. 7) are broad and include "(a) providing good government of its community, (b) providing for services, laws and other matters for community benefit, (c) providing for stewardship of the public assets of its community, and (d) fostering the economic, social and environmental well-being of its community." S. 8 provides broad areas in which to legislate and confers natural person powers upon municipalities.

and others through *statutes*. Granting more authority through a statute is arguably similar to what has been done in Canada. Third, the difference between the two kinds of states is further muddied by the fact that some Dillon's Rule states have begun to delegate authority in more permissive ways (rather than in detailed itemized lists). Furthermore, the principle of home rule can be undermined if states pass legislation in particular fields to pre-empt local action (narrowing the scope of local laws that would not conflict with state law). In fact, there has been an increase in the use of pre-emption in the last decade in the United States. States have overridden progressive municipal bylaws in a variety of areas including gun control, tobacco regulations, living wage regulations, sanctuary city policies, municipal civil rights law, LGBTQ anti-discrimination rights, posting nutritional information in restaurants, and anti-plastic and environmental protection legislation (Hirschl 2020a, 5).

Differences between the status of American and Canadian municipalities have been emphasized in part because dominant accounts have stressed that provinces either do not have constitutions or that their constitutions are not sufficiently rigid to provide protection for municipalities. This is because of the nature of the principle of parliamentary sovereignty in Westminster systems in which the "constitution" of the province and the laws are whatever the parliament of the day legislates. This idea has led some experts to argue that municipal home rule is impossible in Canada. However, new ideas of parliamentary sovereignty have emerged that legitimize self-imposed limitations on a legislature's ability to legislate. These legal mechanisms are called "manner and form" limitations (they are like flexible amending formulas adapted to Westminster-style parliaments). The legislated limitation on amalgamations in British

Columbia (discussed above) is one example. Manner and form mechanisms in municipal legislation could become a way of securing degrees of municipal home rule in Canada (Good 2019).

CITY CHARTERS IN CANADA

Since the enactment of the Baldwin Act, the use of general or "omnibus" municipal acts rather than special legislation to delegate power to municipalities has been the norm in Canada (in contrast to the United States). Since the 1990s, there has been an increasing recognition that large cities differ from other municipalities and that systems of granting authority should reflect this by taking a municipal system's largest cities outside of the general Municipal Act and delegating authority separately – through a city charter. In Canada, when provincial legislation is tailored to a single municipality, it is called a city charter. The term is sometimes misapplied, and one could say that it is contested in some ways. In 2000, Toronto's city solicitor defined a municipal charter as a law that "codifies the laws applicable to the particular city and contains powers and responsibilities not given to other municipalities in the province concerned" (City of Toronto 2000, 3).

The move toward city charters represents a shift away from the Baldwin Act, which consolidated special municipal legislation into a general-purpose act. Nevertheless, city charters, like general municipal acts, are quite comprehensive in scope insofar as they treat a variety of subjects in a single act. Moreover, one might see them as an extension of the long-standing principle of needing to treat urban and rural places differently in law, a precedent also established in the Baldwin Act since, to date, they have only been enacted to govern the largest city or cities in a particular province. However, if they become widespread among cities and highly asymmetrical, they will represent a significant legal shift.

The idea of a city charter is to empower municipalities and to acknowledge their unique needs. In the early 2000s, Toronto, which is Canada's largest city and municipality, did not have separate legislation governing it, and a movement began to pass "charter" legislation to govern it. However, some legislation that is labelled charter legislation is not particularly empowering, such as the Halifax Regional Municipality Charter (2008), which does not include either natural person powers or spheres of jurisdiction although it is certainly empowering compared to the former act (particularly after amendments were made to it). It is also somewhat confusing that British Columbia's general local government legislation is called a "Community Charter." The word charter was likely used to emphasize the legislation's intent to empower municipalities. As a separate piece of legislation, the Vancouver Charter, which dates to colonial times (1886), is a charter, but it is notable that it is not as legally empowering as British Columbia's general legislation (see Taylor's and Dobson's 2020 survey). This legislation governs the core municipality in Canada's third largest city outside of the general municipal legislation (the Community Charter), but it is not as progressive in terms of legal permissiveness as the general legislation insofar as it relies on express powers rather than spheres of jurisdiction and has not introduced natural person powers. Saint John, New Brunswick, has a unique legal status as it was incorporated by a royal charter in 1785 at a time when municipal incorporation was rare and, to our knowledge, done individually. This is likely where the term charter originates (in the idea of a royal charter) (see Tindal et al. 2017, 145). Another example of a "charter city" is Winnipeg, whose charter dates back to 1972, when amalgamation occurred, and was amended in 2002 to consolidate a variety of powers into fourteen broad spheres of jurisdiction (Tindal et al. 2017).

As Canada's largest municipality and the core municipality in its largest metropolitan area, Toronto was a notable omission among charter cities until the Stronger City of Toronto for a Stronger Ontario Act (2006), which took effect in 2007. This act was passed within the context of a municipal autonomy movement that developed in Toronto in the late 1990s, following a forced municipal amalgamation and a "disentanglement" process (an attempt to clarify and real-locate service responsibilities between the province and the city). The transfer of responsibilities was not fiscally neutral and led to "downloading" of fiscal burdens to the City of Toronto. These reform initiatives, as well as the general tendency of other orders of government to ignore the urban consequences of their policy-making, led to an urban autonomy movement calling for a city charter (see Good 2009, chapter 7).

As a separate act meant to empower a single municipality, the City of Toronto Act (2006) is a charter. However, as Sancton (2016) notes, the legislation does not contain many additional powers that were not also included as amendments to the Municipal Act in 2006. For instance, spheres of jurisdiction, power to delegate decision-making to community councils, and an acknowledgement that municipalities could enter into agree-ments with the federal government in their areas of jurisdiction were all included in both the City of Toronto Act (2006) and amendments to the Municipal Act in 2006. Toronto was granted additional financial tools, including the authority to introduce new taxes on alcohol, motor vehicle ownership, land transfer, tobacco, amusement, parking, billboards, and road pricing/congestion (Tindal et al. 2017, 206). Although motor vehicle and land transfer taxes were introduced when David Miller (2003–10) was mayor, the former was rescinded when Rob Ford was elected mayor in 2010. Some experts consider Toronto to have failed the test of political willingness to use its taxation authority instead of going to the province for money when needed (Tindal et al. 2017, 207). Sancton (2016) notes that Toronto's jurisdiction and authority are similar to other Ontario municipalities despite the high hopes surrounding the reform. The real significant question is not whether a munic-ipality has a charter or not but what jurisdiction it possesses and the extent to which the municipality is treated *asymmetrically*.

Comparatively speaking, the other significant difference is whether the "charter" is en-trenched constitutionally. As Andrew Sancton (2016) notes, charters do not limit provincial authority in municipal affairs because they are not entrenched in provincial constitutions. In contrast, in the United States, both the establishment of commissions to reform city charters and the ratification of amendments are usually subject to approval through a local referendum (Sancton 2016, 1). As discussed above, I propose that manner and form limitations could play this role in municipal legislation in Canada (see Good 2019). However, to my knowledge, such mechanisms have not been introduced into city charters. Rather, it is British Columbia's Community Charter (2003) that has broken new ground in using this form of limitation on provincial authority in municipal affairs (see discussion above). This difficulty of entrenching protections of municipal institutions and authority in flexible constitutions is common to countries operating in the British tradition of constitutionalism – most of the Anglo cases. In Britain, this debate has arisen in a variety of areas of constitutionalism including human rights, devolution (to Scotland and Wales), and local government. This debate will be engaged further in the concluding chapter of this volume.

THE FEDERAL-MUNICIPAL RELATIONSHIP AND "NATIONAL" URBAN POLICY

Although many federal decisions have important urban and local implications, an explicit federal role in urban and municipal affairs has been limited due to s. 92 (8) of the Constitution. The federal role in urban affairs, in other words a "national" urban policy, has varied through time but, in general, institutions for sustained engagement (in particular a department and minister) and continued political will have been lacking. Under Trudeau Sr., there was a short-lived Ministry of State for Urban Affairs in 1971. However, it was disbanded in 1979. The next major turning point in federal-municipal relations occurred under Liberal prime minister Paul Martin (2003–6), who promised a New Deal for Cities and Communities. Among his initiatives were the introduction of a GST rebate for municipalities (2004 budget) as well as the gas tax transfer (2005 budget). He also established a "Cities Secretariat" in the Privy Council Office[10] and named John Godfrey as parliamentary secretary responsible for cities in 2003 and then minister of state for Infrastructure and Communities in 2004.[11] Nevertheless, although some previous initiatives continued, the Conservative governments under the leadership of Stephen Harper (2006–15) endorsed a new approach to federalism that they called "open federalism." "Open federalism" stressed the importance of clear lines of jurisdiction and respecting provincial jurisdiction, including in municipal affairs. Federal interest in urban affairs and a relationship with municipalities has increased again with the election of Liberal governments led by Justin Trudeau (2015–present). However, this interest has not translated into an explicit urban policy. Rather, Trudeau has pursued urban policy through a variety of forms of multilevel governance in areas such as infrastructure funding, immigration policy (by continuing to fund Local Immigration Partnerships and by providing special funding for refugee resettlement in 2018), urban Indigenous capacity building, and other areas (Bradford 2018). As this book is being published, a major debate in federal politics is how the federal government should incentivize municipalities to remove barriers to building more housing, such as zoning rules, by using the federal "spending power" – the ability to spend money in any area of authority.

Historically, tri-level agreements have been a way to collaborate among governments in a way that respects provincial jurisdiction for municipal affairs. Tri-level agreements are written (formalized) intergovernmental agreements that include the federal, provincial, and municipal governments as signatories. Prominent past examples are Winnipeg's Core Area Initiative and the Vancouver Agreement, both of which dealt with multiple areas of policy to address issues in an area of the city experiencing stress – Winnipeg's core and Vancouver's Downtown Eastside. There have also been tri-level relationships established in immigration policy agreements in Ontario (discussed further in chapter 12).

There has been a global increase in interest in national urban policy in the twenty-first century across the countries in the Global North and South (Friendly 2016) as urbanization progresses across the world. A recent study offers examples of such policies in Latin America (Brazil, Chile, Mexico), Europe (Belgium, Czech Republic, France, Germany, Netherlands, Switzerland, United Kingdom), Africa (Ghana, Morocco, South Africa, Uganda), Asia (China, Korea) and Oceania (Australia) (Friendly 2016). In this global context, Canada stands out as an exception in a recent OECD study that found that Canada was one of only five countries out of thirty-five that "does not show any evidence of a National Urban Policy adoption" (OECD 2017 in Bradford 2018, 4). However, as Neil Bradford argues, although Canada lacks an explicit urban policy, the Trudeau government (and past governments to various degrees) has implicit urban policies: "Instead of explicit urban development strategies, Canadian government support for cities has emerged largely as the by-product of many 'aspatial' policies and sectoral programs for the economy, environment and society" (2018, 7). These interventions are framed in multilevel terms and take different forms – they involve federal-provincial agreements with municipal involvement (e.g., the National Housing Strategy), direct federal-municipal funding or community planning (e.g., Urban Programming for Indigenous Peoples), or collaborative federal-provincial-municipal work on policy adaptation (e.g., federally funded intersectoral governance arrangements in the immigration policy field called Local Immigration Partnerships, which are discussed in chapter 12) (Bradford 2018). Nonetheless, as stated above, the continuation of such an implicit agenda is not guaranteed. Rather, it depends on the political will of the federal government of the day.

From a legal perspective, some provinces address federal-municipal relations in enabling legislation which could shape the dominant forms that tri-level collaboration might take and the extent to which an implicit urban policy is possible in some provinces. For instance, Quebec forbids agreements between municipalities and the federal government in s. 3 (11) of its Act Respecting the Ministère du Conseil exécutif. On the other hand, s. 1 (4) of Toronto's "Charter," the City of Toronto Act (2006), explicitly grants the city authority to enter into agreements with the federal government on matters relating to the city's jurisdiction. This power, as discussed above, was also given to all Ontario municipalities in 2006.

Although Canada may indeed have an implicit national urban agenda, a number of scholars have begun calling for a sustained and institutionalized federal role in urban affairs. This debate will be addressed further in the concluding chapter of the volume.

THE COURTS' ROLE IN INTERPRETING MUNICIPAL LAW

Although debates about municipal autonomy have been worked out politically (and through policy-making processes) in Europe, the courts have played a decisive role in establishing the contours of municipal autonomy in North America (Hirschl 2020b, 101).

In Canada, recent court decisions continue to support an interpretation of municipalities as mere creatures of the provinces when conflicts between municipal governments and citizens, on the one hand, and provinces, on the other, have emerged during periods of restructuring. The unilateral imposition of amalgamation on Metro Toronto (now the City of Toronto), despite municipalities' and citizens' opposition, and the more recent reduction of Toronto City Council by nearly half in the middle of the 2018 election are two prominent examples of such conflicts. In these instances, the "creatures of the province" doctrine ultimately prevailed.

However, since provinces began introducing changes to municipal legislation in the mid-1990s, the courts have been more willing to support municipalities in conflicts against other parties (including corporations). In other words, they appear to be taking the provincial delegation of increased authority to municipalities seriously and interpreting the legislation more broadly, moving beyond Dillon's Rule.

The Supreme Court of Canada has also recognized that municipalities further the principle of subsidiarity, a principle linked with federalism in recent court jurisprudence. For instance, in a widely cited decision in favour of the Municipality of Hudson, Quebec, which involved a dispute with a pesticide company over a bylaw banning the use of pesticides, the courts cite this principle. More specifically, they define subsidiarity as "the proposition that law-making and implementation are often best achieved at a level of government that is not only effective, but also closest to the citizens affected and thus most responsive to their needs, to local distinctiveness, and to population diversity" (114957 Canada Ltée [Spraytech, Société d'arrosage] v. Hudson [Town], 2001, para. 3).

The appellants in the case were two lawn care/landscaping companies that used pesticides. The companies argued that the City of Hudson did not have the authority (under the law that delegates powers to municipalities in Quebec – The Cities and Towns Act) to ban the use of pesticides. In Canada, the environment is not listed as a head of power, but the courts have decided that it is a joint area of federal-provincial jurisdiction, and the two levels of government had passed legislation to regulate the use of pesticides. Furthermore, even though municipal restrictions on the use of pesticides were stricter than provincial and federal laws, they did not contradict them. Although the Cities and Towns Act did not specifically delegate the power to regulate pesticides to cities and towns, the bylaw was upheld as a legitimate exercise of power under the "general welfare" provisions of this statute, showing the potential of such broadly stated powers to expand municipalities' legal autonomy. One study of this process stresses the important policy impact that this decision had, calling the conflict in Hudson as well as the municipality's ultimate Supreme Court of Canada victory "the mouse that roared," creating a cascading effect as municipalities across the country enacted bylaws regulating pesticides (Pralle 2006, 179). A lesson here is that municipalities could be important lawmakers in areas like environmental policy-making if given the legal clarity and latitude to innovate and respond to the preferences of their residents.

Nevertheless, although the courts have acknowledged the subsidiarity principle in relation to municipalities, the courts have been clear that this does not mean that municipalities are more than "creatures of the provinces" (Hirschl 2020b). In his concurring opinion in *Spraytech v. Hudson*, Justice LeBel states:

> A tradition of strong local government has become an important part of the Canadian democratic experience. This level of government usually appears more attuned to the immediate needs and concerns of the citizens. Nevertheless, in the Canadian legal order, as stated on a number of occasions, *municipalities remain creatures of the provincial legislatures* [emphasis added] (114957 Canada Ltée [Spraytech, Société d'arrosage] v. Hudson [Town], 2001, para. 49).

Thus, although the courts recognize the importance of local government to Canada's democratic tradition, the doctrine of creatures of the provinces inspired by Dillon's Rule stands. This was again confirmed in the Supreme Court's decision in *Toronto (City) v. Ontario*, although strikingly, as noted above, a substantial minority dissented (four out of nine justices) and stated explicitly that municipalities are more than "creatures of the provinces" (Toronto [City] v. Ontario 2021, para. 116).

CONCLUSION: CANADIAN MUNICIPAL SYSTEMS IN COMPARATIVE PERSPECTIVE

As discussed in chapter 1, urbanization has changed human habitats across the globe with fundamental implications for urban governance, and Canada is no exception. In chapter 8, Mévellec and others refer to a distinct "Canadian municipal model" characterized by two main features which are related: provincial control in municipal affairs and a limited, apolitical conception of municipal politics (see also Chiasson and Mévellec 2014). These characteristics are expressed in municipalities' self-conception as service providers to property, in a low level of participation in municipal elections, and in a conception of the local representative as "gifted amateurs who refuse both a political understanding of their role and their integration into political parties" (248). They also note that this conception may be changing – in other words, we may be witnessing an increased politicization of municipal politics.

As we saw above, elements of control by central governments and the lack of a robust independent politics are common to municipalities in other Anglo democracies. Municipalities are legal "creatures" of the central state and ultimately subject to their "sovereign" will. American states with home rule provisions are a partial exception to this rule. However, as mentioned above, state pre-emption has increased in American cities in areas such as sanctuary cities and minimum wage legislation, for instance. In Canada, there is progress on the legal empowerment of municipalities in municipal legislation in many provinces, and the courts have also interpreted municipal authority more generously in response. However, Canadian cities and other municipalities remain fundamentally "creatures of the provinces" in the face of a provincial will to intervene as Canadians have witnessed in recent years even in Canada's largest cities. Moreover, they have not been delegated significant additional financial resources to support an evolving role.

Although variation exists both within Canada and among Western democracies, constitutional weakness is common in "old world" constitutions of the Global North (Hirschl 2020a, 2020b). These constitutions have not adapted to the global phenomenon of urban agglomeration and the rise of megacities. Indeed, as discussed above, it is in the Global South, including, for instance, South Africa, that the most significant innovation in addressing the place of municipalities in constitutions has occurred (Hirschl 2020a, 2020b). The South African constitution has entrenched some of the home rule principles that have appeared in Canadian provincial legislation in the country's federal constitution, protecting them against unilateral change by parliaments in the country.

Municipalities' constitutional space and independence as an order of government are particularly vulnerable in Anglo democracies where parliamentary sovereignty reigns. Furthermore, although the underrepresentation of urban places (dilution of the urban vote in parliaments) in national and sub-national governments is common to many countries, Canadian cities, like other Anglo cities, do not possess the traditions of *cumul de mandats* of the Franco model or established rules for intergovernmental relations (in the Northern and Middle European model) that incorporate city perspectives into these governments' policy-making. Following Sellers, Lidström, and Bae (2020), Martin Horak (chapter 4) notes that Northern European countries combine "nationalized" infrastructures of local government to support integrated urban policy-making as well as local autonomy. These integration mechanisms include integrated party systems and common training for civil servants across orders of government.

In Canada, the dominance of the constitutional doctrine of "creatures of the provinces" limits the extent to which the federal government engages in urban policy-making, at least in an *explicit* way (Bradford 2018). This doctrine is reinforced by the political reality that Canada is a multinational federation with the French homeland concentrated in Canada's second largest province – Quebec. Indeed, a central question for students of urban and municipal politics is whether Canada needs a national urban policy, and if so, what kind? Another crucial question is whether such a policy is politically possible. In chapter 4, Martin Horak argues that the prospects for such nationalized multilevel policy-making are slim in Canada.

This chapter has established a foundation for understanding Canadian municipalities' status in the constitution and law in a broad comparative perspective, as well as how their status has varied through time. With this grounding in place, we now turn to a discussion of the comparative method and explore theories and approaches that have influenced the study of Canadian urban politics. We will discover a rich terrain of comparative work in Canada that furthers our understanding of the causes, consequences, and, importantly, the *normative position* of Canadian municipalities in Canada's democratic practices.

NOTES

1 Their categories have been used by other studies since then, including Bäck, Heinfelt, and Magnier (2006).

2 This may be less true of some large American cities like New York City, particularly those that have not adopted institutions inspired by the nineteenth century reform movement.

3 In addition to the consent of both the House of Commons and the Senate, Canada's general amending formula requires the consent of two-thirds of the provinces representing at least 50 per cent of the population to make constitutional changes.

4 The roots of local government in Canada begin earlier with the French regime and the establishment in Quebec of the short-lived "syndics d'habitation" in (1647–61) and in the mid-1750s with the establishment of the Courts of Sessions. These were governor-in-council-appointed bodies that performed administrative and judicial duties and included propertied grand juries of middle and upper middle-class residents (Higgins 1991, 52). The Courts of Sessions were also adopted in Lower Canada after the British Conquest in 1760 (52).

5 For example, the City of Saint John, New Brunswick, which was granted a royal charter of incorporation in 1785.

6 In 1982, the Canadian Constitution was "patriated" with the entrenchment (inclusion of) constitutional amending formulas (along with other significant constitutional amendments). This meant that significant constitutional amendments no longer had to be enacted by the UK Parliament at the request of the prime minister of Canada.

7 Another attempt in 1974 also failed in a referendum and another was withdrawn due to lack of support in 2013 (Hirschl 2020b, 7).

8 In British Columbia, unincorporated places participate in local government through regional governmental bodies called regional districts.

9 Note that Vancouver is governed by a "charter," separate provincial legislation that only applies to Vancouver.

10 The Privy Council Office is a central agency at the apex of power that advises cabinet and the prime minister on policy.

11 Furthermore, he created an External Advisory Committee on Cities in 2004.

REFERENCES

114957 Canada Ltée (Spraytech, Société d'arrosage) v. Hudson (Town), 2001 SCC 40.

Abu-Laban, Yasmeen, and Christina Gabriel. 2002. *Selling Diversity: Immigration, Multiculturalism, Employment Equity, and Globalization*. Peterborough, ON: Broadview Press.

Act Respecting the Ministère du Conseil exécutif, Québec Official Publisher, c. M-30, updated to December 1, 2021. https://www.legisquebec.gouv.qc.ca/en/pdf/cs/M-30.pdf.

Bäck, Henry, Hubert Heinelt, and Annick Magnier. 2006. "Introduction." In *The European Mayor: Political Leaders in the Changing Context of Local Democracy*, edited by Henry Bäck, Hubert Heinelt, and Annick

Magnier, 7–20. Wiesbaden: VS Verlag für Sozialwissenschaften. https://doi.org/10.1007/978-3
-531-90005-6_1.

Bourinot, John George. 1887. *Local Government in Canada: An Historical Study*. Baltimore: John Hopkins
University.

Bradford, Neil. 2018. "A National Urban Policy for Canada? The Implicit Federal Agenda." RPP Insight,
November 2018, no. 24. https://irpp.org/research-studies/national-urban-policy-canada-implicit
-federal-agenda/

Braid, Don. 2019. "After Tax Fiasco, the Province Should Fire City Council." *Calgary Herald*, May 29,
2019. https://calgaryherald.com/news/politics/braid-after-tax-fiasco-the-province-should-fire-city
-council.

Bulpitt, Jim. 1983. *Territory and Power in the United Kingdom: An Interpretation*. Manchester: University of
Manchester Press.

Cameron, David, and Richard Simeon. 2002. "Intergovernmental Relations in Canada: The Emergence of
Collaborative Federalism." *Publius* 32, no. 2 (Spring): 49–71. https://doi.org/10.1093/oxfordjournals
.pubjof.a004947.

Chiasson, Guy, and Anne Mévellec. 2014. "The 2013 Quebec Municipal Elections: What Is Specific
to Quebec?" *Canadian Journal of Urban Research* 23, no. 2 (Winter): 1–17. https://www.jstor.org
/stable/26189248.

City of Clinton v. Cedar Rapids and the Missouri River Rail Road Company, Supreme Court.
7 January 1884.

City of Toronto. 2000. *Power of Canadian Cities: The Legal Framework*. Report prepared by the City
Solicitor, City of Toronto, June 2000 (updated October 2001). https://www.toronto.ca/ext/digital
_comm/inquiry/inquiry_site/cd/gg/add_pdf/77/Governance/Electronic_Documents/Other_CDN
_Jurisdictions/Powers_of_Canadian_Cities.pdf.

Côté, André, and Michael Fenn. 2014. "Provincial-Municipal Relations in Ontario: Approaching an
Inflection Point." In *IMFG Papers on Municipal Finance and Governance*, no. 17. Toronto: Institute on
Municipal Finance and Governance.

Crawford, K. Grant. 1954. *Canadian Municipal Government*. Toronto: University of Toronto Press. Kindle.
https://doi.org/10.3138/9781442653283.

Dewoghélaëre, Julien, Raul Magni Berton, and Julien Navarro. 2006. "The *Cumul des Mandats* in
Contemporary French Politics: An Empirical Study of the *XIIᵉ Législature* of the *Assembleé Nationale*."
French Politics 4, no. 3 (December): 312–32. https://doi.org/10.1057/palgrave.fp.8200104.

Dollery, Brian E., Joseph Garcea, and Edward C. LeSage Jr. 2008. "Introduction." In *Local Government
Reform: A Comparative Analysis of Advanced Anglo-American Countries*, edited by Brian E. Dollery, Joseph
Garcea, and Edward C. LeSage Jr., 1–15. Cheltenham: Edward Elgar.

Dupré, J. Stefan. 1967. *Intergovernmental Finance in Ontario: A Provincial-Local Perspective. A Study Prepared
for the Ontario Committee on Taxation*. Toronto: Queen's Printer.

East York (Borough) v. Ontario (Attorney General), 1997 CanLII 12263 (ON SC).

Edmonds, Penelope. 2010. "Unpacking Settler Colonialism's Urban Strategies: Indigenous Peoples in
Victoria, British Columbia, and the Transition to a Settler-Colonial City." *Urban History Review* 38,
no. 2 (Spring): 4–20.

Ford, Doug. 2018. "Priority Lies in Ending Toronto's Council Gridlock." *Toronto Sun*, September 12,
2018. https://torontosun.com/opinion/columnists/ford-priority-lies-in-ending-toronto-councils
-gridlock.

Friendly, Abigail. 2016. "National Urban Policy: A Roadmap for Canadian Cities." In *IMFG Perspectives*, no. 14. Toronto: Institute on Municipal Finance and Governance. https://imfg.munkschool.utoronto .ca/research/doc/?doc_id=357.

Good, Kristin R. 2009. *Municipalities and Multiculturalism: The Politics of Immigration in Toronto and Vancouver.* Toronto: University of Toronto Press.

———. 2019. "The Fallacy of the 'Creatures of the Provinces' Doctrine: Recognizing and Protecting Municipalities' Constitutional Status." In *IMFG Papers on Municipal Finance and Governance*, no. 46. Toronto: Institute on Municipal Finance and Governance. https://imfg.munkschool.utoronto.ca /research/doc/?doc_id=523.

Government of Alberta. n.d. "Strengthening Local Elections and Councils." New and Proposed Legislation. Accessed June 13, 2024. https://www.alberta.ca/strengthening-local-elections-and-councils.

Graham, Katherine A., Susan D. Phillips, with Allan M. Maslove. 1998. *Urban Governance in Canada: Representation, Resources, and Restructuring.* Toronto: Harcourt Canada.

Guest, Denis. 1980. *The Emergence of Social Security in Canada.* Vancouver: UBC Press.

Haddow, Rodney. 2002. "Municipal Social Security in Canada." In *Urban Policy Issues: Canadian Perspectives*, edited by Edmund P. Fowler and David Siegel, 2nd ed., 90–107. Toronto: Oxford University Press.

Halifax Regional Municipality Charter. 2008. Statutes of Nova Scotia, c. 39. https://nslegislature.ca /sites/default/files/legc/statutes/halifax%20regional%20municipality%20charter.pdf.

Hesse, Joachim Jens, and Laurence J. Sharpe. 1991. "Local Government in International Perspective: Some Comparative Observations." In *Local Government and Urban Affairs in International Perspective: Analyses of Twenty Western Industrialised Countries*, edited by Joachim Jens Hesse, 603–21. Baden-Baden: Nomos Verl.-Ges.

Higgins, Donald. 1991. "Local Government and Urban Affairs in International Perspective: The Canadian Case." In *Local Government and Urban Affairs in International Perspective: Analyses of Twenty Western Industrialised Countries*, edited by Joachim Jens Hesse, 45–76. Baden-Baden: Nomos Verl.-Ges.

Hillhouse, Albert Miller. 1936. *Municipal Bonds: A Century of Experience.* New York: Prentice-Hall.

Hirschl, Ran. 2020a. "Cities in National Constitutions: Northern Stagnation, Southern Innovation." In *IMFG Papers on Municipal Finance and Governance*, no. 51. Toronto: Institute on Municipal Finance and Governance. https://imfg.munkschool.utoronto.ca/research/doc/?doc_id=540.

———. 2020b. *City, State: Constitutionalism and the Megacity.* New York: Oxford University Press. https:// doi.org/10.1093/oso/9780190922771.001.0001.

Horak, Martin. 1998. "The Power of Local Identity: C4LD and the Anti-Amalgamation Mobilization in Toronto." Research Paper 195, Centre for Urban and Community Studies, University of Toronto, November, pp. 44. https://hdl.handle.net/1807/94452.

Hunter v. City of Pittsburgh, Supreme Court, November 18, 1907.

Isin, Engin. F. 1992. *Cities without Citizens: The Modernity of the City as a Corporation.* Montreal: Black Rose Books.

John, Peter. 2001. *Local Governance in Western Europe.* London: Sage Publications. https://doi. org/10.4135/9781446217788.

Levi, Ron, and Mariana Valverde. 2006. "Freedom of the City: Canadian Cities and the Quest for Governmental Status." *Osgoode Hall Law Journal* 44, no. 3 (Fall): 409–59. https://doi.org/10.60082 /2817-5069.1281.

Lucas, Jack, and Alison Smith. 2019. "Which Policy Issues Matter in Canadian Municipalities? A Survey of Municipal Politicians." The School of Public Policy Publications, University of Calgary, *SPP*

Research Paper 12, no. 8, March, pp. 25. https://www.policyschool.ca/wp-content/uploads/2019
/03/Canadian-Municipalities-Lucas-Smith.pdf.

Magnusson, Warren. 1986. "Bourgeois Theories of Local Government." *Political Studies* 34, no. 1 (March):
1–18. https://doi.org/10.1111/j.1467-9248.1986.tb01869.x.

———. 2005. "Are Municipalities Creatures of the Provinces?" *Journal of Canadian Studies* 39, no. 2
(Spring): 5–29. https://doi.org/10.1353/jcs.2006.0019.

———. 2015. *Local Self-Government and the Right to the City.* Montreal: McGill-Queen's University Press.
https://doi.org/10.1515/9780773597280.

Mabileau, Albert. 1994. *Le système locale en France.* 2nd ed. Paris: Montchrestien.

Municipal Government Act, RSA 2000, c M-26. https://canlii.ca/t/567fm.

People ex rel. Leroy v. Hurlbut, 24 Mich. 44 (1871).

Pralle, Sarah. 2006. "The "Mouse That Roared": Agenda Setting in Canadian Pesticides Politics." *The Policy
Studies Journal* 34, no. 2 (May): 171–94. https://doi.org/10.1111/j.1541-0072.2006.00165.x.

Russell, Jon D., and Aaron Bostrom. 2016. "Federalism, Dillon Rule and Home Rule." White Paper: A
Publication of the American City County Exchange, American City County Exchange, January, pp. 10.

R. v. Greenbaum, [1993] 1 S.C.R. 674

Sancton, Andrew. 2006. "Why Municipal Amalgamations? Halifax, Toronto, Montreal." In *Canada: The
State of the Federation 2004*, edited by Robert Young and Christian Leuprecht, 119–37. Montreal:
McGill-Queen's University Press.

———. 2009. "Introduction." In *Foundations of Governance: Municipal Government in Canada's Provinces*,
edited by Andrew Sancton and Robert Young, 3–19. Toronto: University of Toronto Press.

———. 2015. *Canadian Local Government: An Urban Perspective.* 2nd ed. Don Mills, ON: Oxford
University Press.

———. 2016. "The False Panacea of City Charters? A Political Perspective on the Case of Toronto."
The School of Public Policy SPP Research Papers 9, no. 3. University of Calgary, January.

Sansom, Graham. 2009. "Commonwealth of Australia." In *Federal Systems*, edited by Nico Steyler, 8–36.
Vol. 6 of *A Global Dialogue on Federalism.* Montreal: McGill- Queen's University Press.

Simeon, Richard, and Ian Robinson. 2004. "The Dynamics of Canadian Federalism." In *Canadian Politics*,
edited by James Bickerton and Alain-G. Gagnon, 4th ed., 101–26. Peterborough, ON: Broadview Press.

Smith, Alison, and Zachary Spicer. 2018. "The Local Autonomy of Canada's Largest Cities." *Urban Affairs
Review* 54, no. 5 (September): 931–61. https://doi.org/10.1177/1078087416684380.

Smith, Jennifer. 2004. *Federalism.* Vancouver: UBC Press.

South Africa. 1996. "Constitution of the Republic of South Africa." No. 108 of 1996. https://www.gov
.za/sites/default/files/images/a108-96.pdf.

Swift, Nick, and Guy Kervella. 2003. "A Complex System Aims to Bring French Local Government
Closer to the People." City Mayors: Local Government in France. http://www.citymayors.com
/france/france_gov.html.

Taylor, Zack. 2019. *Shaping the Metropolis: Institutions and Urbanization in the United States and Canada.*
Montreal: McGill-Queen's University Press. https://doi.org/10.1515/9780773558427.

Taylor, Zack, and Alec Dobson. 2020. "Power and Purpose: Canadian Municipal Law in Transition." In
IMFG Papers on Municipal Finance and Governance, no. 47. Toronto: Institute on Municipal Finance and
Governance. https://tspace.library.utoronto.ca/bitstream/1807/99216/1/imfgpaper_no47_Power
_and_Purpose_Taylor_Dobson.pdf.

Tindal, C. Richard, and Susan Nobes Tindal. 2000. *Local Government in Canada.* 5th ed. Toronto: Nelson
Thomson Learning.

———. 2009. *Local Government in Canada*. 7th ed. Toronto: Nelson Education Limited.

Tindal, C. Richard, Susan Nobes Tindal, Kennedy Stewart, and Patrick Smith. 2017. *Local Government in Canada*. 9th ed. Toronto: Nelson Education.

Toronto (City) v. Ontario (Attorney General), 2021 SCC 34.

Vipond, Robert. 1985. "Constitutional Politics and the Legacy of the Provincial Rights Movement in Canada." *Canadian Journal of Political Science* 18, no. 2 (June): 267–94. https://doi.org/10.1017/S0008423900030250.

Wollmann, Hellmut. 2000. "Local Government Systems: From Historic Divergence Towards Convergence? Great Britain, France, and Germany as Comparative Cases in Point." *Environment and Planning C: Government and Policy* 18, no. 1 (February): 33–55. https://doi.org/10.1068/c9867.

CHAPTER THREE

Understanding Canadian Urban Governance Comparatively: Methods, Theories, and Contributions

Kristin R. Good

INTRODUCTION

Comparative politics can be understood as a method and as a field of study. Most fundamentally, comparison is a *method* for exploring similarities and differences among cases. For instance, one definition of comparative method is the "rules and standards and procedures for identifying and explaining differences and similarities between cases … using concepts that are applicable in more than one case or country" (Halperin and Heath 2020, 231). The field of comparative politics uses comparative methods to ask and answer a variety of political questions. It emerged and has evolved from the application of methodologies that compared *countries* to one another. The field of comparative politics is interested in the extent to which trends in one country are generalizable to others and why. However, in this volume, we unpack and disaggregate countries to compare cities, city-regions, and municipalities, both within countries and internationally.

In an increasingly globally connected world, a major debate in urban politics is how much national contexts matter to urban politics. Some scholars argue that cities are connected with each other globally in ways that defy national boundaries. However, in our view, although national institutions have had to adapt to changes brought about by globalization, they still matter. Jefferey Sellers (2005) argues that we need to unpack the national scale, conceptualizing it as an "infrastructure" that shapes but does not determine local action in cities. National infrastructures include constitutions and the way that institutions are configured, policies in a variety of areas, and a country's political culture. By comparing multiple cities in one country with multiple cities in another, we can begin to see the effects of these national infrastructures. Within-country comparisons can highlight how aspects of city contexts shape urban politics and governance despite a similar national infrastructure, and cross-national comparisons can highlight how aspects of national infrastructures lead to common urban policies and governance arrangements in cities in the same country. In federal systems such as Canada, such infrastructures are further layered with both federal and provincial (sub-national) infrastructures potentially influencing municipal and city governance. In fact, as we discovered in chapter 2, in federal systems in Anglo democracies, municipal systems are most directly influenced by sub-national governments, which have been assigned constitutional responsibility for establishing and managing municipal systems.

Comparative urban political science research has flourished in Canada in the last few decades. This work sheds light on fundamental questions such as the constitutional status of municipalities, the design of municipal systems and institutions, and the quality of democratic governance in Canada. Furthermore, this work has developed new concepts to understand local variations in political cultures and how demographic change influences cities' political cultures, and applies Canadian-made concepts to urban places and policy. Collectively, this scholarship highlights both the potential and the limitations of municipal systems and institutions as service providers, policy-makers, and, ultimately, democratic institutions. Through an examination of seminal contributions in the field by Canadian scholars and by scholars whose ideas have been influential in Canada, we lay out an exciting and vibrant area of study and debate.

DESIGNING COMPARATIVE URBAN RESEARCH: RESEARCH DESIGNS AND THE ROLE OF THEORY

A central goal of comparison has been to establish causal relationships, test existing theories, and develop new theories and hypotheses – in other words, to *explain* political phenomena. As such, comparison has frequently been used as a research strategy to control the number of factors under consideration through the careful selection of cases. Two dominant strategies have been employed in comparative research – the "most similar" and "most different" systems designs (Denters and Mossberger 2006). In the most similar systems design, the researcher selects cases that are highly similar except with respect to the factors that are hypothesized to have a causal effect (independent variables) on the phenomenon under study (called the dependent variable). Arend Lijphart (1975, 163) argues that selecting comparable cases is fundamental to the comparative method and, importantly, "selecting intranation cases" is identified as an important strategy for the selection of comparable cases since cases within the same national context tend to be "most similar" (159). The idea is that one can explain variation in the dependent variables (the political or policy phenomenon of interest) with differences in variables of interest if the cases are sufficiently similar and "control for" rival explanatory factors or existing explanations. For instance, in *Municipalities and Multiculturalism* (2009), I use the logic of a most similar systems design to explore the relationship between ethnic configurations of municipalities (immigrant settlement patterns) and variations in municipalities' responsiveness to immigrants and ethnocultural minorities. By selecting some of Canada's most significant immigrant-receiving destinations, and therefore cases that all have large immigrant and ethnocultural minority populations, I control for the proportion of immigrants in the municipal population, eliminating this as an alternative explanation (and because past studies had established the significance of proportion of immigrants in a municipality's population as an explanation of a greater level of multicultural policy activity). My cases fall into two groups: "biracial" and "multiracial." The former represents cases where a concentration of a visible minority group has settled in the municipality; the latter represents a more diverse group of immigrants, most of whom are also visible minorities, settling in these otherwise highly similar cases located in Metro Vancouver and the Greater Toronto Area. I find that municipalities in biracial demographic contexts (places where a single visible minority population has concentrated in large numbers) are more responsive to immigrants and ethnocultural minorities because (among other reasons) there tends to be backlash from long-standing residents in places where this visible minority group has settled and begun to change the norms of the majority population, pushing the question of multiculturalism onto municipal agendas. Furthermore, these municipalities are more responsive because the collective action problem (ability to cooperate) is easier to overcome in these less diverse locales.

In a most different systems design, variables are controlled by selecting different cases and tracing similar processes of change or outcomes within them. The logic is that if similarities or similar processes can be identified in such cases, then the systems-level variables that differ among the cases – like national institutions and other country-level variables – can be excluded as causal factors. David Hugill (discussed below) uses the logic of a most different systems design to highlight similar Indigenous experiences of migration to Minneapolis and Winnipeg, tying them to global processes of colonialism. As Denters and Mossberger (2006, 553) observe, most different systems designs "emphasize the applicability of phenomena across a range of settings."

There is a variety of approaches to comparison and strategies used to design comparative research. Although many associate the comparative method with an in-depth examination of a small number of cases (Lijphart 1975; Ragin 1987), the comparative analysis of large quantitative data sets, including surveys, has contributed significantly to our understanding of municipal politics in comparative perspective. In Canada, comparative elections and voting behaviour literature has grown significantly in recent years, making significant contributions to our understanding of local democracy. To use only a few examples, such studies have identified the size and sources of the incumbency advantage of candidates in Canadian municipal elections (Lucas 2019) and the effect of ward versus at-large electoral institutions on the representational focus of municipal councillors (Koop and Kraemer 2016). A recent volume comparing voting behaviour in eight major cities in Canada finds that voters' economic conservatism and retrospective evaluation of the performance of the local economy matter most to voter choice in Canadian mayoral elections (Lucas and MacGregor 2021).

Qualitative and quantitative methods have different strengths and weaknesses. By virtue of examining a limited range of cases in relation to one another, the findings of qualitative forms of comparison are limited in their *reliability*, in other words, the extent to which they are generalizable. However, the concepts and categories used in quantitative research can lack *validity* in the sense that some of the nuances and *accuracy* of the categories are lost in attempts to apply concepts to new cases.

For this reason, *mixed methods approaches* that combine qualitative and quantitative analyses have become common as research strategies in comparative analysis. Such studies combine the benefits of qualitative studies to understanding policy and causal processes more accurately with the generality of "large N" (large number of cases) statistical analysis. For instance, Williamson's (2019) path-breaking study of local immigration politics in the United States (discussed more in chapter 12) first uses case studies to identify the political dynamics involved in local immigration policy-making in midsized American cities and suburbs (including the emergence of anti-immigrant measures). Then, after finding that discussion or adoption of anti-immigrant measures in three suburban cases tended to be followed by immigrant-friendly measures, she used survey data to quantify how frequently a variety of different policies, such as anti-immigrant measures, are adopted at the municipal level in midsized cities (suburbs), showing that they are rare. This approach allowed her to show the political dynamics involved and explore their causes while also establishing the generality of her findings in the American context.

THE ROLE OF THEORY IN COMPARATIVE RESEARCH

Another complementary way to reduce the number of factors under consideration in a comparative analysis is to apply theory to one's work. In other words, cases can be selected with a view of exploring the generality of a theory, testing it, and refining it, or they can be chosen in order to offer a coherent interpretation of a particular case or set of cases. Since theories were developed based on past research, in a sense, theory-driven research increases the number of cases at play in the analysis (when they have been confirmed in past studies or have provided powerful interpretations of political phenomena in the past). For this reason, theoretically driven case studies might be seen as a form of comparative study since the new case is being compared implicitly to the previous cases to which it was applied.

Although theory can help researchers to make sense of urban complexity, it also limits the questions that researchers can ask. Furthermore, students of urban research must acknowledge that existing bodies of theory and knowledge have been shaped by researchers that are unrepresentative of the diversity of urban populations, identities, and perspectives, as well as parts of the world. As Theresa Enright notes, there are "imperial implications of generalized theories" and "extreme geographic asymmetries of power-knowledge that undergird academic production today" (Enright 2020, 30). These asymmetries of power and knowledge apply globally between regions of the so-called Global North and Global South. In a global field of knowledge asymmetries, the commonly employed most similar systems design often centres Western cases and theoretical perspectives, neglecting the urban governance of cities in the Global South.

Asymmetries in who has defined the field of urban politics (and comparative urban politics) are also relevant *within* countries, shaping whose politics matter, whose perspective is incorporated, and whose knowledge and experiences are centred. For instance, in Canada, urban theory could benefit enormously from incorporating Indigenous perspectives and knowledge into urban theorizing – perspectives that have been largely missing from the field to date (see Tomiak et al. 2019).

Such considerations have led some to call for more open-ended comparative inquiries and for comparative designs to address interpretive goals. Such comparisons embrace the complexity of urban places and employ the method as a heuristic device to spark the theoretical imagination. This kind of research explores how a concept is expressed in different locales and develops concepts and theories by examining cities *in relation to one another*. This perspective acknowledges that the research process is not neutral but is affected by the positionality of the researcher, is subject to interpretation, and that power relations are central to interpretation. Such comparisons can also be used to *centre a particular explanation or perspective* that has been silenced in dominant accounts. In these comparisons, the goal is to offer an *interpretation* of a particular process or phenomenon. The language of variables is discarded because although there are often underlying explanatory claims, a definitive test of alternative explanations is often not offered but rather the objectivity and neutrality of those dominant explanations are problematized. David Hugill's (2019) comparison of Indigenous Peoples' experience in Winnipeg and Minneapolis, discussed below, is an example of such a comparative approach that contributes to unsettling dominant accounts of Indigenous alienation from urban places in the Prairies.

The remainder of this chapter provides an overview of influential theories, concepts, and approaches to comparison in the field of urban politics, highlighting their contribution to understanding Canadian cities. We discuss studies that have had major impacts in the field and highlight work that centres new and innovative perspectives that have been marginalized. The goal is to introduce some of the most important studies of comparative city politics and governance that include a Canadian case to illustrate the value of comparative analysis to understanding Canadian urban politics as well as to introduce key ideas that have influenced the study of Canadian urban political systems. As we will discover, most Canadian urban scholars are institutionalists. This consistent institutional focus contrasts starkly with the evolution of the American urban politics literature that developed theories of community power in the 1950s and 1960s – the debate between the pluralists and the elitists – as well as political economy perspectives such as the concept of the city as a growth machine (inspired by Marxism) and urban regimes. These theoretical perspectives were widely employed and engaged comparatively in the United States and will be discussed further below. More recently, Canadian urban scholarship has made important contributions to understanding how the political culture and normative context of cities matter to their governance.

THEORETICAL APPROACHES TO STUDYING CANADIAN URBAN POLITICS

Institutionalisms in Canada

CONSTITUTIONAL INSTITUTIONALISM IN CANADA: DEBATING INSTITUTIONAL DESIGN

Institutions are "the rules, structures and norms that create and enforce cooperative behaviour among individuals and groups" (Davies and Trounstine 2012, 52). Institutional analysis is the foundation of the discipline of political science (Peters 2019, 1). It was democratic institutions (including constitutions) and differences among them that were the first political scientists' focus as political science became a separate discipline distinct from economics and sociology. Historically, like the field of Canadian political science more generally, the study of local and urban politics in Canada has been focused on formal institutions (Eidelman and Taylor 2010, 312). This approach continues to be employed productively in Canadian urban political science and by legal scholars. Comparative urban scholars Rikke Berg and Nirmala Rao (2005, 1) call this approach "constitutional institutionalism," which "defines institutions as formal structures, including rules and regulations reflected in the legislative framework that provide the frames for the behaviour of individuals operating within these structures." Such studies explore if and how differences in formal structures affect a variety of outcomes. The rich Canadian urban scholarship also tends to take the historical evolution of institutions seriously and to incorporate an explicitly normative analysis into their work.[1]

In Canada, the institutional orientation both in the field in general and in urban politics is in part due to the power of contemporary reform debates to drive research agendas not only at the local level but in the field of Canadian politics more generally. Many Canadian political scientists have been interested in contributing to public debates, making important empirical contributions in areas as diverse as amalgamations (Sancton 2000), the design and reform of municipal systems (Garcea and LeSage 2005), and the constitutional status, significance, and possibilities of municipal and local government in Canada (Good 2009, 2019; Hirschl 2020; Sancton 2008).

Debates about the constitutional status of municipalities have risen to prominence in Canada and have inspired some recent work in the formal or constitutional-institutionalist vein. As discussed in chapter 2, beginning in the mid-1990s, legal changes to empower municipalities were enacted and a debate about city charters emerged in Canada, a development that has inspired institutional research evaluating and documenting these developments (Garcea and LeSage 2005; Taylor and Dobson 2020). Other work explores the possibilities and limitations of creating constitutional space for Canadian municipalities in light of Canada becoming a highly urban country. In 2008, two important books were published on the subject, one by Toronto-based philanthropist Alan Broadbent, an advocate of greater municipal empowerment, and the other by Andrew Sancton, one of Canada's preeminent scholars of local government. In *Urban Nation*, Broadbent (2008) makes a strong argument for why urbanization necessitates change to cities' status in the Canadian Constitution and the importance of place-based policy-making. He concludes with a radical proposal for constitutional change that includes creating city-provinces out of Canada's three largest metropolitan areas – Toronto, Montreal, and Vancouver – and merging the Atlantic provinces! One of two major works discussed in this section, Andrew Sancton's (2008) *The Limits of Boundaries* is in part a response to Broadbent and the movement for constitutional status for "Toronto," a city whose boundaries are particularly contested in Canada. According to Sancton (2008), the question of what constitutes "Toronto" – in other words, where its boundaries are and/or would be established for the purposes of devolving significant autonomy to the city – is a difficult but fundamental question that has been left unaddressed by the movement. The other contribution discussed here is Ran Hirschl's (2020) *City, State.* Together, these works attest to the fundamental importance of analyzing constitutions and institutions as a strategy of comparative research.

Andrew Sancton's (2008) *The Limits of Boundaries* explores boundary-making across the world and through time to argue that cities cannot be self-governing due to the "problem of boundaries." Sancton's argument unfolds through a broad historical overview of boundary drawing for sovereign states that shows that political boundaries have usually been drawn in an arbitrary rather than principled way. He explores various forms of "self-governing" for cities, from a sovereign state (Singapore) to a sub-national unit of a federation (e.g., Hamburg and Berlin, which are both *Land* governments in Germany, the equivalent of provinces) and through metropolitan government institutions. His central point is that self-government for cities is unattainable because we do not have principled ways of establishing permanent boundaries around cities or metropolitan areas, and even if we did, as dynamic forms of human settlement, cities often outgrow their boundaries. Sancton uses this broad historical and global overview of boundary-making to inform debates about urban and municipal autonomy in Canada, exploring the political and practical difficulties of establishing boundaries around Toronto and arguing that securing agreement from various interests would be impossible. Sancton offers a rich analysis of a crucial question of constitutionalism and public policy. His goal is not to explain, but through a rich survey and description of cases, he establishes the *generality* of the problem of boundaries through time, around the world, and in different institutional contexts (for city-states and metropolitan governments). In addition, he also offers a normative assessment of what he considers to be the implications of urbanization. In his view, the assumption that municipalities are growing in importance because cities are growing is false. He argues instead that central governments (and, in Canada, provinces in particular) have a greater role to play in governing urban places instead – from above or at a larger territorial scale.

Another excellent example of the strength of the constitutional-institutionalist approach to comparison comes from Ran Hirschl's (2020) *City, State*. Through a remarkably thorough global sweep of the place of municipal governments and cities in national constitutions, he is able to show that countries (including Canada) in the Global North are suffering from constitutional stagnation as they have failed to adapt to global urban agglomeration. Broadly speaking, countries in the Global South, which have established their constitutions more recently, have recognized municipalities. South Africa emerges as a global example of innovation in his book. Indeed, Anglo countries, such as Canada and Australia, are among the most stagnant. He considers the seventy-third and seventy-fourth amendments to India's Constitution, the 1988 constitutional recognition of cities in Brazil, and the South African Constitution's recognition of cities as an order of government to be the most significant global attempts to address urbanization. Importantly, he also identifies three factors that influence whether cities gain recognition in a country's constitution:

> (i) a necessity factor – an acute need to think creatively about urban agglomeration in large, densely populated countries where much of the world's urban expansion world-wide has taken place; (ii) a constitutional fact – a constitutional order's amenability, whether formal or informal, to change in response to the astonishing rise of megacities; and, (iii) a political factor – the interplay of power holders' incentives alongside national and sub-national governments' interests in enabling or subverting megacity emancipation. (Hirschl 2020, 13)

Importantly, Hirschl's work offers research design lessons for scholars. Looking beyond the usual cases studied by scholars of comparative constitutionalism by including countries in the Global South, particularly from Asia, Latin America, and Africa, Hirschl (2020, 13) identified "truly cutting-edge constitutional thought and innovation" reflected in the Constitutions and national debates about local democracy and urbanization in these countries.

Several chapters that follow in part 3 of this book focus on comparisons of constitutional-institutional differences in municipal systems and governance. The constitutional-institutional strain of literature pushes us to describe and critically assess the influence of formal structures on the quality of local democracy and other outcomes.

HISTORICAL INSTITUTIONALISM: EXPLAINING INSTITUTIONAL TRAJECTORIES

Historical institutionalism has been an important strain of institutionalism in both comparative politics and Canadian political science. This approach posits that earlier decisions about policy and the governmental system narrow the options in the future. Political scientists refer to this as path dependence, which holds that institutions and policies continue down a particular path unless that path is interrupted by a significant event or force that sends them down another trajectory (Peters 2019, 24), called a critical juncture in the literature. An excellent example of such an institutional study that has generated important insights about Canada is Zack Taylor's (2019) *Shaping the Metropolis*. In this study, Taylor begins with broad observations about differences between Canadian and American cities: first, he notes that American metropolitan areas are more complex than Canadian metropolitan areas, a term that he prefers to "fragmented," which is often used and has negative connotations. Second, Canadian cities have a more compact urban form than American cities. Finally, Canadian and American cities have different relationships with upper levels of government, in other words, their forms of multilevel governance vary.

Then, Taylor (2019) recounts how Canadian provinces and American states took different approaches at different historical junctures. In the early phase of the establishment of municipal systems, Canadian provinces, as we discuss in chapter 2, enacted general legislation. In contrast, American states enacted legislation to govern single municipal corporations – ad hoc municipal charters. In the reform period (1880–1929), American states implemented home rule to break apart corrupt local-state party networks whereas in Canada provinces increased their level and capacity of supervision. During the Depression and the World Wars, the federal government intervened in American cities, pre-empting state action, and in Canada, provincial supervision increased, both of finances and in general. According to Taylor, these periods set the institutional foundations of the local government systems in both countries. The next period, which Taylor (2019) calls "machinery in action" (1945–75), is when rapid urbanization occurred, the response to which was shaped by these established institutional differences. In Canada, provincial supervision increased, and in the United States, the federal government played a lead role in encouraging intermunicipal collaboration, using it as a condition for spending on infrastructure investments in cities related to growth, renewal, and housing (Taylor 2019, 46). The legacy of home rule also mattered, which led local governments to establish more single-purpose districts as service providers since they could get around legal limitations on capital borrowing in suburbs in the United States (46). Taylor argues that this period led to more effective metropolitan planning in Canadian cities than in the United States and a lower level of complexity in municipal systems (including fewer single-purpose districts or agencies, boards, and commissions than in the United States). According to Taylor, the current era, which he argues began in 1975, is one in which political cultures shifted, including a shift in the level of trust in government. In this period, provincial action in metropolitan land-use and infrastructure planning was inconsistent; in the United States, federal incentives to support metropolitan coordination declined, and states did not fill the gap in this respect (47). Thus, through comparison of two cases in each country – Toronto and Vancouver in Canada and Minneapolis-St. Paul and Portland in the United States – he shows how the institutional foundations of Canadian municipal systems created conditions for more effective metropolitan planning, but also how changes in political culture (or the normative context) matter (namely the willingness of citizens to trust provincial governments to intervene).

Like many institutional analyses, Taylor (2019, 312–15) draws lessons about institutional design from the study, arguing that we must take provinces and states' roles seriously as enablers of robust local government systems. He argues for balance between respect for local (municipal) autonomy and a provincial/state role in setting standards at a larger scale and ensuring equity across jurisdictions. For him, too much focus on home rule might de-incentivize provincial or state action in metropolitan government or as enablers of strong local government. Through a thorough historical and comparative analysis of municipal systems in two similar Anglo countries, Taylor generates powerful insights to inform current constitutional debates.

Influential Theoretical Ideas about Institutions, Political Behaviour, and Community Power in the American Urban Politics Literature

RATIONAL CHOICE INSTITUTIONALISM IN URBAN THEORY: TIEBOUT AND THE CITY LIMITS THESIS

Rational choice theory is a body of theory that begins with the assumption that individuals are self-maximizing agents, essentially seeking to further their own self-interest. As Guy Peters (2019, 14–19) describes, this body of theory initially developed as part of the behavioural revolution in social sciences and represented a move away from institutional theory toward the study of individual behaviour, driven by individuals' self-interest. These perspectives diverged with institutional analysis, which does not centre individual actors in its analysis, instead focusing on broad patterns of political development (as depicted above), or which considers individual behaviour to be driven by institutional norms and what is considered appropriate rather than by a strategic calculation – what Peters calls "normative institutionalism" (2019, 24).

Rational choice approaches to the study of urban politics in Canada have influenced the debate about municipal behaviour and metropolitan governance. Such approaches impute rationality upon municipal governments, conceptualizing them as in competition with one another for residents that will further the interests of the municipality, which is characterized like a type of firm.

The Tiebout Hypothesis. As Guy Peters notes, rational choice theories are often motivated by showing how a social welfare function can be achieved without the imposition of hierarchical or coercive means (essentially without being imposed by government) (Peters 2019, 58). For instance, the highly influential Tiebout hypothesis (Tiebout 1956) posits that by competing with each other for residents, municipalities are incentivized to offer a bundle of services and taxes that are attractive to prospective residents. Residents, who are also conceived as rational actors, are assumed to move within metropolitan areas to places that provide the right bundle of services for them, leading to responsive and efficient service provision. Such ideas underpin debates about municipal fragmentation and consolidation (through amalgamations, for instance) with the Tiebout hypothesis viewing fragmentation as a way of ensuring that services are highly tailored to local populations and that residents only receive the services that they are willing to pay for (by voting with their feet so to speak). As we see in chapter 6, a major concern of the municipal finance literature is to ensure that there is a match between who pays for and who benefits from services, which is thought to increase service efficiency and equity by making "the best use of available resources to improve people's lives" (See also Bird and Slack 2014).[2] An implicit assumption (which Slack mentions explicitly in chapter 6) is that municipal governments should not be in the business of redistribution (social policy) and that redistribution will happen at other levels of government.

However, as Michael Howell-Moroney (2008) argues, the Tiebout hypothesis does not address "spillover" effects (the way that policy decisions in one jurisdiction affect other jurisdictions) among fragmented jurisdictions in metropolitan areas. In particular, he points out that upper-class residents may choose to live in affluent developments on the urban fringe, contributing to sprawl and the concentration of poverty in urban cores. Sorting is not only motivated by preferences for particular services but also by a desire for exclusive communities (Howell-Moroney 2008, 98).

The City Limits Thesis. In his highly influential book *City Limits*, Paul Peterson (1981) offers a rational choice and institutionalist theory of city (municipal) policy-making and of the nature of local politics. He conceptualizes cities as rational actors in the American intergovernmental system whose decisions are determined mainly by their jurisdictional constraints as well as the constraints of their competitive position in relation to other municipalities as the lowest level of government in the United States. Peterson argues that since they exist in a situation of limited jurisdiction and at a smaller scale, the powers that they do have are influenced to a large degree by socioeconomic and political factors at larger scales (Peterson 1981). Essentially, Peterson (1981, 22) conceptualizes cities as self-maximizing, rational actors that seek to improve their economic, social, and political status relative to other cities. According to him, cities will use their limited jurisdiction, including zoning laws, level of spending, tax rates, and ability to provide land and a low-regulation environment to attract business and human capital (27–8). His assumptions about cities' "rationality" led him to predict that cities will focus on developmental policies, that is, policies that are in their economic interest and avoid redistributive policies for the same reason.

Furthermore, Peterson downplays the significance of other grassroots forces, depicting local politics as a form of politics that is unable to sustain partisan politics and that is generally devoid of sustained group politics (117–18), in other words, as apolitical. With Marxism-inspired growth machine theorists, discussed below, he describes developmental politics as a "consensus" (133) but attributes it to the strategic behaviour of municipalities within the context of external forces (a particular constitutional-institutional system in which municipalities have jurisdictional and other limits) that create incentives for cities to compete with one another instead of to the ongoing boosterism of local actors like the "rentiers" of the growth machine (discussed more below).

Although Peterson's analysis misses important elements of local politics, his depiction of cities as self-interested, competitive, and strategic actors in a system of "open borders" captures elements of local immigration policy-making discussed in chapter 12 of this volume. For instance, although rare, we see evidence of American cities using their bylaw-making and enforcement powers to deter undocumented migrants from settling in their cities. Farmer's Branch, Texas, passed three such ordinances, including an enactment that prohibited landlords from renting to undocumented migrants (Vicino 2013, 56). However, the research on local immigration policy-making also suggests that what constitutes a developmental policy varies among municipalities, with immigrant-friendly policy-making now widely considered a way to attract and retain human capital (see chapter 12 of this book). In both Canada and the United States, members of the business community are among the most vocal supporters of immigration, and many municipal corporations see this as in their interest as well.

In other ways, though, this chapter and others challenge the notion that city politics is as limited as Peterson suggests. Many of the powers that he stresses as fundamental to national governments (and as limits to cities), such as border control through the issuance of passports or currency, have also become constrained in a global, interdependent world in which migrant flows are increasingly difficult to control. Cities are, in fact, finding innovative ways to integrate migrants whose status is undocumented through measures such as municipal identifications. In another example provided in chapter 13, municipalities are adopting measures to contribute to reconciliation with Indigenous Peoples in Canada despite their lack of jurisdiction and legal uncertainty about their obligations to Indigenous Peoples. Although the idea that forms of city citizenship are emerging is highly contested, such experimentation, coupled with the increasing constraints facing national governments, raises serious points of debate about Peterson's highly influential conception of local politics. The notion that municipal politics cannot sustain a partisan form of politics and that group politics is unimportant to local policy-making is also increasingly challenged as we see in chapters 8 (on municipal elections) and 14 (on challenging anti-Black racism), for instance. Nevertheless, although local policy-making may be less constrained and more political than Peterson suggests, the level of consensus around policies that grow municipal populations, including through immigration, also lends credence to Peterson's notion that cities possess a "unitary interest." Does this seminal work still offer insights into the nature of local politics? Moreover, can these insights be applied to Canadian cases? In other words, is there value in thinking about Canadian municipal politics in this way (and making an implicit comparison with American cities since the theory was developed in that context)?

An earlier debate in the American urban politics literature recognized the importance of local politics in an era that might be seen as a "golden age" in the study of urban politics in the United States – the community power debate of the 1950s and 1960s.

THE COMMUNITY POWER DEBATE

In contrast to Peterson's conception of municipal politics and policy-making as fundamentally different and limited, in the 1950s and 1960s, many American scholars believed that studying individual cities in-depth (conducting case studies) could shed light on the general nature of American democracy. In this body of literature, two important works with conflicting findings about the extent to which power was concentrated in an elite or dispersed more widely initiated what became known as the "community power debate." Floyd Hunter's (1953) elitist study of Atlanta, Georgia, used reputational methods to identify community decision-makers by asking an initial group of elites to list who was most powerful in the city and then to interview individuals who were consistently at the top of the list to understand their connections and influence on policy-making. He found that there was a "powerful and coherent cadres of perceived policymakers" that consisted mainly of senior business executives (Harding 2009, 38–9). Among elected officials, only the mayor was in this decision-making group (38–9). One powerful critique of Hunter's study was that he did not show how this group of local elites actually influenced particular decisions at the local level.

Robert Dahl's (1961) *Who Governs?* is a pluralist work that established that power is more *dispersed* in the United States than Hunter's depiction suggested. He examined decision-making in urban development, education, and political nominations, finding that a form of stratified pluralism existed in New Haven, Connecticut (Judge 1995, 19). In the pluralist framework, although some actors are more influential in local politics, different elites lead in different policy areas, and elected officials are guided by the preferences of citizens (perceived or expressed) (19). In addition, pluralists argue that although resources are unequal, influence is not cumulative; in other words, "no minority group is permanently excluded from the political arena or suffers cumulative inequalities" (16). All groups have some resources, and therefore, also some influence, even if it is unequal.

Writing in 1995, in his review of pluralist thought, American urban scholar David Judge argued that "a reassessment of the importance of Dahl's work is underway" and that there has been a rapprochement between the left and pluralist theory (Judge 1995, 32). To him, pluralism seemed to fit as a model to understand the rising significance of a wide range of identity groups to local politics, including gender and ethnic identities (32).

Whereas pluralism continues to be an influential theory in urban politics not only on its own but also because of the way it influenced theories that came later, it suffers from fundamental flaws. Some elitists pointed out that the agenda-setting process is not addressed in pluralist accounts, including the question of non-decisions; for instance, some elitist critics note that the capitalist (business) class's broad interests are always represented even in the absence of group pressure. As we will discuss further below, growth machine theory makes the question of agenda setting central to urban analysis, arguing that all cities govern for growth. More recent critiques also discussed below point out that pluralism ignored the presence of structural racism and exclusion in the United States, a particularly relevant critique in the current context of the Black Lives Matter movement. According to Thompson, the fact that race riots occurred in New Haven shortly after *Who Governs?* was published and that African American exclusion and demobilization was not addressed in the study (Thompson 2009, 188) shows how pluralism was a normative ideal that only applied to the privileged white population. This work did not consider race as a structural and historically rooted form of power but instead viewed African Americans through an "ethnic politics" lens whereby they were perceived as a group that would integrate into city politics as waves of immigrants had in the past (188).

GROWTH MACHINE THEORY

One important response to the community power debate came from Harvey Molotch and John Logan,[3] who argued that the most pertinent question is not "who governs?" but rather is "for what?" Their Marxism-inspired theory might be placed within the elitist tradition of community power. Their primary research question asks: What are the primary goals of municipal politics? Their answer is that American cities govern in the interest of growth above all else, and they theorize "an apparatus of interlocking progrowth associations and governmental units" – in other words a type of urban coalition that they call a "growth machine" (Logan and Molotch 1987, 32). This type of coalition dominated in American cities in the 1960s, 1970s, and 1980s, through a period of urban development called the urban renewal period when so-called slums were cleared to make way for expressways and so-called renewal, a phenomenon that is discussed critically in chapter 14 on race and urban politics. Growth machine theory argues that growth is not only one of many equally important goals of cities; rather, it is a consensus and an ideology that pervades all aspects of urban politics (Logan and Molotch 1987). As the authors describe: "Although they may differ on which particular strategy will best succeed, elites use their growth consensus to eliminate any alternative vision of the *purpose of local government or the meaning of community*" (51, emphasis added).

Like elitist theory, growth machine theory emphasizes the power of the business community – and, in particular, a segment of business owners that own land and are involved in land development, whom they call the "rentiers." The rentiers are city boosters who want growth to be connected not only with making profits (with cities' exchange values) but also with their use values – as places that provide employment, good services, and have strong cultural industries, for instance (Logan and Molotch 1987). The growth machine accomplishes this by fostering a competitive spirit in city dwellers, with the ultimate goal being a local public that unquestionably supports development (Logan and Molotch 1987). They have a number of natural allies with whom they share a common interest in growth (Harding and Blokland 2014, 96): First, businesses that benefit directly from the development process, including developers, financiers, construction interests, and professionals with a direct interest in development such as architects, planners, and real estate agents; second, actors who benefit indirectly because development boosts demand for their products and services such as local media and utility companies; third, organizations with local connections – like universities, cultural institutions, professional sports clubs, labour unions, the self-employed, and local retailers (if interests coincide).

Although little research exists on growth politics and the influence of local actors in Canadian cities compared with the American literature, we see in chapter 10 that growth is also a central focus of local leaders in Canada as highlighted by Canadian and American leaders' common and "longstanding fascination with the construction and public subsidy of sports stadiums" to attract or retain professional sports franchises that are seen as important to civic pride and city boosting. The concept of cities as growth machines also resonates with the insights of James Lorimer's (1978) important book entitled *The Developers*, which argues that growth was also unchallenged in Canadian cities in the early post-war period. However, his account draws attention to the multilevel aspect of growth governance. Developers' (instead of residents') preferences shaped the types of housing and commercial buildings built in Canadian cities, but they did so with the support of all levels of government (federal, provincial, and municipal) as well as Canada's financial institutions. He explores not only the local coalition behind the rise of what he calls the "corporate city" and "corporate suburb" but also how the broader institutional context in Canada shaped the possibilities that developers and the development industry worked within. The consequences were significant – suburbanization, increased reliance on automobiles, and housing that was less affordable than it could have been. He argues that because municipalities could no longer afford to (or chose not to) service new land, developers were able to control which land would be developed. Developers created large stocks of land, called land banks, serviced it themselves, and marked it up dramatically, controlling where development would occur while making excessive profits (Lorimer 1978). Developers also benefited from government subsidies and intervention in the rapid expansion of downtown office buildings (Lorimer 1978). In his analysis, all levels of government and banks influenced the development process – the banks injected capital into this industry instead of others, the federal government (through the CMHC) backed mortgages, and municipalities used their powers of expropriation to help developers assemble land to pursue their developments. Developers also benefited from government assistance, including municipal assistance, in the rapid expansion of downtown office buildings in Canada. We see a similar dynamic of extraction of benefits and pressure on municipalities to succumb to the demands of owners of sports franchises, discussed in chapter 10.

Although there was resistance by residents in neighbourhoods subject to so-called renewal (Lorimer 1978, 228) as we discover in chapter 14, developers' urban renewal projects often targeted racialized neighbourhoods disproportionately, in some cases demolishing entire communities as in Africville, a historic Black settlement in Halifax.

Growth continues to dominate local agendas in North American municipalities; however, changes in the economy (including globalization) as well as changing ideas of economic development now shape these coalitions. For instance, one highly popular theory of how cities grow is offered by Richard Florida (2002, ix), whose work has been highly influential in North America. He argues that a specific "class" – the "creative class," which includes scientists, engineers, architects, designers, writers, artists, musicians, and others who use creativity in their work – drives economic growth. The creative class prefers places that are "diverse, tolerant and open to new ideas" (249); what he refers to as the 3Ts of economic development – technology, talent, and tolerance must all be present (249). The popularity of his ideas has influenced municipal growth strategies, leading municipalities to pursue policies that they expect to attract this class. His ideas provide one rationale for municipalities' entry into the field of local immigration policy-making (see Good 2009). This work does not challenge the idea that municipalities focus on growth – it simply argues that a city's use value is what attracts the human capital that, in turn, drives growth. In chapter 10, Spicer argues that a focus on "quality of life factors and the advantage of settling in communities that are diverse and well-educated" is emphasized by Canadian leaders more than American leaders in their efforts to attract digital infrastructure for smart city development because provinces regulate the types of financial inducements municipalities can provide more strictly than in the United States, where local leaders have greater freedom to provide tax breaks and "direct cash inducements."

Chapter 11 on climate change draws our attention to how growth at any cost is increasingly challenged. Chapters 14 and 15 also provide perspective on how the benefits of growth are highly uneven. Focusing on the continued influence of structural racism and colonialism in cities underscores the extent to which not all forms of diversity are equally valued, even in places that have bought into Richard Florida's ideas (see Rutland 2018, loc. 262).

If one considers the growth machine idea in relation to scholarship on settler colonialism, we can see how the profits made by landowners have occurred on the ancestral and often unceded lands of Indigenous Peoples. This process involved the displacement of Indigenous Peoples onto rural reserves and the erasure of cities' Indigenous histories. As chapter 13 discusses, the relationships between Indigenous Peoples and municipalities are shifting, and efforts at decolonization are underway in some places. Should such efforts progress, the concept of land as a means to turn a profit could clash with Indigenous conceptions of land's purpose, offering another challenge to a consensus about "value free development" or development at all costs (Logan and Molotch 1987). To what extent are Canadian cities growth machines? Who are the contemporary actors who support growth, and who are challengers to the growth agenda? Are growth machine coalitions similar across cities or do they vary by city?

Indeed, although growth machine theory continues to resonate because a great deal of local politics continues to be driven by growth politics, intercity competition, and local boosterism, it also has several limitations, such as how it cannot explain variation in local political agendas. Furthermore, growth agendas can take many forms, and resistance to focusing on growth varies by city. This is where our next theory – urban regime theory – has more currency.

URBAN REGIME THEORY

Urban regime theory was a dominant theoretical paradigm in the American urban politics literature beginning with Clarence Stone's (1989) seminal study of Atlanta entitled *Regime Politics*, which is widely seen as the starting point for contemporary regime analyses (Mossberger and Stoker 2001). *Regime Politics* is case study of Atlanta in 1946–88 that examined how local leaders constructed and maintained a biracial coalition that was able to pursue urban redevelopment in a highly volatile era of American politics – the rise of the civil rights movement and the dismantling of legal segregation under Jim Crow. Together, the largely white business community pursued its urban renewal objective of downtown redevelopment in exchange for support of desegregation and jobs for middle-class Blacks.

Urban regime theory resonated in the United States in part because it offered a concept of power and a view of local agency that could refocus the theoretical debate about local community *control* between the elitists and pluralists. The study of urban regimes offered a social-production model of power defined by *a capacity, a set of actors*, and *relationships* that support that resource sharing.

In the 1980s, many urban scholars agreed that American local politics was developmental and focused largely on urban renewal objectives, which were perceived to be questions of land use (Stone 2015). Urban regime theory accepted much of this account of the political economy, arguing, however, that how and whether these developmental purposes were pursued depends on the possibilities for collaboration across sectors *in a particular city context*. For instance, in Atlanta, after trying (without success) to have the core city's boundaries extended to increase the white population, the business community chose *pragmatically* to put aside its racist and segregationist views to be able to pursue downtown redevelopment in a municipality where the demographics favoured the Black community. In essence, the white business community supported desegregation and Atlanta became the "City Too Busy to Hate" (its city motto) based on a strategic alliance with the business community offering jobs for middle-class Blacks in exchange for municipal support from the Black majority city council.

Thus, although urban regime theory shifted the focus of urban power to social production, it did not completely abandon the question of stratification or control in urban societies, acknowledging that the business community possesses a form of systemic power because it is resource rich and, therefore, an attractive coalition partner. Nevertheless, although regime theory theorizes the systemic power of the business community and explains why co-operation emerged biracially in Atlanta, it does not provide an account of institutionalized white privilege and structural racism. As we discuss further below, such an account requires thinking about how the state contributes to perpetuating privilege and structural racism.

Urban regime theory became the dominant theoretical paradigm in American urban politics literature. Regime studies proliferated, and a debate emerged about whether the concept had been "stretched," losing its precision and core meaning (Mossberger and Stoker 2001).

Whether the concept can travel to Canada has also been a subject of debate (Cobban 2003a, 2003b; Leo 2003). Judith Garber and David Imbroscio also argue that growth politics in Canada is directed at the province, not at the city level, due to differences in American and Canadian legal contexts, what they call differences in "constitutional regimes" (1996, 597). Others such as Horak (1998) and Good (2009) applied the concept to their studies of Toronto's anti-amalgamation movement and local immigration policy-making, respectively. Good (2009) adapted the concept to acknowledge the importance of multi-scale governance relations. Some European scholars also argue that the urban regime concept is an abstraction of the American political economy, noting that institutional differences shape local politics differently in Europe (Pierre 1999). Thus, the term "urban governance" is more commonly employed in Canada and in Europe, with leading urban governance theorist Jon Pierre conceptualizing regimes as one type of urban governance (that has emerged in the United States). Yet, key insights from urban regime theory remain relevant, including the importance of acknowledging the business community's systemic power based on its advantage in terms of providing resources to local communities as well as the strategic and pragmatic orientation to co-operation among local leaders who assemble governance arrangements.

Urban Governance Theory and Multilevel Governance

URBAN GOVERNANCE: THE IMPORTANCE OF INSTITUTIONS AND NORMS TO GOVERNANCE

Urban scholars in Europe have developed a rich literature on "urban governance," which "looks at the interplay between state and society and the extent to which collective projects can be achieved through a joint public and private mobilization of resources" (Pierre 2011, 5). Although work on governance is widespread, the literature focuses on the role of *government* in governance processes, which is new (5). As Bradford and Bramwell argue, government continues to be relevant in urban governance arrangements, but "its role changes from provider of solutions to enabler or partner in joint problem solving" (2014, 14). In this capacity, "new roles and instruments come into focus: catalyst, convener, facilitator, and partner" (14). The term "metagovernance" has been introduced to capture the way "specific types of institutionalized governance networks are created, managed and steered by government officials" (Doberstein 2013, 587).

Jon Pierre, a central contributor to this work, usefully draws attention to institutions in two senses – first, as structures and sources of organizational continuity that "define the range of choice and behaviour of the organization's members" and as "norm, value, rules and practices" (2011, 6). Both types of institutions mould and constrain behaviour (Thelen and Steinmo 1991) and are related because norms become institutionalized in formal structures, which become their "carriers" (Pierre 2011, 6; see also Peters 2019). In Pierre's (2011, 15) view, urban regime theory blurs the role of *formal institutions* in governance processes. According to Pierre, examining formal institutions is important not only because it is the only way in which local governments are held accountable by citizens (through the democratic process) but also because they provide clues as to who wields power in cities because institutions reflect *embedded norms*. Pierre develops a typology of modes of urban governance, arguing that the modes have dominant goals, which he labels "managerial governance, corporatist governance, pro-growth governance and welfare governance" (2011, 8). According to him, the pro-growth orientation is more common in the United States (as reflected in the concept of American cities as growth machines) than in Europe although it has spread globally in recent years.

Pierre's point that institutions and the broader institutional context (e.g., various levels of government) matter to local governance and that norms can develop is in alignment with Canadian scholars' historical approaches to institutional analysis. However, both Canadian and American scholars challenge Pierre's typology, which emphasizes single dominant focuses. For instance, Canadian urban governance scholars Neil Bradford and Allison Bramwell argue that urban governance goals do not fit neatly into economic, social, or environmental categories implied by the categories of pro-growth and welfare governance, for instance (for examples of this phenomenon, see also Sellers 2002; Savitch and Kantor 2002). They suggest that "hybrids" that combine different types of goals (e.g., economic, social, and environmental) are more common (Bradford and Bramwell 2014). Bradford and Bramwell argue that we should think about governance in terms of the scope and level of institutionalization of the governance arrangements or forms of co-operation, identifying three types: "institutionalized collaboratives," "sector partnerships," and "project partnerships" (2014, 17). Through comparison of Canadian cities, these Canadian scholars have made a significant contribution to the international governance literature.

MULTILEVEL POLITICS AND GOVERNANCE

It is increasingly recognized that the localist perspective on urban governance – in other words, a perspective that views the local scale as independent of the larger intergovernmental system – is an incomplete picture. Urban governance has always been a multilevel process of interaction between levels of government and organizations operating at a variety of scales. The term *multilevel governance* emerged more recently (originally in Europe to describe the layering of authority brought about by the European Union) and has been used somewhat indiscriminately to describe all types of multilevel processes or politics (Alcantara, Broschek, and Nelles 2016).

In chapter 4 of this book, Martin Horak defines multilevel governance "as a set of practices that operate across state scales, through which multiple autonomous actors – including but not necessarily limited to governments – coordinate resources and authority in order to address governing tasks that each of them cannot address by acting alone." For Horak, multilevel governance is a "set of governing *practices*" that "emerge *in* a political system where resources and authority are divided among multiple actors at different scales." For this reason, multilevel governance practices emerge even in unitary states, which divide authority between a central government and local governments (see chapter 4). He proposes a threefold typology of multilevel governance based on variation in "*who* is involved (actors), *what* they do (roles), and *how* they interact (modes)."

Multilevel governance is a type of governance that has become more widespread due to global economic, social, and political changes, as well as urbanization. For instance, work on the political economy of cities argues that the reorganization of capitalism is leading to a rescaling of authority and influencing how "state spaces" are organized with an increasing focus on cities by all levels of government (Brenner 2004). This work suggests that changes in multilevel relations and policy-making are motivated by the territorial reorganization of capitalism to a hierarchical system of world cities. Governments at all levels now understand that major cities are crucial to competing globally. Therefore, all governments must address the complex urban policy challenges in cities. Another relevant trend is what Alcantara, Broschek, and Nelles (2016, 36) call the "resurgence of territorial politics," involving the "appreciation, empowerment and even creation of governmental or quasi-governmental tiers" at the local, regional, and supranational levels (e.g., the EU, USMCA). Furthermore, changing political cultures and patterns of mobilization in cities, as well as ideas about democratic legitimacy, have led governments to include organizations in civil society in decision-making (Alcantara, Broschek, and Nelles 2016). A fundamental characteristic of multilevel governance, according to these authors, is its non-hierarchical and inclusive nature (Alcantara, Broschek, and Nelles 2016).

Canadian scholars have made significant conceptual and empirical contributions to the literature on multilevel politics in a variety of policy areas (see, for instance, Horak and Young 2012; Peters 2012; and other books in the same series as well as Leo 2006). For instance, Smith's (2022) study of homelessness policy in four major cities in Canada (Calgary, Montreal, Toronto, and Vancouver) demonstrates the role of a variety of types of ideas in shaping governance relationships to address homelessness in Canada. Specifically, three kinds of ideas matter: ideas about whose role it is to provide social protection, ideas about the city's role (whether it is seen primarily as a service provider or as a government with a more comprehensive role), and ideas about the definition of homelessness (Smith 2022, 17). Multilevel politics and Canadian contributions to the vast international literature are so important to the study of urban politics in Canada that we have devoted a foundational, conceptual chapter to this topic (chapter 4).

Political Culture and the Roots of Collective Action

The study of political culture is the study of a political community's "fundamental orientations and assumptions about politics" (Stewart 2002, 24). It "refers to the shared values, orientations, and attitudes that define various social groups (such as nations, regions, and groups of people that share ethnic or religious backgrounds)" (Harell and Deschâtelets 2014, 229). In their seminal book, *The Myth of the North American City*, Goldberg and Mercer (1986) argue that major differences in cities and municipal institutions can be traced to social, civic, or public values (which they use interchangeably). For instance, they distinguish Canadians and Americans along an "individualism" versus "collectivism" axis and an "assimilationism" versus "multiculturalism" axis. They tie these broad differences to variation in urban density, levels of fragmentation of local government institutions and systems, patterns of intergovernmental relations, forms of metropolitan government, and urban finance (Goldberg and Mercer 1986, 142–4). For instance, they argue that Canadians prefer living in central cities because of their collective orientation and support for multiculturalism, which results in higher densities in Canadian cities than in the United States. In the United States, racially mixed but segregated cities push more Americans to the suburbs; they also have a greater cultural preference for suburban and rural living (146–7). With respect to institutions and institutional change, they argue that differences in political culture explain why provinces were able to consolidate municipal systems through reforms such as major amalgamations, whereas "resistance in American cities to municipal integration is well known, and the thought of this being imposed by any of the states with no local say is anathema" (144).

Although dated, this interpretation of the evolution of Canadian municipal institutions and the development of cities is impressive in its scope. However, such a depiction of Canadians' view of local government lacks nuance as it belies the fact that prominent figures in Canada's early constitutional development (as discussed in chapter 2) valued local institutions. Furthermore, Canada's (as well as other countries') political cultures appear to be shifting. As discussed above, Taylor (2019) notes a general shift in the normative context of governance (since the 1990s) that has made it more difficult for provinces to pursue (and, depending on one's perspective, impose) programmatic reforms. Furthermore, as we saw in chapter 2, state governments in the United States appear more willing to intervene in local affairs by passing laws that pre-empt local action in specific policy spheres. Such a national perspective also absorbs community-level diversity in perspectives across Canada, including in more recent Canadian history of municipal reform. The reaction of Toronto residents, from the C4LD's response (Horak 1998) to a forced municipal amalgamation to the more recent Charter City Toronto movement (Charter City Toronto, n.d.), suggests that cities may vary in the extent to which citizens are deferential to provincially imposed municipal reforms.

COMPARATIVE APPROACHES TO LOCAL "CIVIC CULTURES" AND POLICY STYLES IN METROPOLITAN AREAS

The literature on local "civic cultures" has identified *different political-cultural environments at the local scale*, even in places with common formal local institutions (see Nelles 2012). Reese and Rosenfeld argue that local political cultures matter – the "fine distinctions in local civic culture, the habitus of how interests are balanced, problems defined, symbols interpreted, goals envisioned, and decisions made … have the greatest and perhaps most subtle effects on public policy" (2002, 43).

In her study of regional co-operation, Jen Nelles (2012) compares four metropolitan regions – Toronto and Waterloo in Canada and Frankfurt Rhein-Main and Rhein-Neckar in Germany. This comparison allows her to assess the impact of different factors (including city size and national context) on regional co-operation. She finds that while institutions (the capacities of local actors) and opportunities (external events and interventions) shape the intensity of co-operation in these city-regions in significant but unpredictable ways, "civic capital" has a consistently positive effect on co-operation (Nelles 2012, 19):

> Civic capital is a shared perception of a region. It is the idea that there exists a metropolitan region defined, independently from political formulations and structures, by the space within which individuals and other actors organize and experience their social, economic, and professional existence in urban space. It is based on the assumption that how people collectively define and experience a metropolitan region can influence the political calculus of decision-makers and their political will to engage at that scale. Civic capital is the measure of the extent to which an urban community has a collective perception of a metropolitan space. It is nothing more than the idea of a region. But ideas can be powerful. (Nelles 2012, 44)

From a practical perspective, civic capital emerges from local leaders who mobilize local networks and have a particular scalar perspective that is oriented to the metropolitan regional scale (Nelles 2012, 45–6). The analysis reveals that civic capital is stronger in smaller places (Waterloo in Canada and Rhein-Neckar in Germany both have higher levels of civic capital than Toronto and Frankfurt Rhine-Main), allowing for more bridging among policy issues and across municipalities (171). Nelles is also able to observe differences in *policy styles* in the two national contexts (more radical policy shifts in Germany compared with incrementalism in Canada), arguing that these differences may be due to national infrastructures (173). More recently, Jen Nelles and David Wolfe (2022) have revisited the idea of civic capital, situating it relative to literature on urban institutions, urban governance, social capital, and place leadership to address the question of how particular social and political qualities of place create supportive environments for urban economic development.

Anthony Perl, Matt Hern, and Jeffrey Kenworthy's (2020) comparative study of mobility infrastructure in Montreal, Toronto, and Vancouver underscores a national policy style that may complement Nelles's (2012) contention of Canadian incrementalism, which they describe as ambivalent, equivocal, and pragmatic. They draw on Carolyn Tuohy's notion of "institutional ambivalence" – noting that a distinctive feature of "Canadian institutions is their capacity to embody conflicting principles within structures ambiguous *enough to allow for ad hoc accommodations over time*" (Tuohy 1992, xvii, 4, emphasis added). They identify a common tendency in these Canadian cities in *different* regions noting that they have all accommodated both global aspirations and local preferences as well as allowed different development paradigms to co-exist in tension with one another – car dependence, walkability, and transit-oriented development (Perl, Hern, and Kenworthy 2020, 31). For instance, Montreal's enthusiastic embrace of urban expressways connecting to routes that serve the Island of Montreal and beyond was offset by a full build-out of its metro network and the preservation of many walkable inner-city neigh-bourhoods that paralleled the creation of an automobile-dependent suburbia.

POLITICAL CULTURE, DIVERSITY, AND DEMOGRAPHIC CHANGE

A strictly national perspective on political culture such as Goldberg and Mercer's (1986) not only hides regional, provincial, and community diversity, it also absorbs and erases the per-spectives of minorities and their place in shaping Canadian political culture. Debra Thompson (2008) argues that both institutions and paradigmatic approaches to political science, such as the mainstream literature on political culture upon which Goldberg and Mercer draw, purport to be colour-blind and, in doing so, reinforce racial inequities. For instance, she points out that immigration is considered a major source of change in political cultures (with histories of immigration used to explain provincial differences in political culture in seminal works such as Nelson Wiseman's) but that more recent waves of immigration by racialized minorities are conceptualized as having little impact because the political culture is now "too established" (Wiseman 2008, 41, quoted in Thompson 2008, 539). Yet, as she also points out, research on regional political cultures finds significant differences in the political cultures of urban places, which is where most immigrants, many of whom are racialized minorities, settle (see Hen-derson 2004, 53). Kristin Good's (2009) work on how immigrant settlement patterns have influenced local community dynamics and municipal activity in multiculturalism policy also suggests that immigration continues to change Canada's political culture(s).

Such work also erases the influence of Indigenous political culture, conceptualizing cities' political culture as only (or mainly) influenced by waves of settlers. As we discuss below, in-stances of the political and cultural resurgence of Indigenous Peoples in urban places, particu-larly in Prairie cities (see Tomiak et al. 2019), suggest that Indigenous agency is a significant influence on the political culture of cities, an influence that will likely only grow as urban Indigenous populations come to form a large percentage of the major cities across the country but particularly in the West's Prairie cities.

Thus, immigration and deep, historically entrenched forms of diversity shape the political cultures of city-regions. The linguistic bifurcation between francophones and anglophones has had a significant impact on the political culture of Moncton, New Brunswick, as evident in dif-ferent "identity projects" in the metropolitan area (Bourgeois and Bourgeois 2005). Alcantara and Nelles (2016) find a positive trend of increased collaboration through intergovernmental agreements between Indigenous governments and municipalities and identify a number of factors conducive to collaboration, factors that influence actors' willingness and capacity to act collectively. One such factor is what they call "community capital," which captures whether there is a shared "civic identity," defined as an "understanding that, despite differences, the two (or more) communities are part of a shared region" with "social integration" (loc. 1031). Ultimately, they find that willingness to collaborate is more important than capacity (resources), which underscores the importance of local political cultures to collective action.

In sum, Canadian scholars have made significant contributions to our understanding of how variations in local political cultures shape urban governance and municipal policy in Canadian cities. Canadian scholars have used comparison to develop a rich set of concepts that characterize aspects of cities and contribute to explaining patterns of political behaviour and decision-making. They identify dominant policy styles/orientations (e.g., institutional ambivalence), ethnic configurations that introduce different intercultural dynamics (e.g., backlash in response to immigration in "biracial" versus "multiracial" contexts), and various forms of local and regional capital that shape how actors imagine the city, including its boundaries and social identity. The next section offers a critical perspective on Canadian political culture, including its particular expression in cities.

Incorporating the Politics of Structural Racism and Colonialism into Urban Politics

Racism is not just about individual attitudes and beliefs; it is also about how norms and discriminatory rules are inscribed in institutions and continue to have a racist impact. Structural or systemic racism refers to "the macrolevel systems, social forces, institutions, ideologies, and processes that interact with one another to generate and reinforce inequities among racial and ethnic groups" (Gee and Ford 2011, 116). Institutional rules can empower individuals with racist attitudes, and discriminatory norms can also be *embedded in the rules themselves*. It is through activism, the grassroots struggles of marginalized communities, that the racist structures and their impact may become evident.

Canadian urban scholars have made important contributions to critically examining how discriminatory norms are embedded in municipal laws (bylaws) and governance practices. For instance, in her *Everyday Law on the Street*, Marianna Valverde (2012) critically explores municipal law and its enforcement, showing that both bylaws and enforcement practices are infused with cultural norms that disadvantage marginalized or minority communities. In some cases, the norms underpinning laws are discriminatory. A mundane example includes a property standards bylaw that requires a particular kind of lawn maintenance that is at odds with some cultural preferences for, for example, vegetable gardens in their front yards (Valverde 2012, 52). Reflecting on property standards bylaws, Valverde observes that the "cultural preferences of middle-aged, middle-class, married folks who own and lovingly tend a piece of urban property are constantly reinscribed in law both by the petty legislators who draw up ordinances and by the judges who interpret them" (49). Similarly, zoning generally reflects a clear normative preference for single-family homes over homes with secondary suites that can accommodate extended families in a way that is common in some cultures more than others.

In other cases, it is the processes of enforcement or policy implementation that enable racism. For instance, Valverde (2012) finds that Toronto's municipal bylaws are enforced unevenly, with higher noise levels permitted in marginalized neighbourhoods, by applying vague concepts such as "reasonableness" in nuisance bylaws. In another example, discussed in chapter 12, a comparative study of local immigration policies finds that the enforcement of housing bylaws in the United States has been deployed as an "anti-immigrant" measure in American suburbs (Williamson 2019, 95). The complaints-driven nature of bylaw enforcement practices can enable racist individuals to inflict harm on their neighbours.

What Michael Lipsky (2010) calls "street-level bureaucrats" have a significant level of discretion in how they implement policy decisions and services. Although such discretion can be used to be more responsive to local citizens, it can also be influenced by systemic racism and enable individuals with racist attitudes to harm others. The uneven employment of street checks by police to stop Black residents in cities across North American and British cities, discussed in chapter 14, is but one example of how rules and practices, and ultimately, the discretion of street-level bureaucrats, might channel individual racism or societal systemic racism embedded in local political cultures or organizations.

Another crucial example of institutional racism can be seen in the educational practices and outcomes for Black students in schools in major cities such as Toronto. Black students are more likely to be streamed into non-university pathways than others, contributing to a higher incidence of dropping out of high school. Such findings have led to the introduction of Black-focused schools, discussed in chapter 15 (see Thompson and Wallner 2011 for an overview of the debate leading up to the establishment of Afrocentric schooling in Toronto). And, unlike the pluralist notion that the power dynamics in different policy areas are distinct and disadvantages do not accumulate, institutional racism in one area bleeds over into other policy areas – *disadvantages are cumulative*. For instance, critical race scholars have written about the school-to-prison pipeline "to refer to the disciplinary policies and patterns of socialization utilized within school settings to differentially target minority students (particularly young African Canadian males) away from educational success, and towards incarceration" (Swain and Noblit 2011, cited in Bernard and Smith 2018, 151). The way in which racism leads to reinforcing forms of disadvantage may become evident in cities and in the everyday struggles of marginalized residents against discriminatory policy implementation by a variety of street-level bureaucrats, making cities important sites for the comparative study of power from the ground up.

In his *Displacing Blackness*, Ted Rutland (2018) shows how a normative assumption about the mobility of residents in the Halifax Regional Municipality led to further disadvantaging the African Nova Scotian community. The plan proposed growth centres to restrict development on the periphery of this vast municipality that combines urban, suburban, and rural places. He shows that planning norms were based on a white, middle- or upper-class experience of mobility across the municipality and did not acknowledge the "nonnormative and nonmarket histories of Black communities" that had settled on the periphery of the region due to deep structural racism (Rutland 2018, 280). Instead, planning norms look at these communities through the lens of sprawl, and these norms reinforce the disadvantage already faced by the Halifax Regional Municipality's peripheral, historic Black settlements. As Rutland articulates, "the Halifax Regional Municipality Planning, unable to recognize the particular nonnormative and nonmarket histories of Black communities, could find no reason to support a form of settlement (peripheral and dispersed) that Black residents had established and developed under the constraints of anti-Blackness. Perversely, planning could only see this form of settlement as a "a wasteful 'choice,' parasitic upon the economic lives of the broader population" (280).

Canada also has a long history of anti-Asian racism that continues to shape its urban politics. In the late nineteenth century, there was a strong anti-Chinese movement in British Columbia, where many Chinese immigrants were concentrated, as reflected in protests and a multitude of provincial anti-Asian bills, which were passed and then disallowed by the federal government on jurisdictional rather than human rights grounds (Fernando 2006). Vancouver experienced anti-Asian rioting in its early history, including on February 24, 1887, soon after its incorporation in 1886 (Yan 2023, 151). Open anti-Chinese racism was also a Canada-wide phenomenon until after the Second World War, supported by prime ministers, major newspapers, and reflected in various provincial laws disenfranchising residents with Chinese ancestry (until as late as 1951 in Saskatchewan) as well as in federal legislation restricting Chinese immigration (Fernando 2006). The City of Vancouver's history of racial violence also includes the removal of Japanese Canadians from coastal British Columbia to internment camps in the interior after Japanese attacks on Pearl Harbor during the Second World War, including from a Vancouver neighbourhood known to Japanese residents as Paueru Gai (Masuda et al. 2023). Nevertheless, although racism was less overt in later decades in Canadian history, structural anti-Asian racism persisted and was resisted by Chinese Canadian (and women-led) activism to protect a Chinese neighbourhood in Vancouver called Strathcona from "slum" clearance efforts (Lee 2007), a common racialized urban renewal strategy in the 1950 and 1960s in Canadian cities, discussed more in chapter 14 on combatting anti-Black racism. As Shanti Fernando (2006) argues in her comparison of Chinese Canadian and Chinese American mobilization in Toronto and Los Angeles, structural racism continues to present barriers to full political participation and power sharing for Chinese residents of both Toronto and Los Angeles even though their numbers are growing and their educational attainment often surpasses that of white residents. Chinese residents are perceived as unable to meet the norm of "whiteness," and discourses of "foreignness" persist with exclusionary effects (Fernando 2006).

Thus, work on race and diversity in Canadian cities demonstrates that power relations and, therefore, politics infuse the nature of municipal law and decision-making as well as its implementation. One form that power takes is normative – how the experience and cultural preferences of privileged residents are inscribed in law and policy-making in ways that lead to the marginalization of minorities. In the next section, we see the power of normative orders in processes of colonialism that are both manifested and challenged in Canadian cities.

COLONIALISM, DECOLONIZATION, AND RECONCILIATION IN CANADIAN CITIES

Although Indigenous Peoples face structural racism in cities like other racialized groups, as First Peoples with rights to land and other distinct legal and constitutional rights, they have a unique relationship with the Canadian state and have been subject to colonialism. In Canada, path-breaking research by both Indigenous and non-Indigenous scholars has begun to explore the relationship between cities and settler colonialism, defined as "sites where settlers have come to constitute a sizeable demographic majority independent of ties with any metropolitan sponsor and assert a sovereignty distinct from that of the metropolitan core" (Tomiak et al. 2019, loc. 304). Due to this, settler colonialism is about a settler population occupying the land itself and displacing Indigenous Peoples (loc. 304).

Tomiak et al. (2019) offer the concept of "settler city" to capture the way that settler colonialism operates at multiple scales and to highlight the particular role that the city plays in broader processes of colonialism through forced assimilation, brutality, and by attempting to disconnect the city from broader Indigenous struggles (loc. 421).

A fundamental element of power in urban places can be seen in an ongoing process of erasure – of replacing Indigenous names, languages, and traces of culture and history in urban places with settler institutions and cultural pieces, some of which are symbols of brutality for Indigenous Peoples like the statue of Edward Cornwallis in Halifax (Halifax Regional Municipality 2020). "Erasure" is one foundational manifestation of how the normative underpinning of institutions can be taken for granted and reinforce the privilege and culture of some groups over others. As we discuss in chapter 13, urban communities in Canada and other settler countries like Australia and New Zealand originated as Indigenous gathering places and spaces. In Canada, the "colonial spatial imaginary" places Indigenous Peoples in remote rural reserves, and cities are considered fundamentally non-Indigenous spaces (Tomiak et al. 2019, loc. 229). Nevertheless, Indigenous residents have been reclaiming city spaces in a variety of ways that point to the analytical importance of two additional forms of power in cities – resistance and resurgence. Indigenous scholars have made important contributions to our understanding of the various ways that colonialism is manifest in Canada as well as to our understanding of resistance and resurgence as forms of power in a colonial context. Drawing upon a rich body of Indigenous political theorizing, Julie Tomiak et al. (2019) discuss these two forms of Indigenous power in urban contexts. While resistance describes "movements and embodied practices [that] focus on addressing and fighting against settler colonial and state violence" and "react to" and "engage the settler state," "resurgence" involves "movements and embodied practices focused on rebuilding nation-specific Indigenous ways of being and actualizing self-determination"

(Tomiak et al. 2019, loc. 255). Corntassel and Bryce underscore the importance of "everyday practices of resurgence and decolonization" arguing that "Indigenous resurgence is about reconnecting with homelands, cultural practices, and communities and is centered on reclaiming, restoring, and regenerating homeland relationships" (2012, 153). Furthermore, resurgence requires moving away from strategies aimed at "state affirmation and approval [and] toward a daily existence conditioned by place-based cultural practices" (153). According to Tomiak et al. (2019), the resurgence of Indigenous Peoples can be seen by examining Indigenous grassroots initiatives and community organizations in Canadian cities. There are many such initiatives in Prairie cities, some of which have large concentrations of Indigenous Peoples. One example is Kinew, which is an Indigenous-led housing cooperative located in Winnipeg (Tomiak et al. 2019, loc. 273). Children of the Earth School, an Indigenous-focused school, is another Winnipeg example. Doug Anderson and Alexandra Flynn (2020) describe a variety of little-known practices associated with urban Indigenous cultural resurgence in Toronto in a park along the Humber River, including "full moon ceremonies" held by women, building purification lodges, naming ceremonies, planting and harvesting, fishing, lighting ceremonial fires, and others (Anderson and Flynn 2020, 116–17). As will be discussed further in chapter 12, Indigenous leaders and organizations in Winnipeg have also contributed significantly to Indigenous-newcomer relations, a form of intercultural relations aimed at recentering Indigenous community leaders as hosts in Canadian cities that reflect Indigenous resurgence in Winnipeg since Indigenous community leaders are leading such efforts.

What can comparison offer to our understanding of structural racism and colonialism on the one hand, and to resistance and resurgence on the other? Although scholars who study structural racism and colonialism stress the importance of context to understanding these processes, comparison can be fruitful in highlighting similarities in how such processes work in different contexts. In his comparative study of Minneapolis and Winnipeg, Hugill traces similar experiences of Indigenous migration to these cities in the post-1940s period. He notes a similar concentration of Indigenous people in particular neighbourhoods in both cities, especially in Minneapolis, where urban Indigenous residents concentrated in Southside Philips, a neighbourhood that became a focal point for cultural and political life so much so that it is "often described as a de facto 'urban reservation'" (Hugill 2019, loc. 1806). He notes that in both cities, concentration occurred for a combination of reasons, including both exclusion and the desire to build community. Spatial concentration, in turn, provided a greater capacity for the communities to organize in both cases. He notes that the American Indian Movement (AIM) was born in Minneapolis in 1968, a movement that built on a culture of grassroots organizing in which Indigenous women played a central role (Hugills 2019).[4] A similar vibrancy of Indigenous activism is evident in Winnipeg in its Idle No More mobilizations and in a long history of resistance (Hugill 2019). Hugill (2019) argues that in addition to highlighting the pervasiveness of colonialism in North American cities, the comparison offers an alternative interpretation of Indigenous marginality and segregation in cities, challenging a dominant explanation that focuses on the failure of Indigenous individuals to adjust to city life, ignoring colonialism as a process that continues to shape power relations in the present. He concludes that comparison can be deployed to non-imperial ends, observing that "while this [comparative] approach risks conflating heterogenous phenomena into an overtly coherent frame, it also offers opportunities to challenge the naturalization of settler hegemonies *by revealing their proximity to other historical formations*" (Hugill 2019, loc. 2089). He does this in two ways: first, by showing that settler colonialism operates in two different national and city contexts to produce similar negative outcomes for Indigenous Peoples; second, he highlights that resistance (and resurgence) rather than marginality is evident in both places. In this way, Hugill's comparative work centres Indigenous agency and downplays the idea that settler society can be taken for granted – that the relevant question is one of integration into a settler-defined city. Furthermore, the similar findings in his two cases in different national contexts show that settler colonialism is a global process (Gabriel Piterberg 2008, 55, cited in Hugill 2019, loc. 1755).

Although colonialism's impacts continue to be significant, local and urban places are also important sites of evolving relationships between Indigenous Peoples and non-Indigenous peoples as well as between Indigenous governments and municipalities. The Truth and Reconciliation Commission released its six-volume report in 2015, including ninety-four calls to action or recommendations to move the relationship between Indigenous Peoples and the Canadian state to more friendly relations. Nevertheless, there is debate about whether reconciliation is possible or whether it amounts to assimilation (Borrows and Tully 2018, 4). The concept of resurgence "is often used to refer to Indigenous Peoples exercising powers of self-determination outside of state structures and paradigms" (3). For this reason, John Borrows and James Tully (2018, 4–5) distinguish between "separate resurgence" and "resurgence-reconciliation" or "transformative reconciliation," which are relationships between Indigenous Peoples and settlers that are informed by "robust" practices of resurgence. They suggest that what this means in practice must be left open-ended and that we must examine concrete examples of relationships critically and in a dialogical way that involves listening and learning how different participants use the word. According to them, "Learning how to use the words reconciliation and resurgence in this intersubjective and interdependent dialogical way is akin to Indigenous storytelling. It is also said to be the way good treaty negotiation were begun in the early contact period" (11). Such a dialogical approach might also inform *how* and *to what end* we compare urban phenomena – through attention to and critical examination of relationships between Indigenous Peoples and settler populations in urban places and city-regions. There is evidence to suggest that positive relationships that one might conceptualize as moves toward reconciliation are occurring at the local level and at the grassroots. In *A Quiet Evolution*, Christopher Alcantara and Jen Nelles (2016, loc. 434–43) document the existence and proliferation of intergovernmental agreements between Indigenous Peoples and local governments, particularly since the 2000s. These agreements "commit the signatories to dialogue and engage in the joint governance of regional affairs, such as joint management, relationship building, and decolonization types (as opposed to municipal service delivery)" (loc. 435). Their main objectives were to document and categorize the agreements as well as to identify factors associated with their emergence (using theory and an inductive, empirical approach). Although they note that their intention was not to assess these agreements from a normative perspective, they observe that, in contrast with national and provincial media coverage of conflict and contention, "many Indigenous and local governments are quietly engaging in what seems to be highly productive and beneficial international partnerships" (loc. 211). Furthermore, they make the choice to centre what they admit is a rare type of agreement, which they label "decolonizing" as a distinct form of relationship building – "Agreements that outline the basis of a partnership with reference to historical rights and values and specifically attempt to situate a partnership in the context of that history" (loc. 580). Studies such as these highlight the potential of comparative urban and local studies to contribute to the dialogical processes of identifying transformative local practices that contribute to reconciliation. It is another example of the rich tradition among Canadian urban scholars in the constitutional-institutional tradition of describing, explaining, and ultimately evaluating formal institutions from a normative perspective in order to contribute to democratic governance in Canada.

CONCLUSION

Canadian urban scholars have made substantial contributions to our understanding of municipalities and the urban governance process through comparative analysis. Institutional approaches, including the "constitutional-institutional" approach, have been a preferred approach to many of these studies. However, important contributions have also been made to our understanding of urban governance and multilevel governance processes as well as to political culture literature, including our understanding of the (political-cultural) foundations of collective action. Other studies have documented how the role of municipalities is changing in response to urbanization, such as an emerging role in immigration policy-making and climate change. Another strain of literature has increased our understanding of local democracy in Canada through comparison and the development and engagement of survey-based research. Collectively, these contributions show the value of both sub-national and international comparisons to understanding urban governance in Canada, helping us see how national infrastructures shape those processes. They also identify possible best practices and, in some cases, potentially transformative governance practices, such as the intensification of a variety of intergovernmental agreements between Indigenous governments and municipalities. Canadian studies demonstrate that explanation is not the only goal of comparison. Rather, most Canadian scholars bring an explicitly normative perspective to their empirical analyses in addition to offering an explanation of institutional processes, patterns of collective action, and other important topics.

In chapter 4, we turn to a discussion of multilevel governance, an area of theory to which many Canadian scholars, including the chapter's author, have made significant contributions. A central part of both understanding and possibly also reimagining municipalities' place in Canada's democratic system will involve evaluating how municipalities are currently integrated (or not) into a coherent national infrastructure of urban policy-making and, ultimately, whether that should be the aim. The next chapter provides important conceptual tools to engage with that debate.

NOTES

1 Together, the formalism, historicism, and normative bent in many Canadian studies would place them in Peters's category of "old institutionalism" (Peters 2019).
2 As Bird and Slack (2014, 364) argue: "trying to rectify fundamental distributional problems by inefficiently pricing scarce local resources is a bad idea that at best may produce a little more equity at a high price in efficiency terms."
3 The concept of "growth machine" was developed first by Harvey Molotch in an article in 1976 and elaborated on further by John Logan and Harvey Molotch's (1987) seminal book entitled *Urban Fortunes*.
4 These initiatives included the development of the first urban Indian Health Boards, community schools, and activism on a range of other issues (Hugill 2019, loc 1886).

REFERENCES

Alcantara, Christopher, and Jen Nelles. 2016. *A Quiet Evolution: The Emergence of Indigenous-Local Intergovernmental Partnerships in Canada*. Toronto: University of Toronto Press. Kindle. https://doi .org/10.3138/9781442625884.

Alcantara, Christopher, Jörg Broschek, and Jen Nelles. 2016. "Rethinking Multilevel Governance as an Instance of Multilevel Politics: A Conceptual Strategy." *Territory, Politics, Governance* 4, no. 1 (January): 33–51. https://doi.org/10.1080/21622671.2015.1047897.

Anderson, Doug, and Alexandra Flynn. 2020. "Rethinking 'Duty': The City of Toronto, A Stretch of the Humber River, and Indigenous-Municipal Relationships." *The Alberta Law Review* 58, no. 1: 107–32.

Berg, Rikke, and Nirmala Rao. 2005. "Institutional Reforms in Local Government: A Comparative Framework." In *Transforming Local Political Leadership*, edited by Rikke Berg and Nirmala Rao, 1–14. New York: Palgrave MacMillan. https://doi.org/10.1057/9780230501331.

Bernard, Wanda Thomas, and Holly Smith. 2018. "Injustice, Justice, and Africentric Practice in Canada." *Canadian Social Work Review* 35, no. 1: 149–57. https://doi.org/10.7202/1051108ar.

Bird, Richard M., and Enid Slack. 2014. "Local Taxes and Local Expenditures in Developing Countries: Strengthening the Wicksellian Connection." *Public Administration and Development* 34, no. 5 (December): 359–69. https://doi.org/10.1002/pad.1695.

Borrows, John, and James Tully. 2018. *Resurgence and Reconciliation: Indigenous-Settler Relations and Earth Teachings*. Toronto: University of Toronto Press.

Bourgeois, Daniel, and Yves Bourgeois. 2005. "Territory, Institutions and National Identity: The Case of Acadians in Greater Moncton, Canada." *Urban Studies* 42, no. 7 (June): 1123–38. https://doi.org/10.1080/03056240500121123.

Brenner, Neil. 2004. *New State Spaces: Urban Governance and the Rescaling of Statehood.* Oxford: Oxford University Press.

Broadbent, Alan. 2008. *Urban Nation: Why We Need to Give Power back to the Cities to Make Canada Strong.* Toronto: HarperCollins Canada.

Bradford, Neil, and Allison Bramwell, eds. 2014. *Governing Urban Economies: Innovation and Inclusion in Canadian City-Regions.* Toronto: University of Toronto Press. https://doi.org/10.3138/9781442617223.

Charter City Toronto. n.d. "Charter City Toronto: A Project to Empower Toronto and Large Ontario Cities." Accessed June 16, 2024. https://www.chartercitytoronto.ca/.

Cobban, Timothy. 2003a. "The Political Economy of Urban Redevelopment: Downtown Revitalization in London, Ontario, 1993–2002." *Canadian Journal of Urban Research* 12, no. 2 (Winter): 231–48. https://www.jstor.org/stable/44320772.

———. 2003b. "Timothy Cobban's Reply to Christopher Leo's Comment 'Are There Urban Regimes in Canada?'" *Canadian Journal of Urban Research* 12, no. 2 (Winter): 349–52. https://www.jstor.org/stable/44320778.

Corntassel, Jeff, and Cheryl Bryce. 2012. "Practicing Sustainable Self-Determination: Indigenous Approaches to Cultural Restoration and Revitalization." *The Brown Journal of World Affairs* 18, no. 2 (Spring/Summer): 151–62. https://www.jstor.org/stable/24590870.

Dahl, Robert A. 1961. *Who Governs? Democracy and Power in an American City.* New Haven, CT: Yale University Press.

Davies, Jonathan S., and Jessica Trounstine. 2012. "Urban Politics and the New Institutionalism." In *The Oxford Handbook of Urban Politics*, edited by Karen Mossberger, Susan E. Clarke, and Peter John, 51–70. Oxford: Oxford University Press. https://doi.org/10.1093/oxfordhb/9780195367867.013.0004.

Denters, Bas, and Karen Mossberger. 2006. "Building Blocks for a Methodology for Comparative Urban Political Research." *Urban Affairs Review* 41, no. 4 (March): 550–71. https://doi.org/10.1177/1078087405282607.

Doberstein, Carey. 2013. "Metagovernance of Urban Governance Networks in Canada: In Pursuit of Legitimacy and Accountability." *Canadian Public Administration* 56, no. 4 (December): 584–609. https://doi.org/10.1111/capa.12041.

Eidelman, Gabriel, and Zack Taylor. 2010. "Canadian Urban Politics: Another 'Black Hole'?" *Journal of Urban Affairs* 32, no. 3: 305–20. https://doi.org/10.1111/j.1467-9906.2010.00507.x.

Enright, Theresa. 2020. "Beyond Comparison in Urban Politics and Policy Analysis." *PS: Political Science & Politics*, in "Symposium, Toward an Urban Policy Analysis," special issue, 53, no. 1 (January): 29–32. https://doi.org/10.1017/S1049096519001367.

Fernando, Shanti. 2006. *Race and the City: Chinese Canadian and Chinese American Political Mobilization.* Vancouver: UBC Press. https://doi.org/10.59962/9780774855136.

Florida, Richard. 2002. *The Rise of the Creative Class.* New York: Basic Books.

Garber, Judith A., and David L. Imbroscio. 1996. "'The Myth of the North American City' Reconsidered: Local Constitutional Regimes in Canada and the United States." *Urban Affairs Review* 31, no. 5 (May): 595–624. https://doi.org/10.1177/107808749603100502.

Garcea, Joseph, and Edward C. LeSage Jr., eds. 2005. *Municipal Reform in Canada: Reconfiguration, Re-empowerment and Rebalancing.* Toronto: Oxford University Press.

Gee, Gilbert C., and Chandra L. Ford. 2011. "Structural Racism and Health Inequities: Old Issues, New Directions." *Du Bois Review: Social Science Research on Race* 8, no. 1 (Spring): 115–32. https://doi.org/10.1017/S1742058X11000130.

Goldberg, Michael A., and John Mercer. 1986. *The Myth of the North American City: Continentalism Challenged*. Vancouver: UBC Press. https://doi.org/10.59962/9780774857031.

Good, Kristin R. 2009. *Municipalities and Multiculturalism: The Politics of Immigration in Toronto and Vancouver*. Toronto: University of Toronto Press. https://doi.org/10.3138/9781442690417.

Halifax Regional Municipality. 2020. "Report of the Task Force on the Commemoration of Edward Cornwallis and the Recognition and Commemoration of Indigenous History." July 21, 2020. https://cdn.halifax.ca/sites/default/files/documents/city-hall/regional-council/200721rc11110.pdf.

Halperin, Sandra, and Oliver Heath. 2020. *Political Research: Methods and Practical Skills*. 3rd ed. Oxford: Oxford University Press.

Harding, Alan. 2009. "The History of Community Power." In *Theories of Urban Politics*, edited by Jonathan S. Davies and David L. Imbroscio, 2nd ed., 27–39. Thousand Oaks, CA: Sage Publications.

Harding, Alan, and Talja Blokland. 2014. *Urban Theory: A Critical Introduction to Power, Cities and Urbanism in the 21st Century*. London: Sage.

Harell, Allison, and Lyne Deschâtelets. 2014. "Political Culture(s) in Canada: Orientations to Politics in a Pluralist, Multicultural Federation." In *Canadian Politics*, edited by James Bickerton and Alain-G. Gagnon, 6th ed., 229–48. Toronto: University of Toronto Press.

Henderson, Ailsa. 2004. "Regional Political Cultures." *Canadian Journal of Political Science* 37, no. 3 (September): 595–615. https://doi.org/10.1017/S0008423904030707.

Hirschl, Ran. 2020. *City, State: Constitutionalism and the Megacity*. New York: Oxford University Press. https://doi.org/10.1093/oso/9780190922771.001.0001.

Horak, Martin. 1998. "The Power of Local Identity: C4LD and the Anti-Amalgamation Mobilization in Toronto." Research Paper 195, Centre for Urban and Community Studies, University of Toronto, November, pp. 44.

Horak, Martin, and Robert Young. 2012. *Sites of Governance: Multilevel Governance and Policy Making in Canada's Big Cities*. Montreal: McGill-Queen's University Press. https://doi.org/10.1515/9780773586918.

Howell-Moroney, Michael. 2008. "The Tiebout Hypothesis 50 Years Later: Lessons and Lingering Challenges for Metropolitan Governance in the 21st Century." *Public Administration Review* 68, no. 1 (January–February): 97–109. https://doi.org/10.1111/j.1540-6210.2007.00840.x.

Hugill, David. 2019. "Comparative Settler Colonial Urbanisms: Racism and the Making of Inner-City Winnipeg and Minneapolis, 1940–1975." In *Settler City Limits: Indigenous Resurgence and Colonial Violence in the Urban Prairie West*, edited by Heather Dorries, Robert Henry, David Hugill, Tyler McCreary, and Julie Tomiak, loc. 1682–2200. Winnipeg: University of Manitoba Press. Kindle. https://doi.org/10.1515/9780887555893-005.

Judge, David. 1995. "Pluralism." In *Theories of Urban Politics*, edited by David Judge, Gerry Stoker, and Harold Wolman, 11–34. London: Sage.

Koop, Royce, and John Kraemer. 2016. "Wards, At-Large Systems and the Focus of Representation in Canadian Cities." *Canadian Journal of Political Science* 49, no. 3 (September): 433–48. https://doi.org/10.1017/S0008423916000512.

Lee, Jo-Anne. 2007. "Gender, Ethnicity, and Hybrid Forms of Community-Based Activism in Vancouver, 1957–1978: The Strathcona Story Revisited." *Gender, Place & Culture* 14, no. 4 (August): 381–407. https://doi.org/10.1080/09663690701439702.

Leo, Christopher. 2003. "Are there Urban Regimes in Canada? Comment on Timothy Cobban's 'The Political Economy of Urban Redevelopment: Downtown Revitalization in London, Ontario, 1993–2002.'" *Canadian Journal of Urban Research* 12, no. 2 (Winter): 344–8. https://www.jstor.org/stable/44320777.

Leo, Christopher. 2006. "Deep Federalism: Respecting Community Difference in National Policy." *Canadian Journal of Political Science* 39, no. 3 (September): 481–506. https://doi.org/10.1017/S0008423906060240.

Lijphart, Arendt. 1975. "The Comparable-Cases Strategy in Comparative Research." *Comparative Political Studies* 8, no. 2 (July): 158–77. https://doi.org/10.1177/001041407500800203.

Lipsky, Michael. 2010. *Street-Level Bureaucracy: Dilemmas of the Individual in Public Services.* 30th anniversary expanded ed. New York: Russell Sage Foundation.

Logan, John R., and Harvey L. Molotch. 1987. *Urban Fortunes: The Political Economy of Place.* Berkeley, CA: University of California Press.

Lorimer, James. 1978. *The Developers.* Toronto: James Lorimer.

Lucas, Jack. 2019. "The Size and Sources of Municipal Incumbency Advantage in Canada." *Urban Affairs Review* 57, no. 2 (March): 373–401. https://doi.org/10.1177/1078087419879234.

Lucas, Jack, and R. Michael McGregor. 2021. "Conclusion." In *Big City Elections in Canada*, edited by Jack Lucas and R. Michael McGregor, 211–29. Toronto: University of Toronto Press. https://doi.org/10.3138/9781487528577.

Masuda, Jeffery R., Aaron Franks, Audrey Kobayashi, Trevor Wideman, and the Right to Remain Research Collective. 2023. "Urban Rights Praxis of Remaining in Vancouver's Downtown Eastside." In *White Riot: The 1907 Anti-Asian Riots in Vancouver*, edited by Henry Tsang, 167–78. Vancouver: Arsenal Pulp Press.

Molotch, Harvey. 1976. "The City as Growth Machine: Toward a Political Economy of Place." *The American Journal of Sociology* 82, no. 2 (September): 309–32. https://doi.org/10.1086/226311.

Mossberger, Karen, and Gerry Stoker. 2001. "The Evolution of Urban Regime Theory: The Challenge of Conceptualization." *Urban Affairs Review* 36, no. 6 (July): 810–35. https://doi.org/10.1177/10780870122185109.

Nelles, Jen. 2012. *Comparative Metropolitan Policy: Governing Beyond the Local Boundaries in the Imagined Metropolis.* Oxon: Routledge.

Nelles, Jen, and David Wolfe. 2022. "Urban Governance and Civic Capital: Analysis of an Evolving Concept." *Territory, Politics, Governance.* Published in Latest Articles, November 4, 2022. https://doi.org/10.1080/21622671.2022.2123031.

Perl, Anthony, Matt Hern, and Jeffrey Kenworthy. 2020. *Big Moves: Global Agendas, Local Aspirations, and Urban Mobility in Canada.* Montreal: McGill-Queen's University Press. https://doi.org/10.1515/9780228002949.

Peters, B. Guy. 2019. *Institutional Theory in Political Science: The New Institutionalism.* Cheltenham, UK: Edward Elgar Publishing.

Peters, Evelyn J. 2012. *Urban Aboriginal Policymaking in Canadian Municipalities.* Montreal: McGill-Queen's University Press. https://doi.org/10.1515/9780773587441.

Peterson, Paul E. 1981. *City Limits.* Chicago: University of Chicago Press.

Pierre, Jon. 1999. "Models of Urban Governance: The Institutional Dimension of Urban Politics." *Urban Affairs Review* 34, no. 3 (January): 372–96. https://doi.org/10.1177/10780879922183988.

———. 2011. *The Politics of Urban Governance.* Houndmills, Basingstoke, Hampshire, UK: Palgrave Macmillan.

Piterberg, Gabriel. 2008. *The Returns of Zionism: Myths, Politics and Scholarship in Israel.* London: Verso.

Reese, Laura A., and Raymond A. Rosenfeld. 2002. *The Civic Culture of Local Economic Development.* New York: Sage. https://doi.org/10.4135/9781452229447.

Ragin, Charles C. 1987. *The Comparative Method: Moving Beyond Qualitative and Quantitative Strategies.* Berkeley: University of California Press.

Rutland, Ted. 2018. *Displacing Blackness: Planning, Power, and Race in Twentieth-Century Halifax.* Toronto: University of Toronto Press. Kindle. https://doi.org/10.3138/9781487518233.

Sancton, Andrew. 2000. *Merger Mania: The Assault on Local Government.* Montreal: McGill-Queen's University Press. https://doi.org/10.1515/9780773568914.

———. 2008. *The Limits of Boundaries: Why City-Regions Cannot Be Self-Governing.* Montreal: McGill-Queen's University Press. https://doi.org/10.1515/9780773574977.

Savitch, H.V., and Paul Kantor. 2002. *Cities in the International Marketplace: The Political Economy of Urban Development in North America and Western Europe.* Princeton, NJ: Princeton University Press. https://doi.org/10.1515/9780691186504.

Sellers, Jefferey M. 2002. *Governing from Below: Urban Regions and the Global Economy.* Cambridge: Cambridge University Press. https://doi.org/10.1017/CBO9780511613395.

———. 2005. "Re-placing the Nation: An Agenda for Comparative Urban Politics." *Urban Affairs Review* 40, no. 4 (March): 419–45. https://doi.org/10.1177/1078087404272673.

Smith, Alison. 2022. *Multiple Barriers: The Multilevel Governance of Homelessness in Canada.* Toronto: University of Toronto Press. https://doi.org/10.3138/9781487548742.

Stewart, Ian. 2002. "Vanishing Points: Three Paradoxes of Political Culture Research." In *Citizen Politics: Research and Theory in Canadian Political Behaviour*, edited by Joanna Everitt and Brenda O'Neill, 21–39. Don Mills, ON: Oxford University Press.

Stone, Clarence N. 1989. *Regime Politics: Governing Atlanta, 1946–1988.* Lawrence: University of Kansas Press.

Stone, Clarence N. 2015. "Reflections on Regime Politics: From Governing Coalition to Urban Political Order." *Urban Affairs Review* 51, no. 1 (January): 101–37. https://doi.org/10.1177/1078087414558948.

Swain, Amy E., and George W. Noblit. 2011. "Education in a Punitive Society: An Introduction." *The Urban Review* 43, no. 4 (November): 465–75. https://doi.org/10.1007/s11256-011-0186-x.

Taylor, Zack. 2019. *Shaping the Metropolis: Institutions and Urbanization in the United States and Canada.* Montreal: McGill-Queen's University Press. https://doi.org/10.1515/9780773558427.

Taylor, Zack and Alec Dobson. 2020. "Power and Purpose: Canadian Municipal Law in Transition." In *IMFG Papers on Municipal Finance and Governance*, no. 47. Toronto: Institute on Municipal Finance and Governance.

Thelen, Kathleen, and Sven Steinmo. 1991. "Historical Institutionalism in Comparative Politics." In *Structuring Politics: Historical Institutionalism in Comparative Analysis*, edited by Sven Steinmo, Kathleen Thelen, and Frank Longstretch, 1–32. Cambridge: Cambridge University Press. https://doi.org/10.1017/CBO9780511528125.002.

Thompson, Debra. 2008. "Is Race Political?" *Canadian Journal of Political Science* 41, no. 3 (September): 525–47. https://doi.org/10.1017/S0008423908080827.

Thompson, J. Phillip. 2009. "Race and Urban Political Theory." In *Theories of Urban Politics*, edited by Jonathan S. Davies and David L. Imbroscio, 2nd ed., 188–203. London: Sage.

Tiebout, Charles. 1956. "A Pure Theory of Local Expenditure." *Journal of Political Economy* 64, no. 5 (October): 416–24. https://doi.org/10.1086/257839.

Tomiak, Julie, Tyler McCreary, David Hugill, Robert Henry, and Heather Dorries. 2019. "Settler City Limits." In *Settler City Limits: Indigenous Resurgence and Colonial Violence in the Urban Prairie West*, edited by Heather Dorries, Robert Henry, David Hugill, Tyler McCreary, and Julie Tomiak, 1–25. Winnipeg: University of Manitoba Press. https://doi.org/10.1515/9780887555893-002.

Tuohy, Carolyn J. 1992. *Policy and Politics in Canada: Institutionalized Ambivalence*. Philadelphia: Temple University Press.

Valverde, Marianna. 2012. *Everyday Law on the Street: City Governance in an Age of Diversity*. Chicago: University of Chicago Press. https://doi.org/10.7208/chicago/9780226921914.001.0001.

Vicino, Thomas J. 2013. *Suburban Crossroads: The Fight for Local Control of Immigration Policy*. Lanham, MD: Lexington Books.

Williamson, Abigail Fisher. 2019. *Welcoming New Americans? Local Government and Immigrant Incorporation*. Chicago: Chicago University Press. https://doi.org/10.7208/chicago/9780226572796.001.0001.

Wiseman, Nelson. 2008. *In Search of Canadian Political Culture*. Vancouver: UBC Press.

Yan, Andy. 2023. "Census Making and City Building: Data Perspectives on the 1907 Anti-Asian Riots and the Development of Vancouver." In *White Riot: The 1907 Anti-Asian Riots in Vancouver*, edited by Henry Tsang, 149–66. Vancouver: Arsenal Pulp Press.

CHAPTER FOUR

Multilevel Urban Governance in Canada

Martin Horak

INTRODUCTION

Local governments are at the front lines of governing Canadian cities. To appreciate the significance of local government, we need look no further than the largest local government unit in Canada, the City of Toronto. With over three million people, Toronto has more residents than six of Canada's ten provinces. In 2023, its operating budget was $16.1 billion (City of Toronto 2023a), and it had 41,800 employees (City of Toronto 2023b).[1] The city has a range of important and consequential policy responsibilities. Among many other things, it oversees planning and development for the heart of the Greater Toronto Area, Canada's largest city-region; it owns and manages 166 community recreation centres (City of Toronto, n.d.); it manages the second largest public housing portfolio in North America, with over 60,000 housing units; and it runs a transit system that, before the COVID-19 pandemic, carried about 1.7 million passengers each day.

Yet for all its institutional capacity and responsibilities, the City of Toronto is only one of multiple levels of government involved in urban governance in Toronto. As chapter 2 showed, Canadian local governments are constitutionally within the sphere of responsibility of provincial governments, which have, at times, acted unilaterally with respect to them. Toronto's recent history offers some dramatic examples. The current city was born of a provincially imposed amalgamation in 1997, through which the seven municipalities that made up Metropolitan Toronto were forced to merge into one municipality, over the strenuous objections of many local politicians and residents (Horak 1998). It is ironic that Canada's largest municipality, which has often led calls for more municipal autonomy, is the product of an imposed and largely unwanted merger. More recently, Ontario premier Doug Ford has repeatedly imposed controversial structural changes on Toronto. In 2018, his government cut the size of Toronto's

City Council in half in the middle of the 2018 municipal election campaign; in 2022, it gave the city's mayor the power to overrule council decisions when they conflict with the provincial policy goal of building more housing.

The relationship between the Ontario provincial government and Toronto is much more complex than these examples of unilateral provincial action would suggest, however. Almost every sphere of local government action in Toronto is deeply influenced by provincial legal frameworks. Local planning and development activities, for example, are shaped by provincial laws that prescribe everything from minimum road widths and building standards to the right of citizens to participate in local decision processes about development. In addition, in 2005 the provincial government passed a regional growth management framework for the GTA, the Places to Grow Act (2005), which is aimed at limiting urban sprawl. This framework is substantially reshaping patterns of development across the GTA and has helped to fuel the "upward" growth of dense high-rise developments in the City of Toronto itself. While at times Ontario imposes legal frameworks without municipal input, more often, the process involves negotiation, and sometimes even collaboration, between provincial and local officials.

In recent years we have also seen the rise of joint intergovernmental policy initiatives in Canada that bring together local, provincial, and – increasingly – federal governments to address a specific urban policy problem or issue. In Toronto, for example, the revitalization of the long-derelict waterfront has been led since 2001 by Waterfront Toronto, an agency with funding and representation from all three levels of government (Eidelman 2013). While formal tri-level agencies such as this are rare, less institutionalized coordination is quite common. For instance, the construction of new transit lines in Toronto – such as the Eglinton-Crosstown light rail line, due to open in 2024 – is largely bankrolled by other levels of government, and immigrant settlement policies have been guided since 2005 by a series of Memorandums of Understanding between the Government of Canada, the Province of Ontario, and the City of Toronto.

As the case of Toronto shows, then, local governments – even large, institutionally powerful ones – "will always only be part of a multi-level system of government for cities" (Sancton 2008, 32). This is true not only in Canada, but around the world. Although scholars of urban politics in North America tend to focus on the local scale, there is increasingly a recognition that if we view urban politics through a purely local lens, we can miss many of the important factors that shape it (Sellers 2005).

This chapter examines multilevel urban governance in Canada, focusing on its evolution over the past three decades. As we saw in chapter 1, Canadian cities have undergone a social and economic transformation in recent decades. Their population has grown (in many cases quite rapidly), while immigration, economic globalization, and the shift to a post-industrial economy have increased urban social diversity and inequality. Together, these changes have produced complex, new urban policy problems and political demands. Meanwhile, as discussed in chapter 2, a decline in intergovernmental financial transfers to local governments in the 1990s tightened political and fiscal constraints on local policy-making as Canadian cities entered the new millennium.

As we will see, the contours of multilevel urban governance have shifted significantly in response to these broader changes. The provincial-municipal relationships that dominated multilevel urban governance in the late twentieth century still exist, but alongside them we have seen the rise of federal funding for local infrastructure, the emergence of new forms of multilevel urban policy coordination, and increased reliance in some policy fields on resources and input from local non-governmental actors. The degree to which these changes have produced effective responses to urban policy problems varies by city and by policy field. Drawing on cross-national comparisons, the chapter suggests that the fact that federal, provincial, and municipal political systems operate quite separately from each other in Canada is an enduring challenge for urban governance. The integration of parties, interest groups, and administration across levels of government is weaker in Canada than in most other democracies, complicating sustained multilevel coordination. Before we turn to these matters, however, we foreground our analysis with a discussion of some key concepts in the study of multilevel urban governance.

GOVERNANCE AND URBAN POLITICS

What Is Governance?

The concept of "governance" has become ubiquitous in the study of urban politics, both at the local scale and in a multilevel context. But what exactly is governance? Like many widely used social science concepts, its definition is the subject of debate. While we cannot explore this debate fully here, we do need a clear working definition for our purposes. One way to do this – following Stoker (1998) – is to contrast "governance" with "government." In classic democratic theory, "government" refers to a single, integrated set of state institutions that has a monopoly on public authority. A government receives inputs from society through elections and other processes of consultation and communication, and it translates these inputs into policies and programs, drawing on its own resources and authority to do so. There are, however, many public policy challenges that cannot be addressed by one government acting alone. These range from place-specific urban problems that are too big and complex to be handled by local governments – such as building big transit infrastructure or integrating new immigrants in a global city – to problems that cross jurisdictional boundaries, such as climate change.

When the scope, scale, or complexity of policy challenges surpasses the governing capacity of any single government, multiple actors – governments, societal organizations, and/or private-sector businesses – need to *coordinate* their authority and resources to develop a response. This is the essence of "governance" as we will use the term in this chapter. For our purposes, then, "governance" is a set of *practices* through which multiple autonomous actors – including, but not necessarily limited to governments – work to coordinate resources and authority to address governing tasks that they cannot address by acting alone.

In theory, governance is a logical solution to the problem of fragmented authority. Many writers go even further than this, embracing governance as a more inclusive and collaborative alternative to the top-down exercise of government authority. Yet in practice, governance is often messy and difficult, for two reasons. First, voluntary coordination requires that different autonomous actors have shared – or at least compatible – goals. But precisely because they are autonomous, they may have different goals. In the case of a public-private partnership to build a new sports stadium, for instance, the government's goal of developing new infrastructure must be squared with the private-sector partner's goal of making a profit (Erie, Kogan, and MacKenzie 2010). Non-profit groups, for their part, may be accountable to a board and/or a community to whom they have a specific mission, which may differ from the policy goals of governments with whom they interact. Likewise, when governance arrangements bring together different governments – say, a provincial government and a municipality – each is accountable to a different electorate. Even if the governments share policy goals at one point in time, an election or changing political priorities at one level of government may cause goal alignment to fall apart.

A second and related challenge for governance is that it is often *asymmetrical* – that is, some actors hold more power or resources than others. When this is the case, more powerful actors may be able to skew outputs to favour their particular goals. At the extreme, if one actor is so powerful that it can force others to do its bidding, it may be more expedient for that actor to simply *impose* its will rather than pursue the messy task of consensual coordination. As our discussion of Toronto showed, given the weak legal standing of Canadian municipalities, provincial governments have in fact often used unilateral imposition, not governance, in dealing with local governments. These challenges and limitations notwithstanding, governance practices are common in contemporary politics, and nowhere more so than in the urban realm.

Three Arenas of Urban Governance

Many analysts have remarked on a broad shift from government to governance in national public policy and administration across wealthy industrialized nations since the 1980s, spurred by the desire to leverage non-governmental resources in an era of budget constraint, as well as by increased demands for citizen and private-sector participation in policy processes (Bevir 2010). In urban politics, however, governance practices were common long before this national-level shift. This is because urban politics is fundamentally different from national politics. As Clarence Stone puts it, "cities are not the nation-state writ small" (2015, 122). Local governments are at the front lines of governing cities, but local governments are not sovereign, and they have limited powers and resources in comparison with national governments. People, goods,

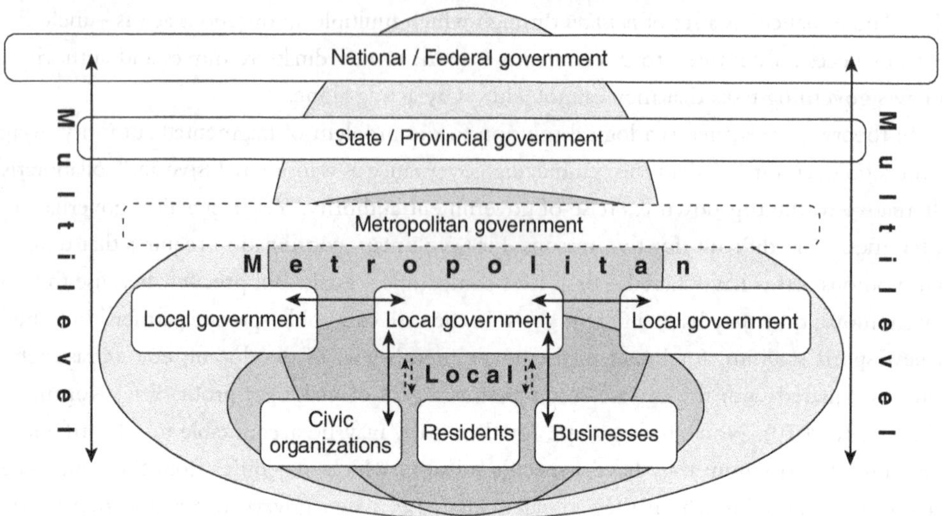

Figure 4.1. Three Arenas of Urban Governance
Source: Author.

and investment flow freely across local government boundaries. Many large city-regions are divided among multiple local government units. For all these reasons, local governments – although they are at the front lines of governing cities – are rarely able to tackle big, complex urban problems on their own. As a result, governance practices of many kinds are an enduring feature of urban politics.

Within the geographical and political confines of any one country, we can think of urban governance as operating in three arenas, illustrated in figure 4.1. The first is the *local* arena. In this arena, local government can respond to many local needs and demands using its own powers and resources. These relationships are represented in figure 4.1 by the black dashed arrows. However, when local governments lack the resources or expertise to respond to local needs and demands on their own, they may develop formal or informal governance partnerships with local businesses or civil society organizations – represented in the diagram with the solid black arrows in the bottom centre. You may recognize this idea from the discussion of "urban regime theory" in chapter 3 of this book, since urban regimes are one form – although by no means the only form – of local governance. Local governments in cities around the world often engage in local governance practices, which range from public-private partnerships to build stadiums, transit systems, and other infrastructure, to negotiated arrangements with community organizations to deliver services to immigrants, the elderly, or other specific populations.

The second arena of urban governance is *metropolitan* (which is the main subject of the next chapter). While some large metropolitan areas – such as Calgary, Halifax, and Ottawa in

Canada – have a single local government unit that covers all or most of the urban area (the dashed box in figure 4.1), it is more common to have numerous municipalities in one large urban area. The City of Toronto, for example, is only one of twenty-five municipalities in the Greater Toronto Area. Whenever multiple municipalities exist, some policy fields might benefit from regional coordination – such as regional growth planning, public transit, or water provision. Where metropolitan governments do not exist, coordination can be pursued through metropolitan governance practices (the horizontal black arrows in figure 4.1), in which policies and resources in metropolitan-wide fields of activity are coordinated through agreements among area municipalities or through the creation of special purpose governing organizations such as metropolitan transit, police, or sewage authorities.

The final arena of urban governance, which we focus on in this chapter, is the *multilevel* one. In most countries around the world – and certainly in all industrialized democracies – governmental powers and resources are formally divided among two or more levels of government, or what political geographers call "state scales." In unitary countries, there are two basic state scales – national and local; in federal countries, there is also a third, sub-national (state or provincial) scale. To some extent, governments at each scale can operate independently of each other in policy fields where they have exclusive jurisdiction and the resources necessary to make and implement policies. However, the legal and constitutional *division* of authority among governments also frequently brings about a need for *coordination*.

Even though they have distinct spheres of authority, governments at different state scales depend on each other in many ways. This is perhaps most obvious in the case of local governments, which rely extensively on central governments (be they national, federal, provincial, or state) to provide necessary legal frameworks and financial resources for local policies and programs. However, the reverse is also true: Central governments frequently need to communicate and coordinate with sub-national and local governments. For example, the Canadian federal government under Justin Trudeau, which has committed to significant investment in "green" infrastructure such as public transit systems, cannot deliver this without support from local governments, which are directly responsible for transit and land-use planning.

In Canada and beyond, there are many policy fields – ranging from housing and immigrant settlement to climate action and economic development – in which relevant powers and resources are distributed across different levels of government, so coming up with effective policy responses requires ongoing coordination across state scales. In addition, in many policy fields, non-governmental actors (ranging from private companies to non-profits and community groups) also play a key role, so multilevel governance often involves both multiple levels of government *and* non-governmental actors. As we will see later when we discuss multilevel urban governance in Canada, there is wide variation by policy field and over time in terms of who participates, what they bring to the process, and how they interact. In the next section, we develop conceptual tools that allow us to make sense of this variation.

MULTILEVEL GOVERNANCE: A THREE-DIMENSIONAL ACCOUNT

Scholars have long debated the meaning of "multilevel governance" (MLG), and the concept has been defined in many different ways (see Piattoni 2009). The concept was initially developed to study the process of European integration, and as such, its scalar focus extended to supra-national institutions such as the European Union (Hooghe and Marks 2003). In the study of Canadian urban governance, the term has generally been confined to the domestic arena, however, and that is how we will use it in this chapter. Even given this specification, the term is used in various ways by different scholars, and its content often remains a bit fuzzy. Does MLG refer to a political system or a set of processes or practices? Who is involved in MLG?

In a recent article, Alcantara, Broschek, and Nelles (2016) try to break through the definitional debate by proposing a narrow definition of MLG. They define it as a mode of policy-making in which governments *and* non-governmental actors at different scales work closely together to "co-produce" policies – that is, to share responsibility for developing and implementing them. However, this definition conflates the "who" of MLG (actors) and the "how" (modes of interaction) when, in reality, these two dimensions do not necessarily vary together. Co-production sometimes happens without non-governmental actors, while interaction between governments and non-governmental actors does not always take the form of co-production. In other words, MLG is a *multidimensional* concept whose various dimensions do not always co-vary. Instead of narrowing our definition, then, it may thus be better to retain a broad view of MLG but distinguish among its different dimensions and develop an account of how these can vary. This is the approach that we will pursue here.

Building on our discussion of "governance," we will conceptualize MLG as a set of practices that operate across state scales, through which multiple autonomous actors – including but not necessarily limited to governments – coordinate resources and authority to address governing tasks that each of them cannot address by acting alone. It is important to note that in this definition, MLG is not a political *system*, but a set of governing *practices*. These practices emerge *in* a political system where resources and authority are divided among multiple actors at different scales. Since even unitary countries divide authority between at least two state scales (national and local), MLG is widespread in contemporary politics and policy-making. Within any multilevel political system, we find varied practices of multilevel governance. We can make sense of these varied practices by developing a three-dimensional typology that focuses on *who* is involved (actors), *what* they do (roles), and *how* they interact (modes).

Actors and Roles in MLG

To classify the actors involved in MLG and the roles that they play, we will adapt a typology developed by Horak (2012, 340–2; see also Lucas and Smith 2019). Writing about Canadian urban politics, Horak identifies four basic kinds of actors in MLG: *local governments*, *provincial governments*, the *federal government*, and *non-governmental actors* (which include both non-profits and business actors) (Horak 2012, 341). Any one actor can in turn play one or more of four roles in MLG processes. First, an actor can engage in *policy advocacy* – "lobbying for a particular framing of the problem in a given policy area, and/or advocating for a particular set of solutions to a given problem" (341). Second, an actor can engage in *resource provision* – providing money, fixed assets (such a land), and knowledge or expertise. Third, an actor can be involved in *policy development* – the process of deciding how to respond to a policy problem. Finally, an actor can be involved in *implementing* policies and programs that have been developed through MLG processes.

With four kinds of actors and four roles, there are clearly many possible combinations. What explains who is involved in MLG in Canadian cities, and how they are involved, across different policy fields and initiatives? There is no simple answer to this, but we can identify two important considerations. The first is the distribution of authority and resources among actors (Lucas and Smith 2019). For instance, local governments have legal authority over transit and urban planning in Canada, so they invariably play an important role in planning and building new light rail and subway systems. Since building transit is very expensive and local government resources are limited, provincial and/or federal governments sometimes step in with funding (Horak 2021). Business actors may also be involved if governments adopt a public-private partnership model, but other non-governmental actors typically play little role. By contrast, in the field of homelessness, local non-profits often play a central role on the ground, so policy development and implementation rely extensively on governmental collaboration with these organizations (Smith 2022). By the same token, as we will see later, the distribution of resources and authority across levels of government can also change over time; as a result, the role that each level of government plays in any one policy field is dynamic and subject to change.

A second key consideration that affects who is involved in MLG processes and how is the *salience* – that is, the political importance – of a particular policy problem. This factor is particularly important in the case of government actors. To be involved in MLG in a particular policy field, governments must care about the problem being addressed. This may not always be the case – even if they are necessary partners for any policy solution. Government priorities shift over time not just because policy problems change, but also due to changing societal preferences, ideological currents, and structural pressures. As a result, whether and how different levels of government are involved in any one policy field can also shift over time.

For instance, access to decent housing for families with limited incomes has been a problem in Canadian cities for many decades. Between the 1960s and the 1980s, during the heyday of the welfare state, the federal government financially supported the construction of subsidized housing. However, this support was cut in the 1980s and 1990s as deficit reduction became a top priority, and neo-liberal ideas emphasizing market mechanisms over government redistribution became politically dominant. It is only in the last few years, when the housing affordability crisis in Canada has deepened and has begun to affect middle-class residents, that the rising political salience of housing issues has pushed the federal government to once again roll out financial support (albeit limited) for subsidized housing construction.

Table 4.1. Modes of Multilevel Governance

Characteristics	Negotiation	Co-production	Metagovernance
Policy goals	Distinct	Shared	Distinct
Actors	Governments	Governments, non-government actors	Governments, non-government actors
Mechanisms	Conferences, lobbying	Multilevel partnerships, special purpose authorities	Legal frameworks, conditional funding
Products	Intergovernmental agreements, policy commitments	Joint policy outputs	Local co-production

Modes of MLG: Intergovernmental Negotiation, Co-production, and Metagovernance

As we have seen, MLG arises when actors at different scales interact to coordinate resources and/or authority. The *way* in which they interact is what we will call the *mode* of MLG. Building on foundational work by Scharpf (2001), Hooghe and Marks (2003) and Jessop (2004), as well as more recent scholarship by Doberstein (2013) and Taylor (2021), we can identify three modes of multilevel interaction: *negotiation*, *co-production*, and *metagovernance*. Table 4.1 presents a schematic comparison of the main defining characteristics of these three modes.

NEGOTIATION

Multilevel *negotiation,* as we conceptualize it here, is similar to what scholars of federalism would call intergovernmental relations. It is grounded in the separate, legally defined authority of each level (or scale) of government. Each government has its own responsibilities and pursues its own policy goals, but since policies at different scales affect each other, governments negotiate to ensure that the policies of their counterparts support (or at least do not hinder) their own policy goals. While non-governmental organizations sometimes provide input into multilevel negotiation, the main actors are governments. Both federal-provincial and provincial-local relations are commonly pursued through various forms of negotiation in Canada. Since municipalities are under provincial jurisdiction, there is little scope for direct negotiation between local and federal governments. Tri-level negotiation does occur in federal countries where local governments have their own constitutional standing. In Canada, however, negotiation is usually *either* federal-provincial *or* provincial-municipal.

Annual intergovernmental conferences and meetings are important institutional mechanisms for multilevel negotiation in Canada. This is true of both federal-provincial negotiation, which features an annual First Ministers' Conference and a Premiers' Conference (Cameron and Simeon 2002, Schertzer 2020), and provincial-municipal negotiation (Lucas and Smith 2020), which we will discuss in detail later. Participants at such meetings discuss a wide range of issues; to prepare for them, political representatives of sub-national and local governments sometimes work collectively to develop positions and lobby higher-level governments. At the same time, there is also near-continuous negotiation among levels of government in individual policy fields, featuring a variety of roundtables, intergovernmental councils, and other venues in which civil servants at different levels of government meet to discuss specific issues.

Negotiation is a mode of MLG that involves limited coordination across state scales. The products of negotiation include intergovernmental agreements, memorandums of understanding, or commitments by one level of government toward another. Negotiation does not result in the joint exercise of governmental authority across state scales. Rather, after a limited round of interaction, the governments involved go back to the work of governing at their respective state scales, making and implementing policies in their own sphere of authority.

While multilevel negotiation rests on a division of authority among state scales, it does not necessarily take place on a level playing field. On the contrary, the division of authority and resources across scales is often quite asymmetrical. This is the case in provincial-municipal relations in Canada, where municipalities are often junior partners in an unequal relationship. Indeed, in constitutional terms, the authority of provinces over municipalities is virtually absolute, so when push comes to shove, provinces can dispense with negotiation and instead simply *impose* directives on municipalities or take unilateral action such as downloading policy responsibilities without local consent. Since imposition involves the centralized exercise of authority, it is **not** a mode of MLG, but it *is* a recurring mode of action in provincial-municipal relations, as we will see in detail in the next section of this chapter.

By maintaining a separation among levels of government, multilevel negotiation maximizes political accountability and allows governments at different scales to pursue their own priorities. But as we have already noted, relevant governmental authority is widely distributed across scales in many urban policy fields. Effective policy responses may thus require deeper and more sustained coordination than negotiation allows, pushing actors toward *co-production*.

CO-PRODUCTION

In contrast to negotiation, co-production is a mode of MLG that features a *joining* of power and resources across state scales. Much of the research on MLG in Canadian cities focuses on co-production initiatives, in fields that range from immigrant settlement (Leo and August 2009) and transit (Horak 2021) to homelessness (Doberstein 2016; Smith 2022). Since co-production involves a deeper and more sustained coordination than negotiation, a prerequisite is that the actors involved must have shared – or at least complementary – policy goals. While co-production does not *necessarily* include non-governmental actors, it can more easily include them since it is not built on the separate legal authority of actors, and in practice it often does.

Local and provincial governments almost always play a role in multilevel co-production in Canadian cities; while the federal government is not always involved, many of the most visible co-production initiatives in Canadian cities are tri-level ones.

To pursue co-production, actors must build new venues that enable them to work together toward common policy goals. These venues range from intergovernmental committees and other multilevel decision-making mechanisms embedded within existing structures to what Hooghe and Marks call "task-specific jurisdictions" (2003, 237)[2] – special purpose governing bodies with representation from more than one level of government, through which the partners jointly exercise power. While the products of negotiation are agreements and mutual commitments among governments, the products of co-production are *joint* policy outputs – programs and projects produced and implemented in a coordinated way (Piattoni 2010).

In contrast to negotiation, which can deal with very broad issues, co-production initiatives typically pursue a time-limited project in a particular place – such as a waterfront cleanup project, a downtown revitalization initiative, a local homelessness reduction strategy, or an Olympic bid. This narrow, place-specific focus is related to the need for agreement on goals. The more specific the initiative, the more likely it is that the actors involved can identify and sustain shared goals, and therefore agree to share authority with others.

Co-production is a normatively attractive idea. It holds out the promise of joint action across scales that can address difficult urban policy problems (Bradford 2007). Yet it is not without its limitations. The most obvious problems stem from the need for goal alignment. Governments at different scales respond to different electoral constituencies, so developing and maintaining shared policy goals can be difficult. Indeed, co-production initiatives in Canada often fail because the goals of participants diverge due to a change in government (or in political priorities) at one scale (Horak 2012, 361–3). Furthermore, like negotiation, co-production does not necessarily take place on a level playing field, and those actors with more resources or authority can have an outside influence on the direction of joint outcomes (Horak 2012). Finally, co-production can create accountability problems since if multiple actors are collectively responsible for a policy output, it is difficult to know whom to hold responsible when things go wrong. A third mode of MLG – *metagovernance* – responds in part to these problems.

METAGOVERNANCE

Metagovernance literally means the governance of governance. Unlike negotiation and co-production, metagovernance is built on the distinct powers and resources available to non-local governments. In metagovernance, a non-local government (such as the federal or provincial government) assumes the role of *metagovernor*. The metagovernor identifies a set of policy goals – more affordable housing, more transit, new services for immigrants – and uses its legislative and/or fiscal power to establish rules and incentives that encourage local governmental and nongovernmental actors to work together to pursue these goals. The purpose of metagovernance, then, is to *incentivize local co-production* in pursuit of policy goals identified by the metagovernor.

The goals of the metagovernor and local actors need not be the same. To align goals across governing scales, metagovernance relies on incentivization, *not* unilateral imposition. Its aim is not to force unwilling local actors into action but rather to empower them to act together (Taylor 2021). As a result, metagovernance works best when the metagovernors identify broad policy goals but provide local actors with flexible powers and resources to achieve these goals in a way that fits well with local conditions and policy preferences (Doberstein 2013).

Metagovernance steers a middle course between the *thin* coordination of negotiated MLG and the *thick* coordination of multilevel co-production. It adopts a *nested* approach to coordination, in which the metagovernor sets broad goals and establishes a framework of rules and incentives that encourage local actors to co-produce locally appropriate responses to those goals. Although the term metagovernance is quite new, the practices that it describes have long been used by some provincial governments in Canada. As we will see later on, the Canadian federal government is also increasingly turning to metagovernance in the urban arena in order to overcome the limitations of negotiation and multilevel co-production.

However, metagovernance is not a panacea for complex urban policy challenges. It is only likely to be viable under certain circumstances. The metagovernor must have the necessary powers, resources, and motivation. Quite often, it might be more politically expedient to pursue another course of action, such as doing nothing or imposing a top-down solution in a unilateral way. Meanwhile, at the local level, metagovernance initiatives rely on pre-existing trust and consensus among local actors, and they tend to work best in contexts where local actors already have a history of productive collaboration (Doberstein 2016b).

We have identified three modes of interaction in MLG: negotiation, co-production, and metagovernance. As with actors and roles, there is no simple overall explanation for variance in the modes of MLG. We can identify some general tendencies based on our discussion so far. For instance, negotiation is more likely in policy fields where there is only a limited need for co-operation and when the policy goals of governments at different scales do not fully align. Multilevel co-production, by contrast, tends to arise when actors at different scales agree on a very limited, specific set of policy goals. However, modes of MLG can also shift over time, even within one policy field – from negotiation to co-production and then back to negotiation, or from multilevel co-production to metagovernance. Perhaps the best way to understand how the many variable parts of MLG fit together in Canadian urban politics is to review the recent history and practice of MLG in urban Canada. That is what we turn to now.

PROVINCIAL-MUNICIPAL SYSTEMS AND URBAN POLITICS IN CANADA

Unlike their counterparts in most other democracies, Canadian municipalities have no direct, legally recognized relationship with the national government. Rather, the formal intergovernmental relationships of Canadian municipalities are with provincial governments only. As a result, from a legal perspective, multilevel urban governance in Canada is, first and foremost, a matter of provincial-municipal relations. In this section, we will discuss the legal and institutional structure of provincial-municipal relations, comparing across provinces to reveal both commonalities and differences. The structure and practice of provincial-municipal relations vary both across provinces and over time, as does the extent to which provincial governments use their power to unilaterally impose provincial priorities on local governments. Notwithstanding, as we shall see, the structure of provincial-municipal relations usually provides only weak and unstable channels through which *urban* municipalities can articulate their distinct interests and needs to other levels of government.

Provincial Legislation, Regulation, and Supervision

The foundation of the provincial-municipal relationship is provincial legislation that sets out the structure, powers, responsibilities, and financing arrangements of municipal governments. Such legislation has historically been quite prescriptive and restrictive compared with most other democratic countries, although as we will see later, this has begun to shift in recent years. While the powers and resources granted to municipalities (discussed in chapter 2) are broadly similar across provinces, there is considerable diversity in how the municipal system is structured. Two provinces (Saskatchewan and Quebec) govern rural and urban municipalities separately, through different pieces of legislation. While in most provinces there is only one level of local government, in three provinces – British Columbia, Ontario, and Quebec – most of the population is governed by two tiers of elected local government. Upper-tier local governments – called "regional districts" in British Columbia, "counties" or "regional municipalities" in Ontario, and "municipalités régionales de comté" in Quebec – usually have councils composed of representatives from lower-tier municipalities and are responsible for planning and other regional-scale services. By contrast, in some provinces there are substantial areas – usually rural ones – that have no elected local government at all. The extreme case is New Brunswick, where until a major reform in 2023, more than 30 per cent of the population lived in areas with no local government (Taylor and Taylor 2024).

In addition to municipal legislation, countless other provincial laws, regulations, and policy frameworks – local elections laws, planning and building codes, environmental regulations, policing standards, infrastructure maintenance standards, and so on – affect almost every aspect of municipal activity. Ironically, even as provincial governments have broadened the legal scope of municipal authority in recent years, other legislation and regulation that shape and restrict municipal action have proliferated. For example, in 2005 Ontario passed the Accessibility for Ontarians with Disabilities Act (AODA); to comply with its provisions, municipalities must make their services (such as transit and parks) accessible to those with physical disabilities. Manitoba and Nova Scotia followed suit with accessibility legislation in 2013 and 2017 respectively, and several other provinces are currently developing similar acts.

Recent years have also seen the rise of new provincial regulation in policy fields as diverse as the management of local infrastructure assets, emergency planning, employment equity, and environmental standards for building. Canadian provincial governments thus continuously exercise what Lucas and Smith (2020, 438) call a "supervisory" or "regulatory" role with respect to municipal governments.

The effects of extensive provincial supervision and regulation on local governments are complex. On the one hand, provincial regulations can play an important role in supporting local policy capacity. For example, since the early twentieth century, most Canadian provinces have banned "bonusing" – the practice of giving away incentives to developers (tax breaks, free land, etc.) to attract investment (Cobban 2013, 88). While this limits the policy choices that municipalities have, it prevents the kind of destructive "race-to-the-bottom" competition for investment among municipalities that occurs in American states that allow bonusing (Mast 2020). More generally, as Taylor (2019) argues in his comparative historical study of American and Canadian urban development, the comprehensive planning regulations developed by Canadian provinces have, over time, produced cities that are more compact, integrated, and livable than American cities that have developed with little top-down planning regulation. Other provincial regulations – such as those that require municipalities to set aside funds for future infrastructure needs, or those that mandate public involvement in planning processes – also arguably support local policy capacity.

At the same time, provincial regulation clearly restricts local choices in Canadian municipalities. As Andrew Sancton (2015, 251–4) observes, a significant proportion of what municipalities do involves fulfilling provincial mandates and responding to provincial directives. Sometimes provincial governments give municipalities resources to fulfill such mandates and directives, but at other times, they do not. For example, while Ontario's AODA is a ground-breaking piece of legislation, it comes with no dedicated funding for local implementation, which has created a significant budget headache for many municipalities as they try to make services accessible. Another common problem with provincial regulation from the municipal point of view is that while local needs and the capacities of local governments vary widely, many regulations are one-size-fits-all. A study of emergency management in Canadian municipalities, for example, found that some small rural municipalities do not have the resources to meet provincial emergency planning requirements, whereas large urban municipalities that have long had emergency plans in place see little benefit in the provincial regulations (Henstra 2013).

Provincial-Municipal Interaction: Institutions and Modes

So far, we have taken a top-down view of provincial-local relations in Canada. This view may suggest that there is little room for MLG of any kind, and that the long-standing characterization of Canadian municipalities as "policy-takers," beholden to and directed by provincial governments, is accurate. Provincial laws and regulations certainly do structure and limit the local policy space, but Canadian municipalities nonetheless make their own important

Table 4.2. Provincial-Level Municipal Associations in Canada

Province	Association(s)
British Columbia	Union of British Columbia Municipalities (UBCM)
Alberta	Alberta Urban Municipalities Association (AUMA), Rural Municipalities of Alberta (RMA)
Saskatchewan	Saskatchewan Association of Rural Municipalities (SARM), Saskatchewan Urban Municipalities Association (SUMA)
Manitoba	Association of Manitoba Municipalities (AMM)
Ontario	Association of Municipalities of Ontario (AMO)
Quebec	Fédération québécoise des municipalités (FQM) – rural, Union des municipalités du Québec (UMQ) – urban
Prince Edward Island	Federation of Prince Edward Island Municipalities (FPEIM)
Nova Scotia	Union of Nova Scotia Municipalities (UNSM)
New Brunswick	Union of Municipalities of New Brunswick (UMNB) – English / Association francophone des municipalités du Nouveau Brunswick (AFMNB) – French
Newfoundland	Municipalities Newfoundland and Labrador (MNL)

decisions in fields ranging from planning and development to library services and parks and recreation. As Good (2021) argues, municipalities are fundamentally important democratic venues that provide local spaces for political voice and choice. As such, they are by no means passive implementers of provincial legislation and regulation. As Lucas and Smith put it, "Canadian municipal politicians have the capacity to leverage media profiles, electoral mandates, implementation responsibilities, and even infrastructure ownership … into a level of involvement in public policy issues that goes well beyond what one would expect from a 'creature of the province'" (2019, 272). Municipalities and the politicians who lead them have their own interests vis-à-vis provinces, such as securing provincial funding or regulatory support for local priorities, and they regularly articulate these.

Perhaps the most important institutional mechanism for articulating the collective interests of municipalities is the municipal association. The landscape of municipal associations across Canadian provinces is quite diverse. As table 4.2 shows, most provinces have one main association that represents all municipalities, but Alberta, Saskatchewan, and Quebec have separate associations for rural and urban municipalities, while New Brunswick has separate associations for English and French-speaking municipalities. In Ontario, the Association of Municipalities of Ontario (AMO) represents all municipalities except Toronto, which withdrew from the AMO in 2004 and now represents its interests individually to the provincial government.

Municipal associations develop positions on behalf of their membership base and lobby and negotiate with the provincial government. The focal point for the activity of municipal associations is their annual meeting, which brings together representatives of all member municipalities, as well as provincial cabinet ministers. Municipal sector representatives pass resolutions that call on the provincial government for action, and local and provincial politicians hold meetings to discuss specific issues (Lucas and Smith 2020, 436–7). Outside the annual conference, municipal associations participate in various provincial policy consultation committees, ensuring that the municipal voice is heard.[3] In recent years, municipal associations in Quebec and Ontario have succeeded in convincing provincial governments to establish new mechanisms for intergovernmental dialogue – the Table Québec-municipalités and the annual Ontario-AMO memorandum of understanding process. The intent is to limit the possibility of arbitrary provincial action with respect to municipalities by agreeing on shared priorities and formalizing the limits of acceptable provincial intervention.

While municipal associations are the primary vehicle through which local politicians articulate their priorities to provincial governments, provincial ministries of municipal affairs sometimes advocate for municipalities as well. As David Siegel writes about Ontario's Ministry of Municipal Affairs and Housing, "one of the ministry's prime roles is to represent the interest of municipalities in cabinet and ensure that municipalities have the legislative powers and financial and other resources needed to carry out their mandate" (2009, 37). Furthermore, the fact that municipal action is so heavily regulated by the province means that there is a dense web of interaction between provincial and local administrators in specific policy fields as well. However, while the flow of bureaucratic correspondence between local and provincial officials – applications for funding, performance reports, provincial administrative decisions, etc. – is constant, actual opportunities for local administrators to raise issues with their provincial counterparts tend to be limited and fleeting (Lucas and Smith 2020, 437).

Where do provincial-local interactions in Canada fit in terms of the modes of MLG that we identified earlier? Given the full legal authority that provinces have over municipalities, it is unsurprising that the top-down *imposition* of laws and mandates is quite common. However, there are political consequences to imposition, and municipalities actively defend and lobby for their own interests. In practice, then, most provincial-local interaction occurs through an asymmetrical system of *negotiation* in which municipalities are the junior partners. This system of negotiation is weakly institutionalized. Mechanisms for ongoing policy dialogue between provinces and municipalities are weak, and governing bodies that bring together provincial and local representatives are relatively uncommon. That said, there are differences in provincial-local interaction styles by province. British Columbia, in particular, has a history of more collaborative relations with municipalities. The right of municipalities to be consulted in provincial policy processes is enshrined in British Columbia's Community Charter, and *co-production* initiatives are more common than in other provinces. In addition, the BC system has long featured elements of *metagovernance* – such as the Regional Districts, introduced in the 1960s to encourage collaboration among municipalities in service delivery (Cashaback 2001).

The Interests of Urban Municipalities in the Provincial-Municipal System

Canada is an overwhelmingly urban country. Most of the country's population growth occurs in cities, and over half of Canadian residents live in the ten largest urban areas (Statistics Canada 2022). As detailed in chapter 1, Canadian cities have undergone a social and economic transformation in recent decades, spurred by economic globalization and the shift to a post-industrial economy. Canadian cities are now more multi-ethnic, multicultural, and multiracial than a generation ago; they are also more socially unequal. In addition, as Canada's large cities have become more directly connected to the global economy, their relative economic clout has increased. They concentrate wealth, dominate production in post-industrial sectors of the economy, and serve as gateways to the global economic system.

These social and economic changes have produced or accentuated a range of complex policy challenges, such as housing unaffordability and homelessness, the need to provide services to an increasingly ethnoculturally diverse population, and the need to maintain and expand transportation infrastructure. Many of these challenges are beyond the jurisdictional and/or fiscal capacity of municipal governments. Some of them are what Head and Alford (2015) call "wicked problems" – complex challenges that necessitate a response that spans traditional policy domains and spatial scales. At the same time, urban problems manifest differently in different places, meaning that effective public responses to them need to be grounded in, and tailored to, local conditions.

Despite the growing demographic and economic importance of urban Canada, as well as the concentration of complex policy challenges in cities, existing provincial-municipal systems have historically provided weak opportunities for urban municipalities to lobby for intergovernmental support for urban priorities. There are several interrelated reasons for this. First, urban municipalities face a collective action dilemma. While most people live in urban municipalities, rural municipalities are more numerous, and their voices carry a lot of weight in unified municipal associations. The extreme case is in Manitoba, where the City of Winnipeg is home to more than 60 per cent of Manitoba's population but is only 1 of 137 members of the Association of Manitoba Municipalities. As we saw, urban municipalities have formed separate associations in some provinces. But this does not fully address the problem, since different kinds of urban municipalities – midsized cities vs. large global cities, booming cities vs. declining ones – also often have different interests.

In democratic countries where the same political parties exist across levels of government, local political leaders can sometimes bypass this collective action dilemma by using intergovernmental party networks to secure benefits and support for their municipality. In France, local politicians can even simultaneously hold office at other levels of government, ensuring a strong upward conduit for local priorities (Brunet-Jailly 2007). In addition, in numerous countries – such as Germany and Scandinavian countries – the existence of a unified administrative state, where civil servants at all levels of government receive the same training, can provide an administrative avenue for the articulation of local needs. By contrast, the Canadian intergovernmental system is remarkably *dis-integrated* in both political and administrative terms. Local government is officially non-partisan (with a few exceptions), and local administrators are not part of a unified civil service across levels of government.

The political and administrative dis-integration of Canadian intergovernmental systems means that urban politicians, as well as municipal administrators, lack the stable channels of upward influence that their counterparts in other countries can use to leverage the population strength, economic significance, and institutional clout of a large urban municipality. Writing in 1995, Goldsmith observed that "notwithstanding the existence of partisan politics at the provincial level, their formal virtual absence at the local level gives little access to local elites [at the provincial level]" (243). Twenty-five years later, reporting on the results of a survey of local mayors across Canada, Lucas and Smith note that "in general, the intergovernmental relationships described in these responses were informal, ad hoc, and short-lived" (2020, 437).

Canadian urban municipalities are thus in a comparatively weak negotiating position in relation to provincial governments. As a result, provincial attention to local government concerns, and especially the needs of urban municipalities, has tended to be driven by *provincial* politics and policy aims. Research on subjects ranging from municipal amalgamations in Nova Scotia, Quebec, and Ontario (Sancton 2006) to regional growth management in the Greater Toronto Area (Eidelman 2010) shows that major provincial interventions in local affairs are often motivated by provincial electoral and policy considerations. Since the turn of the millennium, however, a combination of local activism and political change at other levels of government has shifted the dynamics of multilevel urban governance in Canada, creating space for new forms of interaction.

THE EVOLUTION OF MULTILEVEL URBAN GOVERNANCE IN CANADA

Restructuring and Response: Local Autonomy and Federal Engagement

The post-war welfare state consensus lasted longer in Canada than in many other Western countries, but when change came, it came swiftly. During a few short years in the 1990s, the federal government signed the North American Free Trade Agreement, rolled out massive cuts in transfer payments to provinces, and decisively shifted Canada toward a post-welfare-state model informed by neo-liberal ideas about smaller government and market-led growth (discussed more in chapter 2). These changes had significant impacts on local governments, nowhere more so than in urban areas.

Many provinces responded to federal transfer payment cuts by in turn cutting their own transfers to municipalities. Country-wide, intergovernmental transfers shrunk from 45.5 per cent to 17.9 per cent of municipal revenues between 1990 and 2000 (Tindal et al. 2017, 182). In Ontario, the Conservative provincial government of Mike Harris downloaded new responsibilities to municipalities in a way that disadvantaged big cities (City of Toronto 2002). Meanwhile, imposed municipal amalgamations in Ontario, Nova Scotia, and (between 2000 and 2003) Quebec, largely driven by provincial political priorities and widely opposed at the local level, put further stress on municipalities (Sancton 2006). Restructuring and cutbacks aside, provincial governments preoccupied with managing economic change paid little attention to local and urban policy concerns in the 1990s, as one recent study shows (Peterson, Lucas, and Klain 2019).

Urban municipalities across Canada emerged from the 1990s with more responsibilities and fewer resources than before. Decreased intergovernmental support meant that expensive but essential infrastructure, ranging from social housing to public transit, saw little investment, producing a growing infrastructure deficit. At the same time, the decline of the welfare state and the emergence of the post-industrial economy deepened socio-economic inequality in cities, which in turn often led to increased socio-spatial segregation into rich and poor neighbourhoods (Hulchanski 2010). The silver lining in this rather bleak picture was that more Canadians than ever before lived in large cities, so the political fortunes of provincial and federal governments were increasingly influenced by urban voting patterns. This demographic shift put weight behind emerging multilevel demands by urban municipalities.

Local governments in Canadian cities faced a revenue squeeze at the very same time as they were broadening the scope of their developmental ambitions. While promoting local economic development has long been central to city politics in Canada (Magnusson and Sancton 1983), globalization encouraged local policy-makers to look beyond Canada in seeking to promote their cities as places to live, work, and invest. Waterfront redevelopment schemes, support for local arts and culture, and bids for mega-events such as the Olympics – all of these were now being leveraged as a means to put Canadian cities on the global urban map (Kipfer and Keil 2002). In pursuing such new developmental efforts, local leaders turned to partnerships with private business interests, but also to other levels of government.

Shortly after the turn of the millennium, a bottom-up push for urban governance reform, led by large urban municipalities, began to gather steam across several provinces. This push had two basic components: a call for provinces to grant more legal autonomy and fiscal resources to municipalities, and a campaign to get the federal government involved in supporting urban policy priorities. Both efforts had an impact. In terms of autonomy, since 2000 all provinces except for Nova Scotia and Newfoundland have amended municipal legislation to give local governments broader spheres of authority (Taylor and Dobson 2020). In addition, several cities – including Toronto, Edmonton, Calgary, and Montreal – that had previously been governed by general-purpose legislation got their own special governing legislation. Most scholars suggest, however, that the impact of these changes has been limited (Good 2019) – in part because municipalities have been reluctant to test the limits of their broader authority, and in part because provincial governments "remain reluctant to cede independent decision-making authority when their electoral self-interest is at stake" (Taylor and Bradford 2021, 46).

On the fiscal front, advocates of local autonomy point out – rightly – that municipal "revenue tools" remain highly constrained, with property taxes and local service fees accounting for virtually all locally raised revenues. Nonetheless, the fiscal position of municipalities has generally improved since the turn of the millennium. This is largely a result of the re-emergence of intergovernmental grants to municipalities after the nadir of the 1990s (Taylor and Bradford 2021, 41–2). While most grants come from provincial governments, the federal government has also rolled out significant funding. Although municipalities are under provincial jurisdiction and the provinces have historically opposed any federal move to develop local or urban policies (Spicer 2011), the federal government can use its *spending power* to fund activity in policy fields that are not within its jurisdiction. Canadian municipalities maintain a lobbying presence in Ottawa through the Federation of Canadian Municipalities (FCM), and in the early 2000s, the FCM's Big City Mayors' Caucus, led by mayor of Toronto David Miller, launched a lobbying campaign aimed at securing long-term urban funding commitments from the federal government, with a primary focus on funding for infrastructure (Horak 2008, 24).

Between 2003 and 2005, the governing federal Liberal Party, under the leadership of Paul Martin, responded to these demands. In a context where the Liberals increasingly relied on an urban base of support (Armstrong, Lucas, and Taylor 2022), Martin promised a "new deal for cities," which was eventually rebranded to "cities and communities" to broaden the electoral appeal (Horak 2008, 24, 32–3; Bradford 2007, 9–10). The primary outcomes were a Gas Tax Fund (which was renamed the Canada Community-Building Fund in 2021) that transfers a portion of the federal gas tax directly to municipalities, and a series of "contribution programs" that co-fund local infrastructure with matching contributions from provincial and local governments. As figure 4.2 shows, both types of programs have since become well established, with spending peaking in 2010–11 due to recession-era economic stimulus funding, and growing again recently under the Liberals, who returned to power in 2015 after a decade of Conservative government. In recent years, the Liberals have heavily emphasized public transit, making it by far the largest single category of infrastructure funding. It is also a distinctly urban type of infrastructure. Recent research suggests that the focus on transit reflects the fact that the federal Liberal Party has a more distinctly urban base of support than it has ever had in the past (Horak and Helmer 2021; Armstrong, Lucas, and Taylor 2022).

The rise of federal involvement in local and urban issues in recent years has not been limited to infrastructure. Recent initiatives in other policy fields include a $40 billion National Housing Strategy, which features various spending programs ranging from funding for affordable housing construction and homeless shelters to a first-time home buyers' incentive; the Innovation Superclusters program, which funds locally based coalitions of businesses,

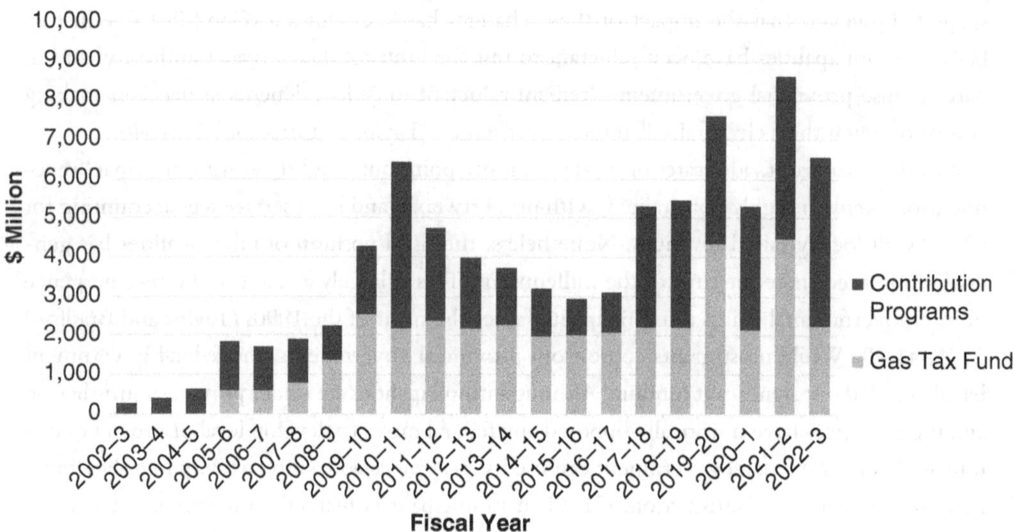

Figure 4.2. Federal Infrastructure Funding Transfers by Fiscal Year, 2002–23
Source: Author's calculations based on Infrastructure Canada data.

research institutions, and local governments in five city-regions to grow post-industrial economic clusters; and programs aimed at supporting new immigrants and urban Indigenous populations through funding for local government-NGO partnerships. More recently, as part of the "Safe Restart Agreement" announced in July 2020, the federal government pledged $4.3 billion to help municipalities deal with the financial impact of COVID-19, again with a focus on public transit systems, which were hit hard by falling fare revenues (Government of Canada 2020). As Bradford points out, although Canada lacks explicit federal urban policies such as exist in most other wealthy democratic countries, this proliferation of federal programming amounts to the emergence of an "implicit" federal urban agenda (Bradford 2018).

Multilevel Urban Governance in Canada: Negotiation, Co-production, and Metagovernance

Over the past twenty years, multilevel urban governance in Canada has become more varied in form. Not only does it now often involve the federal government, but it also often involves local non-governmental actors, especially in policy fields that focus on vulnerable or marginalized populations, such as the homeless, new immigrants, and urban Indigenous Peoples. These are fields in which resources are scarce, and on-the-ground knowledge is essential. They are also policy fields in which the federal government has become increasingly involved, and where, by reaching out directly to community partners through metagovernance initiatives, the federal government can sidestep constitutional limits on its local engagement.

Multilevel urban politics in contemporary Canada is highly varied in terms of the actors involved and the roles that they play. Drawing on the Horak (2012) typology presented earlier in this chapter, Lucas and Smith (2019) analyze actors and roles across eighteen multilevel policy fields, drawing on a Canada-wide survey of mayors. They find that different levels of government play leading roles in different cases and that the roles played by different actors vary significantly as well. Interestingly, such variation is driven more by differences across policy fields than by different provincial or local contexts (290), which echoes findings from earlier work on multilevel politics in Canada (Horak and Young 2012) that also noted wide variation in actors and roles by policy field.

In this increasingly complex landscape, is co-production replacing negotiation as the dominant mode of multilevel governance in Canadian cities? The short answer is no. On the one hand, as we have seen, both the federal government and local non-governmental actors have become more deeply involved multilevel urban governance in numerous policy fields, so provincial-municipal negotiation is not as dominant as it once was. On the other hand, building sustained coordination and joint action remains difficult, and stable multilevel co-production initiatives are uncommon. In fact, there seems to be a trend *away* from co-production in recent years.

For example, federal "contribution programs" that co-fund local infrastructure, which emerged in the mid-2000s, initially involved all three levels of government in making decisions about which local projects would receive funding. Criticized as an example of federal micro-management, the programs were restructured after 2015, and the federal role in project decisions was removed (Jacques and Ferland 2021; Horak and Helmer 2021). Another prominent and recent instance of multilevel co-production is Waterfront Toronto, an agency that is jointly governed and funded by the federal, provincial, and municipal governments. Created in 2008 as part of an unsuccessful bid to attract the Olympics to Toronto, the agency has had significant success in revitalizing parts of Toronto's long-idle port lands. However, it has faced increasing challenges over time as tri-level funding has dried up, and the agency has had to find new ways of funding its work within the tight fiscal and authority limits imposed on it by governments that are reluctant to delegate too much power to an agency that they cannot fully control (Eidelman 2013).

The perennial underlying challenge for co-production, as noted earlier, is that governments at different spatial scales respond to different electorates. As a result, even if joint policy goals are identified at one point in time, agreement on goals may not last. This challenge exists in all democratic settings, but in Canada it is exacerbated by the fact that political party systems and administrative systems are not aligned across spatial scales. Despite its appeal in principle, co-production is thus likely to remain a relatively uncommon mode of multilevel urban governance in Canada. This does not mean, however, that we are moving back toward an era when multilevel urban governance is all about provincial-municipal negotiation. While provincial-municipal negotiation remains vitally important, the more complex governance landscape that includes the federal government and local societal actors is here to stay. In this context, there are signs of increased reliance on the third mode of MLG – metagovernance.

The federal government has developed two models of urban metagovernance in recent years. One uses federal-provincial agreements to incentivize local action in a particular policy field. For example, federal-provincial immigration policy agreements provide funding and logistical support for "Local Immigration Partnerships" (LIPs). LIPs bring together local non-profits and local governments to support the community integration of newcomers. Federal funding programs for local infrastructure are likewise implemented through federal-provincial agreements that stipulate the criteria that fundable projects must meet and who must be involved in implementing them (Infrastructure Canada 2021). A second model, which largely bypasses provincial and local governments, has emerged with the "Innovation Superclusters" program and federal programming for Indigenous Peoples living in cities. In these fields, the federal government provides funds directly to local non-governmental actors, who then collaborate with each other under terms outlined by federal program requirements (Bradford and Taylor 2021, 44–5).

As we saw earlier, historically many provinces have regulated local affairs with a heavy hand, using detailed regulation and oversight, sometimes imposed without consultation. As we noted earlier, there have also long been elements of a metagovernance approach in some provinces, such as British Columbia's Regional Districts. More recently, provincial metagovernance initiatives – such as the Local Health Integration Networks established by the Liberals in Ontario in 2006 – have emerged in other provinces as well. However, the long history of top-down provincial management in most provinces means that significant inertia limits the spread of metagovernance. This inertia exists among provincial administrators and politicians who are reluctant to let go of detailed management of local affairs; however, importantly, it also exists among local government administrators and politicians, who often hold on to what Siegel and Tindal (2006, 40) call a "comfortable subordination" in which problems and policy failings can be blamed on the province. In this context, detailed provincial regulation and supervision are likely to remain common in Canadian urban politics for the foreseeable future.

MAKING MULTILEVEL URBAN GOVERNANCE WORK: CANADA IN CROSS-NATIONAL PERSPECTIVE

Serving Local Needs? Multilevel Urban Politics and Local Priorities

Multilevel governance in Canada clearly focuses more on urban issues today than it did a couple of decades ago, with increased funding and policy attention for urban-centred concerns such as affordable housing, transit infrastructure, and immigrant integration, both at the federal levels and in most provinces. While this rise of policy attention is in part a result of bottom-up activism by urban political leaders in the early 2000s, the increasing electoral significance of urban constituencies has also played a role. Provincial and federal governments that rely on an urban support base are naturally more likely to pay attention to urban policy issues. While the degree of reliance on urban votes varies across provincial governments, recent work on the rural-urban divide in federal politics shows that the support base of the federal Liberal Party has become strikingly urban in recent decades (Armstrong, Lucas, and Taylor 2022), which might help to explain increased federal attention to urban policy issues since 2015.

However, increased attention to urban concerns in general does not necessarily mean that provincial and federal policies and programs are responsive to *local* priorities and needs in Canadian cities, for two reasons. First, insofar as provincial and federal attention reflects political pressures and priorities at those levels, it may not take account of the priorities of local governments in general, or of local preferences in places that are not deemed to be politically important. Second, and relatedly, place-specific needs and preferences vary from one city to another, so to be locally responsive, multilevel support must be *tailored* to different local conditions in different places. The degree to which this happens in Canadian cities varies, and some cities have more success in securing support for their needs than others.

A 2012 study of multilevel politics in six policy fields across ten large Canadian cities found that several characteristics of individual urban municipalities affect their relative success in securing federal and/or provincial support for local priorities (Horak and Young 2012). First – and unsurprisingly, given our discussion above – the electoral importance of a city at other levels of government matters. Second, the study found that the "conception of local government … held by local officials" is also important. If local politicians conceive of local government as a "minimalist" provider of local services, they are less likely to lobby for multilevel support than if they see local government as a "comprehensive" steward of local well-being. Finally – and relatedly – municipalities that have a strong administrative capacity in policy development and intergovernmental affairs are more likely to be able to act strategically in the multilevel political arena to secure benefits for distinct local priorities (Horak 2012, 365).

Even if local actors secure multilevel support for local policy initiatives, these initiatives must then be implemented; and in complex governance-based policy fields that involve multiple actors, successful implementation can be a real challenge. Recent work suggests that there is a strong element of *path dependence* that shapes the prospects for successful local implementation. Specifically, places in which there is a pre-existing local history of collaborative action are more likely to implement complex governance-based initiatives successfully. For example, in a study of the local governance of homelessness in Toronto, Calgary, and Vancouver, Doberstein (2016b) found that local actors in Vancouver were able to draw on a history of collaborative work at the regional scale to make more effective use of available resources than their counterparts in Toronto and Calgary. Likewise, a recent comparative study of the development of rapid transit infrastructure in Vancouver and Toronto (Horak 2021) found that a history of regional collaboration among local governments on transit issues in Vancouver has allowed actors there to use multilevel funding for transit to build new rapid transit lines much more quickly than in Toronto, where there is no history of formal regional collaboration on transit, and the question of what to build where is the subject of ongoing political wrangling.

The Canadian Experience in Cross-National Context: Is the Grass Really Greener?

Multilevel urban governance in Canada has evolved significantly over the past twenty years. Long-standing practices of provincial-municipal negotiation have been joined by federal funding for local and urban concerns and the increased involvement of local non-governmental actors in many policy fields. While intergovernmental negotiation remains an important mode of interaction, federal and provincial governments have also experimented with co-production initiatives and are increasingly deploying metagovernance approaches to address local and urban policy concerns. Nonetheless, as chapter 2 shows, many urban politics scholars and city advocates maintain that the Canadian system must be fundamentally restructured to better serve a largely urban population – be it through the granting of stronger resources, legal autonomy, or immunity from provincial intervention to local governments (Good 2021), or through the development of more explicit federal urban policies (Bradford 2018). Yet cross-national experience suggests that there are challenges associated with both these paths.

The multilevel context for urban governance in the United States – discussed in detail in chapter 2 – is in some ways similar to that in Canada since local governments are under state (not federal) jurisdiction and raise most of their own revenues, and partisan politics is weakly integrated across scales. However, in many American states, home rule gives municipalities greater legal autonomy than their Canadian counterparts, as well as protection from state-level interventions such as forced amalgamations. In addition, as chapter 6 explores further, American municipalities have access to a broader range of local revenue sources than Canadian ones.

In many senses, then, local governments in American cities are more autonomous than Canadian ones. Yet the degree to which American urban municipalities can translate this autonomy into actual governing capacity varies greatly, precisely *because* of the decentralized nature of the multilevel system. Over time, the combined effects of high dependence on locally raised revenues, the fragmentation of metropolitan areas into many local government units, and a laissez-faire attitude toward urban affairs in state legislatures have produced a patchwork of have and have-not municipalities. Wealthy municipalities have the capacity to provide good services to their populations and offer residents real policy choices; poorer municipalities struggle to attract investment and maintain basic services. In this sense, as Taylor puts it, the American system of multilevel urban politics grants only an "illusory independence" to local governments – an autonomy that "rewards wealth while punishing poverty" (Taylor 2021, 5).

If the American example illustrates the problems that can come from a highly decentralized urban governing system, evidence from other countries shows the challenges associated with centralized national urban policies. In England, for instance, there is no intermediate level of government between the national and the local. With the growth of the welfare state in the twentieth century, managing nationally designed and funded programs became one of the main functions of local government in England. The national government has long had a strong suite of locally focused programs, but until the 1990s, these programs (such as public housing and urban renewal) were designed without local input and implemented in a largely top-down manner (Keating 1991). Mounting criticism of this approach led the national government to develop a more flexible approach in the 2000s, focusing on "partnerships" and "deals" that are negotiated with individual municipalities. While this has allowed national urban programs to be tailored more to local conditions, it has also been criticized as highly ad hoc and inefficient, and many in the local government sector complain that there are no channels through which local governments can collectively discuss needs and priorities with the national government, so the system is still effectively centrally controlled since the representation of local interests in the multilevel arena is highly fragmented (McEwen et al. 2020).

Decentralization and strong central action in urban affairs thus both come with challenges. In the decentralized system of the United States, the policy capacity of urban governments depends on local economic circumstances; in England's more centralized system, local governance is shaped by decisions made far away at the national level. Can the circle be squared? Are there multilevel systems that empower urban governments without leading to winner-takes-all inter-local competition, and in which national and regional governments support local governing capacity without dictating the terms? The discussion of South African urban governance in Ran Hirschl's (2020) recent comparative survey of cities and constitutionalism is illuminating in this regard. Hirschl shows that, while its cities continue to face major policy challenges, South Africa has legally and fiscally empowered urban governments in a way that has enhanced urban governing capacity and responsiveness. However, what is notable is that local empowerment was accompanied by a comprehensive, nationally led series of structural reforms in the 1990s that replaced the fragmented local government landscape of apartheid-era cities with consolidated metropolitan authorities and developed a suite of national programs that provided resources and policy support to these new metropolitan authorities (Cameron 2005). Arguably, it is these reforms and national programs – which amount to a comprehensive system of national urban metagovernance – that have given local governments in South Africa's cities the capacity to make use of their new legal and fiscal powers and responsibilities.

The South African example suggests that building better multilevel urban governing systems is not about local empowerment alone, nor is it about stronger national urban policies. Rather, it is about recognizing that urban governance is a matter of what Sellers, Lidström, and Bae (2020) call "multilevel democracy." Contemporary democratic governance, they argue, is inherently multilevel. As a result, the quality of democratic processes and outputs at *all* spatial scales in a country is shaped by a "institutional infrastructure of multilevel democracy" that organizes relationships between local, regional, and national political institutions and actors (Sellers, Lidström and Bae 2020, 23). Sellers, Lidström, and Bae identify three types of multilevel governance infrastructures in stable democracies: nationalized, local elitist, and civic localist. Based on a comparative analysis of policy outputs over time, as well as a meta-analysis of survey data on government performance, they argue that the best governance outcomes – both locally and nationally – are produced by what they call a "nationalized infrastructure of multilevel democracy," (2020, 33) which is characteristic of small northern European countries such as Denmark, Sweden, and the Netherlands.

A nationalized infrastructure of multilevel democracy is one in which local governments have broad powers and strong fiscal resources, but in which local governance is also strongly integrated with national systems through political parties and civil society organizations (such as interest groups and social movement organizations) that span spatial scales. The combination of empowered local governments and strong partisan and civil society links among scales "can both sustain broad local political incorporation and link local democracy to inclusion at the national level. This combination thus offers the strongest prospects for full democratic inclusion as well as effective public policy" (47).

In countries with nationalized infrastructures of multilevel governance, Sellers, Lidström, and Bae suggest, the distribution of governing capacity among spatial scales is not a zero-sum game. "Institutionalized support from higher levels can give local governments legal, administrative, and fiscal capacities they would otherwise lack … What is given to the local level, therefore, need not be taken away from higher levels. Lower-level governments could be empowered by governments at higher levels to undertake elements of an expanded state activity that also strengthens the capacity of higher-level authorities" (58). For this reason, they conclude, countries with nationalized infrastructures "have come closest to reconciling the inherent tensions between local and national democracy" (341).

Reframed in terms of our earlier discussion of modes of MLG, Sellers, Lidström, and Bae's (2020) comparative research suggests that political systems that combine empowered local governments with strong partisan and civil society links among local, regional, and national scales of democratic activity support both multilevel co-production and the national metagovernance of local and urban affairs. Strong and systematic links among governing scales – both in politics and in civil society – can foster multilevel support for local and urban needs and priorities without sacrificing responsiveness to local priorities and preferences.

CONCLUSION: THE FUTURE OF MULTILEVEL URBAN GOVERNANCE IN CANADA

Sellers, Lidström, and Bae's (2020) work demonstrates the value of systematic, cross-national research on multilevel politics. For Canadians, their conclusions highlight the importance of strong multilevel links in political and civil society, which can facilitate interest articulation and policy coordination across scales. However, Canada is *not* a country where such links exist, nor is it likely to become one. Indeed, in Sellers, Lidström, and Bae's (2020) account, Canada (along with the United States) has a "civic localist" infrastructure of multilevel politics, characterized by low levels of multilevel integration. As we suggested earlier, it is precisely this dis-integration that has historically impeded the upward articulation of urban interests in Canada's governing system. At the same time, Canada's dis-integrated system, in which political dynamics at each level of government are sui generis, also exacerbates the difficulties of co-production, which relies on shared goals and mechanisms across state scales.

Any multilevel political system develops over a long period of time, and its basic contours shift only slowly and incrementally. As Sellers, Lidström, and Bae (2020, 339) document in detail, the three types of multilevel infrastructures that they identify have deep historical roots that date back hundreds of years. For the foreseeable future, then, a dis-integrated system of inter-scalar political relations is bound to remain the norm in Canada. Provincial constitutional supremacy over municipalities, non-partisan local government, and other foundational elements of Canada's system are not going to disappear overnight. Sustained multilevel co-production is likely to remain rare, and other forms of multilevel coordination will continue to be challenging, leading provincial governments to resort to unilateral action from time to time.

That said, the past twenty years have seen urban issues taking a more prominent place in multilevel politics in Canada. The result has been the emergence of a new, more complex, multilevel urban governance – one that is messy, unstable, and uneven in its success, but that has also produced considerable policy innovation, along with successful experiments with new modes of multilevel interaction. The steady increase in the demographic weight of large cities, the emergence of rural-urban partisan divides in federal and (in some cases) provincial politics, and the place of cities as sites of emerging social needs and new political demands are likely to ensure that urban concerns remain on provincial and federal agendas in the decades to come. Translating this political salience into more responsive, effective urban governance will require, above all, an understanding by policy-makers at all spatial scales that governing cities is an inherently multilevel enterprise.

ACKNOWLEDGEMENTS

Many people contributed valuable feedback that made this a better chapter. They include the volume editors, two anonymous reviewers, Jack Lucas, Zack Taylor, students in my 2021–2 Globalization and Urban Politics class, and the participants in a May 2022 session on multilevel governance in Canada at the Institute for Comparative Federalism in Bolzano, Italy. Financial support was provided by the European Union's Horizon 2020 research and innovation program (grant agreement no. 823961).

NOTES

1 By comparison, as of 2022 the provincial government of Manitoba employed 12,500 people (Manitoba Public Service Commission 2022).
2 To be precise, Hooghe and Marks's "task-specific jurisdictions" is a broader concept that includes not only multilevel governing bodies, but special-purpose authorities of all kinds, including things such as metropolitan planning organizations and police boards (Hooghe and Marks 2003, 237).
3 For a detailed discussion of the activity of municipal associations in Canada, see Shott (2017).

REFERENCES

Alcantara, Christopher, Jörg Broschek, and Jen Nelles. 2016. "Rethinking Multilevel Governance as an Instance of Multilevel Politics: A Conceptual Strategy." *Territory, Politics, Governance* 4, no. 1 (January): 33–51. https://doi.org/10.1080/21622671.2015.1047897.

Armstrong, David A., II, Jack Lucas, and Zack Taylor. 2022. "The Urban-Rural Divide in Canadian Federal Elections, 1896–2019." *Canadian Journal of Political Science* 55, no. 1 (March): 84–106. https://doi.org/10.1017/S0008423921000792.

Bevir, Mark. 2010. *Democratic Governance.* Princeton: Princeton University Press.

Boland, Philip. 1999. "Contested Multi-level Governance: Merseyside and the European Structural Funds." *European Planning Studies* 7, no. 5 (October): 647–64. https://doi.org/10.1080/09654319908720543.

Bradford, Neil. 2007. *Whither the Federal Urban Agenda? A New Deal in Transition.* Ottawa: Canadian Policy Research Networks.

———. 2018. "A National Urban Policy for Canada? The Implicit Federal Agenda." *IRPP Insight,* no. 24 (November). https://irpp.org/research-studies/national-urban-policy-canada-implicit -federal-agenda/.

Brunet-Jailly, Emmanuel. 2007. "Municipal-Central Relations in France: Between Decentralization and Multilevel Governance." In *Spheres of Governance: Comparative Studies of Cities in Multilevel Governance Systems,* edited by Harvey Lazar and Christian Leuprecht, 125–62. Montreal: McGill-Queen's University Press.

Cameron, David, and Richard Simeon. 2002. "Intergovernmental Relations in Canada: The Emergence of Collaborative Federalism." *Publius: The Journal of Federalism* 32, no. 2 (Spring): 49–72. https://doi.org/10.1093/oxfordjournals.pubjof.a004947.

Cameron, Robert. 2005. "Metropolitan Restructuring (and More Restructuring) in South Africa." *Public Administration and Development: The International Journal of Management Research and Practice* 25, no. 4 (October): 329–39. https://doi.org/10.1002/pad.383.

Canada. 2020. "Safe Restart Agreement." Last modified September 16, 2020. https://www.canada.ca /en/intergovernmental-affairs/services/safe-restart-agreement.html.

Cashaback, David. 2001. *Regional District Governance in British Columbia: A Case Study in Aggregation.* Ottawa: Institute on Governance.

City of Toronto. 2002. "Provincial Auditor Confirms Downloading Is Not Revenue Neutral." Press release, January 3, 2002 (removed from website in 2021). Archived June 26, 2021, at the Wayback Machine. https://web.archive.org/web/20210626215846/https://wx.toronto.ca/inter/it/newsrel. nsf/382b8dfa7ac9b7dd85257aa70063f75b/266ace90a98791d385256df60045f0f2?OpenDocument.

———. 2023a. *2023 City of Toronto Budget Summary.* https://www.toronto.ca/wp-content /uploads/2023/05/95f8-2023-City-of-Toronto-Budget-Summary.pdf.

———. 2023b. "Quarterly Workforce Statistics – March 2023." https://www.toronto.ca/city-government/data-research-maps/workforce-statistics/.

———. n.d. "Recreation Centres Listings." Accessed May 10, 2024. https://www.toronto.ca/data/parks/prd/facilities/recreationcentres/index.html.

Cobban, Timothy. 2013. *Cities of Oil: Municipalities and Petroleum Manufacturing in Southern Ontario, 1860–1960*. Toronto: University of Toronto Press. https://doi.org/10.3138/9781442663138.

Doberstein, Carey. 2013. "Metagovernance of Urban Governance Networks in Canada: In Pursuit of Legitimacy and Accountability." *Canadian Public Administration* 56, no. 4 (December): 584–609. https://doi.org/10.1111/capa.12041.

———. 2016. *Building a Collaborative Advantage: Network Governance and Homelessness Policy-Making in Canada*. Vancouver: UBC Press. https://doi.org/10.59962/9780774833264.

Eidelman, Gabriel. 2010. "Managing Urban Sprawl in Ontario: Good Policy or Good Politics?" *Politics & Policy* 38, no. 6 (December): 1211–36. https://doi.org/10.1111/j.1747-1346.2010.00275.x.

———. 2013. *Three's Company: A Review of Waterfront Toronto's Tri-government Approach to Revitalization*. Toronto: Mowat Centre for Policy Innovation.

Erie, Steven P., Vladimir Kogan, and Scott A. MacKenzie. 2010. "Redevelopment, San Diego Style: The Limits of Public – Private Partnerships." *Urban Affairs Review* 45, no. 5 (May): 644–78. https://doi.org/10.1177/1078087409359760.

Good, Kristin R. 2019. "The Fallacy of the 'Creatures of the Provinces' Doctrine: Recognizing and Protecting Municipalities' Constitutional Status." In *IMFG Papers on Municipal Finance and Governance*, no. 46. Toronto: Institute on Municipal Finance and Governance.

———. 2021. *Reconsidering the Constitutional Status of Municipalities: From Creatures of the Provinces to Provincial Constitutionalism*. Montreal: Institute for Research on Public Policy.

Head, Brian W., and John Alford. 2015. "Wicked Problems: Implications for Public Policy and Public Management." *Administration & Society* 47, no. 6 (August): 711–39. https://doi.org/10.1177/0095399713481601.

Henstra, Dan, ed. 2013. *Multilevel Governance and Emergency Management in Canadian Municipalities*. Montreal: McGill-Queen's University Press. https://doi.org/10.1515/9780773589537.

Hirschl, Ran. 2020. *City, State: Constitutionalism and the Megacity*. New York: Oxford University Press. https://doi.org/10.1093/oso/9780190922771.001.0001.

Hooghe, Liesbet, and Gary Marks. 2003. "Unraveling the Central State, but How? Types of Multi-level Governance." *American Political Science Review* 97, no. 2 (June): 233–43. https://doi.org/10.1017/S0003055403000649.

Horak, Martin. 1998. *The Power of Local Identity: C4LD and the Anti-Amalgamation Mobilization*. Toronto: Centre for Urban and Community Studies.

———. 2008. *Governance Reform from Below: Multilevel Politics and Toronto's "New Deal" Campaign*. Global Dialogue Series, no. 4. Nairobi: UN-Habitat.

———. 2012. "Conclusion: Understanding Multilevel Governance in Canada's Cities." In *Sites of Governance: Multilevel Governance and Policy Making in Canada's Big Cities*, edited by Martin Horak and Robert Young, 339–70. Montreal: McGill-Queen's Press. https://doi.org/10.1515/9780773586918-013.

———. 2021. "Building Rapid Transit in Canada: The Problem of Governance." *Anuario De Derecho Municipal*, no. 14 (June): 243–58. https://doi.org/10.37417/ADM/14-2020_09.

Horak, Martin, and Jesse Helmer. 2021. "Program Design and Distributive Politics in Canadian Infrastructure Transfers," working paper, Canadian Urban Politics Workshop, April 12, 2021.

Horak, Martin, and Robert Young, eds. 2012. *Sites of Governance: Multilevel Governance and Policy Making in Canada's Big Cities*. Montreal: McGill-Queen's University Press. https://doi .org/10.1515/9780773586918.

Hulchanski, J. David. 2010. *The Three Cities within Toronto*. Toronto: Cities Centre.

Infrastructure Canada. 2021. "Provincial-Territorial Agreements and Letters." https://www .infrastructure.gc.ca/prog/agreements-ententes/index-eng.html.

Jacques, Olivier, and Benjamin Ferland. 2021. "Distributive Politics in Canada: The Case of Infrastructure Spending in Rural and Suburban Districts." *Canadian Journal of Political Science /Revue canadienne de science politique* 54, no. 1 (March): 96–117. https://doi.org/10.1017 /S0008423920000955.

Jessop, Bob. 2004. "Multilevel Governance and Multilevel Metagovernance. Changes in the EU as Integral Moments in the Transformation and Reorientation of Contemporary Statehood." In *Multi-level Governance*, edited by Ian Bache and Matthew Flinders, 49–79. Oxford: Oxford University Press. https://doi.org/10.1093/0199259259.003.0004.

Keating, Michael. 1991. *Comparative Urban Politics: Power and the City in the United States, Canada, Britain, and France*. Aldershot: Edward Elgar.

Kipfer, Stefan, and Roger Keil. 2002. "Toronto Inc? Planning the Competitive City in the New Toronto." *Antipode* 34, no. 2 (March): 227–64. https://doi.org/10.1111/1467-8330.00237.

Leo, Christopher, and Martine August. 2009. "The Multilevel Governance of Immigration and Settlement: Making Deep Federalism Work." *Canadian Journal of Political Science/Revue canadienne de science politique* 42, no. 2 (June): 491–510. https://doi.org/10.1017/S0008423909090337.

Lucas, Jack, and Alison Smith. 2019. "Multilevel Policy from the Municipal Perspective: A Pan-Canadian Survey." *Canadian Public Administration* 62, no. 2 (June), 270–93. https://doi .org/10.1111/capa.12316.

———. 2020. "Municipalities in the Federation." In *Canadian Federalism: Performance, Effectiveness and Legitimacy*, edited by Herman Bakvis and Grace Skogstad, 4th ed., 427–52. Toronto: University of Toronto Press.

Magnusson, Warren, and Andrew Sancton. 1983. *City Politics in Canada*. Toronto: University of Toronto Press. https://doi.org/10.3138/9781487575908.

Manitoba Public Service Commission. 2022. *Annual Report 21/22*. Winnipeg: Manitoba Public Service Commission. https://www.gov.mb.ca/csc/publications/annrpt/pdf/2021-22_annualrpt_en-fr.pdf.

Mast, Evan. 2020. "Race to the Bottom? Local Tax Break Competition and Business Location." *American Economic Journal: Applied Economics* 12, no. 1 (January): 288–317. https://doi .org/10.1257/app.20170511.

McEwen, Nicola, Michael Kenny, Jack Sheldon, and Coree Brown Swan. 2020. "Intergovernmental Relations in the UK: Time for a Radical Overhaul?" *The Political Quarterly* 91, no. 3 (July–September): 632–40. https://doi.org/10.1111/1467-923X.12862.

Peterson, Jacqueline, Jack Lucas, and Andrew Klain. 2019. "Cities and Places in Provincial Policy Agendas." *Canadian Public Administration* 62, no. 2 (June): 249–69. https://doi.org/10.1111 /capa.12317.

Piattoni, Simona. 2009. "Multi-level Governance: A Historical and Conceptual Analysis." *Journal of European Integration* 31, no. 2 (March): 163–80. https://doi.org/10.1080/07036330802642755.

———. 2010. *The Theory of Multi-level Governance: Conceptual, Empirical, and Normative Challenges*. New York: Oxford University Press.

Sancton, Andrew. 2006. "Why Municipal Amalgamations? Halifax, Toronto, Montréal." *Municipal-Federal-Provincial Relations in Canada*, edited by Robert Young and Christian Leuprecht, 119–38. Kingston: Institute for Intergovernmental Relations.

———. 2008. *The Limits of Boundaries: Why City-Regions Cannot Be Self-Governing*. Montreal: McGill-Queen's University Press.

———. 2015. *Canadian Local Government: An Urban Perspective*. 2nd ed. Toronto: Oxford University Press Canada.

Scharpf, Fritz W. 2001. "Notes toward a Theory of Multilevel Governing in Europe." *Scandinavian Political Studies* 24, no. 1 (March): 1–26. https://doi.org/10.1111/1467-9477.00044.

Schertzer, Robert. 2020. "Intergovernmental Relations in a Complex Federation." In *Canadian Federalism: Performance, Effectiveness and Legitimacy*, edited by Herman Bakvis and Grace Skogstad, 4th ed., 165–94. Toronto: University of Toronto Press.

Sellers, Jefferey M. 2005. "Re-placing the Nation: An Agenda for Comparative Urban Politics." *Urban Affairs Review* 40, no. 4 (March): 419–45. https://doi.org/10.1177/1078087404272673.

Sellers, Jefferey M., Anders Lidström, and Yooil Bae. 2020. *Multilevel Democracy: How Local Institutions and Civil Society Shape the Modern State*. Cambridge: Cambridge University Press. https://doi.org/10.1017/9781108672337.

Shott, Alison. 2017. "The Composition of Municipal Associations and Policy Requests to Provincial Governments: Selected Cases." *Canadian Public Administration* 60, no. 1 (March): 111–34. https://doi.org/10.1111/capa.12204.

Siegel, David. 2009. "Ontario." In *Foundations of Governance: Municipal Governance in Canada's Provinces*, edited by Andrew Sancton and Robert Young, 20–69. Toronto: University of Toronto Press. https://doi.org/10.3138/9781442697874-004.

Siegel, David, and C. Richard Tindal. 2006. "Changing the Municipal Culture: From Comfortable Subordination to Assertive Maturity – Part I." *Municipal World*, March 2006: 37–40. https://www.municipalworld.com/articles/changing-the-municipal-culture-part-1/.

Smith, Alison. 2022. *Multiple Barriers: The Multilevel Governance of Homelessness in Canada*. Toronto: University of Toronto Press. https://doi.org/10.3138/9781487548742.

Spicer, Zac. 2011. "The Rise and Fall of the Ministry of State for Urban Affairs: Exploring the Nature of Federal-Urban Engagement in Canada." *Canadian Political Science Review* 5, no. 2 (January): 117–26. https://doi.org/10.24124/c677/2011149.

Statistics Canada. 2022. "Focus on Geography Series, 2021 Census of Population." https://www12.statcan.gc.ca/census-recensement/2021/as-sa/fogs-spg/page.cfm?lang=E&topic=1&dguid=2021A000011124.

Stoker, Gerry. 1998. "Governance as Theory: Five Propositions." *International Social Science Journal* 50, no. 155 (March): 17–28. https://doi.org/10.1111/1468-2451.00106.

Stone, Clarence. 2015. "Reflections on Regime Politics: From Governing Coalition to Urban Political Order." *Urban Affairs Review* 51, no. 1 (January): 101–37. https://doi.org/10.1177/1078087414558948.

Taylor, Zack. 2019. *Shaping the Metropolis: Institutions and Urbanization in the United States and Canada*. Montreal: McGill-Queen's University Press. https://doi.org/10.1515/9780773558427.

———. 2021. "From Local Autonomy to the Metagovernance of Place." Paper presented at Canadian Political Science Association Annual Meeting, June 2021.

Taylor, Zack, and Jon Isaac Taylor. 2024. "Boundary Battles in New Brunswick." In *Municipal Boundary Battles*, edited by Sandeep Agrawal, 185–211. Edmonton: University of Alberta Press.

Taylor, Zack, and Neil Bradford. 2021. "Governing Canadian Cities." In *Canadian Cities in Transition*, edited by Markus Moos, Ryan Walker, and Tara Vinodrai, 6th ed., 33–50. Toronto: Oxford University Press.

Tindal, Richard, Susan Tindal, Kennedy Stewart, and Patrick Smith. 2017. *Local Government in Canada*. 9th ed. Toronto: Nelson Education.

PART THREE

Comparing Local Institutions

CHAPTER FIVE

Metropolitan Governance and Institutional Responses to Urbanization

Jen Nelles

INTRODUCTION

Canada is a metropolitan nation. As of 2023, over 29 million Canadians (approximately 72 per cent of the population) lived in a major metropolitan area (Statistics Canada 2024). While these regions appear as orderly entities on a map (see figure 5.1) they are, in reality, a relatively chaotic jumble of jurisdictions, regimes, and arrangements. The reason for this is that the boundaries on that map represent how we perceive metropolitan areas in this country – defined using statistical constructs – and not actual political spaces subject to coordinated rule. These statistical constructs exist because we recognize that metropolitan spaces are worth measuring, in part because we understand that local boundaries are permeable and that there are policy issues that require (or would at least benefit from) coordination across the fragmented landscape of political units. Yet the political reality of metropolitan government and governance is far more complex than the image that these maps portray.

To confront multi-dimensional regional challenges, Canadian jurisdictions have tended to turn to formal institutional reforms. Due to the strength and engagement of Canadian provinces in municipal affairs, these reforms have been driven by provincial governments and have been hotly contested by local authorities and civic groups. However, because reforms and experiences vary by province, the Canadian experience has proved an interesting lab for metropolitan experimentation that is often difficult to implement elsewhere (most notably, for our neighbour to the south, the United States). Although these are, in most cases, ongoing experiments, a consensus is emerging that institutional reforms have fallen short of policy objectives. The growth and evolution of urban regions in Canada and around the world and the rising complexity of shared urban problems suggest that the problem of metropolitan coordination will continue to engage and challenge urban scholarship.

This chapter explores the rationale for metropolitan coordination, outlines the range of approaches that various governments have used to manage policy across jurisdictional boundaries, and discusses the advantages and disadvantages of each. It then details some of the most notable Canadian experiments with metropolitan regionalism: the cases of Vancouver, Winnipeg, Toronto, and Montreal. These cases are then contrasted with the metropolitan traditions in the United States, France, and the United Kingdom. It concludes with some observations about how we can conceptualize the Canadian approach in comparative perspective.

(WHY) DO WE NEED A METROPOLITAN APPROACH?

In many countries, including in many places in Canada, there is no formal level of government between the municipal and state/provincial scales. Yet, economic, social, and political life is anchored in and dependent on urban agglomerations under the jurisdiction of multiple local authorities. Consider this: in many large metropolitan regions, it is difficult to tell when you are crossing from one municipality to another – urban spaces blend together almost seamlessly. On major roadways, there may be signs welcoming you to a new jurisdiction, but aside from that, there would be few clues that you had crossed a largely invisible but politically significant frontier. Places may look similar, but they are governed by a different set of decision-makers and a different government, representing different interests and objectives than their neighbours.

While there are certain advantages to this kind of political fragmentation, in practice, it makes governing in certain policy areas quite difficult. Proponents of regionalism focus on five core rationales for policy coordination across local boundaries: externalities, economies of scale, efficiency, competitiveness, and fiscal equity concerns.

Coordination across jurisdictional boundaries is necessary because decisions made in one municipality can adversely affect neighbouring municipalities. If one municipality sites schools and parkland near its jurisdictional boundaries and its neighbour locates polluting heavy industry next door, that decision will negatively impact the experience of those using the parks and school facilities. In this scenario, the first municipality must deal with the externalities – the smog, noise, traffic, etc. – generated by the decisions of the second municipality to build its industry next to the park. This example is a simple one, but externalities come in all sorts of forms. Coordination is required to ensure that roads align, transit schedules coincide, natural resources remain unpolluted, and shared values are upheld. Simply put, communicating with neighbouring municipalities is a necessary part of being a good neighbour and mitigating the impact of others' decisions on your own community.

There are also economic reasons to consider coordinating across local boundaries. Sometimes services and infrastructure are too expensive for one community to provide alone. In that case, it can make sense to expand the service area to include more municipalities and provide the service collectively. Things like fire protection and other emergency services, trash collection, or expensive infrastructure like sewers and transit are among the most common areas in which multiple municipalities will engage in some form of agreement to provide.

These agreements are often driven by the cost advantages of economies of scale but can also be more administratively efficient. If local governments are required to provide certain services and fulfill specified roles, that means that each political jurisdiction must duplicate the services of its neighbours. There are lots of great reasons for localities to maintain control over those functions, not least of which is to retain autonomy over, and the ability to differentiate, the cost/services package that may be attractive to residents (see our discussion of Tiebout in chapter 3). However, that duplication of library systems or bus services can also be resource intensive. Working across regional boundaries can reduce the degree of duplication as well as contribute to cost management.

In the wake of globalization and the subsequent elevated competition between international city-regions for capital, talent, and prestige, policy-makers have increasingly invoked the logic of competitiveness as a justification for regionalism. The argument is that investors and workers first select the metropolitan region that they want to locate in before settling on a location within that region. Thus, metropolitan regions must put their best foot forward in order to sustain growth. In response, some metros have developed international marketing partnerships – coalitions of municipalities that sponsor trade missions and produce promotional material (see, for example, Toronto Inc. or Montréal International). In others, the competitiveness imperative is interpreted more broadly to include collaboration on regional quality of life issues – housing, transportation, parks, immigration, etc. – to boost international attractiveness. Often, the logic of international competitiveness is among the justifications for regional political restructuring or reorganization (such as in the creation of the Toronto Megacity).

Politically fragmented metropolitan regions are also prone to wide variations in socio-economic advantage and disadvantage. Some jurisdictions concentrate wealth while others exist in states of decline or distress. The distribution of costs and benefits for regional stewardship often fall unequally across neighbouring jurisdictions. Frequently, central cities must shoulder the burden of sustaining resources and amenities – arts and cultural institutions, infrastructure such as airports – that are widely used, but not paid for, by residents throughout the region. These issues of regional equity concerns are common justifications for regional approaches, particularly in the realm of regional redistributive practices such as tax base sharing.

Ultimately, all metropolitan areas could benefit from some degree of regional coordination, but regionalism is not appropriate for every policy area. As a result, a variety of approaches have emerged to the challenges and opportunities of governing in metropolitan regions.

WHAT IS A METROPOLITAN REGION?

"A region … is an area safely larger than the last one to whose problems we found no solutions" (Jacobs 1961, 410).

It can be very difficult to define precisely what a region is. Ask any individual and you're likely to get a slightly different answer about the location of the boundaries of "their" metropolitan area. The above quotation has a little fun with the idea of the ephemeral region. However, by necessity, policy-makers in most countries have developed systems to specify the boundaries of metropolitan regions and measure them.

At their simplest, metropolitan regions are urbanized areas formed by the expansion, and accretion, of numerous neighbouring localities around a denser urban core (or around multiple dense urban cores) that have developed a degree of integration between them. In practice, metropolitan regions are typically defined by a minimum population density for a given geography and/or based on the strength of commuting ties between those geographies. Commuting patterns have emerged as the standard by which the degree of integration is determined.

Different formal definitions for metropolitan areas have been adopted in jurisdictions around the world. What follows is a small selection of different approaches. Note that these are purely statistical definitions, and while they tend to be made up of building blocks based on administrative divisions (such as cities, counties, or their equivalents), they often do not represent territories of political governance.

Canada: Census Metropolitan Areas (CMAs)
Statistics Canada
Municipalities

CMAs are urban agglomerations with a minimum of 100,000 inhabitants formed by one or more adjoining contiguous municipalities centred on a core municipality with a population of at least 50,000. Adjacent municipalities are included in the CMA if (a) at least half of the resident labour force works in the core municipality; and/or (b) at least 25 per cent of the labour force employed in the municipality lives in the core. See figure 5.1 for a map of Canadian CMAs (Statistics Canada 2015).

USA: Metropolitan Statistical Areas (MSAs)
Office of Management and Budget
Counties/county-equivalents

MSAs are built outwards from a central county, which must have an urbanized area with a population of at least 50,000. Adjacent counties are included in the MSA if (a) at least 25 per cent of the workers living there work in the central county or work in other counties that are part of the MSA, or (b) at least 25 per cent of employees working in the county commute from the centre or other counties that are part of the MSA (Federal Register 2010).

European Union: Larger Urban Zones (LUZs)

Eurostat

Local administrative units (these vary by country)

LUZs are built around urban centres, which must have a minimum of 1,500 inhabitants per square kilometre and 50,000 inhabitants. The LUZ region must have a population of at least 250,000. Adjacent local administrative units are included in the region if at least 15 per cent of the employed population commutes to the urban centre for work. Each LUZ is equivalent to a NUTS 3/ITL3 region – the smallest European regional division on the Nomenclature of Territorial Units for Statistics (NUTS) or International Territorial Level (ITL) scale – or is made up of an agglomeration of NUTS 3 regions (Eurostat 2012).

While these definitions capture how different countries have grappled with the complexity of describing metropolitan regions statistically, the reality is that coordination almost never occurs at these neat and idealized scales. The following section explores the different ways that cross-boundary policy has been coordinated across metropolitan spaces.

A FRAMEWORK OF APPROACHES TO GOVERNING METROPOLITAN REGIONS

Government vs. Governance (Revisited)

One of the ways to think about and compare different approaches to regional policy coordination is to consider the institutional structure of the arrangement, the actors involved, and the power dynamics between them. Who is at the regional table? Who is driving the process? How are decisions made? Depending on the answers to these questions, an approach to regional policy coordination will fall somewhere on a spectrum between government and governance solutions.

Government approaches lie at one end of the spectrum. Broadly, government approaches involve the creation of new governing structures by the state or the adaptation of existing state structures, usually through some process of legislative decision-making or, more rarely, executive order. The structures that result are typically staffed by public officials, their institutions and authorities are derived from and codified in state statute, and they are located within and subject to state hierarchies. Decisions and actions are usually also shaped by and subject to a hierarchical structure that is often described as "top-down."

At the other end of the spectrum, governance approaches have quite a different character. Solutions that lie closer to this end of the spectrum have more flexible institutional

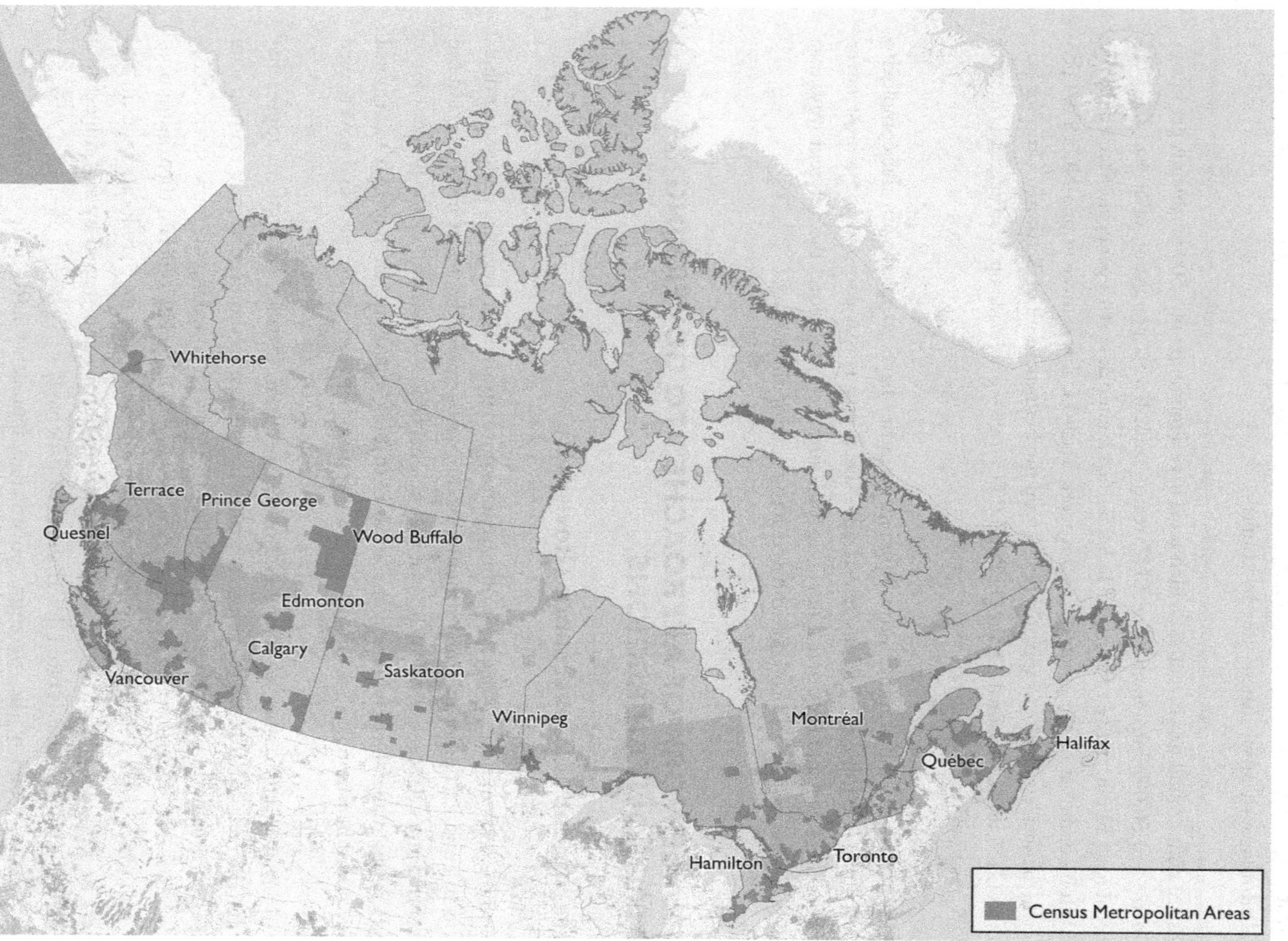

Figure 5.1. CMAs of Canada
Map created by Elvis Nyanzu (2023), "CMAs of Canada" based on 2021 Canadian Census Boundary Files, QGIS.

arrangements, include non-governmental actors among core decision-makers, and approach decision-making as a process of negotiation and consensus-building.

In truth, very few approaches to regional policy coordination are typified by either of these extremes. Rather, most exist somewhere on the spectrum and many exhibit characteristics of both. For instance, a formal government may engage with non-governmental actors in its decision-making process, or a non-governmental organization may include government representatives in theirs. The state may mandate and empower an organization made up of a mix of public and private actors but specify limits on their decision-making autonomy. Non-governmental organizations may adopt formal organizational structures and majority rule.

While these distinctions can be difficult to process in the abstract, we discuss the following examples of existing approaches to regional policy coordination from "most like governmental" to "most like governance" to demonstrate these concepts in action and show the breadth of potential solutions to the "regional problem."

Regional Solutions in Theory and Practice

TRANSFER OF FUNCTIONS TO THE STATE OR PROVINCE

One of the simplest ways to deal with the regional issue is to transfer local responsibilities to a level of government that has a larger territorial scope – usually the state or province. This makes intuitive sense. If a problem exceeds the ability or jurisdiction of a single local government, the level of government located directly above in the governmental hierarchy almost certainly has adequate institutional capacity and territorial jurisdiction. If that's not the case, then the level above that surely will.

In its description of this regional solution, the U.S. Advisory Commission on Intergovernmental Relations cites the following examples of transfers of functions: the state or province providing water supply and major trunk lines throughout a region while local distribution is left to municipalities; a similar relationship with respect to regional versus local roads; tiered responsibilities for acquisition and administration of recreational spaces. The commission was careful to point out, as these examples make clear, that transferring specified aspects of a function, rather than the entire responsibility for that function, has been much more common. It states that "usually the transfer of 'aspects' of functions involves a shift in the relative responsibility of the State and the localities with reference to functions which they have long shared, rather than the State's assumption of the function for the first time" (ACIR 1962, 46).

Although this approach is frequently characterized as a neutral transfer of functions – which implies the willing participation of local authorities in relinquishing authority over a specific area of regional interest – in practice, it is the state or provincial governments that often take the decisive step to initiate a regional solution on behalf of their subordinate local governments. As such, these solutions can often seem (and may be) policy impositions rather than the products of a mutual agreement to "shift relative responsibility."

The Province of Ontario's 2005 Places to Grow regional planning initiative is a good example of the ambiguity of this kind of approach. Municipalities in Canada have jurisdiction over land-use planning, which they can use to encourage or limit development within their territorial boundaries. Although provincial governments have considerable constitutional power over local land use, large-scale interventions in metropolitan and regional land-use planning have been rare (Filion 2003, Eidelman 2010). This, coupled with the lack of incentives for local governments to coordinate plans across jurisdictional boundaries, has characterized Ontario as having a "culture of regional non-planning" (White 2007, 44). The Places to Grow Act gave the provincial government authority to designate any geographic region of the province as part of a growth plan area, to develop a growth plan for those areas in consultation with local officials and stakeholders, and to develop growth plans for any part of Ontario (Ontario 2005). Ultimately, the act led to the first regional plan for the Greater Toronto Region, and for other urban regions in the province, in over thirty years.

Significantly, the act has been perceived as an important moment in local-provincial relations and as an instance of the transfer of functions discussed above. Macdonald and Keil (2012, 128) portray the act as an example of the "upscaling of traditional urban-regional regulation in Southern Ontario" wherein the province "takes back and fully occupies the space of regional planning." And while Eidelman (2010) demonstrates that voters, particularly in the Greater Toronto Area, supported the initiative, local governments have been very vocal in their opposition to measures that effectively limited their ability to expand areas for urban development.

This case demonstrates the difficulties with this particular approach to solving regional policy coordination issues. Even in the context where senior levels of government are statutorily permitted to intervene to transfer or undertake local functions, they are typically wary of doing so. Interfering with local autonomy, even if it is limited, does not come without cost. In the Places to Grow case, the Ontario government had the support of the electorate and was, therefore, emboldened to proceed in the face of municipal opposition. In many cases, that equation balances differently, and the political consequences of superseding local authority can be significant. That is particularly the case in places with strong traditions of local autonomy, such as the United States (see Taylor 2019 for an excellent discussion of these dynamics in the United States). On the plus side, however, this strategy can be effective. Removing responsibility for coordination from local governments enabled the province to establish regional planning where there previously had been none.

HARMONIZE FUNCTIONAL AND POLITICAL BOUNDARIES

While the previous approach effectively makes regional issues someone else's problem (usually a state or provincial government), it is possible to retain local jurisdictional control and establish the capacity to act regionally by aligning local political boundaries with those of the region in question. In other words, by turning the local government into a larger, *region sized* local government. This type of boundary harmonization can be accomplished in three different ways: (a) annexation, (b) consolidation, and (c) amalgamation.

Annexation. Municipal annexation occurs when a municipality incorporates the territory of a neighbouring local government or an unincorporated area into its own jurisdiction. Generally, it is a form of incremental urban expansion where the boundaries of a city grow bit by bit as it expands into neighbouring territory.

Annexation is of limited practicality in confronting modern regional issues. First, where annexation is permitted (not everywhere), legislation typically requires that the target communities consent to incorporation, and that consent can be very difficult to secure. In Canada, annexation is subject to provincial approval. Second, many regional problems involve areas much larger than a core municipality and the communities on its fringes. As such, properly aligning boundaries would require multiple annexations, compounding the difficulty of securing the required consent.

For these reasons, the annexation option is not frequently exercised at a large scale. Its use in most urbanized nations peaked in the nineteenth and early twentieth centuries. In the nineteenth century, before the advent of most annexation legislation, large cities like New York, Philadelphia, Pittsburgh, Boston, and Chicago, in what is described as their "imperial" phase, used this strategy to grow rapidly (Teaford 2006). Annexation remains a popular strategy to adjust municipal boundaries in the United States, outside of the densely urbanized Northeast. Edwards estimates that between 1990–2005 over 61,000 annexations took place in the United States (2008, 199). Canadian cities have also pursued annexation as a means of boundary expansion although, as in the American context, the pace and scale of territorial growth has slowed. Montreal annexed fifty-one municipalities between 1881 and 1921. Edmonton undertook nineteen separate annexations between 1947 and 1980. Calgary has been particularly aggressive in using annexation to expand its territory and most recently exercised this strategy in 2011 (Sancton 2015). While all of these municipalities used annexation to their advantage to expand their boundaries, few did so with the intent of aligning political boundaries to confront regional challenges. Contemporary annexations are driven by the imperative of securing greater territory for development and revenue generation.

City-County Consolidation. City-county consolidation is a type of amalgamation (see the following subsection) in which a county and one or more cities within its boundaries merge to become a single government. In this situation, the individual municipal governments cease to exist, and the functions of city and county governments are combined at the county scale. The result is a unique form of government that has "elements of city and county governments but is actually neither" (Martin and Schiff 2011, 168). This strategy can solve a lot of problems – consolidation increases the size of what had previously been city's policy influence to a much larger scale; if there were multiple cities, then it can erase the political boundaries that may have been barriers to regionalism. Furthermore, it makes a lot of fiscal sense in counties that are mostly urban where municipal fragmentation has led to municipalities providing duplicate local services.

In their expansive study of city-county consolidation in the United States, Leland and Thurmaier (2010) listed forty consolidated governments, the most recent of which occurred in 2008. The 2003 merger of Louisville and Jefferson County, Kentucky, is the most recent consolidation of a major American city (see Savitch and Vogel 2004 for a historical overview of this case).

A version of city-county consolidation has also happened from time to time in Canada in the formation of regional municipalities. The creation of the Halifax Regional Municipality in 1996 – merging the City of Halifax, City of Dartmouth, Town of Bedford, and County of Halifax – is one of the most high-profile examples in the Canadian context. However, city-county consolidation is relatively rare in Canada, which has tended to favour larger-scale amalgamations involving multiple municipalities and counties/county-equivalents or the creation of two-tier government solutions that leave existing municipalities intact (see the following section).

For all of its apparent simplicity and promise, city-county consolidation is relatively rare due to the weight of local opposition. Most citizens like their local governments, and local governments rarely have an interest in supporting their own elimination. Furthermore, researchers and policy-makers dispute that city-county consolidation has been able to deliver the collective benefits promised (Carr and Feiock 2004).

Amalgamation. Amalgamation involves the consolidation of multiple municipalities and/or counties to create a single larger urban government. Because amalgamations usually involve the abolition of many municipalities, this is one of the most drastic and contentious strategies for aligning political boundaries with those of some ideal region.

New York City's transformation in 1898 from a collection of counties into the five boroughs governed by the single city government we know today is a historically significant amalgamation. Governments all over the world have used amalgamation to reform and align regional boundaries. Wollmann (2004) describes the emergence of unitary municipalities (*Einheitsgemeinden*) in the German provinces (*Lander*) of Hessen and Nordrhein-Westfalen in the 1960s and 1970s. In his book *Merger Mania*, Sancton (2000) surveys significant contemporary amalgamations in the United Kingdom, Australia, New Zealand, Greece, and Denmark in the 1990s. Some of these involved very far-reaching, nationally directed municipal reorganizations, but most amalgamations have occurred sporadically and focused on specific target regions. In the 1990s and early 2000s, Canada experienced a wave of amalgamations focused most intensely in the provinces of Ontario (Toronto, Ottawa, Hamilton, and Sudbury) and Quebec (Montreal and Quebec City). We discuss these instances further in our analysis of the Canadian metropolitan experiment as this strategy has been applied in many of the major metropolitan regions in the country.

These examples notwithstanding, amalgamation is relatively rare. As demonstrated in the previous strategies, local governments, no matter their national context, tend to oppose measures designed to eliminate them. Even where senior governments are able to initiate an amalgamation, it takes a great deal of political will to accomplish in the face of such opposition. The high-profile de-amalgamation of Quebec's merged municipalities in the 2000s serves as a cautionary tale about the durability of these new municipal forms and the determination of local opponents.

Whereas city-county consolidation and annexations have territorial limitations (the boundaries of the county and the boundaries of neighbouring municipalities, respectively), amalgamations can, and do, take place at a very large scale. As such, amalgamations can be very effective mechanisms for the consolidation of a territory large enough to internalize regional issues. That said, the result is relatively inflexible – if the scale of the regional problems change or the population grows quickly, the regional boundaries selected are quickly obsolete (Sancton 2008). Finally, the effectiveness of amalgamation has been challenged from many quarters in Canada and beyond (Schwartz 2009; Dollery and Crase 2004).

ADD ANOTHER LAYER OF GOVERNMENT

In the two previous sections, an existing level of government either takes responsibility for a local function of regional significance or local authorities are abolished and replaced by a single-tier government responsible for the entire territory. But what if a senior level of government wants to establish a regional government without engaging in the politically fraught process of eliminating local governments? In that case, it can simply create another regional layer of government to address issues of collective concern at that scale. There are two broad ways of doing that: two-tier governments and special-purpose districts.

Two-Tier Governments. In Canada, we call these two-tier governments because this strategy involves creating an upper-tier regional government and retaining the lower-tier local governments. In practice, this approach can manifest in two slightly different forms: as a metropolitan multi-purpose district or as a metropolitan federation.

A metropolitan multi-purpose district is a special authority, set up by an existing government, to perform a number of services in all or most of a metropolitan area. The use of the term "district" allows for some flexibility in this definition. For instance, some multi-purpose districts have directly elected representatives – such as Portland Metro in Oregon. In other cases, such as with the Metro Council in Minneapolis-St. Paul, Minnesota members are appointed by senior levels of government. In both of these cases, certain planning and service delivery functions are performed at the metropolitan scale, while localized service delivery and policy-making remain a municipal function. The Winnipeg Unicity (1961–70) briefly employed this model until it was amalgamated.

Students of Canadian urban politics will be more familiar with the metropolitan federation. In a federation structure the upper-tier, or metropolitan, government council is composed of representatives from the constituent local governments. This is in contrast to the metropolitan district model, which may be made up of representatives of the municipalities, but they do not need to be sitting members of constituent municipal councils. Some of the most frequently cited examples of the metropolitan federation model are Canadian cases such as Metro Toronto (1953–98) and the Metro Vancouver Regional District. New Brunswick adopted Regional Service Commissions (RSCs) in 2013. More recently, the Métropole du Grand Paris (MGP) was designed around a metropolitan federation model when it was established in 2016. In the United Kingdom, the Greater Manchester Combined Authority unites representatives of the ten municipalities in the region in this regional tier with responsibility for public transportation, skills development, housing, waste management, environmental issues, and planning permissions.

Whatever its particular form, the two-tier model has some important advantages. It allows for regional coordination in policy areas that make sense to tackle at a regional scale while also allowing municipalities autonomy over issues best addressed at the local level. It also allows senior levels of government to sidestep the politically perilous act of abolishing municipal governments. However, two-tier solutions are still not easy to establish. Local authorities still object to having functions delegated away from them, and critics dispute the cost-effectiveness of adding additional layers of government. Furthermore, while Metro Toronto has been idealized as a model that "works" (particularly by urbanists in the United States), it was, in practice, an unwieldy structure prone to internal conflicts whose dysfunction contributed to the arguments of pro-amalgamation forces in the 1990s. That is, the division of powers between two different levels of government is rarely the frictionless and efficient process that the architects envisioned. A movement has emerged in Ontario – tipped off by the passage of the Hazel McCallion Act in June 2023 – to reverse decades of two-tier government by dissolving the upper-tier regional municipalities. The act (Bill 112) provided for the dissolution of Peel Region, which would have enabled Mississauga, Brampton, and Caledon to become single-tier municipalities independent from regional government by 2025. The Act was subsequently modified by Bill 185 in June 2024 to reverse the dissolution of Peel and remove some planning responsibilities from upper tier municipalities in Durham, Halton, Niagara, Peel, Waterloo, and York Regions and Simcoe County. The dissolution provoked a broader discussion about regional government reform in Ontario that, at the time of writing, was still ongoing. Much will be learned from this latest era of two-tier regionalism in the province.

Special Purpose Districts. Special purpose districts are independent units of government created to perform one or more local functions for the region as a whole. The most common districts manage ports, sewage, parks, water supplies, and transportation infrastructure. These authorities commonly focus on a single-issue area and are delegated whatever tools are deemed appropriate for fulfilling that function (such as various revenue-raising powers or regulatory authority). The members of special purpose districts can be democratically elected or appointed by elected officials in other levels of government. Often, these districts include non-governmental members.

Special purpose districts are one of the most flexible regional governing structures – they can span any geography; their members can be whomever the convening government decides; they can have any kind of power their creators are willing to delegate to them (or have very few) – and they are often seen as neat, technocratic solutions to otherwise spatially and politically messy problems. For this reason, special purpose districts occur in almost every country. One example is the Metropolitan Transit Authority (MTA), which controls and operates the various transit networks (subways, buses, ferries, and some commuter rail) in part of the New York Metropolitan region. Its board is partially appointed by the governor of New York with the rest of the seats filled by appointees selected by the New York City mayor.

In Canada, we refer to local special purpose districts as agencies, boards, and commissions, or ABCs (Lucas 2013). TransLink performs a similar function as the MTA in Metro Vancouver. It is governed by a mayor's council, which has a seat for each of the region's twenty-one mayors, and a board of directors made up primarily of members of the private sector. In the Greater Toronto Area, the regional dimension of public transportation and roads is controlled by Metrolinx, an agency created by the Ontario provincial government. Interestingly, Metrolinx no longer includes any representatives from the municipalities within its service area as a response to the polarizing influence of the elected officials on its original board structure (Addie 2017).

These examples highlight the flexibility of the special purpose district structure and show how special purpose districts can fall in any number of places along the government-governance spectrum. Where they are principally controlled by local governments, they can be positioned closer to the government side of the spectrum. Where their membership includes other actors or is dominated by them, they are closer to the governance side. The magnitude of their authority and autonomy can also tilt these bodies closer to one end or the other – those with more formal "government-like" powers toward government and those whose purpose is regional brokerage toward governance.

This structural flexibility is one of the reasons that special purpose districts are such a popular response to regional complexity. While general purpose governments, such as the two-tier arrangements described in the preceding section, will struggle to secure agreement about the appropriate governing scale for their entire portfolio of functions, focusing on a single issue allows a more tailored definition of the relevant region and flexibility of institutional design to (in theory) strike a balance between representation and effectiveness. Special purpose districts are comparatively easy to create. They can be very effective. Depending on how they are structured, they can help to overcome political parochialism. However, they also have numerous drawbacks. As Lucas notes: "ABCs provide very important services, spend large sums of money, and raise serious questions about democratic accountability" (2013, 2). Their diverse structures and origins make it difficult for the public to understand the limits of ABC powers, and lines of oversight are not always clear. Lyons (2015) raises questions about their effectiveness. Defaulting to the creation of multiple, overlapping special purpose districts to resolve regional issues risks fragmenting responsibility to agencies with little incentive for cross-sectoral co-operation and that operate with a single-mindedness to the detriment of comprehensive regional approaches.

ENGAGE IN REGIONAL INTERGOVERNMENTAL COOPERATION

What if local governments want to work together to address collective issues or coordinate policies across jurisdictional boundaries without the permanence, prescription, or structures associated with establishing a formal regional government? What if local governments would prefer to structure their own partnership without the interference or leadership of senior levels of government (that many of the previous examples require)? Further along the governance spectrum, there are several options available for bottom-up, horizontal, and locally driven regional collaboration.

In many countries, local governments are permitted to join together to discuss, provide services, or implement policies in any area that they have statutory jurisdiction. That is, whatever they are permitted to do themselves they are often also empowered to do in partnership with peer jurisdictions. This type of partnership can take various forms; however, the most common are regional intergovernmental organizations (RIGOs), interlocal agreements, and informal agreements.

We address each in turn below. However, we want to specify that solutions in this section are specifically intergovernmental in nature. While other types of actors may have a role in the resulting partnerships, the types of arrangements that we discuss in this section are led by governments. This distinguishes this type of solution from the even broader regional civic organizations located further along the government-governance continuum and discussed in the following section.

Regional Intergovernmental Organizations. Regional intergovernmental organizations (or RIGOs) are regional organizations made up of a majority of local governments that engage with a relatively broad range of policy areas for the purpose of improving policy coordination and resolving cross-boundary issues. These organizations are relatively formal but voluntary partnerships between local governments and usually have attributes such as a permanent address, dedicated staff, bylaws that stipulate meeting schedules and voting rules, and websites. Such organizations go by all sorts of different names – Councils of Governments, Associations of Governments, Regional Planning Commissions, Regional Partnerships, Mayors' Caucuses, to name just a few – and so can be difficult to identify without researching their specific structures.

However, organizations like RIGOs are relatively common. In their recent study of RIGOs in the United States, Miller and Nelles (2019) identify 477 active organizations. A notable exemplar of this type of organization is the Atlanta Regional Commission (ARC). Per its website, ARC functions as the regional planning and intergovernmental coordination agency for the eleven-county Atlanta region, helps to focus the region's leadership, attention, and resources on critical issues, and serves as a regional convener, bringing diverse stakeholders to the table to address the most important issues facing metro Atlanta (Atlanta Regional Commission 2017). ARC is among the most active RIGOs and engages in regional transportation planning, healthy community development, environmental and resource management, planning for age and aging, business recruiting and training, regional data provision, and disaster and emergency planning.

These voluntary regional organizations also exist outside of the United States. In the Paris region the Forum Métropolitain du Grand Paris brings together local and regional governments (communes, intercommunalités, départements, and région) to collectively discuss and address metropolitan issues across jurisdictional boundaries (Forum Métropolitain du Grand Paris 2017). In Canada, examples include organizations such as the Edmonton Metropolitan Region Board (EMRB) and the Calgary Regional Partnership (CRP). The EMRB was created by the province of Alberta in 2008 to bring together local elected officials across the Edmonton region to create a collective growth plan detailing how the region can grow responsibly. The organization focuses on six core policy areas. The CRP is a collaborative network of eleven municipalities in the Calgary region. It hosts collective discussions about growth strategies, transportation and mobility issues, natural resources and service provision, and employment.

This type of organization is relatively common because of the flexibility of its structure. This approach enables local governments to come together on their own terms for collective benefit, which is particularly useful in places where senior levels of government lack the power or political will to intervene in local government affairs. It can be relatively easier to secure the buy-in of member municipalities as these organizations can be flexibly structured to minimize impingement on local autonomy (e.g., by requiring consensus decisions or making compliance voluntary). Even where RIGOs are encouraged or imposed by senior levels of government, their internal structures – voting, decision-making, membership requirements – are often left to members to negotiate. This structural flexibility also applies to which policy areas the organization engages with. Members can select the issues upon which they are willing to work together to avoid potentially controversial and conflictual areas.

There are, of course, downsides to this flexibility. Their voluntary nature means that they will not necessarily be established in every region. Because these organizations often lack formal powers (e.g., to compel compliance) their effectiveness is often questioned. Such organizations have also been criticized for their potential to magnify the power of certain members relative to others in decision-making processes (particularly suburban members over urban ones, see Rickabaugh 2018) and for lack of transparency and accountability.

Interlocal Agreements. While RIGOs are a mechanism for more formalized, permanent, and usually multilateral and multi-purpose regional policy coordination, interlocal agreements offer municipalities a much more limited option for policy engagement beyond their jurisdictional boundaries. Interlocal agreements can take many forms, but they often manifest as bilateral, limited-term contracts for service provision. For instance, a municipality may contract with a neighbour to purchase fire protection services under a specified set of terms and for a given duration of time. In another example, municipalities may enter into an agreement to construct and maintain infrastructure – water and sewer systems, for instance. In his survey of interlocal agreements in Canada, Spicer (2015) found that contracts of this nature were the most common form (representing 85 per cent of the agreements that he found) and that they focused most frequently on sharing emergency services.

Interlocal agreements are attractive alternatives to other forms of regional organization because the risk to participants is lower, and they are more easily justified to constituents. Because these often take the form of a contract, with clear and legally binding stipulations that leave very little to interpretation, parties to interlocal agreements have a reasonable expectation that their partner will behave as specified. Such agreements also typically carry stipulations about legal recourse should a partner defect, agreed-upon dispute resolution mechanisms, and may also include other types of escape clause should either of the partners want to terminate the agreement for cause. As they are often negotiated for finite periods of time, neither of the partners is locked in forever, and the end date of the contract offers an opportunity to renegotiate terms.

These deals can be easier to negotiate than membership in a multi-purpose organization because each agreement typically focuses on only one area of service delivery (multi-service agreements happen but are much rarer). If partners find it difficult to agree to terms on snow removal, that will not prevent them from doing so with emergency services if they're different deals. If a municipality does not want to discuss a partnership for garbage collection, there's no need to pursue it. However, agreeing to join a multi-purpose organization means that municipalities may be forced to discuss or partner on issues that they would prefer to avoid. This separation of issues can also make partnerships of this nature more palatable to constituents. It may be easier to convince residents of the benefit of economies of scale related to the provision of a service than of the benefits of subverting local interests to regional ones on a broader scale. Finally, as many of these agreements involve simple cash-for-service transactions, there is little risk that either municipality will have to sacrifice policy autonomy over any area of their jurisdiction as a result.

These agreements are not, however, particularly useful vehicles for metropolitan policy coordination. For one, they tend to focus on service provision. While engaging in collaborative service provision or contracting for a service can spark dialogue about broader issues (for instance, a transit partnership could lead to more coordination on land-use planning), they are rarely intended to do so. As such, service provision may become more efficient but regional policy will be elusive. Furthermore, these agreements also tend to be bilateral. This may result in the proliferation of one-to-one relationships between local governments in a region in place of broader region-wide coordination. While some have speculated that these agreements are a good place to start building interlocal relationships as a prelude to more widespread co-operation, this kind of cooperative intensification is very rare. If the region is small (two members) or if the goal is limited policy coordination, then interlocal agreements are an excellent mechanism. However, if policy-makers seek broader policy integration, then such agreements may create policy silos and preferential interlocal relationships that might discourage regional co-operation.

Informal Co-operation. Whereas interlocal agreements tend to be institutionalized – in contracts of memorandums of understanding – there are other alternatives that are even more informal. Informal partnerships can include an agreement to share information or to inform neighbours of intentions in specific policy areas. In some cases, this kind of oral or "handshake" agreement may be used for service sharing between local governments and function as informal interlocal agreements (see Spicer 2016). These partnerships are often forged between individuals who occupy similar positions in neighbouring municipalities (mayors, city managers, planning directors, etc.).

In theory, informal agreements can be incredibly powerful tools – individuals may be able to exercise considerable influence over other communities' decisions simply by being transparent about concerns. Sharing information can create strong bonds of trust and deepen connections between local governments. However, these relationships can also be quite precarious. Informal agreements are not legally binding. If a partner decides not to share crucial information at a critical juncture, or not consult their neighbour as agreed, that trust can erode quickly. No formal penalties bind partners to their word. Furthermore, because they are typically relationships built by individuals, they frequently dissolve when those individuals no longer occupy that office.

While regional researchers suspect that this type of relationship is fairly widespread, because they are informal no one has a very accurate idea of how many there are, whether they are effective, or what policy areas they affect. Theoretically, these types of relationships could be very useful mechanisms for low-level regional coordination (involving information exchange and influence). They could even lead to the development of some of the more formalized alternatives discussed so far. However, as these impose no permanent costs on partners, and may be quite effective on their own, some have posited that these more informal partnerships could discourage the emergence of more formalized relationships (see Nelles 2012). Whatever their impact – potential or real – informal relationships are the most decentralized and "bottom-up" type of regional governance approach. These networks simply cannot be imposed or created by a central actor but must emerge through repeated interactions between individuals and a process of establishing credibility and trust.

RELY ON CIVIC ORGANIZATIONS TO RAISE REGIONAL AWARENESS

Regardless of what other forms of regional problem-solving exist (or do not exist), civic associations often identify and strategize solutions to metropolitan challenges. These organizations are primarily driven by the private sector, although most include local governments among their members. As such, they have little to no authority to implement policy recommendations but can be effective coalitions to secure political action from relevant governments.

Civic organizations include Chambers of Commerce, industry associations, interest groups, or any other group that has formed to represent the interests of its members in the public sphere. While those interests can be parochial and locally focused, on occasion broad-based coalitions emerge at the regional scale to secure regional benefit. In the New York metropolitan region, the Regional Plan Association (RPA) has been active in advocating for regional issues since 1922. In Toronto, CivicAction engages in regular forums and advocacy at the metropolitan scale. Among other organizations, San Francisco has the San Francisco and Bay Area Planning and Urban Research Association (SPUR). These, and many other organizations like them, are all made up of a wide range of members from business, education, government, and other civic groups.

While these groups do not have any formal power to implement regional policy, they can be very influential in shaping regional agendas. The RPA, for instance, has released four regional plans for the New York City metropolitan area, and many of their recommendations have ended up inspiring local and state policies. Nelles (2012) argues that these organizations exert this type of influence both directly and indirectly. Their advocacy and lobbying activities are a form of direct influence – aimed at shaping specific public policies. However, they can also be very effective at disseminating the idea that policies should be considered at a regional scale, through their membership and the resonance of their message to region residents. This can, indirectly, create a constituency that wants and expects its leaders to be receptive to "thinking regionally" and, as such, influence the willingness of leaders to come to the table to coordinate policies.

While regional civic associations can be useful mechanisms for stimulating regional action, stimulation is the limit of their ability. They cannot compel action. That is probably a good thing. These membership organizations are not democratically elected, nor are they accountable to anyone but their members. They may not be adequately representative and may even be exclusionary. That they can have influence over local governments is useful in promoting regionalism, but they are often subjected to criticism (from all sides) about what kind of regionalism they stand for and for whom.

This survey of regional solutions provides a good overview of the alternatives available to policy-makers that have emerged in response to regional issues. Students of regionalism often ask which one is "the best." The fact of the matter is that it depends. If there is agreement on one thing in the realm of regional scholarship, it is that one-size-fits-all solutions are not appropriate. Much depends on local contexts and the policy areas under consideration. Furthermore, these alternatives are not mutually exclusive. The discerning reader will note that we present examples from many of the same regions across several different categories. Another point of agreement in the scholarship is that we are likely to continue to debate the comparative merits of these alternatives for as long as there are externalities (and other rationales for regionalism). No "best practice" will emerge, in part because of the fundamental tensions inherent in each of these solutions.

FUNDAMENTAL TENSIONS

Each approach to regionalism has different strengths and weaknesses. In this section, we survey a selection of what we characterize as fundamental tensions.

Institutionalization versus Autonomy

Many favour solutions located closest to the government end of the spectrum, such as amalgamation or two-tier regional governments. These have the advantage of being institutionalized. They are actual governments that usually have formal powers such as revenue-raising and rule-setting abilities. They have a formal slot in the hierarchy of governmental power and, as such, can compel those below them (more local governments or citizens) to act in accordance with their agendas. For those who support this approach to regional coordination, this power means that things will get done. Such an empowered regional entity has a greater chance of marshalling the resources necessary to support its agenda (it can impose taxes, fees, or require transfers from member governments) and of shaping the behaviour of governments and citizens than the voluntary partnerships that characterize the governance end of the spectrum.

For all of these advantages, this degree of institutionalization is difficult to achieve because local governments typically resist policies that will curtail their autonomy. To local governments, consenting to amalgamation or a layering of authority (such as with the introduction of a regional tier) means relinquishing control over areas of local jurisdiction. For instance, a regional tier of government in charge of land-use planning may require that local plans be consistent with their guiding documents. In this case, even though local governments have not lost all control, their autonomy to plan as they see fit for their constituencies is constrained. While there are certainly cases where local governments might agree to accept a reduction of autonomy in exchange for some benefit (as is the case with special purpose districts), it is rare that all local governments in a region would agree to lose power across a variety of policy areas simultaneously. As such, when senior levels of government pursue solutions closer to the government end of the spectrum – and it must be senior levels as local governments lack the authority to create their own level of government by themselves – they typically must do so in the face of (sometimes very vocal) local opposition. Even where senior levels of government are empowered to reorganize local governments, as in Canada and many parts of the United States, this opposition is not trivial and thus reduces the attractiveness of solutions on the government end of the spectrum.

This trade-off between institutionalization and autonomy partly explains the attractiveness of special purpose districts. In these cases, governments accept carefully negotiated constraints on their autonomy in very circumscribed areas, often with seats on governing boards. This narrow focus makes it easier to secure support as local autonomy is not so broadly threatened.

Autonomy versus Effectiveness

Local autonomy is most protected in approaches on the governance end of the spectrum. At this end, regional arrangements rely on partnership, co-operation, and consensus and usually have no formal powers to compel their members to act in the collective interest beyond the soft powers of influence and persuasion. Even when a regional organization is able to secure the consensus of its members, there is no guarantee that they will uphold it in practice and not act in their own best interests.

The advantage of these looser governance approaches is that they are easier to enact. Following the logic of the previous example, local governments are more willing to come together when they perceive fewer restrictions on their own policy autonomy. Voluntary organizations that generate non-binding decisions epitomize this kind of freedom and are, consequently, more likely to secure local government buy-in than more restrictive options.

However, logically, this freedom implies some significant disadvantages for organizational effectiveness. This type of organization is often accused of generating "lowest common denominator" policies. That is, they only engage with the (much smaller) pool of policies that members are willing to consider in a collective forum, leaving more contentious and controversial regional issues unresolved. While agreement on small issues should not be dismissed, the perception is that these approaches are less likely to subject the big stuff to regional consideration. When consensus is required, the results will, by definition, be those that everyone could agree to – hence the indictment that these structures yield to the lowest common denominator. Even where decisions are determined by other voting conventions, these organizations lack the formal power to implement policies. They must rely on their membership to conform to the group's agenda. Unfortunately, this compliance is not always forthcoming. Although there is some evidence to suggest that voluntary organizations, such as RIGOs, can be quite effective, critics of these kinds of governance approaches tend to focus on the tension between autonomy and effectiveness as a most damning drawback.

Institutionalization versus Flexibility

Supporters of more institutionalized, governmental forms of regional policy coordination can certainly claim at least theoretical superiority in terms of organizational effectiveness. However, they also have to contend with the not insignificant constraint to organizational flexibility. Organizations that are designed to be more institutionally empowered tend to also have clearly fixed boundaries and mandates. This can limit their ability to actually address metropolitan issues as the boundaries of the "region" can vary by issue area. Crucially, their ability to address regional issues that extend beyond their own fixed boundaries is as compromised as any other local government's.

Regional issues come in all shapes and sizes. Some will involve a subset of region members more than others. For instance, consider a regional government arrangement charged with environmental planning that contains a mix of coastal and landlocked local governments. Coastal governments may be concerned about water issues – flood management, habitat conservation, water pollution, etc. – that are not priorities for the rest of the governments in the region. These coastal governments may find their interests subsumed by those of the landlocked governments who have no interest in additional regulations to protect resources that are not shared. In this case, the regional scale of environmental planning can act as a constraint on meaningful action at the sub-regional scale.

As complex as sub-regional coordination can be in such circumstances, the more pressing concern is when regional issues transcend even the boundaries of the regional government. Even the most prescient policy-maker will struggle to draw regional boundaries that perfectly encompass all of the regional externalities and issues that local governments will face, now and in the future. Consider the case of Metro Toronto. Even as the province established the metropolitan level of government in 1953, communities outside of that boundary were developing. Today, what used to be the metropolis of Toronto is just a kernel of a vast urbanized region – the Greater Toronto and Hamilton Area (GTHA) – and metropolitan issues affect actors far outside its political borders. This case demonstrates how the rigid regional borders that characterize solutions nearer to the government end of the spectrum limit the effectiveness of more institutionalized approaches over the long term. What is now just the City of Toronto must navigate regionalism just as any other local government in the region.

The less institutionalized and more flexible governance approaches are not immune to the complexity of shifting regional boundaries (or multiple definitions of a region). They, too, must contend with their geographical limitations. However, they are more frequently structured to accommodate the addition (or subtraction) of members without formal institutional reforms and may be more willing to adapt (and embrace) shifting coalitions of interests.

Flexibility versus Accountability

Approaches that are further toward the governance end of the spectrum tend to be the most flexible in terms of membership and scope. However, when different actors come together to make regional policy, lines of accountability become blurry (especially when non-governmental actors are involved).

Many of the arguments against more flexible governance arrangements for regional policy coordination could be levelled against any organization that is not democratically elected. In the event of policy failure, who is held accountable? There are other concerns as well about the composition of regional organizations, including questions about who is allowed a seat at the table in collective decision-making and who controls that process. More flexible governance approaches are attractive and valuable because they can engage a broad constituency and include participants that have traditionally existed outside of the policy process, but that is no guarantee that these organizations will be inclusive.

These tensions are the reason that there is no one magic solution to governing metropolitan regions. Some are just impossible to implement in some places. Others are very common but are implemented with varying degrees of effectiveness. In many Western liberal democracies, the creation of special purpose authorities and RIGOs are the two most common approaches. Canadian provinces have, however, experimented relatively widely with approaches closer to the government end of the spectrum.

THE METROPOLITAN EXPERIMENT IN CANADA

The choice of the term "experiment" in reference to Canada's metropolitan evolution is a deliberate one. Each of the different responses to regional issues detailed in the preceding section has been attempted in Canada, at one time or another. In this sense, Canadian metropolitan regions can be seen as laboratories for structural experimentation and innovations in governing. Despite this variety of approaches, the most notable, internationally renowned, and some might even say notorious exercises in metropolitan governance have all been on the government end of the spectrum.

One thing that we can say about the Canadian metropolitan experiment is that there's no natural, or inevitable path toward regionalism. As we will see, Canadian metropolitan areas all began in the same place but have moved through a range of quite different approaches. Just because the two-tier governments in Toronto and Winnipeg were ultimately amalgamated does not mean that Vancouver's two-tier structure is destined to do so. And, as Montreal teaches us, amalgamated structures are not necessarily destined to stay amalgamated. If there is a contemporary trend it may be that Canadian regions are in the process of experimenting on the governance side of the spectrum. In this section, we highlight some of the most prominent entries in the Canadian metropolitan experiment.

The Notable Canadian Cases

We recognize that in focusing on these most visible cases we are necessarily giving short shrift to a whole range of approaches that live at the governance end of the spectrum. While there is no shortage of literature on these cases, we focus on these as particularly notable contrasts to the international experience (described in the following section). Also note that these cases are not presented in chronological order but organized by the progression of their metropolitan governing approaches.

VANCOUVER: MAKING TWO TIERS WORK

When confronted with a regional policy coordination pickle, establishing a two-tier structure is a great place to start. As we have noted, such a structure has many of the desirable qualities of amalgamated regional governance while retaining some functions at the local scale (and, therefore, containing some of the opposition that would have arisen otherwise). Such was the logic employed by the British Columbia minister of Municipal Affairs, Dan Campbell, as he established regional districts for the urban regions of the province, including Vancouver, in 1967. According to Tennant and Zirnhelt's colourful account of the early days of regional government in Vancouver and British Columbia, the regional districts were established less as a response to a specific set of regional problems but rather "to provide a framework for orderly development of local government in the future" (1973, 127) and, in the absence of counties, to establish authorities to which the province could decentralize certain functions (Taylor 2015). However, when it came to Vancouver, one major motivation was to harmonize the activities of the proliferation of single function regional boards.

Until that point, regional coordination in the Vancouver area occurred in the form of special purpose districts for sewage, water, hospitals, planning, parks, and more. Once the Metropolitan Vancouver Regional District (MVRD) – then, the Fraser-Burrard Regional District and later the Greater Vancouver Regional District (GVRD) – was established, it became the entity responsible for those functions once undertaken by separate special purpose authorities as well as the proper repository of any new regional functions that might subsequently emerge. Among its current functions are collaboratively planning for and delivering regional-scale services – drinking water, wastewater treatment, and solid waste management – regulating air quality, creating plans for urban growth, managing the regional parks, and providing affordable housing (see Metro Vancouver 2018).

The organization was governed by a council representing the fourteen municipal members as well as three representatives of unincorporated areas. The council employed a weighted voting system that assigned multiple representatives and multiple votes to some areas, such as Vancouver and its larger suburbs, according to population. It has since expanded to incorporate twenty-one-member municipalities, one electoral area, and one treaty First Nation.

Even though scholarship tends to classify the MVRD as a second-tier regional government it has never been a pure instance of this form. It has several features that complicate this classification. First, even at its inception, the MVRD was not billed as government; rather, for largely political reasons it was characterized as a multi-purpose metropolitan district. Second, it was created with the unique feature (since removed) that the participating municipalities could opt out of any decisions taken by the joint authority, which is not a typical characteristic of regional governments. Third, the organization was built, and still operates, as a voluntary organization. Also unusual is its governance structure, which contains four separate corporate entities – the Metro Vancouver Regional District, the Greater Vancouver Sewerage and Drainage District, the Greater Vancouver Water District, and the Metro Vancouver Housing Corporation – each with a different set of members. Apart from a few responsibilities mandated by provincial statute, the services that the regional tier provides are those that participants agree they should provide (British Columbia Ministry of Community Services 2006). Perhaps this more flexible governance-like construction has been the key to its resilience over time. Although the organization is not without critics, it is generally regarded as one of the most successful sustained two-tier models in North America.

WINNIPEG AND TORONTO: TWO TIERS TO AMALGAMATION

While in some places like Vancouver the two-tier government form of regional coordination has been stable over time, in other places like Toronto and Winnipeg it paved the way for amalgamation.

In Winnipeg the period between two-tier and single-tier solutions was relatively short – the Corporation of Greater Winnipeg lasted for only a decade. The Manitoba provincial governments established the Corporation over twelve municipalities after "decades of pressure by local authorities in the region to provide the machinery for inter-jurisdictional coordination" (Lightbody 1971, 492). Responsibilities attributed to this second tier included equalization of tax assessment, major arterial routes, public transportation, waste and sewage disposal, and long-range planning. While the province was very careful not to characterize the establishment of the metropolitan tier as a prelude to amalgamation, Lightbody acknowledges that an evolutionary lens might be appropriate. At the very least, in its decade of operation, the Corporation was regarded as a misunderstood and disliked structure, but people had become used to the idea of metropolitan government, which laid the foundations for the Unicity.

The NDP government proposed and then enacted the amalgamation of the twelve municipalities that became known as the Unicity. The province was driven, in part, by concerns about the impact of internal fragmentation on equity. Although the province perceived amalgamation as a logical evolution and institutionalization of an already united community of governments, the municipalities objected. Despite this, the province prevailed and passed Bill 36: the Unicity came into existence in 1972.

One of the fundamental tensions associated with formally fixing "metropolitan" boundaries is that those boundaries often do not make sense for very long. Predictably, the urbanized region around Winnipeg continued to expand beyond the jurisdiction of the Unicity, which ultimately forced it to reckon with regional problems with other tools. In 2005, the province enabled the Partnership of the Manitoba Capital Region – a structure that enables cross-boundary co-operation through intermunicipal agreement – which united the City of Winnipeg with fifteen neighbouring municipalities.

Toronto's metropolitan experience has had a similar, if longer, arc. The Municipality of Metropolitan Toronto (Metro) was established in 1953 and remains one of Canada's earliest and most studied (and celebrated) instances of metropolitan government. This metropolitan innovation initially emerged as a response to service coordination problems in the areas of transportation, water, sanitation, and sewage, although questions of equity also entered the conversation. Amalgamation, annexation, and special purpose districts were all on the table in the thirty-year run-up to Metro's creation, but the two-tier model prevailed. Metro became responsible for major roads, public transportation, property assessment, regional water distribution and sewage, and later police services.

While Metro enjoyed some successes, particularly in the areas of infrastructure and service expansion, it was never a harmonious structure. Despite successive waves of institutional reforms, it was plagued by chronic infighting between tiers of government. Additionally, as in Winnipeg, urban growth rapidly breached Metro's boundaries such that by the 1960s it was largely obsolete as a genuinely metropolitan instrument of governing. In 1967, the provincial government confronted this by establishing a ring of two-tier structures – regional municipalities – in the surrounding, fast-growing urban areas. While this effectively established "metropolitan" scale government as a standard for much of Southern Ontario, it also decisively stopped debate about the expansion of Metro Toronto.

The era of fractious intergovernmental relations and ongoing debates about the future of Metro came abruptly to an end with the 1998 amalgamation and creation of the Megacity of Toronto. The provincial Progressive Conservative government that presided over the amalgamation cited cost savings, alignment with principles of local services, and political dysfunction, among other reasons for the reforms. It also goes without saying that political restructuring occurred over the vocal opposition of local governments, residents, and interest groups and in contravention of the results of a 1997 referendum on the subject. Two decades later, citizens and pundits have come to accept the reality of the Megacity – so much so that almost no one uses that moniker any longer – but are also quick to note that the promised efficiencies and cost savings have fallen short of expectations.

Today, Toronto is the dominant centre of a large metropolitan region – the Greater Toronto and Hamilton Area (GTHA) – with a population of over seven million spread out over thirty contiguous cities, towns, and regional municipalities. In short, neither Metro Toronto nor its amalgamated successor managed to provide a durable solution for regional policy coordination. As in Winnipeg, Toronto now participates in a variety of metropolitan partnerships to confront regional issues. Among these is CivicAction, a partnership of elected officials and civic leaders to address challenges in the region. This partnership sits as close to the governance end of our spectrum as two-tier solutions do to the government side. By virtue of its economic and physical importance in Ontario, the province has also been active in addressing regional issues, on a case-by-case basis, from the top-down. It has taken an activist role in regional transit issues through the metropolitan transit authority – Metrolinx – and intervened to enact sustainable planning and green belt legislation.

Both Toronto and Winnipeg have been here before. In the past, regional challenges were resolved by provincial governments keen on boundary alignment and, ultimately, amalgamation. That is unlikely to happen again – at least in the medium run. Instead, both metros are exploring the potential of metropolitan governance.

MONTREAL: AMALGAMATION, DE-AMALGAMATION, RIGO

Truthfully, the subtitle of this section is misleading. The history of regionalism in the Montreal metropolitan region is far more complex and nuanced than the amalgamation/de-amalgamation storyline implies. First, the Montreal region has been the site of various experiments in regionalism, of which amalgamation (and the creation of other regional structures) is only one. Second, from a metropolitan governance standpoint, the amalgamations in the Montreal region are of secondary importance to the more broadly metropolitan Montreal Metropolitan Community (MMC) that was created at the same time. That this more interesting structure is often outshined by the more controversial government restructuring is a shame and a missed opportunity in the study of Canadian metropolitan governance.

Scholarship has been generally pessimistic about Montreal's metropolitan governance evolution. Fischler and Wolfe (2000, 90), for instance, evoke a "long saga of half-failed [metropolitan] reforms." The earliest significant attempt at metropolitan governance was the Montreal Metropolitan Commission, which existed in 1935–59. It was created to monitor and regulate suburban municipal borrowing and later added responsibilities for tax base sharing and joint planning. By most accounts, this tier had very little influence beyond administration, it never evolved into a regional planning organization, and even its core functions were dormant by the 1940s. The commission was succeeded by another weak attempt at revenue sharing and assessment coordination that also yielded few regional policies of note (the Montreal Urban Corporation).

The Montreal Urban Community (MUC) was established in 1969 in the wake of a police strike that brought inequities in the distribution of costs and benefits of regional services to the fore. The MUC could be described as a weak second-tier structure. It was governed by the council of the City of Montreal and one delegate from each of the twenty-nine other municipalities on the Island of Montreal, and it was assigned responsibility for police, real estate assessment, water and sewage, garbage, planning, public transportation, and other services. The structure was institutionally weak insofar as it relied on the consensus of members to actually engage in those assigned functions and because it had very little legal capacity to actually do any of them (Thibert 2015; Sancton 1985). Furthermore, actors on the Island of Montreal took city-suburban rivalry to a new level when suburban communities organized a Suburban Mayors' Caucus to represent their interests within the MUC. Needless to say, the MUC's accomplishments were limited (see Thibert 2015 for a detailed discussion of its successes in green space protection and regional park creation). In 1978, the province institutionalized regional planning across the province with the creation of regional county municipalities – roughly equivalent to the regional municipality model in Ontario – such that the MUC was surrounded by twelve new regional planning authorities.

By the 1990s, a financial downturn had weakened the City of Montreal and its surrounding region. Municipalities were seen as ill-equipped to handle the challenges of globalization, their proliferation was fiscally inefficient, they were obstacles to resolving intermunicipal inequities, and their fragmentation was a weakness to the region's international competitiveness. In 2000, the provincial government, led by the Parti Québécois, passed legislation to restructure the metropolitan region. This reorganization was undoubtedly the most complex in Canadian metropolitan history. First, it involved the amalgamation of all of the municipalities on the Island of Montreal into a single City of Montreal. However, in the process of abolishing the existing municipalities, the legislation also created a new lower tier of twenty-seven "boroughs" in an effort to preserve local character through the administration of local services (though these existed without revenue-raising capacity). In 2001, the new amalgamated City of Montreal was then included in a new and much broader metropolitan structure – the Montreal Metropolitan Community (MMC). This RIGO covered the territory of the 1996 CMA with representation from eighty-two municipalities within eleven regional county municipalities in the region (population of over four million in 2016). The MMC is responsible for regional transportation and planning, and it has programs in economic development, environmental management, and affordable housing.

Accounts of this ambitious set of reforms – what Sancton (2015) describes as a three-tier model – tend to focus on amalgamation. As in other Canadian cases, amalgamation was opposed and contested by local authorities but forced through by the province nonetheless. Unlike the other cases, opposition to amalgamation became a central element of the Liberal's platform as they swept to victory in the 2003 provincial election. In the next year, the Charest government passed three bills that established mechanisms for de-amalgamation and further regional restructuring. De-amalgamation was not a return to the pre-2000 status quo. Only fifteen municipalities were able to meet the requirements for demerger and these still had to participate, albeit as more independent entities, in collective service provision through the Montreal Agglomeration Council.

Lost in this focus on the politics of amalgamation are evaluations of the effectiveness of the more metropolitan MMC. Tomàs (2012) notes that the MMC's legitimacy has been challenged by the amalgamation/de-amalgamation struggle and that persistent opposition from certain suburban municipalities has slowed the evolution of this tier. That said, there is evidence that the MMC and its mission have gradually been accepted by its members. While it still has institutional limitations, a constrained agenda, and has seen its share of conflict, some have noted that members are learning to live together and have been able to develop mechanisms to overcome divisions and get deals done, when appropriate (Douay and Roy-Baillargeon 2015).

Explaining the Canadian Metropolitan Approaches

The preceding cases describe different trajectories of metropolitan reform across the most notorious Canadian cases. Such brief descriptions unfortunately limit discussion of the unique political and historical contexts that shaped each one but do enable us to draw out some important common themes:

PROVINCES ARE DOMINANT IN METROPOLITAN AFFAIRS

The most staggering similarity between all of these cases is that metropolitan reforms were always initiated by the provincial governments. There are legal and practical reasons for this. Governed, as they are, by the Baldwin Act, municipal governments lack the statutory authority to formally reorganize themselves. As such, any major institutional changes must originate from their provincial masters, even if they are at the request of the municipalities. However, it should be noted that none of these reforms (nor any that we are aware of) was instituted by the provinces as a response to a clear consensus about how municipalities in metropolitan regions wanted to organize themselves. Certainly, different actors within these regions had preferred alternatives, but they were rarely the same as their neighbours'. Central cities, for instance, often favoured annexation of or amalgamation with contiguous jurisdictions. Quite naturally, neighbouring municipalities typically opposed such proposals. Central cities prefer two-tier arrangements that preserve their political dominance relative to more numerous suburban interests. Suburbs do not. While there has often been consensus that a metropolitan solution would be beneficial, in the absence of agreement about what that should look like it has often fallen to the province to step in and arbitrate. It is important to note that provinces have also organized metropolitan affairs to suit their own agendas, regardless of municipal input. Metropolitan reorganizations and policies are highly visible and have been used to send political messages, leveraged as part of election platforms, pushed through to show that something was being done, and enacted as parts of ideological programs. Whatever their motivations, Canadian provinces have been, and will remain, core players in the evolution of the metropolitan experiment.

GOVERNMENT APPROACHES ARE GIVING WAY TO GOVERNANCE APPROACHES

Overwhelmingly, provinces have tended to favour government approaches to issues of metropolitan policy coordination. They have the power and have shown the willingness to implement government solutions, so they have experimented with various forms throughout the twentieth century. In part, this preference was driven by a desire for effective structures coupled with less concern for issues of local autonomy than in other places (such as the United States). In part, government solutions were perceived as best practices of that era. Occasionally, as in the Montreal case, stronger institutions were the logical response to the failure of weaker structures.

It is notable that, for a variety of reasons, every case discussed here has ultimately adopted metropolitan solutions closer to the governance end of the spectrum. That is, even where government restructuring occurred to address some of the challenges of regional coordination, governments still find the need to engage in collaboration and coordination with other governments and stakeholders to address metropolitan-scale issues. In some cases (Toronto and Winnipeg), this is because amalgamated structures no longer adequately cover the territory of the metropolitan region (if they ever did). In others, more flexible and limited structures were the only politically feasible solution (Montreal). In Vancouver, the regional district model has proved incredibly durable, in part because of its adaptability to change and local concerns. The most common practice, at the moment, is for the province to mandate the creation of a RIGO endowed with little legal authority and the responsible for the coordination of a variety of regional activities. In this role, the province is a metropolitan enabler rather than an enforcer.

Time will tell if the evolving governance approaches are effective mechanisms for regional policy coordination, or at least effective enough. As noted previously, these forms also have weaknesses and must navigate pitfalls. Although provincial governments appear less apt to invoke the large-scale institutional reforms that characterized the twentieth-century experiments, they still regularly establish special purpose districts (such as Toronto's regional transportation agency, Metrolinx) and impose regional policies (like Toronto's greenbelt). As metropolitan regions continue to grow and change, provinces will likely be central to the ongoing experiment.

Each of these metropolitan experiments has been contested and, on balance, their successes have been limited. Each has succumbed, in various ways, to the tensions inherent to their forms. If there were a result to these experiments, I think it would be that there is no best practice. Each approach has its strengths and challenges.

INTERNATIONAL COMPARISONS

The United States: Invisible Regions?

In the United States, there have been very few high-profile examples of regional government – two, to be exact. Both the Minneapolis-St. Paul (Minnesota) and Portland (Oregon) regions have second-tier metropolitan governments called Metro (or Met) Councils despite the fact that they have different origins, structures, and ambits. While these regional governments have been held up as ideals by scholars of American regionalism, similar structures have failed to materialize or even be seriously debated in other states. The result is that regionalism is something that occurs very much under the radar.

This general reticence to establish formal metropolitan governments is attributable to a strong political culture of local autonomy paired with a lack of political will on behalf of state governments to override local interests (even when they are statutorily empowered to do so). No institution embodies the American tendency to individualism, wariness of centralized government, and defence of local autonomy better than home rule. While both Canadian and American local authorities have traditionally been governed by legal frameworks that subordinate local governments to provincial and state governments (the Baldwin Act and Dillon's Rule, respectively), home rule has granted American jurisdictions some measure of freedom to govern their own affairs without state intervention since 1875 (see our discussion of home rule in chapter 2).

However, although regional government is an unlikely proposition, American regions have adopted a variety of mechanisms to coordinate policies across jurisdictional boundaries. For instance, recent research found 477 active RIGOs and several other types of multi-functional cross-boundary organizations. American jurisdictions have also enthusiastically adopted special purpose authorities – water districts, utilities, flood control districts, fire protection districts, etc. – as an alternative to establishing multi-purpose governing authorities. There are over 51,000 special purpose governments active in the United States today (Hogue 2012).

France: Governing Metropolitan Regions from the Centre

The French state is quite centralized, and while it has recently loosened its control over the specifics of regional policy, it has remained quite active in directing the spatial and political structures of subordinate levels of government. Specifically, the French government has been very active in organizing and reorganizing metropolitan governments. This typically involves the creation of new layers of government (and very seldom involves the dissolution of old iterations), resulting in the creation of what some have described as a millefeuille (Torre and Bourdin 2015).

While France has regional governments, these are roughly equivalent to large states or provinces. Beginning with a series of regional structural and decentralizing reforms initiated in 1992, metropolitan development and planning have been conducted through federated governments, broadly titled établissements publics de coopération intercommunale à fiscalité proper (EPCI-FP) and often referred to as intermunicipal organizations (intercommunalités). There are four variations of EPCI-FP stratified by population: communities of communes, agglomeration communities (> 50,000 inhabitants), urban communities (> 250,000 inhabitants), and metropolitan areas (> 650,000 inhabitants). There are presently 1,266 active EPCI-FP (Doré 2018). The governance landscape is also complicated by the proliferation of various types of special purpose authorities (*syndicats mixtes*) and a variety of other voluntary governance structures.

The recent reforms of the Paris regional and metropolitan governments, and the creation of the MGP, are among the most recent exercises in metropolitan reconceptualization and reterritorialization. In a nation built on égalité, the capital was often minimized in policies that sought to spread growth and prosperity around, while the state exercised control over key administrative and technical bodies (Kantor et al. 2012; Bourdeau-Lepage 2013). As a result, successive administrations have made their mark on the territorial and political organization of the Paris region. The MGP is a departure from the French tradition of layering new authorities to suit differing territorial and political needs. It was conceived to consolidate and replace existing joint authorities and profoundly change the balance of power in the planning and development of the capital.

In 2014 legislation was passed mandating the creation of the MGP. According to its website (Métropole du Grand Paris: Mission de Préfiguration 2015), as of January 1, 2016, the MGP encompassed 124 municipalities and 3 departments in the densest central part of the region and governed seven million inhabitants. This reform replaces nineteen existing intermunicipal partnerships and merges the municipality and department of Paris into a single structure. This new body is responsible for regional coordination of economic, social, and cultural development, housing, the environment, and quality of life. The series of reforms of which the reorganization of Paris was a part also required the merger and reduction in the number of EPCI-FPs and included clarifications of their roles and responsibilities in an effort to render the millefeuille more legible, efficient, and functional.

Ultimately, the French government regularly exercises its authority with respect to local affairs and has proved perennially willing to intervene in issues of metropolitan governance, particularly in support of its own policy goals.

The United Kingdom: Top-Down and Bottom-Up Metropolitanization

The highly centralized British state has been sporadically active in metropolitan affairs. Aside from a few blanket reforms (the creation of regions) and several targeted interventions with respect to the governing of the capital region of London, the British government has pursued a weak metropolitan policy: the local level was largely left to deliver services while the centralized state focused on the affairs of "high" politics.

In recent years this has changed. The emergence of a national focus on metropolitan regions dates to New Labour's devolution agenda of the late 1990s. These reforms included measured devolution to Scotland, Wales, and Northern Ireland, the introduction of a regional tier (Regional Development Agencies or RDAs), and the reconceptualization of the government of the city of London. By 2009, national focus shifted away from regions to focus on empowering city-regions. This culminated in the institutional changes that provided the legal framework within which metropolitan governance could emerge. Shaw and Tewdwr-Jones (2017) argue that the government's decision to pursue this strategy was influenced by the success of the voluntary Association for Greater Manchester Authorities dating back to the 1980s.

The 2010s saw another upheaval for local and metropolitan governance under the Conservatives. The abolition of the RDAs was one plank in a platform aimed to further devolve responsibilities to local and metropolitan scales. Central among these initiatives were the City Deals – individual negotiations with cities to devolve specific powers in exchange for assuming more responsibility for delivering growth locally – and the introduction of Combined Authorities (CAs) – further legal frameworks for city-regional policy coordination. Due to its long history with regionalism, the GMCA was among the first to be established (2011) with jurisdiction over economic development and transportation. By 2014, CAs had been established in five other metropolitan areas (West Yorkshire, Sheffield, Liverpool, Tees Valley, and the North East), and in the following year, the government expanded the areas in which the CAs could exercise jurisdiction. These developing authorities are essentially RIGOs to the extent that they are voluntary in nature and have specifically negotiated governance structures, despite the fact that they now control vast budgets and responsibilities for crucial service delivery and development support.

This approach to regionalism is aptly described as both top-down and bottom-up to the extent that metropolitan structures have not been imposed and are, at least nominally, optional. The structure and powers allocated to each city, through the City Deals, and to each CA have been highly variable and dependent on the strength and capabilities of local coalitions. This has led scholars to comment that the current approach to metropolitan governance in the UK is "bespoke" or, less charitably, "asymmetrical" and "disorganized."

CONCLUSION

This survey demonstrates the wide range of strategies that can be employed to address metropolitan issues. While no two applications of regional approaches are the same, it is possible to discern nationally specific variations in metropolitan coordination that are profoundly affected by distinctive institutions, political cultures, and unique national and regional histories.

The Canadian experiment falls somewhere between the relatively hands-off American experience and the more centralized and interventionist French and British approaches. This is partly tied into how much local democracy is valued, as well as possible tradeoffs between efficiency and effectiveness and local autonomy. As we argue above, the Canadian approaches to metropolitan coordination have been firmly driven by the provincial governments, often against the objections of local governments. This has been possible because of institutions that enshrine the provinces as the ultimate arbiters of municipal and, by extension, metropolitan affairs and empower them to intervene as they see fit. The provinces are able and willing to exercise this political fiat in part because the Canadian political culture does not privilege local autonomy quite as highly as in the American context. Across the country, the timing and shape of specific metropolitan interventions were the product of the unique confluence of local circumstances, but it is remarkable how similar the broad trajectories have been – a pendulum swinging from government to governance solutions.

We use the image of the pendulum deliberately here. While it seems that the harsh lessons of metropolitan government reforms have permeated the national consciousness, resulting in the increasing popularity of approaches closer to the governance end of the spectrum, that does not mean that more intense structural reorganization will not come back into vogue or, indeed, be seen as the only viable solution. Much will depend on how effective, flexible, and resilient contemporary solutions are to persistent and emerging metropolitan challenges. Much will also depend on the receptiveness of local governments to the idea of coordinating across jurisdictional boundaries and the degree to which provinces are willing to encourage the emergence of metropolitan institutions. Whether a truly metropolitan mindset (Iveson and Eidelman 2023) will emerge from this era of regional experimentation in Canada remains to be seen.

REFERENCES

ACIR. 1962. *A Commission Report: Alternative Approaches to Governmental Reorganization in Metropolitan Areas*. Washington, DC: Advisory Commission on Intergovernmental Relations.
Addie, Jean-Paul D. 2017. "Governing the Networked Metropolis: The Regionalization of Urban Transport in Ontario." In *Governing Cities through Regions: Canadian and European Perspectives*, edited by Roger Keil, Pierre Hamel, Julie-Anne Boudreau, and Stefan Kipfer, 121–41. Waterloo: Wilfred Laurier University Press. https://doi.org/10.51644/9781771122610-008.
Atlanta Regional Commission. 2017. "Planning for the Future and Providing Services Today to Improve Quality of Life in our Region." https://cdn.atlantaregional.org/wp-content/uploads/arc-brochure-final-2023-2.pdf.
Bourdeau-Lepage, Lise. 2013. "Introduction. Grand Paris : projet pour une métropole globale." *Revue d'Économie Régionale & Urbaine*, no. 3 (August): 403–36. https://doi.org/10.3917/reru.133.0403.
British Columbia Ministry of Community Services. 2006. *Primer on Regional Districts in British Columbia*. Victoria: British Columbia Ministry of Community Services.
Carr, Jered B., and Richard C. Feiock, eds. 2004. *City-County Consolidation and Its Alternatives: Reshaping the Local Government Landscape*. Armonk, NY: M.E. Sharpe.
Dollery, Brian, and Lin Crase. 2004. "Is Bigger Local Government Better? An Evaluation of the Case for Australian Municipal Amalgamation Programs." *Urban Policy and Research* 22, no. 3 (September): 265–75. https://doi.org/10.1080/0811114042000269290.
Doré, Gwénaël. 2018. "Le boulversement territorial en France : analyse et enjeux." *Population & Avenir* 1, no. 736: 4–7. https://doi.org/10.3917/popav.736.0004.
Douay, Nicolas, and Olivier Roy-Baillargeon. 2015. "Le Transit-Oriented Development (TOD), vecteur ou mirage des transformations de la planification et de la gouvernance métropolitaines du Grand Montréal?" *Flux* 3–4, nos. 101–2: 29–41. https://doi.org/10.3917/flux.101.0029.

Edwards, Mary M. 2008. "Understanding the Complexities of Annexation." *Journal of Planning Literature* 23, no. 2 (November): 119–35. https://doi.org/10.1177/0885412208322921.

Eidelman, Gabriel. 2010. "Managing Urban Sprawl in Ontario: Good Policy or Good Politics?" *Politics & Policy* 38, no. 6 (December): 1211–36. https://doi.org/10.1111/j.1747-1346.2010.00275.x.

Eurostat. 2012. *Defining Urban Areas in Europe*. Brussels: Eurostat.

Federal Register. 2010. *2010 Standards for Delineating Metropolitan and Micropolitan Statistical Areas*. Office of Management and Budget. Washington, DC: National Archives and Records Administration. https://www.federalregister.gov/d/2010-15605.

Filion, Pierre. 2003. "Towards Smart Growth? The Difficult Implementation of Alternatives to Urban Dispersion." *Canadian Journal of Urban Research* 12, no. S1: 48–70. https://www.jstor.org/stable/44387636.

Fischler, Raphaël, and Jeanne M. Wolfe. 2000. "Regional Restructuring in Montreal: An Historical Analysis." *Canadian Journal of Regional Science* 23, no. 1 (Spring): 89–114.

Forum Métropolitain du Grand Paris. 2017. "Qui sommes-nous ?" Accessed January 30, 2020. Archived November 30, 2022, at the Wayback Machine. https://web.archive.org/web/20221130112440/http://www.forumgrandparis.fr/nous-connaitre/qui-sommes-nous.

Hogue, Carma. 2012. *Government Organizations Summary Report: 2012*. Government Division Briefs. Washington, DC: U.S. Census Bureau.

Iveson, Donald, and Eidelman, Gabriel. 2023. *Toward the Metropolitan Mindset: A Playbook for Stronger Cities in Canada*. Toronto: University of Toronto School of Cities. https://schoolofcities.utoronto.ca/the-metropolitan-mindset/.

Jacobs, Jane. 1961. *The Death and Life of Great American Cities*. New York: Random House.

Kantor, Paul, Christian Lefèvre, Asato Saito, H.V. Savitch, and Adam Thornley. 2012. *Struggling Giants: Governance and Globalization in the London, New York, Paris and Tokyo City Regions*. Minneapolis: University of Minnesota Press.

Leland, Suzanne M., and Kurt Thurmaier, eds. 2010. *City-County Consolidation: Promises Made, Promises Kept?* Washington, DC: Georgetown University Press.

Lightbody, James. 1971. "The Reform of a Metropolitan Government: The Case of Winnipeg, 1971." *Canadian Public Policy/Analyse de politiques* 4, no. 4 (Autumn): 489–504. https://doi.org/10.2307/3549974.

Lucas, Jack. 2013. "Hidden in Plain View: Local Agencies, Boards, and Commissions in Canada." In *IMFG Perspectives*, no. 4. Toronto: Institute on Municipal Finance and Governance.

Lyons, Joseph. 2015. "Local Government Structure and the Co-ordination of Economic Development Policy." *Canadian Journal of Political Science* 48, no. 1 (March): 173–93. https://doi.org/10.1017/S0008423915000220.

Macdonald, Sara, and Roger Keil. 2012. "The Ontario Greenbelt: Shifting Scales of the Sustainability Fix?" *The Professional Geographer* 64, no. 1 (February): 125–45. https://doi.org/10.1080/00330124.2011.586874.

Martin, Lawrence L., and Jeannie Hock Schiff. 2011. "City–County Consolidations: Promise Versus Performance." *State and Local Government Review* 43, no. 2 (August): 167–77. https://doi.org/10.1177/0160323x11403938.

Metro Vancouver. 2018. "About Us." *Metro Vancouver*. Accessed February 23, 2022. https://metrovancouver.org/about-us.

Métropole du Grand Paris: Mission de Préfiguration. 2015. "Le Métropole du Grand Paris." Accessed December 9, 2018. Archived March 16, 2016, at the Wayback Machine. https://web.archive.org

/web/20160316165008/http://www.prefig-metropolegrandparis.fr/La-Metropole-du-Grand-Paris
/Le-projet-de-constitution.

Miller, David Y., and Jen Nelles. 2019. *Discovering American Regionalism: An Introduction to Regional Intergovernmental Organizations.* New York: Routledge. https://doi.org/10.4324/9781351242653.

Nelles, Jen. 2012. *Comparative Metropolitan Politics: Governing beyond Local Boundaries and the Imagined Metropolis.* London: Routledge.

Ontario. 2005. Places to Grow Act, 2005, S.O. 2005, c. 13.

Rickabaugh, James. 2018. "Finding the Unique Balance: Local Government Representation on the Boards of Regional Intergovernmental Organizations." PhD diss., Graduate School of Public and International Affairs, University of Pittsburgh. https://d-scholarship.pitt.edu/id/eprint/35737.

Sancton, Andrew. 1985. *Governing the Island of Montreal: Language Differences and Metropolitan Politics.* Berkeley, CA: University of California Press. https://doi.org/10.1525/9780520310766.

———. 2000. *Merger Mania: The Assault on Local Government.* Montreal: McGill-Queen's University Press. https://doi.org/10.1515/9780773568914.

———. 2008. *The Limits of Boundaries: Why City-Regions Cannot Be Self-Governing.* Montreal: McGill-Queen's University Press. https://doi.org/10.1515/9780773574977.

———. 2015. *Canadian Local Government: An Urban Perspective.* Don Mills, ON: Oxford University Press.

Savitch, H.V., and Ronald K. Vogel. 2004. "Suburbs without a City: Power and City-County Consolidation." *Urban Affairs Review* 39, no. 6 (July): 758–90. https://doi.org/10.1177/1078087404264512.

Schwartz, Harvey. 2009. "Toronto Ten Years after Amalgamation." *Canadian Journal of Regional Science* 32, no. 3 (Autumn): 483–92. https://idjs.ca/images/rcsr/archives/V32N3-Schwartz.pdf.

Shaw, Keith, and Mark Tewdwr-Jones. 2017. "'Disorganised Devolution': Reshaping Metropolitan Governance in England in a Period of Austerity." *Raumforschung und Raumordnung – Spatial Research and Planning* 75, no. 3 (June): 211–24. https://doi.org/10.1007/s13147-016-0435-2.

Spicer, Zachary. 2015. "Regionalism, Municipal Organization, and Interlocal Cooperation in Canada." *Canadian Public Policy/Analyse de politiques* 41, no. 2 (June): 137–50. https://doi.org/10.3138/cpp.2014-078.

———. 2016. "Governance by Handshake? Assessing Informal Municipal Service Sharing Relationships." *Canadian Public Policy/Analyse de politiques* 42, no. 4 (December): 505–13. https://doi.org/10.3138/cpp.2015-079.

Statistics Canada. 2015. "Census Metropolitan Area (CMA) and Census Agglomeration." *Census Dictionary.* Ottawa: Statistics Canada.

———. 2024. "Table 17-10-0148-01: Population Estimates, July 1, by Census Metropolitan Area and Census Agglomeration, 2021 Boundaries." Released May 22, 2024. https://doi.org/10.25318/1710014801-eng.

Taylor, Zachary Todd. 2015. "The Politics of Metropolitan Development: Institutions, Interests, and Ideas in the Making of Urban Governance in the United States and Canada, 1800–2000." PhD diss., Department of Political Science, University of Toronto (3744188). https://hdl.handle.net/1807/69520.

Taylor, Zack. 2019. *Shaping the Metropolis: Institutions and Urbanization in the United States and Canada.* Vol. 11 of McGill-Queen's Studies in Urban Governance. Montreal: McGill-Queen's University Press. https://doi.org/10.1515/9780773558427.

Teaford, Jon. 2006. *The Metropolitan Revolution: The Rise of Post-Urban America.* New York: Columbia University Press.

Tennant, Paul, and David Zirnhelt. 1973. "Metropolitan Government in Vancouver: The Strategy of Gentle Imposition." *Canadian Public Administration* 16, no. 1 (March): 124–38. https://doi .org/10.1111/j.1754-7121.1973.tb02113.x.

Thibert, Joel. 2015. *Governing Urban Regions through Collaboration: A View from North America*. Farnham, UK: Ashgate.

Tomàs, Mariona. 2012. "Exploring the Metropolitan Trap: The Case of Montreal." *International Journal of Urban and Regional Research* 36, no. 3 (May): 554–67. https://doi.org/10.1111/j.1468-2427.2011.01066.x.

Torre, André, and Sébastien Bourdin. 2015. *Big Bang Territorial: La réforme des régions en débat*. Paris: Hachette Book Group.

White, Richard. 2007. "The Growth Plan for the Greater Golden Horseshoe in Historical Perspective." *Neptis Paper on Growth in the Toronto Metropolitan Region*. Toronto: Neptis Fondation.

Wollmann, Hellmut. 2004. "The Two Waves of Territorial Reform of Local Government in Germany." In *Redrawing Local Government Boundaries: An International Study of Politics, Procedures, and Decisions*, edited by John Meligrana, 106–29. Vancouver: UBC Press. https://doi.org/10.1515/9780774850940-008.

CHAPTER SIX

Municipal Finance

Enid Slack

Local governments in Canada deliver a wide range of public services to residents and businesses, including public transit, local roads, water, sewers, solid waste collection and disposal, police and fire protection, as well as parks, libraries, cultural facilities, public health, social services, and affordable housing.[1] Increasingly, local governments have been taking on added responsibilities in response to changing demographics, the impact of climate change, federal immigration policies, the housing affordability crisis, the pandemic, increasing income inequality, and more. Yet, the revenues to pay for all these responsibilities have stayed pretty much the same for decades – property taxes, user fees, and intergovernmental transfers. Not only may these revenues not be sufficient to meet the growing need, but they may not be appropriate to pay for the different types of services municipalities deliver. For example, some local services (such as social services and social housing) entail redistribution from higher-income households to lower-income households, and property taxes and user fees may not be the best way to do that.

As this chapter will indicate, the ongoing challenge facing municipalities is to determine how to pay for the vast array of services and infrastructure they provide. Should they charge the costs to users (through some form of user fee or special levy), local taxpayers (through property or other taxes), or should they be paid by provincial or national taxpayers (through transfers or revenue sharing)? What is the role of federal and provincial governments in local affairs?

This chapter tries to answer these questions by looking at the experience of municipalities in Canada and comparing it to other municipalities around the world. The first section, "How Should We Pay for Municipal Services and Infrastructure?," sets out a theoretical model for who should pay for municipal services and infrastructure. The second section, "Municipal Finance in the Canadian Intergovernmental System," describes the finances of municipalities in Canada and includes a quantitative overview of municipal revenues and expenditures. The third section, "A Closer Look at Municipal Revenues in Canada," provides more details about specific revenue sources. The fourth section, "How Do Municipal Expenditures and Revenues in Canada Compare to Other OECD Countries?," compares expenditures and revenues of Canadian municipalities with those in other OECD countries, followed by a comparison of the degree of local fiscal autonomy in major international cities in the fifth section, "Local Fiscal Autonomy: How Does Canada Compare with Other Countries?" The sixth section, "How Are Canadian Municipalities Faring?," briefly summarizes how well Canadian municipalities are faring in terms of their fiscal health. The seventh section, "Clarifying Federal-Provincial-Municipal Roles and Responsibilities," addresses the importance of clarifying federal, provincial, and municipal responsibilities and makes the case for a mix of taxes for municipalities. The final section looks at the enduring debates in municipal finance.

How Should We Pay for Municipal Services and Infrastructure?

How local governments pay for services depends, at least in part, on what services they are providing. As the European Charter of Local Self-Government (Article 9, para. 2) states, "local authorities' financial resources shall be commensurate with the responsibilities provided for by the constitution and the law." Another way to say this is that finance should follow function (Bahl and Bird 2018).[2]

Before looking at what sources of funds Canadian municipalities use to pay for expenditures, we start by asking the question about the funding model they should use. Both theory and experience point to a funding model that links expenditure and revenue decisions. Many authors have emphasized the importance of establishing a clear connection between expenditure and revenue decisions (often referred to as the Wicksellian Connection after Swedish economist, Knut Wicksell).[3] The best way to design a local revenue system is first to decide what services should be delivered locally and then to put into place the local revenue system (a combination of user fees, taxes, and transfers) that will best induce local decision-makers to finance precisely that package of expenditures that their residents want.

User fees are appropriate to pay for those services where the beneficiaries can be identified and those who do not pay can be excluded from the service. One critical feature needed to ensure that local governments deliver the right services is to allocate the costs associated with providing a service as directly as possible to those individuals, firms, neighbourhoods, and groups that enjoy the benefits of the service (Bazel and Mintz 2014). From the perspective of efficiency, and arguably also from that of equity, the first rule of sensible local finance is therefore "wherever possible, charge" (Bird and Slack 2014). Good user charges not only produce revenue, but they also promote economic efficiency – that is, the best use of available resources to improve people's lives.[4] User fees also provide information on which services should be provided, in what quantity and quality, and to whom. People seldom like paying for what they get from the government, but financing local public services by properly designed user charges remains the best way to ensure that people get what they want (and are willing to pay for) rather than what someone else decides they should have.

When public services are not priced, or they are underpriced (such as water or roads), consumers tend to use more services than they would be willing to pay for if they had to face the full cost. Failing to charge properly also imposes hidden costs. The initial waste of resources that could be put to more socially valued uses can also lead to still further waste as governments pour additional resources into infrastructure in response to demands for more and better services from both current users and those who think they deserve to be similarly subsidized. As an example, when governments do not charge for the use of roads, they are subsidizing car ridership. The result is that the roads become crowded and the political pressure to widen them to combat congestion increases. Finally, since virtually all public services that are not paid for by user charges end up being financed by taxes that almost invariably impose additional efficiency costs, the initial waste of resources arising from inefficient pricing is again multiplied.[5]

User fees cannot be charged for all municipal services, however. When the beneficiaries of services cannot easily be identified (or cannot be excluded if they do not pay), other ways of paying for services and infrastructure may be appropriate. Some local public services may, for example, generate collective benefits that are enjoyed by residents as a group. Benefits from services such as fire protection, neighbourhood parks, local streets, and street lighting cannot easily be assigned to individual beneficiaries, so it is difficult to levy specific fees or charges for them. But it is generally possible to impose some form of local benefit-based taxation such as the property tax to finance such services. Property taxes serve the same purpose as user charges by permitting people to express their collective demand for services. Viewed as a generalized local user charge, the local property tax can be seen as an appropriate way to finance not only current local public services but also local infrastructure that has a short life, such as office computers or automobiles (Kneebone and McKenzie 2003).[6] Moreover, when infrastructure projects increase land values, various forms of land value capture may be used as a financing mechanism, and development charges (charges on developers of new subdivisions to pay for infrastructure necessitated by the development) may be appropriate to cover the growth-related capital costs associated with new development or redevelopment.[7]

For services that have a redistributive component, such as social housing or social assistance, a progressive tax such as the income tax or a sales tax with compensation for low-income households is appropriate. Regardless of what one thinks of the property tax, at least in the current Canadian context, it is less progressive than an income tax.[8]

When benefits (or costs) from locally provided services spill over municipal boundaries but local provision is still considered desirable, a federal or provincial transfer may also be appropriate. Positive spillovers (externalities) occur if residents of neighbouring jurisdictions receive a service for free or at less than the cost of providing it. For example, roads constructed in one jurisdiction may be used by residents of another jurisdiction without paying for them. One result may be that the providing jurisdiction spends less on roads than it should because it has no incentive to consider benefits accruing to those outside the jurisdiction.[9] Matching revenues to expenditures requires matching on a geographic basis both to share costs equitably among all beneficiaries and to ensure that due allowance is made for external benefits.

Finally, the appropriate way to cover the costs of infrastructure projects with a long life (forty to fifty years, for example) is usually to spread the tax impact over time for reasons of both equity and efficiency. Much of the discussion about how best to "finance" (as opposed to "fund," that is, to pay for) infrastructure focuses on this timing issue. Although users should pay to the extent possible, there are, of course, many ways in which infrastructure investment can and should be financed. But what is critical is not to let the financing decision obfuscate what is really going on in terms of who is paying and responsible for what. Funds that are borrowed must still be paid back. The key question remains: how much should users pay? And how much should taxpayers – local, provincial, federal, current, or future – pay?[10]

Table 6.1 provides an overview of some of the different types of services and infrastructure that municipalities provide and some suggestions for the appropriate source of revenues. Of course, some services or infrastructure exhibit more than one of the characteristics in the table. For example, social services are redistributive, but their benefits can also spill over municipal boundaries. For this reason, it may be appropriate to pay for these services using more than one revenue source.

MUNICIPAL FINANCE IN THE CANADIAN INTERGOVERNMENTAL SYSTEM

The Constitution sets out the division of powers between the federal and provincial governments. Local institutions have no sovereign constitutional powers and are only mentioned in the Constitution as one of the responsibilities of the provinces.[11] In terms of revenues, the Constitution gave the federal government comprehensive powers to raise money "by any mode or

Table 6.1. Linking Revenues to Expenditures

Characteristics of Service/Infrastructure	Types of Service/Infrastructure	Revenue Source
Private good – can identify beneficiary and exclude those who do not pay	Water, sewers, garbage collection, transit	User fees
Public good – cannot exclude individual beneficiaries	Police, fire, local parks, streetlights	Property tax, sales tax
Redistributive	Social housing, social assistance	Income tax, sales tax with compensation for low-income households
Spillover – benefits cross municipal boundaries	Roads, social services, culture	Federal or provincial transfers
Increases land value	Transit, parks	Land value capture
Growth-related infrastructure	Water, sewers, roads	Development charges
Large-scale infrastructure	Roads, bridges	Borrowing

system of taxation," whereas the provinces were given authority to levy "direct taxation within the province" for provincial purposes. Municipalities are limited to the taxing authority that is delegated to them by provincial governments, which have the exclusive authority to make laws in relation to municipal institutions (Philipps et al. 2019). The result has been that municipalities are largely restricted to levying property taxes and user fees as well as receiving transfers from the provincial and federal governments. With respect to taxation, municipal governments accounted for 8.6 per cent of all taxes collected in Canada in 2022, the federal government accounted for 45.6 per cent, and provincial governments for 45.8 per cent of all taxes (Statistics Canada 2024).

Provincial governments play a much larger role than the federal government in the affairs of municipal governments in Canada.[12] In terms of municipal finance, they determine what responsibilities are assigned to local governments and which revenues they can raise. Municipalities are not permitted to budget for an operating deficit, and if over the course of the year they do run a deficit, they are required to cover it immediately in the next fiscal year. Provincial governments also restrict the amount that municipalities are permitted to borrow to meet capital expenditures. For example, in Ontario (except for Toronto), the rule is that debt charges cannot exceed 25 per cent of own-source revenues. Last, provincial governments provide transfers to municipalities. Some of these transfers are unconditional (that is, they can be spent on whatever the municipality chooses) while others are conditional (they have to be spent on the specific functions set out by the province).

Table 6.2 shows the distribution of municipal expenditures by province for 2020. Although the types of expenditures are fairly similar across provinces – municipal governments spend on police, fire, transportation, water and waste management, recreation and culture, and housing – there are some notable differences. For example, municipalities in Ontario spent almost one-quarter of their budget on social services whereas municipalities in most other provinces spent little or nothing. In these other provinces, the provincial government is responsible for social services. Municipalities in Ontario and Nova Scotia stand out because they spend more on health than municipalities in other provinces. Municipalities in Quebec and Alberta spent almost one-quarter of their total expenditures on transportation, which is considerably more than the average of 18 per cent for the country (see table 6.2). British Columbia municipalities spend more of their budgets on recreation and culture than municipalities in other provinces. On average, municipalities devote 11 per cent of their budget to policing, but this estimate ranges from less than 1 per cent in Newfoundland and Labrador to over 19 per cent in New Brunswick.[13]

It is difficult to compare the distribution of expenditures over the last decade because expenditure data has not been disaggregated for the earlier years. However, for the general categories, it appears that the largest growth is in economic affairs, which mainly includes transportation, but also some other sub-categories.

In terms of municipal revenues, table 6.3 shows the distribution by province for 2020. The main sources of revenue for municipalities in Canada are the property tax (44 per cent of revenues, on average, across the country), followed by provincial and federal transfers (almost

Table 6.2. Distribution of Municipal Expenditures by Province, 2020, %

Municipal Expenditures	Newfoundland and Labrador	Prince Edward Island	Nova Scotia	New Brunswick	Quebec	Ontario	Manitoba	Saskatchewan	Alberta	British Columbia	Canada (incl. territories)
General Public Services	30.0	26.8	30.2	16.7	28.8	10.0	29.0	24.7	16.8	17.4	16.9
Public Order and Safety											
Police Services	0.6	14.4	12.4	19.3	8.3	11.0	14.0	12.7	11.7	15.2	11.1
Fire Protection	6.7	10.3	6.3	7.3	4.3	5.2	6.9	6.8	7.6	9.0	5.8
Other	3.7	2.1	5.4	1.0	2.7	1.2	3.8	2.1	1.4	2.6	1.8
Total	11.0	26.8	24.0	27.70	15.4	17.3	24.7	21.6	20.7	26.8	18.7
Economic Affairs											
Transportation	20.9	13.4	13.0	13.7	24.0	16.6	13.3	5.6	23.9	7.7	17.6
Other Affairs	0.6	1.0	0.2	0.9	2.6	0.8	0.9	6.9	1.7	0.1	1.4
Total	21.5	14.4	13.2	14.6	26.6	17.4	14.2	12.5	25.7	7.8	19.0
Environmental Protection											
Waste Management	5.9	0.0	6.5	6.2	3.8	3.5	2.0	2.8	5.2	6.3	4.1
Wastewater Management	1.7	4.1	0.8	6.0	3.7	4.4	4.4	4.9	1.8	7.1	4.1
Other	1.7	0.0	0.5	0.8	0.5	1.6	2.2	2.4	0.2	0.0	1.0
Total	9.3	4.1	7.7	12.94	8.0	9.5	8.6	10.1	7.1	13.4	9.3
Housing and Community Amenities											
Housing and Community Dev.	2.8	3.1	1.9	5.0	2.1	3.1	4.6	3.1	3.4	5.2	3.2
Water Supply	10.1	9.3	6.3	8.2	3.9	3.5	9.6	12.5	5.6	8.4	4.9
Street Lighting	2.3	2.1	2.1	2.7	0.6	0.4	1.1	0.6	0.8	0.9	0.7
Other	0.3	0.0	0.0	0.1	0.0	0.4	0.0	0.0	0.4	0.0	0.2
Total	15.5	14.4	10.3	16.0	6.6	7.4	15.3	16.2	10.2	14.6	9.0
Health											
Outpatient Services	0.0	0.0	0.0	0.0	0.0	3.3	0.0	0.0	0.4	0.0	1.6
Public Health	0.0	0.0	5.4	0.0	0.0	1.9	0.3	0.1	0.0	0.0	1.1
Other	0.0	0.0	0.1	0.0	0.0	0.1	0.0	0.1	0.0	1.0	0.2
Total	0.0	0.0	5.4	0.0	0.0	5.3	0.3	0.2	0.4	1.0	2.9
Recreation and Culture	12.7	13.4	9.2	12.2	10.7	8.9	7.7	14.6	16.0	18.3	11.3
Social Protection											
Old Age	0.0	0.0	0.0	0.0	0.0	3.9	0.0	0.0	0.0	0.0	1.9
Family and Children	0.0	0.0	0.0	0.0	0.1	5.2	0.0	0.0	0.1	0.0	2.5
Housing	0.0	0.0	0.0	0.0	3.2	5.2	0.2	0.0	2.1	0.1	3.4
Social Exclusion	0.0	0.0	0.0	0.0	0.0	9.3	0.0	0.0	0.0	0.0	4.5
Other	0.0	0.0	0.0	0.0	0.4	0.5	0.0	0.0	0.9	0.8	0.5
Total	0.0	0.0	0.0	0.0	3.8	24.1	0.2	0.1	3.1	0.8	12.9
Total Expenditures	100.0	100.0	100.0	100.0	100.0	100.0	100.0	100.0	100.0	100.0	100.0

Note: Totals may not add up to 100 per cent due to rounding.

Source: Statistics Canada, "Table 10-10-0024-01: Canadian Classification of Functions of Government, by General Government Component (x 1,000,000)," https://doi.org/10.25318/1010002401-eng. Contains information licensed under the Open Government Licence – Canada.

25 per cent) and user fees (almost 20 per cent). Provincial and federal transfers range from a low of 12 per cent of revenues in BC municipalities to a high of 54 per cent in Prince Edward Island. Transfers account for over 30 per cent of total municipal revenues in Ontario, where social services are cost-shared with the provincial government. User fees represent a somewhat smaller percentage of municipal revenues in Quebec, where water is paid for out of property tax revenues. Lot levies (also known as development charges) are significant in Ontario, Saskatchewan, Alberta, and BC. Last, land transfer taxes (the bulk of the category of property-related taxes) are levied by municipalities in Quebec and Nova Scotia, and by the City of Toronto in Ontario.

Figure 6.1 shows how the distribution of municipal revenues in Canada has changed – or not – over the past decade. Property taxes have accounted for just under half of total revenues throughout the period and user fees remain just under one quarter of revenues. Intergovernmental transfers have ranged from 17 to 20 per cent of total revenues over the decade, except for 2020 where they rose to 25 per cent of total revenues in response to the pandemic.

Statistics Canada data shows that municipalities in all provinces levy property taxes (on residential and non-residential properties), but "other taxes" are not disaggregated. Table 6.4 shows some of the other taxes that municipalities levy in some (but not all) provinces across Canada.

In terms of fiscal powers, in addition to the information in tables 6.3 and 6.4, Vancouver is permitted to borrow on its own authority without the approval of the BC Municipal Finance Authority; it can impose specialized development cost levies; and more recently, it can impose

Figure 6.1. Distribution of Municipal Revenues, Canada, 2009–20
Source: Statistics Canada, "Table 10-10-0020-01: Canadian Government Finance Statistics for Municipalities and Other Local Public Administrations (x 1,000,000)," https://doi.org/10.25318/1010002001-eng. Contains information licensed under the Open Government Licence – Canada.

Table 6.3. Distribution of Municipal Revenues by Province, 2020, %

Municipal Revenues	Newfoundland and Labrador	Prince Edward Island	Nova Scotia	New Brunswick	Quebec	Ontario	Manitoba	Saskatchewan	Alberta	British Columbia	Canada (incl. territories)
Property Taxes	50.3	28.2	57.2	54.5	59.9	38.9	42.4	32.1	42.2	45.1	44.2
Property-related Taxes	0.0	0.0	2.1	0.0	3.4	1.4	0.0	0.0	0.1	0.0	1.3
Lot Levies and Motor Vehicle Taxes*	3.0	0.0	0.4	0.9	1.6	7.0	3.2	10.3	7.0	7.9	5.9
Other Taxes	2.4	0.5	0.4	0.1	0.0	0.1	0.9	2.3	2.9	1.0	0.7
User Fees	21.5	16.0	16.5	19.2	13.7	19.5	24.5	28.0	17.6	30.6	19.8
Other Revenue	1.1	1.0	1.9	4.5	4.7	2.8	1.9	3.2	4.5	3.4	3.4
Total Own-Source Revenues	78.4	45.6	78.5	79.2	83.3	69.6	72.9	75.9	74.3	88.1	75.2
Intergovernmental Transfers	21.6	54.4	21.4	20.8	16.7	30.3	27.1	24.1	25.7	11.9	24.8
Total Revenue	100.0	100.0	100.00	100.0	100.0	100.0	100.0	100.0	100.0	100.0	100.0

* The actual category is "taxes on use of goods and permission to use goods or perform activities" and includes lot levies and motor vehicle taxes.
Note: Totals may not add up to 100 per cent due to rounding.
Source: Statistics Canada, "Table 10-10-0020-01: Canadian Government Finance Statistics for Municipalities and Other Local Public Administrations (x 1,000,000)," https://doi.org/10.25318/1010002001-eng. Contains information licensed under the Open Government Licence – Canada.

Table 6.4. Selected Additional Municipal Revenues by Province

Revenues	BC	AB	SK	MB	ON	QC	NB	NS	PE	NL
Accommodation Tax				X	X			Halifax Only	X	St. John's Only
Land Transfer Tax				X	Toronto Only	X		X		
Vehicle Registration Tax					Toronto Only (Discontinued)					
Billboard Tax				Winnipeg Only	Toronto Only					
Electricity and Natural Gas Consumption Tax				Winnipeg Only						
Poll Tax									X	

Source: Adapted from Taylor and Dobson (2020), table 5.1.

a tax on vacant housing. Both Edmonton and Calgary can levy supplementary assessments on property that has changed from farm to another use but only Calgary can establish its own debt servicing policies (such as determining its debt limit), run operating deficits for up to three years, and impose off-site infrastructure levies. Unlike other municipalities in Manitoba, Winnipeg may borrow without the approval of the Manitoba Municipal Board. The City of Toronto has the power to levy taxes not available to other municipalities in Ontario, but there are many exclusions, including taxes on income, payroll, wealth, sales of goods and services, road tolls, and more. It levies a vacant home tax. Montreal has separate legislation but no additional financial powers.

A CLOSER LOOK AT MUNICIPAL REVENUES IN CANADA

The property tax has been the central source of municipal revenues in Canada since before Confederation. But municipalities do levy other taxes and charges, and they receive transfers from the federal and provincial governments. This section provides some details on select municipal revenues in Canada.[14]

PROPERTY TAX

The property tax is calculated by multiplying a tax rate or rates times the assessed value of property. In most provinces, properties are assessed on the basis of market value. There are generally at least two classes of property – residential and non-residential – with different tax rates applied to each, and in some provinces, there are more property classes.

Property tax policy is far from standardized across the country because the provincial legislation that governs property taxation differs from province to province.[15] Different municipalities may be subject to different policies on how tax rates are set, for example.[16] In some provinces – such as Alberta, Nova Scotia, Prince Edward Island, and Newfoundland and Labrador – municipalities are free to set their own property tax rates without provincial restrictions. In others, the provincial government directly controls or limits tax rates on some property classes.[17]

Residents and businesses in different provinces in Canada may have access to different exemptions and incentives, and to different tax breaks, schemes, and programs meant to address the supposedly regressive and volatile nature of the property tax. Finally, all but two provinces levy their own property tax, ostensibly as a source of funding for public schooling, although the revenue from this tax goes directly to the province as general revenue.

Regardless of the details, the property tax generally satisfies many characteristics of a fiscally sound local tax. Its base is largely immobile – the residential portion cannot be exported to taxpayers in other jurisdictions – and therefore relatively efficient because distortions in economic behaviour are minimized.[18] It is at least partly effective in funding services for which the collective benefits accrue to the local community; hence, it satisfies the fairness criterion based on benefits received. Revenues are relatively stable and predictable, which has served municipalities well during the pandemic as it has in recessions. It is highly visible, too, so it makes local governments accountable for the tax levied.

Although the property tax is a good tax for local governments, it is relatively inelastic (it does not grow automatically as the economy grows), and because it is highly visible, it is politically contentious. Moreover, there is the perception among municipal officials, taxpayers, and some analysts that the property tax is regressive, meaning that it represents a greater percentage of income for lower-income individuals than for higher-income individuals. However, a number of studies have disputed that property taxes are regressive (for a summary of studies, see Kitchen and Tassonyi 2012). The answer depends on how one views the nature of property taxes.

If the property tax is viewed as an excise tax, its burden is regressive because it takes a higher percentage of a lower household's annual income than of a higher household's annual income, because lower-income households spend a greater proportion of their income on housing. If it is viewed as a capital tax, its burden is likely to be progressive because higher-income households are likely to own a disproportionately large share of the stock of capital. If it is viewed more as a user charge, it pays for those services that provide collective benefits to the local community. According to this view, the property tax is a benefit tax. Benefit taxes are not based on ability to pay, which is the commonly accepted base for measuring regressivity. Rather, they are based on the link, sometimes direct but often indirect, between the benefits one receives from local public services and the taxes paid for these services.

Regardless of one's views of the incidence of the property tax (who bears the burden), policy-makers are often concerned about its impact on taxpayers who are asset rich but income poor, such as the elderly on fixed incomes. For this reason, many jurisdictions have introduced tax deferral programs or other property tax relief schemes to address this problem to some extent.

Another potential downside of a local property tax is that it may be more expensive to administer than other local taxes (income, sales, fuel, for example) that can be piggybacked onto existing provincial taxes. This cost may be a small price to pay, however, if local governments are to have autonomy and flexibility in setting tax policy – important ingredients of responsible, efficient, and accountable local governments (Bird 2011b).

Some have argued that the property tax is sufficient to fund municipal services: other taxes are not needed. A study of Alberta municipalities, for example, found that the property tax can do the job (Dahlby and McMillan 2019). Furthermore, if the provincial education portion of the property tax were eliminated, municipalities would have more than enough tax room to finance their services now and well into the future. A study of the City of Toronto's finances noted that property tax revenues have grown more slowly than inflation since 2000 and that the tax burden per household has fallen over this time (IMFG 2018). A study of the Greater Toronto Area concluded that there is room to increase residential property taxes in most municipalities in the region (Tassonyi, Bird, and Slack 2015).

The real question, however, is not whether the property tax is *adequate*, but whether it is the *best* tax for funding all city services. As noted earlier, municipalities increasingly engage in social housing, public health, immigration settlement, and social services that have a redistributive element. Because the property tax is not appropriate for services of a redistributive nature, some authors have called for a mix of taxes for Canadian municipalities (Kitchen and Slack 2016). For example, it might be more appropriate for municipalities to fund redistributive services from more progressive taxes such as the income tax or a value-added tax that includes mitigation for low-income households in the design.

LAND TRANSFER TAX

The municipal land transfer tax is an alternative source of revenue to pay for municipal services that allows municipalities to rely less on the property tax. Municipalities in three provinces, plus the City of Toronto, are permitted to levy a land transfer tax. This tax is levied on the selling price of the house when it is transferred from one owner to another and is paid by the purchaser. Although the tax can generate substantial revenues, it is not considered by economists to be a good local tax for a number of reasons. First, the tax bears no relationship to the benefits received from local services. Second, it is not related to ability to pay because there is no direct relationship between homebuyers and their income or wealth (Clayton 2015). Third, the land transfer tax imposes a burden on those who buy property while placing no direct burden on those who remain in their existing property, providing an incentive for those who remain in their homes to demand additional municipal services, knowing that new homebuyers will disproportionately pay for city services. Finally, and perhaps most significantly, the tax provides a disincentive for people to move, thereby resulting in potential inflexibilities in the labour market and encouraging people to stay in properties of a size and location that they might not otherwise have chosen.

In terms of its impact, two empirical studies on housing prices in Toronto concluded that sales of single-family homes in the city fell by 16 per cent after the implementation of the land transfer tax, with the most pronounced effect in areas with relatively low sales values. Another study suggested, however, that the decline in housing sales in Toronto in 2008 can also be attributed to macroeconomic factors and market regulations (Haider, Anwar, and Holmes 2016). There is some evidence that homeowners chose to renovate rather than relocate because of the tax (Dachis, 2012; Dachis, Duranton, and Turner 2008). In terms of the impact of the tax on mobility, it was estimated that about 3,500 families that would have moved did not do so because of the tax (Dachis, Duranton, and Turner 2008). The impact on housing prices and mobility led one study to conclude that revenue generated by the land transfer tax is far less than the economic cost in terms of the billions of dollars of economic activity and thousands of jobs lost in the city since its inception (Altus Group Economic Consulting 2014).

HOTEL AND MOTEL OCCUPANCY TAXES

An occupancy or room tax is a levy imposed on hotel and motel stays. This tax, it can be argued, compensates cities for services provided to tourists and visitors (for example, additional police and fire protection, and highway and public transit capacity needed to meet weekend or peak convention and tourist demands). The advantage of a hotel and motel occupancy tax over income and sales taxes is that it falls primarily on visitors who use services but do not otherwise pay for them.

Several cities in Canada levy hotel or motel occupancy taxes (see table 6.4). In some cities, the tax is mandatory, but in other cities, a voluntary destination marketing fee is levied by those hotels that wish to participate. As with other taxes, cities piggyback onto the existing provincial sales tax on hotel and motel rooms through the addition of a few percentage points rather than setting up their own administrative structure.

A tax on hotel and motel rooms in selected cities and not in competing communities provides an incentive for individuals to stay in hotels and motels in those cities without the tax. The extent to which differential tax rates would actually deter visitors from renting rooms is uncertain, however. If the demand for hotel and motel rooms is sensitive to price, then noticeable losses may occur. Since convention arrangements are often highly cost-sensitive, the impact on the convention business might be significant.

USER FEES

As noted earlier, wherever possible, municipalities should charge directly for services. Appropriately designed user fees allow residents and businesses to know how much they are paying for the services they receive from local governments. When appropriate fees or prices are charged, citizens can make efficient decisions about how much to consume, and governments can make efficient decisions about how much of the service to provide.

Economic efficiency dictates that prices or fees should equal the marginal cost of providing the goods or services; that is, where the price per unit of output equals the cost of the last unit consumed. Current practice in setting user fees, however, almost always deviates from what is fair, efficient, and accountable (Fenn and Kitchen 2016; Kitchen and Tassonyi 2012). The tendency is to set fees to generate revenue rather than to allocate resources to their most efficient use.

Transportation is an example of the need for more efficient pricing in Canadian cities. Motor vehicles occupy valuable space while moving and while parked. Yet neither road usage nor parking spaces are currently rationed with effective pricing structures. Without efficient prices, users cannot tell how much it costs to use an automobile and lack incentives to make efficient decisions about how often to use them, where to live and work, and so on. This lack of efficient pricing has been a primary cause of highway congestion, environmental degradation, lost productivity, and reduced economic activity in many large cities and urban areas in Canada (Kitchen and Lindsey 2013).

Municipal efforts to increase reliance on user fees are often criticized on the grounds that user fees are regressive. For some services, however, the opposite is often true – those who benefit most from underpriced services are often those who use them the most, and these beneficiaries are often in higher-income groups. By not charging the marginal cost of water, for example, those who are heavy consumers of water – for watering lawns, washing cars, filling swimming pools, and so on – are frequently in the higher-income groups. Nevertheless, to address the perceived inequity from efficient pricing systems for low-income households, relatively simple pricing systems, such as low initial "lifeline" charges, can be applied, as is done in a number of Canadian cities.

Although Tassonyi and Kitchen (2021) are in favour of targeting relief to those who need it most, they argue that it is more equitable to address income distribution issues with income transfers from federal and provincial governments that have access to broader tax bases than by changing the design of fees. Where user fees are discounted for some users, such as for transit, the relief should be based on income, which is a measure of ability to pay and not age (seniors or children, for example) or other factors (Tassonyi and Kitchen 2021).

Development Charges

Development charges provide significant revenues to municipalities in Ontario, Saskatchewan, Alberta, and British Columbia. A development charge (known as development cost charges in British Columbia and off-site levies in Alberta) is a one-time levy on developers to finance the off-site, growth-related capital costs associated with new development or, sometimes, redevelopment. Charges are levied for works constructed by the municipality, and the funds collected must be used to pay for the infrastructure made necessary by the development. The rationale for charging developers for growth-related capital costs is that "growth should pay for itself" and not be a burden on existing taxpayers (Slack 2002, 15; Found 2019, 18). Growth-related costs have traditionally included hard costs for roads, water, and sewage systems and, in some jurisdictions, also include soft costs for services such as libraries, recreation centres, and schools. Development charges are used to pay for transit in Ontario municipalities (although there are restrictions on its application) but not in British Columbia.

Efficient development charges vary by type of property (residential, commercial, or industrial), density of the development (single units versus apartments), and distance from existing services. In this way, the charge captures the extra cost of the infrastructure required by the new growth. Marginal cost pricing is better at linking revenues and expenditures for specific developments than average cost pricing, but most Canadian municipalities impose the same charge on all properties in any class, regardless of location. Although easier to calculate, this postage stamp approach to charges means that municipalities levy the same charge on residential dwellings in low-density neighbourhoods as in high-density neighbourhoods, even though the marginal cost per property of infrastructure projects in low-density areas is higher (Blais 2010). One result of this approach can be urban sprawl (Slack 2002). Moreover, developments close to existing infrastructure pay the same charge as developments far away, even though the costs are higher for the more distant developments. Although it may be difficult to calculate the growth-related infrastructure costs for individual properties, costs could be calculated by neighbourhood to discourage inefficient development patterns (Kitchen and Tassonyi 2012).

LAND VALUE CAPTURE

The idea behind land value capture is to recoup some or all of the unearned increment in private land values arising from a public investment (such as a new transit line or transit station) that benefits (indirectly) property owners adjacent to the infrastructure.[19] Under tax increment financing (TIF), for example, property tax revenue from the designated area is divided into two categories for a specific period of time (long enough to recover all costs of public funds used to redevelop the property, usually between fifteen and thirty years). Taxes based on pre-developed, assessed property values are retained by the municipality for general use. Taxes on increased assessed values arising from redevelopment (the tax increment) are deposited in a special fund to repay bonds that have been issued to finance public improvements in the redeveloped area. In other words, increases in property tax revenue from the redevelopment of an area are dedicated to financing public improvements in that area.

TIFs are widely used in the United States, but they are less common in Canada, although often talked about.[20] In Manitoba, cities are permitted to use TIFs but do not currently do so.

Legislation in Alberta permits municipalities to use a form of TIF known as the community revitalization levy. Ontario municipalities may use tax increment equivalent grants (TIEGs), but these are not the same as TIFs because they involve a subsidy component.[21]

Two studies in the Greater Toronto Area looked at the potential use of TIFs for major transit investments. One study concluded that if TIFs had been used to finance the Sheppard subway line in 2006, it would not have been able to cover all capital costs (Haider and Donaldson 2016). This result is not that surprising given the low ridership on that subway line. Another study of the proposed SmartTrack proposal for the City of Toronto suggested that there would be sufficient commercial development in the city to fund the proposed $2.6 billion investment (Found 2016). The jury is still out on the ability of TIFs to finance major infrastructure projects, but to the extent they do so, they may provide one way to match benefits (to property owners) to the taxes they pay.

FEDERAL AND PROVINCIAL TRANSFERS

According to the Constitution, the federal government has no role in municipalities. Through its spending power, however, it can direct funds wherever it likes, and over the years, some federal governments have chosen to spend money in cities. As Bradford (2018) notes, these programs amount to an "implicit" federal urban agenda.

Infrastructure Canada, for example, provides several programs for municipal infrastructure (Canada 2024). The Canada Community-Building Fund (formerly known as the Gas Tax Transfer) is an example of a tri-level agreement to fund infrastructure. It provides provinces and territories with permanent funding for local infrastructure investments, allocated on a per capita basis with payments flowing to designated signatories – provinces, territories, municipal associations, and the City of Toronto. In 2012, the fund was indexed to grow at 2 per cent per year. Although its spending power has allowed the federal government to pursue an implicit urban policy, federal spending has not been without controversy. Some provinces feel that the federal government is encroaching on provincial jurisdiction.

Over the years there have also been examples of trilateral and bilateral agreements through which the federal government has helped fund municipal services. A recent example has been in response to the large operating deficits faced by municipalities because of the impact of COVID-19. The federal government announced a $19 billion agreement between Ottawa and the provinces to provide support, in part, to municipalities to cover deficits. Specific funds were allocated, on a matching basis with the provinces, for transit systems that have been impacted by a drop in ridership. Another example of federal funding is the National Housing Strategy, which comprises spending programs that range from funding for affordable housing construction and homeless shelters to a first-time home buyers' incentive. More recently, the federal government introduced the Housing Accelerator Fund for local initiatives to build more homes.

Federal funding can be justified under a few circumstances. For example, it may be needed where the benefits of municipal services or infrastructure spill over municipal and provincial boundaries. In those circumstances, the appropriate transfer is conditional and matching. Federal funding is also appropriate where there are national objectives to be met such as immigration settlement, investment in productivity-enhancing infrastructure, and responding to climate change. Although it is easy to justify federal funding for major projects, it is difficult to justify it for small local infrastructure projects. Of course, the federal government has greater fiscal capacity than provincial or local governments, and the resulting fiscal imbalance, clearly evident during COVID-19, is also a reason for federal funding.

The bulk of transfers to local governments in Canada come from provincial governments, however. Transfers can be economically justified to the extent that local expenditures spill over municipal boundaries, as noted above with respect to federal transfers. For example, if 10 per cent of the benefits of a road cross over municipal boundaries, it is appropriate that the province pick up 10 per cent of the costs. Higher-level governments in Canada often finance as much as a third or half of the cost of infrastructure when few projects seem likely to provide regional, let alone national, benefits to this extent.

Even to the extent they may be justified, transfers tend to distort local decision-making by lowering the price of some services. Often, municipalities are required to spend the funds they receive according to the guidelines of senior governments and not according to their own interests (Slack 2011, 2016b). Sometimes they are required to provide matching funds, which may be beyond the capacity of some municipalities. Funding from senior governments can lead to inefficient local revenue decisions. When transfers cover a large proportion of costs, there may be little incentive to use proper pricing policies for services. For this reason, any grants should ideally require recipient governments to implement efficient pricing and taxation policies (Boadway and Kitchen 2014). Such requirements would, of course, reduce local fiscal freedom but may nonetheless be justified as improving local accountability by encouraging local governments to make the best use of their resources.

Intergovernmental transfers can also be justified on equity grounds. Local funding of services will mean that there will be differences in the ability of local governments to deliver services. Some municipalities are unable to provide an adequate level of service at reasonable tax rates whereas other municipalities can. This inability to provide an adequate level of service may occur because the costs of services are higher, the need for services is higher, and/or the tax base is smaller. To address this imbalance, equalization grants based on expenditure needs and fiscal capacity allow those municipalities with small tax bases and greater costs and needs to be able to provide a comparable level of services by levying tax rates that are comparable to other jurisdictions.

Six provinces provide some form of equalization grants to municipalities, but these do not generally constitute the major component of grants – in most provinces, the majority of provincial-local transfers are conditional.[22] In only two provinces (Nova Scotia and New

Brunswick) has the equalization grant formula explicitly recognized both expenditure need and fiscal capacity; the other provinces only take account of fiscal capacity, although population size is sometimes used as a proxy for expenditure need.[23] The two provinces that have included explicit measures of expenditure need in the grant formula differentiated their equalization grants by classes of municipalities because of wide divergences in expenditures and revenue-raising capacities of different types of municipalities.[24]

Even the best-designed transfers, however, are likely to reduce accountability to some extent. When the level of government that is making spending decisions (a municipality, for example) is not the same as the level of government that raises the revenues to pay for them (a senior level of government), accountability is blurred. Moreover, transfers are rarely a stable and predictable source of revenue. If fiscal pressures lead senior governments to reduce transfers, for example, local governments must either increase taxes, increase borrowing (that is, increase future taxes), or cut spending.

HOW DO MUNICIPAL EXPENDITURES AND REVENUES IN CANADA COMPARE TO OTHER OECD COUNTRIES?

At 9 per cent of GDP, municipal expenditures in Canada sit in the middle of the pack of OECD countries (see figure 6.2). The countries with the highest ratio of municipal expenditures to GDP are mainly in Northern Europe. Although it is difficult to get disaggregated data on municipal expenditures, OECD data does show that these countries have a high proportion of municipal expenditures on social protection relative to total expenditures: Denmark – 56 per cent; Norway – 29 per cent; Sweden – 26 per cent; and Finland – 25 per cent (International Monetary Fund 2024). As will be noted below, municipalities in these countries depend heavily on income taxes and very little on property taxes. This matching of progressive taxes to redistributive services corresponds with the model of municipal finance set out earlier.

Cities in many parts of the world levy a wider variety of taxes to pay for local services than do Canadian cities. Property, income, and sales taxes are the most common taxes levied, but the property tax is not nearly as significant in terms of revenues as it is in Canada and a few other countries. Table 6.5 shows the distribution of local tax revenues for thirty-four OECD countries for the three main taxes – income, sales, and property – as well as user fees, other revenues, and intergovernmental transfers.

Income taxes accounted for more than 50 per cent of local tax revenue in thirteen countries.[25] Sales taxes are the most important local tax source in three countries, and they provided 10 per cent or more of local taxes in twelve countries. Although local governments in all of the countries levy property taxes to some extent, these are the most important local revenue source in only twelve countries. They accounted for more than 10 per cent of local taxes in thirty countries, but more than 90 per cent of local taxes in only six countries (Australia,

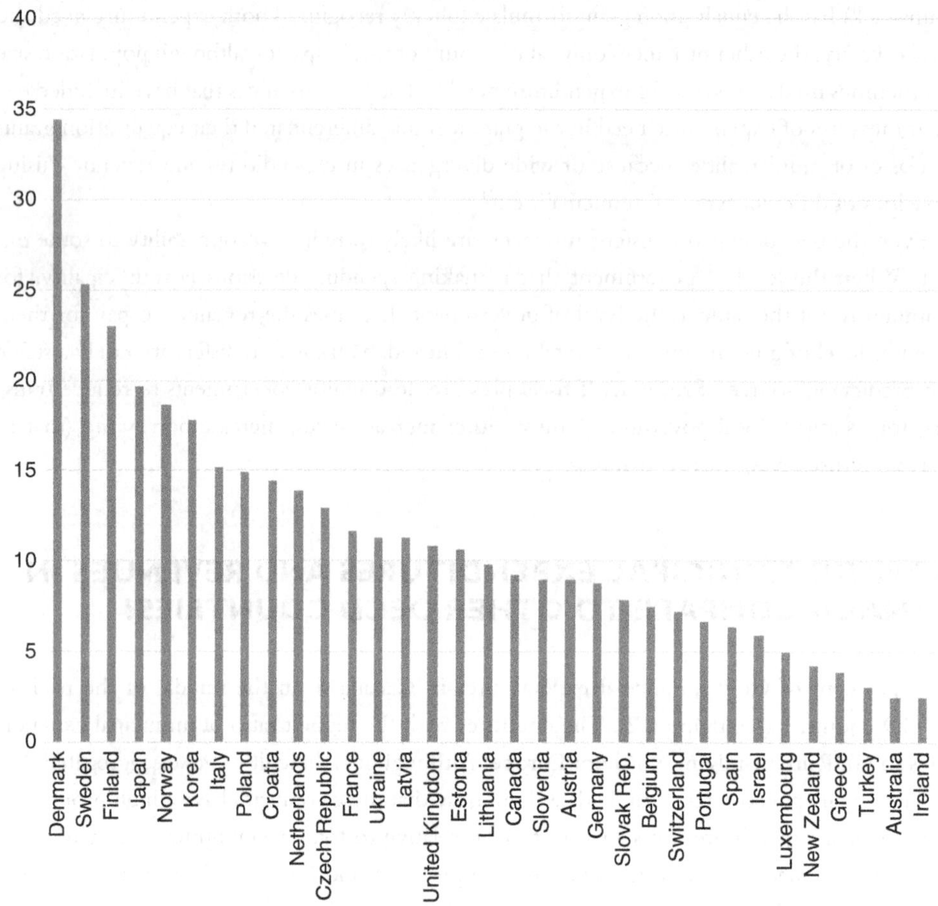

Figure 6.2. Municipal Expenditures as % of GDP, Selected Countries, 2020
Source: IMF Government Finance Statistics, 2020.

Canada, Greece, Israel, New Zealand, and the United Kingdom). Countries with a balanced local revenue structure – in the sense that it is not dominated by one tax – are Italy, Korea, Portugal, and Spain.

With a few exceptions, wherever local taxes are a comparatively high percentage of total tax revenue and GDP, and where local governments spend significant amounts on social protection, local governments tend to rely more heavily on local income taxes. For example, Nordic countries, where local taxes are generally more than 10 per cent of GDP, rely heavily on income taxes, whereas property taxes are more important in countries where local taxes account for less than 3 per cent of GDP. These countries tend to be ones that, in the past, were part of the British Commonwealth or significantly influenced by the British Empire (see chapter 2 for more on the Anglo model). Local sales taxes are usually less important in federal countries than

Table 6.5. Relative Importance of Municipal Revenues by Source, Selected OECD Countries, 2018, %

Countries	Income	Sales	Property	Other Taxes	User Fees	Other Revenues	Total Own-Source Revenues	Intergovernmental Transfers
Federal								
Australia	0.0	0.0	38.7	0.0	27.0	20.6	86.3	13.7
Austria	11.4	1.8	2.2	0.0	15.9	6.1	37.5	62.5
Belgium	10.1	2.6	16.6	0.0	11.7	10.5	51.5	48.5
Canada	0.0	7.5	47.7	0.0	22.0	3.2	80.4	19.6
Germany	30.8	3.0	4.5	0.2	15.5	6.7	60.7	39.3
Mexico	0.0	0.3	10.6	2.3	6.3	3.7	23.1	76.9
Switzerland	49.5	0.2	9.6	1.4	16.9	11.6	89.2	10.8
Regional Country								
Spain	9.1	19.4	22.3	0.1	9.7	3.7	64.2	35.8
Unitary								
Chile	0.0	23.6	17.8	0.0	1.4	6.0	48.8	51.2
Czech Republic	22.0	21.6	1.7	0.1	12.3	3.1	60.8	39.2
Denmark	32.0	0.0	4.0	0.0	4.7	0.5	41.1	57.6
Estonia	0.0	0.5	2.3	0.0	9.1	1.7	13.6	86.4
Finland	42.5	0.0	3.7	0.0	21.4	2.6	70.3	29.7
France	4.1	19.3	29.6	0.3	15.5	1.5	70.3	22.2
Greece	0.0	1.7	23.1	0.0	9.4	0.9	35.1	62.1
Hungary	0.0	28.2	6.1	0.0	10.4	2.6	47.4	52.6
Iceland	63.6	2.4	12.8	0.0	8.7	3.6	91.0	9.0
Ireland	0.0	0.0	18.9	0.0	26.4	3.6	48.9	44.5
Israel	0.0	7.8	33.7	0.0	4.3	12.9	58.6	41.4
Italy	6.9	16.3	7.6	0.4	9.4	4.4	45.0	55.0
Japan	23.6	12.1	12.4	1.1	5.9	4.6	59.6	40.4
Korea	6.3	14.2	7.8	3.2	6.0	5.6	43.1	56.9
Luxembourg	32.3	1.3	1.2	0.1	15.6	0.9	51.4	48.3
Netherlands	0.0	1.2	4.9	0.0	12.7	4.7	27.9	72.1
New Zealand	0.0	4.5	50.3	0.0	17.0	14.	86.0	14.0
Norway	32.4	0.3	4.8	0.0	13.7	4.8	55.9	44.1
Poland	20.9	2.3	8.3	0.5	7.5	1.6	41.2	50.2
Portugal	10.7	19.1	12.5	0.7	15.0	5.3	63.4	27.3
Slovak Republic	0.0	1.3	5.7	0.0	15.3	1.5	23.8	73.5
Slovenia	31.0	3.5	6.2	0.0	17.4	1.6	59.7	38.2
Sweden	53.2	0.0	0.0	0.0	8.5	2.8	64.6	33.7
Turkey	0.0	3.8	6.7	0.0	10.3	12.5	33.2	66.8
United Kingdom	0.0	0.0	17.9	0.0	14.6	3.6	36.1	63.9

Notes: Income taxes include individual, corporate, and payroll taxes; sales taxes include general consumption taxes, value-added taxes, specific taxes on goods and services (fuel, hotel, and motel occupancy taxes), and taxes on use of goods or permission to use goods or perform activities; property taxes include taxes on property and recurrent taxes on net wealth; other taxes include a miscellaneous collection of taxes; total taxes include central government, state government, local government, and social security funds.
Source: IMF Government Finance Statistics, https://data.imf.org/?sk=a0867067-d23c-4ebc-ad23-d3b015045405.

they are in unitary countries. The reason is that states and provinces collect considerable sales tax revenue, making it less likely that this source of revenue is available to local governments.

LOCAL FISCAL AUTONOMY: HOW DOES CANADA COMPARE WITH OTHER COUNTRIES?

Local fiscal autonomy refers to the extent to which local governments rely on locally raised revenues for funding (rather than receiving transfers from federal or provincial governments) and on the control they have over their taxes. Simply stated, local governments that depend heavily on transfers from senior levels of government have less fiscal autonomy than those that rely more on own-source revenues (taxes, user fees, etc.). Even with transfers, however, there can be more or less local autonomy depending on the type of transfer (Blöchliger and Kim 2016). As noted earlier, unconditional transfers have no strings attached to the use of funds; they can be spent on any expenditure function or used to reduce local taxes and thus result in more local autonomy.[26] Conditional transfers, however, result in less local autonomy because the donor government has a say over where the funds can be spent.[27]

In terms of reliance on own-source revenues versus intergovernmental transfers, a comparison of eight international cities in table 6.6 shows that Toronto, Tokyo, Paris, New York, and Frankfurt seem to have the most fiscal autonomy (own-source revenues account for more than 70 per cent of total revenues) and Berlin and London have the least (at about 30 per cent of total revenues).

Although municipal taxes per capita in Berlin appear to be significant, a large portion of those taxes are shared taxes over which the city has little control. In the case of shared taxes, the national or provincial/state government determines the tax base, sets the tax rate, and shares the revenues with cities. If the cities do not have the ability to set the tax rate, there is no local autonomy for shared taxes: cities are simply given a share of the revenues, and it is simply a transfer.

Although a city that relies more heavily on taxes is assumed to have more local fiscal autonomy than a city that relies more heavily on intergovernmental transfers, local fiscal autonomy also refers to the freedom that local governments have over their own taxes. A truly local tax is one for which the local government can:[28]

- decide whether to levy the tax or not;
- determine the precise base of the tax;
- set the tax rate;
- administer (assess, collect, enforce) the tax;
- keep all the revenue collected; and
- grant tax allowances or reliefs to individuals and firms.

Table 6.6. Own-Source Revenues, Shared Taxes, and Intergovernmental Transfers

City (Year)	Own-Source Revenues, %	Shared Taxes, %	Intergovernmental Transfers, %
Toronto (2015)	82.0		18.0
London (2015)	31.2		68.8
Berlin (2014)[*]	30.3	36.5	33.2
Frankfurt (2015)	71.1	15.7	13.2
Madrid (2015)[*]	48.3	5.7	46.0
New York (2015)	74.0		26.0
Paris (2015)[†]	83.7		16.3
Tokyo (2015)[*]	81.9	12.5	5.6

[*] Shared taxes in Berlin and Madrid appear under taxes; in Tokyo, transferred national taxes appear under transfers.
[†] The business value-added tax in Paris (18 per cent of total municipal revenues) is a local tax, but the city has no discretion over the tax rate, which is set by the central government.
Source: Reprinted from Slack (2017), table 5. From the author's calculations based on tables in Slack (2016a).

The ability of local governments to set their own tax rates is the most important element of fiscal autonomy.[29] International experience tells us that the most responsible and accountable local governments are those that raise their own revenues and set their own tax rates (Bird 2011a). Unless local governments can alter the tax rates, they will not have local autonomy or the accountability that comes with it. Local tax rate setting also provides predictability for local governments and gives them the flexibility to change rates in response to different circumstances.

Tax autonomy can also lead to greater efficiency in the public sector. It provides voters with some ability to decide on tax levels and, in that way, makes them more aware of public service outcomes. Some limited empirical research on the impact of tax autonomy suggests that it also has a positive impact on the efficiency of municipal spending (Blöchliger and Pinero-Campos 2011). With tax autonomy, local decision-makers are inclined to use their own resources more wisely than if their funding comes from another level of government, and thus, local government is expected to be smaller (Martinez-Vazquez, Lago-Penas, and Sacchi 2015). Using panel data for nineteen OECD countries, Liberati and Sacchi have shown that tax decentralization based on taxes used solely by local governments (e.g., the property tax) facilitates local spending control, but this is not necessarily the case for taxes where the base is shared with other levels of government (e.g., income and sales taxes) (Liberati and Sacchi 2013).

Toronto is less dependent on intergovernmental transfers than many other major cities but, with the exception of London, it has fewer tax options than the other cities. New York is less reliant on state transfers and can levy many different taxes, although the city still needs permission from the state government to implement some new taxes. Tokyo and Paris rely heavily on own-source revenues but may not have much control over their tax sources. Frankfurt and Berlin have access to more tax sources than many of the other cities, but a portion of these taxes is shared, and the city does not have the ability to set the tax rates. Madrid relies relatively heavily on property taxes but also shares in revenues from the personal income tax, value-added tax, and selected excise taxes.

Although Canadian cities have considerable fiscal autonomy when measured as the percentage of total revenues that are own-source revenues (as shown in table 6.6), compared to other cities around the world, they tend to have fewer tax options. And, given the increasing range of responsibilities at the local level noted earlier, this lack of diversity in tax options may increasingly be a problem.

HOW ARE CANADIAN MUNICIPALITIES FARING?

The question of how well Canadian municipalities are faring is a difficult one to answer in part because there is limited comparable data on measures of fiscal health. Nevertheless, some efforts to date suggest that, on average, Canadian municipalities have been doing well (Bird and Slack 2015). An analysis of the fiscal health of the City of Toronto prior to the pandemic, for example, suggested that it is sound by most measures – expenditures per capita adjusted for inflation have not increased very much over the last decade, property taxes per capita adjusted for inflation have been declining, and debt is manageable (Slack and Côté 2014; IMFG 2018). Similar analyses in other provinces show similar findings (Bird and Slack 2015).

Even for cities that appear to be doing well, however, the story may not be so favourable. The reason is that their apparent fiscal health may have been achieved at the expense of their overall health, which has less to do with whether they balance their budget (which they must do by law) than with the quantity and quality of the services they provide and the state of their infrastructure. A city that balances its budget, has modest tax increases from year to year, and has little or no debt may seem fiscally healthy, but its infrastructure may be crumbling. Infrastructure investment is needed both to maintain a state of good repair and to invest in the new. Infrastructure needs present a huge financial challenge to municipalities in Canada.

There is much discussion about the poor state of municipal infrastructure in Canada – roads are congested, transit systems are in need of major investments, bridges are crumbling, water treatment plants need to be replaced, and more. Yet, we have not progressed very far in measuring the state of urban infrastructure (roads, transit, housing, water pipes, etc.), nor in understanding what is needed to maintain it or increase it to meet future needs. Perhaps the most often cited estimate of that infrastructure deficit is $123 billion, which was put forward by the Federation of Canadian Municipalities back in 2007. More recent information for the Province of Ontario suggests that approximately 45.3 per cent of municipal assets in that province are not in a state of good repair, and the capital spending needed to bring them up to a state of good repair in 2020 was about $52 billion (FAO 2021).

Although the public discourse appears to have adopted these and similar numbers of other organizations, Fenn and Kitchen (2016) caution against taking some of these numbers at face value. In some cases, for example, estimates are based on surveys conducted by associations with a vested interest in making the number significant enough to attract federal and provincial funding. Moreover, where deficits have been estimated, it is assumed that existing taxing and pricing policies for the services delivered by the assets will continue; there is no estimate of infrastructure needs if more effective demand management or conservation-based pricing policies were adopted, for example. As noted earlier, efficient prices for services such as road use, water, and wastewater would reveal the true demand for infrastructure because people would know the cost of providing those services and they would give an indication of the efficient supply. Pricing water correctly, for example, would mean people would use less water and reduce the need for water treatment plants. Tolls on major highways, another example, would discourage road use and lessen the need to build more roads. In other words, efficient pricing would likely reduce the estimates of the infrastructure deficit.

Notwithstanding the above concerns, there is little doubt that municipal governments, on average, have underinvested in infrastructure. Much more work needs to be done to understand the state of municipal infrastructure in Canada and to measure the overall fiscal health of municipalities. And, of course, who should pay for the infrastructure is another question that needs to be addressed.

CLARIFYING FEDERAL-PROVINCIAL-MUNICIPAL ROLES AND RESPONSIBILITIES: WHO DOES WHAT AND HOW DO WE PAY FOR IT?

Although municipalities deliver a wide range of services in their jurisdictions, as noted earlier, they do little of this alone. Provinces are involved in almost every aspect of local service delivery through cost-sharing, policy setting, regulations, or other forms of intervention. In Ontario alone, more than 280 provincial statutes and countless provincial regulations, policy frameworks, and service standards affect how municipalities deliver services (Wilson 2019). Indeed, the current cost-sharing arrangements between the province and municipalities have been described as a "tangled web" of overlapping obligations (Côté and Fenn 2014, 4). When federal government funding is added to the mix, the web becomes even more entangled.

How do we determine the roles and responsibilities that should be assigned to the different orders of government? Some experts make the case for decentralization to local governments: as a general rule, services should be assigned to the lowest level of government where efficiency and equity can be achieved (Bahl and Bird 2018; Boadway and Shah 2009). This concept is sometimes referred to as the subsidiarity principle. As Bahl and Bird have written, "people are more likely to get the package of public services they want, if not necessarily what others think they should want, under a decentralized system than under a centralized system" (2018, 9).

Local governments are sites for innovation. Emerging policy solutions can be more easily tested at a small scale before they are adopted by others. Decentralization can feed this innovative capacity by creating more room for experimentation. Decentralization to local governments also fosters the involvement of local organizations in policy-making, including businesses, residents' groups, arts organizations, and environmental groups. These organizations, the argument goes, are more likely to have access to local governments than to higher levels of government. Removing local governments from policy-making and decision-making can thus reduce the voice of these organizations (Horak 2012).

Centralizing functions (to the provincial or federal level), on the other hand, may be warranted and desirable under certain circumstances. For example, centralization is often warranted to ensure common service standards, such as in health care and education (Boadway and Shah 2009). Centralization can result in economies of scale (where the cost per unit of output falls with increasing scale) and help ensure fairness. Some services, such as social services, are redistributive in nature, and the most effective and equitable way to fund redistributive services is through a progressive tax, such as an income tax, which is currently levied only at the provincial (and federal) levels in Canada.

Finally, as noted earlier with respect to the example of roads that cross municipal boundaries, centralization can address spillover effects. Centralizing responsibility, or at least leaving some oversight at a higher level of government, ensures the optimal level of service for the region; decentralization, meanwhile, can lead to municipalities making service decisions based on the needs of local residents only.[30]

Deciding who does what is a matter of balancing the need for uniform standards on the one hand with the desire for local input and innovation on the other. It is also a matter of balancing competing priorities and adapting to the particular context of a region or the demands of delivering a particular service. In some cases, it may be beneficial to disentangle provincial and municipal involvement by assigning responsibility to one government or the other. Some services, though, may benefit from greater coordination and co-operation among orders of government.[31]

A study on clarifying provincial-municipal responsibilities in Ontario recommends a principles-based approach to sorting out who does what between municipalities and provinces – what municipalities do best, what the province does best, where they can work together, and what resources cities need to meet their responsibilities (Eidelman, Hachard, and Slack 2019).

The study recommended the following principles to clarify provincial and local responsibilities:[32]

1 **Take a collaborative approach:** Rather than using a top-down approach, collaboration that engages municipalities, the business communities, and service providers would ensure greater buy-in.

2 **Follow the pay-for-say principle and avoid unfunded mandates:** A government's input into how a service functions should be matched with a corresponding responsibility to pay for that service. Unfunded mandates, whereby provincial regulations require local government to perform certain actions without providing money to meet those requirements, should be avoided.

3 **Consider local revenue capacity:** Any proposal to increase municipal service responsibilities should consider whether local governments have the necessary and appropriate resources to meet those responsibilities.

4 **Respect local and regional differences:** The costs of delivering services are not the same across each province. A review should take account of differences between regions. Asymmetrical arrangements may be required.

5 **Look forward, not backward:** A review of provincial-municipal responsibilities should look ahead to future challenges, such as how the aging population or climate events might affect local service costs.

In a federal country such as Canada, COVID-19 has highlighted how the division of powers among the federal, provincial, and local governments plays out in the face of a public health crisis. In particular, the federal government has used its spending powers to assist provinces and municipalities that face considerable fiscal pressure to address critical responsibilities but lack the necessary revenue sources to meet them. This misalignment of revenues and expenditures is particularly acute for municipalities that rely mainly on property taxes and user fees. It is time to revisit the role of all orders of government: to this end, the Fiscal Federalism Policy Network (formerly the Intergovernmental Fiscal Relations Commission) was established to rethink the architecture of fiscal federalism in Canada (Béland, Dahlby, and Orsini 2020).[33]

A rethink of fiscal federalism needs to consider the possibility of a mix of local taxes, especially for large Canadian cities. A portfolio of taxes would give cities more flexibility to be internationally competitive and to respond to local conditions such as changes in the economy, evolving demographics and expenditure needs, the impact of climate change, rising inequality, changes in the political climate, and other factors. As an example, elected local politicians might choose to levy sales taxes for local services that are enjoyed by commuters and visitors.[34] An employee-based personal income tax (often referred to as a payroll tax) would tax commuters. Property taxes might be chosen where there is a need for a more stable revenue source. A mix of taxes would also allow cities to increase or stabilize revenue while maintaining equity (Bahl 2011; Kitchen 2016; Slack 2011).[35]

A single tax, such as the property tax, almost always creates local distortions, some of which may be offset by other taxes. For example, the property tax may discourage investment in housing.[36] An income tax, on the other hand, may encourage investment in owner-occupied housing because the imputed income of owner-occupied housing is not taxed in Canada. With a range of tax sources, distortions in one tax may be counteracted by distortions in other taxes.

Finally, relying on many sources means that a city can set lower tax rates for any single tax to levy a given amount of revenue. Since the burden of a tax increases with the tax rate (that is, the distortions increase as the tax rate increases),[37] a more diversified system should yield a given amount of revenue more efficiently with a smaller negative impact on the overall tax base (Chernick, Langley, and Reschovsky 2010).[38]

Recalibrating our federal fiscal structure will hopefully put municipalities and provinces on better footing, but there will still be areas where coordination between orders of government will be required. Going forward, such coordination needs to be trilateral, rather than bilateral (Slack and Hachard 2020). In the aftermath of COVID-19, the OECD urged national governments to "introduce, activate or reorient existing multi-level coordination bodies that bring together national and subnational government representatives, in order to minimise the risk of a fragmented crisis response" (OECD 2020, 68).

Canada has a history of establishing trilateral agreements in areas such as homelessness and urban development, but these agreements are the exception rather than the rule (Bradford 2020). Decisions taken on immigration, infrastructure, and public health, to name a few examples, have significant effects on municipalities. In cases where there is insufficient funding for programs, municipalities often bear the cost of filling gaps in services. Municipalities, particularly large cities, should not need to wait to see what arrangements the provinces and the federal government agree to in areas such as infrastructure, public health, and immigration. They need to be part of the discussion or, as it is often stated, they need a seat at the federal-provincial policy-making table.[39]

CONCLUSION: THE ENDURING DEBATE ON MUNICIPAL FINANCE

Municipalities are on the front lines when it comes to delivering the services that people use every day. Yet, Canadian municipalities are constrained by provincial legislation in terms of what they can do. Financially, they are restricted by provincial governments to using primarily property taxes, user fees, and provincial transfers. Compared to municipalities in many other countries, Canadian municipalities have fewer taxes to rely on.[40]

Throughout the 2000s, provincial governments have increasingly recognized municipalities as democratic and accountable orders of government, empowered them through legislative change, and, to some extent, expanded their fiscal resources (Taylor and Bradford 2020). Moreover, several major cities in Canada are governed by separate legislation or city charters (including, for example, Vancouver, Edmonton, Calgary, Toronto, and Montreal). As is evident in this chapter, however, even with more powers and separate legislation and charters, there is some question as to whether the expansion of fiscal resources has kept pace with the increasing role of local governments.[41]

When the Constitution stated that municipal institutions were the responsibility of provincial governments back in 1867, most people did not live in cities. Now, over 80 per cent of Canadians live in cities. In recent years, many of the issues facing Canadians have also changed, including the need to provide social services and social housing, integrate immigrants, mitigate the impact of climate change, reduce inequality, combat urban sprawl, respond to the opioid crisis, and more. Many of these issues have been described in other chapters. As this chapter has suggested, the property tax and user fees, the main sources of revenue for local governments for many decades, may no longer be sufficient or the best source to address the new challenges that they face. For example, they may not be sufficient to provide disaster relief, and they may not be appropriate to deliver affordable housing.

Thus, the enduring debate in municipal finance in Canada surrounds what municipalities should be doing and how they should pay for it. What services are best delivered at the local level and what resources do local governments need to deliver them? What role should the federal and provincial governments play in local affairs?

Although there is general agreement that there is a vertical fiscal imbalance in this country – meaning that revenues do not match expenditures for the different orders of government – there is an ongoing debate about how to improve the fiscal situation of local governments. Some argue, for example, that municipalities need more sources of revenue to meet their obligations – perhaps access to income or sales taxes, for example. Others argue that municipalities have sufficient sources of revenue and can meet expenditure requirements without new taxes. Some, often municipalities themselves, suggest that local governments need more transfers from the federal and provincial governments. Some believe that the provincial government should take over some responsibilities that are now at the local level because they have more appropriate tax sources to pay for them. Yet others believe that municipal governments just need to find expenditure efficiencies.

Regardless of what one thinks about how to solve the fiscal problems of municipalities, it is important to start the discussion by revisiting who does what and how to pay for it. Over the years, many provinces have undertaken exercises to clarify municipal roles and responsibilities, but this analysis needs to be done on a regular basis because circumstances are always changing. Particularly if municipalities are not going to be able to levy new taxes, we need to think about what services they should be responsible for delivering. Should they be delivering social services and social housing, for example, if their main source of revenue is the property tax? As noted earlier in this chapter, it is important that municipal revenue sources match the full range of municipal expenditure responsibilities. That may mean that some responsibilities should be transferred from municipalities to provincial governments, or it may mean that municipalities should be given access to new revenues. The federal government cannot change municipal expenditure responsibilities or revenue-raising powers, but in those areas where there is a national interest, it may be appropriate to provide funding. All three orders of government thus need to be involved in addressing the fiscal problems being faced by Canadian cities.

NOTES

1 See chapter 2 for more information on what local governments do.
2 This section draws heavily from Slack and Bird (2019).
3 See, for example, Bird and Slack (2014) and Kitchen and Slack (2016).
4 An important assumption underlying this argument is that our present political and fiscal system places the key responsibility for distributive outcomes almost entirely on higher levels of government.
5 Taxes can result in distortions in economic decisions. For example, income taxes distort the work/leisure choice, excise taxes impact consumption decisions, and property taxes may distort the decision about where to live.
6 A local sales tax or personal income tax could also play a role in paying for services with public good characteristics (Kitchen and Slack 2016), especially in larger metropolitan areas where many who benefit from local services may not reside in the local tax jurisdiction.
7 Land value capture and development charges are described more fully later in this chapter.
8 The issue of regressivity of the property tax is discussed further in the section on property taxes.
9 Other ways to internalize externalities may be by providing the service at a metropolitan or regional level or by having the provincial government do it.
10 For a much more detailed discussion of this question, see Bird and Slack (2017).
11 This chapter does not go into a discussion of whether the Constitution should be amended to give original powers to municipalities in Canada. For that discussion, see IMFG (2020).
12 In addition to the provincial legislation that applies to all municipalities in a province, some municipalities have specific legislation in a separate specific law: Vancouver, Calgary, Edmonton, Toronto, Winnipeg, and Montreal (Taylor and Dobson 2020). Special legislation does not seem to have increased the revenue raising powers of the affected cities in a significant way, however (Taylor and Dobson 2020; Kitchen 2016).
13 A study of municipal police budgets in seven major Canadian cities found that police expenditures have been rising steadily for many years even though police employment has been stable and crime rates have been declining (Smart 2020). The exception is Toronto, where employment and per capita spending have been declining since 2010. Nevertheless, criminality and crime clearance rates continue to evolve similarly in Toronto as in the other major cities (Smart 2020).
14 This section reviews taxes that are levied by municipalities in more than one province, so vehicle registration taxes, billboard taxes, electricity and natural gas consumption tax, and poll taxes are not included. Business taxes are a supplement to the property tax and have been included in the discussion of property taxes.
15 For a detailed account of the characteristics of the property tax in different provinces and an examination of the broader issues around property taxation in Canada, see Kitchen, Slack, and Hachard (2019).
16 In four provinces – Alberta, Manitoba, Quebec, and Newfoundland and Labrador – municipalities can levy an additional business occupancy tax, which may be based on assessed value, rental value, or some other measure. In the other provinces, the business occupancy tax has been eliminated.
17 For more details on tax rate setting for the property tax, see Kitchen, Slack, and Hachard (2019).
18 The same is not true of the non-residential property tax, however, which can be exported to other jurisdictions. For a discussion of the economic impact of non-residential property taxes in Ontario, see Smart (2012).

19 Land value capture can also be used when the municipality permits an increase in height or density, which will also have a positive impact on land values. The sale of building rights is one method to capture the increase in land value under these circumstances. See Moore (2013) for a discussion of the sale of building rights (also known as density bonusing).

20 TIFs in the United States have generated a fair amount of criticism. For a good discussion of TIFs, see Youngman (2011).

21 The Province of Ontario passed TIF legislation in 2006 but never enacted regulations. Under a TIEG, municipalities can designate an area or the entire municipality as a community improvement project area. They can then implement a community improvement plan (CIP) with grants and/or loans which can, if the municipality chooses, be calculated on a tax increment basis. In other words, the municipality can offer developers a grant or loan that is based on the higher property tax that is generated from development.

22 For more details on provincial-municipal equalization transfers in Canada, see Bird and Slack (2021).

23 Starting in 2023, the annual increase in equalization funding in New Brunswick is based on the growth rate of the municipal tax base relative to the provincial tax base.

24 Without these groupings, expenditure levels and revenue-raising capacity would over-emphasize fiscal needs and fiscal capacity in the formula because of the significantly higher expenditures levels and tax base in the largest cities.

25 The source for the estimates in this paragraph is the same as in table 5.

26 In some cases, unconditional transfers are given on a per-capita basis. In other cases, unconditional transfers provide equalization, as noted earlier.

27 Conditional grants are fungible, however, in the sense that, even though they come with strings attached, there is no guarantee that the recipient will spend the funds on what the donor government intended. This is particularly true for large cities, which are more likely to be spending substantial funds already in the area specified by the donor government.

28 See Bird (2011) and Blöchliger and Rabesona (2009).

29 In some countries (such as Norway, Korea, and Japan) where sub-central governments have the authority to set tax rates, they set the same tax rate across the country (see Blöchliger and Rabesona 2009).

30 Other possibilities for addressing externalities include road tolls or amalgamation of municipalities affected by the spillover. See Kitchen and Slack (2016).

31 Multilevel governance carries significant possible benefits, including the ability to profit from pooled resources while still creating opportunity for local input. However, risks of sacrificing accountability and wasting resources also exist (see Horak 2012).

32 The report also suggested that, in the case of Ontario, a review of who does what should begin with health and social services (which includes public health, ambulance services, long-term care, social housing, social assistance, and childcare) because, as noted earlier, cost sharing is common for these services in Ontario and the lines of accountability are blurred. The Who Does What series at IMFG reviews many of these services (IMFG, n.d.)

33 For more information on the Fiscal Federalism Policy Network, see Canada West Foundation (2020).

34 US evidence suggests that the cost of inner-city services used by people who live in the suburbs and commute to work exceeds, sometimes substantially, what they pay for inner-city services. Local income and consumption-based taxes could be used to alleviate this disparity. See Chernick (2002) and Chernick and Tkacheva (2002).

35 Many of the revenue sources set out above are practical only when employed on a metropolitan-wide or region-wide basis and hence require some form of metropolitan or regional government. In a jurisdictionally fragmented area, local property taxes and user charges are probably the only feasible own-source revenues.

36 The property tax will also have an impact on decisions about where to live or work, where to locate a business, and other economic decisions.

37 For example, a residential property tax may discourage investment in housing improvements; a retail sales tax may discourage consumption of goods, etc. A mix of taxes can reduce the distortion of any one tax by keeping each tax rate low.

38 The authors also argue that greater revenue diversity means a more complex tax system that most people do not understand and thus there may be less resistance to tax increases.

39 For more on intergovernmental relations, see chapters 2 and 4 in this volume. For a discussion of municipalities having a seat at the table, see Hachard (2022).

40 Large Canadian cities do, however, enjoy more fiscal autonomy than many other cities around the world because of their greater reliance on own-source revenues compared to intergovernmental transfers.

41 Municipalities also still face governance challenges. See, for example, Hachard (2020).

REFERENCES

Altus Group Economic Consulting. 2014. *Economic Implications of the Municipal Land-Transfer Tax in Toronto* (prepared for the Ontario Real Estate Board).

Bahl, Roy. 2011. "Financing Metropolitan Areas." In *Local Government Finance: The Challenges of the 21st Century, Second Global Report on Decentralization and Local Democracy, by United Cities and Local Governments*, 285–308. Cheltenham, UK: Edward Elgar.

Bahl, Roy, and Richard M. Bird. 2018. *Fiscal Decentralization and Local Finance in Developing Countries*. Cheltenham, UK: Edward Elgar. https://doi.org/10.4337/9781786435309.

Bazel, Philip, and Jack M. Mintz. 2014. "The Free Ride Is Over: Why Cities, and Citizens, Must Start Paying for Much-Needed Infrastructure." *SSP Research Paper* 7, no. 14: 1–31. Calgary: University of Calgary School of Public Policy. https://doi.org/10.11575/sppp.v7i0.42466.

Béland, Daniel, Bev Dahlby, and Steve Orsini. 2020. "COVID-19 Will Force a Change to Canada's Fiscal Arrangements." *Policy Options*, May 7, 2020. https://policyoptions.irpp.org/magazines /may-2020/covid-19-will-force-a-change-to-canadas-fiscal-arrangements/.

Bird, Richard, M. 2011a. "Subnational Taxation in Developing Countries: A Review of the Literature." *Journal of International Commerce, Economics and Policy, World Scientific* 2, no. 1 (June): 131–61. https://doi.org/10.1142/S1793993311000269.

———. 2011b. "Are There Trends in Local Finance? A Cautionary Note on Comparative Studies and Normative Models of Local Government Finance." In *IMFG Papers on Municipal Finance and Governance*, no. 1. Toronto: Institute on Municipal Finance and Governance.

Bird, Richard M., and Enid Slack. 2014. "Local Taxes and Local Expenditures in Developing Countries: Strengthening the Wicksellian Connection." *Public Administration and Development* 34, no. 5 (December), 359–69. https://doi.org/10.1002/pad.1695.

———. 2017. *Financing Infrastructure: Who Should Pay?* Montreal: McGill-Queen's University Press. https://doi.org/10.1515/9780773552449.

———. 2021. "Provincial-Local Equalization in Canada: Time for a Change?" In *IMFG Papers on Municipal Finance and Governance*, no. 57. Toronto: Institute on Municipal Finance and Governance.

Bird, Richard M., and Enid Slack, eds. 2015. *Is Your City Healthy? Measuring Urban Fiscal Health.* Toronto: Institute on Municipal Finance and Governance and Institute of Public Administration of Canada.

Blais, Pamela. 2010. *Perverse Cities: Hidden Subsidies, Wonky Policy, and Urban Sprawl.* Vancouver: UBC Press. https://doi.org/10.59962/9780774818971.

Blöchliger, Hansjörg, and Junghun Kim. 2016. *Fiscal Federalism 2016: Making Decentralization Work.* Paris: OECD and Korea Institute of Public Finance. https://doi.org/10.1787/9789264254053-en.

Blöchliger, Hansjörg, and José Maria Pinero Campos. 2011. *Tax Competition between Sub-Central Governments.* Paris: OECD.

Blöchliger, Hansjörg, and Josette Rabesona. 2009. *The Fiscal Autonomy of Sub-central Governments: An Update.* Paris: OECD.

Boadway, Robin, and Anwar Shah. 2009. *Fiscal Federalism: Principles and Practices of Multiorder Governance.* Cambridge: Cambridge University Press. https://doi.org/10.1017/CBO9780511626883.

Bradford, Neil. 2018. "A National Urban Policy for Canada? The Implicit Federal Agenda." *IRPP Policy Insight*, no. 24. Montreal: Institute for Research on Public Policy.

———. 2020. "Policy in Place: Revisiting Canada's Tri-level Agreements." In *IMFG Papers on Municipal Finance and Governance*, no. 50. Toronto: Institute on Municipal Finance and Governance.

Canada. 2024. "For Partners & Builders." Infrastructure Canada. Last updated April 9, 2024. https://www.infrastructure.gc.ca/partners-partenaires-eng.html.

Canada West Foundation. 2020. "About: Fiscal Federalism Policy Network (FFPN)." July 30, 2020. https://cwf.ca/research/publications/fiscal-federalism-policy-network/.

Chernick, Howard. 2002. "The Effect of Commuters on the Fiscal Costs of the District of Columbia." Mimeograph, 36 pages.

Chernick, Howard, and Olesya Tkacheva. 2002. "The Commuter Tax and the Fiscal Cost of Commuters in New York City." *State Tax Notes* 25, no. 6 (August): 451–6. https://ssrn.com/abstract=321081.

Chernick, Howard, Adam Langley, and Andrew Reschovsky. 2010. "Revenue Diversification and the Financing of Large American Central Cities." In *IMFG Papers on Municipal Finance and Governance*, no. 5. Toronto: Institute on Municipal Finance and Governance.

Clayton, Frank A. 2015. *City of Toronto's Land Transfer Tax – Good, Bad or Merely Tolerable?* Toronto: Ryerson University, Centre for Urban Research and Land Development.

Côté, André, and Michael Fenn. 2014. "Provincial-Municipal Relations in Ontario: Approaching an Inflection Point." In *IMFG Papers on Municipal Finance and Government*, no. 17. Toronto: Institute on Municipal Finance and Governance. https://tspace.library.utoronto.ca/bitstream/1807/81250/1/imfg_paper_17_cote_fenn_May_22_2014.pdf.

Dachis, Benjamin. 2012. *Stuck in Place: The Effect of Land Transfer Taxes on Housing Transactions.* Toronto: C.D. Howe Institute. https://doi.org/10.2139/ssrn.2169978.

Dachis, Benjamin, Gilles Duranton, and Matthew Turner. 2008. *Sand in the Gears: Evaluating the Effects of Toronto's Land Transfer Tax.* Toronto: C.D. Howe Institute.

Dahlby, Bev, and Melville McMillan. 2019. "What Is the Role of Property and Property-Related Taxes? An Assessment of Municipal Property Taxes, Land Transfer Taxes, and Tax Increment Financing." In *Funding the Canadian City*, edited by Enid Slack, Lisa Philipps, Lindsay M. Tedds, and Heather L. Evans, 45–73. Toronto: Canadian Tax Foundation and Institute on Municipal Finance and Governance.

Eidelman, Gabriel, Tomas Hachard, and Enid Slack. 2019. "In It Together: Clarifying Provincial-Municipal Responsibilities in Ontario." *Ontario 360 Policy Papers*, January 23, 2020. https://on360.ca/policy-papers/in-it-together-clarifying-provincial-municipal-responsibilities-in-ontario/.

Fenn, Michael, and Harry Kitchen. 2016. *Bringing Sustainability to Ontario's Water System: A Quarter Century of Progress, with Much Left to Do.* Report prepared for the Ontario Sewer and Watermain Construction Association.

Financial Accountability Office of Ontario (FAO). 2021. *Municipal Infrastructure: A Review of Ontario's Municipal Infrastructure and an Assessment of the State of Repair.* Toronto: Queen's Printer for Ontario.

Found, Adam. 2016. *Tapping the Land: Tax Increment Financing for Infrastructure.* Toronto: C.D. Howe Institute. https://www.cdhowe.org/public-policy-research/tapping-land-tax-increment-financing-infrastructure.

———. 2019. "Development Charges in Ontario: Is Growth Paying for Growth?" In *IMFG Papers on Municipal Finance and Governance*, no. 41. Toronto: Institute on Municipal Finance and Governance.

Hachard, Tomas. 2020. "It Takes Three: Making Space for Cities in Canadian Federalism." In *IMFG Perspectives*, no. 31. Toronto: Institute on Municipal Finance and Governance.

———. 2022. "A Seat at the Table: Municipalities and Intergovernmental Relations in Canada." In *IMFG Papers on Municipal Finance and Governance*, no. 59. Toronto: Institute on Municipal Finance and Governance.

Haider, Murtaza, and Liam Donaldson. 2016. "Can Tax Increment Financing Support Transportation Infrastructure Investment?" In *IMFG Papers on Municipal Finance and Governance,* no. 25. Toronto: Institute on Municipal Finance and Governance.

Haider, Murtaza, Amar Anwar, and Cynthia Holmes. 2016. "Did the Land Transfer Tax Reduce Housing Sales in Toronto?" In *IMFG Papers on Municipal Finance and Governance*, no. 27. Toronto: Institute on Municipal Finance and Governance.

Horak, Martin. 2012. "Conclusion: Understanding Multilevel Governance in Canada's Cities." In *Sites of Governance: Multilevel Governance and Policy Making in Canada's Big Cities*, edited by Robert Young and Martin Horak, 349–70. Montreal: McGill-Queen's University Press. https://doi.org/10.1515/9780773586918-013.

IMFG. 2018. "A Check-up on Toronto's Fiscal Health, 2018." Toronto: Institute on Municipal Finance and Governance, University of Toronto. https://imfg.munkschool.utoronto.ca/research/a-check-up-on-torontos-fiscal-health-2018/.

———. 2020. "Charting a New Path: Does Toronto Need More Autonomy?" In *IMFG Forum*, no. 10. Toronto: Institute on Municipal Finance and Governance.

———. n.d. "Who Does What Series." Accessed May 22, 2024. https://imfg.munkschool.utoronto.ca/who-does-what-series/.

International Monetary Fund. 2024. "Government Finance Statistics (GFS)." IMF Data. Last updated May 18, 2024. https://data.imf.org/?sk=a0867067-d23c-4ebc-ad23-d3b015045405.

Kitchen, Harry. 2016. "Is 'Charter-City Status' a Solution for Financing City Services in Canada – Or Is That a Myth?" *SPP Research Papers* 9, no. 2. Calgary: The School of Public Policy, University of Calgary.

Kitchen, Harry, and Enid Slack. 2016. *More Tax Sources for Canada's Largest Cities: Why, What, and How?* Toronto: Institute on Municipal Finance and Governance, University of Toronto.

Kitchen, Harry, and Robin Lindsey. 2013. *Financing Roads and Public Transit in the Greater Toronto and Hamilton Area.* Report for the Residential and Civil Construction Alliance of Ontario. https://rccao.com/research/files/RCCAO_JAN2013_REPORT_LOWRES.pdf.

Kitchen, Harry, Enid Slack, and Tomas Hachard. 2019. "Property Taxes in Canada: Current Issues and Future Prospects." In *IMFG Perspectives*, no. 27. Toronto: Institute on Municipal Finance and Governance.

Kitchen, Harry M., and Almos Tassonyi. 2012. "Municipal Taxes and User Fees." In *Tax Policy in Canada*, edited by Heather Kerr, Ken McKenzie, and Jack Mintz, 9:1–34. Toronto: Canadian Tax Foundation.

Kneebone, R.D., and McKenzie, K.J. 2003. "Removing the Shackles: Some Modest, and Immodest, Proposals to Pay for Cities." In *Paying for Cities: The Search for Sustainable Municipal Revenues*, edited by Paul Boothe, 43–77. Edmonton: Institute for Public Economics, University of Alberta.

Liberati, Paulo, and Agnese Sacchi. 2013. "Tax Decentralization and Local Government Size." *Public Choice* 157, nos. 1–2 (October): 183–205. https://doi.org/10.1007/s11127-012-9937-9.

Martinez-Vazquez, Jorge, Santiago Lago-Penas, and Agnese Sacchi. 2015. "The Impact of Fiscal Decentralization: A Survey." International Center for Public Policy Working Paper 15-02. Vigo: Universida de Vigo. https://doi.org/10.2139/ssrn.2633869.

Moore, Aaron. 2013. "Trading Density for Benefits: Toronto and Vancouver Compared." In *IMFG Papers on Municipal Finance and Governance*, no. 13. Toronto: Institute on Municipal Finance and Governance.

OECD. 2020. *The Territorial Impact of COVID-19: Managing the Crisis across Levels of Government*. June 16, 2020. https://read.oecd-ilibrary.org/view/?ref=128_128287-5agkkojaaa&title=The-territorial-impact-of-covid-19-managing-the-crisis-across-levels-of-government.

Philipps, Lisa, Enid Slack, Lindsay M. Tedds, and Heather L. Evans. 2019. "Introduction." In *Funding the Canadian City*, edited by Enid Slack, Lisa Philipps, Lindsay M. Tedds, and Heather L. Evans, 1–20. Toronto: Canadian Tax Foundation and Institute on Municipal Finance and Governance.

Slack, Enid. 2002. *Municipal Finance and the Pattern of Urban Growth*. Commentary no. 160. Toronto: C.D. Howe Institute.

———. 2011. "Financing Large Cities and Metropolitan Areas." In *IMFG Papers on Municipal Finance and Governance*, no. 3. Toronto: Institute on Municipal Finance and Governance.

———. 2016a. *International Comparison of Global City Financing*. London: London Finance Commission.

———. 2016b. "Local Finances and Fiscal Equalization Schemes in Comparative Perspective." In *Das Teilen beherrschen, Analysen zur Reform des Finanzausgleichs 2019*, edited by René Geißler, Felix Knupling, Sabine Kropp, and Joachim Weiland, 283–312. Berlin: Nomos. https://doi.org/10.5771/9783845259284-283.

———. 2017. "How Much Local Fiscal Autonomy Do Cities Have? A Comparison of Eight Cities around the World." In *IMFG Perspectives*, no. 18. Toronto: Institute on Municipal Finance and Governance.

Slack, Enid, and André Côté. 2014. "Is Toronto Fiscally Healthy? A Check-up on the City's Finances." In *IMFG Perspectives*, no. 7. Toronto: Institute on Municipal Finance and Governance.

Slack, Enid, and Richard M. Bird. 2019. "Municipal Taxation in Canada' Federal System: Linking Taxes and Expenditures?" In *Funding the Canadian City*, edited by Enid Slack, Lisa Philipps, Lindsay M. Tedds, and Heather L. Evans, 21–43. Toronto: Canadian Tax Foundation.

Slack, Enid, and Tomas Hachard. 2020. "Now, with a Deal Made to Help Cities, the Work Begins." *Policy Options*, August 17, 2020. https://policyoptions.irpp.org/magazines/august-2020/now-with-a-deal-made-to-help-cities-the-work-begins/.

Smart, Michael. 2012. "The Reform of the Business Property Tax in Ontario: An Evaluation." In *IMFG Papers on Municipal Finance and Governance*, no. 10. Toronto: Institute on Municipal Finance and Governance.

———. 2020. "Defund This." *Finances of the Nation*, June 30, 2020. https://financesofthenation.ca/2020/06/30/defund-this/.

Statistics Canada. 2024. "Table 10-10-0015-01: Statement of Government Operations and Balance Sheet, Government Finance Statistics (x 1,000,000)." Data. Last updated March 25, 2024. https://doi.org/10.25318/1010001501-eng.

Tassonyi, Almos, and Harry M. Kitchen. 2021. "Addressing the Fairness of Municipal User Fee Policy." In *IMFG Papers on Municipal Finance and Governance*, no. 54. Toronto: Institute on Municipal Finance and Governance.

Tassonyi, Almos, Richard M. Bird, and Enid Slack. 2015. "Can GTA Municipalities Raise Property Taxes? An Analysis of Tax Competition and Revenue Hills." In *IMFG Papers on Municipal Finance and Governance*, no. 20. Toronto: Institute on Municipal Finance and Governance.

Taylor, Zack, and Alec Dobson. 2020. "Power and Purpose: Canadian Municipal Law in Transition." In *IMFG Papers on Municipal Finance and Governance*, no. 47. Toronto: Institute on Municipal Finance and Governance.

Taylor, Zack, and Neil Bradford. 2020. "Governing Canadian Cities." In *Canadian Cities in Transition: Understanding Contemporary Urbanism*, edited by Markus Moos, Tara Vinodrai, and Ryan Walker, 33–50. Don Mills, ON: Oxford University Press.

Wilson, Matthew. 2019. "Municipal Money Matters: Our Fiscal Future." Presentation to AMO Annual Conference, August 19, 2019. https://web.archive.org/web/20200108114130/http://www.amo.on.ca/AMO-PDFs/Events/19/Monday/MoneyMatters-Conference-fiscal-issues-session.aspx.

Youngman, Joan. 2011. TIF at a Turning Point: Defining Debt Down. Cambridge, MA: Lincoln Institute of Land Policy.

CHAPTER SEVEN

Local Leadership and Forms of Municipal Government

Kristin R. Good, Kate Graham, and Jesse Helmer

It is often said that local government is "closer" or "closest to the people" among governments in Canada. This phrase is generally intended to describe the more personal or proximate nature of local representation and municipal services; that city hall is geographically closer to where most people live than are other legislative houses; that people are more likely to actually know and interact with their elected officials as they work within their community; or, that municipal governments provide the more "day to day" services that residents rely upon with high frequency such as water, wastewater, garbage disposal, roads, transit, parks, and more.

Closer also can refer to the more accessible and familiar style of local governance. Municipal council meetings are generally open for anyone to attend, and residents can walk into most city halls in the country without barrier or obstruction. The same cannot be said about visits to provincial or territorial legislatures or Parliament Hill, where advanced invitations are sometimes required, and visitors are met with extensive security screenings and highly limited facility access. Unlike at the local level, many of the most important discussions within provincial, territorial, and federal governments – such as cabinet conversations – are not only entirely inaccessible but also hold no public record. For many Canadians, the prime minister seems like something of a celebrity who lives and works far away; the mayor, on the other hand, may live right around the corner and eats, shops, and enjoys the same local amenities they do.

In every Canadian city, the mayor is an important figure, but their formal power varies significantly across cities and is a current subject of debate in Canada. Mayors lead elected councils, some are described as chief executives of their municipal corporations, and they are generally the most well-known local officials. Since leaders at the provincial and federal levels are elected indirectly and big-city mayors are elected directly by the entire city, they are elected by more people than any federal or provincial politician in Canada. Consider that in Toronto's mayoral election in 2022, former mayor John Tory (2014–23) received 342,158 votes to become mayor (City of Toronto 2022) whereas in the 2021 federal election, Justin Trudeau, Canada's prime minister, was elected in his riding of Papineau (in Quebec) with only 22,848 votes, becoming prime minister by virtue of leading the party deemed most likely to be able to hold the confidence of the House of Commons (Elections Canada, n.d.). In times of celebration and crisis, mayors are the voices of their cities on the provincial, national, and international stage. They are praised for their communities' successes and blamed for their failures. In many ways, the mayor is "the living symbol of [their] city" (Ruchelman 1969, 4).

Despite the significance of the position, remarkably little is known about the role of Canadian mayors, including as leaders of municipal councils. In Canada, local institutions are not only different from other orders of government by being closer to the people and more transparent. Many are also characterized by a lack of clear division between and articulation of distinct executive and legislative powers on local councils, making many mayors institutionally "weak."

This differs from both American mayor-council systems in which mayors possess clear executive authority as well as Westminster parliamentary forms of government at the federal and provincial levels in Canada, under which a cabinet of ministers appointed by the governor general on the advice of the first minister (prime minister or premier) possesses clear executive authority, debating and making decisions in private. At these parliamentary levels, the first minister has become so powerful that some argue that they now often bypass not only Parliament but also the cabinet as a decision-making body (Savoie 1999). In stark contrast with Westminster-style parliamentary governance in Canada, with some limited exceptions, including matters related to personnel, land acquisition, and negotiations, meetings of municipal councils are open to the public, and decisions are subject to council debate and approval.

However, as Kate Graham (2018) observes, there is no uniform job description for mayors; in fact, there are more than fifty pieces of provincial legislation in Canada prescribing duties of mayors, not including municipal bylaws and policies. Although many Canadian mayors are weak in terms of formal structures of government (Sancton 1994), there are important variations in mayoral power in Canada, with mayors in Montreal (and other cities in Quebec) and Winnipeg possessing significant additional power relative to councillors. More recently, several large municipalities in Ontario were granted what is known as strong-mayor powers, including extensive power to shape the city's administration, propose the budget, and veto council decisions. Moreover, as we discuss here, some mayors become stronger and more influential through their personality, popularity, and their coalition-building efforts. This strength does not come from a strong-mayor system; instead, it comes through the leadership efforts of Canadian mayors who are sometimes able to overcome their institutional weaknesses through coalition-building on councils, developing relationships with leaders in civil society (establishing governance relationships), and networking with other mayors in a variety of national (or even international) municipal associations. Mayors are key actors in creating and maintaining the multilevel governance relationships conceptualized by Martin Horak in chapter 4. Furthermore, although many elections are non-partisan in Canada, some mayors lead coalitions of electors in independent local parties in British Columbia and Quebec (discussed more in chapter 8), provinces that are home to some of Canada's largest cities and municipalities (both urban and suburban).

This chapter explores the origin and evolution of Canadian systems of local leadership, highlighting important questions that continue to animate debates over the institutions and practices that govern mayor and council roles. We interrogate how Canadian municipal forms compare with each other and with international jurisdictions. Are Canadian mayors generally weak, and if so, would strengthening their formal powers be a desirable reform? What are the potential trade-offs involved in this kind of institutional change? Is there a clear trend toward a particular form of city government internationally, and what can this teach us about what may lie ahead for Canadian experiments with decision-making structures?

The chapter begins by providing an overview of municipal council forms in Western liberal democracies, outlining what Poul Erik Mouritzen and James Svara, leading scholars of the forms of local government, call the four "constitutions of local governments" (Mouritzen and Svara 2002, 3). Next, we discuss the popular conception of Canadian forms of local government as weak-mayor systems, and then we look at a wide variety of mayoral powers in Canada. Specifically, we draw on original research conducted by Kate Graham (2018) to examine the role of the mayor in the largest Canadian cities by population in each province: Vancouver, British Columbia; Calgary, Alberta; Saskatoon, Saskatchewan; Winnipeg, Manitoba; Toronto, Ontario; Montreal, Quebec; Saint John, New Brunswick; Halifax, Nova Scotia; Charlottetown, Prince Edward Island; and St. John's, Newfoundland and Labrador. We argue that although many municipalities reflect features of council-manager systems and have institutionally weak mayors, there are also important exceptions and extensive variation in how power is constituted in municipal governing structures. Following this, the chapter describes examples of strong mayoral leadership in the absence of strong executive powers, arguing that big-city mayors can use their platforms to build coalitions and the capacity to address significant policy challenges even in areas beyond their jurisdictional authority. The final section takes up the debate raised most recently by reforms in Ontario about whether strong-mayor powers are required to govern big cities in Canada. The chapter concludes with a summary of main points and with brief observations about international trends in reforming mayoral powers.

MUNICIPAL CONSTITUTIONS IN COMPARATIVE PERSPECTIVE

As Poul Erik Mouritzen and James H. Svara (2002) observe, it is challenging to categorize municipal council forms based on existing governmental models in particular countries because they evolve through time and retain the same label (55). Therefore, discussion of forms must consider ideal types that vary significantly across countries, within countries, and over time.

Mouritzen and Svara (2002, 55–6) identify four ideal types:

1 **The strong-mayor form,** in which "the elected mayor controls the majority of the city council and is legally and in actuality in full charge of all executive functions. The CEO serves at the mayor's will and can be hired and fired without the consent of any other politicians or political bodies. The mayor can hire political appointees to help with any function."

2 **The committee-leader form,** in which "One person is clearly 'the political leader' of the municipality – with or without the title of mayor. He or she may or may not control the council. Executive powers are shared. The political leader may have responsibility for some executive functions but others will rest with collegiate bodies, that is, standing committees, composed of elected politicians and with the CEO. In this form, there is a more even blending of the three principles [discussed below] than in other forms."

3 **The collective form:** "The decision center is one collegiate body, the executive committee that is responsible for all executive functions. The executive committee consists of locally elected politicians and the mayor, who presides. In this form, greater emphasis is given to the laymen principle (albeit a select body of laymen), and political leadership and professionalism are accommodated to it."

4 **The council-manager form:** "All executive functions are in the hands of a professional administrator – the city manager – who is appointed by the city council, which has general authority over policy but is restricted from involvement in administrative matters. The council is a relatively small body, headed by a mayor who formally has presiding and ceremonial functions only. In this form, emphasis is given to professionalism with constricted layman rule and limited political leadership."

According to Mouritzen and Svara (2002), all council forms reflect different balances between the principles of *laymen rule*, *political leadership*, and *professionalism*. *Laymen rule* is the principle that "citizens elected for political office should be involved effectively and intensively in making decisions," a foundational notion in any representative democracy (51). A representative is a link between citizens and government, serving as their advocate and "informal ombudsman" to improve the municipality's responsiveness to citizen concerns (51). However, the extent to which they can play their role varies by council form, with Mouritzen and Svara noting that "in some American and Australian cities … council members are not permitted by charter to communicate with any staff member other than the city manager," limiting their roles as ombudsmen with staff (51). This rule is common to council-manager forms of local government and applies in some Canadian municipalities. For instance, s. 34 (2) of the Halifax Regional Municipality Charter specifies that council's communication with the administration should go through the chief administrative officer unless it is for the purposes of obtaining or providing information, which could no doubt be interpreted creatively to advocate on behalf of citizens but limits this interaction nonetheless.

Mouritzen and Svara (2002, 52) observe that *political leadership* is the principle that elected officials should inject value choices, energy, passion, dynamism, and innovation into policy-making: "politicians make a distinctive contribution by raising controversial issues, proposing innovative plans and projects, setting direction, generating resources, making compromises, and mobilizing citizens – in short, making things move."

The principle of *professionalism* underscores the importance of expertise and a long-term strategy for policy-making. The organization of the administrative aspect of municipal governments varies considerably across local government forms. The administration of many cities is headed by a chief administrative officer or city manager, a generalist that provides administrative guidance in all of the areas of municipal policy and action. These administrators are unlike those at any other level of government in a variety of ways, such as their high level of unmediated interaction with elected officials. In some places, the chief administrator directly controls the administration rather than serving as an adviser to politicians, as is the case at other levels (Mouritzen and Svara 2002, 9–10). Furthermore, due to their proximity to communities, like elected officials, they have extensive interaction with residents and a variety of groups in civil society (business groups and NGOs, for instance) (10). Writing about the role of the CAO in the Canadian context, David Siegel argues that a strong CAO "has the ability to move the municipality forward by interacting in a mutually influential way with and motivating council, external stakeholders, and organizational subordinates" (2015, loc. 788). He describes the leadership task as operating in three directions – "down," "up," and "out" – where leading down refers to the traditional role of leading subordinates (staff) in the organization, leading up refers to the CAO's relationship with council, and leading out refers to their relationship with stakeholders in civil society, other orders of government, and the media (in other words, a leading role in *governance*) (loc. 829, 841).

Different governmental systems strike different balances among these three principles. We provide examples of each form below, paying particular attention to strong-mayor and council-manager systems, the two municipal constitutions most dominant in the United States and most influential in debates about council forms in Canada.

Strong-Mayor Forms

Municipalities that fall into the Franco category of local government, discussed in chapter 2, tend to share a preference for strong mayors. Examples include France, Spain, Portugal, and Italy. Mouritzen and Svara (2002) also place the United States' mayor-council forms in this category.

The mayor is a focal point of the French system of local government, the "cornerstone of French territorial administration" (Berg and Rao 2005, 12). In France, mayors generally hold all executive powers, from the power to create and introduce the budget for council approval to the power to control the administration. They are supported by council-selected deputy mayors who are nonetheless controlled by the mayor since they determine which powers to delegate to them (Mouritzen and Svara 2002, 57). French mayors have become even more powerful since reforms toward decentralization were introduced in 1992 and some have been empowered with formal powers by communities of municipalities (in forms of regional governance), which has led to the emergence of a kind of "supermayor" of a collectivity of municipalities (Berg and Rao 2005, 12). In the United Kingdom, directly elected metro-mayors that govern combined local authority areas (and that coexist with local authority mayors in some cases) took office in May 2017 after signing devolution agreements with the government, and others have followed since then (Sandford 2022, 17), joining the list of strong mayors. Examples include a metro-mayor for Greater Manchester and for the Liverpool City Region.

In Spain, mayors also possess extensive executive powers: they chair council, create its agenda, formulate the budget, advise the municipality's administration, and implement council policies (Mouritzen and Svara 2002, 57). They also appoint executive committees in communities larger than 5,000 and generally control the committee system (57). Moreover, the party system in Spanish municipalities provides further support to mayors as they come from parties with majority support on local councils in close to two-thirds of cases (57). For these reasons, Mouritzen and Svara describe Spanish municipalities as "very close to the strong-mayor type" (57).

The Central and Eastern European countries of Poland and Hungary also have executive mayors that fall into the strong-mayor category (Bäck, Heinelt, and Magnier 2006, 34). In their assessment of reforms in local council forms in eleven countries in Europe, Rikke Berg and Nirmala Rao (2005, 9) note that some European countries such as the Netherlands, Germany, and Britain have taken radical steps to strengthen the executive with "moves away from 'parliamentary' to more presidential models of government, or toward the concentration of powers in smaller executives."

In the American literature, the terms "strong mayor" and "weak mayor" refer to variants of the mayor-council form, reflecting the extent to which executive authority is concentrated in the office of the mayor or shared with council. They do not refer to the difference between mayoral-council and council-manager forms in that literature (as some Canadians assume – see Graham 2018). A mayor-council form of "strong mayor" has extensive executive authority, including the unilateral ability to appoint and dismiss city managers and department heads, prepare budgets, and direct the efforts of departments. A "weak-mayor" model is characterized by a fragmentation of power, a more limited ability to appoint or remove staff (as some are directly elected and/or appointed by other officials), and a more limited role in preparing the budget. In the United States, "weak mayors" are those in mayor-council forms who lack integrated administrative control over the operation of city government (Svara 1990, 47). However, when placed in a broader comparative perspective, the American mayor-council system is considered a form of strong-mayor system since it emphasizes (to relative degrees) the principle of political leadership (and subordinates laymen rule and professionalism to this principle). Given its emphasis on the principle of political leadership, American municipalities with mayor-council forms are also more likely to hold partisan elections. Finally, Kate Graham (2018) underscores another important design feature of American mayor-council systems: they are based on the principle of checks and balances, whereby the council serves as a check on the executive power of the mayor (see also Ridley and Notling 1934, 1; Svara 1994, xxi).

New York City is an example of a mayor-council system. S. 1 of the New York City Charter describes the mayor as the city's chief executive officer with the power to appoint and remove heads of departments, including "heads of administrations, departments, all commissioners and all other officers not elected by the people" (s. 6). These include the heads of more than forty agencies running police, fire, education, sanitation, health, and other services (Bergin 2021). The mayor also controls public schools. In addition, New York City's mayor appoints deputy mayors who hold "such duties and responsibilities as the mayor determines" (s. 7), a commonality with French mayors' powers described above. Furthermore, New York City's mayor possesses general powers described as "all the powers vested in the city, except as otherwise provided by law," is "responsible for the effectiveness and integrity of city government operations," and has the powers of a "finance board" (in s. 8). The mayor oversees budget preparation, which is then subject to negotiation with the city council (Bergin 2021). The mayor can also propose bylaws to either be passed by council or enacted through executive order (Bergin 2021). They possess a veto over legislation passed by council, which can only be overridden by a two-thirds majority vote of the council (Bergin 2021). Additionally, New York City mayors manage relationships with state and federal governments and oversee major planning functions and housing policy. An example of a mayoral intervention in housing policy was former New York City Mayor de Blasio's (2014–21) Mandatory Inclusionary Housing initiative that was enacted through changes to zoning regulations (Bergin 2021). As a journalist describes the role, New York City's mayor "also functions as the chief influencer with a citywide and national bully pulpit," noting that "the job is often referred to as the second most important, and difficult job, in American politics and government" (Bergin 2021). Importantly, there are significant constraints on the mayor's power to raise taxes. Specifically, the mayor needs council's approval to raise property taxes and the state's approval for increases to other city taxes, such as the "Millionaire's Mansion" tax (a land transfer tax on properties sold in the city that are valued over US$1 million) and personal income taxes (Bergin 2021).

Committee-Leader Form

The committee-leader form is employed by Denmark, Sweden, and Great Britain, although English mayors who are elected may be considered strong mayors (Bäck, Heinelt, and Magnier 2006, 34).[1] In Denmark, the city council is organized into an executive committee, and standing committees are elected by city council on a "proportional basis" (based on the partisan composition of council). A finance committee prepares the budget, and standing committees are responsible for the immediate administration of areas in their purview (Mouritzen and Svara 2002, 60). Although the mayor can oversee the administration and is accountable for the implementation of municipal policies, they cannot override the standing committees (60). In 1998, the mayors in three of Denmark's largest cities, Copenhagen, Aalborg, and Odense, possessed stronger executive powers (cabinets) and chose to move to the more collective form of decision-making described here (committees) (Berg 2005, 85).

Collective Form

Belgium and the Netherlands employ the collective form of municipal government, in which power rests with an executive committee elected by council that possesses executive authority (Mouritzen and Svara 2002, 61). Crucially, municipal executive committees in both places act on behalf of a central or provincial government in some areas, and the mayors are appointed by these governments (62). In the case of Belgium, the mayor is appointed by the Crown upon recommendation from council and from among elected members of council (62). In the Netherlands, the mayor is also appointed by the central government and is an outsider (not an elected member of council) (62). This direct connection to the centre stands out among the council forms.

Council-Manager Form

The final form is the council-manager form. It is employed in Australia, where elected representatives (council) possess *"undivided authority to determine the policy of the municipality"* and *"the city manager has full executive authority over the administrative organization"* (Mouritzen and Svara 2002, 64, emphasis added). Ireland also employs this system and has ceremonial mayors (Bäck, Heinelt, and Magnier 2006, 34). The mayor is weak and "presides over council and performs ceremonial functions" (Mouritzen and Svara 2002, 64). In fact, there is a rotation of the mayoralty among councillors on a yearly basis in many municipalities in Ireland (64).

The council-manager form is now the predominant form of local government in the United States. According to Graham (2018), this model is based on the principle of unity. Power is concentrated in a legislative body (council as a whole) which controls the executive (led by an appointed professional manager, not the mayor) (Svara and Watson 2010). There are no checks and balances in this form, as the appointed manager serves at the pleasure of the council and has no power to check the council (Svara 1994).

The City of Austin, Texas, is an example of a city that is governed using a council-manager system. As the city's official website describes, the "Mayor *and* City Council are responsible for all legislative functions of the City" (emphasis added) and "they appoint a professional City Manager who operates much like a CEO in private-sector businesses and who is tasked with carrying out City Council's legislative and policy objectives" (City of Austin, n.d.). The City of Austin shifted from a "commissioner" system to the council-manager system in 1924 with five members elected at large and with the mayor selected by councillors at their first meeting (Blodgett and Hogg, n.d.). The model has evolved over time as the size of council expanded: councillors are now elected by district, and the mayor is now elected at large (Blodgett and Hogg, n.d.). The city manager's extensive responsibilities in the City of Austin are also listed on the city's website and are worth listing here as they illustrate the extensive power vested in American city managers in the council-manager system. The Austin city manager is responsible for:

- Preparing a $4.2 billion budget for Council consideration and managing its passage
- Managing a City staff of more than 14,000 including overseeing recruiting and hiring
- Directing operations
- Recommending policies and programs to City Council, and carrying out Council policies
- Spearheading key initiatives. (City of Austin, n.d.)

Note that the city manager (not the political leadership) prepares the budget and is responsible for providing leadership on key issues.

Another distinguishing feature of the council-manager systems is that these systems tend to be adopted in places with a non-partisan tradition, which is exceptional when one canvasses local elections globally. The link between council-manager systems and non-partisan elections is logical given that they privilege the principle of professionalism over politics or "political leadership."

PARTISANSHIP AND LOCAL LEADERSHIP

As we discuss more in chapter 8, in Canada only two (of ten) provincial jurisdictions – British Columbia and Quebec – allow partisan affiliations to be listed on local election ballots, a common measure used to distinguish between partisan and non-partisan elections.[2] However, even in these provinces, local parties are independent rather than connected with parties at other levels. In some cases, they are also significantly less cohesive and described by some as electoral "slates" rather than parties. A strong tradition of non-partisanship is also present in other settler Anglo countries such as the United States and Australia, but it is not present in England, where parties dominate. The existence of parties and their level of cohesiveness is crucial to understanding mayoral power as well as how representation works on council. It is also crucial to understanding Canada's form of multilevel democracy which, as Martin Horak elaborates upon in chapter 4, is highly dis-integrated (see Sellers, Lidstrom, and Bae 2020 for a comparative perspective). However, this lack of integration could allow local governments to tailor their services and decisions to the local context in ways that would be difficult in more "nationalized" systems of multilevel democracy. For instance, in the view of Colin Copus et al. (2013), national party systems can infringe upon local autonomy, noting that local governments tend to develop common, national positions on questions of local development that may be in tension with the principle of local self-government. Furthermore, unlike in systems where a mayor leads a party with a majority on council, in non-partisan contexts, mayors cannot count on support from fellow partisans to lead. Thus, partisanship influences the nature of mayoral leadership (and the CAO's role – see Siegel 2015) in fundamental and multiple ways.

The prevalence of non-partisanship in North America and Australia stands out compared to Europe,[3] where national political parties dominate local elections (Copus et al. 2012, 211; Aars and Ringkjob 2005, 178). One study of the role of national parties in local elections that examined party membership in sixteen countries (fifteen European countries and Israel) found that 94.2 per cent of councillors in municipalities with populations larger than 100,000 held national party memberships (Razin 2013, 54). These figures were as high as 100 per cent in Sweden, Norway, and France (93.8 per cent), Germany (91.2 per cent), and the United Kingdom (95.8 per cent) – all had rates of national partisanship above 90 per cent (54).

Nevertheless, by some measures, partisanship appears widespread at the local level, not only internationally but in Canada as well. Indeed, Peter John and Martin Saiz (1999) find that an average of 77 per cent of mayors in eighteen liberal democracies held national party memberships and that 100 per cent of Canadian mayors were members of parties *at other levels of government*.[4] In the United States, the figure was 86.9 per cent, and in Australia, only 45.8 per cent (50). Nevertheless, according to their measure of local party strength based on mayoral perceptions – which included measures that could potentially capture the informal influence of party politics in formally non-partisan elections including "mentioning one's party in an election," "party's electoral activity," and "more frequent meetings with party officials after the election" – Canada's local party strength was the lowest at 12.89 per cent (53–4). The only other two countries that fell below 60.73 per cent were Australia (23.58 per cent) and the United States (23.66 per cent) (54). This suggests that although Canadian mayors are partisan, a strong non-partisan culture exists at the local level in Canada that leads them to downplay their partisanship. Contrast this with European local politics, where "an *explicit sentiment* or *formal rules* that exclude national parties from being involved in local politics are not part of European local democracy" (Razin 2013, 54).

THE REFORM MOVEMENT IN NORTH AMERICA AND ITS INFLUENCE ON CANADIAN MUNICIPAL INSTITUTIONS

The American reform movement had an enduring influence on Canadian municipal institutions, including the "bundle" of institutional design elements associated with the council-manager form of municipal government. For instance, experts writing on local government are "almost unanimous" in ascribing the origins of municipal non-partisanship in Canada to the influence of ideas from the American reform or Progressive movement that began in the late nineteenth century (Anderson 1972, 5). In the United States, the Progressive Era reforms were presented as rational and merit-based solutions to the political corruption and patronage associated with partisan politics in party-boss-led "machine" cities such as New York City and Chicago. Although corruption also existed in Canadian local governments, the American-style local political machines did not exist in Canada (Tindal et al. 2017, 254). The later adoption of the universal municipal franchise in Canada removed the incentives to develop political machines to mobilize and incorporate the working class and immigrants and to reward their loyalty with patronage appointments (Taylor 2014, 60).

However, other factors may have contributed to municipal reformers' receptiveness to reform institutions and the associated *apolitical conceptions of local democracy* at the turn of the twentieth century, including its low rate of urbanization, the relative homogeneity of its cities, and the level of provincial control over municipalities in Canada (Anderson 1972, 9), all of which may have made more appealing an administrative conception of the municipality guided by the principle of "efficiency" rather than politics.[5]

The largely white, male, property-owning reformers were inspired by conceptions of municipalities as publicly run businesses. Thus, they proposed to attempt to make a clear separation between politics and administration and to empower expert managers to manage local service delivery. Reforms proposed and implemented by the Progressives in Canada included the non-partisan ballot, the city manager system, and the at-large election (Anderson 1972, 16). In at-large systems, the city is not divided into wards or districts (territorial subdivisions) for the purposes of electing councillors but, rather, is treated as a single constituency for the election of both the mayor and councillors. Thus, in such systems, voters vote for as many councillors as there are positions on council. In theory, such systems encourage councillors (and not only the mayor) to adopt a city-wide perspective on issues since the link between a particular neighbourhood or geographical area of the city and a councillor is absent. It avoids the politics of Nimbyism or opposition to development in one's backyard, allowing development decisions that benefit the city as a whole to proceed.

Nevertheless, such systems are arguably less politically responsive since they do not capture the territorial and political diversity of their municipalities. Among the most important critiques of such systems is that they dilute minority votes. Indeed, in the United States, many of the reforms associated with the initial establishment of council-manager systems, including at-large electoral systems, were designed to disempower the working class and immigrants (Judd and Swanstrom 2015, 97). Political parties and the machine politics that they engaged in were also vehicles for the political incorporation of immigrants and minorities. Drawing on the cases of Chicago and San Jose, as well as other examples of machine and reform local governments, the American political scientist Jessica Trounstine (2008) argues that both machine and reform coalitions employed biasing strategies to maintain their dominance over time. Changing the rules of the game was a key strategy of reform coalitions. In other words, in both cases, the institutions and practices of democracy were biased in favour of particular interests – upper classes and non-minorities in the case of council-manager systems and immigrants and party supporters in the case of machines. We must, therefore, always be aware that how we design municipal institutions could have the effect of empowering some groups and interests at the expense of others.

Historically, many Canadian municipalities adopted the at-large method of election but gradually changed to ward-based systems (Graham, Phillips, and Maslove 1998, 97). Currently, at-large elections are the default option only for municipalities in British Columbia (Sancton 2015, 189). The enduring influence of the Progressive movement's reform ideas on Canadian municipal systems can be seen in the pervasiveness of non-partisan ballots, the influence of council-manager systems, and the prevalence of the ideal of non-partisanship in local political cultures.

ARE CANADIAN MUNICIPAL CONSTITUTIONS "WEAK-MAYOR SYSTEMS"?

In Canada, there has been less interest in labelling municipal government forms than in the United States, which has an established tradition of defining its forms of local government, dating back to the late nineteenth century (Graham 2018).[6] However, they are often described as weak-mayor systems, and to the extent that they fall into a category of local government form, the consensus is that Canadian local governments use a type of council-manager form (Plunkett 1992; Fenn and Siegel 2017).

Mayors are members of council, reflecting the unity principle described above (see Graham 2018), and executive and legislative power is shared in these systems. A textbook on municipal government in Canada describes Canadian municipalities' form of government as follows:

> Perhaps the most distinctive feature of council as a governing body is that it combines both executive and legislative responsibilities. As an executive body it initiates proposals for municipal action, makes a myriad of specific decisions – such as hiring a particular employee – and supervises the administration of the policies and programs of the municipality. As a legislative body, it makes by-laws which are the laws governing its citizens. (Tindal and Tindal 2000, 259–60)

Others remark on the limited powers of local mayors. For instance, the role of the mayor in Canada is described as "remarkably limited" with "no strong mayors in Canada" (Sancton 2015, 228–9). The power of the mayor is often described as being no greater than that of any other member of council (Crawford 1954, 56; Lightbody 2006, 156), with duties described as primarily procedural and administrative in nature (Rogers 2009).

Reflecting the principle of equality among councillors, even seemingly popular mayors like Naheed Nenshi (2010–21) have found themselves on the losing side of council votes on major issues of policy (Farkas 2013), a phenomenon that would lead to the fall of a government at other levels since it would indicate loss of confidence in the government. Nenshi's "win rate" (for either voting for or blocking a council motion in 2010–13) was only 60.3 per cent (Farkas 2013, 10). Indeed, eleven councillors had higher win rates, and only three had lower win rates (10). More recently, the mayors of Calgary and Guelph were on the losing side of votes on the budget in 2021 (Kelcey 2022). Specifically, in Calgary, despite mayor Jyoti Gondek's position against a request by the Calgary Police Service for a C$6 million addition to its budget because "she felt that the police service had not yet delivered on commission goals regarding 'anti-racism work' and 'call diversion' of social or health emergencies to other agencies," council voted 11–4 in favour of the increase (Kelcey 2022, 1). Kennedy Stewart (2023), the former mayor of Vancouver, describes the difficulties of governing with a divided council as an independent mayor with five centre-right NPA councillors who had run with his opponent, the current mayor Ken Sim, in 2018 (Stewart 2023, 111). He also describes the resignation of key staff, including his city manager, attributing the resignation to tensions with councillors (111).

Some responsibilities of mayors may actually serve to limit their power in practice. For instance, they may be "handicapped in giving leadership to … [their] council because some of the other members may be potential competition for the mayoral chair and they may not be anxious to see his proposals succeed" (Crawford 1954, 56). Furthermore, mayors usually preside over meetings, but as Sancton notes, "this gives them little in the way of special advantage" and, in fact, "often puts mayors at a disadvantage" because they must vacate their chair to participate in debates (Sancton 2015, 230). This thinking informed Toronto Council's decision to delegate authority (with the mayor's permission) to two councillors through the establishment of the positions of speaker and deputy speaker to chair council debates in Toronto following the passage of the City of Toronto Act in 2006 (City of Toronto, n.d.). In Winnipeg, although the mayor chairs the first meeting of council, s. 67 of the Winnipeg Charter provides for the election of a presiding officer and deputy presiding officer from among the members of council who are not part of the executive policy committee (Winnipeg's mayor-appointed executive committee).

However, a characterization of Canadian mayors as weak and one among equals is not straightforward. The mayoralty in every Canadian city is established and empowered through legislation of the city's respective provincial government, generally titled the Municipal Act or something similar. Some provinces have more than one primary municipal statute, specific to particular municipalities, types of municipalities, or geographic areas of the province. In some provinces, mayors are literally defined as the chief executive officer of their respective municipalities (e.g., in Vancouver and Charlottetown). This term is found in legislation in British Columbia, Ontario, and Prince Edward Island. Other provinces use terms such as chief elected official (Calgary), the chief officer (Winnipeg), the official head (St. John's) and, in one case, the president of council (Vancouver) (see Graham 2018, table 4). These terms creatively avoid the term executive. Some provinces provide no such titles. Curiously, there is no obvious relationship between the terminology used and the provision of formal power or authority by Canadian provinces to mayors. For instance, the City of Vancouver calls its mayor a chief executive officer (and president of council) but does not provide the powers necessary to control council or the bureaucracy as discussed below.

Table 7.1 reproduces a table in Kate Graham's (2018) work on mayoral leadership in Canada. It provides a comparison of provincially enumerated powers and responsibilities of mayors in major cities in all ten Canadian provinces. This table does not include the recently enacted changes in Ontario to establish strong mayors in some cities in Ontario, including Toronto. These powers are described separately below. The three basic and shared duties of mayors spanning all provinces are presiding over meetings (or having the option of presiding over meetings), calling meetings, and signing official documents (Graham 2018).

The role of presiding over meetings reflects the concept of the ceremonial mayor described above, which exists in Ireland's council-manager system, for instance. Nevertheless, for years, some Canadian mayors have held powers and responsibilities also held by American mayors in mayor-council systems, including overseeing employee conduct, temporarily suspending employees and officers, and temporarily suspending council decisions. Four provinces provide mayors with unilateral power to make appointments. For example, s. 59(1) of the City of Winnipeg Charter Act (2002) states that "the mayor must appoint (a) a deputy mayor; (b) an acting deputy mayor; (c) the chairpersons for the standing committees … and (d) members of the executive policy committee." Winnipeg's executive committee is called the Executive Policy Committee, and its composition and size (with a maximum of eight members, half of a sixteen-member council) are determined by the mayor. These appointments may be an important lever for securing and rewarding political support from other council members, particularly where appointments are accompanied by financial compensation.

In the United States, strong mayors in mayor-council systems possess the power to veto council decisions. Section 60 of the Winnipeg Charter gives Winnipeg's mayor the power to suspend a council bylaw (which can be overridden by a majority vote in council at a subsequent meeting) – in other words, a suspensive veto. Montreal's mayor also possesses a suspensive veto, granting the power to suspend a bylaw passed by council to ensure that it is reconsidered (Municipal Code of Québec, CQLR c C-27, s. 142(3)).

Kate Graham (2018) finds that, in several major cities in Canada, councils have provided mayors with additional powers through procedural bylaws. Before the more recent introduction of provincially legislated strong-mayor powers, an example of this was Toronto Council's delegation of the power to the mayor to appoint the deputy mayor and the chairs of standing committees who, in turn, would sit on the executive committee.[7] However, not all executive committees empower the mayor to a significant degree. For instance, the procedures of council in the Halifax Regional Municipality (established in Administrative Order 1, a bylaw passed by council) establish an executive committee that does not provide executive authority to the mayor (HRM Administrative Order 1 – The Procedure of Council). Instead, it includes

Table 7.1. Comparison of Provincially Enumerated Mayoral Powers by City

Mayor Powers	Vancouver, BC*	Calgary, AB	Saskatoon, SK	Winnipeg, MB*	Toronto, ON*	Montreal, QC*	Saint John, NB	Halifax, NS*	Charlottetown, PEI*	St. John's, NL*
Mayor Presides Over Meetings (or Has Option to)	X	X	X	X	X	X	X	X	X	X
Mayor Calls Special Meetings at Own Discretion	X	X	X	X	X	X	X	X	X	X
Mayor Signs Bylaws, Contracts, Cheques, etc.	X	X	X	X	X	X	X	X	X	X
Mayor Makes Specified Appointments	X	X	X	X	X	X			X	
Mayor Appoints Deputies, Committees and/or Chairs	X			X	X	X			X	
Mayor "Provides Leadership" (or Equivalent)	X				X		X			
Mayor "Provides Direction" (or Equivalent)	X					X	X			
Mayor "Communicates Information" (or Equivalent)	X				X	X	X	X		X
Mayor "Makes Recommendations"	X				X	X				X
Mayor "Reflects the Will of Council"	X									
Mayor "Prosecute and Punishes All Negligence"										X
Mayor Oversees Employees' Conduct	X			X		X				X
Mayor Temporarily Suspends Employees or Officers	X			X		X				X
Mayor Suspends Council Decisions for Limited Period				X		X				

*Denotes cities with city-specific legislation.
Source: Republished from Graham (2018), table 6.

the mayor as chair, but its composition is determined by council. The other members are the deputy mayor (who serves as the committee's vice chair and who is also elected by council) and a member of each standing committee, the composition of which is also determined by council. Of note as well is the fact that one of the committees is the "Committee of the Whole on Budget," which essentially means that the *entire council* constitutes the budgetary committee (and this is neither the mayor's responsibility nor the responsibility of the executive committee).

Local practices and norms can also serve to either empower or disempower mayors. For example, the mayor of Winnipeg has issued mandate letters to council colleagues when appointing them to committees, akin to common practice in parliamentary systems (City of Winnipeg Media Release, November 2016). Locally established practices can also have the effect of disempowering mayors. In some cases, procedural bylaws limit the participation of the mayor during council deliberations. In the City of Saskatoon and City of Calgary, for example, the mayor must vacate the chair in order to participate in debate or make a motion. This may explain why former City of Calgary mayor Naheed Nenshi was on the losing side of so many council votes as discussed above.

Until the recent empowerment of some Ontario mayors (discussed more below), Ontario's general municipal act placed significant limits on mayoral power despite language describing the mayor's role as "to act as the chief executive officer of the municipality." Specifically, s. 226.1 states that the mayor's role is to "uphold and promote the purposes of the municipality," encourage public participation in the municipality, act as a representative both within and outside the municipality, and to "participate in and foster activities that enhance the economic, social and environmental well-being of the municipality and its residents" – responsibilities that are vague. Importantly, the act did not give Ontario mayors the power to control municipal administration, a crucial power of strong mayors, nor the ability to execute decisions. This role was reserved for officers and employees of the municipality in s. 227 and 229 of the act, which empowered "the municipality" to appoint a chief administrative officer with the following responsibilities:

(a) exercising general control and management of the affairs of the municipality for the purpose of ensuring the efficient and effective operation of the municipality; and

(b) performing such other duties as are assigned by the municipality. (Ontario Municipal Act 2001)

These powers have now been transferred to some Ontario mayors in a new part of the act entitled "Special Powers and Duties of the Head of Council." Ontario mayors with these powers are now the strongest in the country *in relation to councils and staff*, and for some scholars they are the only examples of truly strong mayors in Canada.

Legislation to introduce strong-mayor powers was enacted in 2022 when the Ontario government led by Doug Ford passed the Strong Mayors, Building Homes Act (2022), followed by the Better Municipal Government Act (2022), which together provided unprecedented powers to the mayors of Toronto and Ottawa in relation to council and city staff. These powers were extended to twenty-six other mayors in Ontario in June 2023 through ministerial regulations. In relation to council, the legislation provides the mayor of Toronto with clear executive authority to create and disband council committees and prepare and propose the budget. Furthermore, the mayor has the ability to veto council's amendments to the budget, which can only be overridden by a two-thirds supermajority vote of council. The mayor has also been granted the power to veto city bylaws *that conflict with provincial priorities* (which also can be overturned by a two-thirds majority vote of council).[8] In a particularly controversial innovation of the Ford government (enacted by the Better Municipal Governance Act 2022),[9] mayors and the heads of the regional councils of the Region of Niagara, the Region of Peel, and the Region of York have been empowered with the ability to introduce and pass bylaws that reflect provincial priorities with only one-third support from council. In relation to the city's administration, the legislation also confers substantial powers: the power to appoint the city manager, senior staff such as municipal managers and the chairs and vice-chairs of agencies, boards, and commissions, as well as the power to reorganize the city's functions (see City of Toronto, n.d.). These make Ontario mayors using these powers[10] among the most powerful in the country in relation to council and the administration. However, as discussed below, what is unknown is whether these powers will lead to greater provincial interference in local affairs since mayoral vetoes are tied to provincial priorities and the balance of power between provincial governments and municipalities is so uneven.

Ontario urban mayors are not the only mayors with formal strength in Canada. As discussed above, Winnipeg's mayor, who is called the CEO in the City of Winnipeg Charter Act, is also powerful. They appoint the city's executive committee and have been long considered to wield more power than other mayors in Canada, along with Montreal's mayor, who not only chairs the city's executive committee but also leads a political party. Nevertheless, as Sancton correctly argues, Winnipeg's mayor is not a strong mayor in the American sense of the term (the strongest of the mayor-council forms) because of their *lack of full control over the administration* (Sancton 2015, 231). In Winnipeg, council appoints the chief administrative officer (as per s. 96 of the City of Winnipeg Charter Act), who is then supervised by the executive committee (in s. 62.1). The mayor can suspend the CAO for up to three days (s. 92.1) but only council can dismiss them (s. 98.2). Nonetheless, as discussed below, the extent to which mayors are strong even in this respect in the United States varies considerably as the strong and weak variants of the mayor-council system suggest.

According to Andrew Sancton (2015, 231–2), Montreal's form of government is unique and closest to a parliamentary system. Executive committees in Quebec have historically been the strongest in the country; Montreal's executive committee has wielded significant power since the 1960s (217). The members are nominated by the mayor, approved by council, and "have special responsibilities for part of the municipal bureaucracy in the same way that cabinet ministers do" (217). Nevertheless, according to Sancton, the power of executive committees has declined in Quebec in part because they now meet in public and have included members of other parties since 2010 (217).

In Sancton's (2015, 271) view, the other way in which Canadian municipal councils deviate from the American council-manager system is insofar as Canadian city managers tend to be weaker. Furthermore, "the actual authority granted to the [city manager or equivalent] varies significantly," and "there are no major Canadian municipalities in which the city manager or CAO has as much authority as envisioned by the original designers of the council-manager plan" (271).

The judgment that Canadian cities fall into a weak-mayor category and that strong mayors of the American variety do not exist in Canada is often made with an idealized model in mind. However, as alluded to above, there is wide variation within each of the dominant American models, including the mayor-council systems in the United States. Additionally, significant adaptations have been made to the council-manager form that reflect the principle of political leadership discussed above to increase the political responsiveness of the municipal form (Frederickson, Logan, and Wood 2003, 7) and, in some cases, strengthen the mayor's power. These include the direct election of mayors (instead of having them selected by councils), having the mayoral position paid and established as a full-time position, providing staff for mayors and councillors, having councillors elected by district instead of at large, and even "in some cases, mayoral involvement in the budget preparation and department head selection and direction" (7). Mayor-council systems have also been reformed in incremental ways in the United States, further muddying the distinction between the mayor-council and council-manager systems. Such reforms took place both in the Progressive period (late nineteenth to early twentieth century), in which the council-manager systems were first introduced, and after it (7). For instance, the appointment of CAOs in mayor-council systems is a major development in the direction of the principle of professionalism. Charles Adrian describes the CAO as "a compromise between the manager plan and the strong mayor government, and as a means of providing professional administration without eliminating the mayor as the symbolic head and chief policymaker of the city" (Adrian 1961, 446, quoted in Frederickson, Logan, and Wood 2003, 9). As early as 1931, San Francisco appointed a CAO (Adrian 1988), and civil service reforms away from patronage and toward merit-based staffing were also becoming a general norm during the Progressive period (Frederickson, Logan, and Wood 2003, 9). By 1972, 24 per cent of mayor-council cities already had a CAO, a figure that jumped to over 50 per cent by 2000 (9). Furthermore, CAOs have more power in appointments and budgeting in many mayor-council systems than is generally recognized, and councils often participate in their selection with more than half (51 per cent) being selected jointly by the mayor and council (Svara 1999 in Frederickson, Logan, and Wood 2003, 10). There is also a trend toward longer mayoral terms in order to facilitate administrative stability. Another study finds that there are seven different subcategories when considering the two higher order or "ideal" categories of mayor-council and council-manager: "classic council-manager, council-manager with at-large mayor, council-manager with empowered mayor, strong-mayor-council with CAO, stronger mayor-council without CAO, weak mayor-council with CAO, and weak mayor-council without CAO" (DeSantis and Renner 2002, 103). This hybridity reflects the need to balance the principles of political leadership, laymen rule, and professionalism outlined above by Mouritzen and Svara (2002). How to strike this balance is a debate that continues within Canada, the United States, and globally.

Factors other than what is written into municipal laws influence the power of mayors on local councils. The presence of political parties, the size and composition of council, budget and staffing resources, and leadership roles on various external organizations (regional governments, universities, police boards, and other municipal boards and commissions) can further add to (or detract from) the executive-type power of the mayor. In addition to the obvious, recent, and untested case of strong mayors in Ontario, upon closer examination, the mayors of some Canadian cities may in fact be closer to the strong-mayor end of what may be best conceived as a spectrum rather than a distinct form. In sum, Canadian mayors can and do have a range of executive-type powers, so they do not fit uniformly into a definition of a weak-mayor system.

Furthermore, the broad ambiguity of the role can create conditions where mayors, in practice, can be "strong." As Higgins observes:

> Because of the vagueness of their specified powers and duties, their relationships with other members of council can vary greatly even within a particular city when the occupant of the mayor's chair changes. The extent to which a mayor is pre-eminent in council depends much on the personality of the particular incumbent. If the mayor has a forceful personality and has developed a network of close working relationships with other members of council, then the incumbent mayor may acquire informally a position of strong leadership in council and be able to exercise the powers of a strong chief executive. (Higgins 1977, 96)

As we discover in the next section, these coalition-building efforts may extend across levels of government, into civil society, and even to the international level, explaining how mayors develop the capacity to punch above their weight in a variety of important areas of policy.

MAYORAL POWER BEYOND INSTITUTIONS

There is no municipal, provincial, territorial, or federal legislation in Canada that would suggest that local actors such as mayors are engaged in issues like the regulation of controlled substances, immigration, climate action, and more. In fact, most of the defined duties of actors like mayors focus on the formal governance activities at city hall such as chairing meetings, signing bylaws, and having responsibility for things like declaring emergencies. However, mayors and other local leaders spend a great deal of time working to mobilize diverse groups of people inside and beyond their cities on issues of mutual concern. Canadian local leaders are actively engaged in networks at the city, regional, provincial, national, and international scales and are able to exercise power and influence in sometimes unexpected ways. Table 7.2 provides examples of how Canadian mayors have exercised leadership both within and beyond their cities.

In the United States, there are also numerous examples of local leaders coming together on issues that are generally considered federal or state level matters. A well-known example is the National League of Cities (NLC), which has convened American urban leaders for a century. Today NLC represents 2,725 member American cities, towns, and villages, and they operate a large suite of programs aimed at mobilizing people within and across cities (National League of Cities, n.d.). The REAL program (Race, Equity, and Leadership) offers hands-on toolkits to help communities address systemic oppression – including toolkits for organizing protests and launching successful petitions.

Internationally, there is an increasing number of convening coalitions targeted at local leaders. Sometimes these exist within countries or regions, such as the United States Conference of Mayors or the Council of Capital City Lord Mayors in Australia. Sometimes they are continental, such as the Covenant of Mayors for Climate and Energy in the European Union; sometimes they are international, such as the Global Parliament of Mayors. Similar networks exist among networks of other local actors such as city managers or leaders of particular policy or service areas.

One example of how this works in practice can be found in the City of Toronto (and former mayor John Tory's) response to the Syrian refugee crisis. On September 2, 2015, a three-year-old boy drowned as his family attempted to flee Syria by boat. A heartbreaking photograph of the boy's lifeless body washed up on the beach went viral, prompting calls for needed action to support refugee families from leaders around the world. On September 3, Toronto mayor John Tory called a press conference, immediately filling a room with local and national media. With uncharacteristically teary remarks, Mayor Tory urged the federal government to "act quickly" (Pete 2015). The following day, September 4, the Big City Mayors' Caucus – a group of twenty-two mayors from Canada's large cities, convened by the Federation of Canadian Municipalities – issued a press release with a clear statement: "Canadian cities are ready to address this crisis" (FCM 2015). Each of the mayors identified the specific numbers of Syrian refugees their cities could support. This happened to fall during a federal election. All of the major party leaders began to articulate plans to dramatically increase the number of refugees they would welcome – plans which transpired into reality shortly after, with more than 44,000 Syrian refugees welcomed to Canada since that time. In a twelve-month period, 36,135 Syrian refugees were resettled in Canada, with 29,695 in fifteen cities that are members of the Federation of Canadian Municipality's Big City Mayors' Caucus (Garcea 2016, 154). Within this group, close to half were initially resettled in Toronto, Vancouver, and Montreal (154).

Table 7.2. Examples of Local Leadership by Canadian Mayors, within and beyond Their Cities

Mayors	Within City	Beyond City
Vancouver: Kennedy Stewart (2018–22)	Created and chaired a Mayor's Overdose Emergency Task Force, examining causes and solutions to support people struggling with addictions and succeeded in having drugs decriminalized in Vancouver	Chaired the committee of mayors for Metro Vancouver region, advocating provincially and federally on issues like housing and transportation
Calgary: Naheed Nenshi (2010–21)	Created Mayor's Civic Engagement Committee, which produced the 3 Things for Calgary to engage youth in setting the strategic direction for the city	Part of the Bloomberg Harvard City Leadership program connecting mayors and local leaders in the United States and beyond
Toronto: John Tory (2014–23)	Led local COVID-19 recovery response including convening community task forces, doing daily press conferences from his home, and hosting a press event when he received his vaccine	Worked closely with Toronto Global to convene regional leaders to promote economic growth for the region, including a bid on Amazon HQ2
Montreal: Valérie Plante (2017–present)	Appoints members and leads Montreal's executive committee, including assigning members with portfolio responsibilities	Appointed as Global Ambassador for Local Biodiversity by Local Governments for Sustainability
Halifax: Mike Savage (2012–24)	Chaired group of local community and business leaders to promote new stadium (after two previous community-led efforts failed)	Chaired the Big City Mayors' Caucus, including mayors of twenty-two large Canadian cities to advocate for urban issues to the federal government

Source: Authors.

Immigration and international relations are decidedly federal matters in Canada (immigration is a joint federal-provincial responsibility, with federal paramountcy to be specific – see chapter 12 for more on this topic). Why are mayors holding press conferences and issuing calls to the federal government on this topic? Often it is because the problems that cities face are evident on the ground, and the organizations that can help solve them are also in the community and known by local leaders such as mayors. Local leaders are aware of and able to tap into policy knowledge and capacity at the local level. The Federation of Canadian Municipalities in general, including the Big City Mayors' Caucus, also plays a significant role in the diffusion of policy ideas in the local immigration policy realm as illustrated in the example of John Tory's leadership on immigration policy. In Canada, federally funded Local Immigration Partnerships and national conferences evaluating them play a role in building capacity to settle immigrants and in policy idea sharing (called policy diffusion in academic circles). Mayors chair these partnerships in some cities, such as Vancouver. This example shows that mayors are able to develop coalitions and engage in multilevel relations (with other levels of government and sometimes also at the international scale) to lead in areas that are formally outside their jurisdictions. Toronto and other Canadian cities' response to the Syrian refugee crisis is but one of many examples of how Canadian mayors can and do lead beyond their cities – and engage in issues not traditionally considered to be local matters.

In the United States, an important part of leading and building capacity in immigration policy at the local level is membership in organizations and coalitions of cities such as Welcome America (a non-profit that works with others and municipalities), more general coalitions such as Cities for Action (which brings together mayors and leaders from county governments), and regular national meetings of municipalities. As we discover in chapter 12, municipalities in the United States are developing immigrant affairs offices to help them lead in this area, and mayors are an important influence on their focus and scope (De Graauw 2019, 173–4). They are significantly more common in mayor-council systems; indeed, 81 per cent are housed in municipalities that have adopted this local government form (171) that emphasizes the principle of political leadership. Coalition-building across sectors and among cities is a crucial aspect of capacity-building in this area as cities that have created these offices tend to belong to one or both of these inter-city networks (171).

Former Vancouver mayor Kennedy Stewart's (2018–22) leadership on drug policy in Vancouver provides another example of a mayor leading in an area of particular salience to a city (but with broader national implications) by mobilizing the community and intergovernmental networks to a significant policy effect. As he describes in his recent book *Decrim* (Stewart 2023), through coalition-building among community groups and local organizations such as the Vancouver Police, as well as by leveraging his political networks as a former member of Parliament, he was able to achieve the decriminalization of drugs within the City of Vancouver's boundaries and in British Columbia. This was despite his institutional weakness as an independent mayor on a divided council with weak mayor powers.

Thus, although many Canadian mayors operate in forms of municipal government that do not provide them with the formal authority to be strong political leaders, some are able to become strong despite their constraints and achieve significant policy results. They do this through coalition-building and by combining the policy knowledge and the capacity of multiple networks. As leaders close to the ground, they are positioned to bring together these networks and often bring a pragmatism to decision-making inherent in a desire to solve problems (drug poisonings due to unsafe supply in the case of former mayor of Vancouver Kennedy Stewart) and see opportunities (how Toronto's refugee resettlement and settlement infrastructures could address an international refugee crisis in the case of former mayor of Toronto John Tory) that are so readily apparent "on the ground" and in their immediate environment. Still, as political scientists, we know that institutions matter. Would local leadership efforts be enhanced by strong formal mayoral powers in Canada? The next section turns to that debate inspired by recent reforms in Ontario.

REFORM DEBATES – DO BIG-CITY MAYORS NEED STRONG-MAYOR POWERS?

Should mayors be given more formal power? And, if so, why and how? The debate about how to institutionalize power on municipal councils in Canada is both an enduring and contemporary one. Since councils and their forms are established in provincial legislation, reform can be accomplished more easily than changes to some elements of political institutions at other levels that would require a constitutional amendment. However, what kind of process ought to guide fundamental changes to the "constitutions of local government" (Mouritzen and Svara 2002) is a crucial question as well.

The Ford government's recent legislation in Ontario granting some municipalities strong mayoral power has raised many questions about the pros and cons of this kind of institutional change. The stated rationale behind Ontario's efforts to empower big-city mayors was to address the housing crisis and to enable mayors of the largest and fastest growing places in Ontario to, in the words of Steve Clark, minister of Municipal Affairs and Housing, "deliver on the housing commitments they have made" (CBC 2023). Is there reason to believe that strong-mayor powers could help address the housing crisis? As Taylor and Horak (2022, 2) argue, there are multiple reasons for the current housing affordability crisis: government reluctance to invest in social housing and protect current affordable housing stocks and a variety of market forces that have driven up housing costs. Taylor and Horak argue that "while local planning and zoning are part of the puzzle, the notion that broad, systemic constraints will be overcome by allowing big-city mayors to overrule majorities of democratically elected councillors is a fallacy" (2).

Instead, they suggest that the Ontario reforms are a veiled attempt and political move to shift responsibility for the housing crisis to cities, which raises the question of who is accountable for policy decisions in a multilevel governance system. They point to an interesting comparative case of the Conservative government in the United Kingdom experiencing a rebellion of its backbenches (one hundred backbench MPs revolted) when they proposed to impose "high housing delivery targets on local authorities in hope of expanding the housing supply by 300,000 units annually" (3). The backbench MPs were motivated by NIMBY (not in my backyard) reactions from their constituents, and the government's policy now allows for less housing to be built if building more would "significantly change the character" of their neighbourhood or area (3). With strong mayors in place in some municipalities in Ontario, the province has created an alternative culprit should constituents react against decisions to increase development and housing supply in their district or failure to deliver on affordable housing. However, in the shorter term the province has also suggested that municipal decision-making processes are plagued by red tape unnecessarily slowing down housing development, thus laying blame on municipalities for the current crisis.

However, as housing policy expert Alison Smith observes, there is a misalignment in Ontario between governments with the authority and those with the resources to address affordable housing. Ontario is the only province to have transferred authority for administering social housing to municipalities in the 1990s, and it did not follow the transfer of responsibility with the necessary funding (which amounted to "downloading" the fiscal burden). As she notes, "when it comes to providing deeply affordable housing (housing that is affordable for people who are on social assistance), rent-geared-to-income housing (usually capped at 30 per cent of someone's income), and supportive housing for people who are or are at risk of being un-housed, municipalities cannot act on their own" (Smith 2023, 9). It is a multilevel governance challenge that requires collaboration among governments and stakeholders. Although the impact of strong-mayor powers is untested, she points out that strong-mayor powers could lead to decisions about housing being made by "a small number of people" and "behind closed doors" as mayors and provinces negotiate provincial priorities and their implementation (9). This could extend executive federalism, a process whereby the provincial and federal ministers (including first ministers) negotiate major policy changes outside of legislative bodies where they are subject to debate (9).

However, strong-mayor powers could also lead to a greater level of political accountability at the local level. As we saw above, such systems privilege political leadership as a governing principle. Although the council-manager form is most popular in the United States, especially in cities with populations under 250,000, two-thirds of large cities (with populations over 500,000) use the mayor-council form of government with strong mayors (Chapple 2023, 5). Indeed, seventeen out of the United States' twenty-five largest cities (nearly three-quarters) employ mayor-council forms (New York City, n.d.). Although they disagree with specific elements of the Ford government's reforms and its framing as a response to the housing crisis, Taylor and Horak (2022, 3) also note that strengthening the Canadian mayor's powers is "not entirely without merit" since the current process based on consensus-building in a non-partisan environment with a ward-based council can be "slow and messy." They stress the possible benefits of a stronger executive for policy coherence and democratic accountability (3).

Similarly, a recent article by Brian Kelcey (2022), an urban policy consultant who served as budget adviser to former Winnipeg mayor Sam Katz (2004–14) from 2005–8, makes a case for stronger mayoral power, arguing that they ought to be granted the "power to propose." Kelcey's proposal does not deviate significantly from current practices in places such as Winnipeg (and was likely informed by his experience in that jurisdiction):

1   Replace mayors in their roles as impartial presiding officers with an elected councillor, so mayors are free to engage in every debate;
2   Allow mayors to direct public servants (in writing) to help develop mayoral proposals for council's consideration, and;
3   Award mayors (or acting mayors) the sole authority to propose draft budgets to their council. (Kelcey 2022, 3)

Kelcey (2022) notes that points two and three would empower mayors to work with staff to develop draft budgets that are consistent with mayoral priorities. In his evaluation of the Ford government's reforms, Gabriel Eidelman (2023) also sees placing the preparation of the budget in the mayor's hands as a positive change that brings it more in line with the mechanisms of political accountability for spending that exist at other levels of government. He notes that council passed Toronto's budget for 2023 virtually unaltered even though it was short almost C$1 billion, hoping that other orders of government would fill the gap. As Eidelman (2023, 10) describes: "The formal budget process begins with a presentation by the city manager, who tables the staff-recommended 'preliminary' or 'draft' operating and capital budgets. And in most cases, despite months of debate in committees, council usually passes the staff-proposed budget with almost no meaningful changes." He argues that in this type of process, nobody is clearly accountable for this shortfall – staff can blame council, councillors can in turn blame staff for their advice, and mayors can "take their pick" in attributing the decision to someone else (10). He notes that the mayor only gains the power to *propose* the budget. However, if council proposes amendments, the mayor has also been empowered to veto them (subject to a two-thirds majority vote of council to override the veto). However, there would be a political cost to a mayor who did not take reasonable and popular council input into account. As Eidelman notes, for staff, this change clarifies whose vision is to be implemented, places city-wide priorities over local concerns, and "would match the public's expectations that the job of the mayor is to lead" (10). In his view, the power to hire and fire senior staff would further result in an administration more responsive to the mayor's vision.

However, others point to a risk of politicizing the public service (Taylor 2023a; Graham and Grant 2023) and to the higher likelihood of corruption (Graham and Grant 2023). Furthermore, although lines of accountability may be clearer, they note that radical shifts in policy as new mayors are elected and appoint new CAOs and department heads could have an impact on staff morale (Graham and Grant 2023). Unsurprisingly, the concern about politicization of the administration is shared by the Canadian Association of Municipal administrators (CAMA), the professional association that represents chief administrative officers (CAMA, n.d.). The association entered the debate on strong mayors in Ontario, arguing that "even a 'strong' mayor needs a strong CAO" and noting that the strength of CAOs varies considerably across the country (7). The association notes the importance of the CAO and other senior staff to the quality of local decision-making:

> While the CAO and management staff need to be sensitive to local concerns as they carry out their duties, the nature of their tenure gives them a different perspective compared to their council counterparts that face re-election. Senior staff members derive their legitimacy from specialized professional expertise and career experience. It also imposes on them an obligation to consider the long term, as well as future residents and other, non-voting stakeholders, like the disenfranchised and the business community. (CAMA, n.d., 6)

They are articulating the importance of the principle of professionalism in local governance. The organization argues for statutory protection of the CAO, the development of policies to guide the use of strong-mayor powers before issues arise, as well as council involvement in the recruitment and performance-review processes (13–14). As we saw above, the mayor's role in relation to CAOs also varies considerably even in strong-mayor (mayor-council) systems in the United States (with councils often playing a significant role in hiring and dismissing CAOs even in this system). Many American strong-mayor systems have tempered strong political leadership with a check by the council and a strong CAO (incorporating the principles of laymen rule and professionalism).

Which of the American systems performs better from a policy perspective? A US study of the performance of council-manager systems, compared to mayor-council systems, found that although council-manager systems have lower voter turnout, senior executive staff tend to spend more time in their role as managers and tend to favour more comprehensive policy solutions that have broader benefits city-wide (Carr 2015). Despite that greater stability in personnel and preference for comprehensive policy solutions, there was little difference between the two systems in terms of operational effectiveness, responsiveness, or the quality of public services offered (Carr 2015). Thus, there does not appear to be a clear consensus on which system is preferable from a policy perspective. This could be due to the fact that so many systems make incremental compromises among the three principles of laymen rule, political leadership, and professionalism that deviate from their original form.

Finally, it is worth underscoring that the strong-mayor reforms enacted in Ontario are fundamentally different from American strong-mayor systems insofar as they introduce provincial priorities as standards for mayoral decision-making, which can be changed and expanded through ministerial regulations. Indeed, the Better Governance Act gives the minister of Municipal Affairs and Housing a wide ability to change the democratic process, especially the budgetary process, through regulation. This means that significant further changes to democratic decision-making could be made unilaterally by the minister and without the involvement of the provincial legislature. The centralization reflected in this aspect of Ontario's reforms reflects similarities with the collective forms as institutionalized in Belgium and the Netherlands, where the central government is involved in the appointment of the mayor.

Both the recently legislated reforms in Ontario as well as the ongoing ability to change the process through regulations stand in sharp contrast to changes in local government forms in the United States, where referendums have been held. A recent Brookings Institution report indicates that twenty-six large cities in the United States have held such referendums "to fully change their form of government" and "half of these referendums were successful" with mayor-council systems adopted in ten cities to replace council-manager systems and only two cities choosing to move from mayor-council to council-manager systems (Harkness et al. 2017, 36). The necessity of broad public debate and robust democratic processes to change the fundamental rules of decision-making at the local level may seem obvious in major cities in the United States. The fact that more Ontarians and Canadians are not outraged by such unilateral action by provincial governments reflects the ongoing hegemony of the "creatures of the provinces" concept as a discourse in Canada (Good 2019) and the failure of Canadians to value their right to local self-government (Magnusson 2005).

CONCLUSION

There is a variety of forms of local government across the world that strike different balances between the principles of political leadership, laymen rule, and professionalism. There is less discussion in Canada about the form of municipal government, but the consensus seems to have been that Canadian mayors are formally weak and that municipal systems are variations of or have been influenced by the council-manager form. Nevertheless, as this chapter shows, the form of municipal government is difficult to pin down, and Canadian mayors are not universally weak. Following Graham (2018), it may be more accurate to conceptualize mayoral forms as a spectrum rather than as types. Winnipeg and Montreal's form of government provides substantial powers to the mayor above ordinary councillors. More recently, the number of strong mayors in Canada has been increased substantially with Ontario's recent legislation making mayors of major cities among the strongest in the world in relation to their councils, with extensive veto powers and the power to propose and enact legislation with only one-third of the elected council's support. However, these powers have been introduced in a way that has the potential to lead to greater provincial interference in municipal affairs and ultimately less power for mayors who disagree with members of the political executive at the provincial level. This suggests that the spectrum metaphor must also acknowledge a variety of unique elements and a diversity of democratic practices in Canada as well.

A major debate in Canada, implied in the concept that Canadian mayors are weak but brought to the forefront in recent reform debates in Ontario, is whether municipal institutions ought to grant mayors more formal power to lead. Internationally, there does not appear to be a clear trend in terms of reforms toward establishing strong-mayor systems. However, strengthening mayoral power in large cities appears to be more common as the disproportionate switch from council-manager to mayor-council forms in large American cities (discussed in the previous section) suggests. Nonetheless, more generally, the council-manager form has become the predominant model in the United States; it was also adopted in New Zealand in the 1980s (Wallis and Dollery 2000). When one considers that Australian municipalities also use a council-manager form and that it has significantly influenced Canadian municipalities, we can see the dominance of this way of organizing authority in Anglo municipalities, especially settler Anglo countries. Interestingly, with its parliamentary model and stronger mayors, Quebec is a distinct society in this respect as it is in many other areas of constitutionalism. However, as Andrew Sancton (2021, 217) argues, even Quebec's mayors are no longer as powerful as they once were.

As we saw above, France, Germany, and the Netherlands have also strengthened the role of their mayors in recent decades (Berg and Rao 2005, 9). In addition, directly elected mayors have been introduced in some municipalities in England with mayors of major cities and city-regions becoming significantly more powerful. Nonetheless, a move toward reducing the concentration of power is also evident in reforms to local councils in some countries such as Denmark (Berg and Rao 2005). Not all reforms have been radical, with many European countries making incremental adaptations to existing systems (Berg and Rao 2005, 9).

As in Europe, in the United States and Canada, many reforms happen incrementally. Take the example above of Austin, Texas, where councillors are now elected by district, the mayor is elected at large, and the council size has increased. These changes all represent concessions to political leadership and laymen rule while still retaining a foundation of professionalism (with a strong city manager in place). The same could be said of many Canadian council forms that also include these features, having evolved through time to give a greater nod to the principle of political leadership.

The council form that is appropriate may depend on other factors such as the size of the municipality and the existence of political parties. Council needs to be able to make decisions and to act strategically, particularly as cities become larger. As urbanization has progressed, cities have also taken on more responsibilities, often in areas not formally delegated to them as the example of mayoral leadership in immigrant integration and drug policy mentioned above illustrate. This arguably requires a strong ability to act strategically.

A major part of a mayor's ability to lead is determined by their abilities to mobilize a diverse range of actors around an urban agenda and may involve multiple levels of government, sometimes with competing or even conflicting policy goals. The previous chapter by Martin Horak on multilevel governance offers important insights into some of the practical challenges of leadership within this context. Canadian mayors have been leading in important areas such as the resettlement of Syrian refugees, drug decriminalization, the environment, and public health (especially evident during the COVID-19 pandemic). In order to understand their ability to lead, we must understand their institutional context and also the informal processes through which they are able to influence Canadian public policy.

The responsiveness of municipalities in some communities may be enhanced by strengthening mayors' formal powers, especially in large cities. The lines of democratic accountability may also be clarified. However, the fact that mayors have become such important actors on both national and international scales only underscores the democratic importance of these choices. In our view, decisions about municipal constitutions ought to be made through a decision-making process that encourages broad public debate. Furthermore, the desire to achieve a specific policy goal like building more housing should not overshadow the fundamental constitutional debates inherent in balancing political leadership, laymen rule, and professionalism in municipalities in Canada.

NOTES

1 There are a variety of types of directly elected mayors in England, including local authority elected mayors, the mayor of London, and "metro-mayors" that govern "combined authorities" (Sandford 2022, 14).

2 Although local partisan politics in British Columbia has a much longer history, partisan ballots were introduced by Harcourt in 1992 (Smith and Stewart 2009, 300). Legislation recognizing municipal

political parties in Quebec municipalities with populations greater than 100,000 was passed in 1978, and its scope was broadened in both 1979 and 1998 (Belley et al. 2009, 108).

3 In 2001 in the United States, 77 per cent of city elections employed a non-partisan ballot (Svara 2003, 14).

4 Their data comes from the Fiscal Austerity and Urban Innovation Project.

5 The non-British immigrant population in cities was comparatively low, and immigrants that began to arrive in large numbers in 1896 were encouraged to settle in rural areas (Anderson 1972, 9). Furthermore, French Canadians in both Quebec and New Brunswick were largely confined to rural areas in those provinces (9). Finally, the Indian Act (1876) consolidated a system of reserves that segregated Indigenous Peoples in rural communities, displacing them from their lands in cities.

6 Today there are at least four forms of local government in the United States: the mayor-council system, the council-manager system, the commission system, and the town meeting system (DeSantis and Renner 2002, 95) and there are variants of all four. Almost all local governments in the United States today use one of the first two – the mayor-council form (34 per cent) and the council-manager form (55 per cent) (National League of Cities, n.d.).

7 Before recent reforms, council only appointed *one* member of the executive committee, but when the committee was initially established, it was more equally co-appointed by council and the mayor.

8 See the Strong Mayors, Building Homes Act, 2022, S.O. 2022, c. 18, Bill 3.

9 See the Better Municipal Governance Act, 2022, S.O. 2022, c. 24, Bill 39.

10 The use of these powers in Ontario remains an emerging development as this volume is being written. In some cases, the incumbent mayor has vowed not to use any of the strong-mayor powers – importantly including Ottawa's Mayor Sutcliffe (elected shortly after the new powers were extended) and Toronto's Mayor Chow (elected in June 2023 through a by-election following the resignation of Mayor Tory). The powers were only used in Toronto for a few months of Mayor Tory's tenure, and under extenuating circumstances as he announced a sudden resignation the week before the budget was tabled by the mayor through the new strong-mayor arrangements. In response to the strong-mayor powers being extended to twenty-six other communities, several other mayors and/or councils have made formal commitments to resist or not use the new powers extended by the province.

REFERENCES

Aars, Jacob, and Hans-Erik Ringkjob. 2005. "Party Politicisation Reversed? Non-Partisan Alternatives in Norwegian Local Politics." *Scandinavian Political Studies* 28, no. 2 (June): 161–81. https://doi .org/10.1111/j.0080-6757.2005.00126.x.

Adrian, Charles. 1961. "Recent Concepts in Large City Administrations." In *Urban Government: A Reader in Politics and Administration*, edited by Edward C. Banfield, 256–65. New York: The Free Press of Glencoe.

———. 1988. "Forms of City Government in American History." In *The Municipal Year Book*. Washington, DC: International City/County Management Association.

Anderson, James D. 1972. "Nonpartisan Urban Politics." In *Emerging Party Politics in Urban Canada*, edited by Jack K. Masson and James D. Anderson, 5–25. Toronto: McClelland and Stewart.

Bäck, Henry, Hubert Heinelt, and Annick Magnier. 2006. "Introduction." In *The European Mayor: Political Leaders in the Changing Context of Local Democracy*, edited by Henry Bäck, Hubert Heinelt, and Annick Magnier, 7–20. Vol. 10 of *Urban and Regional Research International*. Wiesbaden, Germany: VS Verlag für Sozialwissenschaften. https://doi.org/10.1007/978-3-531-90005-6_1.

Belley, Serge, Laurence Bherer, Guy Chiasson, Jean-Pierre Collin, Pierre Hamel, Pierre J. Hamel, and Mathieu Rivard with Julie Archambault. 2009. "Quebec." In *Foundations of Governance: Municipal Government in Canada's Provinces*, edited by Andrew Sancton and Robert Young, 70–137. Toronto: University of Toronto Press. https://doi.org/10.3138/9781442697874-005.

Berg, Rikke, and Nirmala Rao. 2005. "Institutional Reforms in Local Government: A Comparative Framework." In *Transforming Local Political Leadership*, edited by Rikke Berg and Nirmala Rao, 1–14. New York: Palgrave Macmillan. https://doi.org/10.1057/9780230501331.

Berg, Rikke. 2005. "From Cabinets to Committees: The Danish Experience." In *Transforming Local Political Leadership*, edited by Rikke Berg and Nirmala Rao, 85–100. New York: Palgrave Macmillan. https://doi.org/10.1057/9780230501331.

Bergin, Brigid. 2021. "What Does the Mayor of New York City Do?" *Gothamist*, February 2, 2021. https://gothamist.com/news/what-does-mayor-new-york-city-do.

Blodgett, Terrell, and Mike Hogg. n.d. "City of Austin Government Structure: A Comparative Analysis." https://services.austintexas.gov/edims/document.cfm?id=224455.

CAMA/ACAM. n.d. "The Role and Significance of the Chief Administrative Officer Position in Canadian Municipal Government: A CAMA 'White Paper' on Ontario's Strong Mayor Legislation and the Pivotal Role of the CAO in Providing Good Governance." Accessed July 19, 2023. https://www.amcto.com/sites/default/files/2023-04/CAMA%20Strong%20Mayors%20White%20Paper%20-%20Final%20English%20-%20March%2023%202023_0.pdf.

Carr, Jered B. 2015. "What Have We Learned about the Performance of Council-Manager Government? A Review and Synthesis of the Research." *Public Administration Review* 75, no. 5 (September–October): 673–89. https://doi.org/10.1111/puar.12415.

CBC. 2023. "Ontario Expanding 'Strong Mayor' Powers to Cities across the Province." *CBC News*, June 16, 2023. https://www.cbc.ca/news/canada/toronto/municipal-affairs-meeting-ontario-big -city-mayors-1.6878776.

Chapple, Karen. 2023. "The American Strong Mayor: Similarities and Differences." In Taylor 2023b, 5–6.

City of Austin. n.d. "Office of the City Manager." https://www.austintexas.gov/department/city-manager.

City of Toronto. 2022. "Clerk's Office, Declaration of Results." https://www.toronto.ca/wp-content /uploads/2022/10/9085-FinalDeclaration-of-Results-for-the-2022-Toronto-Municipal-Election.pdf.

City of Toronto. n.d. *The Roles of the Mayor and City Council*. Accessed February 23, 2024. https:// www.toronto.ca/wp-content/uploads/2017/12/94af-roles-of-the-mayor-city-council-learning -guide-brochure.pdf.

City of Winnipeg Charter Act, SM 2002, c 39.

Copus, Colin, Melvin Wingfield, Kristof Steyvers, and Herwig Reynaert. 2012. "A Place to Party? Parties and Nonpartisanship in Local Government." In *The Oxford Handbook of Urban Politics*, edited by Karen Mossberger, Susan E. Clarke, and Peter John, 210–30. New York: Oxford University Press. https://doi.org/10.1093/oxfordhb/9780195367867.013.0011.

Crawford, K. Grant. 1954. *Canadian Municipal Government*. Toronto: University of Toronto Press. https://doi.org/10.3138/9781442653283.

de Graauw, Els. 2019. "City Immigrant Affairs Offices in the United States: Taking Control of Immigrant Integration." In *The Routledge Handbook of the Governance of Migration and Diversity in Cities*, edited by Tiziana Caponio, Peter Scholten, and Ricard Zapata-Barrero, 216–27. Abington: Routledge. https://doi.org/10.4324/9781351108478-17.

DeSantis, Victor S., and Tari Renner. 2002. "City Government Structures: An Attempt at Clarification." *State & Local Government Review* 34, no. 2 (Spring): 95–104. https://doi.org/10.1177 /0160323X0203400202.

Eidelman, Gabriel. 2023. "Making the Mayor More Accountable." In Taylor 2023b, 10–12.

Elections Canada. n.d. "Past Results: Papineau. Official Voting Results – General Election (September 20, 2021)." Voter Information Service. https://www.elections.ca/Scripts/vis /PastResults?L=e&ED=24055&EV=99&EV_TYPE=6&PROV=ON&QID=-1&PAGEID=28.

Farkas, Jeromy Anton. 2013. *Growing the Democratic Toolbox: City Council Vote Tracking*. September 20, 2013. Kelowna, BC: Manning Foundation for Democratic Education.

Federation of Canadian Municipalities (FCM). 2015. "Cities Mobilizing for Action on Syrian Refugee Crisis." Big City Mayors Caucus. September 4, 2015. https://fcm.ca/en/news-media/news-release /cities-mobilize-action-syrian-refugee-crisis.

Fenn, Michael, and David Siegel. 2017. "The Evolving Role of City Managers and Chief Administrative Officers." In *IMFG Papers on Municipal Finance and Governance*, no. 31. Toronto: Institute on Municipal Finance and Governance.

Frederickson, George, Brett Logan, and Curtis Wood. 2003. "Municipal Reform in Mayor-Council Cities: A Well-Kept Secret." *State & Local Government Review* 35, no. 1 (December): 7–14. https:// doi.org/10.1177/0160323X0303500101.

Garcea, Joseph. 2016. "The Resettlement of Syrian Refugees: The Positions and Roles of the Federation of Canadian Municipalities and its Members." *Canadian Ethnic Studies* 48, no. 3 (Fall): 149–73. https://doi.org/10.1353/ces.2016.0030.

Good, Kristin R. 2019. "The Fallacy of the 'Creatures of the Provinces' Doctrine: Recognizing and Protecting Municipalities' Constitutional Status." In *IMFG Papers on Municipal Finance and Governance*, no. 47. Toronto: Institute on Municipal Finance and Governance. https://imfg .munkschool.utoronto.ca/research/doc/?doc_id=523.

Graham, Kate. 2018. "Leading Canada's Cities? A Study of Urban Mayors." PhD diss, University of Western Ontario. Electronic Thesis and Dissertation Repository (5745). https://ir.lib.uwo.ca/etd/5745.

Graham, Kate, and Jason Grant. 2023. "Strong Thoughts on Strong Mayors." *Municipal World*, January 2023, 13. https://www.municipalworld.com/articles/strong-thoughts-on-strong-mayors/.

Graham, Katherine A., Susan D. Phillips, and Allan M. Maslove. 1998. *Urban Governance in Canada*. Toronto: Harcourt Brace.

Halifax Regional Municipality Charter, Statutes of Nova Scotia. 2008, c. 39. https://nslegislature.ca /sites/default/files/legc/statutes/halifax%20regional%20municipality%20charter.pdf.

Harkness, Alaina, with Bruce Katz, Caroline Conroy, and Ross Tilchin. 2017. *Leading Beyond Limits: Mayoral Powers in the Age of New Localism*. Washington, DC: Brookings Institute. https://www .brookings.edu/articles/leading-beyond-limits-mayoral-powers-in-the-age-of-new -localism/.

Higgins, Donald J.H. 1977. *Urban Canada: Its Politics and Government*. Toronto: Macmillan.

John, Peter, and Martin Saiz. 1999. "Local Political Parties in Comparative Perspective." In Saiz and Geser 1999, 44–73. https://doi.org/10.4324/9780429037351-3.

Judd, Dennis R., and Todd Swanstrom. 2015. *City Politics*. 9th ed. New Jersey: Pearson Education.

Kelcey, Brian. 2022. "To Lead in the 21st Century, Canadian Mayors Need the Power to Propose." *Policy Options*, January 12, 2022. https://policyoptions.irpp.org/magazines/january-2022/to -lead-in-the-21st-century-canadian-mayors-need-the-power-to-propose/.

Lightbody, James. 2006. *City Politics, Canada*. Peterborough, ON: Broadview Press. https://doi.org /10.3138/9781442602038.

Magnusson, Warren. 2005. "Protecting the Right of Local Self-Government." *Canadian Journal of Political Science* 38, no. 4 (December): 897–922. https://doi.org/10.1017/S0008423905040436.

Mouritzen, Poul Erik, and James H. Svara. 2002. *Leadership at the Apex: Politicians and Administrators in Western Local Governments*. Pittsburgh, PA: University of Pittsburgh Press. https://doi.org/10.2307/jj.11498450.

Municipal Code of Québec, CQLR c C-27.

National League of Cities. n.d. "About NLC." Accessed August 1, 2024. https://www.nlc.org/about/.

New York City. n.d. "Twenty-Five Largest U.S. Cities by Population: Form of Government." Accessed on July 19, 2023. https://www.nyc.gov/assets/quadrennial/downloads/pdf/tables/Forms-of-Government.pdf.

Ontario Municipal Act, 2001, S.O. 2001, c. 25.

Pete, Don. 2015. "Torontoians Urged to Step Up and Help Refugees." *Toronto Sun*, September 4, 2015. https://torontosun.com/2015/09/04/torontonians-urged-to-step-up-to-help-migrants.

Plunkett, Thomas J. 1992. *City Management in Canada: The Role of the Chief Administrative Officer*. Toronto: Institute of Public Administration of Canada.

Razin, Eran. 2013. "Councillors and Their Parties." In *Local Councillors in Europe*, edited by Björn Egner, David Sweeting, and Pieter-Jan Klok, 51–62. Vol. 14 of *Urban and Regional Research International*. Wiesbaden: Springer VS. https://doi.org/10.1007/978-3-658-01857-3_3.

Ridley, Clarence E., and Orin F. Nolting. 1934. *The City Manager Profession*. Chicago: University of Chicago Press.

Rogers, Ian MacFee. 2009. *The Law of Canadian Municipal Corporations*. Toronto: Thompson Reuters Canada.

Ruchelman, Leonard I. 1969. *Big City Mayors: The Crisis in Urban Politics*. Don Mills, ON: Oxford University Press.

Saiz, Martin. 1999. "Do Political Parties Matter in U.S. Cities?" In Saiz and Geser 1999, 171–90. https://doi.org/10.4324/9780429037351-9.

Saiz, Martin, and Hans Geser, eds. 1999. *Local Political Parties in Political and Organizational Perspective*. Boulder, CO: Westview Press.

Sancton, Andrew. 1994. "Mayors as Political Leaders." In *Leaders and Leadership in Canada*, edited by Maureen Mancuso, Richard G. Price, and Ronald Wagenberg, 174–89. Toronto: Oxford University Press.

———. 2015. *Local Government in Canada: An Urban Perspective*. Don Mills, ON: Oxford University Press.

Sandford, Mark. 2022. "Directly-Elected Mayors." House of Commons Library, Research Briefing, November 11, 2022. United Kingdom Parliament. Archived November 14, 2022, at the Wayback Machine.https://web.archive.org/web/20221114150249/https://commonslibrary.parliament.uk/research-briefings/sn05000/.

Savoie, Donald J. 1999. "The Rise of Court Government in Canada." *Canadian Journal of Political Science* 32, no. 4 (December): 635–64. https://doi.org/10.1017/S0008423900016930.

Sellers, Jefferey M., Anders Lidström, and Yooil Bae. 2020. *Multilevel Democracy: How Local Institutions and Civil Society Shape the Modern State*. Cambridge: Cambridge University Press. https://doi.org/10.1017/9781108672337.

Siegel, David. 2015. *Leaders in the Shadows: The Leadership Qualities of Municipal Chief Administrative Officers*. Toronto: University of Toronto Press. Kindle.

Smith, Alison. 2023. "Intergovernmental Relations and the Housing Connection: Downloading Political Responsibility." In Taylor 2023b, 9–10.

Smith, Patrick J., and Kennedy Stewart. 2009. "British Columbia." In *Foundations of Governance: Municipal Government in Canada's Provinces*, edited by Andrew Sancton and Robert Young, 282–313. Toronto: University of Toronto Press. https://doi.org/10.3138/9781442697874-009.

Stewart, Kennedy. 2023. *Decrim: How We Decriminalized Drugs in British Columbia*. Madeira Park, BC: Harbour Publishing.

Svara, James H. 1990. *Official Leadership in the City: Patterns of Conflict and Cooperation*. New York: Oxford University Press. https://doi.org/10.1093/oso/9780195057621.001.0001.

Svara, James. 1999. "U.S. City Managers and Administrators in a Global Perspective." In *The Municipal Year Book*. Washington, DC: International City/County Management Association.

Svara, James H., and Douglas J. Watson. 2010. "Introduction: Framing Constitutional Contests in Large Cities." In *More than Mayor or Manager*, edited by James H. Svara and Douglas J. Watson, 1–24. Washington, DC: Georgetown University Press.

———. 1994. *Facilitative Leadership in Local Government: Lessons from Successful Mayors and Chairpersons in the Council-Manager Form*. San Francisco: Jossey-Bass.

———. 2003. *Two Decades of Continuity and Change in American City Councils*. Report commissioned by the National League of Cities. Archived November 4, 2021, at the Wayback Machine. https://web .archive.org/web/20210304054028/https://wanty.com/wp-content/uploads/2018/01/NLC-City -Councils.pdf.

Taylor, Zack. 2014. "If Different, Then Why? Explaining the Divergent Political Development of Canadian and American Local Governance." *International Journal of Canadian Studies* 49 (January): 53–80. https://doi.org/10.3138/ijcs.49.53.

———. 2023a. "Conclusion." In Taylor 2023b, 1–4.

———, ed. 2023b. "Strong(er) Mayors in Ontario – What Difference Will They Make?" In *IMFG Forum*, no. 13. Toronto: Institute on Municipal Finance and Governance.

Taylor, Zack, and Martin Horak. 2022. "Strong Mayor Powers in Ontario are a Gross Violation of Democratic Principles." *Policy Options*, December 16, 2022. https://policyoptions.irpp.org/magazines /december-2022/strong-mayor-powers-in-ontario-are-a-gross-violation-of-democratic-principles/.

Tindal, C. Richard, and Susan Nobes Tindal. 2000. *Local Government in Canada*. 5th ed. Toronto: Nelson Thomson Learning.

Tindal, Richard, Susan Nobes Tindal, Kennedy Stewart, and Patrick J. Smith. 2017. *Local Government in Canada*. 9th ed. Toronto: Nelson Education.

Trounstine, Jessica. 2008. *Political Monopolies in American Cities: The Rise and Fall of Bosses and Reformers*. Chicago: University of Chicago Press. https://doi.org/10.7208/chicago/9780226812830.001.0001.

Wallis, Joe, and Brian Dollery. 2000. "Local Government Reform in New Zealand." Working Paper Series in Economics, University of New Zealand School of Economic Studies.

CHAPTER EIGHT

Municipal Elections and Political Incorporation

Anne Mévellec, Brandon Bolduc, Guy Chiasson, and Veika Donatien

In July 2018, less than three months before the October 22 municipal elections, newly elected Ontario premier Doug Ford announced that the number of seats on the Toronto city council was going to be brought back from forty-seven to twenty-five. This decision, which became the Better Local Government Act, overturned a previous motion voted by Toronto's council to actually increase the number of wards and councillors. Many in Toronto, including the incumbent mayor John Tory, saw this move as an attack on local democracy and were particularly critical of this decision for "changing the rules" in the middle of the ongoing election campaign. Yet some councillors also agreed that the reduction in the number of seats on Toronto's council was necessary. While such highly conflictual changes are not the usual way in contemporary Canadian local democracy, this event serves as a reminder that local democracy and how it is organized and practised is a political question, meaning that it might be subject to debate and differing (both local and provincial) views and understanding.

The political nature of local democracy has not gone unnoticed by historians who study the birth of municipal democracy in the mid-nineteenth century. As discussed in chapter 2, the Baldwin Act of 1848 is widely considered the birth certificate of local democracy in Canada. While forms of local government (the Courts of Quarter Sessions) existed in several cities in British North America, decision-making was mainly reserved for persons appointed by the colonial power. The novelty of the Baldwin Act was that decision-makers were elected in all municipalities in the territory that later became the province of Ontario. Many consider that a majority of the mechanisms of local democracy put in place by the Baldwin Act were replicated by the laws of other provinces in the following decades. This interpretation suggests that local democracy was crafted without much debate and followed similar patterns across provinces. Nicol (1997, 21) offers a fairly different interpretation that reinstates the political nature of local democracy in its infancy. In her words, Canadian local democracy was "an ongoing project well into post-Confederation years, and even after Confederation, systematic legislation controlling municipal institutions was yet to emerge in many of Canada's new provinces."

While the political nature of Canadian local democracy has been confirmed by historians of the nineteenth century, very little research has done the same for more recent times. We think that Canadian local democracy is currently undergoing significant changes. These transformations are fuelled by evolving conceptions and ongoing debates. Most of these debates are much less visible and more subtle than the Ford government's strong-arm reforms of 2018. Little media attention has been given to them, and even urban political science has not paid much notice to these less visible ongoing changes (Eidelman and Taylor 2010). Unpacking these changes and their consequences can shed new light on the politics of contemporary Canadian local democracy.

This is what we propose to do in this chapter by exploring the ongoing changes to local democracy in current Canadian municipalities, and more particularly in the main metropolitan areas of the country. It is useful to consider, as a starting point, that in the twentieth century Canadian cities have embodied a distinct democratic model from the one prevailing in other countries. This conception is particularly rooted in the idea that municipal affairs would be "by nature" apolitical, implying a managerial conception of the role of cities and the absence of political parties from the local arena. However, some aspects of this Canadian model are now contested, and changes put in place in some municipalities have contributed to its partial unravelling. While some of these changes, including the rise of local political parties in major cities in British Columbia and Quebec, date back to the 1960s, others are more recent. Because these changes result from debates both at the local and provincial level, they have proceeded at different paces in different cities and provinces, and cross-city comparisons are useful in capturing this ongoing renewal of Canadian local democracy. Moreover, municipalities are also proving to be agents of change, sometimes initiating their own forays into areas of intervention that are non-traditional for Canadian municipalities. It is argued here that the affirmation of large cities as levels of government in their own right is also linked to certain transformations in local democracy. We will first briefly present the Canadian municipal democratic model, historically grounded in a democracy of property owners. In the following sections, we will show how this initial model needs to be reviewed in light of the transformations that can be seen in Canada's major cities (Toronto, Montreal, Vancouver, and Ottawa). These transformations concern the institutional context, the profile of elected officials and their professionalization, as well as the more general politicization of the municipal level.

THE TRADITIONAL CANADIAN MUNICIPAL "DEMOCRATIC MODEL"

Elsewhere, we have asserted the presence of a "Canadian municipal model" that was associated with two main characteristics: provincial control of local municipalities and a "depoliticized view of municipal politics" (Chiasson and Mévellec 2014). The idea that Canadian municipal practice is distinct from other countries also has some bearings in terms of democracy. In other terms, local democracy in Canada has traditionally aligned along three trends: (1) Canadian municipalities see themselves as public service providers to property owners as opposed to spaces for democratic participation; (2) electoral participation in Canadian cities remains very weak, especially when compared to participation in European municipal elections; (3) and elected officials see themselves as *gifted amateurs* who refuse both a political understanding of their role and their integration into political parties. These interconnected trends form the backbone of what we will call here the "Canadian democratic model." Each of these trends, which have played their part in shaping a particularly depoliticized Canadian local democracy, will be further elaborated in the following paragraphs.

A Property-Owner's Democracy

When the provinces, beginning with Ontario's Baldwin Act, instituted municipal democracy, it was largely with a view to encourage the development of property services (Andrew 1999). The role of municipalities, as conceived by provincial legislation, was to ensure the construction and maintenance of infrastructure and services that would primarily benefit property owners (water, sewer, road construction, fire department, etc.) and that would be paid for by them through property taxes. In keeping with this understanding of the municipality as a property service authority, the democracy put in place has largely been a democracy of owners. As a general rule, to vote or stand as a candidate in municipal elections, certain property ownership requirements must be met. This situation allowed Quebec women, when they were property owners, to obtain the right to vote (but not to run for municipal office) as early as 1892. It would be several decades before these restrictions were lifted. It was not until 1912 that all Montreal residents were able to vote, and as Maillé and Tardy (1988, 54) point out, it was much later (1968) that residents of all Quebec municipalities would be able to vote, whether they were homeowners or residents. In Ontario, it was not until 1958 that the law allowed all citizens to vote at the municipal level, leaving it up to municipalities to implement this new provision. Thus, it was by referendum that several cities, including Toronto, expanded their constituencies (Rowat 1969, 19). It is significant that this conceptualizes democracy as primarily in service to property rather than as a space for public debate. Municipal franchise based on property ownership is rooted in the British model – maintained in New Zealand until 1986 and still partially in place in Australia and Canada (Sawer 2007). This is a far cry from the German model of "free towns" or the French municipalities created from 1789 onwards whose function was to represent the interests of the local community (Wollmann 2000). Despite the extension of suffrage during the twentieth century, this land/ownership concept has remained firmly entrenched, as we will see below. This idea is reflected in many ways in the concrete expression of Canadian municipal democracy, whether it be in the typical functioning of municipal councils or in the electoral practices discussed in the following sections.

Weak Electoral Participation – Not Really the Expected "Training Ground for Democracy"

According to Dahl (1967), the local level offers the opportunity for citizens to become genuinely involved in public affairs for the good of their community. Vandelli (2000) evokes in the European context the idea of a "base cell for all democracies." Paradoxically, the proximity of the municipal level to the population does not seem to encourage electoral participation at this tier of government. Indeed, data shows that on average only 40 per cent of Canadian voters exercise their right to vote at the municipal level (Couture, Breux, and Bherer 2014). In this respect, the Canadian situation seems to follow the general trend of low voter turnout in Western countries, regardless of the elections. In the United States, the rate of participation in municipal elections is not only in continuous decline but is sometimes only half the rate observed for national elections. It is thus around 25 per cent of the urban electorate of major Californian cities that choose their councillors (Hajnal and Lewis 2003). In the case of Los Angeles County, on average 21.3 per cent of eligible voters turned out to the polls in the previous five elections (table 8.2). Therefore, Canada is closer to this American model since we observe lower rates of participation in municipal elections than at other levels of government. As table 8.1 confirms, electoral participation in the 2000 elections in Montreal, Toronto, Vancouver, and Ottawa is slightly higher than the American average but rarely surpasses the 50 per cent mark. These figures are substantially lower than local electoral participation usually found in major European cities (see table 8.2, perhaps with the exception of London), where municipal participation better resists downward trends (Gendźwiłł and Kjaer 2021). In many South American countries, voting is compulsory for municipal elections for the majority of constituents, which explains such high levels of participation in cities like São Paulo. For others like the city of Bogotá, the voter turnout is not too far off that of European cities.

Hajnal and Lewis (2003) point out the negative effects that low participation can have. First of all, according to them, it is a missed opportunity for many citizens who could take advantage of the proximity of the municipal government to socialize in politics. Following Dahl (1961), their trust and confidence in their government will determine its stability. Second, as at other levels of government, the fewer voters that vote, the greater the participation bias is likely to be on the selection of elected officials and the public policies they put forward.

Several researchers have tried to explain the puzzle of low voter turnout. Several hypotheses, largely inspired by the US literature, resonate in the Canadian context. Participation is potentially related to the size of municipalities (Denters et al. 2014; Kouba, Novak, and Strnad 2021; McDonnell 2020; Oliver 2000), or to social capital, more specifically with community rootedness and civic engagement (Nakhaie 2006). The lack of interest in municipal politics could also be attributed to information deficits. Weak media coverage, coupled with the absence of national partisan labels, can contribute to making citizens' choices more difficult and discouraging participation beyond the initiated (Couture, Breux, and Bherer 2014; Cutler and

Table 8.1. Voter Turnout Rates in Canadian Municipal Elections

City	Year	%	Year	%	Year	%	Year	%	Year	%
Montreal	2002	49.00	2005	35.00	2009	39.40	2013	43.30	2017	42.50
Toronto	2003	38.33	2006	39.30	2010	50.55	2014	54.67	2018	41.00
Vancouver	2005	32.45	2008	30.79	2011	34.57	2014	43.40	2018	39.36
Ottawa	2003	33.00	2006	54.00	2010	44.00	2014	39.92	2018	42.55

Voter turnout rates provided by the following sources: Montreal (Ministère des Affaires municipales et de l'Habitation du Québec, n.d.); Toronto (City of Toronto, n.d.); Vancouver (City of Vancouver, n.d.); Ottawa (City of Ottawa, n.d.).

Table 8.2. Voter Turnout in Some Major European, American, and Latin American Cities

City	Year	%	Year	%	Year	%	Year	%	Year	%
Paris	1995	53.05	2001	64.13	2008	56.67	2014	58.41	2020*	36.70
London	2000	34.00	2004	37.00	2008	45.00	2012	38.00	2016	46.00
Barcelona	2003	59.24	2007	49.62	2011	52.99	2015	60.59	2019	66.20
Los Angeles	2001	27.92	2005	24.49	2009	15.63	2013	18.37	2017	20.10
Chicago	2003	33.70	2007	33.08	2011	42.30	2015	34.03	2019	35.45
São Paulo[†]	2004	85.45	2008	82.46	2012	80.10	2016	78.16	2020	85.84
Bogotá	2003	43.51	2007	47.87	2011	47.41	2015	51.55	2019	54.99

[*] The municipal elections of March and June 2020 were held in the context of the pandemic, which mainly explains the low voter turnout.

[†] São Paulo's voter turnout is higher because of compulsory voting for all literate citizens from eighteen to seventy years old for all elections in Brazil as it is in many South American countries such as Argentina, Uruguay, Peru, and Bolivia (subject to a small financial penalty) (Superior Electoral Court 2022).

Voter turnout rates provided by the following sources: Paris (Ministry of Interior of France); London (London Elects, n.d.); Barcelona (Government of Catalonia); Los Angeles (City of Los Angeles); Chicago (Chicago's Board of Election Commissioners); São Paulo (Regional Electoral Tribune of São Paulo); Bogotá (Registraduria Nacional Del Estado Civil).

Matthews 2005). Other work focuses instead on the "property owner" variable. Following the American work of Oliver, Ha, and Callen (2012), the profile of the municipal electorate thus combines the following typical characteristics: owner, older, richer, and more educated than the average electorate (Breux and Valette 2020). The "property owner" variable is, moreover, validated by McGregor and Spicer (2016), who tested the "Homevoter" hypothesis in Vancouver. Their study confirms that voting in the city is highly correlated with property ownership. Thus, the weight of ownership is still important in the functioning of Canadian municipal democracy even though non-property owners obtained the right to vote decades ago.

The low voter turnout rings even more true for some groups. In the United States, Latino and Asian Americans vote half as much as whites and only slightly more than Blacks in municipal elections (Hajnal and Trounstine 2005). In Canada, several studies have shown that those who vote and run for office are typically older white males, which can be linked to property ownership. The low participation rates of newly arrived Canadians (De Graauw and Andrew 2012) and young people (Dostie-Goulet et al. 2013; Breux and Valette 2020) thus contribute to characterizing Canadian municipal democracy as struggling to reach categories of the population that are potentially less concerned about property service issues (Mévellec, Donatien, and Chiasson 2020).

Many initiatives to try to boost voting in municipal elections do exist. The main municipal associations, organized on a provincial basis, are launching campaigns in that direction, aimed, for example, at young people ("Je m'implique" in the case of the province of Quebec). In addition, certain devices, such as internet voting, have been presented as an avenue of solution. However, Goodman (2014), using the case of Markham (Ontario), shows that it is mostly middle-aged and already active voters who take advantage of them. If internet voting has the potential to attract younger voters with noncommittal voting records, this has not yet been clearly demonstrated.

Local Worthies and the Gifted Amateur

Describing the traditional Canadian municipal democratic model also involves looking at the characteristics of elected municipal officials. Two main elements influence the profile of elected officials: electoral boundaries and the importance of property ownership. The figure of the local worthy is well established in this tradition. Moreover, Canadian municipal elected officials seem to have long embodied the figure of the "gifted amateur," a notion that encapsulates the idea of an elected official devoted to a mission of "service" rather than one that is fully embedded in a political perspective.

AN ELECTORAL SYSTEM THAT FAVOURS THE WORTHIES

Two main voting systems, at large and by ward, have been used in Canadian cities. The second is the most common in midsized and larger cities and has often been in place since the creation of the municipalities. In this case, the municipality's territory is divided into wards for which one or two councillors (or aldermen) are elected. Only the position of mayor is elected at large by all the voters in the municipality. The voting system is a first-past-the-post system, so the candidate who receives the most votes is automatically elected. However, in the early twentieth century, due to pressure from local reformist movements, many cities put in place boards of control. These boards of control were meant to serve as an executive body of a limited number of controllers who were elected at large. This coexistence of opposing electoral models – a board of control and mayor elected at large and a council elected on a district basis – did not prove durable in some cities such as Halifax (Roper 1985), but in Ontario many cities only gave up their board of control and returned to a ward model in the 1960s and 1970 (Sproule-Jones and Becker 2005), even as late as 2010 in the case of London. The municipality of London once again attracted considerable attention when it chose a ranked ballot electoral system for the 2018 election (Anderson and Stephenson 2021). This system, while remaining within the bounds of the ward model, gives voters the possibility to rank up to three candidates for the mayor and ward councillor, departing from the Canadian norm of first-past-the-post elections. However, in 2020 the Ontario provincial government, through its Supporting Ontario's Recovery and Municipal Elections Act, revoked the possibility for cities to use ranked ballots and forced London's return to a first-past-the-post system in 2022 (City of London 2022).

Several municipalities have adopted an entirely at-large system and still have this approach. Of the large cities, only Vancouver is organized in this way: voters choose ten councillors from the list of candidates on the ballot; the mayor is also elected at large. Koop and Kraemer (2016), in a study on a number of major cities in Canada, test the hypothesis that ward or at-large voting systems tend to promote different "representational focus of councillors" (433). They show that councillors in an at-large system likely focus on city-wide representation; conversely, ward councillors are more concerned about the representation of their geographic area, but they also mention the two geographic focuses when describing their mandate. According to critics, some minority groups are less well represented by at-large elections, and the need for candidates to get elected on a city-wide basis makes it more difficult for less well-known persons as well as candidates with fewer resources to be voted in. On the other hand, the ward system is dismissed by some as favouring parochialism and struggling to integrate city-wide concerns.

Ward voting also strongly localizes electoral competition, giving an advantage to candidates already known in their nearby communities – an advantage that is hardly offset by media coverage. In general, Cutler and Matthews (2005, 36) argue that "municipal elections provide voters with less political information (i.e., information relating to issues, candidates and the like)" than national elections. This makes it potentially more difficult for newcomers to become known to voters. In connection with this, the fame of the incumbents gives them a significant advantage in the elections, similar to what is observed in the United States (Lucas 2019). Thus, the incumbency advantage proves to be very strong at the municipal level, contributing to a small number of people "confiscating" the mandates.

The predominance of ward voting in most major Canadian cities has favoured the presence of municipal elected officials that correspond to what would be considered a "notable" in the literature from France (Abelès 1989), or in other words, a "worthy" or "dignitary." Those elected to municipal offices are most often elected because of their social characteristics, which prevail over their political ones. It is, therefore, the ability to rely on a social network that can be mobilized during the campaign that makes it possible to win. We thus speak of "notables," not necessarily in the sense of higher socio-professional categories but rather in terms of social capital.

This notable profile was also favoured by the absence of provincial political parties at the municipal level, a point to which we will return later. While political parties can help generate candidacies within their ranks while providing resources to campaign and eventually win, in their absence, candidates run in their own name, relying primarily on their reputation and social network. This has encouraged a male presence on city councils as men have traditionally had significant social capital that has enabled them to gain political power (Bjarnegård 2013).

GIFTED AMATEURS

In connection with the figure of the "worthy," the Canadian municipal model is also traditionally based on the figure of the "gifted amateur" that Steyvers and Verhelst (2012) put forward in a European context. The "gifted amateur" is an elected official who sees their role as being rather technical and as far removed as possible from political debates. Exercising their mandate on a part-time basis, compensated but not salaried, they see themselves, above all else, as at the service of their constituents (Mévellec and Tremblay 2018). Thus, the gifted amateur perceives their role as an extension of social involvement rather than as a profession (hence the expression "amateur") that would be practised full-time with some professional knowledge and skills.

Distrust of the figure of the professional politician on the local scene has deep roots in Canada. As Graham, Phillips, and Maslove (1998) have well documented, the reform movements of the early twentieth century opposed the corruption of municipal governments in the United States and Canada. For the reformers, this clientelism prevented the establishment of a professional municipal administration where decisions were based on the knowledge of the new experts in urbanization (urban planners, engineers, etc.). Thus, from the reformist point of view, it was necessary to depoliticize the city and ensure that elected officials and political parties did not thwart the management of the city by experts. For this reason, one of the legacies of the reform movements was a municipal democracy that valued a central place for experts from the municipal bureaucracy and elected officials who were independent, that is, not linked to political parties.

The predominance of independent elected officials sets Canada apart from other countries. In countries where national political parties are present on the local scene, vertical career movements are common, and roles in municipal politics often serve as stepping stones toward national office, as we can observe in the United States, Italy, France, or the Czech Republic (Dodeigne, Krukowska, and Lazauskienė 2018). The Canadian experience is quite remote from this type of political path, each level being relatively independent (Docherty 2011). On a few occasions, the major political parties have attempted to gain a foothold by running candidates under their banner. For example, the Liberal Party ran candidates for mayor of Toronto in 1969 (Fowler and Goldrick 1972). However, the lack of results ultimately meant that the independent model resisted this incursion of the major parties into the local arena and vertical integration.

The idea of a "Canadian democratic model" not only implies that cities in different provinces shared some common traits but also that these traits contributed to making the Canadian version of local democracy pretty specific. As this chapter has shown, this is not to say that these traits were not shared with some cities in other countries, but that, perhaps more than elsewhere, the Canadian version of local democracy strongly resisted politics.

While this democratic model prevailed in Canadian cities for the post-war period, there are now some more or less visible signs of change in different aspects of this model and how democracy in Canadian cities can be portrayed. The contours of municipal democracy are changing, and this is what we will illustrate in the next sections.

INSTITUTIONAL TRANSFORMATION: NEW APPEAL FOR MUNICIPAL POLITICS?

As mentioned previously, Canadian municipal governments have historically been considered mostly as simple service providers. This is reflected in the traditional activities that have been passed down by provinces over the past centuries, such as public infrastructure, waste management, water treatment, etc. In fact, based on s. 92 of the British North America Act of 1867, Canadian local governments can be formally qualified as legal "creatures of the provinces" through the control exercised by provincial governments over the distribution of responsibilities (Mévellec, Chiasson, and Fournis 2017). Lacking tangible political power, localities in the twentieth century are characterized as politically invisible (Andrew 2000, 67). It is from this minimalist conception of municipalities that many of the key elements that constitute the Canadian democratic model arose. However, this vision is somewhat challenged by a series of reforms that have taken place since the late 1990s. These reforms, which vary in nature from province to province, have had a converging effect in strengthening the role of cities. Can this new situation in the Canadian governmental hierarchy influence democracy? We believe so.

Municipal Reorganization: Municipal Assertion at the Expense of Democracy?

As noted above, municipalities, regardless of size, were traditionally considered a minor order of government. However, this situation of legal dependency was quickly out of step with the generally held idea that cities, and particularly metropolises, were fully participating in the deployment of a new economy that was less reliant on manufacturing goods and more service oriented – what some would call a post-Fordist city (Lever 2001). In a similar vein, Sassen (1991) refers to "global cities" as those that manage to capture the higher functions (e.g., financial, managerial, legal, or planning services) of the global economy and that are very polarized in terms of class. The phenomenon of metropolization includes both the transformation of the urban fabric in and around large cities and the establishment of a metropolitan framework on a global scale, which in turn anchors economic development. This has led to a new interest in very large cities on the part of the provinces and even the federal government.

In Canada, several models of metropolitan organization coexist between provinces and sometimes even within the same province. Created in 1968, the Metro Vancouver Regional District (originally known as the Greater Vancouver Regional District) is an example of great institutional stability. Conversely, Ontario and Quebec have chosen a very different path by significantly revising the municipal map and municipal organization through amalgamation. These amalgamations had important consequences for municipal democracy.

First, municipal mergers were largely carried out with very little citizen involvement. They were not really part of the election platforms of the governing parties (Mike Harris's Conservative Party in Ontario, Lucien Bouchard's Parti Québécois in Quebec) on which voters could have voted. Moreover, the implementation method relied mainly on experts (government agents, transition committees), offering few means for citizens to express themselves on both the merits and the terms of the mergers. Recourse to legal challenges failed as the provinces had full rights over municipal organization (Milroy 2002). In the case of Quebec, it was not until the arrival of a new government (Jean Charest's Liberal Party in 2003) that the citizen's voice was invited through the organization of referendums on the dismemberment of the new cities created in 2001.

Second, municipal mergers reduced the size of municipal councils and increased the number of citizens represented by each councillor. As indicated above, electoral boundaries by ward have potential implications for the representation of certain communities, such as francophones in Ottawa. These risks do not seem to have been considered by the reformers. Little work has been done on the effects of mergers on representation; however, Kushner and Siegel (2003) showed that the accessibility of elected officials was not particularly diminished. Fewer elected officials are now elected, but they also get higher salaries, more full-time staff, and new resources such as political staff (Meloche and Kilfoil 2017). Only Montreal has kept a large council like European cities, whereas the rest of Canada has opted for small city councils as is usually the case in American cities.

Third, in the case of Montreal, the reforms of the turn of the 2000s paradoxically made it more difficult for citizens to understand territorial organization. The first reform involved the creation of a new large city on the scale of the Island of Montreal organized around nineteen boroughs, as well as the creation of the Montreal Metropolitan Community on the scale of the metropolitan census region. This was followed by the demerger of certain municipalities and the creation of a coordinating body, the "communauté d'agglomération." There are therefore four levels in this institutional *mille-feuille*. On election day, the citizen must, depending on their borough of residence, vote for up to four people to represent them: the mayor of Montreal, a city councillor for Montreal, the mayor of their borough, and one borough councillor. In the case of the Ville-Marie borough, the mayor of Montreal sits as the borough mayor. All this makes for a fairly complex electoral process. One could ask to what extent this layered voting is difficult to fully grasp for citizens or if it affects the accountability of elected officials.

However, beyond obvious changes to the size of city councils, mergers have also created a context for other, perhaps less visible changes. In the case of Ottawa, Caroline Andrew (2005) has argued that the merger opened a window for "political creation." The creation of the new City of Ottawa made it necessary to review the services offered by the city as well as how those services should be offered. Along the same lines, Alain Faure (2003) suggested that the merger in Montreal would increase the political clout of the mayor of the new city, not only locally but at the provincial level. While this has not been studied much in other major cities that underwent mergers, we suspect that these changes in bigger cities have created a favourable context for a municipal shift from "policy-takers" to "policy-makers." The international literature, however, remains divided on the democratic effects of municipal mergers. In terms of the classic size/democracy issue, some authors see mergers as a source of empowerment for legislatures while others note a tendency to technocratize local authorities.

Policy-Takers, Policy-Makers, and Local Democracy

Taylor and Dobson (2020) describe the provincial-municipal relationship as one of "enduring tension," during which phases of centralization and decentralization follow one another, but also during which the role of municipalities is multiple: "In certain domains, municipalities are policy takers, functioning as the field offices of provincial ministries; in others, they are policy-makers, devising innovative solutions to local problems" (8). Without going back over the series of legislative amendments that have expanded the scope of municipal jurisdiction, notably in Alberta, Ontario, and more recently in Quebec (discussed in chapter 2), it is important to note that in these provinces at least municipalities are moving away from their initial status as "creatures of the provinces" delineated to a limited number of property-related jurisdictions and toward a model of "governments of proximity" in the terms used by the Quebec government. More generally, cities are becoming more involved in human services and not just the traditional property services.

Beyond the decentralization reforms that gave cities new powers, cities are acting more and more on a widened policy agenda that they themselves are creating. They are increasingly investing in quality of life to attract the creative class – the highly skilled workforce that companies in the knowledge-based sectors (high-tech, finance, education, science, engineering, etc.) are looking for (Florida 2002). Cities are also the sites of contemporary social issues as Andrew (2001) has already pointed out. Thus, poverty, homelessness, housing, integration, and Indigenous presence are cross-cutting issues on which they have no choice but to act. Canadian cities are also confronted with issues such as security threats, immigration, and climate change. These transnational challenges have pushed many cities to voluntarily adopt action plans and innovative policy measures in order to respond to these issues, thus becoming "policy-makers." In Canada, Toronto, Montreal, and Vancouver are members of the C40 Cities Climate Leadership Group, an international organization for helping cities share experiences and resources, as well as develop common strategies to respond effectively to climate change. Therefore, many big Canadian cities are adopting diverse forms of foreign policies, something that was traditionally reserved for senior levels of government.

The political transformation of Canadian cities' traditional role and the widening of the policy agenda may have multiple repercussions for local democracy. A number of hypotheses could be tested. First, the addition and consideration of these new issues by local governments could attract new interest in municipal politics. In fact, Breux and Vallette (2020) have demonstrated that young voters do not go to the polls as often in municipal elections compared to other general elections for higher levels of government given the notable lack of quality information and or accessibility, as well as the absence of political projects. This last element relates to the lack of political issues that stimulate and motivate voter turnout, especially that of non-property owners. That being said, the widening of the municipal policy agenda to include topics like climate change, social justice, and security may incentivize certain groups to participate in the electoral process. However, current data does not give obvious signs of these changes in terms of voter turnout, which has remained fairly stable (and fairly low) in most recent elections in major Canadian cities. Second, as will be seen in the two following sections, with a growing range of political issues on the agenda, new types of candidates may also be tempted to pursue a career in local politics.

LOCAL ELECTED OFFICIALS: SIGNS OF PROFESSIONALIZATION

In this section, we look first at some of the characteristics of local elected officials in Canada's major cities and then at some transformations in the conditions under which municipal elections and the exercise of mandates take place.

Local Political Representation in Recent Municipal Elections

The municipal level has served as a laboratory for American theorists who have studied the distribution of power in society. The work of Hunter and then Dahl is thus at the source of the elitist and pluralist schools of thought that structure part of the political science debate. As discussed in chapter 2, the common question they tried to answer was: Who governs? For Hunter (1953), certain groups can be considered as elites since they have significant capital, whether social or economic, enabling them to claim power and impose their agenda on the community. Conversely, for Dahl (1961, 1967), power is more dispersed in the community, with a variety of sources. In fact, power cannot be confiscated by one group or the other. A third school proposes, notably with the work of Polsby (1963), to focus attention on community power, that is, to identify signs of political power not only in the formal institutions dedicated to it but also in the different spheres that make up society. Today, the literature has moved away from this initial debate to focus instead on the ability of municipal elected officials to deliver. As a result of Stone's work on urban regimes, the central preoccupation now is the local collaboration schemes that create the capacity to govern. But there is another question that is crucially important and is expressed in terms of identity politics.

On this topic, there is little Canadian work that documents the profiles of elected municipal officials in general. This is why in the following lines we return to only one of the dimensions of political representation, highlighting the unfinished representativeness of Canadian municipal councils. In this sense, elements related to descriptive representation (Pitkin 1967) are presented here.

FEMINIZATION IN PROGRESS

The municipal level has sometimes been described as more "women friendly." Two main categories of argument would explain this. First, the costs of entering municipal politics (financial costs, severity of competition) are lower than at other levels. Second, women may be more attracted to municipal jurisdictions (Trimble 1995), which are themselves closer to everyday quality of life issues. However, these arguments have been challenged in several contexts, including Germany (Eder, Fortin-Rittberger, and Kröber 2016) and Canada (Tolley 2011; Tremblay and Mévellec 2013). Indeed, although the election of the first woman municipal councillor took place in 1917 in Calgary (Hannah Gale), the data confirms that the municipal level does not fare particularly well compared to other levels of representation, since in 2009 the presence of women on municipal councils remained below 30 per cent (Tremblay and Mévellec 2013). However, their presence is not only important in terms of descriptive representation but also substantive representation. Recent studies have indeed shown that their presence has consequences on municipal public policies (Koop and Conrad 2021), confirming work on American (Holman 2017) and Brazilian (Funk and Philips 2019) cities. The under-representation of women seems to be changing, however, and women's participation in municipal affairs is being confirmed, particularly in some large cities. Several examples can be presented here. They confirm both a slow but steady trend toward the feminization of municipal councils. As such, in 2017 Montreal elected for the first time a parity council (composed of 53 women out of a total of 103 members, i.e., 51.4 per cent). Vancouver has the highest proportion of women, with eight women councillors out of a total of ten council members. Toronto and Ottawa are currently more at the beginning of the parity zone, with eight out of twenty-five (32 per cent) and eight out of twenty-three (34 per cent) women board members, respectively. Halifax did achieve parity when eight women and eight men were elected on its council in the 2020 municipal elections. This recent increase in the number of women in large Canadian cities seems to validate the hypothesis put forward by Gidengil and Vengroff (1997) that women are more successful in getting elected in large urban centres because of their diverse populations and "more progressive" politics.

These results, however, call for several nuances. While women make up a significant portion of elected municipal officials, they hold only a small proportion of key positions, particularly that of mayor. The percentage of women "mayors" thus remains well below the parity zone. Breux, Couture, and Koop (2019) have shown that for the one hundred largest cities in Canada, only 16 per cent of all mayoral candidates were women. Similarly, in the United States only 23 per cent of the mayors of cities with more than 30,000 inhabitants are women (CAWP 2020) – only 10 per cent in Latin America (Martínez 2014). However, the symbolic nature of some electoral victories cannot be overlooked. In this sense, the mayoral elections of Valérie Plante in Montreal (in 2017 and 2021) and Jyoti Gondek in Calgary (in 2021) are visible examples of women breaching the glass ceiling of their municipality. They joined a select group of first woman mayors with Anne Hidalgo in Paris, Manuela Castrillon in Madrid, and Lori E. Lightfoot in Chicago. Beyond the "role models" Valérie Plante and Jyonti Gondek could provide for the next generation, the trend toward feminization remains slow. Yet, recent pan-Canadian data (Lucas et al. 2021) confirms what others had already identified in a more partial way (Tremblay 2014): "women are, on average, more likely than men to win municipal elections in Canada," regardless of the size of the municipality. This confirms that the solution lies in increasing the number of women candidates.

In order to do this, it is important to know the barriers that seem to stand in front of women. Several analysts, including Gavan-Koop and Smith (2008), have identified the lack of regulation of election financing as one of the major barriers to women's election in Vancouver. This view is consistent with a body of literature on the conditions for women's electoral success and financial resources (see, among others, Trimble and Arscott 2003; Kushner, Siegel, and Stanwick 1997). Consistent with this literature, reforms to election financing would make electoral competition more affordable for some women (Trimble and Arscott 2003). As McAllister (2004, 61) summarized, the issue of financing is twofold: (1) it may hinder the candidacy of people who do not have the necessary network to accumulate substantial electoral funding; (2) following Lightbody (1993), she points out that donors are probably inclined to give their money to candidates who share at least some of their interests, thereby limiting the diversity of candidate profiles. The recent situation in Vancouver invites consideration of this argument because the implementation of local election financing reform in British Columbia in 2018 coincided with an increased presence of women in the 2018 election. However, the lack of hindsight does not yet suggest a clear link between these two events.

A LONG OVERDUE ETHNOCULTURAL DIVERSITY

The presence of ethnocultural minorities on councils is another important element to consider when analyzing the composition of local political personnel in large cities and its representativeness. According to Statistics Canada, large cities are the most diverse jurisdictions in the country. In Montreal, the proportion of immigrants living in the city is 33.4 per cent. This percentage is 23.6 per cent in Ottawa, 46.3 per cent in Toronto, and 46.6 per cent in Vancouver according to data from 2016 (Statistics Canada 2017). It is fair to ask whether the demographic mosaic is reflected in the municipal councils in the last election. To put it bluntly, the data challenges the general notion that members of ethnocultural communities are better represented politically at the municipal level than at other levels of government (Collin et al. 2008, 8).

In Montreal, in 2017, 25 per cent of the 86 (out of 103) councillors who responded to a survey declared belonging to a visible minority. The situation is not much different in Ottawa, where four out of twenty-three (17 per cent) of municipal councillors consider themselves as part of an ethnic minority. In Toronto, proportions are higher as immigrants or children of immigrants occupy nine out of the twenty-five seats on council, which amounts to 36 per cent. However, Siemiatycki (2008, 23) still argues that Toronto's elected politicians do not reflect the city's population profile and that the "politics of difference" in Toronto are considerably more ambiguous and interesting than the city's self-styled reputation for unproblematic integration. In Vancouver, minorities are not as well represented. Bloemraad (2008) argues that compared to other levels of government, the City of Vancouver is less open to ethnocultural minorities. In 2018, 90 per cent of elected municipal officials were of European descent. In addition, in 2020, for the first time in thirty-two years, the council had no Asian representatives (McElroy 2020), even though more than a quarter of the city's population belongs to this ethnic community (Statistics Canada 2017). This contrasts with Vancouver's reputation as one of the most ethnocultural diverse cities in Canada (Collin et al. 2008, 17). Recent results show both a decline in inclusive representation in some places and (rather timid) advances in others: a certain inconsistency in the trends traditionally observed is emerging.

As demonstrated, the challenges for minorities' representation are differentiated according to the urban agglomeration considered and are highly contextualized. The findings are similar in the United States (Hajnal and Trounstine 2005). These challenges may be exacerbated or mitigated by voting patterns, low turnout, at-large or ward systems, the size of constituencies, or the presence of municipal political parties. Therefore, the question that arises is whether these peculiarities of the municipal political field have an impact on the under-representation/ political representation of certain groups traditionally excluded from the political field.

Critics argue that Vancouver's electoral processes and territorial organization of the vote do not help the representation of groups traditionally excluded from politics (Gavan-Koop and Smith 2008). Large electoral areas and the limited number of positions available in some cities increase campaign costs and reduce the opportunities for an ethnocultural group to effectively influence the outcome of an election (38). This argument suggests that immigrant and minority communities favour candidates from their own communities and that the high residential concentration of immigrants in a given electoral district could confer an electoral advantage to minority candidates through identity considerations. However, these positions are not always unanimous. While the idea is validated in some works on the City of Toronto (Siemiatycki and

Saloojee 2002; Siemiatycki and Matheson 2005), other authors (e.g., Saggar 1998) studying the issue in the British context urge caution and consider it more of a perception. Immigrant and minority communities do not necessarily vote for candidates with the same ethnic or identity characteristics. The obstacles to the election of minority groups are, therefore, differentiated according to the urban agglomeration under consideration. To this end, understanding the political offer from minorities requires contextualized and more in-depth analyses.

Changes in Electoral Conditions and Terms of Office

Thus, the issues of representativeness are linked to the institutional conditions of access but also to the exercise of mandates. In this section, we return in particular to the crucial issue of municipal election financing, which is involved in the selection of candidates, as well as the principles and practices concerning the exercise of mandates, particularly wages and training.

RECENT REFORMS IN LOCAL ELECTION FINANCING

The recent municipal elections in the four cities surveyed were all held under the auspices of new legislation. Indeed, the 2010s were a particularly fertile period for electoral reform and local campaign financing in Canada. The aim of these reforms was to respond to the growing demands in Western democracies for greater control over election spending and financing (OECD 2016). They also reflect ongoing dissatisfaction with electoral control mechanisms. In Vancouver, the 2018 municipal elections were conducted under the control of the Local Elections Campaign Financing Act of 2014. In Montreal, the reformers introduced amendments to the Municipal Elections and Referendums Act in 2013 and 2016 regarding financing. Ontario municipalities have also seen reform of the local electoral system. In June 2016, the Municipal Elections Act of 1996 was amended by Bill 181, the Municipal Elections Modernization Act. Then, in May 2017, the new Bill 68, Modernizing Ontario's Municipal Act, which governed the final 2018 elections in Toronto and Ottawa, was passed.

While the scope of these reforms varies from one jurisdiction to another, several factors specific to the municipal political scene justify putting them on the agenda. These include the proven risks of collusion between firms and local politicians and the repeated corruption scandals that mar local institutions (Hudon and Garzón 2016). In addition, there are factors such as the growing increase in election expenses for candidates and the overall cost of elections due to the professionalization of campaigns, which disadvantages the participation of certain groups in electoral contests (Gavan-Koop and Smith 2008), or factors related to the very characteristics of the local political field (restricted local electoral base, presence of independent candidates with limited resources, etc.). There is also a trend toward convergence of municipal standards with those defined for higher levels of government (Pelletier 2014). This harmonization is leading to a gradual tightening of the rules enacted in the name of the principles of political equity and transparency: limitations on individual contributions, a ban on corporate contributions, limits on election expenses at very low thresholds, restrictions on third-party advertising, and the imposition of heavier sanctions on offenders.

The issue of local election financing is not only Canadian, as illustrated by billionaire Michael Bloomberg, who invested US$108 million in 2009 in his campaign to become mayor of New York for a third time (Foreman 2014). Corrupt electoral practices, particularly in connection with the awarding of local public contracts, have been identified in Paris (Lalam 2012) as well as in Italian cities (Coviello and Gagliarducci 2017). Moreover, even when important advances in electoral regulation are made, they do not always concern the municipal level. This is particularly the case in Latin America, where local elections are still considered less important (Londoño and Zovatto 2014, 129). In such circumstances, the implementation of electoral regulations at the local level remains a real challenge when considering the steps recently taken by Canadian municipalities.

In spite of a convergence in objectives, values, and general orientations, provincial reforms are characterized by varied instruments, selected according to the always specific provincial political configurations, and unevenly involving public electoral subsidies, the authorization of third-party advertising, or the imposition of individual contribution rates.

Opinions differ on the potential impacts of these new rules on political life. Some observers believe that they are likely to result in low voter turnout and reduced interest in local elections (Fisher and Eisenstadt 2004; Ansolabehere and Snyder 2000). Others, however, argue that they promote equality of citizens in getting elected and facilitate the emergence of new individuals and groups traditionally excluded from political arenas (Ohman 2014). The debate remains open pending the availability of adequate empirical data to assess the actual effects of the implementation of these new regulations in Canadian cities.

PROFESSIONALIZING TERMS IN OFFICE: REMUNERATING AND TRAINING ELECTED MUNICIPAL OFFICIALS

If the conditions of access to the term in office are important, so are the conditions of exercise of these terms. Elected officials in large Canadian cities generally set their own compensation, to which must be added other types of additional payments depending on their responsibilities. Canada's large cities can be distinguished from the municipal world in general by the degree of professionalization they exhibit. Max Weber (1965) defined political professionalization as the ability to live for politics and of politics, that is, to derive one's main income from it. The monetary dimension is closely associated with the exclusive nature of the political mandate (i.e., not having to exercise another profession to support oneself). Moreover, professionalization requires municipal office-holders to master different types of knowledge.

Although elected municipal officials in Canada's major cities most often serve on a full-time basis, it is important to remember that the local political office is still attached to the image of service to the community in the form of volunteerism (Steyvers and Verhelst 2012). However, the international literature highlights at least three phenomena potentially related to the payment of elected officials. First, higher remuneration would help to attract candidates with higher levels of education or professional occupations that are considered more competent. Ensuring good salaries would, therefore, potentially broaden the pool of candidates beyond the traditional worthy figure. However, the existing work does not allow for an unequivocal link. Second, remuneration is associated with the behaviour of elected officials, that is, their performance once in office. Higher salaries would make the term of office a coveted position, providing an incentive for elected officials to seek re-election. This quest would, in turn, have an impact on the way they exercise their term (notably regarding the number of legislative proposals, success, or accountability) but also on their longevity in politics (possibly leading to forms of term confiscation). However, the efficient wages thesis tested on Italian mayors (Gagliarducci and Nanninici 2013) concludes that there are effects on selection rather than on performance. Third, remuneration is sometimes associated with the fight against corruption. The authors, however, do not agree on the scope of better wages. According to Benito, Guillamón, and Bastida (2015), this seems to discourage some Italian mayors from participating in a system of corruption; others such as La Porta et al. (1999) are much more nuanced. To sum up, on this aspect, as on that of recruitment and performance of political work, salary is only one dimension of a complex phenomenon.

To conclude this section, we add to the Weberian definition of professionalization that of Gaxie (2001), for whom it is also important to take into consideration the knowledge and know-how possessed by elected officials in the exercise of their mandates. The recognition that the municipal political mandate comes with a certain number of skills is another element that should help Canadian society move away from the idea that municipal elected officials are gifted amateurs. This is an underdeveloped research theme. It should be noted that provincial municipal associations, like their American counterparts, offer a wide range of training programs designed to equip elected officials: training in municipal finance, political communication, use of social networks, urban planning, municipal budgeting, and so on. It also should be noted that only Quebec has imposed mandatory content on the ethics and professional conduct of elected municipal officials, which they must acquire during the first year of their term in office, regardless of the size of their municipality (Mévellec and Grenier 2016). In addition, "transition teams" are being set up along the lines of those found at other levels of government. As noted by Spicer and Graham (2016), Toronto mayor John Tory, elected in 2014, had no municipal experience. The Transition Advisory Committee allowed the new mayor to be briefed on the political and administrative functioning of the city, including the functioning of council, recruitment procedures, and strategies to get his platform passed through council. This type of approach illustrates the complexity of the task of mayors in large cities and the need for them to rapidly acquire a body of knowledge and know-how to fully exercise their role as elected officials.

POLITICIZATION OF MUNICIPAL POLITICS

In the last section of this chapter, we wish to emphasize the fundamentally political character of the municipal level, which today moves away from the traditional, supposedly apolitical model, returning to the need to consider municipal affairs as an expression of politics. Politicization can be promoted by the local political parties that are now found in greater numbers in cities of Quebec and British Columbia, but it can also take other channels.

This politicization is, first of all, related to the range of responsibilities of cities. Those defending the traditional minimalist conception of municipal politics might argue that there's no liberal or conservative way to pave a street (Lightbody 2006, 240). Yet, the expansion of the local policy agenda to include social or environmental issues complicates political debates and discredits the factual perspective of the decision-making process. The decision to pave a street includes multiple micro and macro political choices that reflect new concerns, such as environmental, security, and equity issues, which can be ideological and value based (Béland, Cattapan, and Schwartz 2017). The already mentioned widening of the local policy agenda also contributes to the politicization of local governance.

The politicization of Canadian cities does not take the form, as elsewhere, of partisanization, that is, a process whereby politics is primarily exercised through political parties. Thus, unlike in American or most European cities, elected municipal officials are elected as independents. However, it is important to note that in some cases, political parties managed to have a lasting presence in the major cities of Quebec and British Columbia. These are not integrated with the provincial parties but are referred to as local political parties (specific to a city), as can be found in Sweden, the Netherlands, and Denmark (Reiser and Holtmann 2008). The Non-Partisan Association (whose name is quite evocative of a desire to dissociate itself from political parties) has been running candidate slates since 1936 in Vancouver, which makes it the eldest of local political parties. Apart from this rather peculiar experience, it was only much later, in the 1960s, that local political parties in Quebec City and Montreal made the first breakthroughs in city politics dominated by independent elected officials. Originating in urban social movements, the Montreal Citizens' Movements (Léveillée and Léonard 1987) and Le Progrès civique (1962–2001) in Quebec City managed to defeat previous municipal administrations close to the business classes. Today, Quebec's electoral legislation continues to favour the presence of municipal political parties, allowing them, for example, to raise electoral funds throughout their mandate, whereas independents can only do so during the election year itself. Numbering 138 (as of July 2024), they are minimally campaign vehicles grouping candidates around a modest platform although they may also sometimes result from a more entrenched citizen movement (Chiasson, Gauthier, and Andrew 2011). In any case, their presence has an impact on the number of candidacies, which has been steadily increasing since 2011 in Quebec, and on the feminization of candidacies, whereas national political parties have generally been seen as obstacles to the presence of women (Tremblay 2014). Finally, when they have a sufficient number of elected members on council, their presence favours forms of parliamentarization (Mévellec and Tremblay 2013) that reveal the existing cleavages within the elected assemblies. The presence of local political parties in cities in British Columbia and Quebec and the fairly long-standing provincial legislation that allows these parties to exist (and offer some support) can be seen as early breaches in the Canadian municipal model. Other provincial governments have not followed this path, and the independent elected official remains the norm in municipal politics outside of British Columbia and Quebec.

While the rise of local political parties has favoured politicization in some cities in Quebec and British Columbia, it can also emerge in cities where there are no political parties. A telling example of this would be the debates on women's safety in cities. Whitzman (2002) has shown how, in the 1980s and 1990s, women's groups managed to push for women's safety on the political and administrative agenda of the City of Toronto. In that case, as in the case of Ottawa (Andrew 2000, 2007) and other cities in Canada and elsewhere, safety for women successfully became a recognized political reference point for urban planning by the city. In more recent times, local debates about "defunding the police" have confirmed that municipal politicization can very well emerge in contexts where independent councillors are the norm. As is the case in many North American cities, local movements have strongly advocated for reducing municipal police budgets to better fund social services. In Ottawa, for instance, a summer 2021 proposal to raise the 2022 police budget by 3 per cent generated very sustained opposition by a number of civil society groups in public consultations held by the Police Service Commission. A number of Ottawa city councillors also expressed their opposition to the measure. Similar politically charged debates around police budgeting can also be found in Toronto. These recent municipal debates might be exceptionally charged, but they serve as a powerful reminder that important contemporary political issues are to be debated locally. While this was not well recognized when the Canadian municipal democratic model was dominant, it has become a more recognizable part of Canadian municipal democracy in the past decades.

CONCLUSION

This chapter started by pointing out that local democracy is a political question. While the political nature of the nascent Canadian municipal democracy in the nineteenth century could be taken for granted, our intent was to show that local democracy in major Canadian cities of the twenty-first century remains political.

The idea of a Canadian municipal democratic model suggests that, for a good part of the twentieth century, municipalities in different provinces often shared many common traits not necessarily found in cities outside of Canada. These traits – a property-owner democracy, low turnouts in elections, representation dominated by white, middle-aged males following the gifted amateur – have fairly deep roots in the Canadian urban experience. However, reinstating the politics of local democracy can help to appreciate that these might not be eternal and that changes might occur in how local democracy is conceived and practised in Canada. Our analysis of four major Canadian cities has shown that they are undergoing transformations in at least some of the traits of the old Canadian model. As we could see, these changes are usually fairly slow and not particularly spectacular. Some of these transformations will be more apparent in certain cities (e.g., in terms of representativeness), suggesting that specific local institutional conditions are important drivers for change along with broader trends.

In our view, these changing trends give us a better understanding of the political nature of local democracy in two ways. First, they confirm that previous forms of property-owner-dominated democracy are challenged and subject to debates both at the local and provincial levels. Second, the new trends uncover the political nature of municipal representation and decision-making. In both ways, these trends seem to contribute to the reinvention of what could be considered the new Canadian municipal democratic model and recast some of its international specificity. While these changes are undoubtedly significant, municipal reliance on property taxes still imposes limits on the ability of local government to tackle the social, economic, and environmental challenges of our times. More secure municipal access to funding sources beyond the property tax still seems an important condition for increasing local governing capacity as well as a far-reaching municipal democracy. In closing, this chapter should be seen as an invitation to take more seriously the municipal level as an important site of Canadian democracy in the making, not only in terms of representation but also in terms of collective choices and, therefore, public policy.

REFERENCES

Abélès, Marc. 1989. *Jours tranquilles en 89 : ethnologie d'un département français.* Paris: Odile Jacob.

Anderson, Cameron D., and Laura B. Stephenson. 2021. "London." In *Big City Elections in Canada,* edited by Jack Lucas and R. Michael McGregor, 127–46. Toronto: University of Toronto Press. https://doi.org/10.3138/9781487528577-009.

Andrew, Caroline. 1999. "Les métropoles canadiennes." In *Dislocation et permanence : l'invention du Canada quotidien,* edited by Caroline Andrew, 61–80. Ottawa: University of Ottawa Press.

———. 2000. "Resisting Boundaries? Using Safety Audits for Women." In *Gendering the City,* edited by Kristine Miranne and Alma Young, 157–68. Lanham, MD: Rowman and Littlefield.

———. 2001. "The Shame of (Ignoring) the Cities." *Journal of Canadian Studies* 35, no. 4 (Winter): 100–10. https://doi.org/10.3138/jcs.35.4.100.

———. 2005. "Les fusions municipales : ouvertures ou obstacles pour les femmes ?" In *Femmes et politiques : L'État en mutation,* edited by Dominique Masson, 273–95. Ottawa: Presses de l'Université d'Ottawa.

———. 2007. "La gestion de la complexité urbaine ; le rôle et l'influence des groupes en quête d'équité dans les grandes villes canadiennes." *Téléscope* 13, no. 3 (Spring): 60–7.

Ansolabehere, Stephen, and James M. Snyder Jr. 2000. "Soft Money, Hard Money, Strong Parties." *Columbia Law Review* 100, no. 3 (April): 598–619. https://doi.org/10.2307/1123496.

Béland, Daniel, Alana Cattapan, and Elizabeth Schwartz. 2017. "Paying Attention to the Mundane Policy Issues." *Policy Options*, December 5, 2017. https://policyoptions.irpp.org/magazines/december-2017/paying-attention-to-the-mundane-policy-issues/.

Benito, Bernardino, Maria-Dolores Guillamón, and Francisco Bastida. 2015. "Determinants of Urban Political Corruption in Local Government." *Crime, Law and Social Change* 63, no. 3 (May): 191–210. https://doi.org/10.1007/s10611-015-9563-9.

Bjarnegård, Elin. 2013. *Gender, Informal Institutions and Political Recruitment: Explaining Male Dominance in Parliamentary Representation*. New York: Palgrave Macmillan. https://doi.org/10.1057/9781137296740.

Bloemraad, Irene. 2008. "Diversity and Elected Official in the City of Vancouver." In *Electing a Diverse Canada: The Representation of Immigrants, Minorities, and Women*, edited by Caroline Andrew, 46–69. Vancouver: UBC Press. https://doi.org/10.59962/9780774814874-005.

Breux, Sandra, Jérôme Couture, and Royce Koop. 2019. "Influences on the Number and Gender of Candidates in Canadian Local Elections." *Revue Canadienne de science politique/Canadian Journal of Political Science* 52, no. 1 (March): 163–81. https://doi.org/10.1017/S0008423918000483.

Breux, Sandra, and Salomé Valette. 2020. "Voter à l'échelle municipale au Québec : significations et portée chez certains jeunes électeurs." *Revue Jeunes et Sociétés* 5, no. 1 (July): 50–70. https://doi.org/10.7202/1070525ar.

Center for American Women and Politics (CAWP). 2020. "Women Mayors in U.S. Cities 2020." Accessed April 26, 2022. https://cawp.rutgers.edu/levels_of_office/women-mayors-us-cities-2020.

Chiasson, Guy, and Anne Mévellec. 2014. "The 2013 Quebec Municipal Election." *Canadian Journal of Urban Research* 23, no. 2 (Winter): 1–8. https://www.jstor.org/stable/26189248.

Chiasson, Guy, Mario Gauthier, and Caroline Andrew. 2011. "Les élections municipales de 2009 à Gatineau : quel modèle de démocratie urbaine ?" In *Les élections municipales au Québec : enjeux et perspectives*, edited by Laurence Bherer and Sandra Breux, 265–87. Québec: Presses de l'Université Laval.

City of London. 2022. "Method of Voting." May 4, 2022. https://london.ca/government/council-civic-administration/elections/method-voting.

City of Ottawa. n.d. "Previous Elections and Appointment Processes." Accessed April 26, 2022. https://ottawa.ca/en/city-hall/elections/previous-elections-and-appointment-processes.

City of Toronto. n.d. "About Election – Voter Statistics." Accessed April 26, 2022. https://open.toronto.ca/dataset/elections-voter-statistics/.

City of Vancouver. n.d. "Previous Elections." Accessed April 26, 2022. https://vancouver.ca/your-government/previous-elections.aspx.

Collin, Jean-Pierre, Sandra Breux, and Laurence Bherer. 2008. *La participation et la représentation politique des membres des communautés ethnoculturelles au sein des instances démocratiques municipales*. Montreal: Groupe de recherche sur l'innovation municipale.

Couture, Jérôme, Sandra Breux, and Laurence Bherer. 2014. "Analyse écologique des déterminants de la participation électorale municipale au Québec." *Canadian Journal of Political Science/Revue canadienne de science politique* 47, no. 4 (December): 787–812. https://doi.org/10.1017/S0008423914001152.

Coviello, Devio, and Stefano Gagliarducci. 2017. "Tenure in Office and Public Procurement." *American Economic Journal: Economic Policy* 9, no. 3 (August): 59–105. https://doi.org/10.1257/pol.20150426.

Cutler, Fred, and J. Scott Matthews. 2005. "The Challenge of Municipal Voting: Vancouver 2002." *Canadian Journal of Political Science/Revue canadienne de science politique* 38, no. 2 (June): 359–82. https://doi.org/10.1017/S0008423905040151.

Dahl, Robert A. 1961. *Who Governs? Democracy and Power in an American City*. New Haven, CT: Yale University Press.

———. 1967. "The City in the Future of Democracy." *The American Political Science Review* 61, no. 4 (December): 953–70. https://doi.org/10.2307/1953398.

de Graauw, Els, and Caroline Andrew. 2012. "Immigrant Political Incorporation in American and Canadian Cities." In *Immigrant Geographies of North American Cities*, edited by Carlos Teixeira, Wei Li, and Audrey Kobayashi, 179–206. Don Mills, ON: Oxford University Press.

Denters, Bas, Michael Goldsmith, Andreas Ladner, Poul Erik Mouritzen, and Lawrence E. Rose. 2014. *Size and Local Democracy*. Cheltenham, UK: Edward Elgar. https://doi.org/10.4337/9781783478248.

Docherty, David. 2011. "The Canadian Political Career Structure: From Stability to Free Agency." *Regional & Federal Studies: Moving through the Labyrinth: Political Careers in Multi-level Systems* 21, no. 2 (May): 185–203. https://doi.org/10.1080/13597566.2011.530018.

Dodeigne, Jérémy, Joanna Krukowska, and Aistė Lazauskienė. 2018. "The Mayors' Political Career: Between Local and National Ambition." In *Political Leaders and Changing Local Democracy: The European Mayor*, edited by Hubert Heinelt, Annick Magnier, Marcello Cabria, and Herwig Reynaert, 109–47. Cham: Palgrave Macmillan. https://doi.org/10.1007/978-3-319-67410-0_4.

Dostie-Goulet, Eugénie, André Blais, Patrick Fournier, and Elisabeth Gidengil. 2013. "L'abstention sélective, ou pourquoi certains jeunes qui votent au fédéral boudent les élections municipales." *Canadian Political Science Journal/Revue canadienne de science politique* 45, no. 4 (December): 909–27. https://doi.org/10.1017/S0008423912001084.

Eder, Christina, Jessica Fortin-Rittberger, and Corinna Kröber. 2016. "The Higher the Fewer? Patterns of Female Representation across Levels of Government in Germany." *Parliamentary Affairs* 69, no. 2 (April): 366–86. https://doi.org/10.1093/pa/gsv021.

Eidelman, Gabriel, and Zack Taylor. 2010. "Canadian Urban Politics: Another 'Black Hole'?" *Journal of Urban Affairs* 32, no. 3 (August): 305–20. https://doi.org/10.1111/j.1467-9906.2010.00507.x.

Faure, Alain. 2003. "Montréal, l'Ile laboratoire. Les politiques publiques à l'épreuve du bien commun urbain." *Revue Canadienne d'études urbaines/Canadian Journal of Urban Research* 12, no. 1 (Summer): 35–57. https://www.jstor.org/stable/44320748.

Fisher, Justin, and Todd A. Eisenstadt. 2004. "Introduction: Comparative Party Finance, What Is to Be Done?" *Party Politics* 10, no. 6 (November): 619–26. https://doi.org/10.1177/1354068804046910.

Florida, Richard. 2002. *The Rise of the Creative Class: And How It's Transforming Work, Leisure, Community and Everyday Life*. New York: Basic Books.

Foreman, Sean D. 2014. "The Political Environment for Mayors in the 21st Century." In *Local Politics and Mayoral Elections in 21st Century America: The Keys to City Hall*, edited by Sean D. Foreman and Marcia L. Goldwin, 3–17. New York: Routledge. https://doi.org/10.4324/9781315740089.

Fowler, Edmund. P., and Michael D. Goldrick. 1972. "Patterns of Partisan and Non-Partisan Balloting." In *Emerging Party Politics in Urban Canada*, edited by Jack K. Masson and James D. Anderson, 45–59. Toronto: McClelland and Stewart.

Funk, Kendall D., and Andrew Q. Philips. 2019. "Representative Budgeting: Women Mayors and the Composition of Spending in Local Governments." *Political Research Quarterly* 72, no. 1 (March): 19–33. https://doi.org/10.1177/1065912918775237.

Gagliarducci, Stefano, and Tommaso Nannicini. 2013. "Do Better Paid Politicians Perform Better? Disentangling Incentives from Selection." *Journal of the European Economic Association* 11, no. 2 (April): 369–98. https://doi.org/10.1111/jeea.12002.

Gavan-Koop, Denisa, and Patrick J. Smith. 2008. "Gendering Local Governing: Canadian and Comparative Lessons – The Case of Metropolitan Vancouver." *Canadian Political Science Review* 2, no. 3 (August): 152–71. https://doi.org/10.24124/c677/200826.

Gaxie, Daniel. 2001 "Les enjeux citoyens de la professionnalisation politique." *Mouvements* 5, no. 18: 21–7. https://doi.org/10.3917/mouv.018.0021.

Gendźwiłł, Adam, and Ulrik Kjaer. 2021. "Mind the Gap, Please! Pinpointing the Influence of Municipal Size on Local Electoral Participation." *Local Government Studies* 47, no. 1 (January): 11–30. https://doi.org/10.1080/03003930.2020.1777107.

Gidengill, Elisabeth, and Richard Vengroff. 1997. "Representational Gains of Canadian Women or Token Growth? The Case of Quebec's Municipal Politics." *Canadian Journal of Political Science /Revue canadienne de science politique* 30, no. 3 (September): 528–44. https://doi.org/10.1017 /S0008423900015997.

Goodman, Nicole J. 2014. "Internet Voting in a Local Election in Canada." In *The Internet and Democracy in Global Perspective*, edited by Bernard Grofman, Alexander H. Trechsel, and Mark Franklin, 7–24. Cham: Springer. https://doi.org/10.1007/978-3-319-04352-4_2.

Graham, Katherine A., Susan D. Phillips, with Allan M. Maslove. 1998. *Urban Governance in Canada.* Toronto: Harcourt Brace.

Hajnal, Zoltan, and Jessica Trounstine. 2005. "Where Turnout Matters: The Consequences of Uneven Turnout in City Politics." *The Journal of Politics* 67, no. 2 (May): 515–35. https://doi .org/10.1111/j.1468-2508.2005.00327.x.

Hajnal, Zoltan L., and Paul G. Lewis. 2003. "Municipal Institutions and Voter Turnout in Local Elections." *Urban Affairs Review* 38, no. 5 (May): 645–68. https://doi.org/10.1177/1078087403038 005002.

Holman, Mirya R. 2017. "Women in Local Government: What We Know and Where We Go from Here." *State and Local Government Review* 49, no. 4 (December): 285–96. https://doi.org /10.1177/0160323X17732608.

Hudon, Pierre-André, and César Garzón. 2016. "Corruption in Public Procurement: Entrepreneurial Coalition Building." *Crime, Law, and Social Change* 66, no. 3 (October): 291–311. https://doi .org/10.1007/s10611-016-9628-4.

Hunter, Floyd. 1953. *Community Power Structure: A Study of Decision Makers.* Chapel Hill, NC: University of North Carolina Press.

Koop, Royce, and Laura Conrad. 2021. "Gender and the Policy Priorities of Canadian City Councillors." *Journal of Women, Politics & Policy* 42, no. 2 (April): 176–87. https://doi.org/10.1080 /1554477X.2021.1842675.

Koop, Royce, and John Kraemer. 2016. "Wards, At-Large Systems and the Focus of Representation in Canadian Cities." *Canadian Journal of Political Science/Revue canadienne de science politique* 49, no. 3 (September): 433–48. https://doi.org/10.1017/S0008423916000512.

Kouba, Karel, Jakub Novák, and Matyáš Strnad. 2021. "Explaining Voter Turnout in Local Elections: A Global Comparative Perspective." *Contemporary Politics* 27, no. 1 (January): 58–78. https://doi.org /10.1080/13569775.2020.1831764.

Kushner, Joseph, and David Siegel. 2003. "Effect of Municipal Amalgamations in Ontario on Political Representation and Accessibility." *Canadian Journal of Political Science/Revue canadienne de science politique* 36, no. 5 (December): 1035–51. https://doi.org/10.1017/S0008423903778950.

Kushner, Joseph, David Siegel, and Hannah Stanwick. 1997. "Ontario Municipal Elections: Voting Trends and Determinants of Electoral Success in a Canadian Province." *Canadian Journal of Political*

Science/Revue canadienne de science politique 30, no. 3 (September): 539–53. https://doi.org/10.1017/S0008423900016000.

Lalam, Nacer. 2012. "France: From Local Elites to National Leaders." In *Corruption and Organized Crime in Europe*, edited by Philip Gounev and Vincenzo Ruggiero, 108–24. London: Routledge.

La Porta, Rafael, Florencio Lopez-de-Silanes, Andrei Shleifer, and Robert Vishny. 1999. "The Quality of Government." *Journal of Law, Economics and Organization* 15, no. 1 (March): 222–79. https://doi.org/10.1093/jleo/15.1.222.

Léveillée, Jacques, and Jean-François Léonard. 1987. "The Montréal Citizen's Movement Comes to Power." *International Journal of Urban and Regional Research* 11, no. 4 (December): 567–80. https://doi.org/10.1111/j.1468-2427.1987.tb00067.x.

Lever, Walter F. 2001. "The Post-Fordist City." In *Handbook of Urban Studies*, edited by Ronan Paddison, 273–83. Thousand Oaks: Sage.

Lightbody, James. 1993. "Cities: The Dilemmas on Our Doorsteps." In *Corruption, Character and Conduct: Essays on Canadian Government Ethics*, edited by John W. Langford and Allan Tupper, 197–216. Toronto: Oxford University Press.

———. 2006. *City Politics, Canada.* Peterborough, ON: Broadview Press. https://doi.org/10.3138/9781442602038.

London Elects. n.d. "Mayor of London & London Assembly Elections Election Results." https://www.londonelects.org.uk/im-voter/election-results.

Londoño, Juan Fernando, and Daniel Zovatto. 2014. "Latin America." In *Funding of Political Parties and Election Campaigns: A Handbook on Political Finance*, edited by Elin Falguera, Samuel Jones, and Magnus Ohman, 128–67. Stockholm: International IDEA.

Lucas Jack. 2019. "The Size and Sources of Municipal Incumbency Advantage in Canada." *Urban Affairs Review* 57, no. 2 (March): 373–401. https://doi.org/10.1177/1078087419879234.

Lucas Jack, Reed Merrill, Kelly Blidock, Sandra Breux, Laura Conrad, Gabriel Edelman, Royce Koop, Daniella Marciano, Zack Taylor, and Salomé Vallette. 2021. "Women's Municipal Electoral Performance: An Introduction to the Canadian Municipal Elections Database." *Canadian Journal of Political Science/Revue canadienne de science politique* 54, no. 1 (March): 125–33. https://doi.org/10.1017/S000842392000102X.

Maillé, Chantal, and Évelyne Tardy. 1988. *Militer dans un parti municipal.* Montréal: Université du Québec à Montréal, Centre de recherche féministe.

Martínez Rosón, and María del Mar. 2014. "Mujeres y política en América Latina." *Iberoamericana* 14, no. 54 (July): 160–3. https://doi.org/10.18441/ibam.14.2014.54.160-163.

McAllister, Mary Louise. 2004. *Governing Ourselves? The Politics of Canadian Communities.* Vancouver: UBC Press.

McDonnell, Joshua. 2020. "Municipality Size, Political Efficacy and Political Participation: A Systematic Review." *Local Government Studies* 46, no. 3 (May): 331–50. https://doi.org/10.1080/03003930.2019.1600510.

McElroy, Justin. 2020. "Local Government in Metro Vancouver is 90% White – But It Doesn't Have to Stay That Way." *CBC News*, June 20, 2020. https://www.cbc.ca/news/canada/british-columbia/metro-vancouver-diversity-solutions-2020-1.5620528.

McGregor, Michael, and Zachary Spicer. 2016. "The Canadian Homevoter: Property Values and Municipal Politics in Canada." *Journal of Urban Affairs* 38, no. 1 (February): 123–39. https://doi.org/10.1111/juaf.12178.

Meloche, Jean-Philippe, and Patrick Kilfoil. 2017. "A Sizeable Effect? Municipal Council Size and the Cost of Local Government in Canada." *Canadian Public Administration/Administration publique du Canada* 60, no. 2 (June): 241–67. https://doi.org/10.1111/capa.12211.

Mévellec, Anne, and Félix Grenier. 2016. "Training Local Elected Officials: Professionalization amid Tensions Between." *Lex Localis – Journal of Local Self-Government* 14, no. 1 (January): 33–51. https://doi.org/10.4335/14.1.33-51(2016).

Mévellec, Anne, and Manon Tremblay. 2013. "Les partis politiques municipaux : la « westminsterisation » des villes du Québec ?" *Recherches sociographiques* 54, no. 2 (May–August): 325–47. https://doi.org/10.7202/1018284ar.

———. 2018. *Genre et professionnalisation de la politique municipale québécoise*. Québec: Presses de l'université du Québec.

Mévellec, Anne, Guy Chiasson, and Yann Fournis. 2017. "De « créatures du gouvernement » à « gouvernements de proximité » : la trajectoire sinueuse des municipalités québécoises." *Revue française d'administration publique* 2, no. 162: 339–52. https://doi.org/10.3917/rfap.162.0339.

Mévellec Anne, Veika Donatien, and Guy Chiasson. 2020. "Municipal/Local Politics: The False Pretences of the Municipal Level in Canada." In *The Palgrave Handbook of Gender, Sexuality, and Canadian Politics*, edited by Manon Tremblay and Joanna Everitt, 249–71. Cham: Palgrave Macmillan. https://doi.org/10.1007/978-3-030-49240-3_13.

Milroy, Beth Moore. 2002. "Toronto's Legal Challenge to Amalgamation." In *Urban Affairs Back on the Agenda*, edited by Caroline Andrew, Katherine A. Graham, and Susan D. Phillips, 157–78. Montreal: McGill-Queen's University Press.

Ministère des Affaires municipales et de l'Habitation du Québec. n.d. Statistiques et archives des résultats des élections municipales. Accessed April 26, 2022. https://www.quebec.ca/gouvernement/gestion-municipale/organisation-municipale/democratie-municipale/elections-municipales/resultats.

Nakhaie, M. Reza. 2006. "Electoral Participation in Municipal, Provincial and Federal Elections in Canada." *Canadian Journal of Political Science/Revue canadienne de science politique* 39, no. 2 (June): 363–90. https://doi.org/10.1017/S000842390606015X.

Nicol, Heather. 1997. "'All of the towns of the Dominion.' Canada's Evolving Urban Framework." In *The Politics of the City. A Canadian Perspective*, edited by Timothy L. Thomas, 17–32. Toronto: International Thomson Publishing Nelson.

OECD. 2016. *Financing Democracy: Funding of Political Parties and Election Campaigns and the Risk of Policy Capture, OECD Public Governance Reviews*. Paris: OECD Publishing. https://doi.org/10.1787/9789264249455-en.

Ohman, Magnus. 2014. "Introduction to Political Finance." In *Funding of Political Parties and Election Campaigns: A Handbook on Political Finance*, edited by Elin Falguera, Samuel Jones, and Magnus Ohman, 1–9. Stockholm: International IDEA.

Oliver, J. Eric. 2000. "City Size and Civic Involvement in Metropolitan America." *The American Political Science Review* 94 no. 2: 361–73. https://doi.org/10.2307/2586017.

Oliver, J. Eric, Shang E. Ha, and Zachary Callen. 2012. *Local Elections and the Politics of Small-Scale Democracy*. Princeton: Princeton University Press. https://doi.org/10.23943/princeton/9780691143552.001.0001.

Pelletier, Maxime. 2014. "Municipal Political Reform in Quebec: The Myth of 'Popular Finance.'" *Journal of Eastern Townships Studies* 43 (Fall): 63–86. http://www.etrc.ca/wp-content/uploads/2016/12/JETS_43-07_Pelletier.pdf.

Pitkin, Hanna Fenichel. 1967. *The Concept of Representation*. Berkeley: University of California Press.

Polsby, Nelson W. 1963. *Community Power and Political Theory*. New Haven, CT: Yale University Press.

Reiser, Marion, and Everhard Holtmann, eds. 2008. *Farewell to the Party Model?* Wiesbaden: Springer VS. https://doi.org/10.1007/978-3-531-90923-3.

Roper, Henry. 1985. "The Halifax Board of Control: The Failure of Municipal Reform 1906–1919." *Acadiensis* 14, no. 2 (Spring): 46–65. https://id.erudit.org/iderudit/acad14_2art03.

Rowat, Donald C. 1969. *The Canadian Municipal System: Essays on the Improvement of Local Government*. Montreal: McGill-Queen's University Press. https://doi.org/10.1515/9780773595231.

Saggar, Shamit. 1998. "Bristish South Asians Elites and Politicial Participation: Testing the Cultural Thesis," edited by Martiniello Marco and Hily Marie-Antoinette, special issue. *Revue européenne des migrations internationales* 14, no. 2: 51–69. https://doi.org/10.3406/remi.1998.1631.

Sassen, Saskia. 1991. *The Global City*. New York: Princeton University Press.

Sawer, Marian. 2007. "Property Voting in Local Government: A Relic of a Pre-democratic Era?" *Representation* 43, no. 1 (April): 45–52. https://doi.org/10.1080/00344890601177123.

Siemiatycki, Myer. 2008. "Reputation and Representation: Reaching for Political Inclusion in Toronto." In *Electing a Diverse Canada: The Representation of Immigrants, Minorities, and Women*, edited by Caroline Andrew, 23–45. Vancouver: UBC Press. https://doi.org/10.59962/9780774814874-004.

Siemiatycki, Myer, and Anver Saloojee. 2002. "Ethnoracial Political Representation in Toronto: Patterns and Problems." *Journal of International Migration and Integration* 3, no. 2 (June): 241–73. https://doi.org/10.1007/s12134-002-1013-8.

Siemiatycki, Myer, and Ian Andrew Matheson. 2005. "Suburban Success: Immigrant and Minority Electoral Gains in Suburban Toronto." *Canadian Issues/Thèmes canadiens*, Summer 2005, 69.

Spicer, Zachary, and Kate Graham. 2016. "Preparing to Lead: Mayoral Transition Planning in Canadian Cities." *Canadian Public Administration/Administration publique du Canada* 59, no. 4 (December): 538–55. https://doi.org/10.1111/capa.12194.

Sproule-Jones, Mark, and Chris Becker. 2005. "The Organization of Municipal Councils in Ontario: A Research Note." *Canadian Journal of Urban Research* 14, no. 2 (Winter): 384–8. https://www.jstor.org/stable/44321040.

Statistics Canada. 2017. "Census Profile, 2016 Census." Catalogue no. 98-316-X2016001, February 8, 2017. https://www12.statcan.gc.ca/census-recensement/2016/dp-pd/prof/index.cfm?Lang=E.

Steyvers, Kristof, and Tom Verhelst. 2012. "Between Layman and Professional? Political Recruitment and Career Development of Local Councilors in a Comparative Perspective (Report)." *Lex Localis – Journal of Local Self-Government* 10, no. 1 (January): 1–17. https://doi.org/10.4335/10.1.1-17.

Superior Electoral Court, International Affairs Unit. 2022. *Practical Guide: 2022 Brazilian Elections*. Brasília: Superior Electoral Court. https://international.tse.jus.br/en/assuntos-internacionais/guia-pratico-para-pessoas-estrangeiras_ingles_digital-1.pdf.

Taylor, Zack, and Alec Dobson. 2020. "Power and Purpose: Canadian Municipal Law in Transition." In *IMFG Papers on Municipal Finance and Governance Papers on Municipal Finance and Governance*, no. 47. Toronto: Institute on Municipal Finance and Governance. https://tspace.library.utoronto.ca/bitstream/1807/99780/1/IMFG_Paper_No47_Power_and_Purpose_Taylor_Dobson.pdf.

Tolley, Erin. 2011. "Do Women 'Do Better' in Municipal Politics? Electoral Representation across Three Levels of Government." *Canadian Journal of Political Science/Revue canadienne de science politique* 44, no. 3 (September): 573–94. https://doi.org/10.1017/S0008423911000503.

Tremblay, Manon. 2014. "Être candidates aux élections municipales et législatives : des courses de haies qui s'apparentent ?" *Canadian Journal of Urban Research* 23, no. 2 (Winter): 38–58. https://www.jstor.org/stable/26189251

Tremblay, Manon, and Anne Mévellec. 2013. "City Hall: Truly More Accessible to Women than the Legislature?" In *Continuing Presence: Women, Elections, and Political Representation in Canada*, edited by Jane Arscott, Linda Trimble, and Manon Tremblay, 19–35. Vancouver: UBC Press.

Trimble, Linda. 1995. "Politics Where We Live." In *Canadian Metropolitics: Governing Our Cities*, edited by James Lightbody, 92–114. Toronto: Copp Clark.

Trimble, Linda, and Jane Arscott, eds. 2003. *Still Counting: Women in Politics across Canada*. Toronto: University of Toronto Press. https://doi.org/10.3138/9781442602144.

Vandelli, Luciano. 2000. "La cellule de base de toutes les démocraties." *Pouvoirs* 95 (November): 5–17. https://revue-pouvoirs.fr/la-cellule-de-base-de-toutes-les/.

Weber, Max. 1965. *Politics as a Vocation*. Philadelphia: Fortress Press.

Whitzman, Carolyn. 2002. "The 'Voice of Women' in Canadian Local Government." In *Urban Affairs: Back on the Policy Agenda*, edited by Caroline Andrew, Katherine Graham, and Susan Phillips, 93–118. Montreal: McGill-Queen's University Press. https://doi.org/10.1515/9780773570146-005.

Wollmann, Hellmut. 2000. "Local Government Systems: From Historic Divergence towards Convergence? Great Britain, France, and Germany as Comparative Cases in Point." *Environment and Planning C: Politics and Space* 18, no. 1 (February): 33–55. https://doi.org/10.1068/c9867.

CHAPTER NINE

Municipalities, Public Services, and the Government-Citizen Interface in Comparative Perspective

John B. Sutcliffe and Sarah Cipkar

INTRODUCTION

Services provided by municipal governments and municipal associations, boards, commissions, and corporations (ABCCs) are essential whether those affected realize they are provided by these municipal bodies or not. Canadians, if to varying degrees, are affected by municipal decisions relating to land use, protective services, garbage collection, recycling, recreational and cultural facilities, the provision of water, road and transportation networks, and many other municipal services. Municipal governments and bodies, moreover, are the part of the governance structure that are closest to residents, and which are often most accessible – again, whether residents realize this or not.

Focusing on municipalities in Canada in comparison with those in the United States and the United Kingdom, this chapter examines three main questions relating to service delivery and citizen engagement. First, what services do municipal governments and municipal bodies provide and why? Second, how are these services provided? And third, to what extent are citizens able to influence the actions of municipal bodies with respect to service delivery? These are complex questions affected by multiple factors. Municipal service provision and citizen engagement with these services are shaped by constitutional and legal frameworks developed over time; political and economic decisions taken at local, regional, and national levels; and economic and social forces that originate both at and beyond the municipal level. The variety of factors affecting municipal service responsibilities helps explain why the three national settings are not identical and further why there is variation within each country. Not all municipal services are delivered in the same way by the same municipal bodies. Similarly, across all three countries, different forms of citizen engagement and participatory mechanisms are employed at different times, in different municipal settings, and in different service areas.

Municipal complexity exists in all three national settings. There are, nevertheless, similar debates in each country regarding the most appropriate scale for municipal service delivery; whether municipal service responsibilities should be prioritized over municipal representative functions; whether services should be delivered by specialized local bodies or municipal governments; and whether and to what extent residents should be involved in establishing services and how they are delivered. The study also highlights the enduring relevance of the typology identified by Good in chapter 2 of this volume. While the municipal systems in Canada, the United States, and the United Kingdom are not identical, they all fall within the "Anglo" category: their municipal governments have limited constitutional status, and there is greater emphasis placed on municipal governments as corporations established to deliver services efficiently rather than as democratic bodies representing and reflecting the interests of their residents. In each case, municipal services, the ways they are delivered, and, sometimes, the mechanisms in place to facilitate citizen engagement are constrained and shaped by senior governments and forces over which municipal bodies have limited control.

MUNICIPAL SERVICES

Municipal services are central to modern life in Canada, the United States, and the United Kingdom.[1] For almost everyone in these three countries, municipal governments and municipal ABCCs provide services that are used every day, particularly those relating to property and the built environment (Sancton 2015a). Municipal governments and bodies shape where we live and how we live. They provide power and water supplies to residences and determine how waste is removed from them. Municipalities build and maintain the roads, sidewalks, and cycle paths that are used to get to work and to places of leisure, and in many cases the municipality owns and operates transit services that supplement or replace private modes of transportation. Municipal or regional bodies often provide or oversee primary and secondary education systems. They also provide the parks, sporting facilities, libraries, and museums that are used for recreation. They may also provide services – such as social housing, homeless shelters, or welfare policies – for vulnerable members of the community in times of greatest need. And, in many cases, they directly provide or fund the police and fire services in their communities. Municipal employees are often the "street-level bureaucrats" that the public is most likely to interact with on a semi-regular basis.[2]

Over time there have been changes in the list of services provided by municipal bodies in all three countries. Prior to the Second World War, social services to support the poor, ill, or aged – to the extent that they existed at all – were often provided by municipal governments or other local organizations in Canada, the United States, and the United Kingdom (Tindal et al. 2016). After the war, senior governments (provincial, state, and national) took on primary responsibility for many social assistance and health programs while sometimes continuing to have municipal bodies deliver the services.

In other areas there has been an expansion of municipal service responsibility. A survey of municipal government services in 1920, for example, would find little to nothing on recycling in any of the three countries. A similar survey in 2020 would reveal that every municipal government has some responsibility for recycling paper, metal, and glass as well as a growing number that mandate the recycling of organic matter. Services directed toward new immigrants and their engagement in the workforce and community (Good 2009), as well as services designed to advance community accessibility, are further examples of additions to lists of municipal services, particularly in larger municipalities. In recent years, municipalities have established policies and departments with the aim of integrating diversity and inclusiveness into their decision-making, and in so doing, achieving more inclusive and equitable service provision.[3] In Canada, some municipalities are taking steps to engage more fully with Indigenous residents in an effort to "decolonize" the municipality (see Anderson and Flynn in this volume).

Not all municipal governments are responsible for the same list of services. This results from differences in the constitutional underpinning of municipal governance and political decisions made based on this constitutional structure, as well as differences in size and structure of municipal governments (see below). If the comparison is limited to large cities across the three countries, it is possible to identify a broad similarity in the services delivered at the municipal level. Nevertheless, differences do exist depending on which municipalities are compared and the province, state, or country in which they are located. Differences become even more apparent when examining the scope of the service and which municipal bodies are responsible for its delivery. Some services are provided by the municipal governments, some by ABCCs (which sometimes include elected municipal councillors on their governing boards), and some by municipal governments co-operating in regional governance networks (Nelles, Gross, and Kennedy 2018).

Table 9.1 compares municipal services in the City of Ottawa, Ontario, in Canada, the City of Liverpool in England, and the City of Columbus, Ohio, in the United States. Although each city has a population of approximately one million, each has a different municipal structure, which impacts service delivery in each case. Ottawa is a unitary authority, Liverpool City Council is one of six lower-tier municipal governments that collectively form the Liverpool City Region Combined Authority, and the City of Columbus is a unitary authority although some municipal services are delivered by county-level bodies (Franklin County). Differences in service provision are evident. With respect to policing, for example, the Ottawa police force is overseen by a seven-member police board, three of whom are members of city council; Liverpool has an elected police and crime commissioner; and the police in Columbus are run by the municipal Department of Public Safety while the mayor appoints the chief of police. Columbus City Council established a Civilian Police Review Board in 2021 in response to public criticism of the force and its actions. Other differences include long-term care homes, some of which are municipally provided in Ottawa but privately provided in Liverpool and Columbus. Similarly, private companies provide utilities in Liverpool. These are provided by publicly owned corporations in Ottawa and Columbus. Education, on the other hand, is directly provided by the municipal government in Liverpool but is overseen by elected school

Service	City of Ottawa (Ontario, Canada)	Liverpool City Council (England, United Kingdom)	City of Columbus (Ohio, United States)
Animal Control	✓	✓	✓
Aviation	Federal government; smaller privately owned airport	✓ Predominantly private ownership. Council owns 10% share.	Columbus Regional Airport Authority (board appointed by mayor)
Child Services	✓	✓	✓
Climate Change and Environment	✓ Climate masterplan	✓ Action on climate change	✓ Climate action plan
Culture	✓	✓	✓
Economic Development	✓	✓ Liverpool City Region Combined Authority	✓ Franklin County Board of Commissioners
Education	School boards	✓	School boards
Electricity	Hydro Ottawa (owned by the city)	Privately provided	Columbus Division of Power (publicly owned)
Equity, Diversity, Inclusiveness	✓	✓	✓
Family Support Services	✓	✓	Franklin County Department of Job and Family Services
Fire	✓	Merseyside Fire and Rescue	✓
Garbage	✓ (Some in-house; some provided by private companies under contract.)	Merseyside Recycling and Waste Authority (Nine councillors from the participating municipalities. Services provided by the private sector under contract.)	✓
Health	Board of Health	Public Health	✓
Hydro	Hydro Ottawa (Owned by city)	United Utilities (Private company)	✓ Columbus City Utilities
Homelessness	✓	✓	
Housing	Ottawa Community Housing Corporation	✓ Limited	Columbus Metropolitan Housing Authority
Library	✓	✓	✓
Long-Term Care Homes	✓	X (Private sector only.)	X
Parking	✓	✓	✓
Parks and Recreation	✓	✓	✓ Columbus and Franklin County Metro Parks Board
Police	Police Services Board (Includes three councillors)	Merseyside Police (Five local policing areas, one in each of the metropolitan boroughs that make up Merseyside. Overseen by Police and Crime Commissioner, which is an elected position.)	✓ Municipal Department of Public Safety. Mayor – appoints chief of police. Civilian Police Review Board est. 2021.

(Continued)

Table 9.1. Continued

Service	City of Ottawa (Ontario, Canada)	Liverpool City Council (England, United Kingdom)	City of Columbus (Ohio, United States)
Neighbourhood/ Community Supports	✓	✓	✓
Recycling	✓ Some in-house. Some provided by private sector under contract.	Merseyside Recycling and Waste Authority	✓
Roads	✓	✓	✓
Social Services	Ontario Works	✓	Franklin County Department of Job and Family Services
Transit	Transit Commission (Six councillors, mayor, and four members of the public.)	Merseyside Travel	Central Ohio Transportation Authority
Tourism	✓	✓	✓ Includes Franklin County Convention Facilities Authority

Source: Data compiled by the authors from various municipal websites.

boards in Ottawa and Columbus. In each case, though, senior governments exert considerable influence over the provision of education in part because of their role in funding education.

Table 9.2 shows the differences between a large unitary authority, Ottawa, and a smaller municipal council, Arnprior (population 9,629), which is one of the seventeen lower-tier councils in Renfrew County, a two-tier municipal structure to the east of Ottawa. Both are in Ontario, Canada. The table identifies that in many cases, municipal services provided in Ottawa are not provided at all in Arnprior or are provided by other bodies under contract with the town, or by the upper-tier municipal structure, the County of Renfrew. The differences are even greater with respect to the scale of service provision in the two settings. In Arnprior, for example, responsibility for mobility is limited to the maintenance of local roads, bike paths, and sidewalks. In Ottawa, it also includes full or partial responsibility for the provision of bus and light rail transit services.

WHAT DETERMINES MUNICIPAL SERVICE RESPONSIBILITIES?

Municipal services and the organizations responsible for delivering them have changed over time as local and national leaders in Canada, the United States, and the United Kingdom have grappled with the same broad questions: What services should be established and delivered at

Table 9.2. Comparison of Municipal Services in the City of Ottawa and the Town of Arnprior

Service	City of Ottawa	Town of Arnprior
Animal Control	✓	✓
Aviation	Federal government; smaller privately owned airport	✓
Child Services	✓	County of Renfrew
Climate Change and Environment	✓ Climate masterplan	County of Renfrew
Culture	✓	✓
Economic Development	✓	County of Renfrew
Education	Elected school boards	Elected school boards
Equity, Diversity, Inclusiveness	✓	✓
Family Support Services	✓	X
Fire	✓	✓
Garbage	✓ (Some in-house; some provided by private companies under contract)	✓ Provided under contract by private company
Health	Board of Health	Renfrew County and District Health Unit
Hydro	Hydro Ottawa (Owned by city)	Hydro One (Corporation with Ontario government as largest share owner)
Homelessness	✓	County of Renfrew
Housing	Ottawa Community Housing Corporation	Renfrew County Housing Corporation
Library	✓	✓
Long-Term Care Homes	✓	X Arnprior Regional Health
Parking	✓	✓
Parks and Recreation	✓	✓
Police	Police Services Board (Includes three councillors)	Ontario Provincial Police contract
Neighbourhood/Community Supports	✓	✓
Recycling	✓ Some in-house; some provided by private sector under contract	✓ Provided under contract by private company
Roads	✓	✓
Sanitation and Water	✓	✓
Social Services	Ontario Works	Ontario Works: administered by County
Transit	Transit Commission (Six councillors, mayor, and four members of the public.)	X
Tourism	✓	✓

Source: Data compiled by the authors from various municipal websites.

the municipal level? Should local variation be permitted, or is it necessary or desirable to have national or regional equity in service provision? What is the most efficient scale for delivering a service? And is the service better delivered by a single-purpose body or by a multi-purpose municipal government? In each case, the answers to these questions have been shaped by a combination of economic and social forces, popular demands, and political decision-making filtered through the constitutional structure and the legislative, legal, and financial decisions that flow from the constitutional framework.

There is, then, variation in municipal services and municipal service delivery both across the three countries and within them. In each case, municipal service responsibility is shaped by municipalities' place within the constitutional structure. The Canadian Constitution, as examined by Good in chapter 2, establishes the division of powers between the federal and provincial levels and, in so doing, establishes municipal bodies as the responsibility of the provinces. And because the functions that municipal governments perform are not entrenched in provincial constitutions, provincial governments determine their functions in provincial statutes (Good 2019; Magnusson 2005). Each province establishes the legislative framework that shapes what municipal bodies do. Provincial governments have the constitutional authority to amend municipal service responsibilities as well as how these services are delivered and funded. As a result, there are interprovincial differences in municipal service responsibilities and "spheres of jurisdiction" (Taylor and Dobson 2020, 17–19). Policing, for example, is a municipal responsibility in many provinces but a provincial responsibility in Newfoundland. Employment and support services to those in financial need are provincially funded and delivered in Quebec and British Columbia. In Ontario, these services are delivered by municipal governments but are primarily, though not exclusively, funded by the Ontario government.

Provincial authority over municipal government does not mean that municipal governments have no role in determining the services they provide. As Graham and Horak identify in this volume, some municipal governments have expanded their service roles into social and environmental areas that go beyond their traditional service delivery roles. In all provinces, there has been movement away from municipal powers being tightly constrained and limited to powers expressly spelled out – Dillon's Rule – to a situation where provincial legislation gives municipal governments more flexibility to act and provide services within their broad sphere of authority (chapter 2). In addition, most provincial governments have given municipalities "natural person" powers, which, while not itself expanding municipal governments' service responsibilities, gives them more flexibility to take actions – such as entering into contracts or purchasing land – necessary to provide services or undertake their designated powers (Tindal et al. 2016; Garcea 2014).[4]

Despite this increased flexibility, municipalities remain constrained by decisions taken at the provincial government level (Magnusson 2005). Provincial governments may download service responsibilities to municipal governments or upload services from the municipal to the provincial level. There are many examples of provincial governments taking these steps or at least proposing to do so (Tindal et al. 2016, 148–55). In the late 1990s, for example, the Conservative government of Ontario downloaded responsibility for social programs, including social housing, to the municipal level. In the 2018 Ontario provincial election, the Conservative Party proposed uploading control of the Toronto Transit Commission from the city to the province but backed away from this commitment once in power. Similarly, in 2020 the Alberta provincial government proposed moving responsibility for some provincial parks to the municipal level before reversing its decision later the same year (Canadian Press 2020).

Provincial governments can also unilaterally restructure municipal boundaries and, in so doing, affect how municipal services are provided. Provincially mandated municipal restructuring in Ontario in the 1990s, for example, reduced the number of municipalities from 850 to 444 (Siegel 2005; Williams and Downey 1999). In enforcing this wide-ranging reform of municipal boundaries, the Conservative provincial government drew a direct link between municipal government size and service responsibility. They argued that consolidation would save taxpayers money by reducing the number of municipal politicians and by allowing services to be delivered more efficiently, claims that were widely challenged at the time and subsequently (Kushner and Siegel 2005; Sancton 1996, 2000, 2005).

This picture of municipalities' constitutional subservience to senior government is evident also in the United Kingdom and the United States. This similarity is not altogether surprising given that all three countries fall within the Anglo category with the municipal government systems in the United States and Canada having been shaped by the British political system. In the United Kingdom, the central government has constitutional authority over local government and has used this authority to introduce both radical and incremental changes at the municipal level; these changes have had a significant impact on municipal services. A clear example of this occurred in 1985 when Margaret Thatcher's Conservative government passed legislation abolishing the upper municipal level in London and other major urban regions and redistributing their service responsibilities to other municipal bodies. At the same time, the Conservative government legislated the complete or partial privatization of services previously provided by municipal governments. In many places, this resulted in the privatization of utility provision and the sale of council houses.

The constitutional situation became more complicated following the 1999 devolution of power and the establishment of the Scottish and Welsh Parliaments. As with Canadian provinces and US states, these parliaments now have responsibility for municipal governments within their national borders, and thus the structures and funding of these governments differ from the situation found in England.[5] Local authorities in England remain under the purview of the central government, which determines their statutory service responsibilities – services that they have to provide – as well as determining and overseeing their discretionary services. In May 2022, for example, the government announced that municipal governments could have the power to enforce moving traffic offences in their municipalities. The power to do so, however, is based on an application process to the central government and is not automatically granted. In addition, the central government limits the amount of money that can be raised using this power and what municipal governments can do with that money (Tyers 2022).

In the United States, municipal governments are established under the purview of the states, and consequently, their number, structure, and service responsibilities vary from state to state and are even more complex than in Canada (Taylor 2019). Variation is evident in the degree to which municipal governments enjoy autonomy from state-level governments. In some states, municipal governments are referred to as "creatures of the states" just as Canadian municipalities are thought of as "creatures of the province." In other states, municipal governments enjoy greater autonomy in terms of amending their city charters and are protected from state-mandated restructuring or reorganization (Sancton 2005; Taylor 2019). One explanation for this is that some state constitutions contain provisions – reflecting traditions of local self-government and specific responses to political and economic events – that provide municipal governments with more autonomy and place limits on state governments' ability to intervene in municipal governance (Taylor 2014; Good 2014). It is important to emphasize, however, that this is not the case in every state. In some cases, the state constitution allows the state government to intervene more easily in municipal affairs as compared to situations where "constitutional" home rule is in place. In these latter states, the constitution more clearly limits the possibility of state interference in municipal affairs. Even the existence of constitutional home rule provisions does not prevent the state governments from intervening – often through funding decisions – and shaping the structure and service responsibilities of municipal governments (Nickels 2016).

In sum, the services that municipal bodies provide in all three countries are shaped and constrained by their constitutional position, which determines their scope for action with respect to the services they deliver and how they are delivered. The constitutional structure also impacts the ability of municipal governments to afford the capital and operating costs associated with the delivery of a service.[6] In Canada, as in the United Kingdom and most US states, municipal governments cannot run annual operating deficits.[7] Senior governments also play a major role in determining how much money municipal governments can raise and from which sources (see chapter 7). In all three countries, municipal governments also rely on grants from senior governments to supplement the money they raise from their own resources. This was particularly evident during the COVID-19 pandemic when municipal governments received large injections of funds from senior governments (Hachard 2020). In many cases, the annual transfer of funds occurs in the form of conditional or targeted grants that limit municipal discretion with respect to service provision.

The most significant financial question is whether municipal governments have sufficient revenues to finance their services. Municipal leaders in all three countries consistently claim that their revenue sources are insufficient; such claims are particularly frequent on the occasions when senior governments have downloaded responsibility for services onto municipal governments, reduced the total amount of grant money directed to municipalities, or during times of economic crisis (Vengroff and Whelan 2001). There is some evidence to support this view. English local governments, for example, saw their overall spending power drop between 2010 and 2019 primarily because of cuts in central government grants. Amin-Smith and Phillips conclude that because of these cuts "local government spending on services has fallen by 21% in real terms since 2009–10" (2019, 2) The occasions when municipal governments in the United States have declared bankruptcy – perhaps most notably in the case of Detroit in 2013 – provide a clear example of the connection between municipal governments' fiscal capacity and their ability to deliver services. The City of Detroit was forced to introduce radical reductions in the services it provided following its declaration of bankruptcy (Binelli 2012; Bomey 2017; Galster 2012).

Even outside of these times of economic crisis, municipal government leaders in all three countries argue that they require more funding, as well as more consistent funding, from senior governments and more flexibility to raise their own sources of revenue. These claims are connected to the prominence of neo-liberalism as a governing philosophy over the past forty years (Harvey 2005; Hackworth 2007). Municipal governments in all three countries have been affected by senior government decisions and global economic forces pushing an agenda that seeks lower government regulation of the marketplace, a business-friendly municipal environment, and services aimed at attracting mobile capital and workers rather than spending on social services that help the most vulnerable members of society (Joy and Shields 2020; Moskowitz 2018; Harvey 2013; Sassen 2001).

There is disagreement about how powerful these pressures are and whether municipal governments or municipal residents can resist a neo-liberal agenda. Jack Hackworth, for example, argues that while all municipal governments have faced pressures to conform to a neo-liberal policy agenda, not all municipalities have responded in the same way (Hackworth 2007; Massey 2007). The existence of "the right to the city" movements provides some evidence to suggest that municipal governments and their residents can resist economic and political forces in pursuit of progressive policies (Harvey 2008, 2013). Municipal governments can take decisions that counter major business economic interests. As Horak and Dantico (2014, 136) identify, municipal governments are able to establish and operate programs "aimed at helping residents of poor, visible-minority neighbourhoods." This is also evident in the list of services provided by municipal governments, which include services aimed at helping the homeless, the unemployed, vulnerable children, and new immigrants (see table 9.1). What is not in doubt, however, is that economic forces and senior government decisions affecting municipal governments' spending capacity directly impact the services they can deliver. Municipal services may be altered by senior government decisions re-evaluating the focus, scale, and cost of these services. Even municipal governments in the US states with home rule provisions are forced to adapt to financial pressures as well as state and federal government funding priorities and decisions.

In sum, municipal service responsibilities in all three countries are affected by economic pressures, social forces, and political decisions that themselves are filtered through the constitutional structure and the place of municipal bodies within this structure. It is this latter point that helps to explain the variations across and within the three countries examined here with respect to both the municipal services that are provided as well as the patchwork of single-tier, multi-purpose municipal governments, two-tier municipal governments, and single-purpose municipal ABCCs that collectively deliver these services.

SERVICE DELIVERY MECHANISMS – HOW SERVICES ARE PROVIDED

An examination of municipal services requires paying attention not only to what services are delivered but also to how these services are delivered and who is responsible for delivering them. These important issues are tied to debates regarding the most appropriate size and form of municipal body for the efficient delivery of services and how this is balanced against municipal governments' representative role and residents' capacity to shape those services.

In-House Service Delivery

Some services are delivered directly to residents by municipal government employees. In these cases, a municipal government determines that it wishes to provide a municipal service – subject to having the legal authority to do so – and pays municipal employees to deliver that service. A municipal government may, for example, build and operate a recreational facility or a community centre. These facilities are run by municipal employees and overseen by the city administration and ultimately city council.

One advantage of this service delivery model is that it provides municipal residents with clarity with respect to who is responsible for the service and who to criticize and potentially punish at the ballot box should they consider the service inadequate. It is worth noting, however, that municipal councillors claim – often correctly – that their capacity to offer a particular service is constrained by senior government regulation and inadequate funding. A second advantage of in-house service delivery is that it allows the municipal government to provide a coordinated service throughout the municipality. Municipal authorities in many large cities, for example, began taking responsibility for providing transit services from private companies in the 1950s and 1960s with the aim of offering a coordinated transit service throughout their city. In 1954, for example, the Toronto Transit Commission took over private bus companies and became the sole public transit provider in Metropolitan Toronto (Small 2009). In-house service delivery also facilitates the examination of how services work together and promotes "joined-up policy-making." As such, municipal governments can make adjustments in one service area if it will assist service delivery in other areas. Promoting the well-being of low-income individuals and families in a community, for example, includes coordinating policies in areas such as the provision of affordable housing, public transportation, recreational services, and mental health services.

Municipal governments do not always have the option of in-house service delivery. In some cases, this is because they are legally prevented from doing so. In other cases, it may be that the costs of in-house delivery are too great. Smaller municipalities in particular may not have the financial and administrative resources to deliver a service directly and so are forced into contracting other organizations to provide the service.

ABCCs: Single-Purpose Municipal Bodies

Many municipal services are delivered by agencies, boards, corporations, or commissions, which are often single-purpose bodies. As Taylor (2014) identifies, this is particularly common in the United States, but it is also a feature of municipal service delivery in Canada and the United Kingdom. The City of Toronto (2020) alone, for example, provides an organizational chart listing over fifty bodies that are involved in delivering municipal services and which often include municipal councillors and officials but which operate separately from the municipal government itself. In each case, then, municipal governments are only one part of a large and complex network of municipal bodies that exist at the local level (Lucas 2013).

In some cases, services such as libraries, policing, and transit are delivered by agencies or boards that are partially separated from the municipal government even though they are partially or wholly funded by municipal governments and have elected councillors and mayors on their decision-making bodies. In Ontario, for example, while larger municipalities pay for their own police force, oversight is in the hands of a police board that includes municipal councillors as well as provincial appointees. (Many smaller municipalities contract the Ontario Provincial Police, the RCMP, or a neighbouring municipality's police force to provide policing for their community.) Municipally owned corporations are another example of this form of service delivery mechanism. Water and electricity, for example, are often delivered by this type of organization (Bel and Fageda 2010; Voorn, Van Genugten, and Van Thiel 2017). These corporations are led by executive boards that include municipal councillors but also appointed members of the community. They receive funding from the municipality but also raise considerable amounts of their budgets from user fees. Ultimately, these organizations, by design, have significant independence from the municipal councils.

Decisions to deliver services through ABCCs may result from municipal decisions or senior government requirements, or they may be the result of historical legacy. In Ontario, for example, provincial legislation requires that police and library services be provided by special-purpose bodies (Taylor and Dobson 2020; Lucas 2013). One purported advantage of single-purpose bodies is that they allow for greater specialization and technocratic expertise in a particular policy sector and remove politics – and possible corruption – from the decision-making. This argument was a key element of the municipal reform era at the turn of the twentieth century in the United States and Canada (Tindal et al. 2016). This delivery mechanism can insulate the service from political control without removing it completely from the oversight of elected politicians. Whether this arm's length relationship with elected municipal governments is considered an advantage or not is subject to debate. In the view of some critics, it can and does reduce the accountability of service providers to the public.

Policing provides an example of these debates as well as differences in the provision of the service in different municipal jurisdictions. In Ontario, for example, police boards have either three or five members (depending on the size of the population). Each board must include members of the municipal council (usually including the mayor), civilians appointed by the municipality, and up to two provincial appointees. The responsibilities of the board include appointing the chief of police, overseeing the objectives and priorities of the police force in consultation with the police chief, and investigating complaints. The police board also helps to determine the budget, which is approved by the municipal council. In reality, however, the powers of the police board are limited. The board cannot intervene in the day-to-day operations of the force, and its financial power over the police force is limited as police forces can appeal funding issues to the Ontario Civilian Police Commission. The relative independence of police forces from political control has resulted in complaints – particularly in the wake of high-profile police killings – that political and public oversight of police forces is too weak (Mukherjee 2018; Tulloch 2017).

In the United States, or at least in some municipal jurisdictions, municipal police forces are departments of city councils. New York City's police department, for example, is governed by Chapter 18 of the city charter. The department is headed by the police commissioner, who serves at the pleasure of the mayor and may be removed by the mayor unilaterally and without cause. A similar situation is evident in Columbus, Ohio (as noted above). City councils also have more power over police force budgets than is the case in Canada. This greater political accountability to elected municipal politicians does not, however, result in less controversy as has been witnessed in the wake of high-profile killings, including that of George Floyd in 2020, and the rise of the Black Lives Matter movement. Across the United States, including in Minneapolis where Floyd was murdered, there have been moves led by both councillors and community groups to "defund the police" and instead create public safety departments that will still include armed law enforcement officers but also social workers, traffic safety responders, and homeless outreach (see Gross and Eligon 2020; Bailey 2021). In many US municipalities, there have also been moves to reduce the mayor's power over the police department and give the elected council a larger oversight role.

Off-loading and Contracting Out

Off-loading and contracting out are two other service delivery mechanisms where services are not delivered directly by a municipal government. Municipal governments can, for example, off-load service delivery to other agencies or to not-for-profit agencies (DeFilippis, Fisher, and Shragge 2006). The provision of social housing, services for the homeless, and care for the elderly are, in some cases, examples of this type of off-loading (Feiock and Jang 2009). Municipal governments might elect to off-load service provisions because of the non-profits' expertise in the policy sector concerned, because it may be cheaper than providing the service directly, and because it is less controversial than contracting the service out to a private sector provider.[8] In many cases, municipalities engage non-profit organizations to provide services through short-term, competitive contracts (Joy and Shields 2020).

Contracting out involves the municipality entering into a legal agreement with private companies to have those companies deliver the municipal service in exchange for financial payment from the municipal government (Fernandez, Ryu, and Brudney 2008).[9] Examples can be found in municipalities across Canada, the United States, and the United Kingdom. Waste collection and recycling are services that are frequently delivered by private companies under a contract with municipal governments. As noted in table 9.1, both the City of Ottawa and City of Liverpool contract out the provision of garbage collection. Margaret Thatcher's Conservative government mandated the contracting out of bus services in the United Kingdom in the 1980s, and it remains the case that most bus services outside of London are provided by the private sector, sometimes working with a municipal government under a franchise agreement (see House of Commons Transport Committee 2019). Some newly incorporated municipalities in the United States have decided to contract out almost all of their services (Bradbury and Waechter 2009).

The assumption underlying the privatization of services is that it is in the best interest of municipal residents, particularly those who pay property tax. Private companies, it is argued, have expertise in the policy sector and can deliver services more cheaply and efficiently than municipal governments because they are subject to competition. It may, in particular, be too expensive for smaller municipalities to provide services directly whereas economies of scale mean that a private company can provide the service and still make a profit. The decision to contract out services, however, is contentious. Critics argue that contracting out does not inevitably result in cost savings and has the potential to reduce the quality of service as the focus of private companies is primarily on profit margins rather than the quality of the service provided. They further argue that it reduces the accountability of service providers to residents and reduces the ability of residents to influence service standards (Schafer and Zhang 2016). Decisions to contract out service responsibility are also a frequent cause of controversy between municipal authorities and municipal trade unions. Indeed, contracting out has sometimes been a central issue leading to municipal strike action, as was the case in Windsor, Ontario, in 2009. In this case, municipalities contested the city's decision to contract with a private waste company for garbage collection.

The push to move municipal service delivery to the private sector is an example of the impact of neo-liberalism on municipal governments. Municipal governments in all three countries have been mandated to model their own service delivery on the practices of the private sector. They have also been told "to do more with less," thus pushing them to contract out service delivery which – so it is claimed – generates cost savings and a reduction in the size and scope of municipal bureaucracies (DeFilippis, Fisher, and Shragge 2006).[10]

Intermunicipal Service Delivery

Services are sometimes delivered by municipalities working collectively. This is, of course, the case with respect to services delivered by the upper tier in two-tier municipalities. In other situations, however, municipal governments contract a different – larger – municipality to deliver the service in question. A smaller municipality may sign a contract with a larger municipality's police board or transit authority to provide policing or transit in their community. In these cases, economies of scale mean that it is cheaper for the smaller municipalities to pay a different municipality to provide the services rather than do so themselves. In so doing, the small municipalities give up some control over services in exchange for savings.

Intermunicipal service delivery is a significant issue because municipal boundaries are not coterminous with the built environment. This is evident in Canada, the United Kingdom, and particularly the United States, where municipal governments are smaller and have more geographically concentrated populations than their Canadian equivalents (Taylor 2019). In all three countries, there are city-regions that contain multiple municipal governments and where service requirements cross municipal boundaries (Nelles, Gross, and Kennedy 2018; Spicer 2015, 2016a; Spicer and Found 2016). Public transit, for example, is frequently required to cross municipal boundaries to facilitate commuting from suburbs to the city centre or reverse commuting from the centre to the surrounding municipalities within city-regions. Indeed, the need to establish integrated transit systems has often been part of provincial decisions to reform municipal government or enforce more integrated planning across city-regions. Regional transit in the Metro Vancouver region, for example, is the responsibility of a provincially created agency: TransLink.[11]

Senior governments have responded to the reality of this urban development in different ways, and it has generated political and academic debate about the most appropriate form of municipal governance for service delivery in these contiguous urban areas (Dreier, Mollenkopf, and Swanstrom 2014; Feiock 2004; Nelles 2013; Sancton 2004). In some cases, the development of urban areas into city-regions and the need for services to be delivered throughout the region has directly shaped the structure of municipal government. In several Canadian provinces, provincial governments have introduced consolidating measures to create larger municipal governments that more closely approximate the size of the built environment (Sancton 2002). This consolidation may take the form of a single-tier municipal structure – as with the 1998 creation of the City of Toronto through the amalgamation of the Municipality of Metropolitan Toronto and its six lower-tier municipalities. In other cases, an upper-tier regional government has been created with the intention of institutionalizing regional co-operation on service delivery (Taylor 2019). As noted earlier, an argument frequently used to support these consolidation efforts is that they will allow services to be delivered more efficiently within the larger urban area. Opponents, on the other hand, have argued that consolidation rarely brings the promised cost savings, weakens local democracy, and reduces the capacity for residents to influence municipal decision-makers (Sancton 1996, 2000; Spicer 2012; Kushner and Siegel 2005).

Consolidation of municipal government in the United States, while not unknown, is less prominent than in Canada. Senior governments in the United States are less likely – and in some cases unable – to intervene in decisions about municipal government structures than are Canadian provincial governments (Sancton 2005; Good 2014; Taylor 2019). Municipal government in the United States, as a result, more closely matches the situation described by a public choice framework, that is, a larger number of smaller municipal governments allowing citizens to choose to reside in the one that more closely matches their desired balance of services and taxes (Tiebout 1956; Nelles 2013). In this context, regional agencies, associations, and boards have been established to deal with the provision of regional services in the city-region (Nelles, Gross, and Kennedy 2018; Sancton 2008; Spicer 2016a; Taylor 2019). As Spicer and Found (2016) identify, these agreements take different forms and are more prominent in the United States than in Canada mainly because metropolitan regions are more fragmented than is the case in Canada and state governments often have less power than provincial governments to enforce change at the municipal level (see also Taylor 2019).[12] One argument made in favour of the US system is that it combines smaller municipal governments that are closer to residents with boards and agencies that coordinate some service delivery over a wider urban region. Critics of this pattern of municipal government structure and service delivery, however, argue that it perpetuates inequality with more affluent municipalities enjoying higher levels of service and being unwilling to contribute to service provision in less affluent parts of the larger city-region (see Dreier, Mollenkopf, and Swanstrom 2014). As Nelles (2012) identifies, the regional cooperative institutions and arrangements that do exist in city-regions are often weak as a result of inter-regional divisions.

There are, then, different ways in which municipal bodies deliver services. Underlying these service delivery models are tensions regarding how to deliver services cheaply and efficiently over larger areas and how to promote equality of service provision while at the same time allowing residents to engage with decision-makers, hold these decision-makers to account, and shape services that are relevant to their local communities. These issues are connected to a more fundamental question about whether municipal governments should primarily be evaluated in terms of their capacity to deliver services efficiently and follow the advice of experts, as democratic governments that make decisions that reflect the views of their residents or, at the very least, governments that make decisions following consultation with residents and in a manner that allows residents to engage in that decision-making process.

CITIZEN ENGAGEMENT

Municipal services have a big impact on the people who live, work, and play within a municipality. As noted earlier, the municipality is the level of government whose services citizens are most likely to use, and municipal employees are the "street-level bureaucrats" with whom citizens are most likely to come into contact. It is also the level of government to which they are most likely to have access. It is, for example, considerably easier to meet with a municipal councillor or a municipal mayor than it is to meet with a member of parliament or the prime minister, although the difficulty rises the larger the municipality. It is also possible for individual residents to participate by making representations at council meetings, something that is not possible at senior levels of government.

Given the diversity evident in municipal bodies and structures across Canada, the United States, and the United Kingdom, it is perhaps inevitable that the interface between residents and the municipality occurs in multiple formal and informal ways in all three countries. That said, there are commonalities with respect to the ways in which residents can engage in municipalities and municipal decisions relating to services. In each country, moreover, the municipal-resident interface raises important, much-studied questions regarding how municipal decisions are made, the extent to which municipal residents influence these decisions, and whether municipalities are accessible, responsive, and accountable to their residents. Underlying all of these is the question of who holds power in a municipality (Dahl 2005; Hunter 1953; Magnusson 2005; Fung 2004; Stone 1989). This section examines different ways in which residents engage with their municipality. Engagement through the electoral process is examined in chapter 8 and is not discussed here. The central focus is on participatory mechanisms and how they constrain or promote differing levels of citizen engagement with municipal government decision-making.[13]

Participation through Direct Action and Advocacy Groups

Residents can participate in advocacy groups and movements that seek to influence municipal decision-making using protests, communications with elected officials, and participation in council meetings (Brown and Hannis 2011). Some of these groups develop from the ground up with the goal of representing the interests of a specific neighbourhood within the municipality or the interests of a specific group. Grassroots groups may exist on an ongoing basis with the aim of tracking and engaging with all municipal decisions and services that impact their neighbourhood or community, or they may form to influence a specific issue. Opposition to proposed development projects has long been a feature of municipal decision-making. Notable examples include the movements spearheaded by Jane Jacobs that opposed highway construction in New York and then successfully mobilized opposition to the proposed Spadina Expressway project in Toronto (Flint 2009). Many municipalities have groups that bring together and seek to represent the interests of public transit users. Bus users in Los Angeles in the 1990s, for example, successfully challenged the transit authority's proposed expansion plans. They were also successful in inserting their voice into transit decisions, including through the creation of a more regularized community engagement process (Grengs 2002). The Black Lives Matter movement is a recent example of advocacy in the United States, Canada, and the United Kingdom that seeks to secure a number of municipal policy changes, including the structure of policing at the municipal level. In so doing, they hope to challenge systemic exclusion from municipal decision-making.

It is often the case that local citizens are most likely to engage with their municipal government when they wish to express their opposition to a proposed municipal project. This engagement takes the form of Not-In-My-Backyard (NIMBY) movements to prevent any municipal project that threatens the engaged citizen's neighbourhood and potentially negatively affects the value of a resident's property, or which has a negative impact on the environment (see Fischel 2001). There are many examples of protests organized by individuals or community groups in opposition to housing developments that they claim are out of place with the existing neighbourhood or threaten the local environment (Poppe and Young 2015). Typically, this means they express opposition to the development of greenfield sites or the construction of apartment buildings in neighbourhoods predominantly comprised of single-family dwellings. There are many examples of this form of citizen engagement in Canada, the United States, and the United Kingdom. Indeed, preservation of "neighbourhood character" and concern for the local environment are prominent parts of planning regulations in many municipal jurisdictions, including Toronto (Bozikovic 2021).

Perhaps the ultimate expression of an individual's opposition to municipal government policy or action is the decision to "exit" the municipality. If an individual feels that municipal changes in their community are too negative, they make the decision to move to one that provides services that more closely fit their needs. This possibility is central to the public choice approach to municipal politics with its emphasis on more and smaller municipalities that provide different mixes of local taxes and municipal services, giving residents the benefit of choice. This argument is closely associated with the work of Charles Tiebout (1956) and his assessment of citizens as consumers of municipal services who make residential decisions based on the services provided and the costs of these services reflected in local taxes (see also Dowding, John, and Biggs 1994). Although this model of municipal residents' behaviour has been subjected to many challenges, it is certainly possible to point to concrete examples of citizens "voting with their feet" and leaving a municipality. In the case of Detroit, for example, the decline of the city over several decades resulted from a vicious cycle: as jobs and people left the city, its tax base declined, leading to a reduction in the quality of services that the city could provide and the abandonment of properties throughout the city, which in turn encouraged more people to relocate to surrounding municipalities (Doucet and Smit 2016; Martelle 2012). This option of leaving the city for the suburbs was not one that was equally available to all Detroit residents, however. Many of the suburban municipal governments and their residents used a variety of legal and illegal actions to prevent African Americans, among others, from buying property in the municipalities (Sugrue 2005).[14] Even today there are neighbourhoods throughout Detroit where residents are trapped in underserviced and declining neighbourhoods (Dreier, Mollenkopf, and Swanstrom 2014; Moskowitz 2018). The example of the metropolitan Detroit area serves as a reminder that community activism is not always supportive of progressive causes.

The effects of structural racism on the provision of services as well as the problematic nature of assuming a mobile, self-maximizing resident or "homo economicus" (Rutland 2018) in racially divided communities is explored further in chapter 14.

Participatory Mechanisms

Alongside elections and referendums, municipal governments use other mechanisms to include citizens in decision-making. The most common mechanisms of this type are information or consultation exercises organized by the municipality with the aim of informing residents of proposed plans and gathering residents' opinions on these proposed decisions. All municipalities in Canada, the United States, and the United Kingdom organize town hall or ward meetings open to all residents to hear directly about ongoing issues related to municipal services.[15] Other mechanisms of this type used by municipalities to listen to their residents include conducting surveys and establishing focus groups. Overall, these forms of interaction depend upon residents' interest in municipal decision-making. Residents decide whether to attend municipal meetings, participate in surveys, or apply to present to meetings of council or a council subcommittee, with a view to influencing particular municipal decisions.

In Canada, the United States, and United Kingdom, there is a general expectation that municipal government should be open and accessible to the public (Kopec and Sheldrick 2020; Sancton 2015b). There is, for example, an expectation that council meetings will be conducted in public rather than *in camera*. The reality of municipal practice has not always lived up to this promised openness, however, and in Canada provincial ombudsman offices have periodically criticized municipalities for their unwarranted use of private meetings. A 2007 Supreme Court of Canada decision, for example, was critical of secrecy in municipal decision-making (Tindal et al. 2016, 328), and in 2013 and 2014, then Ontario ombudsman André Marin criticized a "culture of secrecy" in Ontario municipalities (see Criscione 2014).

Beyond traditional town hall or ward meetings, the number and scope of participatory mechanisms have increased in all three countries with the goal of facilitating increased citizen engagement in municipal decision-making (Bryan 2004; Fung 2004, 2006; Harrison, Munton, and Collins 2004; Pateman 2012; Nabatchi and Amsler 2014; Van de Bovenkamp and Vollard 2019). Several types of mechanism exist, some of which are required by senior governments while others are voluntarily introduced by municipal governments themselves (see Michels 2012). As Arnstein (1969) famously identified, it is possible to classify these engagement mechanisms based on the extent to which they influence final decisions. It is also possible to categorize them along different dimensions including the degree to which they represent the local community, how their participants are selected, how frequently they meet, and whether they cover the full range of a municipality's work, a single policy sector, or a single issue at a particular time (Fung 2006).

Participatory mechanisms that are formally embedded within the institutional structure of government often bring citizens together to debate, deliberate, make recommendations, and, possibly, make decisions on policy issues. These mechanisms have different names – citizen juries, citizen advisory groups, advisory panels, or community or neighbourhood boards – but their underlying rationale is the same: they are designed to facilitate policy learning and deliberation among relatively small groups of citizens who are representative of the wider community and then, to differing degrees, allow that group to influence municipal decision-making (Kamenova and Goodman 2015; McAndrews and Marcus 2015; Sutcliffe and Cipkar 2017). Citizen juries – first used in the United States but now present in Canada and the United Kingdom – provide one example of this form of participatory mechanism. In this type of mechanism, a small group of municipal residents are selected, sometimes randomly from the entire municipality, and sometimes randomly from different groups within the community. The intention is to establish a jury that is representative of either the entire municipality or the users of the service in question. Citizens' juries normally meet intensively over a relatively short period to address the question set for them. Guided by a moderator, the jury hears evidence from academics, policy experts, and municipal decision-makers, and it is allowed to question these witnesses before preparing a final report with recommendations for the municipal council. In 2012, for example, the City of Edmonton used a citizens' jury to deliberate on the issue of internet voting at municipal elections (Kamenova and Goodman 2015).

Citizens' advisory groups are similar insofar as they draw a small group of citizens together to hear from interested parties, meet with city councillors, and debate the issue or issues relevant to their remit. Unlike citizens' juries, these groups usually have shorter meetings over a longer period and focus on a range of issues rather than one or two questions. Some of these panels are formed around a particular municipal policy sector – such as public transit or heritage preservation (Hull 2010; Sutcliffe and Cipkar 2017). Others are formed to provide a voice for neighbourhoods within the municipality as in the New York Community Board system or the neighbourhood associations in Portland, Oregon.[16] In New York City, community boards allow residents to engage and make recommendations on issues relevant to their neighbourhood and on the municipal budget. In each case, they are led by an elected borough president and supported by paid staff.

Other municipal bodies focus on particular groups of people. Many councils, for example, have a youth advisory committee designed to provide a voice to a group that typically demonstrates limited engagement with municipal politics, and it is increasingly common for councils to have advisory groups representing the 2SLGBTQIA+ or Indigenous communities (Fawcett, Walker, and Greene 2015; Bouvier and Walker 2018; Anderson and Flynn, this volume).

Citizens' panels are yet another way to engage with municipal residents. In this mechanism, a large, representative panel of local residents is recruited by the municipal government. These panellists are then asked to complete questionnaires relating to municipal issues or municipal services. In some cases, citizens' panels involve hearings and other opportunities for participants to learn about policy issues prior to providing their opinion on the issue concerned. A related participatory technique is deliberative polling (Rhys, Entwistle, and Guarneros-Meza 2019). In this case, a random sample of the population in a municipality is polled about a public issue. A subset of this group is subsequently provided with information on the issue and then brought together for a period of small group discussion and expert testimony. They are then polled again to assess the extent to which the policy learning has affected their opinions on the issue in question.

Participatory budgeting provides an example of a community engagement mechanism. It began as an experiment in Brazil, has expanded dramatically, and is now used extensively by municipal governments in the United States and the United Kingdom. Although the exact details of how the mechanism works vary from jurisdiction to jurisdiction, central features are present in each case. The mechanism is designed to draw residents into the process of city budgeting through public meetings, small group discussions, and community voting (see Gilman and Wampler 2019). In Boston in 2013–14, for example, the city government set aside $1 million for youth projects, with the possible projects identified through a consultative process and the specific projects selected by youth in a city-wide ballot (Gordon, Osgood, and Boden 2017a). In New York City, the participatory mechanisms in the community board structure allow citizens to be involved in the budgeting process through the selection of some city projects and services, and many other cities are also experimenting with participatory budgeting in some form (Gordon, Osgood, and Boden 2017b). Participatory budgeting is also used extensively in the United Kingdom, sometimes as part of a senior government-mandated requirement to engage citizens in local decision-making (Wilkinson et al. 2019). It is less common in Canadian municipalities although many councils do build extensive community consultation exercises into their budgetary process (see, for example, Johnson 2014), and some municipal bodies have experimented with participatory budgeting (see Petite 2020). Edmonton, Alberta, for example, has used citizen panels to shape budget priorities, and the City of Guelph, Ontario, has had a participatory budgeting process in place for over twenty years (Mao and Adria 2013). In this case, neighbourhood groups meet individually and collectively to determine a list of community projects that will be funded in the budget cycle (Pinnington, Lerner, and Schugurensky 2009).

THE IMPACT OF CITIZEN ENGAGEMENT

Why Do Municipal Governments Introduce Participation Mechanisms?

Municipal governments have in many cases unilaterally determined to support initiatives to consult and engage with residents. Many, for example, provide financial and logistic support for the creation of neighbourhood groups. Senior governments can also mandate the use of participatory mechanisms at the local government level. In the United Kingdom, for example, the 2011 Localism Act (in England) and 2015 Community Empowerment Act (in Scotland) both include requirements for municipal governments to engage with local residents. Similar requirements are evident in the United States and Canada (Brody, Godshalk, and Burby 2003).

The introduction of citizen participation measures – whether mandated or not – has resulted from a widespread agreement that these mechanisms are advantageous, both for municipalities and municipal residents (Irvin and Stansbury 2004). They are often argued to be one way to compensate for the limited public interest – evident in low turnout rates – in municipal elections. In this view, local participative exercises can supplement representative democracy and create more engaged and better-informed citizens. Residents are given the opportunity to develop a deeper understanding of policy issues as they debate proposals over an extended period and, as a result, participation helps to rebuild social capital and popular trust in the political processes and decision-making at the local level (Bonney 2004; Fung and Wright 2001; Hull 2010; Magnusson 2015). It is, for example, possible that residents will be more likely to accept a policy decision as legitimate or consider alternatives to their original views on the policy if they have engaged in consultation and believe that decision-makers have made a genuine attempt to consult the local population.

Alongside these general arguments in favour of popular participation, proponents also assert that there are specific advantages to including public input directly into the policy-making process. One is that this input produces better municipal policies (Burby 2003). Services, so the argument runs, will be improved if those who use them – or need them – are included in the decision-making that establishes the services and their delivery (Brody, Godshalk, and Burby 2003). This, then, is a move away from the idea that residents are passive recipients of municipal services and that determining the type and scope of municipal services should be left to experts in this field. Instead, citizens are, or should be, active participants in the policy-making process, and their knowledge and experiences need to be incorporated into the policy process as this will improve the quality of decision-making (Harris 2002). In sum, experts do not always know best. In the case of public transit, for example, it is sometimes argued that decision-making is too often focused on the needs of wealthy commuters who want access to city centre employment and entertainment districts rather than on the transit needs of less wealthy residents who have limited options with respect to transportation (Grengs 2010; Eisinger 2000; Garrett and Taylor 1999). Including the latter group through engagement mechanisms can result in more equitable access to public transit (Karner and Neimeier 2013).

Does Participation Matter?

A key question is whether these mechanisms matter. Do they allow municipal residents to influence the final municipal decisions reached? Or do participatory mechanisms exist only to inform the public about decisions taken or to provide them with a token opportunity to participate but with limited opportunity to affect final decisions?

Despite their growing prevalence and the arguments made by supporters, public engagement mechanisms do not inevitably improve the interface between residents and municipal governments. In each of the municipal systems examined here, critics challenge the relevance of these mechanisms (Casello et al. 2015; Callahan 2007; see discussion in Irvin and Stansbury 2004). A key factor is the difficulty in determining whether public consultation mechanisms impact the final decisions made by municipal bodies. Even in the case of mechanisms that are designed to go beyond simply informing residents of council decisions and that purport to allow residents to influence those decisions, research indicates that this does not necessarily occur in practice (McAndrews and Marcus 2015). One criticism of participatory budgeting, for example, is that in most cases, it only offers participants the opportunity to make decisions on limited amounts of money that have already been allotted to a particular policy sector or neighbourhood.

There are several reasons why participatory mechanisms may not impact municipal decisions. It is possible, for example, that municipal decision-makers simply ignore ideas presented through public consultation exercises. In a study of community groups, for example, Spicer (2016b) identifies that municipal councillors may oppose empowering such groups because they may see these groups as a rival to the city council itself. Similarly, municipal decision-makers may decide to incorporate only the public input that aligns with the advice provided by municipal staff or the positions they were likely to support even in the absence of that input (Bouchard 2016). In the case of deliberative polling, for example, it is up to the municipal councils to determine whether to incorporate the revised opinions of the participants. In the case of citizen juries, the municipal staff may have an important role in shaping the outcomes to the extent that they select the witnesses and evidence that the jury considers. In sum, it may be that the participation mechanisms are simply "window dressing" for decisions made elsewhere.

It is also important to note that a municipal council's decision to disregard residents' input is not necessarily based on self-interest. Municipal governments may be unable to respond to public engagement because the product of these engagement exercises reveals multiple competing views, thus making it impossible for a council to satisfy them all. Deliberation and debate among municipal residents do not guarantee that they will be able to develop a consensus view. It is also possible that a municipal council may legitimately determine that it is more appropriate for them to rely on the advice of council staff or external consultants rather than the voices of residents (see Fung 2006). This may occur, for example, if they feel that the community engagement has been dominated by particular interests and is not representative of the needs of the community as a whole.

Who Participates?

The latter point raises an issue that proponents of participatory mechanisms face in all three countries examined here: not all residents are able or willing to participate in these mechanisms.

Economic and social inequalities that are present within communities can be replicated in the mechanisms that are designed to engage citizens in municipal decision-making. Various case studies identify that poorer, marginalized groups – such as recent immigrants – are less likely to have the time or money to allow them to engage in municipal participatory mechanisms (Callahan 2007; see chapter 12 in this volume).

Participatory mechanisms may then serve to provide yet another advantage to already advantaged groups within a municipality and lead to municipal decisions that favour these groups to the detriment of disadvantaged residents. Studies of municipal decision-making frequently demonstrate that wealthier residents are more likely than poorer residents to influence municipal decisions (Sutcliffe 2008). This is often seen with respect to decisions on the location of undesirable facilities or services – such as needle exchanges or water treatment facilities – in a community. Municipal decision-makers are often more likely to place these facilities in poorer, disadvantaged neighbourhoods than in wards or communities that are home to wealthier citizens (see chapter 14). With respect to public transit decisions, it is also frequently evident that decision-makers do not prioritize the interests of poorer residents. This, in part, helps to explain the lack of transit equity within many urban regions (Casello et al. 2015; Culver 2017; Lowe and Grengs 2020).

The debate about the inclusiveness of participatory mechanisms at the municipal level fits into a wider debate, evident in all three countries, about the importance of powerful actors and the dominance of a neo-liberal governing framework at the national and local levels. Studies of municipal politics in Canada, the United States, and the United Kingdom identify, at least the possibility, that municipal decision-making prioritizes the interests of powerful actors within the municipality (Hackworth 2007; Leo 2002; Harvey 2005). The powerful interests are often said to include those – such as developers – that are central to the economic prosperity of a municipality and those – such as major business and financial interests – that have flexibility in where they can operate and which can decide to relocate based in part upon local conditions such as the extent of local taxes and the state of local infrastructure. A related possibility is that municipalities must invest in local infrastructure that will encourage the individuals that Richard Florida (2012) refers to as the "creative class" to locate in their municipality, thus limiting the money available to invest in social policies and services directed at marginalized residents.

The common theme in these arguments is that municipal governments are dominated by powerful interests that place substantial limits on their decision-making capacity, which in turn limits the relevance of participatory mechanisms. In this view, municipal governments prioritize services that support business and those who are already advantaged, as opposed to services, such as social housing, that support the less wealthy and less powerful (Pinnington, Lerner, and Schugurensky 2009; Culver 2017). It is certainly possible to identify municipal governments in all three countries that have taken decisions that seem to confirm this assessment (Moskowitz 2018; Sassen 2001; Cobban 2003). Ruppert's study of Toronto, for example, argues that private business interests increasingly dominate governance of the city and, as a result, local government is a "shell emptied of its content" (2000, 285). There are also, for example, many cities that have provided subsidies to professional sports teams to support the construction of new arenas (see chapter 10) or have supported the gentrification of parts of the city while at the same time limiting or reducing services to less affluent residents and communities. Swyngedouw, Moulaert, and Rodriguez highlight situations where cities "hide in their underbelly perverse and pervasive processes of social exclusion and marginalization and are rife with all manner of struggle, conflict, and often outright despair in the midst of the greatest affluence, abundance, and pleasure" (2002, 545).

At the same time, there are also examples of municipal governments – sometimes as a result of pressure from municipal residents – that have taken decisions that do not conform to this picture. In these cases, municipal governments have supported policies that challenge a neo-liberal framework and demonstrate support for the disadvantaged residents within their jurisdiction (Paul 2005). In 2020, for example, popular opposition led to the abandonment of a plan by Google-affiliated Sidewalk Labs to develop former industrial land on Toronto's waterfront, a plan that was originally supported by the Canadian prime minister (see chapter 10). Similar community opposition followed Amazon's 2018 decision to build part of its second headquarters in Long Island City, New York.[17] Despite the support of the New York City mayor, the decision drew opposition from several city councillors, politicians at the state and federal level, and local residents, leading Amazon to reverse its decision (Horowitz 2018). As identified elsewhere in this volume, it is possible that municipalities become sites of resistance to national and global forces as in the case of sanctuary cities in the United States. These are cities, such as San Francisco and Chicago, where the municipal government has voted not to cooperate with federal immigration authorities, particularly in the case of actions against undocumented residents. Indeed, many sanctuary cities provide access to city services to all residents regardless of status and, in some cases, have developed municipal forms of identification to facilitate such access (see Harvey 2013 and chapter 12 for more on this subject).

The fact that different case studies produce different conclusions is perhaps not surprising given the complexity of municipal governance and the variation in types and structures of municipal governments across the three countries.

CONCLUSION

Any comparative examination of municipal government service delivery and the interface between residents and their municipal government faces a major challenge. Not all municipalities are the same. Variation is evident across and within the three countries examined. The constitutional structure within which they are located plays a central role in determining what services municipalities can provide, how they will be paid for, and how they will be provided.

Studying the services that municipalities provide and how they are delivered is therefore difficult. Not all municipalities deliver the same services and certainly not in the same way. In each country, if to differing degrees, municipal service responsibility is affected and constrained by forces that are outside municipal government control. Senior governments, with the partial exception of US states with home rule provisions, have the legal authority to download services to municipal governments or upload them to themselves, and they may make financial decisions that expand or limit municipal governments' service operations. This, in turn, is connected to the wider economic and political forces that affect municipal governments. Municipalities in all three countries have been affected by pressures to provide a local environment that is welcoming for business interests and wealthier residents, as well as pressures to deliver services in a businesslike fashion. Sometimes this means that municipal governments contract service delivery out to private companies, and sometimes it has been used as a rationale for municipal reorganization, one argument being that larger municipalities can take advantage of economies of scale to deliver services more efficiently.

A similar mix of service mechanisms is evident in all three countries. Some municipal services are delivered directly by municipal employees, some are contracted out to the private sector or to non-profit organizations, some are delivered by municipal governments acting collectively or under contract from other municipalities, and some are delivered by organizations that are legally separate from the municipal government but fully or partially funded by municipal governments and have municipal councillors on their governing bodies. In each case, the type of mechanism used has consequences. Off-loading service delivery to not-for-profit organizations, for example, may take advantage of their expertise in the relevant sector but may make it more difficult to coordinate that service with other policy sectors. Services that are delivered by single-issue boards or agencies may allow that service to be insulated from overt political interference and allow a greater role for experts in the field. At the same time, however, they may be less accountable to local residents and may limit the opportunity for decision-makers to incorporate the knowledge and experiences of service users in their decision-making.

In Canada, as in the United States and the United Kingdom, municipal services are the ones that residents are likely to use most often. Despite this, evidence suggests that residents pay relatively limited attention to the municipal level. They are less likely to vote at the municipal level than in elections for the senior levels of government. They are likely to engage with their municipal government directly only when they perceive that a municipal decision will negatively affect their property. Nimbyism is still the most common explanation of citizen engagement with their municipal government.

There is, however, evidence of a change in these patterns. Municipalities in all three countries now use various participation mechanisms to engage municipal residents and incorporate that engagement into their decision-making. These are important experiments in local democracy that have the potential to facilitate greater popular engagement in municipal policies.

There is some evidence to suggest that they are, in some cases, successful in giving a voice to those marginalized by systemic inequalities. It is important, however, to conclude with a degree of caution. Providing citizens with an opportunity to engage directly in municipal decision-making does not guarantee that they will be able to do so, does not guarantee that municipal bodies will listen to their voices, and does not guarantee that the actors who are already privileged will not also be privileged within these participatory mechanisms. Advocates for the inclusion of those disadvantaged by existing municipal structures and services, therefore, cannot assume that participatory mechanisms will by themselves inevitably improve the lot of those marginalized within the municipality. Instead, they must be active in using the citizen-government interface in all its varied forms to advance the interests of all of a municipality's residents.

NOTES

1 The importance of municipal governments is even more evident if we include their power to regulate private service providers. This list can include business owners, taxi services, entertainment venues (through noise bylaws, for example), services aimed at tourists, and property developers.

2 Michael Lipsky (2010) is credited with coining the term to refer to police officers, educators, social workers, and other government employees who act as the interface between members of the public and government.

3 These measures have been taken as a result of internal municipal discussions but also in response to federal and provincial legislation and/or senior government funding opportunities. In June 2021, for example, the Canadian federal government announced funding for municipal infrastructure projects aimed at providing safe and inclusive community spaces.

4 The government of Alberta assigned its municipalities "natural person" powers in 1995. In Ontario, the provincial government introduced this in the 2001 Municipal Act. Nova Scotia and Newfoundland and Labrador have not designated municipal governments with this power (see Taylor and Dobson 2020).

5 Note that unlike the Canadian federal system, the United Kingdom's constitutional structure makes it, at least on paper, possible for the UK central government to abolish the Scottish and Welsh Parliaments, and in so doing regain authority over municipal government. Such a scenario is highly unlikely. The Scotland Act 2016 includes provisions recognizing the Scottish Parliament and Scottish Government as "a permanent part of the United Kingdom's constitutional arrangements," with a referendum required before either could be abolished.

6 A decision to build a recreation centre, for example, requires paying for the facility's construction and a commitment to pay the annual costs of running the centre.

7 The COVID-19 pandemic has changed the situation somewhat. In British Columbia, for example, the provincial government has allowed municipalities to borrow from their capital reserves to fund their operating budgets (Fletcher 2020).

8 Non-profits may, for example, be perceived as having the greater good of the community in mind rather than the focus on profitability that is central to a private company.

9 Municipal governments can also decide to privatize a service entirely by turning it over to a private company. Municipalities may, for example, decide to sell a recreational facility.

10 Contracting out increasingly extends to legal, financial, and planning services within a municipality.

11 The South Coast British Columbia Transportation Authority, referred to as TransLink, was formed through the South Coast British Columbia Transportation Authority Act of 1998.

12 Taylor (2019) identifies this difference, for example, in his comparison of the provincial government role in the creation of Metro Toronto in 1954 and the creation of the Twin Cities (Minneapolis-St. Paul) Metropolitan Council in 1967, in which the state government played a limited role.

13 It is possible to draw a distinction between participatory and deliberative mechanisms. Participatory mechanisms can refer to mechanisms designed to allow decision-makers to hear from citizens whereas deliberative mechanisms allow participants to have a voice and to be involved in making the final decisions in some way. The two terms are used interchangeably here to refer to measures used to allow citizens to have a voice in municipal decision-making that may or may not also let them influence final outcomes.

14 Until late in the twentieth century, for example, many municipalities made homeowners sign "covenants" to prevent them from selling their home to "undesirables"; a list that included Jews and African Americans (see Sugrue 2005).

15 Community groups in all three countries often seek to "pack" the council chambers with supporters with the aim of demonstrating the depth of support to the elected councillors.

16 As Spicer identifies, "after forcibly amalgamating hundreds of municipalities in the 1990s and early 2000s, the government of Ontario promoted community councils to allow restructured communities to retain some control over local affairs" (2016b, 130).

17 In 2017, Amazon announced plans to build a second headquarters. This started a process that resulted in bids from cities and states across North America, bids that included promised tax breaks and other promises of support.

REFERENCES

Amin-Smith, Neil, and David Phillips. 2019. *English Council Funding: What's Happened and What's Next?* London: Institute for Fiscal Studies Briefing Note BN 250.

Arnstein, Sherry R. 1969. "A Ladder of Citizen Participation." *Journal of the American Institute of Planners* 35, no. 4 (July): 216–24. https://doi.org/10.1080/01944366908977225.

Bailey, Holly. 2021. "Minneapolis Rejects Measure to Replace Police Department in First Major Electoral Test of Reform Movement after George Floyd's Murder." *Washington Post*, November 2, 2021. https://www.washingtonpost.com/nation/2021/11/02/minneapolis-mayor-police-vote/.

Bel, Germà, and Xavier Fageda. 2010. "Partial Privatisation in Local Services Delivery: An Empirical Analysis of the Choice of Mixed Firms." *Local Government Studies* 36, no. 1 (February): 129–49. https://doi.org/10.1080/03003930903435856.

Binelli, Mark. 2012. *Detroit City Is the Place to Be: The Afterlife of an American Metropolis.* New York: Metropolitan Books.

Bomey, Nathan. 2017. *Detroit Resurrected: To Bankruptcy and Back.* New York: Norton.

Bonney, Norman. 2004. "Local Democracy Renewed?" *Political Quarterly* 75, no. 1 (January): 43–51. https://doi.org/10.1111/j.1467-923X.2004.00570.x.

Bozikovic, Alex. 2021. "Planning for the Future." *Globe and Mail*, March 6, 2021, O6.

Bouchard, Nancy. 2016. "The Dark Side of Public Participation: Participative Processes That Legitimize Elected Officials' Values." *Canadian Public Administration* 59, no. 4 (December): 516–37. https://doi.org/10.1111/capa.12199.

Bouvier, Noelle, and Ryan Walker. 2018. "Indigenous Planning and Municipal Governance: Lessons from the Transformative Frontier." *Canadian Public Administration* 61, no. 1 (March): 130–4. https://doi.org/10.1111/capa.12249.

Bradbury, Mark D., and G. David Waechter. 2009. "Extreme Outsourcing in Local Government: At the Top and All but the Top." *Review of Public Personnel Administration* 29, no. 3 (September): 230–48. https://doi.org/10.1177/0734371X09332572.

Brody, Samuel D., David R. Godschalk, and Raymond J. Burby. 2003. "Mandating Citizen Participation in Plan Making: Six Strategic Planning Choices." *Journal of the American Planning Association* 69, no. 3 (September): 245–64. https://doi.org/10.1080/01944360308978018.

Brown, Jason D., and David Hannis. 2011. *Community Development in Canada*. 2nd ed. Toronto: Pearson.

Bryan, Frank M. 2004. *Real Democracy: The New England Town Meeting and How It Works*. Chicago: University of Chicago Press. https://doi.org/10.7208/chicago/9780226077987.001.0001.

Burby, Raymond J. 2003. "Making Plans That Matter: *Citizen Involvement and Government Action*." *Journal of the American Planning Association* 69, no. 1 (March): 33–49. https://doi.org/10.1080/01944360308976292.

Callahan, Kathe. 2007. "Citizen Participation: Questions of Diversity, Equity and Fairness." *Journal of Public Management & Social Policy* 13, no. 1 (Spring): 53–68.

Canadian Press. 2020. "Alberta Government Quietly Halts Closure of 17 Provincial Parks Due to COVID-19." *CBC News*, June 23, 2020. https://www.cbc.ca/news/canada/edmonton/alberta-government-quietly-halts-closure-of-17-provincial-parks-due-to-covid-19-1.5624440.

Casello, Jeffrey M., Will Towns, Julie Bélanger, and Sanathan Kassiedass. 2015. "Public Engagement in Public Transportation Projects: Challenges and Recommendations." *Transportation Research Record: Journal of the Transportation Research Board* 2537, no. 1 (January): 88–95. https://doi.org/10.3141/2537-10.

City of Toronto. 2020. "Toronto Agencies and Corporations." Updated May 2020. https://www.toronto.ca/wp-content/uploads/2020/06/9766-Agency-Chart-May-2020.pdf.

Cobban, Timothy. 2003. "The Political Economy of Urban Redevelopment: Downtown Revitalization in London, Ontario, 1993–2002." *Canadian Journal of Urban Research* 12, no. 2 (Winter): 231–48. https://www.jstor.org/stable/44320772.

Criscione, Peter. 2014. "Ontario's Top Watchdog Says Culture of Secrecy Infests Municipal Level." *The Brampton Guardian*, August 27, 2014. https://www.bramptonguardian.com/news/ontario-s-top-watchdog-says-culture-of-secrecy-infests-municipal-level/article_20a87cbb-ea7f-536e-b604-61320ad40ce5.html.

Culver, Gregg. 2017. "Mobility and the Making of the Neoliberal 'Creative City': The Streetcar as a Creative City Project?" *Journal of Transport Geography* 58 (January): 22–30. https://doi.org/10.1016/j.jtrangeo.2016.11.005.

Dahl, Robert. 2005. *Who Governs? Democracy and Power in an American City*. 2nd ed. New Haven, CT: Yale University Press.

DeFilippis, James, Robert Fisher, and Eric Shragge. 2006. "Neither Romance nor Regulation: Re-evaluating Community." *International Journal of Urban and Regional Research* 30, no. 3 (September): 673–89. https://doi.org/10.1111/j.1468-2427.2006.00680.x.

Doucet, Brian, and Edske Smit. 2016. "Building an Urban 'Renaissance': Fragmented Services and the Production of Inequality in Greater Downtown Detroit." *Journal of Housing and the Built Environment* 31, no. 4 (December): 635–57. https://doi.org/10.1007/s10901-015-9483-0.

Dowding, Keith, Peter John, and Stephen Biggs. 1994. "Tiebout: A Survey of Empirical Literature." *Urban Studies* 31, nos. 4–5 (May): 767–97. https://doi.org/10.1080/00420989420080671.

Dreier, Peter, John Mollenkopf, and Todd Swanstrom. 2014. *Place Matters: Metropolitics for the Twenty-First Century*. 3rd ed. Lawrence, KS: University Press of Kansas.

Eisinger, Peter. 2000. "The Politics of Bread and Circuses: Building the City for the Visitor Class." *Urban Affairs Review* 35, no. 3 (January): 316–33. https://doi.org/10.1177/107808740003500302.

Fawcett, R. Ben, Ryan Walker, and Jonathan Greene. 2015. "Indigenizing City Planning Processes in Saskatoon, Canada." *Canadian Journal of Urban Research* 24, no. 2 (Winter): 158–75. https://cjur.uwinnipeg.ca/index.php/cjur/article/view/184/92.

Feiock, Richard C. 2004. "Introduction: Regionalism and Institutional Collective Action." In *Metropolitan Governance: Conflict, Competition and Cooperation*, edited by Richard C. Feiock, 3–16. Washington, DC: Georgetown University Press.

Feiock, Richard C., and Hee Soun Jang. 2009. "Nonprofits as Local Government Service Contractors." *Public Administration Review* 69, no. 4 (July–August): 668–80. https://doi.org/10.1111/j.1540-6210.2009.02016.x.

Fernandez, Sergio, Jay Eungha Ryu, and Jeffrey L. Brudney. 2008. "Exploring Variations in Contracting for Services among American Local Governments: Do Politics Still Matter?" *The American Review of Public Administration* 38, no. 4 (December): 439–62. https://doi.org/10.1177/0275074007311386.

Fischel, William A. 2001. *The Home Voter Hypothesis: How Home Values Influence Local Government Taxation, School Finance, and Land-Use Policies*. Cambridge, MA: Harvard University Press.

Fletcher, Tanya. 2020. "'It Won't Be Enough': Vancouver Mayor Says Provincial Financial Relief Isn't Sufficient." *CBC News*, April 16, 2020. https://www.cbc.ca/news/canada/british-columbia/b-c-financial-relief-for-businesses-municipalities-1.5534657.

Flint, Anthony. 2009. *Wrestling with Moses: How Jane Jacobs Took on New York's Master Builder and Transformed the American City*. New York: Random House.

Florida, Richard. 2012. *The Rise of the Creative Class Revisited*. New York: Basic Books.

Fung, Archon. 2004. *Empowered Participation: Reinventing Urban Democracy*. Princeton: Princeton University Press.

———. 2006. "Varieties of Participation in Complex Governance." *Public Administration Review* 66, no. S1 (December): 66–75. https://doi.org/10.1111/j.1540-6210.2006.00667.x.

Fung, Archon, and Erik Olin Wright. 2001. "Deepening Democracy: Innovations in Empowered Participatory Governance." *Politics & Society* 29, no. 1 (March): 5–41. https://doi.org/10.1177/0032329201029001002.

Galster, George. 2012. *Driving Detroit: The Quest for Respect in the Motor City*. Philadelphia: University of Pennsylvania Press. https://doi.org/10.9783/9780812206463.

Garcea, Joseph. 2014. "The Empowerment of Canadian Cities: Classic Canadian Compromise." *International Journal of Canadian Studies* 49 (January): 81–104. https://doi.org/10.3138/ijcs.49.81.

Garrett, Mark, and Brian Taylor. 1999. "Reconsidering Social Equity in Public Transit." *Berkeley Planning Journal* 13, no. 1: 6–27. https://doi.org/10.5070/BP313113028.

Gilman, Hollie, and Brian Wampler. 2019. "The Difference in Design: Participatory Budgeting in Brazil and the United States." *Journal of Public Deliberation* 15, no. 1 (April): article 7. https://doi.org/10.16997/jdd.318.

Good, Kristin R. 2009. *Municipalities and Multiculturalism: The Politics of Immigration in Toronto and Vancouver*. Toronto: University of Toronto Press. https://doi.org/10.3138/9781442690417.

———. 2014. "Reopening the *Myth of the North American City* Debate: On Comparing Canadian and American Cities." *International Journal of Canadian Studies* 49 (January): 7–29. https://doi.org/10.3138/ijcs.49.7.

———. 2019. "The Fallacy of the 'Creatures of the Provinces' Doctrine: Recognizing and Protecting Municipalities' Constitutional Status." In *IMFG Papers on Finance and Governance*, no. 46. Toronto: Institute on Municipal Finance and Governance.

Gordon, Victoria, Jeffery L. Osgood Jr., and Daniel Boden. 2017a. "The Role of Citizen Participation and the Use of Social Media Platforms in the Participatory Budgeting Process." *International Journal of Public Administration* 40, no. 1: 65–76. https://doi.org/10.1080/01900692.2015.1072215.

Gordon, Victoria, Jeffery L. Osgood Jr., and Daniel Boden. 2017b. *Participatory Budgeting in the United States.* New York: Routledge. https://doi.org/10.4324/9781315535296.

Grengs, Joe. 2002. "Community-Based Planning as Source of Political Change: *The Transit Equity Movement of Los Angeles' Bus Riders Union.*" *Journal of the American Planning Association* 68, no. 2 (June): 165–78. https://doi.org/10.1080/01944360208976263.

———. 2010. "Job Accessibility and the Modal Mismatch in Detroit." *Journal of Transport Geography* 18, no. 1 (January): 42–54. https://doi.org/10.1016/j.jtrangeo.2009.01.012.

Gross, Jenny, and John Eligon. 2020. "Minneapolis City Council Votes to Remove $8 Million from Police Budget." *New York Times,* December 10, 2020. https://www.nytimes.com/2020/12/10/us/minneapolis-police-funding.html.

Hachard, Tomas. 2020. "It Takes Three: Making Space for Cities in Canadian Federalism." In *IMFG Papers on Finance and Governance*, no. 31. Toronto: Institute on Municipal Finance and Governance.

Hackworth, Jason. 2007. *The Neoliberal City: Governance, Ideology, and Development in American Urbanism.* Ithaca: Cornell University Press.

Harris, Neil. 2002. "Collaborative Planning: From Theoretical Foundations to Practice Forms." In *Planning Futures: New Directions for Planning Theory*, edited by Philip Allmendinger and Mark Tewdwr-Jones, 21–43. London: Routledge.

Harrison, Carolyn M., Richard J.C. Munton, and Kevin Collins. 2004. "Experimental Discursive Spaces: Policy Processes, Public Participation and the Greater London Authority." *Urban Studies* 41, no. 4 (April): 903–17. https://doi.org/10.1080/0042098042000194179.

Harvey, David. 2005. *A Brief History of Neoliberalism.* Oxford: Oxford University Press. https://doi.org/10.1093/oso/9780199283262.001.0001.

———. 2008. "The Right to the City." *New Left Review* 53 (September/October): 23–40.

———. 2013. *Rebel Cities: From the Right to the City to the Urban Revolution.* London: Verso.

Horak, Martin, and Marilyn Dantico. 2014. "The Limits of Local Redistribution: Neighbourhood Regeneration Initiatives in Toronto and Phoenix." *International Journal of Canadian Studies* 49 (January): 135–58. https://doi.org/10.3138/ijcs.49.135.

Horowitz, Julia. 2018. "Progressive Backlash against Amazon HQ2 Is Growing. Here's Why." *CNN,* November 10, 2018. https://edition.cnn.com/2018/11/09/tech/amazon-hq2-progressive-backlash/index.html.

House of Commons Transport Committee. 2019. *Bus Services in England outside of London.* Ninth Report of Session 2017–19. London: House of Commons.

Hull, Kristen. 2010. *Effective Use of Citizen Advisory Committees for Transit Planning and Operations: A Synthesis of Transit Practice.* Washington, DC: Transportation Research Board. https://doi.org/10.17226/14388.

Hunter, Floyd. 1953. *Community Power Structure: A Study of Decision Makers.* Chapel Hill, NC: University of North Carolina Press.

Irvin, Renée A., and John Stansbury. 2004. "Citizen Participation in Decision Making: Is It Worth the Effort?" *Public Administration Review* 64, no. 1 (February): 55–65. https://doi.org/10.1111/j.1540-6210.2004.00346.x.

Johnson, Aidan. 2014. "Here's Democracy at Work: Participatory Budgeting Gives You a Real Say on Spending Tax Funds." *Hamilton Spectator*, May 2, 2014, A13.

Joy, Meghan, and John Shields. 2020. "The Political Economy of the Non-profit Sector." In *Canadian Political Economy*, edited by Heather Whiteside, 215–33. Toronto: University of Toronto Press. https://doi.org/10.3138/9781487530907-013.

Kamenova, Kalina, and Nicole Goodman. 2015. "Public Engagement with Internet Voting in Edmonton: Design, Outcomes, and Challenges to Deliberative Models." *Journal of Public Deliberation* 11, no. 2 (December): article 4. https://doi.org/10.16997/jdd.234.

Karner, Alex, and Deb Neimeier. 2013. "Civil Rights Guidance and Equity Analysis Methods for Regional Transportation Plans: A Critical Review of Literature and Practice." *Journal of Transport Geography* 33 (December): 126–34. https://doi.org/10.1016/j.jtrangeo.2013.09.017.

Kopec, Anna, and Byron Sheldrick. 2020. "The Adoption of Open Government by Local Governments in Canada: Obstacles and Possibilities." *Canadian Journal of Urban Research* 29, no. 1 (Summer): 70–93. https://www.jstor.org/stable/26929898.

Kushner, Joseph, and David Siegel. 2005. "Are Services Delivered More Efficiently after Municipal Amalgamations?" *Canadian Public Administration* 48, no. 2 (June): 251–67. https://doi.org/10.1111/j.1754-7121.2005.tb02190.x.

Leo, Christopher. 2002. "Urban Development: Planning Aspirations and Political Realities." In *Urban Policy Issues: Canadian Perspectives*, edited by Edmund P. Fowler and David Siegel, 215–36. Oxford: Oxford University Press.

Lipsky, Michael. 2010. *Street-Level Bureaucracy: Dilemmas of the Individual in Public Services*. 30th anniversary ed. New York: Russell Sage Foundation.

Lowe, Kate, and Joe Grengs. 2020. "Private Donations for Public Transit: The Equity Implications of Detroit's Public-Private Streetcar." *Journal of Planning Education and Research* 40, no. 3 (September): 289–303. https://doi.org/10.1177/0739456X18761237.

Lucas, Jack. 2013. "Hidden in Plain View: Local Agencies, Boards, and Commissions in Canada." In *IMFG Papers on Finance and Governance*. Toronto: Institute on Municipal Finance and Governance.

Magnusson, Warren. 2005. "Are Municipalities Creatures of the Provinces?" *Journal of Canadian Studies* 39, no. 2 (Spring): 5–30. https://doi.org/10.1353/jcs.2006.0019.

———. 2015. *Local Self-Government and the Right to the City*. Montreal: McGill-Queen's University Press. https://doi.org/10.1515/9780773597280.

Mao, Yuping, and Marco Adria. 2013. "Deciding Who Will Decide: Assessing Random Selection for Participants in Edmonton's Citizen Panel on Budget Priorities." *Canadian Public Administration* 56, no. 4 (December): 610–37. https://doi.org/10.1111/capa.12042.

Martelle, Scott. 2012. *Detroit: A Biography*. Chicago: Chicago Review Press.

Massey, Doreen. 2007. *World City*. Cambridge: Polity Press.

McAndrews, Carolyn, and Justine Marcus. 2015. "The Politics of Collective Public Participation in Transportation Decision-Making." *Transportation Research Part A: Policy and Practice* 78 (August): 537–50. https://doi.org/10.1016/j.tra.2015.06.014.

Michels, Ank. 2012. "Citizen Participation in Local Policy Making: Design and Democracy." *International Journal of Public Administration* 35, no. 4 (March): 285–92. https://doi.org/10.1080/01900692.2012.661301.

Moskowitz, Peter. 2018. *How to Kill a City: Gentrification, Inequality, and the Fight for the Neighborhood*. New York: Nation Books.

Mukherjee, Alok. 2018. "Why Anti-Black Racism Persists in the Toronto Police Service." *Globe and Mail*, December 10, 2018. https://www.theglobeandmail.com/opinion /article-why-anti-black-racism-persists-in-the-toronto-police-service/.

Nabatchi, Tina, and Lisa Blomgren Amsler. 2014. "Direct Public Engagement in Local Government." *American Review of Public Administration* 44, no. S4 (July): 63S–88S. https://doi.org /10.1177/0275074013519702.

Nelles, Jen. 2012. "Regionalism Redux: Exploring the Impact of Federal Grants on Mass Public Transit Governance and Political Capacity in Metropolitan Detroit." *Urban Affairs Review* 49, no. 2 (March): 220–53. https://doi.org/10.1177/1078087412458255.

———. 2013. "Cooperation and Capacity? Exploring the Sources and Limits of City-Region Governance Partnerships." *International Journal of Urban and Regional Research* 37, no. 4 (July): 1349–67. https://doi.org/10.1111/j.1468-2427.2012.01112.x.

Nelles, Jen, Jill Simone Gross, and Loraine Kennedy. 2018. "The Role of Governance Networks in Building Metropolitan Scale." *Territory, Politics, Governance* 6, no. 2 (April): 159–81. https://doi.org /10.1080/21622671.2017.1421478.

Nickels, Ashley E. 2016. "Approaches to Municipal Takeover: Home Rule Erosion and State Intervention in Michigan and New Jersey." *State and Local Government Review* 48, no. 3 (September): 194–207. https://doi.org/10.1177/0160323X16667990.

Pateman, Carole. 2012. "Participatory Democracy Revisited." *Perspectives on Politics* 10, no. 1 (March): 7–19. https://doi.org/10.1017/S1537592711004877.

Paul, Darel E. 2005. "The Local Politics of 'Going Global': Making and Unmaking Minneapolis-St Paul as a World City." *Urban Studies* 42, no. 12 (December): 2104–22. https://doi.org /10.1080/00420980500332114.

Petite, Wesley. 2020. "The Promise and Limitations of Participatory Budgeting." *Canadian Public Administration* 63, no. 3 (September): 522–7. https://doi.org/10.1111/capa.12385.

Pinnington, Elizabeth, Josh Lerner, and Daniel Schugurensky. 2009. "Participatory Budgeting in North America: The Case of Guelph, Canada." *Journal of Public Budgeting, Accounting & Financial Management* 21, no. 3: 454–83. https://doi.org/10.1108/JPBAFM-21-03-2009-B005.

Poppe, Will, and Douglas Young. 2015. "The Politics of Place: Place-Making versus Densification in Toronto's Tower Neighbourhoods." *International Journal of Urban and Regional Research* 39, no. 3 (May): 613–21. https://doi.org/10.1111/1468-2427.12196.

Rhys, Andrew, Tom Entwistle, and Valeria Guarneros-Meza. 2019. "Local Government Size and Political Efficacy: Do Citizen Panels Make a Difference?" *International Journal of Public Administration* 42, no. 8 (June): 664–76. https://doi.org/10.1080/01900692.2018.1499774.

Ruppert, Evelyn S. 2000. "Who Governs the Global City?" In *Democracy, Citizenship and the Global City*, edited by Engin F. Isin, 275–88. London: Routledge.

Rutland, Ted. 2018. *Displacing Blackness: Power, Planning, and Race in Twentieth-Century Halifax*. Toronto: University of Toronto Press. https://doi.org/10.3138/9781487518233.

Sancton, Andrew. 1996. "Reducing Costs by Consolidating Municipalities: New Brunswick, Nova Scotia and Ontario." *Canadian Public Administration* 39, no. 3 (September): 267–89. https://doi .org/10.1111/j.1754-7121.1996.tb00133.x.

———. 2000. *Merger Mania: The Assault on Local Government*. Montreal: McGill-Queen's University Press. https://doi.org/10.1515/9780773568914.

———. 2002. "Metropolitan and Regional Governance." In *Urban Policy Issues: Canadian Perspectives*, edited by Edmund P. Fowler and David Siegel, 54–68. Oxford: Oxford University Press.

———. 2004. "Beyond the Municipal: Governance for Canadian Cities." *Policy Options*, February 2004, 26–31.

———. 2005. "The Governance of Metropolitan Areas in Canada." *Public Administration and Development* 25, no. 4 (October): 317–27. https://doi.org/10.1002/pad.386.

———. 2008. *The Limits of Boundaries: Why City-Regions Cannot Be Self-Governing*. Montreal: McGill-Queen's University Press. https://doi.org/10.1515/9780773574977.

———. 2015a. *Canadian Local Government: An Urban Perspective*. 2nd ed. Oxford: Oxford University Press.

———. 2015b. "What Is a Meeting? Municipal Councils and the Ontario Ombudsman." *Canadian Public Administration* 58, no. 3 (September): 426–43. https://doi.org/10.1111/capa.12123.

Sassen, Saskia. 2001. *The Global City: New York, London, Tokyo*. 2nd ed. Princeton, NJ: Princeton University Press. https://doi.org/10.1515/9781400847488.

Schafer, Josephine, and Zhiwei Zhang. 2016. "The Role of Stakeholders in Municipal Contracting Out." *Public Administration Quarterly* 40, no. 4 (Winter): 789–813.

Siegel, David. 2005. "Municipal Reform in Ontario: Revolutionary Evolution." In *Municipal Reform in Canada: Reconfiguration, Re-empowerment and Rebalancing*, edited by Joseph Garcea and Edward C. Lesage Jr., 127–48. Oxford: Oxford University Press.

Small, Kenneth A. 2009. "Transportation: Urban Transportation Policy." In *Making Cities Work: Prospects and Policies for Urban America*, edited by Robert P. Inman, 63–93. Princeton: Princeton University Press. https://doi.org/10.1515/9781400833153-007.

Spicer, Zachery. 2012. "Post-Amalgamation Politics: How Does Consolidation Impact Community Decision-Making?" *Canadian Journal of Urban Research* 21, no. 2 (Winter): 90–111. https://www.jstor.org/stable/26193914.

———. 2015. "Co-operation and Capacity: Inter-Municipal Agreements in Canada." In *IMFG Papers on Finance and Governance*, no. 19. Toronto: Institute on Municipal Finance and Governance.

———. 2016a. "Regionalism, Municipal Organization and Interlocal Cooperation in Canada." *Canadian Public Policy* 41, no. 2 (June): 137–50. https://doi.org/10.3138/cpp.2014-078.

———. 2016b. "A Patchwork of Participation: Stewardship, Delegation and the Search for Community Representation in Post-Amalgamation Ontario." *Canadian Journal of Political Science* 49, no. 1 (March): 129–50. https://doi.org/10.1017/S0008423916000275.

Spicer, Zachery, and Adam Found. 2016. *Thinking Regionally: How to Improve Service Delivery in Canada's Cities*. Toronto: C.D. Howe Institute. https://doi.org/10.2139/ssrn.2855982.

Stone, Clarence N. 1989. *Regime Politics: Governing Atlanta, 1946–1988*. Lawrence, KS: University Press of Kansas.

Sugrue, Thomas J. 2005. *The Origins of the Urban Crisis: Race and Inequality in Postwar Detroit*. Princeton: Princeton University Press.

Sutcliffe, John B. 2008. "Public Participation in Local Politics: The Impact of Community Activism on the Windsor-Detroit Border Decision Making Process." *Canadian Journal of Urban Research* 17, no. 2 (Winter): 57–83. https://www.jstor.org/stable/26193216.

Sutcliffe, John B., and Sarah Cipkar. 2017. "Citizen Participation in the Public Transportation Policy Process: A Comparison of Detroit, Michigan, and Hamilton, Ontario." *Canadian Journal of Urban Research* 26, no. 2 (Winter): 33–51. https://cjur.uwinnipeg.ca/index.php/cjur/article/view/95/48.

Swyngedouw, Erik, Frank Moulaert, and Arantxa Rodriguez. 2002. "Neoliberal Urbanization in Europe: Large-Scale Urban Development Projects and the New Urban Policy." *Antipode* 34, no. 3 (July): 542–77. https://doi.org/10.1111/1467-8330.00254.

Taylor, Zak. 2014. "If Different, Then Why? Explaining the Divergent Political Development of Canadian and American Local Governance." *International Journal of Canadian Studies* 49 (January): 53–79. https://doi.org/10.3138/ijcs.49.53.

———. 2019. *Shaping the Metropolis: Institutions and Urbanization in the United States and Canada.* Montreal: McGill-Queen's University Press. https://doi.org/10.1515/9780773558427.

Taylor, Zak, and Alec Dobson. 2020. "Power and Purpose: Canadian Municipal Law in Transition." In *IMFG Papers on Finance and Governance*, no. 47. Toronto: Institute on Municipal Finance and Governance. https://tspace.library.utoronto.ca/bitstream/1807/99226/1/imfgpaper_no47_Power_and_Purpose_Taylor_Dobson.pdf.

Tiebout, Charles M. 1956. "A Pure Theory of Local Expenditures." *The Journal of Political Economy* 64, no. 5 (October): 416–24. https://doi.org/10.1086/257839.

Tindal, Richard, Susan N. Tindal, Patrick Smith, and Kennedy Stewart. 2016. *Local Government in Canada.* 9th ed. Toronto: Nelson.

Tulloch, Michael H. 2017. *Report of the Independent Police Oversight Review.* Toronto: Queen's Printer for Ontario.

Tyers, Rogers. 2022. "Councils in England Get New Powers over Traffic Offences." House of Commons Library. May 25, 2022. https://commonslibrary.parliament.uk/councils-in-england-to-get-new-powers-over-traffic-offences/.

van de Bovenkamp, Hester M., and Hans Vollard. 2019. "Strengthening the Local Representative System: The Importance of Electoral and Non-electoral Representation." *Local Government Studies* 45, no. 2 (March): 196–218. https://doi.org/10.1080/03003930.2018.1548351.

Vengroff, Richard, and Robert K. Whelan. 2001. "Canadian Municipal Government in an Age of Neoliberalism." *International Journal of Public Administration* 24, no. 6: 503–10. https://doi.org/10.1081/PAD-100104392.

Voorn, Bart, Marieke L. van Genugten, and Sandra van Thiel. 2017. "The Efficiency and Effectiveness of Municipally Owned Corporations: A Systematic Review." *Local Government Studies* 43, no. 5 (September): 820–41. https://doi.org/10.1080/03003930.2017.1319360.

Wilkinson, Catherine, Jo Briggs, Karen Salt, John Vines, and Emma Flynn. 2019. "In Participatory Budgeting We Trust? Fairness, Tactics and (In)accessibility in Participatory Governance." *Local Government Studies* 45, no. 6 (July): 1001–20. https://doi.org/10.1080/03003930.2019.1606798.

Williams, Robert J., and Terrence J. Downey. 1999. "Reforming Rural Ontario." *Canadian Public Administration* 42, no. 2 (June): 160–92. https://doi.org/10.1111/j.1754-7121.1999.tb01066.x.

PART FOUR

Urban Policy Issues in a Global Canada

CHAPTER TEN

The Politics and Governance of Growth and Economic Development

Zachary Spicer

INTRODUCTION

Growth and development are central features in the life of municipal governments. Local decision-makers often devote a significant amount of time, energy, and money to determining how their community should grow and, in turn, attract new residents, jobs, and investment. In this desire for local growth and expansion, these same municipal decision-makers often confront a common challenge in that they do not single-handedly control the economic fate of their communities. In fact, they control few levers to affect the overall economy. Local politicians do not have any control over monetary policy, macro housing policy, or interest rates, among others. Without control over such important factors in managing the economy, municipal decision-makers often devote attention to the issues that they can control, namely local land-use planning, land ownership, economic development strategy, and investment attraction. In doing so, they often hope that the promise of jobs or the promotion of local industry or landmarks, mixed with a bit of luck, will stimulate their local economy and promote the growth of their communities.

This chapter explores the dynamics of local economic development and the politics of growth in a comparative context. In doing so, we set out to answer four core questions:

- Why is economic growth so centrally tied to perceptions of overall community health?
- What tensions are inherent in local economic development?
- What interests must be balanced, and how and why have different jurisdictions chosen different development strategies?
- To what extent are the pressures of globalization experienced similarly or being managed differently?

Additionally, this chapter also seeks to answer questions about differences in approach across jurisdictions. For instance, do American and Canadian economic development practitioners use different tactics or strategies in the face of similar threats and opportunities? What constraints do these actors confront? Are Canadian municipalities more cautious and less likely to provide financial inducements to new firms looking to enter their markets?

To answer these questions, this chapter proceeds in three sections. First, we explore the theoretical work examining the dynamics of growth politics and economic development in local government, identifying the motivation to pursue economic development, along with the types of activities in which local governments engage. Next, we examine the nature of local boosterism, using the long-standing fascination local actors have with the construction and public subsidy of sports stadiums as an example. Despite evidence of weak economic impact, governments have repeatedly devoted heaps of public money to stadium construction, usually under threat of relocation by team owners. This section explores the dynamics of the bargaining processes with private actors, highlighting a series of examples in both Canada and the United States. In the following section, we examine more advanced local economic development efforts, highlighting recent high-profile pursuits of digital infrastructure and highly coveted technology jobs. In doing so, we dive into the dynamics of smart city construction and highlight the aggressive competition over Amazon's HQ2 contest. This section highlights the different strategies that Canadian and American economic development professionals can advance. As a result of stricter provincial regulations on the type of financial inducements municipalities can provide, local Canadian leaders tend to emphasize quality of life factors and the advantage of settling in communities that are diverse and well-educated. In contrast, local American leaders tend to provide financial concessions, such as tax breaks and direct cash injections to potential economic suitors, at a far greater pace. Ultimately, this chapter argues that despite the differences in approach, the economic development strategies of municipalities in both Canada and the United States are prone to capture by powerful financial interests with a stake in directing local investment. In response, communities in both countries need to define their own interests and use economic development as a tool to advance collective well-being on their own terms.

SEEING THE GOOD IN GROWTH

In many municipalities around the world, growth is seen as intrinsically good, rarely questioned, and often supported through a local "booster spirit" (Boorstin 1965). Canada is no exception. To appreciate how and why this is, it is important to understand the nature of local politics, the power dynamics involved with urban growth, and the limitations of local institutions. Much of the existing literature on urban power dynamics and growth has focused on the centrality of land and, specifically, the commodification of land. Logan and Molotch (1987) noted that various local interests come together to develop, market, and enhance the exchange value of property within a community. As discussed in chapter 3, these assemblages, dubbed "growth machines," can be best defined as nested interest groups with common stakes in development who use the institutional fabric, including the political and cultural apparatus, to intensify land use and, as a result, profit (Molotch 1993). In this view, coalitions in urban politics are brought together because of their interest in the growth of a particular place and turn the government into a vehicle to pursue financial goals (Mollenkopf 1987; Elkin 1987). These coalitions become hegemonic in local politics and administration over time, bound together by their interests in maximizing the exchange values of property through the intensification of land use. These coalitions could include a variety of actors, such as property developers, speculators, financial institutions, politicians, or local media. Due to the depth and diversity of the actors involved in growth coalitions, these groupings wield veto power because governing becomes impossible without their participation (Molotch 1993).[1]

In a related vein of literature also discussed in chapter 3, regime scholars detail the interplay between various coalitions and the drive for economic development, growth, and land development. Regime analysis views power as fragmented and regimes as a collaborative mechanism in which local governments and private actors come together to govern a community (Mossberger and Stoker 2001). In doing so, urban regimes bridge the divide between popular control of government and private control of economic resources (Mossberger and Stoker 2001). The collaboration between these groups is based upon social production – both sides bring together fragmented resources and complement the assets of each (Stone 1989). From local government, actors bring legitimacy and policy-making authority, for instance, while the business community brings capital, tax revenue, and financing (Mossberger and Stoker 2001). There can certainly be a monetary flow between both (as demonstrated later in the chapter), where the business community may seek concessions from public bodies.

An important aspect of regime theory is that regimes are not conceptualized as temporary or ad hoc coalitions. Rather they are sustaining, designed for long-term governing capacity, and often outlive city administrations and the key actors that form and sustain them. For instance, Stone's (1989) early and seminal analysis of regimes focused on a development regime in Atlanta that spanned from 1946 to 1988. With this in mind, regimes can be understood as fundamentally reorienting the composition of community life and directing the focus of local politics – in this case on urban development and economic strength.

Stone (1993) argues that there are four different types of regimes: (1) maintenance or caretaker regimes, which focus on routine service delivery and low taxes, (2) development regimes, which are concerned with changing land use to promote growth, (3) middle-class progressive regimes, which emphasize quality of life concerns, such as environmental protection, historic preservation, and affordable housing, and (4) lower-class opportunity expansion regimes, which focus on human investment policy and widened access to employment. As they are usually reliant on ideologically motivated forces, middle-class progressive regimes and lower-class opportunity expansion regimes are the most seldom seen, but the business sector is a key member of both (Stone 1993). The most common types of regimes are development regimes and maintenance regimes.

With a fundamental orientation toward growth and development thanks to the governing coalitions and regimes that focus local governments on the commodification of land and resources, municipalities often actively market themselves to send both internal and external signals of strength and prosperity with the end goal of increasing their competitive position relative to regional and national peers (see Ashworth and Voogd 1990; Smyth 1994; Gold and Ward 1994; Harvey and Young 2012; Duffy 1995).[2] Logan and Molotch elaborate upon this celebration of local growth: "schoolchildren are taught to view local history as a series of breakthroughs in the expansion of the economic base of their city and region, celebrating its numerical leadership in one sort of production or another; more generally, increases in population tend to be equated with local progress" (1987, 61).[3] Caught up in such enthusiasm, it is natural for municipal actors to want their communities to expand and grow.

Given the importance of growth and development to the orientation of local politics, local actors often see other communities as potential competition. Cities are often also severely constrained in their policy choices by both horizontal limitations imposed by state or provincial legislatures (Gamm and Koussser 2013; Frug 1980) and vertical factors, such as competition among neighbours that limits the choices available to local officials, especially when it comes to economic and redistributive issues (Peterson 1981). The threat of competition pushes cities toward policy convergence, which often favours wealthy taxpayers and businesses that have a credible exit option (Einstein and Kogan 2015). According to Peterson (1981), to achieve a competitive advantage, municipalities must use their chief resource, land, to attract as much capital and labour as possible. Peterson (1981) theorized that since cities lacked the ability to regulate labour and capital flows, they are left with only land as the main economic driver of the community, leaving local leaders with little choice but to advance developmental policies and use land to attract resources.

Within this mixed metropolitan "marketplace," we can see a variety of actors – both public (i.e., politicians and bureaucrats) and private ("place entrepreneurs," as Logan and Molotch might term them) – who set and reinforce a competitive mentality within metropolitan areas (see chapter 3). This competition is quite extensive but tends to focus on the outward appearance of a community and the strength of municipal scope and capacity (Lucy and Phillips 2000). In this arena, municipalities seek out a competitive advantage not just locally but globally by competing for certain types of residents, businesses, and non-profit organizations that are more attractive and prized than others because they possess certain strategic resources, such as jobs, property value, income, education, skills, civic virtue, or family support (Deas and Giordano 2002; Kresl 2002; Begg 2002; Asheim and Isaksen 1997; Wolfe and Bramwell 2008; Graham 2002; Florida 2012).

Schneider (1989) provides us with a simplified model of local "buyers" and "sellers." To Schneider, metropolitan areas are just like any type of marketplace where "sellers" (local governments) bring goods to market in the hopes "buyers" will purchase them at a certain price – in this case, those choosing to locate in one jurisdiction over another because one more aligns with their "tastes" (Schneider 1989). These "tastes" could include a preference for a variety of local goods and amenities, such as green space, transit (both local and regional), libraries, and increased police protection, among others (Schneider 1989). The types of goods up for "sale" are diverse, but ultimately if municipalities can get the "buyers" to buy, they can enhance their position and grow. Much of this model is in line with the incentives for private firms: more "sales" will contribute to firm growth. Municipalities often adopt a competitive lens in pursuing these goals, seeing others, especially those with similar goals, as direct competition (Young 2012; Begg 1999; Parkinson and Boddy 2004). Regional co-operation on highly coveted items, such as local investment, is unlikely (Young 2012).[4]

Taking these perspectives into account, three main categories of goods are generally ripe for competition: population, business, and external resources. Municipalities with larger populations are thought to be more attractive to both businesses, who see bigger cities as having a deeper pool of workforce talent and a larger potential market for their goods (Varady and Raffel 1995; Parkinson and Boddy 2004), and individual residents, who view more densely populated cities as having more opportunities, attractions, and social goods (Moore and Begg 2004). Economic development strategy has also increasingly focused on the *type* of population to be attracted in recent years. Richard Florida popularized the notion of the "creative class," which he maintains is a key driving force for economic development in post-industrial cities (see Florida 2002, 2005, 2012). The "creative class" is a group of workers whose jobs are meant to create new forms of economic and creative material. Included are occupations like scientists, engineers, university professors, poets, and architects, as well as "people in design, education, arts, music and entertainment, whose economic function is to create new ideas, new technology and/or creative content" (Florida 2002, 8). These types of professions are termed "knowledge intensive," and the output from their various industries is economically prized (Florida 2002). By locating in a certain community, this class of workers not only changes the economic composition but also the cultural and physical design, making the municipality more attractive to outsiders and further attracting new investment (Florida 2012).

Aside from people, municipalities also covet business and industry as a way to create jobs, which may attract more residents, associated services, and community prestige, and mitigate the impact of larger downturns in the economy (Duffy 1995). Capital is seen as increasingly mobile, providing cities with more incentive to retain and attract new industries (Turok 2005; Graham 2002; Hollands 2008). Finally, municipalities tend to compete for external resources, which could come in the form of placement of federal offices, colleges or universities, prisons, or military bases (Logan and Molotch 1987), or may also centre on infrastructure items, such as the placement of highways or railway tracks, all of which would provide a municipality with better access to raw materials, a gateway to sell goods to other markets, or transportation linkages for community members to reach other cities (Scheiber 1973; Glaab 1962). National and state/provincial governments also distribute various grants and allotments of funding to municipalities, which can be used to subsidize the cost of certain local services or be used to enhance other services (Schneider 1989). This final category can be instrumentally important in creating conditions for economic success in the first two categories. State grants have long been used to attract investment for certain communities or spark economic revival through the relocation of government facilities or the deconcentration of government assets from major population centres (see Christophers 2008; Hackworth 2006). These grants and financial support from senior orders of government may also be used to spark economic activity and restructuring in distressed cities and those suffering from prolonged periods of economic decline.

The goods in each category – population, business, and external resources – contribute to the local assessment base, ultimately enhancing the fiscal position of a municipal government. A larger population base, coupled with a robust business sector, can increase property taxes and, ultimately, local "wealth" (Schneider 1989). Those resources can be invested in the community, creating more opportunity that outsiders may find attractive. Much like a private firm, municipalities will do what they can to enhance this local "wealth," with other municipalities seen as competing firms (Schneider 1989).

The pursuit of growth seems embedded in urban politics. Why is that? Several prominent authors surveyed above have demonstrated that there is a natural orientation toward economic growth and development in local government itself. The nature of coalitions that are built and sustained in local politics tends to involve business interests. Beyond that, the levers that municipalities have to increase the economic health of their communities are centred on land and land development. Municipalities use those resources in close conjunction with the business community to create a stable governing coalition. The focus on development can be best viewed as "baked in" to the politics of cities and fundamental to the maintenance of long-serving governing regimes that include both public and private actors.

THE GROWTH MENTALITY IN ACTION

The theoretical landscape in this area has been well developed over several decades by many prominent thinkers. This section highlights several examples that demonstrate how the growth mentality can motivate municipalities to pursue certain projects over others, sacrifice public capital, and engage in projects that blur the line between the promotion of community and personal interests. The examples below show how the logic behind many of these projects can be convoluted and the outcomes costly.

Few local decisions highlight the dynamics around the growth mentality and boosterism better than stadium construction. Any major sports team requires a large stadium for its operations. The teams, however, rarely fund these construction projects on their own. Instead, teams often draw upon the vanity of municipal governments, playing one municipality against another, to garner public funding for these projects. The threat of relocation is often central in this bargaining process. Having a big-league sports franchise is often central to local identity, signalling to the outside world that a municipality has achieved a certain status, so the potential of losing the team, and that accompanying status, often looms large over negotiations.

The argument in favour of public subsidies involves the promotion of civic pride and some promises of local economic uplift. Sports teams, we are often told, promote a city nationally and internationally, effectively "putting it on the map" and compelling others to acknowledge their elevated status (Trumpbour 2007). Others also argue that stadiums create immense economic benefits, creating not only temporary construction jobs within the community at their outset but sustained business development and attraction opportunities for the local service industry (Wolla 2017). These arguments often harken back to an era when downtown revitalization was a priority for large cities – having a sports arena with a major-league team as a hub was seen to attract those from the surrounding suburbs and encourage them to spend money at adjoining small businesses, such as restaurants or paid parking lots, when taking in a game.

Existing literature has largely shown that the benefits of subsidizing stadiums are minimal (Cagan and deMause 1998) or non-existent (Delaney and Eckstein 2003). The economic impact of stadium construction trumpeted by many supporters of public subsidies, especially construction jobs, has been shown to be highly exaggerated (Baade and Sanderson 1997; Weiner 2000). It is estimated by the *Berkley Economic Review* that the economic impact of an average stadium is US$145 million per year, certainly not insignificant, but none or very little of this money is actually returned to the local government (Berkley Economic Review Staff 2019). Most of the economic impact is directed toward private enterprises – both the team itself as well as smaller private businesses in close proximity, such as bars and restaurants (Wolla 2017). Even with these estimates, the economic impact of stadiums is often significantly less impressive than feasibility studies suggest, partly because sports-related spending tends to "realign economic activity within a city's leisure industry, rather than adding to it" (Baade and Sanderson 1997). Given this impact, some have argued that this is a classic case of allowing team owners and associated private businesses to "socialize the costs and privatize the profits" (Berkley Economic Review Staff 2019).

Despite substantial evidence that stadium subsidies do not often produce the promised economic benefits, numerous cities across North American have continued subsidizing their construction and operation. Trumpbour (2007) argues that a mix of civic pride and a local boosterism in the media increase public support for stadium projects, enabling sports teams to successfully extract concessions from municipal leaders, often under threat of relocation. Even in the face of weak evidence for enhanced economic activity, Trumpbour (2007) argues, local decision-makers agree to subsidize the construction of stadiums to boost local spirit and enhance civic pride. Eventually, the public dollars flow to the project following a predictable formula that relies heavily on local identity, civic pride, and the threat of relocation (Trumpbour 2007).

Empty Threats: The Pittsburgh Penguins Gamble and Win

The Pittsburgh Penguins' lease of the city's Mellon Arena ended at the conclusion of the 2006–7 National Hockey League season. Team ownership described the aging facility as inadequate and the Penguins refused to sign another lease agreement. Instead, the team proposed an agreement with Isle of Capri Casinos that would have seen the company construct a new US$290 million arena in exchange for the state's approval of an adjoining slot machine casino (Robinson 2006). Three companies applied to the state for the rights to build the casino, with only Capri including an agreement to construct a new arena for the Penguins (Cowden 2006). Already passive-aggressively threatening relocation if the state did not comply with the team's desired plan, CEO Ken Sawyer stated that, "this is the best plan for Pittsburgh, it's the best plan for the Penguins, and it is the plan that assures the Penguins stay here" (Cowden 2006).

At the conclusion of the process, Capri's bid was not selected by the state's Gaming Control Board (Robinson 2006). Instead, a firm called PITG was approved for Pittsburgh's only casino licence and pledged US$7.5 million per year for thirty years from casino revenue toward the construction and operation of a new arena (Mauriello and Belko 2006). The money pledged, however, was far less than the US$290 million promised by Capri, leading Penguins' management to describe the offer as "insufficient" (Mauriello and Belko 2006). Upset by the state's decision, team co-owner and former captain Mario Lemieux argued that the team would look for options elsewhere, with Kansas City, Houston, Portland, Winnipeg, and Las Vegas all mentioned as potential relocation sites (Maurello and Belko 2006).[5]

One of the more serious offers came from the Kansas City, Missouri-based Anschutz Entertainment Group, who offered the Penguins' management a rent-free lease agreement for the city's new Sprint Center if they were willing to relocate (CBC Sports 2007). In March 2007, Penguins' co-owner Ron Burkle also led a delegation to Las Vegas to meet with mayor Oscar B. Goodman, who claimed to have five groups interested in building a new arena capable of hosting professional hockey games (Belko 2007). As a third option, Houston mayor Patrick Trahan extended an invitation to discuss relocation with Penguins ownership, with an offer to play in the city's Toyota Centre (Belko 2007).

With news of team owners Lemieux and Burkle actively exploring relocation offers, Pennsylvania governor Ed Rendell, Allegheny County chief executive officer Dan Onorato, and Pittsburgh mayor Luke Ravenstahl all became directly involved in negotiations in the hopes of finding a local funding option for the team (Belko 2007). Despite their presence, a new arrangement could not be reached. The Penguins issued an open letter to Rendell, Onorato, and Ravenstahl, arguing that the team could not stay in Pittsburgh if each level of government did not increase their contribution: "the risk has been magnified by what we perceive as a lack of collaboration from the public sector in the negotiations" (Lemieux and Burkle 2007).

Negotiations proceeded with Lemieux and Burkle stating that the team would be willing to pay US$4 million toward the new arena – US$3.6 million a year in rent and US$400,000 a year in funding for capital expenses (Belko 2007). The team was also willing to pay an additional US$500,000 a year for a new parking garage (Belko 2007).[6] The remaining US$7.5 million put in place by PITG as a result of its winning casino bid and an annual US$7.5 million payment from the state economic development fund would be sufficient to fund the arena's construction (Belko 2007). The impasse involved a dispute in how much the arena would cost, with the team contending it would cost US$290 million and the state believing it could be constructed for US$270 million, the US$20 million difference creating an impasse (Belko 2007). This US$20 million difference was eventually covered by a bond issue (Belko 2007). Once construction began, costs topped the proposed US$290 million budget. In November 2008, it was announced that the costs to build the new Consol Energy Centre had risen by US$31 million (Belko 2008). The Penguins agreed to cover US$15.5 million of the costs, the state contributed US$10 million, and the state sports authority agreed to pay US$5.5 million (Belko 2008).

One year after the agreement was reached and construction began, Penguins' co-owner Mario Lemieux revealed that the team's relocation threats were not sincere. In an August 2008 interview, Lemieux stated that relocation "wasn't a possibility" (Traikos 2012). He continued by stating that "we had to do a few things to put pressure on the city and the state, but our goal was to remain here in Pittsburgh all the way ... those trips to Kansas City and Vegas and other cities was just to go and have a nice dinner, and come back" (Traikos 2012). Despite his insincerity, Lemieux's bargaining tactics evidently worked as the Pittsburgh Penguins received a very favourable deal to build a new arena for their team. A report prepared by TL Hocking & Associates (2012, 12) found that the Penguins were only responsible for 38 per cent of the construction costs for the Consol Energy Centre. The remainder of the funding came from state and local governments. The Penguins are also responsible for an annual US$400,000 maintenance cost, which is paid for entirely through parking fees (TL Hocking & Associates 2012, 12).

New Ownership, New Pressure: Seattle Bids Farewell to Basketball

While the Pittsburgh Penguins were able to successfully threaten city, state, and county officials into primarily funding their arena, relocation does occur. When a local Seattle business magnate was unable to gain a desired set of concessions from local and state leaders, he sold his teams to an out-of-state ownership group to ramp up the threat of relocation, which eventually did lead to relocation.

Seattle's relocation saga began in 2006 with the sale of the National Basketball Association's (NBA) Sonics and the Women's National Basketball Association's (WNBA) Storm by Howard

Schultz's Basketball Club of Seattle corporation to the Professional Basketball Club LLC, an Oklahoma City-based investment consortium led by Clay Bennett. Schultz's group initially threatened to sell the teams at the end of their 2010 lease of KeyArena if the City of Seattle was unwilling to renegotiate their revenue-sharing agreement and fully pay for a US$220 million taxpayer-funded remodelling of the arena (Galloway and Cat Le 2006). Schultz and the team contended that KeyArena was one of the smallest in the league, which, along with being outdated, prevented the team from garnering enough revenue to remain financially viable (Booth 2007). Seattle refused to renegotiate the lease agreement before its expiry, which led Schultz to explore alternatives, including holding informal discussions with the nearby suburbs of Bellevue and Renton to build a new arena in one of those communities (Galloway and Cat Le 2006).

After being unable to reach an agreement with either Seattle or any of its neighbouring cities, Schultz decided to sell the teams to Bennett's group for US$350 million (Galloway and Cat Le 2006). Schultz explained that the sale of the team – four years before his originally threatened sale date – was strategic, arguing that "over the past two years, we have worked with local and state officials to seek a solution to the arena issues ... however, it became more apparent that a new ownership group may be more successful in achieving the remaining goals of the Sonic and Storm" (Galloway and Cat le 2006). Schultz continued by stating that an out-of-state ownership group could place more pressure on local officials and make a relocation threat appear more serious than he could (Galloway and Cat Le 2006).

Despite acknowledging that Bennett's group could more effectively place relocation pressure on the city to pay for a new arena, Schultz included a clause in the sale agreement that the new owners would need to use "good faith best efforts" to secure a local site for the team for a full twelve months after the official sale (Brunner 2008). During the sale, the city contended that they had provided Schultz several offers to renovate KeyArena and that the sale of the team was a surprise. A spokesperson for the city stated that "we presented them with three different offers, proposals, that we felt could get them where they wanted to be in terms of renovating KeyArena and other issues and we got no response on any of those offers" (Galloway and Cat Le 2006).

The new team owners initially stated that they intended to remain in Seattle (Booth 2007). The tone changed, however, when the NBA officially approved the sale of the team to Bennett. After the sale's approval, Bennett gave the City of Seattle one year to create a new plan to house the Sonics and Storm (Washburn 2006). Both teams, Bennett claimed, would need new facilities. Relocation was possible if the city was unable to assemble a plan (Washburn 2006).

Bennett made early efforts to move the team to an area outside the city, funding feasibility studies in both nearby Bellevue and Renton, eventually proposing to construct a US$530 million arena in Renton (Brunner 2007). A request for the state to outlay US$300 million in subsidies for the new facility was included in the proposal (Brunner 2007). The proposal, however, presented a number of challenges. Chief among them was the large public subsidy requested. Additionally, the real estate proposed for the new stadium was not owned by the state or county and would require further negotiations to acquire (Brunner 2007). A state committee rejected the proposal (Brunner 2008). After the decision, Bennett argued he had few options but to move the team. During an interview with local media, Bennett argued that the state legislature's rejection of his proposal was "staggering" and a "debilitating blow" (Brunner 2007). He continued by arguing that "clearly at this time the Sonics and Storm have little hope of remaining in the Puget Sound region" (Brunner 2007).

Shortly after the state's rejection of his Renton proposal, Bennett served notice to the NBA that he planned to move the Sonics to Oklahoma City. Former owner Howard Schultz sued Bennett for breach of contract, arguing that Bennett did not act in good faith during the mandated twelve-month period for finding a local alternative to keep the Sonics in the Seattle area (Brunner 2008). Dennis Daugs, a local Seattle businessman and former minority investor in Schultz's consortium, sent a letter to Bennett stating that he represented a collection of local investors who were willing to buy the team to keep it in Seattle. Seattle council passed an ordinance to hold the team to its lease until its expiry in 2010 (Brunner 2007). Each initiative failed.

In April 2008, the NBA's owners voted to approve the Sonics relocation to Oklahoma City (Allen 2008). Bennett stated that he was "honoured" and "thrilled" with the decision (Allen 2008). Despite his enthusiasm, Bennett still maintained that his original intent was to keep the Sonics in Seattle, stating that "we tried the best we knew how and did the best job I could" (Allen 2008). Shortly after the relocation, Bennett's minority partner in the team, Aubrey McClendon, cast doubt on the investment group's intentions. Speaking with local Oklahoma City media, McClendon stated that "we didn't buy the team to keep it in Seattle, we hoped to come here" (Allen 2007).

As many suspected, it appeared that Bennett only purchased the Sonics in order to move the team and, as Schultz alleged, presented his Renton proposal in order to be rejected. In any case, Washington State and Renton could have gone along with his proposal and contributed US$300 million to a facility located in Renton. Meanwhile Seattle could have agreed to the US$220 million in upgrades to KeyArena while Schultz was the team owner and have avoided the sale to Bennett. In both cases, public officials scoffed at the demands of both owners, called ownership's bluff, and lost their teams to another city.

Nowhere to Go? Hamilton Calls the Tiger-Cat's Bluff

In 2009, it was announced that the Province of Ontario – and more specifically the Greater Toronto Area – had won the right to host the 2015 Pan-American Games. Hamilton sought to host one of the events, hoping to draw some of the provincial infrastructure funding dedicated to the games. Bob Young, the owner of the Canadian Football League (CFL) Hamilton Tiger-Cats, sought to parlay this investment into a new stadium for his team (Kernaghan 2009a).

Young, however, was initially reluctant to invest any of his or his team's money into a new stadium in the city, arguing instead the team could continue to play at the aging Ivor Wynne Stadium as long as the city kept repairing it (Kernaghan 2009b).

Early in February 2009, Young changed his mind and agreed to fund part of the cost for a new stadium, stating that he would bring "millions to possibly tens of millions" to the table (Kernaghan 2009c). The commitment from the provincially funded Toronto 2015 bid committee at this time was to fund 56 per cent of a 15,000-seat track-and-field facility that would cost approximately C$100 million, putting the provincial portion at C$56 million (Kernaghan 2009c). To make the facility usable for the Tiger-Cats, the city would require a 24,000- to 27,000-seat stadium, which would cost approximately C$150 million, leaving the city to address the C$94 million shortfall (Kernaghan 2009c).

While Young agreed to fund part of this cost, his support came with some conditions. Specifically, Young argued the location would need to have suitable highway and rapid transit access and be able to generate revenue (Kernaghan 2009c). He also stated that he would be willing to look outside of the city, namely to adjacent suburban Burlington, Ontario, if his facility conditions were not met.

A city council meeting was set for February 23, 2009, to ask councillors to make financial commitments to the Pan-American Games and choose a site for the new stadium to replace Ivor Wynne (Dreschel 2009a). As the date approached, many city councillors began to cool to the idea of spending nearly C$100 million to build a new stadium. One councillor in particular, Sam Merulla, attacked the costs of the project, arguing that other infrastructure projects required the city's attention more and even attacked the Pan-American Games itself, calling it a "third-rate event with fourth-rate athletes" (Dreschel 2009a).

Hamilton eventually approved C$55 million in funding for a 15,000-seat stadium (Dreschel 2009b). The province, through the Pan-American Games Committee, committed C$57 million in funding, leaving the financial responsibility to increase the size of the stadium to the desired levels of the Tiger-Cats franchise with the team itself (Dreschel 2009b). Through stakeholder consultations that included the Tiger-Cats, city council developed a list of four locations that would be suitable for the new stadium: the west harbour area, Confederation Park, the downtown core, and the airport lands (Dreschel 2009b). Council finally settled on the west harbour – a largely abandoned former port area in northern Hamilton – as its preferred location, with the area surrounding the airport as its second choice if the west harbour area was found to be unsuitable (Dreschel 2009b).

Despite city council selecting its preferred site, Bob Young argued in the local media that the Pan-American Games planners should "think outside the box" and consider other sites, such as Aldershot – an area along the Hamilton-Burlington border (Kernaghan 2009d). Young did muse to a reporter that "I'm OK with any site, as long as it makes sense economically over the long term" (Kernaghan 2009d). Young reiterated those comments in early 2010 as he was attempting the find other local business partners to invest in the C$50 million needed in private capital to complete the project, saying that "we will make it work, whatever the site" (Kernaghan 2010a).

On May 6, 2010, Young and the Tiger-Cats organization reversed its position. In an open letter, Bob Young, referring to himself as the "caretaker" of the franchise, stated that his organization could no longer support the west harbour location, largely because there was no highway access, there was no visibility outside the existing neighbourhood, and very little parking (Young 2010a). Young continued, stating that if the west harbour site went forward, the team would continue to lose money and no longer be economically viable (Young 2010a). Young ultimately asked for a ninety-day moratorium on any stadium decisions so that other sites could be examined (Reilly 2010a).

Hamilton's mayor, Fred Eisenberger, responded to Young's letter, stating, "we are moving full steam ahead on the west harbour site ... we will not waver from that because it is best for Hamilton" (Reilly 2010a). To Eisenberger, the west harbour represented an opportunity to revitalize the harbour area, with the new stadium being a catalyst for future growth. Eisenberger continued: "The statements made by Bob Young only talk about what is best for the Tiger-Cat organization ... there is no mention of the community interest and the community building that we've been talking about" (Reilly 2010a). Eisenberger also noted that arrangements had been made to purchase up to 85 per cent of the properties in the area slated for the stadium to be built on (Reilly 2010a). The remediation costs for cancelling these contracts would be C$3–5 million (Reilly 2010a). Eisenberger also dismissed the idea of a ninety-day moratorium on site selection as well, noting that the Pan-American Games host corporation had a May 17, 2010, deadline for site verification (Reilly 2010a).

Young put forward three alternative sites that he noted had not been fully explored by the city or the club. The first, Confederation Park – an area near the intersection of the Queen Elizabeth Way Highway and the Red Hill Valley Parkway – was initially explored and rejected by city staff (Kernaghan 2010b). The second option was the Aldershot area on the border of Hamilton and Burlington (Kernaghan 2010c). Finally, the last option was Chedoke Park, greenspace that was under protection by the Niagara Escarpment Commission (Kernaghan 2010b).

Tiger-Cats president Scott Mitchell ruled out any return to Ivor Wynne Stadium, stating that the franchise would never be profitable at that location (Edwards 2010). The situation degenerated further as Bob Young began threatening to relocate the team. When asked if there was a risk that the Tiger-Cats would not play in Hamilton in the future, Young responded, "it's absolutely at risk ... if Ivor Wynne falls down and we don't build a viable alternative, where are the Cats going to play?" (Dreschel 2010).

In an effort to break the deadlock, Young came forward with a C$74 million contribution toward a stadium located in Hamilton's east mountain, a growing, suburban area of the city, located at the intersection of two highways (Dreschel 2010). Despite the approval of the site as a viable alternative by council, Mayor Eisenberger was not prepared to abandon the west harbour location (Kernaghan 2010d).

At the beginning of August 2010, the city released a report showing that a stadium built on the east mountain would cost upward of C$55–80 million more than a stadium built at the west harbour site (Reilly 2010b). In the wake of the report, Young published an opinion article in the *Hamilton Spectator*, where he urged the mayor to reconsider his approach to the stadium site (Young 2010b).

Young abruptly changed his position only days later, declaring that the franchise was pulling out of discussions with the city, withdrawing its funding offers, and would serve out the remainder of its lease at Ivor Wynne Stadium, at which point it would "examine all options," which included relocating the team to another city (Elliot 2010). The leading contender to receive the franchise was Quebec City, where city officials indicated they had a "strong interest" in a CFL franchise (Peters 2010a).

Council approved the west harbour location by a vote of 12–3 on August 10, 2011, despite Young's threats (Reilly 2010b). After the vote, Mayor Eisenberger noted that "we'll do our best to encourage them to come back to the table and talk about how we can make it work … that's what we're interested in doing, but we're also all interested in getting a stadium at west harbour for all the right reasons" (Reilly 2010b). When asked to comment on council's decision and Eisenberger's comments, Young stated that "he is making a very big mistake" (Peters 2010b, A01).

Young returned to the bargaining table at the end of August, suggesting that he was willing to examine another site located at Aberdeen Avenue and Longwood Road in the city's west end (Kernaghan 2010e). City staff stated that this would be council's last chance to agree on a site as the Pan-American Games host committee had already extended three previous deadlines (Kernaghan 2010e). The land initially slated for stadium development was owned by McMaster University, who refused to sell, leading the city to examine abandoned rail yards further north on Aberdeen Road as a potential site for the new stadium (Morse 2010).

Young summed up the situation going into discussions about the Aberdeen site: "The city had made its commitment to the west harbour, a location that wouldn't work for running a successful sports marketing operation … so we are open to talking with every other municipality that might be able to help us" (Morse 2010, A03). However, he added honestly that "none of those conversations were overly optimistic either" (A03).

A municipal election in late October 2011 saw mayor Fred Eisenberger voted out of office, largely because of the stadium issue (Thompson 2010). Downtown councillor Bob Bratina was sworn in as the new mayor, but despite the change in leadership, the Aberdeen site was still seen as the most viable option. In December of 2010, however, Tiger-Cats president Scott Mitchell revealed that it would cost C$70–90 million to buy the railroad lands, effectively removing it as a viable option (Reilly 2010c, A1). Bratina introduced a motion in council to investigate the Confederation Park site, but it failed on a 9–6 vote (Reilly 2010d, A3). Frustrated, the Tiger-Cats began revisiting the Aldershot location again and the possibility of relocating to Burlington (Reilly 2010d).

The Tiger-Cats attempted to remove as many barriers as they could for the City of Burlington, arguing that the stadium would not require any additional funding if it were built in Burlington as there would not be a need to acquire additional land (Masters 2011). Burlington city councillors, however, were not as enthusiastic about the plan, arguing instead that the city had already financially committed itself to the redevelopment of the local hospital and a community centre (Peters 2010c). Burlington councillor Marianne Meed Ward called the plan "financial lunacy," arguing that "I don't see a lot of silver lining in it for Burlington … there is every indication the hand will be out to Burlington taxpayers on this project as well" (Peters 2010c).

Faced with a February 1, 2011, deadline from the Pan-American Games host committee, Bratina and Young reached an agreement to retrofit Ivor Wynne Stadium in early January. Young was reserved in his enthusiasm: "It would have been really nice for the city of Hamilton to build a brand new stadium somewhere that has all the facilities of a modern football stadium … but we do not have the funding, and the reality is such that we have to build this on time and on budget" (Brady 2011, S3). Bratina was equally as reserved, stating, "we have to live within our means, and I think this project allows us to do that" (S3).

Even this project, however, had a financial shortfall as funding was still required to complete the renovations. With a firm February 1 deadline to complete the project imposed by the Pan-American Games host committee, the provincial government announced that they would cover a C$22.5 million shortfall (Reilly 2011). With the announcement, Hamilton's protracted stadium debate ended.

The controversy over stadium construction perfectly encapsulates the booster spirit and growth mentality of local decision-makers. Despite evidence showing few economic benefits of publicly subsidizing stadium construction, local officials persist and find new, often dizzying ways to deliver public dollars to private stadium projects. The cases explored above, however, demonstrate that these bargaining processes often take on strange dynamics. In Pittsburgh, team officials bluffed their way to public concessions, even going so far as to visit other potential suitors to force state and local officials in Pennsylvania to acquiesce to their demands. In Washington State, the owner of Seattle's NBA and WNBA franchises could not extract the funding he wanted from public officials, so he sold the teams to an out-of-state buyer to ramp up relocation pressure. In Canada, officials in Hamilton negotiated for years to secure a stadium deal for their franchise, demonstrating that the threat of relocation does have its limits. The common denominator in all of these cases was the threat of relocation. None of the cities examined above wanted to lose their beloved sports franchise, but negotiations took very different directions based on the likelihood of the team actually relocating. The cultural value of possessing a major league sports franchise is a powerful signal about urban vitality and success, leading cities to aggressively negotiate to maintain and acquire them. However, relocation and the threat of missed opportunity are not strategies confined only to stadium negotiations. In fact, a range of private actors can use relocation or the threat of providing economic opportunity to another community to wrest concessions from local actors. The following sections highlight this phenomenon in more contemporary examples involving new technology-oriented enterprises.

TECHNOLOGY AND SMART CITIES: WHO WINS? WHO LOSES?

While stadium politics may be the most glaring example of blind local boosterism, this phenomenon has moved beyond simple large-scale infrastructure projects, like stadiums, toward large-scale projects that are digital in nature. Smart cities are not a new phenomenon by any means, but they have taken on a new imperative in recent years, especially here in Canada where Google-affiliated Sidewalk Labs pushed to create a new smart city along Toronto's eastern waterfront. While the project was eventually abandoned, it does speak to the booster mindset and economic development imperative that many cities pursue at all costs.

The term "smart city" arose from the Smart Growth movement in the 1990s (Hollands 2008; Vanolo 2014). Initial smart city proponents advocated for improved urban planning through policy change to support the use of information and communication technologies and modern infrastructure within cities (Harrison and Donnelly 2011; Albino, Berardi, and Dangelico 2015). Over time, however, the term became synonymous with technology and, eventually, technology-infused urbanism.

In 2010, IBM popularized the term smart city to coincide with their "Smart Cities Challenge" – a pro bono service focused on innovation and opportunity development, widely seen as a business development exercise (Söderström, Paasche, and Klauser 2014). IBM was soon joined in this space by other large technology companies, such as CISCO, and management consulting firms, such as McKinsey, who similarly pitched new technology to cities as solutions to pressing urban challenges (Falconer and Mitchell 2012).

Governments became the primary consumers of technology products. The drive for community intelligence accelerated among local decisions-makers as cities began to label themselves as "smart" after the implementation of functioning ICT infrastructure or e-governance technology (Söderström, Paasche, and Klauser 2014). The label also began to be increasingly applied to communities that had attracted high-tech industries (Söderström, Paasche, and Klauser 2014). Some countries even seized the idea of creating smart cities from scratch rather than integrating ICTs into existing systems of local service delivery.

Cities are often ranked against their global peers for "smartness" and "intelligence," providing an opportunity for recognition on a global level (Giffinger and Gundrun 2010). The centre piece of the smart city pitch from many private firms is generally the local economy, often framed as both a challenge and opportunity. One of IBMs leading documents argues that workforce skills, aptitude, knowledge, creativity, and innovation are more important drivers of economic growth than traditional drivers, such as natural resources, physical labour, or manufacturing prowess (Dirks, Gurdgiev, and Keeling 2010, 1). Integration of ICTs and smart city technology lays the groundwork for attracting this new type of vital workforce talent. Similarly, an IBM study argues that "quality of life and the attractiveness of a city are profoundly influenced by the core systems of a city … therefore these systems are critical for attracting, creating, enabling and retaining this new kind of workforce and the innovation-enabling environment it requires to be productive" (6).

The natural conclusion emerging from the private think pieces on the local economy is that a local government cannot have a robust local economy without laying the groundwork to make the city more attractive to those whose success drives the new economy. Similar narratives have been presented by competitors, such as McKinsey (Boulton et al. 2013) and CISCO (Kim, Mitchell, and Villa 2011): harnessing smart city technology creates the conditions for the right kind of economic development, namely the type that captures emerging economic and labour force trends.

Throughout the process, municipalities are often confronted with a grim future if smart city technology is not part of their local long-term procurement plan. Urban problems, such as pollution, growth, and economic uncertainty are shown to be confronted with inadequate governance tools, such as "broken technologies" and "inadequate systems" (Soderstrom et al. 2014). The adoption of smart city technology is then presented as the way to enhance a local economy, increase competitiveness, and better manage local resources.

Google Attempts to Build a City

In October 2017, Waterfront Toronto, the tri-level agency responsible for the Toronto waterfront, announced that Sidewalk Labs had won the right to pilot their vision at Quayside, a five-hectare parcel of land along the city's waterfront. The land in question, once used for industrial purposes, had sat idle for many years, and Waterfront Toronto had long wanted to breathe new life into the area. As such, Waterfront Toronto sought an "innovation and funding partner" for the initial site, making it clear that a typical urban development firm would not be successful in responding to the request for proposal (RFP). The community that Waterfront Toronto envisioned was technology enabled, leaving only a very narrow list of potential applications able to bid. Google-affiliated Sidewalk Labs was left as one of the only suitable firms.

Founded in 2015 as a subsidiary of Alphabet Inc., Sidewalk Labs describes itself as an urban innovation organization, headed by Daniel L. Doctoroff, the former deputy mayor for economic development of New York City, who facilitated the analogous Hudson Yards development in New York City (Schwab 2017). Sidewalk Labs argues that it aims to improve physical and digital infrastructure in urban spaces by harnessing the connectivity of the platform economy to create a blueprint for the "neighborhood of the future" (D'Onfro 2019). As a result, Sidewalk Labs markets itself as a firm applying technology and digital thinking to land development, conceptualizing what a city would look like if it were built "from the internet up" (Hawkins 2019).

When approaching the Waterfront Toronto RFP, Sidewalk Labs offered a vision of creating one of the world's first purposefully designed "smart" communities, one with sensors and technology embedded throughout. Sidewalk Lab's response to the RFP included technology-driven solutions for the delineated policy areas, with the approach of "viewing [the city] as a platform that integrates the physical environment with digital technology" (Sidewalk Labs 2017). The project itself would encompass at least 3.3 million square feet of residential, office, and commercial space, including Google Canada's new headquarters – all of which would be built around information technology and use environmental data to guide the community's operations and adjust service levels for residents (Bozikovic 2017). Ultimately Sidewalk Labs aimed to balance elements of progressive urbanism, such as multimodal roadways, walkable streets, and green space, with information and communication technology, such as self-driving taxis and buses, cloud-assistant parking, and garbage robots (Bozikovic 2017).

Despite a practically non-existent record of completed projects, in the summer of 2018, Waterfront Toronto's board unanimously selected Sidewalk Labs to head the development of Quayside after a selection process that lasted only six weeks. That led to a year-long consultation phase, which concluded with the firm releasing a 1,524-page draft Master Innovation and Development Plan (MIDP) in June 2019. Sidewalk's total planned investment had risen to US$1 billion as the new proposed development went well beyond the original five hectares of Quayside. Sidewalk Labs had unveiled a second and third phase of the project to create the Innovative Development and Economic Activation (IDEA) District, which expanded to districts adjacent to Quayside and would cover an additional 150 hectares. This addition meant that another fifty thousand residents would be added to Quayside's already planned five thousand. Quayside was therefore positioned, not as *the* development project, but the catalyst for a much larger vision. A much larger proposal was introduced because, as Doctoroff said, "a number of these systems require a greater scale to be proven or make economic sense" (Bickis 2019).

The MIDP was ambitious and controversial, incorporating not only elements of traditional urban design and planning, but also vast amounts of technology, which raised issues about who would collect, store, and own the equally vast amount of data created by the project. Smart cities run on data; in fact, data is best conceived as the lifeblood of smart cities. This rightfully raises questions about how well Sidewalk Labs could achieve the key aspects of Waterfront Toronto's RFP and quell a chorus of criticism that believed the firm was poised to grossly violate privacy and run roughshod over governance standards.

Key to the Quayside project was the "digital layer" that would collect information from those living in and using the site. This raised significant concerns among privacy experts and those in the technology community. The firm pledged to adhere to Responsible Data Use guidelines, which is a framework of self-imposed regulations that mandates transparency about the kind of data collected on individuals, limiting the amount of data collected, and making it practical for people to control their own data. Sidewalk Labs claimed that personal data gleaned from sensors across the community would be de-identified at the source and uploaded to a proposed independent data trust. The overarching commitments made by Alphabet in the MIDP were as follows: no selling personal information, no using personal information for advertising, and no disclosing personal information to third parties without explicit consent (Sidewalk Labs 2017).

Despite this pledge about privacy and third parties, Sidewalk Labs' own documents indicated that the "digital layer" over Quayside would include a robust set of APIs (application programming interfaces), which would provide a "well-designed canvass" for developers to build applications into the community (2017b, 70). The document compared the set of APIs to Apple's App Store, the Google Play Store, or Amazon Web Services, presenting the "digital layer" as an evolving platform that could be added to by a series of actors (2017b, 70). One comes away from the document with an appreciation that the "digital layer" was more of a commercial platform. Presumably, all of these developers would have access to the data stored in the "digital layer" and would be paying some type of licensing fee for such access.

Even within Sidewalk Labs, employees found that their data privacy policies were problematic. In late October 2018, the privacy adviser of Sidewalk Labs, Ann Cavoukian, resigned from her role, citing "concerns over personal data security" policies the firm had in place (O'Shea 2018). According to Cavoukian, the proposed plan addressing privacy was unacceptable, given that there was very little regulation to protect personal identifiable information collected in new smart city projects. This resignation provoked an avalanche of criticism about data collection and security in this project. Other board members, such as Saadia Muzaffar, also resigned, citing several concerns, including transparency (Deschamps 2018).

Smart city developments are not new: they occur all over the world. However, unlike all other global projects, the Quayside project was proposed as an offshoot of one of the world's largest private data firms: Alphabet. Critics argued that the Sidewalk Labs Quayside project was being imposed upon Toronto because the process to approve had been so quick, especially given the scale and scope of the vision Sidewalk Labs had presented, that a competitive bidding process could not have possibly occurred. The project had also been a lightning rod, with some describing it merely as "paving the way for tech billionaires to fulfil their dreams of ruling over cities" (Sadowski 2017).

Even with significant criticism, the project also had prominent public supporters, including academic urbanist Richard Florida, former Toronto mayors Art Eggleton and Barbara Hall, and a host of leaders from the city's philanthropic sector, such as Sharon Avery from the Toronto Foundation and Daniele Zanotti from the United Way of Greater Toronto (Vincent 2019). These leaders were joined by Mark Cohon, the chair of Toronto Global, prominent business leader and philanthropist Alan Broadbent, Sara Diamond, the president of OCAD University, and Anne Sado, the president of George Brown College, in signing a letter calling for Sidewalk Labs to be allowed to pursue its project. While the group did emphasize that there were "some issues and details [that] must still be resolved," they argued that Sidewalk Labs was ultimately "helping us build a better city" (Alberga 2019). The letter continued: "We also believe there are many exciting ideas in this proposal that can help Toronto tackle some of the major challenges we face," noting that the Quayside proposal included plans for green construction and affordable housing (Alberga 2019).

That vision fell to pieces in May 2020 when Sidewalk Labs announced it was cancelling its project and leaving Toronto. Although the project will no longer come to fruition, the inter-jurisdictional and inter-governmental interplay between the private and public sector is informative about the future of the global smart city sector. As the announcement was made that the Quayside project would not be moving forward, the mayor of Toronto, John Tory, said that he regretted the loss of the opportunity but was "heartened" that Sidewalk Labs and Google would both remain in Toronto in some capacity, again demonstrating how highly prized technology jobs remain (O'Neill 2020). Quayside also provided Toronto with bragging rights: the world's largest data firm chose Toronto over others to build a shining new digital community. Google did not choose New York City or Paris or London. Instead, it chose Toronto, indicating (if the project was completed at least) that the city was on its way to becoming a global tech hub and, in the process, significantly boosted its economy and international profile. In this sense, smart city development presents a departure from the economic development strategy with stadiums, instead using the developments as a beacon to signal economic strength through innovation to a new and sought-after class of resident: tech employees and entrepreneurs.

HQ2: A New Race to the Bottom?

In September 2017, Amazon began one of the most highly competitive economic development contests in modern history by announcing the expansion of its existing headquarters in Seattle, Washington. While primarily seen as a technology firm, Amazon has hundreds of physical locations throughout the world to facilitate its logistics operations, the vast majority of which are distribution facilities or warehouses staffed with so-called "unskilled" labourers who facilitate the movement of goods. Amazon was now proposing to build a second headquarters, staffed with primarily high-paying, high-skilled, and highly sought-after technology and management positions. Amazon's second headquarters – more commonly referred to as HQ2 – was seen as a true prize for municipal governments as it promised to be a "full equal" to the firm's first headquarters and came with a promise to spend US$5 billion on construction and employ fifty thousand highly paid technology and management employees upon completion (Day 2017). Amazon wanted to see pitches from municipalities directly, which created fierce competition among local economic development agencies.

The competition for HQ2 eventually drew 238 proposals from across North America. Some cities tried everything imaginable to stand out from the rest of the competition. For instance, Calgary's economic development office launched a campaign promising to fight a bear for Amazon if they won the rights to HQ2 (Gibson 2018). In another pitch, a southern Arizona economic development group sent Amazon CEO Jeff Bezos a twenty-one-foot Saguaro cactus (Day 2017). Not to be outdone, Kansas City mayor Sly James wrote one thousand reviews about Amazon products, giving each a five-star review, while the town council of Stonecrest, Georgia, promised to rename the municipality Amazon, Georgia if it was selected as the location for HQ2 (Liao 2017).

Aside from the gimmicky marketing pitches aimed at standing out from the crowd, the real incentive for Amazon was financial. Every year American cities and states spend up to US$90 billion in tax breaks and cash grants to urge companies to move (Thompson 2018). As such, it was natural for the American-based Amazon to expect these types of concessions when it dangled the most valuable economic development opportunity in a generation in front of state and local officials. These officials did not disappoint. Based on the final bids released, we know some of the financial (and other) details for certain cities that submitted proposals (Miranda, Nguyen, and Mac 2018):

- Atlanta: US$2 billion in financial incentives, US$1.7 billion in tax incentives, US$87 million in local tax credits from the City of Atlanta, a state-university-affiliated education program for company employees called the "Amazon Georgia Academy," and an exclusive lounge with free parking for company executive at Hartsfield-Jackson International Airport, one of the world's busiest airports.
- Boston: US$75 million in funding over ten years to maintain home prices around HQ2, US$13 million in "workforce training grants," and assistance for eligible Amazon employees to purchase a home in the Boston area by providing zero-interest loans.
- Chicago: US$2.25 billion in incentives, half of which would be tax credits, and US$400 million in infrastructure spending to improve roads and sewers for the new proposed site.
- Columbus: 100 per cent property tax abatement over fifteen years, 35 per cent income tax refund over fifteen years, and US$400 million in direct cash incentives over fifteen years. City officials also vowed to create a task force to lower the city's murder rate if it received HQ2.
- Dallas: US$600 million in tax abatements and the construction of a new university called "Amazon U."
- Washington, DC: US$60–80 million per year for fifteen years. Relocation reimbursements of up to US$5,000 per employee and wage reimbursements of up to US$10,000 for each new hire or up to US$30,000 for newly hired veterans. No property tax increase for five years.

New Jersey and Maryland both reportedly offered US$7 billion for HQ2 – the largest proposed corporate incentives in American history (Thompson 2018).

Proposals from Canadian municipalities looked quite different from their American peers. Amazon made it clear that it was looking for a location for HQ2 throughout North America, leaving many Canadian cities salivating at the possibility of having a large, international technology firm move to their community. Canadian municipalities operate in a very different regulatory and legal environment than their American counterparts and are much more restrained in the use of local powers. Provincial legislation guides all municipal financial dealings, including regulations relating to taxing, charging, borrowing, and spending (Arku 2014; Graham, Phillips, and Maslove 1998). These limitations also extend to the field of economic development, where most provincial governments prohibit granting bonuses to private firms and limit the conveyance of economic benefits to private businesses (Gertler 1990; Wolfson and Frisken 2000; Tassonyi 2005). As such, the type of financial incentives that American cities can offer are virtually impossible in most Canadian provinces. As a result, Canadian municipalities often sell the competitiveness of their jurisdiction, such as emphasizing infrastructure investment to stimulate development, special events, site development, marketing policies, and lower rates on industrial and commercial properties than rates in nearby jurisdictions (Reese and Sands 2007; Wolfson and Frisken 2000). Municipalities also often emphasize quality of life factors to attract and retain businesses, such as environmental sustainability, culturally diverse communities, and investments in local services (Arku 2014).

These limitations were displayed in Canadian HQ2 bids. Toronto, for instance, offered no financial incentives at all (Miranda, Nguyen, and Mac 2018). Local officials were unable to and instead highlighted the characteristics of the region's workforce and cultural amenities. Toby Lennox, the CEO of Toronto Global, which represents the business interests of the region's municipalities argued: "Others may provide large subsidies and tax breaks, but like the Province of Ontario, we in the Toronto Region don't want to play that game, and frankly we feel we don't need to play that game" (Miranda, Nguyen, and Mac 2018). The region, as described above, was unable to play "that game" anyway because of the limitations on inducements. One wonders what they may have offered Amazon if they were able to after all.

Even without any financial incentives, Toronto joined twenty other cities as "finalists" in the HQ2 competition, which entitled each city to a personal visit from Amazon staff. Toronto was the only Canadian city to get this far in the competition. Ultimately, Amazon selected to split HQ2 between two locations: the Long Island City community in New York City and the Crystal City and Pentagon City neighbourhoods of Arlington County, Virginia. Once announced, a number of New York City officials came out in opposition to the project, arguing that Amazon should not be receiving a slew of generous financial concessions while the city had yet to fund a number of pressing housing and transportation projects (Warerkar 2018). Many also expressed concern that the presence of HQ2 would also drive already high housing process upward (Warerkar 2018). As pressure mounted, Amazon cancelled the project, opting instead to only pursue the Arlington County site and develop a large distribution centre in Nashville, Tennessee.

Both the HQ2 competition and global desire for cities to become "smart" demonstrate the pressure cities feel to compete. Other peer cities serve as competition and have the potential to take investment, jobs, and economic opportunity. Throughout, private firms are placed in a prized position, acting as both the cause of and the solution to an array of urban ills. Regulations on inducements in economic development do not allow Canadian municipalities to readily compete with each other. This, however, may be a good thing, considering that Thompson (2018) calculates that in the past ten years, Boeing, Nike, Intel, Royal Dutch Shell, Tesla, Nissan, Ford, and General Motors have each received subsidy packages worth more than US$1 billion to either move their corporate headquarters within the United States or to keep their headquarters where they currently are, leading him to argue that these sorts of inducements ought to be illegal. While the type of regulations that Canadian municipalities face will certainly limit competition internally, they may also limit their ability to compete internationally.

CONCLUSION

Institutional context matters when studying the politics and governance of growth and economic development. Local officials in Canada and the United States have very different mechanisms available to promote the growth and development of their communities. Those in the United States are able to draw upon more resources to attract and retain firms, offering financial and tax incentives, drawing upon state-level resources, and applying direct pressure to company officials to undercut potential competitors (and even themselves in some cases). Their Canadian counterparts exist in a world with strict rules in place to control inducements and other financial incentives to attract firms, confined mostly to promotion, planning tools, and pressuring other levels of government.

Even though the tools available differ on either side of the border, the incentives and motivations to pursue growth remain: resource attraction, population growth, community profile, and economic strength, all due to a fundamental orientation of local politics focused on economic development and land commodification. The pathways to achieve these goals were the focus of this chapter. Local actors once focused exclusively on the promotion of local identity fixtures that would boost local fortunes, namely large-scale physical infrastructure projects and sports franchises. Good-paying manufacturing jobs were highly coveted, so the attraction of premier auto manufacturers or industrial development was prized above all others. With good jobs came the recruitment of the right kind of population – people who had the resources to build and beautify the community. Growth for the sake of growth became an enduring mantra for local decision-makers even though the strategy for growth had become more diffuse with the attraction of single large manufacturers replaced by the conditions for knowledge-economy and innovation-economy workers to relocate.

That same mantra remains, but the ways of fulfilling the mantra have changed. Local boosterism remains strong, but technology jobs are now more highly coveted than manufacturing jobs, and attracting a large smart city project or something like HQ2 may serve to enhance a community's profile more now than a new major league sports franchise. Adding an HQ2 or a Sidewalk Labs project can now be seen as a catalyst for future development and the right sort of attraction for highly coveted leaders in the innovation economy. Finding the right fit remains a challenge, however. The relationship between private and public actors can be fraught with difficulty as community interests often conflict with the goals of private interests – displayed clearly in the reaction to New York City (co)winning the HQ2 sweepstakes. While hundreds of other communities were content to sacrifice millions and even billions in tax concessions and give away valuable land to attract Amazon, the reality of doing so jolted the public into revolt once Amazon's interest was reciprocated.

The HQ2 and Quayside sagas, along with a myriad of stadium fiascos, raise an important question about the capacity of local governments to properly adjudicate the worth of such projects. In the case of HQ2 and Quayside, wide-eyed local officials seemingly overlooked community value in their rush to approve these projects. It was the public that applied pressure to two of the world's largest companies and prompted a swift exit. The public, therefore, demonstrated a keen ability to define and safeguard public interest, which raises the stakes for public involvement in adjudicating and governing these projects. It also raises important questions about whom economic development projects are intended to benefit. The existing literature has largely focused on elite conceptualizations of the business class joining coalitions of public decision-makers to direct governments in their favour or on notions of attracting the right type of residents – in this case, the highly educated and affluent. If these efforts are successful, what does it leave for the many who are not included in the benefits of this growth? If some gain, are others left to be displaced? If the current models only direct benefits from economic development in one direction, is there a better, more equitable model that could and should emerge? While local actors often claim to be motivated by enhancing community interest in their pursuit of local growth and development, it is the public who ultimately must articulate what is in the best interest of the community. Who speaks on behalf of the community and articulates the needs of the broader public is a question that political scientists must grapple with as they continue to explore the interplay of urban power, economic development, and growth dynamics.

NOTES

1 It could also be argued that NIMBY (not in my backyard) groups may also wield a form of veto power to block development. This would not necessarily be the same type of veto power conceptualized in the literature, but these groups may seek to block development around property they own and would generally not be opposed to development outside of their immediate area.

2 Some of these efforts may have additional benefits. Richard Florida's work on the "creative class" tells us that there is a correlation between metropolitan growth and success and openness to immigration, artists, members of the LGBT community, and racial integration. In sum, there is also a cultural aspect

to the growth equation, meaning that the promotion of a more tolerant community may very well also have important economic consequences. For more information, see Florida (2005).

3 It should be noted that Logan and Molotch (1987) see competition as both an internal and external process. Groups of local boosters often will do what they can to enhance the position of a city to attract scarce mobile capital, but local business owners will still compete with each other within the locality. See *Urban Fortunes* (Logan and Molotch 1987, 34–5).

4 For an interesting case study in local competition regarding image building, see Lehr and Zubrycki's (2012) chapter on Winkler and Morden, Manitoba, in Harvey and Young's (2012) *Image Building in Canadian Municipalities*.

5 Both Winnipeg and Las Vegas would eventually receive NHL franchises – Winnipeg through relocation of the struggling Atlanta Thrasers and Las Vegas through league expansion.

6 For context, the Pittsburgh Penguins had revenues of US$67 million for the 2006–7 season and US$87 million for the 2007–8 season (Gough 2023).

REFERENCES

Alberga, Hannah. 2019. "Torontonians Are Showing Their Support and Objection to Sidewalk Labs." *BlogTO*, July 4, 2019. https://www.blogto.com/tech/2019/07/torontonians-are-showing-their-support-and-objection-sidewalk-labs/.

Albino, Vito, Umberto Berardi, and Rosa Maria Dangelico. 2015. "Smart Cities: Definitions, Dimensions, Performance, and Initiatives." *Journal of Urban Technology* 22, no. 1 (January): 3–21. https://doi.org/10.1080/10630732.2014.942092.

Allen, Percy. 2007. "Sonics Co-owner McClendon Fined $250K." *Seattle Times*, August 23, 2007. https://www.seattletimes.com/sports/nba/sonics-co-owner-mcclendon-fined-250k/.

Arku, Godwin. 2014. "Competition and Coordination in Economic Development: Examining the Perceptions of Practitioners in Ontario, Canada." *Journal of Urban Affairs* 36, no. 1 (February): 99–118. https://doi.org/10.1111/j.1467-9906.2012.00647.x.

Asheim, Bjørn T., and Arne Isaksen. 1997. "Location, Agglomeration and Innovation: Towards Regional Innovation Systems in Norway?" *European Planning Studies* 5, no. 3 (June): 299–330. https://doi.org/10.1080/09654319708720402.

Ashworth, G.J., and H. Voogd. 1990. *Selling the City: Marketing Approaches in Public Sector Urban Planning.* London: Bellhaven.

Baade, Robert, and Allen Sanderson. 1997. "Subsidizing Stadium: Who Benefits, Who Pays?" In *Sports, Jobs and Taxes*, edited by Roger Noll and Andrew Zimbalist, 119–45. Washington, DC: Brookings Institution.

Begg, Iain. 1999. "Cities and Competitiveness." *Urban Studies* 36, nos. 5–6 (May): 795–809. https://doi.org/10.1080/0042098993222.

———. 2002. *Urban Competitiveness: Policies for Dynamic Cities.* Bristol: The Policy Press. https://doi.org/10.46692/9781847425423.

Belko, Mark. 2007. "Penguins Owners Taking a Look at Las Vegas Today. *Pittsburgh Post-Gazette*, March 7, 2007. https://www.post-gazette.com/local/city/2007/03/07/Penguins-owners-taking-a-look-at-Las-Vegas-today/stories/200703070135.

———. 2008. "New Arena's Cost Rises $31 Million." *Pittsburgh Post-Gazette*, November 13, 2008. https://www.post-gazette.com/sports/penguins/2008/11/13/New-arena-s-cost-rises-31-million/stories/200811130368.

Bell, Gregg. 2008. "NBA Approves Sonics' Move to Oklahoma City." *Seattle Times*, April 19, 2008. https://www.seattletimes.com/sports/nba-approves-sonics-move-to-oklahoma-city/.

Berkley Economic Review Staff. 2019. "The Economics of Sports Stadiums: Does Public Financing of Sports Stadiums Create Local Economic Growth, or Just Help Billionaires Improve Their Profit Margin?" *Berkley Economic Review*, April 4, 2019. https://econreview.studentorg.berkeley.edu /the-economics-of-sports-stadiums-does-public-financing-of-sports-stadiums-create-local -economic-growth-or-just-help-billionaires-improve-their-profit-margin/.

Bickis, Ian. 2019. "Sidewalk Releases Grand Vision for Controversial Toronto Development." *National Post*, June 24, 2019. https://nationalpost.com/pmn/news-pmn/canada-news-pmn /sidewalk-releases-grand-vision-for-controversial-toronto-development.

Boorstin, Daniel. 1965. *The Americans: The National Experience.* New York: Random House.

Booth, Tim. 2007. "SuperSonics Owner Bennett Says He'll File to Relocate Team to Oklahoma City." *San Diego Union Tribune*, November 2, 2007. Online access originally.

Bouton, Shannon, David Cis, Lenny Mendonca, Herbert Pohl, Jaana Remes, Henry Ritchie, and Jonathan Woetzel. 2013. *How to Make a City Great.* New York: McKinsey Cities Special Initiative.

Bozikovic, Alex. 2017. "Google's Sidewalk Labs Signs Deal for 'Smart City' Makeover of Toronto's Waterfront." *Globe and Mail*, October 17, 2017. https://www.theglobeandmail.com/news/toronto /google-sidewalk-toronto-waterfront/article36612387/.

Brady, Rachel. 2011. "City of Hamilton, Ticats End Impasse by Agreeing to Renovate Existing Stadium." *Globe and Mail*, January 12, 2011, S3.

Brunner, Jim. 2007. "Initiative Aimed at Holding Sonics to KeyArena Lease." *Seattle Times*, July 27, 2007. Archived June 28, 2011, at the Wayback Machine. https://web.archive.org/web/20110628185134 /http://seattletimes.nwsource.com/html/localnews/2003808219_keyarena27m.html.

———. 2008. "Breach of Contract Alleged in Sonics Suit." *Seattle Times*, May 21, 2008. Archived June 13, 2008, at the Wayback Machine. https://web.archive.org/web/20080613003345 /http://seattletimes.nwsource.com/html/sonics/2004428236_soni21m.html.

Cagan, Joanne, and Neil deMause. 1998. *Field of Schemes: How the Great Stadium Swindle Turns Public Money into Private Profit.* Monro: Common Courage Press.

CBC Sports. 2007. Kansas City Offers Penguins Free Rent. *CBC Sports*, January 4, 2007. https:// www.cbc.ca/sports/hockey/kansas-city-offers-penguins-free-rent-1.653139.

Christophers, Brett. 2008. "The BBC, the Creative Class and Neoliberal Urbanism in the North of England." *Environment and Planning A* 40, no. 10 (October): 2313–29. https://doi.org/10.1068/a4030.

Cowden, Michael. 2006. "Penguins: Support for Casino Should Be a 'No-Brainer.'" *USA Today*, April 11, 2006. Archived September 18, 2018, at the Wayback Machine. https://web.archive.org /web/20180918090102/https://usatoday30.usatoday.com/sports/hockey/nhl/penguins /2006-04-11-pittsburgh-arena_x.htm.

Day, Matt. 2017. "Amazon Refuses Arizona's Cactus as Bidders for HQ2 Climb to 118." *Seattle Times*, September 19, 2017. https://www.seattletimes.com/business/amazon/amazon -refuses-arizonas-cactus-as-bidders-for-hq2-climb-to-118/.

Deas, Iain, and Benito Giordano. 2002. "Locating the Competitive City in England." In *Urban Competitiveness: Policies for Dynamic Cities,* edited by Iain Begg, 191–210. Bristol: The Policy Press. https://doi.org/10.46692/9781847425423.010.

Delaney, Kevin, and Rick Eckstein. 2003. *Public Dollars, Private Stadiums: The Battle over Building Sports Stadiums.* New Brunswick: Rutgers University Press.

Deschamps, Tara. 2018. "Saadia Muzaffar Resigns from Google's Sidewalk Labs Advisory Panel on Toronto Waterfront Project." *Global News*, October 5, 2018. https://globalnews.ca/news/4519757/saadia-muzaffar-resigns-sidewalk-labs/.

Dirks, Susane, Constantin Gurdgiev, and Mary Keeling. 2010. *Smarter Cities for Smarter Growth: How Cities Can Optimize Their Systems for the Talent-Based Economy*. Somers, NY: IBM Institute for Business Value.

D'Onfro, Jillian. 2019. "Google Sibling Sidewalk Labs Unveils 'Smart City' Plans for Toronto Waterfront." *Forbes*, June 24, 2019. https://www.forbes.com/sites/jilliandonfro/2019/06/24/alphabet-google-sidewalk-labs-smart-city-plans-for-toronto-waterfront/.

Dreschel, Andrew. 2009a. "Pan Am Supporters Ramp Up Sales Spiel." *The Hamilton Spectator*, February 11, 2009, A11.

———. 2009b. "Pan Am Stadium Isn't Just about the Ticats." *The Hamilton Spectator*, November 16, 2009, A15.

Dreschel, Andrew. 2010. "Could Cats Really Leave Hamilton?" *The Hamilton Spectator*, May 19, 2010, A1.

Duffy, Hazel. 1995. *Competitive Cities: Succeeding in the Global Economy*. London: Spon. https://doi.org/10.4324/9780203362310.

Edwards, Drew. 2010. "Ivor Wynne is No Win for Ticats." *The Hamilton Spectator*, May 12, 2010, SP05.

Einstein, Katherine Levine, and Vladimir Kogan. 2016. "Pushing the City Limits: Policy Responsiveness in Municipal Government." *Urban Affairs Review* 52, no. 1 (January): 3–32. https://doi.org/10.1177/1078087414568027.

Elkin, Stephen I. 1987. *City and Regime in the American Republic*. Chicago: University of Chicago Press. https://doi.org/10.7208/chicago/9780226301631.001.0001.

Elliot, Howard. 2010. "Ticats Change the Playbook." *The Hamilton Spectator*, August 10, 2010, A08.

Falconer, Gordon, and Shane Mitchell. 2012. *Smart City Framework: A Systematic Process for Enabling Smart+Connected Communities*. San Jose, CA: CISCO Internet Business Solutions Group.

Florida, Richard. 2002. "Bohemia and Economic Geography." *Journal of Economic Geography* 2, no. 1 (January): 55–71. https://doi.org/10.1093/jeg/2.1.55.

———. 2005. *Cities and the Creative Class*. London: Routledge. https://doi.org/10.4324/9780203997673.

———. 2012. *The Rise of the Creative Class – Revisited and Expanded*. New York: Basic Books.

Frug, Gerald E. 1980. "The City as a Legal Concept." *Harvard Law Review* 93, no. 6 (April): 1057–154. https://doi.org/10.2307/1340702.

Galloway, Angela, and Phuong Cat Le. 2006. Sonics Sold to Ownership Group from Oklahoma City. *Seattle Post-Intelligencer*, July 17, 2006. https://www.seattlepi.com/news/article/sonics-sold-to-ownership-group-from-oklahoma-city-1209167.php.

Gamm, Gerald, and Thad Kousser. 2013. "No Strength in Numbers: The Failure of Big-City Bills in American State Legislatures, 1880–2000." *American Political Science Review* 107, no. 4 (November): 663–78. https://doi.org/10.1017/S0003055413000397.

Gertler, Meric. 1990. "Economic Development." In *Urban Policy Issues: Canadian Perspectives*, edited by Richard A. Loreto and Trevor Price, 35–57. Toronto: McClelland and Stewart.

Gibson, John. 2018. "Calgary Can 'Hold Its Head up' Despite Not Making Amazon HQ2 Short List, Pitch Organizer Says." *CBC News*, January 18, 2018. https://www.cbc.ca/news/canada/calgary/calgary-amazon-short-list-hq2-seattle-toronto-tech-headquarters-jobs-1.4493368.

Giffinger, Rudolf, and Haindlmaier Gudrun. 2010. "Smart Cities Ranking: An Effective Instrument for the Positioning of the Cities?" *ACE: Architecture, City and Environment* 4, no. 12 (February): 7–26. https://doi.org/10.5821/ace.v4i12.2483.

Glaab, Charles, N. 1962. *Kansas City and the Railroads.* Madison: State Historical Society of Wisconsin.

Gold, John R., and Stephen V. Ward. 1994. *Place Promotion: The Use of Publicity and Marketing to Sell Small Towns and Regions.* Chichester: Wiley.

Gough, Christina. 2023. "Pittsburgh Penguins' Revenue 2005–2022." Statistica. Published February 15, 2023. https://www.statista.com/statistics/196880/revenue-of-the-pittsburgh-penguins-since-2006/.

Graham, Katherine, Susan Phillips, and Alan Maslove. 1998. *Urban Governance in Canada: Representation, Resources, and Restructuring.* Toronto: Harcourt Brace.

Graham, Stephen. 2002. "Bridging Urban Digital Divides? Urban Polarisation and Information and Communication Technologies (ICTs)." *Urban Studies* 39, no. 1 (January): 33–56. https://doi.org/10.1080/00420980220099050.

Hackworth, Jason. 2006. *The Neoliberal City: Governance, Ideology and Development in American Urbanism.* Ithaca, NY: Cornell University Press.

Harrison, Colin, and Ian Abbot Donnelly. 2011. "A Theory of Smart Cities." Proceedings of the 55th Annual Meeting of the ISSS, Hull, UK.

Harvey, Jean, and Robert Young. 2012. *Image-Building in Canadian Municipalities.* Montreal: McGill-Queen's University Press. https://doi.org/10.1515/9780773587960.

Hawkins, Andrew J. 2019. "Alphabet's Sidewalk Labs Unveils Its High-Tech 'City-within-a-City' Plan for Toronto." *The Verge,* June 24, 2019. https://www.theverge.com/2019/6/24/18715486/alphabet-sidewalk-labs-toronto-high-tech-city-within-a-city-plan.

Hollands, Robert G. 2008. "Will the Real Smart City Please Stand Up?" *City* 12, no. 3 (December): 303–20. https://doi.org/10.1080/13604810802479126.

Kernaghan, John. 2009a. "Other Cities Eager to Host Track Facility If City Falters." *The Hamilton Spectator,* January 22, 2009, A1.

———. 2009b. "Ticat Dissent Threatens Pan Am Plans." *The Hamilton Spectator,* May 7, 2010, A01.

———. 2009c. "Cats Could Kick in Cash for Pan-Am Stadium." *The Hamilton Spectator,* February 10, 2009, A1.

———. 2009d. "Aldershot Site Worth Pursuing: Young Urges Stadium Planners to 'Think Outside the Box.'" *The Hamilton Spectator,* November 13, 2009, A03.

———. 2010a. "'Build It, We'll Play in It': Cats Owner Backs any Site City Picks for Stadium." *The Hamilton Spectator,* January 14, 2010, A04.

———. 2010b. "Burlington May Be Home to New Stadium." *The Hamilton Spectator,* February 6, 2010, SP02.

———. 2010c. "City Wants to Resume Talks; Stalemate with Ticats Centres around Project Losses." *The Hamilton Spectator,* May 8, 2010, A06.

———. 2010d. "West Harbour Development Isn't Dead: Eisenberger." *The Hamilton Spectator,* July 8, 2010, A06.

———. 2010e. "City and Cats Eye Mac Site." *The Hamilton Spectator,* August 31, 2010, A01.

Kim, Tony, Shane Mitchell, and Nicola Villa. 2011. *Smart + Connected City Services: Cloud-Based Services Infrastructure Enables Transformation of Busan Metropolitan City.* San Jose, CA: CISCO.

Kresl, Peter. 2002. "The Enhancement of Urban Economic Competitiveness: The Case of Montreal." In *Urban Competitiveness: Policies for Dynamic Cities,* edited by Iain Begg, 211–32. Bristol: The Policy Press. https://doi.org/10.46692/9781847425423.011.

Lemieux, Mario, and Ron Burkle. 2007. "Text of the Penguins' Letter to Rendell, Ravenstahl and Onorato." *Pittsburgh Post-Gazette*, March 6, 2007. https://www.post-gazette.com/sports/penguins/2007/03/06/Text-of-the-Penguins-letter-to-Rendell-Ravenstahl-and-Onorato/stories/200703060161.

Liao, Shannon. 2017. "The Eight Most Outrageous Things Cities Did to Lure Amazon for HQ2." *The Verge*, October 19, 2017. https://www.theverge.com/2017/10/19/16504042/amazon-hq2-second-headquarters-most-funny-crazy-pitches-proposals-stonecrest-new-york.

Logan, John R., and Harvey Luskin Molotch. 1987. *Urban Fortunes: The Political Economy of Place.* Berkeley: University of California Press.

Lucy, William H., and David L. Phillips. 2000. *Confronting Suburban Decline: Strategic Planning for Metropolitan Renewal.* Washington: Island Press.

Masters, Mark. 2011. "TiCats Remove Barriers for Stadium to Land in Burlington." *National Post*, January 5, 2011. https://nationalpost.com/sports/cfl/ticats-remove-barriers-for-stadium-to-land-in-burlington.

Mauriello, Tracie, and Belko, Mark. 2006. "PITG Wins Slots Casino License for North Side." *Pittsburgh Post-Gazette*, December 20, 2006. https://www.post-gazette.com/breaking/2006/12/20/PITG-wins-slots-casino-license-for-North-Side/stories/200612200136.

Miranda, Letecia, Nicole Nguyen, and Ryan Mac. 2018. "Here Are the Most Outrageous Incentives Cities Offered Amazon in Their HQ2 Bids." *Buzzfeed News*, November 14, 2018. https://www.buzzfeednews.com/article/leticiamiranda/amazon-hq2-finalist-cities-incentives-airport-lounge.

Mollenkopf, John H. 1987. "The Post-war Politics of Urban Development." *Politics & Society* 5, no. 3 (September): 247–95. https://doi.org/10.1177/003232927500500301.

Molotch, Harvey. 1993. "The Political Economy of Growth Machines." *Journal of Urban Affairs* 15, no. 1 (March): 29–53. https://doi.org/10.1111/j.1467-9906.1993.tb00301.x.

Moore, Barry, and Iain Begg. 2004. "Urban Growth and Competitiveness in Britain: A Long-Run Perspective." In *City Matters: Competitiveness, Cohesion and Urban Governance*, edited by Martin Boddy and Michael Parkinson, 93–110. Bristol: The Policy Press. https://doi.org/10.46692/9781847425911.007.

Morse, Paul. 2010. "Young Likes Aberdeen Site, but 'Far from Optimistic.'" *The Hamilton Spectator*, September 18, 2010, A03.

Mossberger, Karen, and Gerry Stoker. 2001. "The Evolution of Urban Regime Theory: The Challenge of Conceptualization." *Urban Affairs Review* 36, no. 6 (July): 810–35. https://doi.org/10.1177/10780870122185109.

O'Neill, Lauren. 2020. "Here's Why Critics Are Cheering the News That Sidewalk Labs Cancelled Its Toronto Project." *BlogTO*, May 7, 2020. https://www.blogto.com/tech/2020/05/why-critics-cheering-sidewalk-labs-cancelled-toronto-project/.

O'Shea, Sean. 2018. "Ann Cavoukian, Former Ontario Privacy Commissioner, Resigns from Sidewalk Labs." *Global News*, October 21, 2018. https://globalnews.ca/news/4579265/ann-cavoukian-resigns-sidewalk-labs/.

Parkinson, Michael, and Martin Boddy. 2004. "Introduction." In *City Matters: Competitiveness, Cohesion and Urban Governance*, edited by Martin Boddy and Michael Parkinson, 1–10. Bristol: The Policy Press. https://doi.org/10.46692/9781847425911.002.

Peters, Ken. 2010a. "At Death's Door – Again: Tiger-Cats Have Survived Several Extinction Threats." *The Hamilton Spectator*, August 11, 2010, A06.

———.. 2010b. "Don't Risk Driving Ticats Away, Young Warns." *The Hamilton Spectator*, August 12, 2010, A01.

———. 2010c. "Burlington Council Skittish over Aldershot Stadium." *The Hamilton Spectator*, December 29, 2010. Online access originally.

Peterson, Paul. 1981. *City Limits*. Chicago: University of Chicago Press.

Reese, Laura A., and Gary Sands. 2007. "Making the Least of Our Differences? Trends in Local Economic Development in Ontario and Michigan, 1990–2005." *Canadian Public Administration* 50, no. 1 (March): 79–99. https://doi.org/10.1111/j.1754-7121.2007.tb02004.x.

Reilly, Emma. 2010a. "'Moving Full Steam Ahead': Mayor Says City Won't Abandon West Harbour Site for Stadium." *The Hamilton Spectator*, May 7, 2010, A05.

———. 2010b. "West Harbour Wins the Day; Councillors Vote to Put Stadium There Despite Tiger-Cats Pullout." *The Hamilton Spectator*, August 11, 2010, A05.

———. 2010c. "Stadium Sticker Shock Dashes Aberdeen Dream." *The Hamilton Spectator*, December 21, 2010, A1.

———. 2010d. "Mayor Sick of Stadium, Too: Bratina Disappointed, But Calls Burlington 'the Next Best Thing.'" *The Hamilton Spectator*, December 29, 2010, A3.

———. 2011. "Touchdown! Ontario Boots in \$22M." *The Hamilton Spectator*, January 31, 2011. https://www.thespec.com/news/hamilton-region/touchdown-ontario-boots-in-22m/article_4431df12-bc6f-5a85-868b-dfaddb3c58cb.html.

Robinson, Alan. 2006. "Penguins Brass to Discuss Slots Casino Rejection." *USA Today*, December 20, 2006. Online access originally.

Sadowski, Jathan. 2017. "Google Wants to Run Cities without Being Elected. Don't Let It." *Guardian*, October 24, 2017. https://www.theguardian.com/commentisfree/2017/oct/24/google-alphabet-sidewalk-labs-toronto.

Scheiber, Harry N. 1973. "Urban Rivalry and Internal Improvements in the Old Northwest, 1820–1860." In *American Urban History: An Interpretive Reader with Commentaries*, edited by Alexander Callow Jr., 2nd ed., 22–36. New York: Oxford University Press.

Schneider, Mark. 1989. *The Competitive City: The Political Economy of Suburbia*. Pittsburgh: University of Pittsburgh Press. https://doi.org/10.2307/jj.13245890.

Schwab, Katharine. 2017. "How the Chief Architect of 21st Century New York Envisions the Future of Cities." *Fast Company*, September 12, 2017. https://www.fastcompany.com/90139632/how-the-chief-architect-of-new-new-york-envisions-future-of-cities.

Sidewalk Labs. 2017. *Response to Waterfront Toronto RFP*. New York: Sidewalk Labs.

Smyth, H. 1994. *Marketing the City: Flagship Developments in Urban Regeneration*. London: Spon.

Söderström, Ola, Till Paasche, and Francisco Klauser. 2014. "Smart Cities as Corporate Storytelling." *City* 18, no. 3 (May): 307–20. https://doi.org/10.1080/13604813.2014.906716.

Stone, Clarence N. 1989. *Regime Politics: Governing Atlanta, 1946–1988*. Lawrence, KS: University of Kansas Press.

———. 1993. "Urban Regimes and the Capacity to Govern: A Political Economy Approach." *Journal of Urban Affairs* 15, no. 1 (March): 1–28. https://doi.org/10.1111/j.1467-9906.1993.tb00300.x.

Tassonyi, Almos. 2005. "Local Economic Development: Theory and the Ontario Experience." ITP Paper no. 0511. Toronto: University of Toronto.

Thompson, Derek. 2018. "Amazon's HQ2 Spectacle Isn't Just Shameful – It Should Be Illegal." *The Atlantic*, November 12, 2018. https://www.theatlantic.com/ideas/archive/2018/11/amazons-hq2-spectacle-should-be-illegal/575539/.

Thompson, Scott. 2010. "Election May Clear Air Over Stadium." *The Hamilton Spectator*, September 21, 2010, A11.

TL Hocking & Associates. 2012. *Comparison of Operating Costs for Similar Arenas*. Glendale: TL Hocking & Associates.

Traikos, Michael. 2012. "Oilers' Daryl Katz Has Good Reason to be Devious." *National Post*, September 25, 2012. https://nationalpost.com/sports/hockey/nhl/oilers-katz-has-good-reason -to-be-devious-after-seattle-visit.

Trumpbour, Robert C. 2007. *The New Cathedrals: Politics and Media in the History of Stadium Construction*. Syracuse: Syracuse University Press.

Turok, Ivan. 2005. "Cities, Competition and Competitiveness: Identifying New Connections." In *Changing Cities: Rethinking Urban Competitiveness, Cohesion and Governance*, edited by Nick Buck, Ian Gordon, Alan Harding, and Ivan Turok, 25–43. London: Palgrave Macmillan. https://doi .org/10.1007/978-0-230-21203-9.

Vanolo, Alberto. 2014. "Smartmentality: The Smart City as Disciplinary Strategy." *Urban Studies* 51, no. 5 (April): 883–98. https://doi.org/10.1177/0042098013494427.

Varady, David P., and Jeffrey A. Raffel. 1995. *Selling Cities: Attracting Homebuyers through Schools and Housing Programs*. Albany: State University of New York Press

Vincent, Donovan. 2019. "30 Influential Toronto Leaders Pen Letter Supporting Controversial Sidewalk Labs Plan." *Toronto Star*, July 4, 2019. https://www.thestar.com/news/gta/30-influential -toronto-leaders-pen-letter-supporting-controversial-sidewalk-labs-plan/article_7667c87e-cebe -5828-9ed3-b719a35db082.html.

Warerkar, Tanay. 2018. "Queens Officials Come Out against Amazon's HQ2 in Long Island City." *Curbed New York*, November 13, 2018. https://ny.curbed.com/2018/11/13/18090668 /amazon-hq2-long-island-city-opposition-nyc.

Washburn, Gary. 2006. "Sonics Sale Now Official." *Seattle Post-Intelligencer*. October 23, 2006. https:// www.seattlepi.com/news/article/sonics-sale-now-official-1217981.php.

Weiner, Jay. 2000. *Stadium Games: Fifty Years of Big League Greed and Bush League Boondoggles*. Minneapolis: University of Minnesota Press.

Wolfe, David A., and Allison Bramwell. 2008. "Innovation, Creativity and Governance: Social Dynamics of Economic Performance in City-Regions." *Innovation: Management, Policy and Practice* 10, nos. 2–3 (October): 170–82. https://doi.org/10.5172/impp.453.10.2-3.170.

Wolfson, Joanne, and Frances Frisken. 2000. "Local Response to the Global Challenge: Comparing Local Economic Development Policies in a Regional Context." *Journal of Urban Affairs* 22, no. 4 (October): 361–84. https://doi.org/10.1111/0735-2166.00062.

Wolla, Scott A. 2017. "The Economics of Subsidizing Sports Stadiums." *Page One Economics*, May 2017. https://research.stlouisfed.org/publications/page1-econ/2017-05-01/the-economics -of-subsidizing-sports-stadiums/.

Young, Bob. 2010a. "Stadium Plan Means A Future for Ticats." *The Hamilton Spectator*, October 7, 2010, A11.

———. 2010b. "Ticats Need City to Succeed." *The Hamilton Spectator*, August 9, 2010, A15.

Young, Robert. 2012. "Conclusion." In *Image-Building in Canadian Municipalities*, edited by Jean Harvey and Robert Young, 167–96. Montreal: McGill-Queen's University Press.

CHAPTER ELEVEN

Municipalities, Urban Governance, and Climate Change

Tristan Cleveland and Elizabeth Schwartz

On May 9, 2009, New York City staff scooted orange barrels onto Broadway, blocking the street to traffic. Their plan was to test what would happen if they turned a section of Times Square – one of the city's busiest intersections – into public space. They did not have much to decorate the asphalt with aside from a few hundred cheap beach chairs, but the response was dramatic. Pedestrians spilled out from Broadway's tiny sidewalks to fill the seats and enjoy the legroom. Janette Sadik-Khan, former New York transport commissioner, recounts: "Tap dancers strutted and musicians performed as crowds gathered to watch. Hot dog vendors handed out free franks. Some visitors brought baseball gloves and played catch in the suddenly open space" (Sadik-Khan and Solomonow 2017, 98–9). It was an important victory in New York's political struggle to become a sustainable city. Broadway has since been renovated into a permanent public space, shifting one of the city's busiest streets, full of carbon dioxide-emitting cars, into one of its central pedestrian corridors.

The renovation of Broadway is part of a larger story in which major cities have played a leading role in implementing strategies for fighting climate change. Often, the public and scholars focus on the role of national governments in fighting climate change, but these governments have struggled thus far to organize a convincing response to this global crisis. Their greenhouse gas reduction targets in most cases fall short of what is needed to avoid catastrophic climate change, and few, so far, have reduced their emissions even to the level of these limited commitments. Cities offer a promising alternative locus for political efforts to make progress on the issue. Voters who prioritize tackling climate change disproportionately live in cities, which can empower their leaders to act decisively on the issue (Rodden 2019). Many cities have, therefore, set ambitious targets and have made major progress on achieving them.

Vancouver, Toronto, Stockholm, and New York are leaders on climate issues. These cities are similar across multiple dimensions: they are all national and global leaders in terms of climate change mitigation, have large populations, are situated within larger metropolitan areas, are major economic centres within their country and region, and experience a northern climate.

The four cities have, moreover, adopted similar strategies for tackling carbon emissions despite the differences between their national and political contexts. The Canadian cities of Vancouver and Toronto are the largest cities in the provinces of British Columbia and Ontario, respectively, and Toronto is also the capital city of Ontario. Canada is a decentralized federation that grants significant autonomy to provincial governments, including control over local governments. This means that municipal autonomy is granted at the discretion of provincial governments.

New York City is the largest city in both the State of New York and the United States. The United States is also a decentralized federation that grants significant autonomy to state governments. Local governments have more independent legal authority in the United States than in Canada, but much of the formal authority of New York City rests in the state government, including on such topics as transit funding and taxation, as we will see.

Unlike Canada and the United States, Sweden is a unitary country. In other words, there are no provincial or state governments. Local governments enjoy greater authority in Sweden compared to Canada and the United States. Local autonomy is a fundamental principle of the Swedish Constitution, and municipalities and counties are responsible for a wide range of services, including education, elder care, water and sewage infrastructure, health care, and public transportation (Sellers and Lidström 2007, 618). In technical terms, counties and municipalities derive their authority from the central government through the 1992 Swedish Local Government Act that sets out their powers and administrative organization (Government of Sweden 2004).

None of the four cities, of course, have the power or reach of a national government, and yet each one has been able to muster resources at their disposal to make major carbon emission reductions. This chapter examines how and why these cities have been successful in fighting climate change, the barriers they face, and what they have done to overcome those barriers.

WHY CITIES?

"The fight against climate change will be won or lost in cities," argues Marvin Rees (2021), a UK mayor, in a recent op-ed. Cities are particularly well-positioned to tackle two major sources of carbon emissions: transportation and buildings. Transportation causes one-fifth of international greenhouse gas emissions, and personal transportation accounts for roughly half of these emissions (Abraham et al. 2012; International Energy Agency 2013, 8; Sims et al. 2014, 608). The construction and operation of buildings also cause about one-fifth of global greenhouse gas emissions (Lucon et al. 2014). Cities can therefore cut emissions by designing communities in which buildings are more energy efficient and where larger numbers of people walk, bike, and take transit (Sims et al. 2014, 619–20; Brand et al. 2021). Making these changes, however, can evoke stiff opposition because it requires cities to use their scarce space and money for new priorities. In New York, the decision to turn Broadway into a place for pedestrians faced resistance from the city's many auto commuters (Sadik-Khan and Solomonow 2017, 98).

Cities also lack the powers of higher orders of government. Most cannot implement a carbon tax or change the building code. They lack the financial resources of state, provincial, or national governments. Their powers are constrained by state and provincial legislation, particularly in Canada, where there is no constitutional protection for municipal jurisdiction. Municipal governments also have limited geographic reach. They may implement ambitious policies within their boundaries, but if most residents outside that boundary continue to drive to work or live in poorly insulated homes, the region as a whole will not be sustainable. Regional governments that encompass both urban and suburban areas, on the other hand, are often less able to tackle climate change because their voters tend to depend more on driving and are less likely to prioritize policy to limit automobile use (Rodden 2019).

And yet, despite these limitations, the four cities under examination have each made major progress on reducing their carbon emissions. Three of the four have attempted to charge a fee for driving downtown or have set more stringent energy efficiency requirements for buildings, and all four have sought to densify growth around transit and favour active transportation. These policies, moreover, have largely been the product of the initiative of the cities themselves, and in some cases – such as with congestion charges in New York and Vancouver – they pursue them despite the preferences of regional or state governments. That these cities have set similar policies despite the differences in their national contexts suggests the importance of cross-border, horizontal idea exchange within urban networks in setting local policy agendas.

PART 1: PROGRESS

Vancouver, Toronto, Stockholm, and New York have each played an important role in the history of sustainable urban policy. In 1990, Vancouver was one of the first cities to release a report on municipal climate policy, and it has since followed up with ambitious climate change action plans including the 2011 *Greenest City Action Plan* and the 2020 *Climate Emergency Action Plan* (City of Vancouver 2011, 2020). The Toronto region, including surrounding municipalities, has been a leader in efforts to concentrate new growth in compact, mixed-use suburbs (Eidelman 2010). Stockholm helped to invent transit-oriented development, which has since become a central strategy for reducing carbon emissions per person (Cervero 1998). New York's subway system dates from the early twentieth century, and the city was among the first to build transit suburbs (Hall 2002). Today, New York is a leading figure in sustainable transport reform, with a goal of reducing carbon emissions by 80 per cent by 2050, as compared to 2005 levels (New York City, Department of Transportation 2018).

Transportation Planning

All four cities have made major progress on shifting to sustainable modes of transportation, particularly within their city centres. One means by which they have done so is by adopting the principle of "transit-oriented development." In this approach, cities invest in transit infrastructure to incentivize compact residential and commercial development nearby (Cervero and Dai 2014, 128). When successful, transit-oriented development can generate a virtuous cycle: high-quality transit attracts new investment in homes, offices, and businesses near stations, and these new destinations bring more riders to transit, enabling the city to improve transit, which then helps to attract more development (Salat and Ollivier 2017, 68–70; Stojanovski 2020). Transit-oriented development has two major benefits for climate change mitigation: it enables residents to travel long distances via sustainable means and helps to create communities where residents can walk locally for most of their daily needs because a large share of shops and services are close to home (Cervero and Sullivan 2011, 210).

Vancouver met and surpassed many of its sustainable transport targets in 2011, a decade earlier than anticipated – something nearly unheard of in transportation planning (Frank et al. 2012). Rates of driving have continued to drop. As of 2019, cars were used for only 40 per cent of trips within Vancouver, and 96 per cent of recently built homes are well-served by transit (McElhanney 2019, 31; Gordon 2018, 2). In Toronto, 82 per cent of development between 2006 and 2016 was in walkable or transit-oriented communities (Gordon 2018, 2). This has helped Toronto reduce carbon emissions by over 25 per cent since 1990, even as the city's GDP has continued to grow (City of Toronto 2016). Stockholm began building communities around transit stations in the 1950s to avoid traffic and to promote economic growth (Stojanovski, Lundström, and Haas 2012). This historic growth pattern now puts the city in a strong position to continue building homes around transit for the new goal of reducing carbon emissions. Nearly two-thirds of trips made in the city region are now made by transit, walking, or biking, and only 38 per cent of trips are made by car. In the city centre, only 6 per cent of trips are made by car (Bastian and Börjesson 2018, 2–4). In New York City, 67 per cent of people walk, bike, or use transit (U.S. Census Bureau 2019). However, as we will see, all four cities face limits in their ability to shift to sustainable transport particularly because they do not control transportation policy beyond their municipal boundaries.

Green Building

Buildings are a major source of greenhouse gas emissions in urban areas because of their electricity use and their heating and cooling systems. Many practices and technologies can reduce energy use in buildings as well as conserve water, reduce waste, and provide protection against flooding. They can be applied across a building's life cycle, from design and construction to occupation, renovation, and demolition. Even seemingly small changes, like installing double- or triple-paned windows or designing spaces to maximize natural light, can reduce energy use from heating, cooling, and electricity, and therefore reduce carbon emissions from buildings.

Cities have been instrumental in promoting the adoption of these "green building" practices. They are well-positioned to do so because they issue permits for construction and real estate development, and they control the zoning regulations that specify the form of buildings that can be in a particular space. All four cities have taken decisive action on the issue. Vancouver, Toronto, and New York each require developers to meet a set of standards that reduce buildings' energy use and emissions throughout the design and construction processes, and after they are occupied. For example, as of 2022, Vancouver requires new low-rise residential buildings to have additional roof insulation and "zero emissions" equipment for heating, a category that excludes natural gas and oil furnaces (City of Vancouver n.d.). Vancouver and New York have also used their powers to amend the building code to require greener construction.

Roof design provides one particularly fruitful subject for reform. New York City's Climate Mobilization Act (2019) requires new building roofs to include solar panels or greenery (NYC, Local Law 94 2019). Toronto has similarly passed a bylaw requiring green roofs on a range of buildings. In this case, they could not pass the rules under their existing jurisdiction but were able to convince the provincial government to grant them authority to tackle this issue (Schwartz 2016b). Green roofs reduce greenhouse gas emissions by providing thicker insulation while also helping to absorb water during heavy rains and reducing air temperature on hot days. Green building standards have enabled Vancouver to cut emissions from buildings by 10 per cent since 2007 and have helped Toronto reduce its overall emissions by 26 per cent since 1990 (City of Vancouver 2021, 4; City of Toronto 2016, 6).

All four cities also apply yet higher standards to their own municipal buildings. In 2004, Vancouver required all new city-owned buildings to meet the LEED Gold standard, an international certification for sustainable design, and the standards have become increasingly stringent since then (City of Vancouver 2004). Vancouver's leadership in adopting LEED standards has had a major impact: it is now common for governments around the world to require similar standards for city-owned buildings.

While New York, Vancouver, and Toronto focus on the sustainability of individual buildings, Stockholm has taken a more holistic approach. Stockholm aims to shift from a system in which each building heats itself to a *district energy system*, in which centralized plants circulate hot water to nearby buildings through a network of pipes. Eighty per cent of buildings in the city are now linked to district heating, and the city aims to further improve the efficiency of these systems (City of Stockholm 2016). Such improvements cut the greenhouse gas emissions from heating across the whole city by 10.3 per cent in a four-year period (Government of Sweden 2010).

PART 2: BARRIERS AND LIMITATIONS

While cities can show leadership on some climate issues, there are major limits to what they can achieve as the lowest tier of government.

Local Government Autonomy and Capacity

Local governments need some level of autonomy to implement climate action as well as the capacity to act on that autonomy. Sellers and Lidström (2007, 611) find that cities in Canada and the United States enjoy relative autonomy from direct "supervision" by higher levels of government, meaning they have substantial freedom to make their own choices. However, these cities also face significant fiscal and administrative constraints, reducing their capacity to act on their theoretic autonomy. Smith and Spicer (2018) similarly find that Canadian cities face fiscal and legal barriers, reducing their scope for action.

In contrast, Sellers and Lidström (2007) find that Scandinavian local governments, including Stockholm, have substantial policy capacity while also being subject to only a moderate level of supervision. The strength of these local governments, they find, has played an important role in the emergence and persistence of Sweden's extensive egalitarian welfare state policies (622–5). We might therefore expect that Scandinavian municipalities have made greater progress on climate change policies than Vancouver, New York, and Toronto.

However, while Stockholm has made major strides, so too have the other three cities. One potential explanation is that all four cities are highly motivated to work on this specific issue, and they are therefore able to work around constraints and make use of whatever level of autonomy and capacity they have available to them. The limits such constraints impose would likely loom larger for issues on which city governments place lower levels of priority.

Autonomy, moreover, is by nature permissive not prescriptive, which means higher levels of autonomy will only lead to greener policies in those cases where cities want to achieve these goals. Greater municipal autonomy in Ontario would have, for example, enabled Toronto to more easily implement a Green Roof Bylaw without first having to negotiate with the Government of Ontario. Other Canadian and American municipalities, in contrast, are reluctant to implement climate change policy due to the political consequences of imposing costs on real estate developers or upsetting car-dependent residents (Schwartz 2016b; Cleveland 2023).

Rodden (2019) argues that progressive voters, who place greater priority on addressing climate change, are concentrated in city centres, which is one reason major cities are able to take decisive action on climate change. Outside city centres, however, suburban voters rely more on driving, lean more conservative politically, place less emphasis on climate policy, and are more likely to oppose policies that might make driving more difficult or expensive, such as a carbon tax (Taylor and Morris 2015; Filion 2015, 637; Pojani and Stead 2018, 15; Isaksson and

Richardson 2009, 252). While many cities have made major progress on climate mitigation within their municipal boundaries, the picture often looks different in the broader region.

While the majority of development in the City of Vancouver is compact and walkable, 83 per cent of development in the larger urban region was car-dependent between 2006 and 2013 (Gordon 2018, 2). Outside the municipality of Toronto, 99 per cent of growth is car-dependent, and much of New York's larger metropolitan area is similar (Gordon 2018, 2; Morrill 2006; WSP and Parsons Brinckerhoff 2016, 11). Stockholm, too, has seen car-dependent growth in its wider region, though at a smaller scale than the other three cities, as this pattern of development did not begin until the 1970s (Paulsson 2020, 2938; Pojani and Stead 2018, 8).

Electoral pressures in suburban municipalities often mean that climate change action is a low priority for local politicians (Schwartz 2016b). In these municipalities, more autonomy may *allow* progressive climate change policies, but it does not guarantee they will be adopted. City centres may lean left on average, but this is not true of larger urban regions, which constitutes a political barrier to implementing climate policy (Taylor and Morris 2015; Filion 2015, 637; Pojani and Stead 2018, 15; Isaksson and Richardson 2009, 252; Rodden 2019).

A Double-Edged Sword: Geographic Reach vs. Voter Support

The regional populations around Vancouver, Toronto, Stockholm, and New York are all much larger than that of the city centre. The cities can therefore only meaningfully reduce their overall carbon footprint if they act as a region, cooperating with their neighbours rather than focusing only on their own area of jurisdiction (see chapter 5).

None of the four cities has strong institutions of regional governance. The Stockholm County Administrative Board has established a vision for regional growth around transit-oriented, walkable neighbourhoods but has little direct power to implement these plans (Pojani and Stead 2018; Paulsson 2020, 2945; Schmitt et al. 2013, 206). They therefore depend on "informal meetings and discussions" to encourage municipalities to coordinate with each other to translate plans into action (Schmitt et al. 2013, 205). Metro Vancouver's regional plans are similarly non-binding, and the regional transit network is governed by a separate provincial agency that is largely unaccountable to local governments. Workers commute to New York City from three states, complicating efforts to coordinate regional transportation (Bram and McKay 2005).

It is tempting to think that if city governments had broader regional reach, they could better achieve sustainable outcomes. However, it is often the region that influences the city's policy, not the other way around. In 1998, the Province of Ontario amalgamated the City of Toronto with the other six municipalities in the Metro Toronto regional government. From the perspective of the former City of Toronto, the amalgamation shifted the balance of power at city council from transit-oriented voters in the urban core to the much larger population of car-dependent residents in the surrounding region. In 2010, mayoral candidate Rob Ford promised to end the "war on cars" and won the election thanks primarily to the support of voters living in the more suburban areas of the new city (Taylor 2011). In 2012, 81 per cent of cycling trips took place in fourteen central wards (Ledsham et al. 2013). After Ford was elected, the city spent $280,000 to remove bike lanes in the urban centre (Walks 2015, 410–15). Faced with the question of whether to keep or remove the downtown bike lanes, nearly all councillors representing the central wards voted to keep bike lanes, whereas councillors representing car-oriented districts voted to remove them, often arguing that they slowed car traffic during rush hour (City of Toronto 2012).

More recently, Toronto's council voted to rebuild a section of elevated highway that passes through the city's downtown (Pagliaro and Rider 2015; Watson 2018, 58). Most councillors representing the former City of Toronto sought to replace the highway with a ground-level boulevard to open up nearly thirteen acres of land for dense, walkable development. However, the majority of councillors voted to rebuild sections of the highway, which is more convenient for commuters travelling to the centre by car but leaves less land for sustainable redevelopment (Livey 2015, 42–3; Pagliaro and Rider 2015).

Cities face a dilemma. They could make a greater impact on climate issues if their jurisdiction covered more land area, but this would also change the composition of their electorate, which can then undermine their ability to take decisive action on climate change.

By a similar logic, regional, state, and provincial governments would often be better-positioned to tackle climate change issues, but in practice, they tend to be less able to do so due to the preferences of their voters. The New York State government has jurisdiction over the subway system in New York City, and it is in some ways better positioned than the city to build a robust network because it has more access to capital and could integrate the subway into a broader regional transport system. However, the majority of voters in New York State live outside New York City and drive to work. Only 28 per cent take transit (U.S. Census Bureau 2019). The state has therefore tended to invest heavily in highways and has underinvested in transit for many decades, creating a crisis of disrepair (Golden 2014, 12; Nobbe and Berechman 2013, 21; Bresiger 2015, 58–62). The levels of government best able to tackle urban climate mitigation are often least willing to do so because of the priorities and interests of their voters.

Attempts in Stockholm, Vancouver, and New York to implement congestion charges to reduce greenhouse gas emissions have faced similar barriers.[1] Congestion charges are a small fee drivers pay to enter compact areas, which helps encourage drivers to switch to walking, biking, and transit, particularly if the revenue is reinvested in transit (Canada's Ecofiscal Commission 2015, 8). The fate of these policies has often depended on jurisdiction: whether local governments have the power to act unilaterally, or whether they must win the support of regional, car-oriented communities.

In 2006, Sweden implemented a congestion charge in central Stockholm as a temporary trial. However, the national government excluded a key road from the congestion charge to avoid backlash from suburban voters (Isaksson and Richardson 2009, 255). The City of Stockholm then held a referendum on whether to make the congestion charge permanent. The vote excluded nearby municipalities, and some of these municipalities organized their own non-binding referendums in protest. A slim majority in Stockholm voted in favour of the referendum (51 per cent), and the congestion charge was made permanent. However, the average result in the other municipalities was 40 per cent in favour and 60 per cent against (255), demonstrating the strong opposition to the congestion charge in suburban municipalities that held referendums. If the binding referendum had included the whole region, Stockholm's congestion charge might not exist today.

In 2020, Vancouver staff released plans to implement congestion charges, a system the city has unilateral authority to implement. Opponents of the policy argued, unsurprisingly, that authority over the issue should be transferred to the regional government (Chan 2020; Nuttall 2020). They proposed, in other words, to shift decision-making authority from a government whose voters prioritize addressing climate mitigation over driving, to a government whose voters rely more on driving, and who will likely oppose the fee. In 2022, a new mayor was elected in Vancouver who swiftly ended the congestion charge (Chan 2022). His support base was strongest in the outlying areas of Vancouver and weakest in the central area (Griffiths 2022).

New York City, in contrast, needs the consent of the state government to implement a congestion charge, which sealed the fate of Mayor Bloomberg's 2007 congestion-charge proposal. Many more voters in New York State rely on driving to New York City than the people who live in New York City itself, and the idea therefore faced such opposition at the state level that it did not even reach the assembly for a vote (Frug and Barron 2011, xii; Gu et al. 2018, 97).

PART 3: OVERCOMING BARRIERS

Cities are not helpless, however, in the face of barriers to change. New York, Stockholm, Toronto, and Vancouver have had an impact on climate mitigation beyond their boundaries using tools of influence and international collaboration.

Inter-jurisdictional and International Networks

One strategy cities use to overcome the limits of their authority is to partner with other cities within their own countries and abroad through international institutions. Today, cities have formed more than three hundred international networks to help them tackle a wide range of issues, including climate change (Rees 2021). All four of the cities discussed here are members of the C40 Cities network, an organization of local government climate change leaders. To join this network, cities must show that they have met climate change policy and planning leadership standards. Moreover, each of the four cities has been a leader *within* the C40 as a member of the Steering Committee, and mayors of Toronto and New York have served as the elected chair of the organization. These cities can support each other by sharing lessons learned and by promoting each other's work, and together they can bring more visibility to the topic than any one city could on its own. Leading cities can demonstrate the success of their actions to encourage other governments to act, and cities can work together to shape national and international policy to better achieve climate mitigation and adaptation goals.

Soft Power

Even if major cities cannot directly manage regional growth, they do have disproportionate influence over their regions, often through informal channels of power. Each of the four cities are respected and economically successful international urban centres, and therefore can influence other communities who aspire to prestige and prosperity. Many of the communities in Vancouver's region have set a goal to create walkable, transit-oriented city centres, likely due in part to Vancouver's success (City of Surrey 2017; City of Burnaby 2017). These plans have the potential to reduce the stark differences between the city centre's rate of sustainable transportation and that of the region (Gordon 2018, 2). Stockholm County lacks an effective regional system of governance, but its municipalities nonetheless continue to build sustainable, transit-oriented communities, and its carbon emissions per person have decreased as its economy has grown, in part due to the example set by the success of the regional centre (Paulsson 2020; Zakhour and Metzger 2018; Cervero and Sullivan 2011, 214). In the 1970s, the most affluent communities in the United States and Canada were largely car-dependent suburbs, which influenced the model of growth most communities aspired to. Affluence today is increasingly linked to vibrant city centres, which may have a bigger impact on growth outcomes than any specific government policy (Florida 2017, 16–20).

Cities can also shift the political interests of higher orders of government by reframing sustainable policies to be more palatable to car-dependent residents. In the 1990s and early 2000s, Toronto-area advocates worked to convince the provincial government to adopt and implement major legislation to enhance sustainable regional planning and limit urban sprawl. Car-dependent voters are a major voting bloc in Ontario, and no provincial planning policy was likely to pass without their support (Eidelman 2010, 1217–19). Advocates therefore worked to reframe sustainable planning in terms of its positive impacts on car-dependent suburban residents. They argued that if the Toronto region continued to sprawl outwards, traffic would worsen, access to nature would decrease, pollution would rise, and municipal taxes would increase due to the inefficiency of low-density development (Eidelman 2010, 1214, 1222). This framing shifted the political calculus for the issue. In the 2003 election, the concept of smart growth was central. The incumbent Progressive Conservative Party, for whom environmental protection tends not to be a priority, used this term to position themselves in favour of managed suburban growth. Liberal Party strategists went further: for them, committing to smart growth meant promising to limit urban sprawl and plan for sustainable regional development. These campaign promises were calculated specifically to win the support of car-dependent suburban voters (1221–2). After winning the election, the Liberal government went on to develop and enact the Places to Grow Act and the Greenbelt Act, which transformed the regional planning landscape in line with their campaign promises. Cities can shift what is politically possible by shifting voters' perception of their own self-interest.[2]

In 2017, New York again considered implementing a congestion charge, but this time it was the state government who championed the policy, not the city government. New York's subway system faced a crisis level of disrepair and needed a major new injection of funding. While a congestion charge would be unpopular with New York's car commuters, the charge would avoid the need to raise taxes state-wide. Upstate taxpayers outnumber New York City car commuters, and although many are also car-dependent, they tend not to drive into the city. Framing the issue as a financing scheme helped shift the focus away from its impact on drivers and toward ensuring that New York City-area workers pay for New York City-area costs (Norimine 2019; Bliss 2019). Like the Places to Grow Act in Ontario, the New York congestion charge scheme shows that car-dependent voters can become supporters of climate-friendly policy when it is reframed in terms of their interests.

Pilot Projects and Tactical Urbanism

In some cases, voters may not see how they will benefit from sustainable policies, and therefore oppose the changes. In these cases, pilot projects can help demonstrate the benefits.

One fear raised by green building standards is that they will impose excessive costs. However, these policies also substantially reduce energy costs, which can lead to financial savings overall (Koski and Lee 2014). Toronto's Atmospheric Fund sought to demonstrate the long-term financial impacts of green building with a pilot study.[3] In 2008, they partnered with a development company that was planning to build two identical condo towers side by side. They designed one using business-as-usual building practices, and one using green building standards, making it 25 per cent more energy efficient than the Model National Building Code. The savings from reduced heating and cooling saved the occupants enough to recoup the higher initial cost two years ahead of schedule (TAF 2014). This study helped justify the City of Toronto's stricter green building rules because it showed that tighter rules would not cause real estate developers to lose money *or* increase costs for residents and other building occupants.

Stockholm similarly experimented with a pilot congestion charge to demonstrate that the policy could benefit drivers by speeding up traffic (Isaksson and Richardson 2009, 254–5). Most drivers would be willing to pay some amount to make traffic disappear on busy days. Theoretically, if the congestion charge costs less than what drivers would pay to eliminate traffic, the benefits of the fee should outweigh the costs. And indeed, Stockholm's congestion charge did become highly popular among drivers within a few years of it becoming permanent (Gärling and Schuitema 2007; Eliasson et al. 2014).

Beginning in 2007, New York City's transportation commissioner, Janette Sadik-Khan, used temporary experiments to disarm objections to new street-design techniques as we saw in the example of pedestrianizing Times Square. She sought to make streets safer and more comfortable for pedestrians and cyclists, but she faced internal resistance to the projects because they reduced space for cars, and many worried they would have catastrophic impacts on congestion. To address these fears, she conducted temporary experiments, trialling new street designs with paint, planters, and bollards so that the city could directly measure outcomes – a strategy referred to as "Tactical Urbanism" (Lydon, Garcia, and Duany 2015). Sadik-Khan exploited the empirical evidence and data from these projects to demonstrate that specific concerns expressed by many transportation engineers were unfounded, and she slowly shifted the epistemic framework of the organization (Sadik-Khan and Solomonow 2017). She has since written a popular book about these experiments, which may help to shift the culture of transportation engineering more broadly (Sadik-Khan and Solomonow 2017).

Professional Standards

Cities can also affect policy beyond their boundaries by shifting professional best practices. In the 1930s to 1950s, New York City pioneered traffic engineering standards and analysis techniques that prioritized the smooth and efficient movement of automobiles on the road network. These standards shaped cities throughout the world and led traffic engineers to place less priority on the convenience and safety of other modes of transportation, such as walking, cycling, and transit (Caro 1974; Ben-Joseph 2005). In this case, New York's influence undermined sustainable planning, but it suggests the opposite may also be possible: that an influential city could export best practices for mitigating greenhouse gas emissions.

New York City's influential former transportation commissioner, Sadik-Khan, now sits on the Board of Directors of the National Association of City Transportation Officials, an organization created to establish sustainable alternatives to existing car-oriented street-design standards. She and others are thereby reversing New York's historic role in promoting car-oriented standards and are helping to establish a new generation of standards, helping many cities to better mitigate climate change.

Car-oriented engineers held considerable institutional power in Vancouver's public service in the 1960s. In 1972, however, a new municipal party called TEAM was elected to council, campaigning on the promise to implement more pedestrian-oriented planning. They acted explicitly to shift the balance of power within the public service, firing five department managers and the head of the public service, replacing them with staff who supported their goals (Stone 2014, 397). This personnel change led to a permanent shift in the priorities of the organization, institutionalized with a set of design guidelines and planning-review processes that favoured walkable, transit-oriented development (Stone 2014, 397). More recently, generational turn-over in staff in the Engineering Department at the City of Vancouver has meant there is a new cohort of engineers who have redefined their specialty. They see themselves as "transportation engineers" rather than "traffic engineers," and they aim to support all forms of mobility instead of only cars (Schwartz 2016a).

Another successful technique used in Vancouver is to establish environment departments within the municipal administration, which can work to shift which standards are prioritized. Vancouver's Sustainability Office provides direct support to the Engineering Department and other units, helping to shift modes of thinking and implement sustainability strategies and poli-cies. They also fund "embedded" staff within other departments who both forward the aims of those departments and seek to spread an ethos of sustainability (Schwartz 2016b). Overall, the Sustainability Office has helped to institutionalize ideas of sustainability within the city admin-istration and solidify a more climate-friendly organizational epistemology.

This shift in professional culture within Vancouver has since changed professional culture regionally. An engineer at the City of Surrey interviewed on the subject expressed surprise that anyone in his profession would today fail to grasp the importance of planning around pedestrians and transit. He attributes this major shift in thinking, in part, to the fact that engineers in the re-gion go to the same universities and conferences as those in the city centre (pers. comm. 2021).

CONCLUSION

Cities have taken major steps to fight climate change within substantial constraints. Vancouver, Toronto, New York, and Stockholm have all shifted heavily toward sustainable building and transportation. Three of these cities may soon charge a fee for driving in their core. They have all set exacting targets for green building standards. While greenhouse gas emissions for national governments continue to rise, these cities are cutting emissions. Cities have far less power than state, provincial, and national governments, but when their leaders are motivated, they can make imaginative use of the powers they do have to achieve a goal.

Perhaps the greatest limitation on municipal power is that of city boundaries. The four cities have made substantial progress on sustainable design and transportation within their urban cen-tres, where political support for environmental policies is greatest. However, the majority of urban residents now live in vast suburban communities outside the reach of central-city munic-ipal leaders, and these regions have made much less progress on climate change (Gordon 2018). Cities could better shape regional growth if they were amalgamated with their regions, but this would also make these city governments beholden to voters less supportive of decisive action on climate change. In a sense, cities face a difficult dilemma: sacrifice decisiveness in favour of reach, or sacrifice reach in favour of decisiveness. One solution to this dilemma – demonstrated by all four cities – is to instead use networks and soft power to influence their larger regions. They can lead by example, reframe the political narrative, join international networks, and reform standards to shift the behaviour of neighbouring governments. In this way, leading cities have the potential to shift climate policy far beyond their borders.

Of course, none of this means that higher levels of government can relax and let cities tackle climate change alone. National, provincial, and state governments have powers that cities lack. They can amend the building codes for all communities simultaneously, mandate vehicle fuel standards, implement a carbon tax, fund public transit networks, and much more. They face far fewer jurisdictional constraints. Cities will be most successful in fighting climate change if their leadership inspires higher levels of government to act. Cities can accomplish a surprising amount on their own, but they cannot alone end climate change.

NOTES

1 In 2017, the Government of Ontario declined to allow the City of Toronto to implement council-approved road tolls on two major highways leading into the city (Don Valley Parkway and Gardiner Expressway). Road tolls are similar to congestion charges in that they use economic incentives to discourage driving. However, tolls apply to drivers who use specific roads, regardless of destination, whereas congestion charges apply to all traffic in a defined area, irrespective of route taken to get there. The idea of a congestion charge in Toronto was floated by a candidate for city council in 2022 (Achampong 2022) but has not yet been formally raised as a policy option at either the city or provincial level.

2 While soft power can help to shape regional policy, it does not necessarily entrench those policies to the extent that they are not reversible by future governments who embrace previous framings of car-dependent voters' interests. In June 2023, two decades after the election focused on sustainable regional development, Ontario's Progressive Conservative government passed the Helping Homebuyers, Protecting Tenants Act (2023). This legislation includes provisions that almost entirely counteract the anti-sprawl elements of the Places to Grow Act (2005) and Greenbelt Act (2005). For example, while there is implicit reference to transit-oriented development (establishing minimum density targets and requirements to plan for growth in "major transit station areas"), the legislation clearly favours sprawl over intensification. According to John McGrath (2023), whose analysis includes a copy of Government of Ontario briefing materials, the act specifies requirements for development near transit but does not provide any new tools or funding to make it easier to build. In contrast, the new legislation allows municipalities much more leeway to "expand their settlement area boundaries," including those that border the Greenbelt (McGrath 2023). The act also updates the province's Planning Act to help developers to avoid compliance with other provincial rules. In a technical briefing, the government describes the change as helping to "facilitate priority projects and get homes built faster [by] allow[ing] the Minister to exempt downstream approvals (e.g., plans of subdivision) from needing to comply with provincial plans and policies" (McGrath 2023). In other words, the provincial government can override municipalities that require development to be in line with Places to Grow Act and the Greenbelt Act.

3 The Toronto Atmospheric Fund (TAF) was founded in 1991 as a non-profit organization serving the City of Toronto and governed by a board made up of city councillors and members of the public (City of Toronto n.d.). In 2016, the organization received a provincial endowment to enable it to work with municipalities across the greater Toronto region and was rebranded as "The Atmospheric Fund." This regional role was further enhanced by an endowment from the federal government in 2019. The relationship between TAF and the City of Toronto is formally defined in the *Relationship Framework (2013)* (City of Toronto and TAF 2013).

REFERENCES

Abraham, Sarin, K. Ganesh, A. Senthil Kumar, and Yves Ducqd. 2012. "Impact on Climate Change Due to Transportation Sector – Research Prospective." *Procedia Engineering* 38 (January): 3869–79. https://doi.org/10.1016/j.proeng.2012.06.445.

Achampong, Rocco (@Rocco4Toronto). 2022. "Traffic & Congestion Is the Biggest Ward Wide Issue in #SpadinaFortYork …" X (Twitter), September 7, 2022, 10:42 a.m. https://twitter.com/Rocco4Toronto/status/1567501026801946629?s=20.

Bastian, Anne, and Maria Börjesson. 2018. "The City as a Driver of New Mobility Patterns, Cycling and Gender Equality: Travel Behaviour Trends in Stockholm 1985–2015." *Travel Behaviour and Society* 13 (October): 71–87. https://doi.org/10.1016/j.tbs.2018.06.003.

Ben-Joseph, Eran. 2005. *The Code of the City: Standards and the Hidden Language of Place Making.* Cambridge, MA: MIT Press.

Bliss, Laura. 2019. "How New York Finally Passed Congestion Pricing." *Bloomberg News,* March 27, 2019. https://www.bloomberg.com/news/articles/2019-03-27/why-new-york-might -finally-pass-congestion-pricing.

Bram, Jason, and Alisdair McKay. 2005. "The Evolution of Commuting Patterns in the New York City Metro Area." *Current Issues in Economics and Finance* 11, no. 10 (October): 1–7. https://papers .ssrn.com/abstract=845564.

Brand, Christian, Thomas Götschi, Evi Dons, Regine Gerike, Esther Anaya-Boig, Ione Avila-Palencia, et al. 2021. "The Climate Change Mitigation Impacts of Active Travel: Evidence from a Longitudinal Panel Study in Seven European Cities." *Global Environmental Change: Human and Policy Dimensions* 67 (March): 102224. https://doi.org/10.1016/j.gloenvcha.2021.102224.

Bresiger, Gregory. 2015. "Generations of Transit Disaster: The New York City Subways." *Journal of Private Enterprise* 30, no. 3 (Fall): 51–77. http://journal.apee.org/index.php/ajax/GDMgetFile/2015 _Journal_of_Private_Enterprise_vol_30_no_3_parte3.pdf.

Canada's Ecofiscal Commission. 2015. *We Can't Get There from Here: Why Pricing Traffic Congestion Is Critical to Beating It.* Montreal: Canada's Ecofiscal Commission. https://ecofiscal.ca/reports /traffic/.

Caro, Robert A. 1974. *The Power Broker: Robert Moses and the Fall of New York.* New York: Knopf.

Cervero, Robert. 1998. *The Transit Metropolis: A Global Inquiry.* Washington, DC: Island Press.

Cervero, Robert, and Cathleen Sullivan. 2011. "Green TODs: Marrying Transit-Oriented Development and Green Urbanism." *International Journal of Sustainable Development and World Ecology* 18, no. 3 (June): 210–18. https://doi.org/10.1080/13504509.2011.570801.

Cervero, Robert, and Danielle Dai. 2014. "BRT TOD: Leveraging Transit Oriented Development with Bus Rapid Transit Investments." *Transport Policy* 36 (November): 127–38. https://doi .org/10.1016/j.tranpol.2014.08.001.

Chan, Kenneth. 2020. "Business Groups Voice Opposition against City of Vancouver's Plan for Road Tolls." *Daily Hive*, November 2, 2020. https://dailyhive.com/vancouver /downtown-vancouver-businesses-road-tolls-impact.

———. 2022. "It's Official: Vancouver City Council Puts an End to the Road Tolls Plan." *Daily Hive*, November 22, 2022. https://dailyhive.com/vancouver/abc-vancouver-city-council -rejects-road-tolls-decision-final.

City of Burnaby. 2017. *Metrotown Downtown Plan*. The City of Burnaby. https://burnaby.widen.net/s /mmjwrxv6pm/metrotown-downtown-plan.

City of Stockholm. 2016. *Strategy for a Fossil-Fuel Free Stockholm by 2040*. Stockholm: City of Stockholm, City Executive Office. https://www.citiesoftomorrow.eu/sites/default/files/documents/Stockholm_ Strategy-for-a-fossil-fuel-free-stockholm-by-2040.pdf.

City of Surrey. 2017. *Surrey City Centre Plan Update*. Surrey: City of Surrey. https://www.surrey.ca /sites/default/files/media/documents/City%20Centre%20Plan.pdf.

City of Toronto. 2012. City Council. Minutes. 2 October 2012. Minute PW17.9.

———. 2016. *Toronto Environmental Progress Report 2016*. Toronto: City of Toronto.

———. n.d. "Toronto Atmospheric Fund." Agencies & Corporations. Accessed August 4, 2024. https://www.toronto.ca/city-government/accountability-operations-customer-service/city -administration/city-managers-office/agencies-corporations/agencies/toronto-atmospheric-fund/.

City of Toronto, and Toronto Atmospheric Fund (TAF). 2013. *Relationship Framework with City of Toronto*. https://www.toronto.ca/legdocs/mmis/2013/ex/bgrd/backgroundfile-57520.pdf.

City of Vancouver. 2004. "Vancouver City Council Minutes." July 8, 2004. https://council.vancouver. ca/20040708/csbmins.htm.

———. 2011. *Vancouver 2020 A Bright Green Future: An Action Plan for Becoming the World's Greenest City by 2020*. Vancouver: The Greenest City Action Team. https://vancouver.ca/files/cov/bright -green-future.pdf.

———. 2020. *Climate Emergency Action Plan Summary 2020–2025*. Vancouver: City of Vancouver. https://vancouver.ca/files/cov/climate-emergency-action-plan-summary.pdf.

———. 2021. *Climate Emergency Annual Report: 2021 Indicator and Financial Dashboard*. Vancouver: City of Vancouver. https://vancouver.ca/files/cov/2021-ceap-annual-report.pdf.

———. n.d. "Zero Emissions Buildings." Climate Emergency Action Plan. Accessed August 4, 2024. https://vancouver.ca/green-vancouver/zero-emissions-buildings.aspx.

Cleveland, Tristan. 2023. "Urban Intercurrence: The Struggle to Build Walkable Downtowns in Car -Dependent Suburbia." PhD diss., Dalhousie University. https://dalspace.library.dal.ca/handle /10222/82562.

Eidelman, Gabriel. 2010. "Managing Urban Sprawl in Ontario: Good Policy or Good Politics?" *Politics & Policy* 38, no. 6 (December): 1211–36. https://doi.org/10.1111/j.1747-1346.2010 .00275.x.

Eliasson, Jonas. 2014. "The Stockholm Congestion Charges: An Overview." Centre for Transport Studies CTS Working Paper, Stockholm, 7: 42.

Filion, Pierre. 2015. "Suburban Inertia: The Entrenchment of Dispersed Suburbanism." *International Journal of Urban and Regional Research* 39, no. 3 (May): 633–40. https://doi.org/10.1111 /1468-2427.12198.

Florida, Richard L. 2017. *The New Urban Crisis: How Our Cities Are Increasing Inequality, Deepening Segregation, and Failing the Middle Class – and What We Can Do about It*. Toronto: Oneworld Publications.

Frank, Lawrence, Sarah Kavage, George Poulos, and Eric Fox. 2012. *Lessons from the City of Vancouver: How to Accommodate Growth and Create a More Sustainable Transportation System at the Same Time.* Ottawa: Government of Canada, Infrastructure Canada. https://urbandesign4health.com/wp-content/uploads/2013/02/INFC_Vancouver_Study_Final_Report_EN.pdf.

Frug, Gerald E., and David J. Barron. 2011. *City Bound: How States Stifle Urban Innovation.* Ithaca: Cornell University Press.

Gärling, Tommy, and Geertje Schuitema. 2007. "Travel Demand Management Targeting Reduced Private Car Use: Effectiveness, Public Acceptability and Political Feasibility." *The Journal of Social Issues* 63, no. 1 (March): 139–53. https://doi.org/10.1111/j.1540-4560.2007.00500.x.

Golden, Anne. 2014. *Governance of Regional Transit Systems: Observations on Washington, New York, and Toronto.* Washington, DC: Wilson Center.

Gordon, David L.A. 2018. "Canada Is a Suburban Nation." *The Future of the Suburbs: Policy Challenges and Opportunities in Canada* 11, no. 23 (August): 1–4. https://doi.org/10.11575/sppp.v11i0.53000.

Government of Sweden. 2004. *The Swedish Local Government Act.* Ds 2004:31. https://www.government.se/legal-documents/2004/09/ds-200431/.

———. 2010. *Stockholm Action Plan for Climate and Energy 2010–2020.* Stockholm: City of Stockholm, Environment and Health Administration. https://projects.centralbaltic.eu/images/files/result_pdf/COMBAT_result2_Stockholm.pdf.

Griffiths, Nathan. 2022. "Check out Our Interactive Map Showing Poll-by-Poll Election Results for Vancouver." *Vancouver Sun*, October 20, 2022. https://vancouversun.com/news/local-news/this-map-shows-the-results-of-vancouvers-mayoral-race.

Gu, Ziyuan, Zhiyuan Liu, Qixiu Cheng, and Meead Saberi. 2018. "Congestion Pricing Practices and Public Acceptance: A Review of Evidence." *Case Studies on Transport Policy* 6, no. 1 (March): 94–101. https://doi.org/10.1016/j.cstp.2018.01.004.

Hall, Peter A. 2002. *Cities of Tomorrow: An Intellectual History of Urban Planning and Design in the Twentieth Century.* Hoboken, NJ: Wiley-Blackwell.

International Energy Agency. 2013. *Policy Pathways: A Tale of Renewed Cities.* Paris: International Energy Agency.

Isaksson, Karolina, and Tim Richardson. 2009. "Building Legitimacy for Risky Policies: The Cost of Avoiding Conflict in Stockholm." *Transportation Research Part A: Policy and Practice* 43, no. 3 (March): 251–7. https://doi.org/10.1016/j.tra.2008.09.002.

Koski, Chris, and Taedong Lee. 2014. "Policy by Doing: Formulation and Adoption of Policy through Government Leadership." *Policy Studies Journal* 42, no. 1 (February): 30–54. https://doi.org/10.1111/psj.12041.

Ledsham, Trudy, George Liu, Emily Watt, and Katie Wittmann. 2013. *Mapping Cycling Behaviour in Toronto.* Toronto: Toronto Cycling Think & Do Tank, School of the Environment, University of Toronto. https://www.tcat.ca/wp-content/uploads/2023/08/mapping_cycling_behaviour_in_toronto_final_23_may_printer_tl.pdf.

Livey, John. 2015. *Gardiner Expressway and Lake Shore Boulevard East Reconfiguration Environmental Assessment (EA) and Integrated Urban Design Study – Updated Evaluation of Alternatives.* Toronto: City of Toronto. https://secure.toronto.ca/council/agenda-item.do?item=2015.PW4.1.

Lucon, Ottmar, Diana Ürge-Vorsatz, Azni Zain Ahmed, Hashem Akbari, Paolo Bertoldi, Luisa F. Cabeza, Nicholas Eyre, et al. 2014. "Chapter 9 – Buildings." In *AR5 Climate Change 2014: Mitigation of Climate Change. IPCC Working Group III Contribution to AR5*, edited by Ottmar

Edenhofer, Ramón Pichs-Madruga, Youba Sokona, Jan C. Minx, Ellie Farahani, Susanne Kadner, Kristin Seyboth, et al. New York: Intergovernmental Panel on Climate Change and Cambridge University Press. https://www.ipcc.ch/site/assets/uploads/2018/02/ipcc_wg3_ar5_full.pdf.

Lydon, Mike, Anthony Garcia, and Andres Duany. 2015. *Tactical Urbanism: Short-Term Action for Long-Term Change*. Washington, DC: Island Press. https://doi.org/10.5822/978-1-61091-567-0.

McElhanney. 2019. *2019 Vancouver Panel Survey Summary Report*. Vancouver: McElhanney in Association with Mustel Group.

McGrath, John Michael. 2023. "First Impressions: What the Latest Housing Bill Will Mean for Ontario's Renters and Rural Areas." *TVO Today* (blog), April 6, 2023. https://www.tvo.org/article/first-impressions-what-the-latest-housing-bill-will-mean-for-ontarios-renters-and-rural-areas.

Morrill, Richard. 2006. "Classic Map Revisited: The Growth of Megalopolis." *The Professional Geographer: The Journal of the Association of American Geographers* 58, no. 2 (May): 155–60. https://doi.org/10.1111/j.1467-9272.2006.00522.x.

New York City, Department of Transportation. 2018. *Strategic Plan 2017 Progress Report*. New York: New York City, Department of Transportation. https://www.nyc.gov/html/dot/downloads/pdf/Strategic-plan-2017.pdf.

New York City (NYC). 2019. *Local Laws of the City of New York for the Year 2019, No. 94*. https://www.nyc.gov/assets/buildings/local_laws/ll94of2019.pdf.

Nobbe, Patrizia, and Joseph Berechman. 2013. *The Politics of Large Infrastructure Investment Decision-Making: The Case of the Second Avenue Subway Case Study*. UTRC-RF Project No. 49111-16-23. New York: The City College of New York. https://rosap.ntl.bts.gov/view/dot/27119.

Norimine, Hayat. 2019. "How New York Won Congestion Pricing." Sightline Institute, May 10, 2019. https://www.sightline.org/2019/05/10/how-new-york-won-congestion-pricing/.

Nuttall, Jeremy. 2020. "Vancouver Is the First Canadian City to Pursue a Congestion Charge. Is Toronto Next?" *The Toronto Star*, November 22, 2020. https://www.thestar.com/news/canada/2020/11/22/vancouver-is-the-first-canadian-city-to-pursue-a-congestion-charge-is-toronto-next.html.

Pagliaro, Jennifer, and David Rider. 2015. "Gardiner East Will Be a Hybrid Solution, Council Votes." *The Toronto Star*, June 11, 2015. https://www.thestar.com/news/city_hall/2015/06/11/mayor-john-tory-headed-for-decisive-win-on-gardiner-east.html.

Paulsson, Alexander. 2020. "The City That the Metro System Built: Urban Transformations and Modalities of Integrated Planning in Stockholm." *Urban Studies* 57, no. 14 (November): 2936–55. https://doi.org/10.1177/0042098019895231.

Pojani, Dorina, and Dominic Stead. 2018. "Chapter Four – Past, Present and Future of Transit-Oriented Development in Three European Capital City-Regions." In *Advances in Transport Policy and Planning*, edited by Yoram Shiftan and Maria Kamargianni, 1:93–118. Cambridge: Academic Press. https://doi.org/10.1016/bs.atpp.2018.07.003.

Rees, Marvin. 2021. "How Mayors Can Help Save the World." *The Economist*, November 8, 2021. https://www.economist.com/the-world-ahead/2021/11/08/marvin-rees-on-how-mayors-can-save-the-world.

Rodden, Jonathan A. 2019. *Why Cities Lose: The Deep Roots of the Urban-Rural Political Divide*. New York: Basic Books.

Sadik-Khan, Janette, and Seth Solomonow. 2017. *Streetfight: Handbook for an Urban Revolution*. New York: Penguin.

Salat, Serge, and Gerald Ollivier. 2017. *Transforming the Urban Space through Transit-Oriented Development: The 3V Approach*. Washington, DC: World Bank.https://www.worldtransitresearch.info/research/6572.

Schmitt, Peter, Lisbeth Greve Harbo, Asli Tepecik Diş, and Anu Henriksson. 2013. "Urban Resilience and Polycentricity: The Case of the Stockholm Urban Agglomeration." In *Resilience Thinking in Urban Planning*, edited by Ayda Eraydin and Tuna Taşan-Kok, 197–209. Dordrecht: Springer Netherlands. https://doi.org/10.1007/978-94-007-5476-8_12.

Schwartz, Elizabeth. 2016a. "Local Solutions to a Global Problem? Canadian Municipal Policy Responses to Climate Change." PhD. diss, University of British Columbia. https://doi.org/10.14288/1.0300060.

———. 2016b. "Developing Green Cities: Explaining Variation in Canadian Green Building Policies." *Canadian Journal of Political Science* 49, no. 4 (December): 621–41. https://doi.org/10.1017/S0008423916000846.

Sellers, Jefferey M., and Anders Lidström. 2007. "Decentralization, Local Government, and the Welfare State." *Governance* 20, no. 4 (October): 609–32. https://doi.org/10.1111/j.1468-0491.2007.00374.x.

Sims, Ralph, Roberto Schaeffer, Felix Creutzig, Xochitl Cruz-Núñez, Marcio D'Agosto, Delia Dimitriu, Maria Josefina Figueroa Meza, et al. 2014. "Transport." In *Climate Change 2014: Mitigation of Climate Change. Contribution of Working Group III to the Fifth Assessment Report of the Intergovernmental Panel on Climate Change*, edited by Ottmar Edenhofer, Ramón Pichs-Madruga, Youba Sokona, Jan C. Minx, Ellie Farahani, Susanne Kadner, Kristin Seyboth, et al., 599–670. New York: Intergovernmental Panel on Climate Change and Cambridge University Press.

Smith, Alison, and Zachary Spicer. 2018. "The Local Autonomy of Canada's Largest Cities." *Urban Affairs Review* 54, no. 5 (September): 931–61. https://doi.org/10.1177/1078087416684380.

Stojanovski, Todor. 2020. "Urban Design and Public Transportation – Public Spaces, Visual Proximity and Transit-Oriented Development (TOD)." *Journal of Urban Design* 25, no. 1 (January): 134–54. https://doi.org/10.1080/13574809.2019.1592665.

Stojanovski, Todor, Mats Johan Lundström, and Tigran Haas. 2012. "Tram and Light Railway as Key Driver for Sustainable Urban Development: The Swedish Experiences with Transit-Oriented Development (TOD)." Paper presented at BUFTOD 2012, Building the Urban Future and Transit Oriented Development International Conference, Transport Systems in the Context of TOD: Rail, Bus and Inter-Modality, Paris, France, April 2012, 377–408. http://urn.kb.se/resolve?urn=urn:nbn:se:kth:diva-109258.

Stone, John. 2014. "Continuity and Change in Urban Transport Policy: Politics, Institutions and Actors in Melbourne and Vancouver since 1970." *Planning Practice & Research* 29, no. 4 (August): 388–404. https://doi.org/10.1080/02697459.2013.820041.

Taylor, Zack. 2011. "Who Elected Rob Ford, and Why? An Ecological Analysis of the 2010 Toronto Election." Paper presented at the Canadian Political Science Association Conference, Waterloo, Ontario, May 2011. http://www.cpsa-acsp.ca/papers-2011/Taylor.pdf.

Taylor, Brian D., and Eric A. Morris. 2015. "Public Transportation Objectives and Rider Demographics: Are Transit's Priorities Poor Public Policy?" *Transportation* 42, no. 2 (March): 347–67. https://doi.org/10.1007/s11116-014-9547-0.

Toronto Atmospheric Fund (TAF). 2014. "First Green Condo Loan Proves Green Buildings Are Profitable." Toronto Atmospheric Fund, May 28, 2014. https://taf.ca/first-green-condo-loan-proves-green-buildings-profitable/.

U.S. Census Bureau. 2019. "American Community Survey 1-Year Estimates, New York, Census Designated Place." U.S. Census Bureau. https://www.census.gov/data/developers/data-sets/acs-1year.2019.html#list-tab-843855098.

Walks, Alan. 2015. "Stopping the 'War on the Car': Neoliberalism, Fordism, and the Politics of Automobility in Toronto." *Mobilities* 10, no. 3 (May): 402–22. https://doi.org/10.1080/17450101.2014.880563.

Watson, Patrick. 2018. "'Common Sense Geography' and the Elected Official: Technical Evidence and Conceptions of 'Trust' in Toronto's Gardiner Expressway Decision." *Canadian Journal of Sociology = Cahiers Canadiens de Sociologie* 43, no. 1 (March): 49–75. https://doi.org/10.29173/cjs27058.

WSP and Parsons Brinckerhoff. 2016. *Trans-Hudson Commuting Capacity Study: Summary Report.* New York: The Port Authority of New York and New Jersey.

Zakhour, Sherif, and Jonathan Metzger. 2018. "From a 'Planning-Led Regime' to a 'Development-Led Regime' (and Back Again?): The Role of Municipal Planning in the Urban Governance of Stockholm." *disP – The Planning Review* 54, no. 4 (October): 46–58. https://doi.org/10.1080/02513625.2018.1562797.

CHAPTER TWELVE

City Governance and Local Immigration Policy-Making

Kristin R. Good

Although it is often discussed through a country lens, immigration and other forms of migration are mainly urban phenomena, so much so that the International Organization for Migration points out that "urbanization" has almost become synonymous with "migration" (IOM 2018, 227). This is also true in Canada: between 2015 and 2019, 90 per cent of immigrants to the country chose to settle in a Census Metropolitan Area, which Statistics Canada defines as an urban settlement with a population of at least 100,000 (Statistics Canada 2022). A disproportionate number of newcomers live in Canada's top three immigrant destinations – Toronto, Montreal, and Vancouver. Attention to immigration policies' highly uneven spatial consequences and multilevel nature, including the role of local governments, is crucial.

All orders of government play a role in governing the urban dimensions of migration, but since the 1990s we have witnessed the rise of a municipal role in this policy field. One might even describe it as a flood of policy activity in cities across the globe. This chapter explores the global rise of local immigration policy-making, defined as local (municipal) policies concerned with *controlling immigrant flows* and *short-term* and *long-term immigrant integration* (Filomeno 2017). Across the globe, local immigration policies and governance arrangements are a crucial part of immigrant settlement and integration policy infrastructures (see Sellers 2005 on national and policy infrastructures). Furthermore, the way in which immigration and diversity are governed at the local level varies significantly in Canada and abroad, defying the classification of countries according to national models. Distinct modes of urban immigration governance have emerged with many cities incorporating diversity-friendly, "multicultural" approaches regardless of country-level debates.

In Europe, within the context of backlash against multiculturalism in some countries and cities, municipalities are forging new paths in diversity policy in ways that have not completely rejected or replaced past (multicultural) approaches. In the United States, much of the national immigration discourse focuses on enforcement of immigration laws and the challenge of undocumented migration. The failure of successive federal governments to address this challenge has contributed to the rise of local activism. Although illegal immigration relief ordinances and other anti-immigrant measures have received a great deal of attention in the media, many cities continue to offer "sanctuary" to undocumented immigrants in defiance of the federal laws even during the particularly charged Trump era (2017–21). Furthermore, immigrant-friendly and "multicultural" approaches to governing cities such as New York, Los Angeles, and San Francisco persist.

This chapter demonstrates that both sub-national and international comparisons offer crucial insights to our understanding of the changing role of municipalities in local immigration policy-making and diversity policy. It begins by positioning Canada's national immigration policy-making "infrastructure" in international perspective, focusing on how it compares with key developments in the United States and Europe. Next, it discusses the local immigration policy landscape of Canadian cities and provides an account of how they vary. Following this, the chapter examines local immigration policies in American cities and European cities (with a focus on crucial cases in the Netherlands and France) and then makes brief observations about local immigration policy-making in the Global South. Next, the chapter summarizes lessons that can be drawn from existing literature about the factors influencing local immigration policy-making. Finally, it concludes with observations about the broad significance of the global rise of local immigration policy-making.

However, before embarking upon a discussion of local immigration policy-making, we must acknowledge the relationship between immigration, multicultural policy discourses, and settler colonialism. Immigration is a process that involves the ongoing settlement of Canada and the reduction of Indigenous Peoples' demographic weight, which affects power relations. Immigration policy processes can contribute to the ongoing erasure and displacement of Indigenous Peoples both in Canada generally and in Canadian cities. Indigenous scholar Joyce Green argues that to decolonize the Canadian state, "public policies must reflect indigenous histories, imagination, and aspirations as thoroughly as they now reflect colonial priorities" (2003, 54). Green also argues that because of the extensive urbanization of Indigenous Peoples, decolonization "requires new formulae for sharing political and economic power *within mainstream communities*" (54). This means that in settler colonial countries, immigration policy, including *local immigration policy*, ought to reflect not only the settler state's goals but also Indigenous priorities, histories, and community goals. We see evidence of innovation in this respect in cities in Western Canada with Winnipeg constituting a particularly noteworthy case. However, in general, local immigration policy-making focuses on immigrant diversity and takes the "host" community for granted.

LOCAL IMMIGRATION POLICY-MAKING AND COUNTRY CONTEXT: TRENDS AND POLICY INFRASTRUCTURES

Canada: A Proactive Immigration Policy and Positive Multicultural Discourse

Canada is considered a leader in immigration policy, both in policies to select and to integrate immigrants. Historically, the federal government took the lead in immigration policy-making, especially in *selection* but also *immigrant settlement* until the policy field experienced a "federalization" through increasing provincial action in the 1990s (Paquet 2019). Section 95 of the Constitution Act, 1867 establishes immigration as a joint area of federal-provincial jurisdiction with federal paramountcy or pre-eminence.

A key turning point in Canada's immigration policy was the adoption of new regulations in 1967 that established a "point system" by which to assess potential immigrants, eliminating discrimination based on country of origin (Knowles 2016). This policy changed the ethnocultural and racial composition of Canada's immigrant population from largely "white" to a predominance of "visible minority"[1] groups, and in doing so, transformed the ethnocultural composition of Canada's major cities within a generation.

Canada's approach to settlement reflects "two-way street" thinking that acknowledges that not only immigrants but also governments and the host society must adapt to cultural changes brought about by immigration. The foundations of this approach are in a cluster of complementary policies and legislation: the Canadian Multiculturalism Act, the Immigration and Refugee Protection Act, the Employment Equity Act and others, as well as s. 27 of the Charter of Rights and Freedoms (Biles et al. 2012).

Federal integration programs focus on providing language and skills training, facilitating labour market access, and creating welcoming communities (Biles et al. 2012). Short-term programs are the main focus for spending, but there are additional "multicultural" programs focused on the long-term integration of immigrants and diversity (Biles et al. 2012). International comparisons situate Canada among the best-performing countries in terms of legal frameworks to facilitate immigrant integration (Biles et al. 2012) and "multicultural" policy-making (Banting and Kymlicka 2012).

In the 1990s, Canada witnessed a "federalization" of its immigration policy-making as provinces became active in both immigrant selection and integration (Paquet 2019). Despite the concentration of immigrants in major urban centres in Canada, municipal governments are generally not included in these policy discussions. In 2005, municipalities' role in immigration policy was recognized in the Ontario-Canada Agreement on Immigration for the first time despite municipalities' lack of formal jurisdiction (Good 2009).[2] This agreement led to an important innovation in Canadian local immigration governance: the federally funded Local Immigration Partnership (LIP) – a cross-sectoral partnership of local leaders, often hosted by the municipality.

Canadian immigration discourse continues to focus on positive elements; however, there is evidence of growing anti-multicultural and anti-immigrant politics in the Conservative movement in Canada, and the debate about "reasonable accommodation" of cultural and religious practices has intensified in Quebec. Nevertheless, it is worth remembering that these recent flashpoints in the Canadian immigration conversation occur within the context of a country with exceptionally high levels of immigration that, since the 1980s, have remained consistent regardless of downturns in the economy, a policy initiated by the Mulroney Conservatives (Knowles 2016). Both Liberal and Conservative governments since then have continued to plan for high levels of immigration detached from economic considerations and even the ability to provide housing. Canada has also shown leadership in refugee settlement such as during the Syrian refugee crisis when, in the lead-up to the 2015 federal election, the Liberals committed to accepting and settling a large number of refugees in a short period of time, many of whom settled in Canada's major urban centres. The major parties at the federal level recognize that their fates are tied to attracting immigrants to their parties, providing a strong incentive to maintain high levels of immigration when in government and espouse positive discourses. Public opinion in Canada is generally favourable to immigration, and multiculturalism is considered an important part of the Canadian identity.

Some attribute Canadians' positive attitudes toward immigration, multiculturalism, and even the failure of the far right to gain ground in Canada to its multicultural policy infrastructure, including strong hate speech laws (Ambrose and Mudde 2015). Canada's unique ability to control its border (at least comparatively speaking) has also been identified as a contributing factor to Canadians' positive attitudes toward immigrants and immigration. Although there has been more national debate about uncontrolled migration recently due to an unprecedented number of asylum-seeking migrants arriving at the Quebec and Manitoba borders, compared with the United States and EU countries for instance, Canada's borders are relatively secure. For this reason, Canada has been able to select immigrants for their human capital, and there is less fear of the cultural implications of uncontrolled immigration.

United States: A Focus on Enforcement and a "Laissez-Faire" Integration Policy?

In the United States, jurisdiction for immigration is exclusively federal. The roots of the current immigration era are in reforms in the 1960s that ended national-origin quotas and opened immigration to countries in the Global South, including temporary migration agreements with Mexico and Caribbean countries that transformed into streams of undocumented migrants by the 1970s (Bloemraad and De Graauw 2012). Current policies are structured by the 1965 Hart-Cellar Act, which has an emphasis on family reunion and produces an immigration stream that accounts for up to three-quarters of legal immigration in the United States (Bloemraad and De Graauw 2012).

The United States also has a large and growing "undocumented" immigrant population of migrants who have entered the country secretly or who have overstayed legal visas. The undocumented population has grown dramatically since 1990 – a fourfold increase from three to twelve million due in part to economic restructuring under the North American Free Trade Agreement that made it more difficult for Mexican and Latin American agricultural workers to make a living, leading them to migrate (Varsanyi 2010b, 9–10). There was also an increased demand for low-wage and flexible labour among employers, especially in the construction industry and various service industries (9–10). Addressing undocumented migration is such a defining feature of American immigration policy debates that the American public believes that most immigrants are in the country illegally, which is, of course, false (Bloemraad and De Graauw 2012). For many, border enforcement has become a preferred option with which to address this question (Bloemraad and De Graauw 2012). The immigration policy debate in the United States focuses on undocumented migration, and successive administrations have failed to achieve comprehensive immigration reform, a term used in the United States since the early 2000s to describe policies that address multiple objectives simultaneously, including border enforcement, the legalization of undocumented migrants, and the ability to meet labour market needs through immigration (Migration Policy Institute, n.d.). Immigration debates focus on the control of immigration flows and the legacy of these flows rather than measures to facilitate the integration of migrants coming through legal channels.

Many consider the American approach to immigrant *integration* as laissez-faire since the federal government does not have a comprehensive immigrant integration policy or approach (Bloemraad and De Graauw 2012). The exception to this is the refugee population, which has received some settlement support since 1980 (Bloemraad and De Graauw 2012).

Nevertheless, civil rights legislation, which was originally a response to the country's African American population (and civil rights movement), provides a partial infrastructure that benefits immigrants in their long-term integration. Civil rights laws and policy infrastructures have had a major positive influence on the receptivity of small cities to immigrants by requiring municipalities to provide language access to services and recourse to discrimination in housing codes and their enforcement (Williamson 2019). These laws have the effect of incentivizing localities to adopt what Canadians would label "multicultural" policies. In fact, these laws have greater teeth than multicultural policies since municipalities that violate them could face legal or administrative action (including having any federal funding withdrawn).

However, federal immigration law in the United States also provides incentives to create local communities that are unreceptive to immigrants through, for instance, the Illegal Immigration and Immigrant Responsibility Act (1996) that enacted measures to empower state and local police to enforce federal immigration law (Williamson 2019, 10). Since then, a focus on enforcement in the absence of comprehensive immigration reform spans Democratic and Republican presidencies with rates of deportation increasing under both Republican President G.W. Bush and Democratic President Obama.

Partly in response to the federal government's failure to achieve comprehensive immigration reform to address what some perceive as a crisis of undocumented migration and to provide leadership in immigrant settlement, the United States has witnessed a dramatic rise in state and local immigration policy-making. Monica Varsanyi (2010b, 3) describes a "trickle" of such activity beginning in 1994 with California's Proposition 187, which was designed to exclude undocumented immigrants from social services, to a progressive acceleration beginning in the early 2000s with Arizona's Proposition 200, modelled on Prop 187. A staggering total of 1,500 state and local immigration laws were considered and 353 were enacted in 2009 (3) even though immigration is an exclusively federal responsibility. Although the examples here are of anti-immigrant initiatives, it is interesting that American localities have been mainly progressive in their policy efforts as we explore more below.

Europe: A Backlash Against Multicultural Modes of Immigration Governance?

It is impossible to summarize an entire continent's immigration policies and trends. However, a few observations about the European context are in order. One is that there is a widespread perception that "multiculturalism" has failed; this diagnosis has been offered by several European leaders in the last couple of decades, including leaders on the moderate right of the ideological spectrum such as the United Kingdom's David Cameron, Germany's Angela Merkel, and France's Nicolas Sarkozy in 2011. Such diagnoses were fuelled by a series of high-profile events, including the 9/11 terrorist attacks in the United States, the Madrid train bombing in March 2004, the murder of filmmaker Theo van Gogh by a Muslim extremist in 2004, the London terrorist bombings in 2005, the Danish Muhammad cartoon debate in September 2005, riots in Paris in 2005, and a series of high-profile editorials from thought leaders on the left and right condemning multiculturalism (Vertovec and Wessendorf 2010, 4–6). Brexit was an extension and more recent manifestation of this logic.

European scholars have developed typologies of national modes of immigrant integration. Although they vary, many distinguish between "multicultural" modes and "assimilationist" modes. The former mode provides state support for cultural differences, whereas, in the assimilationist mode, the maintenance of cultural differences is left to the private sphere. Canada was the first country to adopt a policy of official multiculturalism at the country level. However, this was followed by European countries such as the Netherlands and Sweden. France is considered to be the typical example of an "assimilationist" mode.

Today, in light of perceived policy failures in places that had adopted "multicultural" modes of governance, an important debate in the comparative immigration policy literature is whether European countries are converging toward a common focus on "civic integration," which is essentially a new way of describing assimilation. For instance, the Netherlands, which was considered a case of a strong commitment to multicultural policies, began pursuing such policies in the 1990s. One well-known immigration scholar goes as far as describing civic integration policies in Europe as "repressive liberalism" (Joppke 2007, 14) because they emphasize the obligations on immigrants to integrate instead of immigrant rights. Although some argue that the Netherlands' civic integration policies have spread across Europe (Joppke 2007), others contend that the shift has been overstated and that the Netherlands is an exceptional case (Banting and Kymlicka 2013). One of the cases that has purportedly been inspired by the Netherlands' adoption of strong civic integration policies is France. However, a move in this direction is less of a shift for France, which is considered to have an "assimilationist" and "republican" approach to immigrant integration. The extent of convergence toward a sole focus on civic integration in Europe is contested, however, with Banting and Kymlicka (2013) arguing that integration programs have been layered upon multicultural ones leading to hybrid approaches rather than a retreat from multiculturalism. Others question the validity of national models, noting, for instance, that even the French model of assimilationism was never monolithic (Schiller 2016, loc. 2366). Indeed, a great deal of variation exists at the local level in European countries (and globally), calling into question the notion of coherent immigration policy paradigms.

LOCAL IMMIGRATION POLICIES

The Local Policy Landscape in Canada

Although there has been a rise in municipal immigration policy-making since the mid-1990s, some Canadian municipalities played a role in local immigration policy-making as early as the 1970s. The former City of Toronto established a translation office in 1975, an equal opportunity policy in 1977, and even a council Committee on Immigrant Settlement & Services in 1979 (Wallace and Frisken 2000). Metro Toronto, the second tier of a two-tier municipality governing the metropolitan area of Toronto at that time (and of which the City of Toronto was a constituent unit), established a "multicultural policy" in 1978 and took on a role in refugee integration with the establishment of the Greater Toronto Task Force on Southeast Asian Refugees (1979) (Wallace and Frisken 2000). We also know that Canada's two largest cities, Toronto and Montreal, introduced significant programs designed to address immigrant integration and diversity in 1988, with the City of Toronto introducing its Multicultural Access Program and the City of Montreal's adoption of the Bureau Intercultural of Montreal (Wallace and Frisken 2000; Tate and Quesnel 1995).

Since these early initiatives, the municipal role has become widespread but uneven in Canada with a range of different policies designed specifically or in part to address immigrant integration. These initiatives range from *symbolic initiatives* to encourage a more welcoming community to highly institutionalized programs and offices with substantial resources devoted to them. *Symbolic initiatives* include hosting or providing funding for multicultural events and festivals as well as efforts to create an inclusive municipal image. The City of Toronto's decision to use "Diversity Our Strength" as its official city motto is a good example of cities adopting inclusive language and symbols. Multicultural festivals such as Toronto's Caribbean Carnival and Winnipeg's Folklorama are common across cities in Canada, often providing opportunities for residents to experience the food, arts, and culture of a multitude of ethnic groups.

Anti-racism policies and initiatives are part of the repertoire of municipal efforts to integrate immigrants. Although such initiatives also address barriers to inclusion for long-standing racialized minorities, they are important to successful immigrant integration since most immigrants are also racialized, "visible" minorities in Canada. A prominent recent example of such an initiative is Toronto's establishment of a separate unit in the City Manager's Office – the Confronting Anti-Black Racism Unit – with four dedicated Black staff people to address "anti-Black racism" in a focused way. This unit reflects an evolution in understanding about the deeply engrained nature of systemic racism in the country. In the 1990s, municipalities in suburbs in Toronto and Vancouver established "race relations" committees in response to large-scale immigration, sometimes to deal with backlash against the demographic changes (Good 2009). These initiatives might be characterized as in the same vein as contemporary "intercultural" initiatives that attempt to "manage" conflict and create bridges across groups without acknowledging the systemic, institutional barriers that perpetuate some forms of racism such as anti-Asian racism and the variants of anti-Black racism that Toronto's new office is designed to address (discussed more fully in chapter 9).

Broadly speaking, addressing access and equity in service delivery might also be considered part of the infrastructure of local immigration policy. Municipal services of all types contribute to successful immigrant settlement, such as recreation and library services, especially when adapted proactively to ethnocultural diversity following a multicultural model of immigrant integration (Good 2009). Measures such as translation and interpretation, offering culturally sensitive and appealing services, and reflecting diversity in communications strategies (by, for instance, engaging with ethnocultural minority communities' media) are examples of this type of policy. The former City of Toronto began to translate and provide interpretation in the 1970s; the current City of Toronto (created through an amalgamation in 1998) currently provides interpretation in 180 languages to residents calling 311, a number dedicated to information on city services and to citizen requests for services (City of Toronto n.d.-d). Although the scope of translation varies, many municipalities across Canada provide some translation and interpretation services.

Some municipalities make efforts to engage immigrants politically through a variety of initiatives like the translation of election materials. More fundamentally, some municipalities (e.g., Toronto and Halifax) have advocated for the extension of voting rights to permanent residents at the municipal level (but without success since provinces must enact the changes). Forms of political engagement in between elections include efforts to incorporate immigrant diversity into decision-making processes through council committees that deal with immigrant- and diversity-related matters. Such committees exist in many municipalities across Canada. An example of a new or reconstituted committee is Winnipeg's Human Rights Committee, which is chaired by the mayor. Municipalities also influence the inclusivity of broader decision-making processes about city services through appointments to agencies, boards, and commissions (ABCs). With this in mind, the Toronto Action Plan to Confront Anti-Black Racism identifies "Outreach, [recruiting, and appointing] diverse people of African descent to City agencies, boards and commissions" as an important action to take to increase the community engagement and leadership of Toronto's communities of African descent (City of Toronto n.d.-c).

Another type of multicultural intervention is to provide grants to community organizations that serve immigrants and have multicultural purposes (Good 2009). In Toronto, such grants predate the current City of Toronto's political institutions (Wallace and Frisken 2000, table 7). The City of Winnipeg provides funding to an innovative settlement agency called IRCOM (Immigrant and Refugee Community Organization of Manitoba), which not only provides settlement services but also operates transitional housing for newcomers. IRCOM was officially established in 1991 but grew out of an organization that began by offering sports and recreation programs to refugee youth with funding from the City of Winnipeg in the mid-1980s (Bucklaschuk 2016, 7–9). According to a study of the organization, after weathering some challenges, IRCOM has become not only a housing organization and an important actor in Winnipeg's settlement sector but also an "important contributor to and champion of community and neighbourhood development" (9).

Employment equity policies and initiatives to address systemic barriers to immigrant and ethnocultural minority access to employment within the municipality and the community are another important part of municipal diversity and immigrant incorporation policy infrastructures. The City of Vancouver has been a leader in this area: it developed an Equal Opportunity Policy in 1977 and then updated it and established an office – the Equal Opportunity Office – with separate staff reporting to the City Manager's Office in 1986 (Good 2009). Some municipalities also contribute to employment equity beyond the municipal corporation by establishing procurement policies with equity objectives. For instance, the City of Toronto has a Social Procurement Program that addresses both "supply chain diversity" and workforce diversity in its procurement practices (City of Toronto n.d.-b).

Beginning in the early 2000s, Canadian municipalities also began to play a more direct role in *immigration* policy (framed directly as such). The City of Toronto appears to have been one of, if not the first, municipalities to use the language of "immigration" in its policy efforts in recent decades, with the establishment of an "Immigration and Refugee Issues Working Group" to engage immigrants and refugees in policy-making and the development of an Immigrant Settlement and Policy Framework (2001) (Good 2009, 60). The policy's main goals were to "attract newcomers," provide the supports necessary to create a sense of belonging among them, and facilitate their integration (City of Toronto 2001). In 2005, then mayor of the City of Vancouver, Larry Campbell, established the Mayor's Working Group on Immigration, acknowledging the city's role in immigrant settlement directly. In 2007 and 2011, respectively, Edmonton and Calgary also developed immigration policies modelled after Toronto's (Tossutti 2012, 617).

A major development in local immigration policy-making in Canada has been the emergence of federally funded LIPs, discussed as an example of "metagovernance" in chapter 4. This program began in Ontario after the Canada–Ontario Immigration Agreement was signed in 2005: it was the first to include municipalities and was especially aimed at the City of Toronto. The Municipal Immigration Committee was established with Citizenship and Immigration Canada (CIC), the Ontario Ministry of Citizenship and Immigration, and the Association of Municipalities of Ontario as co-chairs. This committee identified "attraction and retention" as well as "settlement and integration" as "key municipal priorities" and "highlighted the need to propose new strategies and structures to address complex social issues and service gaps" (Burr 2011, 3). The LIP grew out of this process, first in Ontario in 2008 and then throughout the country.

A LIP is a community-based partnership that serves to foster collaboration among institutions and organizations that contribute to the immigrant settlement process. They do not offer services directly but rather "aim to enhance collaboration, coordination and strategic planning at the community level in order to foster more welcoming and inclusive communities and improve settlement and integration outcomes" (CIC 2014, 3). Secretariats located in host organizations are the "backbone organizations" supporting LIPs. They establish partnership councils, conduct research, and establish strategies, priorities, and action plans, as well as support their implementation. The most common hosts are municipalities (45 per cent) and settlement agencies (CIC 2014, 4). The council is where exchange among sectors occurs. Common members of LIP councils include settlement agencies, municipalities, schools and school boards, employers and employer bodies, newcomers, hospitals, universities, the provincial and federal governments, civil society groups, police services, Francophone organizations, ethnic/religious organizations, and others (4). LIPs are essentially governance arrangements at the city scale that are institutionalized and supported by federal funding.

Another contemporary development in Canadian local immigration policy-making has been the emergence of "sanctuary cities," which is "a loose term that applies to cities refusing to cooperate with federal authorities to enforce national immigration law" (Bauder 2017). This development reflects a foray into the area of immigration "control" (in addition to these policies' effects on integration by providing access to city services for undocumented migrants). Toronto-based Chilean refugees advocated for sanctuary-city bylaws in the 1980s (Solidarity City Network 2013, cited in Bauder 2016, 179), but it was not until 2004 that the City of Toronto and the Toronto District School Board "quietly adopted" "don't ask don't tell" policies regarding migrant status after pressure from Toronto activists (Berinstein et al. 2006; McDonald 2012, cited in Bauder 2016, 179). Subsequently, in February of 2013, the City of Toronto passed a motion that "reaffirmed its commitment to ensuring that Torontonians, regardless of immigration status, have access to City services without fear of being asked for proof of status" and adopted the Access to City Services for Undocumented Torontonians (Access T.O.) (City of Toronto n.d.-a). Since then, at least seven urban municipalities have adopted sanctuary policies (Paquet and Joy 2022). They share common goals of providing information and increasing access to services as well as promoting an inclusive image of their cities (Paquet and Joy 2022). However, in Canada, local sanctuary policies are possibly most distinctive in that they do not provide protection from immigration law enforcement by limiting police forces from cooperating with immigration agencies, and they do not advocate for changes to such policies at the federal level (Paquet and Joy 2022). Vancouver has had an "Access to City Services without Fear" policy since 2016, but activists have withheld the title of "sanctuary city" because it excludes many crucial service areas such as policing (Bauder 2016). As Harsha Walia notes, in Vancouver undocumented migrants are also policed when accessing transit services (Walia 2014). TransLink's transit police also enforce immigration law, collaborating "routinely" with the Vancouver Police Department and the Canada Border Services Agency "to identify and detain people under the pretense of fare evasion" (Walia 2014). As Walia also observes "[t]hey are also the only armed transit police force in the country" (Walia 2014).

Canadian municipalities also play a role in refugee resettlement, a role that grew in response to the Trudeau government's initiative to resettle Syrian refugees. Existing policy infrastructures were brought to bear on the effort in addition to new responses and initiatives tailored to the refugee response effort. Joseph Garcea documents five roles that members of the Federation of Canadian Municipality's Big City Mayors' Caucus played in the resettlement of Syrian refugees: advocacy, the provision of services, response coordination, in-kind contributions, and financial contributions (Garcea 2016, 162). The coordination role included intergovernmental tri-level coordination, interdepartmental coordination, and inter-agency coordination. In Canada's large cities, LIPs played a role in the response by coordinating the efforts of various city-level agencies (166).

Although not widespread enough, some local communities and municipalities have begun to recognize the importance of addressing the implications of urban immigration for urban Indigenous Peoples and "decolonizing" the settlement process through intercultural initiatives aimed at increasing understanding and encouraging positive relations between newcomers and Indigenous Peoples. Indigenous organizations in Winnipeg, such as Ka Ni Kanichihk Inc. (KNK), whose name means "those who lead" in the Ininew (Cree) language, have led in this respect (Ghorayshi 2010). A study of a KNK initiative in Indigenous-newcomer relations concludes:

> Aboriginal community organizations can assert the place and rights of Aboriginal peoples as original occupants of Canada, and re-engage as hosts to orient new waves of newcomers to Canada in ways that generate mutual understanding and respect and the dynamic potential of intercultural urbanism. (Gyepi-Garbrah, Walker, and Garcea 2014, 1797)

Another example of local efforts to build positive intercultural relations between Indigenous residents and newcomers is the Vancouver Dialogues Project (2009–13). This project was a series of dialogues between newcomers and Indigenous Peoples beginning in 2010 that involved a mix of youths and elders in both communities and culminated in a "closing dialogue circle" with the mayor and other distinguished guests (Yu 2011, 306–7). More recently, Winnipeg's LIP, called Immigration Partnership Winnipeg (IPW), has developed an immigration agenda that centres Indigenous perspectives, histories, and goals. It is hosted by Winnipeg's community-based Social Planning Council and includes an Indigenous sector table as part of its governing arrangements. With Indigenous input and guidance, IPW developed educational materials on Indigenous history, culture, and rights for use in the settlement sector (Good 2021). Although limited by the resources available in the community, this initiative is an excellent example of locally based decolonization initiatives that warrant more attention in the local immigration policy literature in settler colonial states.

MUNICIPAL VARIATION IN LOCAL IMMIGRATION POLICY-MAKING IN CANADA

Municipalities vary significantly in their local immigration policy-making. One of the most straightforward ways of thinking about how they vary is to examine how active they are and how many resources have been devoted to the issue. Municipalities that have been the most comprehensive in their approach tend to establish offices and other institutional supports for their role, such as Toronto, Montreal, Vancouver, and Edmonton (Fourot 2013; Good 2009; Tossutti 2012). We know that the core cities in the three most significant immigrant destinations – the City of Toronto, Ville de Montreal, and the City of Vancouver – and other major cities such as Edmonton have one or more (in the case of Toronto) offices with mandates related to immigration and equity (Fourot 2013; Good 2009; Tossutti 2012). For instance, the City of Toronto has several offices with responsibilities related to successful immigrant settlement and integration.

Nevertheless, to the extent that municipalities have assumed a role in this policy field at all, in some municipalities, the immigration "file" is assigned to a staff person with other responsibilities or to a single staff person located in another department such as economic development or social planning, depending on the dominant way immigration and immigrant integration is conceived as a policy challenge. Tossutti (2012) refers to this as a "decentralized" bureaucratic approached to distinguish it from a "centralized" approach reflected in the establishment of a bureau of multicultural affairs or diversity management.

Municipalities use different language or policy paradigms to frame their role in local immigration policy-making, and scholars debate the significance of these differences. Following a European approach to characterizing differences in "national models," some Canadian scholarship distinguishes between three possible models of immigrant integration: an assimilationist model labelled "civic universalism" and two kinds of pluralist models – "multicultural" and "intercultural" (Poirier 2006, 208–9; Tossutti 2012, 611). Civic universalism is a form of assimilationist model that relegates cultural difference to the private sphere, purporting a "neutral" state approach to citizen-state relations. Multicultural and intercultural approaches are both pluralist insofar as they recognize cultural difference in the public sphere, but the latter emphasizes common reference points more (Poirier 2006, 208–9; Tossutti 2012, 611).

The lesson from the studies that characterize municipal differences in this way appears to be that many municipalities mix elements of these models of immigrant settlement (Poirier 2006, 211; Tossutti 2012, 628–9). For instance, Montreal's district-level governments approach services differently with, for instance, one offering separate swimming for Muslim women (a multicultural approach) and another choosing a more universalist approach (Poirier 2006, 211), reflecting the important discretion exercised by "street-level bureaucrats." This hybridity has led some to characterize municipal approaches to local immigration policy-making and diversity as ad hoc and pragmatic (Germain and Alain 2009).

SPATIAL/SCALAR VARIATION

A great deal of variation exists among cities within the same province and even the same metropolitan areas. The core municipalities in large Canadian cities and metropolitan areas, particularly in Canada's most popular immigrant destinations, have the highest levels of activity in local immigration policy-making. Toronto, Vancouver, and Montreal, as well as other major Canadian cities like Edmonton, have all institutionalized their role in immigration policy-making through the establishment of single or multiple corporate-wide units to manage the aspects of the city's role. Some smaller cities and communities across the country, as well as suburbs in Canada's largest cities, have developed more limited capacity in this area. Paquet and Joy's (2022) work on sanctuary cities suggests that they are more common in large (and core) cities although the City of Ajax (a suburban municipality in the Greater Toronto Area) is among the seven cities that they found had adopted sanctuary policies. Given that many immigrants settle directly in suburbs, the variation in Canada's major metropolitan areas is particularly pertinent.

It is interesting that municipalities within the same metropolitan area vary not only in their level of activity but also in the ideational paradigms used to frame their role in immigration. For instance, whereas Montreal has pursued a mainly "intercultural" approach, Laval shifted (in its communications, the adaption of its functions, and in its approach to social relations) from a multicultural to a "republican" approach (essentially an assimilationist approach characterized by an undifferentiated model of local citizenship) in the 1990s after a public engagement process identified community concerns about immigrant integration (Fourot 2013). Highlighting once again the importance of strong leadership, Laval was able to resist the representation of ethnocultural minority interests in favour of an undifferentiated model of local belonging because of the level of political-administrative concentration of power in the mayor (Fourot 2013, 125).

In Toronto, suburbs such as the City of Mississauga and the City of Brampton were largely inactive in 2009 (Good 2009). In contrast, the City of Markham developed a role in "race relations" in part due to controversies that arose in the mid-1990s when a former deputy mayor (Carole Bell) criticized the concentration of Chinese immigrants in the community. Although discussion of what could be characterized as an anti-immigrant politics in Canadian suburbs did not make national headlines, anti-immigration debates emerged in suburbs such as Markham, Ontario, and Richmond, British Columbia, where a single immigrant group concentrated in large numbers. Debates in these Canadian "ethnoburbs" centred on such issues as the language of signage on private businesses and the emergence of Asian-style mall developments. In Richmond, controversy about such issues led to an explicit rejection of the principle of "multiculturalism," which was perceived as emphasizing differences among groups, in favour of a focus on interculturalism, which community members considered to be about creating bridges between groups. However, in many ways the debate was about the "majority" community reasserting cultural and linguistic dominance in the face of becoming a "minority." These policy debates involved reasserting the prominence of English in the communities and are examples of grassroots reactions to the fast-paced and significant demographic changes that are common to many cities across the globe. These reactions were amplified in places like Richmond because some members of the immigrant "minority" had extensive economic power to change the face of local development, and large immigrant numbers led to the "minority" communities becoming the majority (Good 2009). Canadian municipalities such as Richmond and Markham share similarities with American "ethnoburbs" with a concentration of Chinese immigrants in places such as Greater Los Angeles (Li 1999).

In Greater Moncton, immigration policy-making intersects with long-standing divisions among francophones and anglophones in the city and province. These divisions are reflected in and possibly reinforced by the municipal system, which consists of three municipalities with very different linguistic profiles (Good 2013). Although a LIP has been established across the metropolitan area, Francophones established their own separate settlement agency and developed new modes of immigrant integration to address the unique challenges of integrating immigrants into a minority linguistic community (Good 2013). There are ongoing debates about whether francophones' cultural-linguistic concerns and strategic interests in growing their community through immigration are best served by common or separate institutions (Good 2013). The long-standing ethno-linguistic configuration of a municipality and metropolitan community matters to how immigrants are received and integrated and to whether community tensions arise.

International Comparisons

AMERICAN CITIES' LOCAL IMMIGRATION POLICIES

In the United States, New York and Los Angeles are the leading "multicultural cities" based on an analysis of both formal policy-making and governance practices (Qadeer 2016). Services in New York have been available in languages other than English on an ad hoc basis for a long time (rather than as a matter of formal policy) (Qadeer 2016). However, in 2003, Local Law 73 was passed, requiring the Human Resources Administration agency[3] to provide translation and interpretation service in five languages (Qadeer 2016). This local legal regime was extended city-wide in 2008 with Mayor Bloomberg's executive order number 120 (Qadeer 2016). Under the order, city agencies must establish a position of "language access coordinator" to develop and implement access policies. The city also has a Language Access Services program that provides translation and interpretation in six languages costing the city almost US$27 million per year (Qadeer 2016). Los Angeles provides this service through its Language and Culture Resource Center (Qadeer 2016). New York has an extensive municipal administrative infrastructure to support its multicultural goals, including an employment equity policy and an Office of Immigrant Affairs that works on service access and provides training to immigrant entrepreneurs and leaders (Qadeer 2016).

We also see evidence of multicultural modes of governance in many other American cities and their spread to new locales in recent decades. For instance, Immigrant Affairs Offices (IAOs) have spread across the United States in recent decades (De Graauw 2019). New York City's office, which was created in 1984, is the oldest and most well-resourced with over *fifty full-time employees* (De Graauw 2019, 170). Such offices proliferated after 2000, following a period of strong growth in immigration levels to cities, the rapidly changing demographics in these places, and the federal government's failure to achieve comprehensive immigration policy reform (169). In 2016, there were forty-two formal offices dedicated to immigrant affairs in thirty-nine cities in the United States (170). These offices exist in a variety of cities of different sizes and with different migration histories, such as Boston, Chicago, Los Angeles, New York City, and San Francisco, which all have long histories of migration, and newer immigration destinations, such as Atlanta, Nashville, Orlando, and Washington, DC, as well as "re-emerging destinations," such as Baltimore, Buffalo, Denver, Detroit, Portland, and Philadelphia (170). The majority were created after 2005 in cities with lower-than-average national rates of immigration (13 per cent) and functioned with limited resources, typically one or two staff and, therefore, were not as institutionalized as New York City's office (170).

What do these offices do? According to De Graauw (2019), IAOs tend to share common objectives: to create a welcoming environment, make the economic case for immigration, coordinate initiatives across departments, and engage with immigrants in the community. They do this through convening groups and supporting immigration leadership development and organizations. Citing San Francisco, Washington, DC, Houston, and New York City as examples, De Graauw (2019) notes that in the country's largest cities and most significant immigrant destinations, IAOs develop and implement the city's own immigrant integration policies. These include, for instance, language access policies and the municipal ID card legislation discussed below.

Although sanctuary policies have spread internationally, the movement emerged and is strongest in the United States. "Dozens" of American cities have declared themselves to be "sanctuary" cities in the United States (Bauder 2016, 176). The focus began on refugees, but following the mobilization of the faith-based New Sanctuary Movement, it shifted to migrants who have lived for an extended period in the United States and have an established life there (176). Among the signature policies that American sanctuary cities adopt is the "don't ask, don't tell" policy, which "typically prohibit[s] municipal police forces and city service agencies from requesting, recording, or disseminating status information, and den[ies] co-operation with federal immigration authorities unless required by federal or state law" (176). A second signature policy involves providing access to city services through initiatives such as municipal ID programs. San Francisco and New York City have created their own "municipal ID" programs, and many midsized cities in the United States accept the Mexican matricula consular as a form of identification to access city services (De Graauw 2014; Williamson 2019).

Local immigration policies and multicultural initiatives are therefore common in major cities in the United States. What about smaller communities and suburbs? The failure of the federal government to address immigration in a comprehensive way and the problem of undocumented migration in particular have led states and cities (particularly suburbs) to respond with their own policy initiatives. Some such initiatives attempt to "control" local immigration through municipal ordinances. In his *Suburban Crossroads*, Thomas Vicino (2012) studies three of the first suburban "cities" (in terms of their legal status) to address this issue through local legislation – Carpentersville, a bedroom suburb of Chicago, Farmer's Branch, an inner-ring suburb of Dallas, and Hazelton, Pennsylvania, located ninety miles north of downtown Philadelphia. The metropolitan dimension of immigrant policies and politics is increasingly important with pro- and anti-immigrant measures coexisting in major metropolitan areas in the United States.

Anti-immigration policies in American suburbs illustrate how cities' legal authority can be used to create an immigration policy that attempts to "control" immigration in a context of open borders. These "resources" include, for instance, the responsibility for regulating housing and housing codes, the power to impose fines on businesses, and municipalities' role in policing. In Farmer's Branch, three ordinances (including two amendments to an original one) passed unanimously between 2006 and 2008 in response to an increase in the Latino population and the racialized conflict that ensued (Vicino 2012, 56). The first ordinance, Ordinance 2892, "was a comprehensive local law that sought to prohibit landlords from renting to illegal immigrants; declared English as the city's official language; and authorized local police to collaborate with US Immigrant Customs Enforcement (ICE) to detain and remove illegal immigrants from the city" (56). An amendment requiring landlords to verify the legal status of tenants was then enacted through a referendum vote (with 68 per cent support), and in 2007, the city was given responsibility for checking tenants' residency status in single and multi-family dwellings (table 4.5, 82). In 2006, a motion was passed declaring English the official language of Farmer's Branch. Similarly, in Hazelton, the city council enacted the Illegal Immigration Relief Act in 2006 with near unanimous support (a four-to-one vote): this ordinance targeted businesses, landlords, and social service providers that worked with undocumented migrants by threatening to deny commercial licences and impose fines on landlords, as well as by declaring English the official language of the city (57). However, in this case, the ordinance was challenged in the courts and a stay was issued blocking its implementation (57). In 2007, the Village of Carpentersville introduced a bylaw that penalized employers who employed undocumented workers and "[harbored] illegal aliens in the Village of Carpentersville"; it also aimed to "provide for cooperative enforcement of federal immigration laws by the Village police department" (Village of Carpentersville Illegal Immigration Relief Ordinance quoted in Vicino 2012, 56). The bylaw was tabled amidst significant controversy and public debate and failed to be adopted (Vicino 2012, 56).

Although cases such as Carpentersville, Farmer's Branch, and Hazleton received a great deal of attention in American media, these cases are not representative of the broader trend toward accommodation of immigrants in American cities and suburbs. This is true both in large American cities and in the midsized immigrant destinations across the United States. What is probably the most comprehensive study of midsized American cities' local immigration policy-making found that they were mainly accommodating of immigrants, a trend first identified in case studies of Yakima, Washington; Elgin, Illinois; Wausau, Wisconsin; and Lewiston, Maine. This was confirmed by a survey of local government officials in 373 midsized immigrant destinations (Williamson 2019, 20–1). The study identifies an interesting pattern of anti-immigrant measures being enacted, challenged, and then followed by increased municipal inclusion of immigrants. Elgin's path illustrates this dynamic well. This city of 112,000, which is within a forty-five-minute drive of Chicago, experienced rapid growth in its Latino population in the mid-1990s. Given its proximity to Chicago, Elgin provides an interesting comparison with Carpentersville. In the case of Elgin, immigration policy goals were achieved through the municipality's role in housing code enforcement, legitimized by "widespread complaints from residents about overcrowded housing and related quality of life issues, which were attributed to the growth of the Latino population" and a house fire that killed a family living in a basement (Williamson 2019, 52). After complaints of housing discrimination were filed and settled by the city (without the city admitting guilt), a federal investigation was launched which found that "from 1995 to 1998, Hispanics occupied 20 per cent of rental units and constituted 8 per cent of homeowners yet received 64 per cent of the city's housing citations" (54) which, in turn, led to more complaints and settlements. After these episodes, the city not only ended these enforcement practices but also began proactive efforts to adapt municipal governance to its Latino population. For instance, it developed new systems of communication with Latinos, including the establishment of a Hispanic outreach worker, it initiated a "DiverCity" advertising campaign on the back of city buses, and it began providing support to Latino organizations and events such as "Fiesta Salsa" (Williamson 2019). The city experienced another period of restriction from 2008–11, which was then reversed (Williamson 2019). Williamson also found that Lewiston, Maine, and Wausau, Wisconsin, both midsize refugee destinations, also made efforts and devoted considerable resources to respond to the needs of their new immigrant populations (Williamson 2019, 63).

Immigrant-friendly, "multicultural" policies and practices are widespread in midsized American cities. These policies include having some sort of interpretation capacity, translation of documents, efforts to hire bilingual employees, and funding and in-kind support to immigrant organizations (Williamson 2019). Furthermore, anti-immigrant measures are rare: for instance, only 9 per cent of the midsized cities cooperate with the federal government to enforce immigration laws (123) and a staggering 81 per cent of police departments accept the Mexican matricula consular (a Mexican ID) as a form of identification to access city services (88). Most local anti-immigrant measures in the United States are introduced by stealth and indirectly (Varsanyi 2010a). This is done by enacting policies in other spheres of municipal activity to achieve an immigration control or anti-immigrant outcome. These measures include housing measures and anti-trespassing and solicitation ordinances that restrict the ability of day labours to gather in order to facilitate their ability to work informally. Backdoor housing initiatives are the most prevalent form of anti-immigrant policy in midsized cities. Williamson (2019, 76) cites hiring more enforcement officers to enforce housing codes, introducing strict measures regarding maximum occupancy and zoning for a narrow definition of "family" (by excluding extended family) as ways that municipalities pursue anti-immigrant goals by stealth in their housing policies. Still, Williamson (2019) finds that such initiatives were employed in a small minority of cases. An even smaller minority targeted day labourers in their policy efforts, with more municipalities actually funding day labour hiring centres (7 per cent) than creating policies preventing the gathering of day labourers (2 per cent) (Williamson 2019, 81). Thus, despite a nationally charged immigration debate and media attention given to anti-immigrant measures at the local level, the local immigration policy landscape in the United States tends toward accommodation and is generally progressive.

EUROPEAN CITIES: A MORE IDEOLOGICAL POLITICS OF LOCAL IMMIGRATION POLICY-MAKING?

There is a vast literature on the rise of local immigration policy-making in Europe. In light of the debate about shifts in approaches to immigrant integration and the rejection of multicultural paradigms on the continent, it is interesting to note the local variation that exists in many states as well as the widespread adoption of diversity-friendly policies that one might label "multicultural." One study finds the widespread adoption of "diversity" policies in Germany and France like efforts to diversify the local government through recruitment practices and diversity training, adapting services and service delivery to diversity (e.g., through translation of city documents), and symbolic efforts to recognize diversity (Martínez-Ariño et al. 2019). They argue that there is a convergence across German and French cities with respect to the accommodation of diversity (657–8). The diversification of public libraries is a particularly common intervention (three-quarters of cities have adapted libraries to diversity) (658). Importantly, a sizable number of cities have even established separate offices of support for claims of discrimination (more than one-third in France and just under one-third in Germany) (659). It is also notable though that translation of city documents is common in Germany but rare in France (659).

The fact that local multicultural modes of governance exist in states such as the Netherlands and France is particularly remarkable. The Netherlands and France could be considered "crucial" and "least likely" cases (Eckstein 1975), given that one would not expect multicultural policies and modes of practice to be prevalent in cities in the national contexts of strong civic integration policies.

Nevertheless, multicultural policies and modes of governance continue in places like Amsterdam and Rotterdam. Caelesta Poppelaars and Peter Scholten (2008) have suggested that Dutch local governments are more pragmatic in their policy efforts than central governments, continuing to employ multicultural practices despite a shift in national policy toward an (undifferentiated) "citizenship" approach (a variant of what we call "civic universalism" above).

Maria Schiller (2015) argues that a new paradigm has emerged in Europe – the "diversity paradigm" – which is more individualistic and intersectional than the multicultural approaches taken in the past. Nevertheless, she also finds that diversity officers in cities in the Netherlands are pragmatic (including Amsterdam). They are aware of a variety of policy paradigms – including "diversity," "multiculturalism," and "assimilation" – and the tensions among these policies' ideological bases and with national policy. Nevertheless, they chose to draw from them pragmatically to meet the needs of immigrants and to address the diversity of their populations. However, Schiller shows that there are costs to municipalities' "paradigmatic pragmatism" – it creates tensions and uncertainty about how to implement policies and some anxiety among municipal staff, who must navigate these contradictions (Schiller 2015). For instance, as highly individualistic approaches, the assimilationist and diversity paradigms are in tension with a "multicultural" approach that focuses on state recognition and support for the *cultural difference of groups* and that addresses inequalities at the group level (Schiller 2015).

It is therefore notable that there is evidence that some French cities not only adopt individualist diversity policies and anti-discrimination measures (like the anti-discrimination offices mentioned above) but that some also pursue group-based multicultural policies. The City of Marseille is one such example although it may be exceptional in the extent of its multicultural approach. It is credited to former left-wing mayor Robert-Paul Vigouroux (1986–95), who initiated "Marseille Esperance" in 1990 – a city-led initiative to bring religious leaders together at times of conflict or local or national crisis (Moutselos 2020, 7). In 2001, Marseille was the only city in France to have established a department to oversee ethnic relations (Moore 2001, cited in Mitchell 2011, 417). A multicultural approach was continued under the leadership of the right-of-centre mayor Jean-Claude Gaudin (1995–2020) that followed Vigouroux (Moutselos 2020).

"Sanctuary policies" have also emerged in Europe. Like multicultural practices, these policies are largely adopted for pragmatic reasons although some municipalities, such as Barcelona, link them to a rights-based discourse (Marscareñas and Eitel 2019). Pragmatic "sanctuary" policies are reflected in the Netherlands, such as Rotterdam's decision to offer health coverage to undocumented migrants to mitigate public health problems (for instance through coverage of vaccinations) (Marscareñas and Eitel 2019). Rotterdam and Amsterdam have also offered housing to the most vulnerable refugees on a pragmatic basis (Marscareñas and Eitel 2019).

The United Kingdom's "sanctuary" policies do not include the standard (American) policy stance against enforcing national immigration laws (including "don't ask don't tell" policies) and the creation of municipal forms of identification to access services. Instead, they focus on creating welcoming communities for refugees through discursive means rather than the legal aspects of "sanctuary" (Bauder 2016). Sheffield was the first city to be officially named a "City of Sanctuary" in 2007, a status that would then spread across cities and towns in the United Kingdom and Ireland (177). Sanctuary policies in such contexts are about image building (Marscareñas and Eitel 2019).

According to Marscareñas and Eitel (2019), a variety of initiatives to address the needs of refugees emerged when over a million asylum seekers arrived in Europe in 2015 during the "refugee crisis," and many Italian cities responded by developing policies to assist these populations even as a transition or emergency response. In Berlin, the local government took on a role in coordinating efforts that sprung up from the grassroots (Marscareñas and Eitel 2019). Other cities pursued advocacy strategies: Palermo and Naples in Italy criticized the state for its position against maritime rescue whereas others such as Barcelona and Valencia advocated for the opening of their ports to asylum seekers (Marscareñas and Eitel 2019).

A BRIEF NOTE ON LOCAL IMMIGRATION POLICY-MAKING IN THE GLOBAL SOUTH

Although the focus of this chapter has been on local immigration policies in North American and European cities, it is worth noting that 85 per cent of the world's displaced persons reside in countries in the Global South (Marscareñas and Eitel 2019). It is therefore unsurprising that cities in the Global South are also innovating in local immigration policy-making. One study mentions that the Turkish city of Gaziantep, which is near the Syrian border, has become a model for newcomer integration, giving access to a variety of services, including health and education, organizing language instruction, and providing employment assistance (Marscareñas and Eitel 2019). The same study cites Jakarta, Indonesia, as a city that defies the country's policy against allowing refugees to work by also providing language training, access to education, and assistance to find employment (Marscareñas and Eitel 2019). Cities such as Quilicura, which is in the Santiago metropolitan region in Chile, have adopted sanctuary-like policies, including official commitments to provide access to services to all residents regardless of status and celebrations of diversity like "Migrant Fest," which encourages a diverse city identity (Bauder and Gonzalez 2018, 128).

COMPARING LOCAL IMMIGRATION POLICY-MAKING: SOME LESSONS

Leadership Matters

There is evidence that mayoral leadership is important to understanding why municipalities adopt local immigration and diversity policies. Mayors can be important catalysts of change toward diversity policies but can also serve as a form of resistance to change. In Canada, this is evident in Montreal, where the departure of Jean Drapeau (1960–86), coupled with both the election of the Montreal Citizens Movement (MCM) and pressure from civil society groups, led to the emergence of Montreal's intercultural approach (Fourot 2013, 91). In yet another example, the long-standing mayor of Canada's largest suburb (Mississauga), Hazel McCallion (1978–2014), stood against multicultural policy approaches, which has been cited as a reason why Canada's largest suburb failed to adapt its services and governance structures to a dramatic shift in its ethnic composition due to immigration (Good 2009).

The literature on local immigration policies finds that immigrant-friendly policy is more likely in places governed by a left-wing party (De Graauw and Vermeulen 2016). However, this pattern is far from uniform. As we saw above, the multicultural policies of a socialist French mayor of Marseille were continued when a right-wing mayor took over. In Vancouver, parties on both the left and right have supported the city's role in multicultural policy (Good 2009).

Williamson (2019) also finds that immigrant-friendly policies are common not only in Democratic cities but in historically Republican places (in elections at other levels). She argues that the non-partisan reform institutions (council-manager forms of government with weak mayors) employed in many midsized American cities "insulate" cities from partisan politics at other levels, leading even "Republican" cities (and suburbs) to support pro-immigration measures at the city level (Williamson 2019, 19). Nevertheless, other studies note that mayors in mayor-council systems (cities in which the mayor holds executive power, discussed in chapter 7) tend to establish IAOs at higher rates than in council-manager forms of government (De Graauw 2019, 170–1). This suggests that local immigration policy-making is common in American cities regardless of institutions. However, a particularly resource-intensive and visible agency such as an immigrant affairs office is more likely with a more powerful mayor.

The Political Economy of Local Immigration Policy-Making

There is also evidence to suggest that local leaders' choices are shaped by economic and external incentives that are unique to the local level. According to Paul Peterson's (1981) city limits thesis (discussed in chapter 3), municipalities are limited in their authority and must compete for residents and businesses with other cities, which predisposes local leaders to "developmental" policies. Immigration is not simply a "policy field"; it is also a flow that is driving urban growth and economic development. Thus, immigration is intimately tied with growth politics.

Research on local immigration policy-making in Canada also ties such policies to a "growth" agenda and underscores the importance of the business community's support to a municipality's decision to engage in developing such policies (Good 2009). In Canada, national immigration policy discourses portray immigration as the solution to a variety of policy challenges like demographic aging and stress its economic benefits (Hiebert 2006), leading cities of all sizes to compete for immigrants and engage in local policy-making regardless of the number of immigrants in their populations. Cities in Atlantic Canada, a relatively low-immigration region by Canadian standards, have made efforts to attract and retain immigrants (Good 2013). Toronto has also made efforts to attract and retain immigrants (not only to integrate them), and the business community contributes actively to successful immigrant settlement (Good 2009). For instance, business executives in Manulife Financial provided leadership in integrating immigrants into the local workforce in Toronto through a multi-sectoral and regional urban alliance called the Toronto Region Immigrant Employment Council (Good 2009). Somewhat cynically, one could even argue that the true motivation behind immigrant-friendly local immigration policies, including multicultural policies, is to facilitate capitalist accumulation through growth. In fact, in a thought-provoking article, Katharyne Mitchell (1993) argues that Canada's national discourse of "multiculturalism" serves to facilitate the free flow of capital investment in Vancouver by discrediting legitimate political debate about the nature of growth politics in the city, labelling all dissent as racist. Similarly, Paquet and Joy (2022) link Canada's sanctuary policies to an urban competitiveness agenda and the desire of municipalities to signal that they are inclusive.

The leadership and support of the business community also matter in the United States in cities of different sizes. There is a strong correlation between economic growth in metropolitan areas and immigration in the United States (Mollenkopf and Pastor 2019). If business leaders and organizations believe that immigration is important to the local economy, they can play an important role in counteracting anti-immigrant political actors (Mollenkopf and Pastor 2019). Former New York City Mayor Bloomberg's leadership and engagement with business is an important example of this, but this is true more broadly (Mollenkopf and Pastor 2019).

Like in Canada, there are both economic and legal incentives that work toward creating an immigrant-friendly local governance in American cities. Following urban regime theorists (see Stone 1989), Williamson notes that "alliances with businesses that value immigrant labor make [policy] frames emphasizing immigrant economic contributions more accessible and resonant" in midsized American cities (2019, 19), contributing to a policy environment that is more conducive to immigrant-friendly policies. Although residents of a city or the "mass public" may prefer restrictive policies, the ability of elites (including business elites) to mobilize around a pro-immigration agenda leads to a tendency toward such policies, what noted immigration scholar Gary Freeman has called an "expansionary" bias in immigration policy (Freeman 1995, cited in Williamson 2019, 19). Cities are interdependent places, providing incentives for all elites to maintain social order through policy-making that is socially sustainable and to facilitate growth of the city's population and labour pool. Consistent with this theory, Williamson (2019) finds that a pro-immigrant consensus exists among political elites, municipal staff (including city managers), and police chiefs in midsized American cities even though some studies have shown that municipal staff are more likely than political leaders to be responsive to immigrants. Local leaders are also concerned about negative media attention and being labelled "racist" (Williamson 2019). This could also be because such an image could hinder future municipal growth and economic development. Anti-immigrant politics is bad for a city's future development prospects.

There is also evidence that business support of immigration initiatives matters in the European context and that a political economy approach is warranted in understanding what facilitates harmonious ethnocultural relations in cities of immigration. For instance, in Marseille, networks in the business community are more diverse than in Paris, and this is associated with greater support for multicultural policies (Mitchell 2011). The rise of a "diversity" or "diversity management" policy paradigm could also reflect a connection between furthering capitalist development and business interests because this concept emerged in business management literature (Schiller 2016; Abu-Laban and Gabriel 2002). Diversity in these paradigms is conceptualized in a marketized way – as "profitable" (Schiller 2016, loc. 3483).

Demographics and Ethno-racial Configurations

There is evidence that demographics and demographic change matter to local immigration policy-making. Demographics matter in a lot of different ways. The number of immigrants in the municipal population and the municipality's history with immigration matter in terms of whether immigration policies are developed and the types of policies pursued. The earliest adopters of local immigration policy, like Toronto and New York City, have had significant immigrant populations for decades; however, before the 1960s Toronto was homogeneous compared to other major cities in Canada, and despite its size it had a large British Protestant population (Doucet 1999, 12).

The composition of the immigrant population matters as well. For instance, in Canada, municipalities with bifurcated or "biracial" ethnic configurations (municipalities in which a single immigrant group and racialized minority predominates) have produced social conflict and triggering events that pushed the issue of ethnic relations onto the municipal agenda (Good 2005). In Canadian suburbs in Greater Toronto and Greater Vancouver, community backlash is common due to a sense of cultural threat among long-standing residents (Good 2005). Relatedly, there is a tendency to focus on interculturalism objectives (in some cases framed as "race relations") that focus on the English language as a common reference point and to reject a focus on "multiculturalism," which is perceived to emphasize difference (Good 2005). The ethnic configuration also tends to shape the distribution of resources in the community and the complexity of the collective action problem (how difficult it is for minority communities to mobilize for political action). Resources tend to be more concentrated in immigrant communities in ethno-racially bifurcated communities than in municipalities that are more diverse.

In Vancouver and Richmond, the perceived cultural threat of large number of immigrants from China was amplified by the fact that Vancouver has received many of Canada's wealthy business immigrants, whom geographer David Ley (2010) calls "millionaire migrants." In the 1990s, the community dynamics of backlash and controversy around immigration in suburbs such as Richmond and Markham, where large "Chinese" immigrant populations settled in relatively short periods of time, were remarkably similar (Good 2009). The experience of these suburbs is similar to Chinese "ethnoburbs" in the United States, a term developed by geographer Wei Li (1999) based on her study of Monterey Park, California. Ethnoburbs describe concentrations of ethnic groups that, unlike ethnic "ghettos" or "enclaves," are deliberately created by immigrants with economic power. "Ethnoburbs" are common in multicultural cities in the United States and Canada but also across the globe, including in countries in the Global South (Yu and Li 2014).

The American experience also suggests that social conflict and anti-immigrant policymaking (in some cases) are common when there is a sudden influx of a single group of immigrants or refugees in suburbs. Nevertheless, this relationship holds even if the immigrant community is not economically powerful. The "cultural" threat appears to suffice to engender a reaction. We see evidence of this in a wide variety of suburbs in the United States, such as in Carpentersville, Farmer's Branch, and Hazleton, where an influx of Hispanics triggered the emergence of anti-immigrant policy-making (Vicino 2012). A rise in the Latino population was also a precipitating factor in Elgin (Williamson 2019). Lewiston had a similar experience of social and political conflict when a large number of Somali refugees flocked to the community (Williamson 2019).

There are interesting similarities in the policy dynamics in suburbs in Canada and the United States. One notable similarity is that social conflict tends to lead to more action to integrate and include immigrants in the suburbs in question. This is true of Richmond and Markham in Canada and describes the dynamic in Elgin and Lewiston in the United States. In Markham, a community-wide debate about immigration and "race relations" emerged when then deputy mayor Carole Bell criticized the concentration of Chinese immigrants publicly (Good 2009). This triggering event is similar to Lewiston's, which involved a letter written by the then mayor Laurier Raymond asking Somalis to "slow their migration to the 'maxed-out' city" (Williamson 2019, 42). Ultimately, such anti-immigrant episodes have led to a more responsive municipality. These examples also show the important role of political leadership in these conflicts – sometimes as instigators of anti-immigrant rhetoric and policies.

There is evidence that local immigration policies vary depending on the immigration rate, with smaller Canadian cities with low immigration rates pursuing more proactive ways of attracting and retaining immigrants than the larger centres. For instance, in Halifax, Nova Scotia, and Moncton, New Brunswick, economic development agencies have been prominent actors in local immigration politics (Good 2013). These examples also speak to the importance of the business community and to the economic development framing of immigration in many locales.

Also, although different forms of diversity are governed "separately" and in different departmental "silos" at the federal and provincial scales, the governance of immigration and the diversity that it engenders intersect with other forms of diversity, including the interests and identities of Canada's national minorities, in different ways depending on city demographics (Good, Turgeon, and Tridafilopoulos 2014). For instance, francophone minorities outside of Quebec have begun to develop local immigration strategies in cities across the country, such as in Moncton, where a large and growing population of Acadians reside (Good 2013). Similarly, Winnipeg appears to be a leader in decolonizing local immigration policy-making, which may be influenced by its large Indigenous population and numerous Indigenous community organizations, such as KNK, discussed above. The concentration of Indigenous and immigrant youth in North End Winnipeg and the social conflict that ensued led Indigenous community organizations to take a lead role in local immigration governance (Gyepi-Garbrah, Walker, and Garcea 2014). With strong co-leadership from the Indigenous community, IPW has also been a highly innovative actor in efforts to decolonize local immigration policy-making (Good 2021). These examples also suggest the importance of demographics to understanding local immigration policy-making.

British immigration scholar Steven Vertovec coined the term "superdiversity" to describe the complexity of migrant diversity in London (Vertovec 2007). However, superdiversity is not the norm in cities in Canada or abroad. Rather, the extent and types of diversity – whether migrant, multinational, or Indigenous – vary significantly and in ways that influence the way that immigration is discussed and governed.

The Intergovernmental System and Multilevel Governance

The variation that exists in local immigration policy-making in countries around the globe suggests that the intergovernmental system and national constitutions do not determine how local immigration policies are made. There is wide variation in local immigration policies within countries, and it is clear that many local leaders are innovating in this field in the absence of leadership from other orders of government – sometimes even in defiance of their policies. Clearly a "top-down" institutional perspective is inadequate to understand these developments. In Canada and the United States, this means moving beyond a concept of municipalities as "creatures of the provinces/states" and toward a more meaningful account of municipal agency.

The intergovernmental and constitutional system as well as a country's policy context should be seen as a multilevel "infrastructure" of resources upon which local leaders can draw when they choose to create local immigration policies and as incentive structures for particular responses (Sellers 2005). For instance, Canada's federal settlement programs provide material resources to local actors in cities to facilitate immigrant integration and can strengthen those organizations' ability to contribute to local immigration policy-making. Official multiculturalism in Canada also provides "symbolic" resources to local actors engaged in progressive local immigration policy-making by framing diversity as part of Canada's national identity (Bloemraad 2006). Some stress the importance of Canada's official multiculturalism at the federal level in relation to the United States, noting that Canada offers funding for immigrant settlement whereas the American federal government only funds refugee settlement (Bloemraad 2006). Irene Bloemraad (2006) also argues that Canada's multicultural policies elevate the status of immigrants, and the United States "race-based" multiculturalism makes it more difficult for immigrants to integrate. However, this same infrastructure contributes to downplaying the grassroots reality of anti-Black racism in Canadian cities, which affects both historic and immigrant Black communities' integration and equality and leads to the erasure of Indigenous difference. Furthermore, as we have seen, the United States' civil rights infrastructure provides strong incentives to municipalities to adopt what are essentially multicultural policies. These policies are backed up by the possibility of administrative sanction and lawsuits if the requirements of civil rights legislation are not met through policy actions such as translations or if discriminatory housing laws and practices are enacted. Evidence of the influence of this civil rights legislation is widespread in midsized American cities like Elgin (discussed above). However, it has also played a crucial role in New York City's local immigration policy-making. Both Local Law 73 and Executive Order 120 were the result of sustained activism on the part of immigrant rights organizations, which included civil-rights-based lawsuits as a strategy (De Graauw, Gordon and Mollenkopf 2019). For instance, a coalition of community organizations such as NYIC and grassroots organizations such as Make the Road New York targeted municipal, federal, and judicial officials in order to have Local Law 73 passed, which was the strongest legislation of its kind in the United States before the enactment of Executive Order 120 (de Graauw, Gordon, and Mollenkopf 2019, loc. 1062). Indeed, even Bloomberg's Executive Order 120 was a pre-emptive response to strong advocacy and fear that a more expensive and constraining legislative requirement could be imposed on New York City (de Graauw, Gordon, and Mollenkopf 2019, loc. 1093). Local community leaders continue to push for an extension of this policy to city-based pharmacies (loc. 1093). This shows how cities' authority in areas such as regulating business can be crucial to multicultural policy-making.

In the United States, an important part of the "multilevel" infrastructure are national organizations and coalitions of cities: for example, Welcome America, a non-profit organization that works with other non-profits and municipalities across the United States, more general coalitions such as Cities for Action (that brings together mayors and leaders from county governments), and regular national meetings of municipalities. Indeed, 76 per cent of cities with IAOs in 2016 were members of Cities for Action (De Graauw 2019, 171). Although a similar survey does not exist in Canada, the Federation of Canadian Municipalities in general, including the Big City Mayors' Caucus, also plays a significant role in the diffusion of policy ideas in the local immigration policy realm. Furthermore, federally funded LIPs and national conferences evaluating them play a role in policy idea sharing. The Pathways for Prosperity alliance of universities, community organizations, and government partners dedicated to creating more inclusive communities for immigrants is an important actor in this respect.

As we saw above, cities in the Netherlands and France are not following national immigrant integration models even when their role in immigrant integration has been explicitly delegated to them by "upper" levels of government. Some work presents local diversity officers in Amsterdam as struggling with the dissonance between the multicultural policy frameworks that still make sense in cities where ethnocultural groups continue to organize as groups and the direction from the national government to move toward "civic integration" (Schiller 2015). In France, some have noted that multicultural policies and practices are adopted by stealth, "camouflaged through a language of interest in specific 'sensitive' neighbourhoods or religions" (Mitchell 2011, 416), for instance. In Marseille, "the city's politicians thus quote the ideals of secularism but generally practice a form of multiculturalism" (Mitchell 2011, 417). This example suggests a pragmatism among local policy-makers that may characterize local policy-making more generally.

Local Organizations, Local Resources, and Metropolitan Governance

Cities also vary in the extent to which they have resources to address the question of immigrant integration. And, although there are few studies of the urban governance of local immigration, they also vary in their governance relationships. Resources exist in a variety of places such as municipal administrations and non-profit organizations in cities. There is also increasing evidence that business leaders are important actors in local immigration policy-making.

Immigrant-servicing organizations play an especially important role in providing settlement support to and advocating for immigrants. These community resources are unequally distributed across cities and within city regions, which offers some insight into why some municipalities are more active in immigration policy-making than others.

In Canada, the federal government funds immigrant settlement organizations to offer settlement services that are often concentrated in the core cities of the country's most significant immigrant-receiving destinations – Toronto and Vancouver (Montreal's settlement funds come primarily from the province of Quebec). Furthermore, there is significant variation within metropolitan areas in the resources available for settlement and advocacy on immigration issues in Canadian cities. These differences also shape the possibilities for governance relationships in cities and across metropolitan areas (Good 2009).

In the United States, the federal government only provides settlement services to refugees. A comparative study of Ottawa and Newark links Canada's national immigrant settlement infrastructure to the sector's greater level of coherence in its focus, such as the kinds of services that immigrant organizations offer, and to the sector's relationship with government (Sidney 2014, 127). Even though a federally funded "settlement sector" is absent in the United States, there is a variety of other types of community-based organizations with different resources to contribute to the governance of immigration in American cities. Indeed, de Graauw and Vermeulen (2016) identify left-wing governments, a large share of immigrants in the local electorate, their integration into decision-making structures, and the presence of *community infrastructures* to advocate for immigrants in local policy-making as crucial factors explaining local efforts to integrate immigrants in the United States and Europe (De Graauw and Vermeulen 2016). However, like in Canada, these organizations are concentrated in the urban cores of major cities, and there is a general lack of metropolitan co-operation around immigration issues (Mollenkopf and Pastor 2019).

Local Institutions and Institutionalization

Another global trend but also a source of variation in cities is in the development of institutions to support and "steer" the municipal role in immigration policy through the widespread emergence of "immigrant affairs" offices in both Canada and the United States. In Canada, some such offices emerged independently of other orders of government, and they have proliferated recently with federal funding for LIPs, many of which are housed in municipalities. Even Marseille has a department responsible for ethnic relations.

As we discussed in chapter 3, Jon Pierre (2011) offers two definitions of institutions. In one sense, institutions provide "organizational continuity and define the range of choice and behaviour of the organization's members" (6). However, institutions are also informal: in this second sense they consist of "norms, values, rules and practices" (6). Thus, the fact that the responsibility for local immigration policy-making and addressing diversity has been institutionalized in municipalities reflects changing norms of local governance concerning its role and goals (Pierre 2011). Furthermore, how their role in immigration is institutionalized could also shed light on a city's priorities (Pierre 2011). In some cases, economic development agencies have taken a lead role in immigration policy-making, and in others a more corporate-wide and multi-pronged approach is evident. For instance, in Toronto, local immigration policy-making is tied to a decades-old infrastructure of multicultural and "access and equity" policies, whereas in other cities the "immigration function" is less integrated in the municipal institutional matrix. In Europe there is work that discusses evidence of local immigration policy mainstreaming across various departments (Scholten, Collett, and Petrovic 2016). However, to the extent that this is the case, it varies significantly across municipalities.

Municipal Pragmatism? The Role of Ideas in Local Immigration Policy-Making

A common theme in writings about local immigration policy-making is local actors' pragmatic orientation. This policy orientation holds on both sides of the Atlantic. Pragmatic reasons for developing immigrant-friendly policies include economic development objectives and concerns about maintaining public/social order. Studies of local immigration policy-making refer to a "logic of emergency" as a reason for supporting policies of refuge (Mayer 2018) and to cities as governments of "last instance" where "proximity to the politics of exclusion puts them in a peculiar position regarding access to and take-up of rights" (Gebhardt 2016, 850, cited in Mayer 2018, 234). We also see evidence of pragmatism in the strategic behaviour of local politicians (as well as strong leadership!) and other actors who support immigrant-friendly policy even in places with significant public backlash against immigration.

There is also evidence of pragmatism or ad hoc approaches to local policy-making in Canadian cities. In Canada, this takes the form of hybridity in terms of the ideological paradigms guiding municipal policy-makers, which suggests an awareness of and openness to different ideological approaches based on what is possible and perceived to work at the time.

The simplest explanation for municipal hybridity is that municipal policy-makers are adopting policies in an ad hoc and pragmatic fashion (and, essentially, layering them through time) rather than making considered decisions about the paradigms that they adopt.

The comparative literature on local immigration policy-making also suggests that immigration policies might be framed as "civic universalism" (i.e., as culturally or group neutral), not based on ideology but on a pragmatic decision designed to manage the mass public's reaction to the policies. For instance, the development of municipal IDs in San Francisco was presented as a policy directed at all residents of the city in order to sell it to the public (De Graauw 2014). Similarly, in France some local leaders continue to use republican rhetoric while embracing multicultural modes of governance in practice. This suggests that ideas may be less relevant as coherent policy paradigms and ought to be seen as more of a resource that local actors use strategically and in different ways to either frame their local policy efforts to include immigrants in politically palatable ways or to exclude immigrants.

CONCLUSION: THE GLOBAL RISE OF LOCAL IMMIGRATION POLICY-MAKING – A "MULTICULTURAL URBAN FUTURE"?

Both sub-national and international comparisons of Canadian cities' local immigration policy-making make it clear that local politics and leadership matter to local policy-making in Canada and abroad.

Overall, there is evidence that municipalities are capable of significant innovation in this field even in the absence of jurisdiction and the accompanying resources in this policy field. Municipalities are innovating in both immigrant-friendly and anti-immigrant policies with the clearest examples of formal policies in the "anti-immigrant" area coming from American "immigration relief" measures (Vicino 2012). Nevertheless, it is striking that there generally appear to be common incentives at the local level that lead to progressive local immigration policy-making for pragmatic reasons. Municipalities in large urban cores in major metropolitan areas typically have significant and diverse immigrant populations that provide political incentives to be responsive since doing so could mobilize a growing base of political support. More generally, a consensus around the desirability of growth tends to galvanize local elites (including the business community) in support of immigration policies to manage and facilitate economic development. Immigration is a "developmental" policy that facilitates growth by contributing to social cohesion and the attraction and retention of human capital and labour for business activity.

There are also unique features of municipal governments that provide incentives for pragmatic efforts to facilitate immigrant integration in progressive ways. Municipalities are close to the immediate needs of residents and the consequences of forces beyond their control, from inaction on pressing policy concerns to policy failure at other levels. This leads to action in areas regardless of jurisdiction and the use of their resources as well as those of allies to manage policy concerns as they arise.

In the area of immigration, flows of immigrants – whether wanted or not in local communities – are largely beyond local control. If the general public is against the changes in a community, local political officials could decide to respond with anti-immigrant measures, but many would recognize that the changes are irreversible and reason that integration makes the most practical sense to maintain a peaceful and socially sustainable community. They could also recognize that a racist municipal image could jeopardize future growth. Together, the pressing nature of urban and community-level policy challenges and these economic and political incentives create a tendency toward progressive local policy-making, even in places with right-wing or conservative leanings.

Another interesting observation is that multicultural modes of governance are widespread. In his comparative study of Toronto, New York City, and Los Angeles, urban planner Mohammad Qadeer (2016) takes an expansive view of "multicultural" cities in North America, noting that although some (namely Toronto) are "officially multicultural," others (namely New York City and Los Angeles, although the former has become increasingly multicultural in formal policy as well) are multicultural in practice. His conceptualization of the multicultural city encompasses the ways in which ethnocultural diversity is expressed in the three cities' geographic structures, forms of social organization, local economies, and political and "symbolic institutions" (Qadeer 2016, xv). He argues that when one examines the multicultural city in this fulsome way, it is apparent that multiculturalism is not only a formal policy but also a set of practices and processes that come "into existence as a lived reality with the accommodations of diversity" (Qadeer 2016, xvi). This statement alludes to a practical element in the development of such cities. To the extent that multicultural cities' forms of territorial (neighbourhood) and social organization involve organization into ethnocultural groups, either in a positive or negative way, it makes practical sense to address social inclusion, cohesion, or even citizen engagement by engaging with groups. If deep inequalities exist among groups and policy-makers choose to refuse to acknowledge those group-based differences, they risk social unrest.

Mitchell (2011) argues that Paris's failure to address "multicultural" challenges, namely the exclusion of racialized immigrants from power and space in the core city, is why urban riots have happened there. Marseille, which has embraced multicultural modes of governance, avoided urban riots because of its approach. Much more work needs to be done on understanding the outcomes of local immigration policy-making, from their effects on immigrant integration to equity among groups and social cohesion or sustainability.

One outcome worth exploring and disrupting is the extent to which multicultural policy frameworks contribute to the erasure of cities' Indigeneity. More research ought to be conducted in Canadian cities and in cities in other settler colonial contexts to explore Indigenous-newcomer relations and the role of Indigenous communities in local immigration policy, governance, and in welcoming newcomers.

Nevertheless, it is clear that municipalities have become key actors in what is one of the most important current global policy challenges – migration. Whether it is through efforts to address gaps in settlement services, to culturally adapt municipal services to migrants, or to challenge upper levels of governments' monopoly on determining who can legitimately claim the right to live and work on their soil, municipalities in Canada and abroad have taken some bold steps in an area of public policy that is fundamentally implicated in the spatial and economic restructuring of the globe. As such, it is not surprising that some tie municipalities' role in immigration to broader rescaling processes that could transform intergovernmental and, indeed, constitutional systems by empowering municipalities around the world (Good 2009; IOM 2018, 235).

NOTES

1   As noted by Statistics Canada, "Visible minority refers to whether a person is a visible minority or not, as defined by the Employment Equity Act. The Employment Equity Act defines visible minorities as 'persons, other than Aboriginal peoples, who are non-Caucasian in race or non-white in colour.' The visible minority population consists mainly of the following groups: South Asian, Chinese, Black, Filipino, Arab, Latin American, Southeast Asian, West Asian, Korean and Japanese" (Statistics Canada, n.d.).

2   Ontario's 2017 agreement also recognizes local government and commits to consult and cooperate with local government on immigrant settlement.

3   This agency administers important social services in New York City, including food stamps, Medicaid, and welfare.

REFERENCES

Abu-Laban, Yasmeen, and Christina Gabriel. 2002. *Selling Diversity: Immigration, Multiculturalism, Employment Equity, and Globalization.* Peterborough, ON: Broadview Press.

Ambrose, Emma, and Cas Mudde. 2015. "Canadian Multiculturalism and the Absence of the Far Right." *Nationalism and Ethnic Politics* 21, no. 2 (April): 213–36. https://doi.org/10.1080/13537113 .2015.1032033.

Banting, Keith, and Will Kymlicka. 2012. "Canadian Multiculturalism: Global Anxieties and Local Debates." *British Journal of Canadian Studies* 23, no. 1 (May): 43–72. https://doi.org/10.3828 /bjcs.2010.3.

———. 2013. "Is There Really a Retreat from Multiculturalism Policies? New Evidence from the Multicultural Policy Index." *Comparative European Politics* 11, no. 5 (September): 577–98. https:// doi.org/10.1057/cep.2013.12.

Bauder, Harald. 2017. "Sanctuary Cities Like Toronto Are Democracy's Last Stand." *Huff Post*, June 15, 2017. https://www.huffpost.com/archive/ca/entry/sanctuary-cities-like -toronto-are-democracys-last-stand_b_17102376.

Bauder, Harald, and Dayana A. Gonzalez. 2018. "Municipal Responses to 'Illegality': Urban Sanctuary across National Contexts." *Social Inclusion* 6, no. 1: 124–34. https://doi.org/10.17645/si.v6i1.1273.

Berinstein, Carolina, Jean McDonald, Peter Nyers, Cynthia Wright, and Sima Sahar Zerehi. 2006. *"Access not Fear": Non-Status Immigrants & City Services*. Toronto: Centre of Excellence for Research on Immigration and Settlement. https://we.riseup.net/assets/17034/Access%20Not%20Fear%20 Report%20(Feb%202006).pdf.

Biles, John, Annie Carroll, Radostina Pavlova, and Margaret Sokol. 2012. "Canada: Fostering an Integrated Society?" In *International Perspectives: Integration and Inclusion*, edited by James Frideres and John Biles, loc. 1794–2886 of 6749. Montreal: McGill-Queen's University Press. Kindle. https:// doi.org/10.1515/9781553395133-006.

Bloemraad, Irene. 2006. *Becoming a Citizen: Incorporating Immigrants and Refugees in the United States and Canada*. Oakland, CA: University of California Press. https://doi.org/10.1525/9780520940024.

Bloemraad, Irene, and Els de Graauw. 2012. "Immigrant Integration and Policy in the United States: A Loosely Stitched Patchwork." In *International Perspectives: Integration and Inclusion*, edited by James Frideres and John Biles, loc. 4546–5184 of 6749. Montreal: McGill-Queen's University Press. Kindle. https://doi.org/10.1515/9781553395133-012.

Bucklaschuk, Jill. 2016. *The IRCOM Model: Housing and Wrap-Around Supports for Newcomers in Winnipeg*. Winnipeg: Canadian Centre for Policy Alternatives (Manitoba). https://policyalternatives. ca/sites/default/files/uploads/publications/Manitoba%20Office/2016/11/The_IRCOM_Model.pdf.

Burr, Kathleen. 2011. "Local Immigration Partnerships: Building Welcoming and Inclusive Communities through Multi-Level Governance." *Horizons Policy Research Initiative*, February 2011. http://p2pcanada.ca/files/2011/10/Local-Immigration-Partnerships-Building-Welcoming-and- Inclusive-Communities.pdf.

Citizenship and Immigration Canada (CIC). 2014. *Local Immigration Partnerships: Outcomes 2008–2013*. Ottawa: Government of Canada. http://p2pcanada.ca/files/2014/07/Local -Immigration-Partnerships-Outcomes-2008-2013.pdf.

City of Toronto. n.d.-a. "Access to City Services for Undocumented Torontonians." Accessed June 18, 2024. https://www.toronto.ca/city-government/accountability-operations-customer-service /long-term-vision-plans-and-strategies/access-to-city-services-for-undocumented-torontonians/.

———. n.d.-b. "Social Procurement Program." Accessed February 18, 2024. https://www.toronto.ca /business-economy/doing-business-with-the-city/social-procurement-program/.

———. n.d.-c. *Toronto Action Plan to Confront Anti-Black Racism*. Toronto: City of Toronto. Accessed June 18, 2024. https://www.toronto.ca/legdocs/mmis/2017/ex/bgrd/backgroundfile-109127.pdf.

———. n.d.-d. "Translate." Accessed June 18, 2024. https://www.toronto.ca/home/translate/.

de Graauw, Els. 2014. "Municipal ID Cards for Undocumented Immigrants: Local Bureaucratic Membership in a Federal System." *Politics & Society* 42, no. 3 (September): 309–30. https://doi.org/10.1177/0032329214543256.

———. 2019. "City Immigrant Affairs Offices in the United States: Taking Control of Immigrant Integration." In *The Routledge Handbook of the Governance of Migration and Diversity in Cities*, edited by Tizianna Caponio, Peter Scholten, and Ricardo Zapata-Barrero, 216–27. Abington, UK: Routledge. https://doi.org/10.4324/9781351108478-17.

de Graauw, Els., Diana R. Gordon, and John Mollenkopf. 2019. "Immigrant Reception in the Fragmented Metropolis of New York." In *Unsettled Americans: Metropolitan Context and Civic Leadership for Immigrant Integration*, edited by John Mollenkopf and Manuel Pastor, loc. 834–1382 of 7844. Ithaca: Cornell University Press. Kindle.

de Graauw, Els, and Floris Vermeulen. 2016. "Cities and the Politics of Immigrant Integration: A Comparison of Berlin, Amsterdam, New York City, and San Francisco." *Journal of Ethnic and Migration Studies* 42, no. 6: 989–1012. https://doi.org/10.1080/1369183X.2015.1126089.

Doucet, Michael. 1999. "Toronto in Transition: Demographic Change in the Late Twentieth Century." CERIS working paper no. 6. May, 1999.

Eckstein, Harry. 1975. "Case Studies and Theory in Political Science." In *Handbook of Political Science: Political Science: Scope and Theory*, edited by Fred I. Greenstein and Nelson W. Polsby, 94–137. Boston: Addison-Wesley.

Filomeno, Felipe Amin. 2017. *Theories of Local Immigration Policy*. Cham, Switzerland: Palgrave Macmillan. https://doi.org/10.1007/978-3-319-45952-3.

Fourot, Aude-Claire. 2013. *L'intégration des immigrants : Cinquante ans d'action publique locale*. Montreal: Les Presses de l'Université de Montréal. https://doi.org/10.4000/books.pum.8665.

———. 2015. "'Bringing Cities Back In' to Canadian Political Science: Municipal Public Policy and Immigration." *Canadian Journal of Political Science* 48, no. 2 (June): 413–33. https://doi.org/10.1017/S0008423915000785.

Freeman, Gary P. 1995. "Modes of Immigration Policies in Liberal Democratic States." *The International Migration Review* 29, no. 4 (Winter): 881–902. https://doi.org/10.2307/2547729.

Garcea, Joseph. 2016. "The Resettlement of Syrian Refugees: The Positions and Roles of the Federation of Canadian Municipalities and its Members." *Canadian Ethnic Studies* 48, no. 3: 149–73. https://doi.org/10.1353/ces.2016.0030.

Gebhardt, Dirk. 2016. "Re-thinking Urban Citizenship from a Policy Perspective: The Case of Barcelona." *Citizenship Studies* 20, nos. 6–7: 846–66. https://doi.org/10.1080/13621025.2016.1191431.

Germain, Annick, and Martin Alain. 2009. "On the Virtues of Adhocracy: Managing Diversity in Metropolitan Montréal." In *Facing Cultural Diversity: Cities Under Stress*, edited by Alain-G. Gagnon, 105–22. Lyon: Presses universitaires de Lyon.

Ghorayshi, Parvin. 2010. "Diversity and Interculturalism: Learning from Winnipeg's Inner City." *Canadian Journal of Urban Research* 19, no. 1 (Summer): 89–104.

Green, Joyce. 2003. "Decolonization and Recolonization in Canada." In *Changing Canada: Political Economy as Transformation*, edited by Wallace Clement and Leah F. Vosko, 51–78. Montreal: McGill-Queen's University Press. https://doi.org/10.1515/9780773570993-005.

Good, Kristin. 2005. "Patterns of Politics in Canada's Immigrant-Receiving Cities and Suburbs: How Immigrant Settlement Patterns Shape the Municipal Role in Multiculturalism Policy." *Policy Studies* 26, nos. 3–4 (September): 261–89. https://doi.org/10.1080/01442870500198312.

———. 2009. *Municipalities and Multiculturalism: The Politics of Immigration in Toronto and Vancouver.* Toronto: University of Toronto Press. https://doi.org/10.3138/9781442690417.

———. 2013. "Governing Immigrant Attraction and Retention in Halifax and Moncton: Do Linguistic Divisions Impede Cooperation?" In *Canada: Methods and Perspectives on Canadian Politics,* edited by Luc Turgeon, Martin Papillon, Jennifer Wallner, and Stephen White, 292–316. Vancouver: UBC Press. https://doi.org/10.59962/9780774827867-014.

———. 2019. "Municipal Immigration Policymaking in Canadian Cities: The State of the Art." In *The Routledge Handbook of the Governance of Migration and Diversity in Cities,* edited by Tizianna Caponio, Peter Scholten, and Ricard Zapata-Barrero, 216–27. Abington, UK: Routledge. https://doi.org/10.4324/9781351108478-21.

———. 2021. "Decolonizing Local Immigration Policymaking in Canada? Exploring Indigenous Engagement in Local Immigration Partnerships." Paper presented at the Annual Conference of the Canadian Political Science Association, 7 June 2021.

Good, Kristin R., Luc Turgeon, and Triadafilos Triadafilopoulos. 2014. *Segmented Cities? How Urban Contexts Shape Ethnic and Nationalist Politics.* Vancouver: UBC Press. https://doi.org/10.59962/9780774825856.

Gyepi-Garbrah, John, Ryan Walker, and Joseph Garcea. 2014. "Indigeneity, Immigrant Newcomers and Interculturalism in Winnipeg, Canada." *Urban Studies* 51, no. 9 (July): 1795–811. https://doi.org/10.1177/0042098013502826.

Hiebert, Daniel. 2006. "Winning, Losing, and Still Playing the Game: The Political Economy of Immigration in Canada." *Tijdschrift voor Economische en Sociale Geografie* 97, no. 1 (February): 38–48. https://doi.org/10.1111/j.1467-9663.2006.00494.x.

International Organization for Migration (IOM). 2018. *World Migration Report 2018.* Geneva, Switzerland: International Organization for Migration. https://publications.iom.int/books/world-migration-report-2018.

Joppke, Christian. 2007. "Beyond National Models: Civic Integration Policies for Immigrants in Western Europe." *West European Politics* 30, no. 1 (January): 1–22. https://doi.org/10.1080/01402380601019613.

Knowles, Valerie. 2016. *Strangers at Our Gates: Canadian Immigration and Immigration Policy, 1540–2015.* 4th ed. Toronto: Dundurn Press. Kindle.

Ley, David. 2010. *Millionaire Migrants: Trans-Pacific Life Lines.* Chichester, West Sussex: Wiley-Blackwell. https://doi.org/10.1002/9781444319262.

Li, Wei. 1999. "Building Ethnoburbia: The Emergence and Manifestation of the Chinese Ethnoburb in Los Angeles' San Gabriel Valley." *Journal of Asian American Studies* 2, no. 1 (February): 1–28. https://doi.org/10.1353/jaas.1999.0009.

Marscareñas, Blanca Garcés, and Kristin Eitel. 2019. "Sanctuary Cities: A Global Perspective." Barcelona Centre of International Affairs, June 2019. Archived November 1, 2020, at the Wayback Machine. https://web.archive.org/web/20201101063853/https://www.cidob.org/en/articulos/anuario_internacional_cidob/2019/sanctuary_cities_a_global_perspective.

Martínez-Ariño, Julia, Michalis Moutselos, Karen Schönwälder, Christina Jacobs, Maria Schiller, and Alexandre Tandé. 2019. "Why Do Some Cities Adopt More Diversity Policies Than Others? A Study in France and Germany." *Comparative European Politics* 17, no. 5 (November): 651–72. https://doi.org/10.1057/s41295-018-0119-0.

Mayer, Margit. 2018. "Cities as Sites of Refuge and Resistance." *European and Regional Studies* 25, no. 3 (July): 232–49. https://doi.org/10.1177/0969776417729963.

McDonald, Jean. 2012. "Building a Sanctuary City: Municipal Migrant Rights in the City of Toronto." In *Citizenship, Migrant Activism and the Politics of Movement,* edited by Peter Nyers and Kim Rygiel, 129–45. London: Routledge.

Migration Policy Institute. n.d. "Comprehensive Immigration Reform." Accessed January 20, 2021. https://www.migrationpolicy.org/topics/comprehensive-immigration-reform.

Mitchell, Katharyne. 1993. "Multiculturalism, or the United Colours of Capitalism?" *Antipode* 25, no. 4 (October): 263–94. https://doi.org/10.1111/j.1467-8330.1993.tb00220.x.

———. 2011. "Marseille's Not For Burning: Comparative Networks of Integration and Exclusion in Two French Cities." *Annals of the Association of American Geographers* 101, no. 2 (January): 404–23. https://doi.org/10.1080/00045608.2010.545290.

Mollenkopf, John, and Manuel Pastor. 2019. "The Ethnic Mosaic: Immigrant Integration at the Metropolitan Scale." In *Unsettled American: Metropolitan Context and Civic Leadership for Immigrant Integration*, edited by John Mollenkopf and Manuel Pastor, loc. 82–399 of 7844. Ithaca: Cornell University Press. Kindle.

Moore, Damian. 2001. "Marseille: Institutional Links with Ethnic Minorities and the French Republican Model." In *Multicultural Policies and Modes of Citizenship in European Cities*, edited by Alisdair Rogers and Jean Tillie, 123–43. Aldershot, UK: Ashgate.

Moutselos, Michalis. 2020. "What Explains Diversity-Policy Adoption? Policy Entrepreneurs and Advocacy Coalitions in two French Cities." *Ethnic and Racial Studies* 43, no. 11: 2–21. https://doi.org/10.1080/01419870.2020.1751861.

Paquet, Mireille. 2019. *Province-Building and the Federalization of Immigration in Canada.* Toronto: University of Toronto Press. https://doi.org/10.3138/9781487513092.

Paquet, Mireille, and Meghan Joy. 2022. "Canadian Sanctuary Policies in Context." *Canadian Public Administration* 65, no. 4 (December): 629–46. https://doi.org/10.1111/capa.12485.

Peterson, Paul E. 1981. *City Limits.* Chicago: University of Chicago Press.

Pierre, Jon. 2011. *The Politics of Urban Governance.* London: Palgrave Macmillan.

Poirier, Christian. 2006. "Ethnocultural Diversity, Democracy, and International Relations in Canadian Cities." In *Canada: The State of the Federation 2004: Municipal-Federal-Provincial Relations in Canada*, edited by Robert Young and Christian Leuprecht, 201–20. Montreal: McGill-Queen's University Press.

Poppelaars, Caelesta, and Peter Scholten. 2008. "Two Worlds Apart: The Divergence of National and Local Immigrant Integration Policies in the Netherlands." *Administration & Society* 40, no. 4 (July): 335–57. https://doi.org/10.1177/0095399708317172.

Qadeer, Mohammad Abdul. 2016. *Multicultural Cities: Toronto, New York, and Los Angeles.* Toronto: University of Toronto Press.

Schiller, Maria. 2015. "Paradigmatic Pragmatism and the Politics of Diversity." *Ethnic and Racial Studies* 38, no. 7 (May): 1120–36. https://doi.org/10.1080/01419870.2014.992925.

———. 2016. *European Cities, Municipal Organizations and Diversity: The New Politics of Difference.* London: Palgrave Macmillan. https://doi.org/10.1057/978-1-137-52185-9.

Scholten, Peter, Elizabeth Collett, and Milica Petrovic. 2016. "Mainstreaming Migrant Integration? A Critical Analysis of a New Trend in Integration Governance." *International Review of Administrative Sciences* 83, no. 2 (June): 283–302. https://doi.org/10.1177/0020852315612902.

Sellers, Jefferey M. 2005. "Re-placing the Nation: An Agenda for Comparative Urban Politics." *Urban Affairs Review* 40, no. 4 (March): 419–45. https://doi.org/10.1177/1078087404272673.

Sidney, Mara. 2014. "Settling In: A Comparison of Local Immigrant Organizations in the United States and Canada." *International Journal of Canadian Studies* 49 (January): 105–33. https://doi.org/10.3138/ijcs.49.105.

Solidarity City Network. 2013. *A Short History of How We Got There.* Leaflet.

Statistics Canada. 2022. "Canada's Large Urban Centres Continue to Grow and Spread." *The Daily*, February 9, 2022. https://www150.statcan.gc.ca/n1/daily-quotidien/220209/dq220209b-eng.htm.

———. n.d. "Visible Minority of Person." Departmental standard approved August 25, 2021. https://www23.statcan.gc.ca/imdb/p3Var.pl?Function=DEC&Id=45152.

Stone, Clarence N. 1989. *Regime Politics: Governing Atlanta 1946–1988*. Lawrence, KS: University Press of Kansas.

Tate, Ellen, and Louise Quesnel. 1995. "Accessibility of Municipal Services for Ethnocultural Populations in Toronto and Montreal." *Canadian Public Administration* 38, no. 3 (September): 325–51. https://doi.org/10.1111/j.1754-7121.1995.tb01053.x.

Tossutti, Livianna S. 2012. "Municipal Roles in Immigrant Settlement, Integration and Cultural Diversity." *Canadian Journal of Political Science* 45, no. 3 (September): 607–33. https://doi.org/10.1017/S000842391200073X.

Varsanyi, Monica W. 2010a. "City Ordinances as "Immigration Policing by Proxy": Local Governments and the Regulation of Undocumented Day Laborers." In *Taking Local Control: Immigration Policy Activism in U.S. Cities and States*, edited by Monica W. Varsanyi, 135–54. Stanford, CA: Standard University Press.

———. 2010b. "Immigration Policy Activism in U.S. States and Cities: Interdisciplinary Perspectives." In *Taking Local Control: Immigration Policy Activism in U.S. Cities and States*, edited by Monica W. Varsanyi, 1–27. Stanford, CA: Standard University Press.

Vertovec, Steven. 2007. "Super-diversity and Its Implications." *Ethnic and Racial Studies* 30, no. 6 (September): 1024–54. https://doi.org/10.1080/01419870701599465.

Vicino, Thomas J. 2012. *Suburban Crossroads: The Fight for Local Control of Immigration Policy*. Lanham, MD: Lexington Books.

Village of Carpentersville. 2006. *Illegal Immigration Relief Ordinance*. Proposed on September 26, 2006; tabled July 4th, 2006 by the President of the Village Board of Trustees.

Walia, Harsha. 2014. "Sanctuary City from Below: Dismantling the City of Vancouver." *The Mainlander*, June 2, 2014. https://themainlander.com/2014/06/02/sanctuary-city-from-below-dismantling-the-city-of-vancouver/.

Wallace, Marcia, and Frances Frisken. 2000. "City-Suburban Differences in Government Responses to Immigration in the Greater Toronto Area." Research paper no. 197. Centre for Urban and Community Studies, University of Toronto. https://hdl.handle.net/1807/94365.

Williamson, Abigail Fisher. 2019. *Welcoming New Americans? Local Government and Immigrant Incorporation*. Chicago: Chicago University Press. Kindle. https://doi.org/10.7208/chicago/9780226572796.001.0001.

Yu, Henry. 2011. "Nurturing Dialogues between First Nations, Urban Aboriginal, and Immigrant Communities in Vancouver." In *Cultivating Canada: Reconciliation through the Lens of Cultural Diversity*, edited by Ashok Mathur, Jonathan Dewar, and Mike DeGagné, 301–8. Ottawa: Aboriginal Healing Foundation..

Yu, Wan, and Wei Li. 2014. "Globalization, Immigration and Ethnoburbs." In *Segmented Cities? How Urban Contexts Shape Ethnic and Nationalist Politics*, edited by Kristin R. Good, Luc Turgeon, and Triadafilos Triadafilopoulos, 115–39. Vancouver: UBC Press. https://doi.org/10.59962/9780774825856-008.

Indigenous-Municipal Relations in Canadian Cities

Doug Anderson and Alexandra Flynn

ACKNOWLEDGEMENT AND DEFINITIONS

We know that those reading this chapter will have varying levels of knowledge of Indigenous Peoples and communities. We assume that many are new to the topic, with a range of understanding of Indigenous Peoples and their rights under Canadian law, or knowledge of Indigenous laws and traditions. We encourage you to reflect on the Indigenous Peoples and communities where you are located and have added suggested readings at the end of this chapter.

To that end, before turning to the core questions of this chapter, we begin with an acknowledgement of our relationship with Indigenous lands and some key definitions that will be used in our discussions. This chapter was partly written on the territories of the xʷməθkʷəy̓əm (Musqueam), Skxwú7mesh (Squamish), and səlil̓wətaʔɬ (Tsleil Waututh) Coast Salish Peoples, known in Canadian law as Vancouver. It was also written in Toronto, lands that encompass the overlapping territories that include the Mississaugas of the Credit, the Haudenosaunee Confederacy, Treaty 13 Nations, the Wendat, the Petun Nations, and other Indigenous communities. It is said by many to be subject to the Dish with One Spoon Wampum Belt Covenant, a treaty agreement between the Haudenosaunee Confederacy and the Ojibwe and allied nations to peaceably share and care for the resources around the Great Lakes. In addition to the peoples that have resided in these spaces since time immemorial, Indigenous people from diverse nations have long lived in Vancouver and Toronto, as well as in other cities across Canada (Hewitt 2019). We invite you to consult an online tool such as https://native-land.ca to identify the Indigenous lands upon which you are located.

Questions about Indigenous identity and nationhood are also complex, especially in cities, and we cannot address these questions in detail here. We recognize the principle of centring

Indigenous nations and communities in deciding who is Indigenous. We use "First Nations" here to refer to governments that represent Indigenous Peoples, whether recognized as band councils under the Indian Act or by Indigenous Peoples under traditional Indigenous governance systems and laws. The Canadian Constitution recognizes Indigenous Peoples as those who meet the definition of First Nations in the Indian Act, as well as Métis and Inuit. This chapter speaks broadly of Indigenous Peoples in all the above senses. While we refer generally to municipalities, our examples focus on larger cities.

INTRODUCTION AND CONTEXT

This chapter contributes to an understanding of municipal responsibilities in relation to Indigenous communities in Canada by considering the history of Indigenous-municipal relations, exploring the evolution of formal legal structures, and seeking lessons from other countries. In our view, Indigenous and non-Indigenous Peoples have the potential to live and move forward together, with respect and reciprocity, and in harmony with both Indigenous and Canadian laws. The chapter broadly describes how Canadian municipal relationships with Indigenous Peoples have evolved over time, the ways in which formal legal structures govern those relationships, and how these structures are beginning to be challenged. We also look at Indigenous-municipal relationships in other countries as a way to begin considering what can we learn from those contexts.

By "Indigenous-municipal relations," we mean the ways in which municipal governments and Indigenous Peoples engage through evolving systems of governance. This includes:

- Meaningful consultation with First Nations and Indigenous Peoples on matters that affect them;
- Entering into protocols and agreements with First Nations located adjacent to municipal boundaries;
- Having meaningful Indigenous representation on governing bodies; and,
- Various ways in which diverse Indigenous Peoples are reasserting their cultural responsibilities under laws that have existed on their territories since time immemorial (meaning beyond human memory or record).

This brief chapter cannot possibly address what Indigenous laws and cultural responsibilities entail, so this area remains largely unaddressed here. It is important to know that these laws and responsibilities precede the other areas and that their assertion is re-emerging in different places in significant ways. However, to address them, we would need to consider the specific Indigenous Peoples in each urban area, including each of their systems of governance. Given these constraints, we focus here on the evolution of Indigenous-municipal relationships in recent decades in the first three areas above, from a perspective that is still predominately defined through the Canadian state, versus representing specific or general Indigenous views – and that these Indigenous views are in an ongoing process of re-emergence, which may come to change Canadian perspectives in the coming years.

The first part of this chapter explains why relationships between Indigenous Peoples and municipalities matter. We situate the populations of Indigenous Peoples in municipalities, highlighting that more than half of all Indigenous Peoples live in cities. We also explain important concepts concerning Indigenous land and legal interests within municipal boundaries, including urban reserves and treaty lands.

The next section explores how Canada's legal framework affects Indigenous-municipal relationships. The Constitution Act states that matters concerning Indigenous Peoples rest with the federal government and also acknowledges Aboriginal and Treaty Rights. Unwritten constitutional principles, legal cases, and legislation also frame the responsibilities of Canadian governments in relation to Indigenous Peoples (Haida Nation v. British Columbia [Minister of Forests] 2004). While municipalities have historically seen relationships with Indigenous Peoples as falling within federal jurisdiction, local governments have more recently begun to change their governance practices to include Indigenous Peoples and communities in decision-making processes. We explain how municipalities have begun to make changes to modify their governance models (Anderson and Flynn 2020). We also introduce examples of Indigenous-municipal relationships from other parts of the world, including Australia, New Zealand, and Mexico. These cases offer examples within their legal and governance models for how Canadian cities can consider next steps in relationship building.

INDIGENOUS AND FIRST NATIONS INTERESTS IN CANADIAN CITIES

Indigenous-municipal relationships must be understood within a broader understanding of cities as colonial developments. The city as we know it is rooted in Western notions of property law and governance (Nejad et al. 2019). Under Canadian law, municipalities are defined as provincially created public entities with particular mandates and are delegated specific responsibilities. The history of Indigenous displacement from what are now municipalities, and the resulting governance and legal relationships, are rooted in settler-colonialism, erasure, and violence (Coulthard 2007). The spaces that are now cities are the products of colonialism, which created municipal boundaries and authority without considering the impacts on Indigenous communities (Coulthard 2014).

Urban Indigenous Peoples have increasingly integrated important cultural principles and practices into urban services and community life. Indeed, bringing these principles and practices into services addressing the needs of the most oppressed members of the community is arguably consistent with principles of Indigenous law since it serves as a restoration of balance, not just in terms of equity but also of perspective. Significantly, ceremonies outlawed until the 1950s have been taking place for decades in urban centres, servicing those affected by poverty, homelessness, addiction, carceral systems, and other fallout from Canadian policies (Anderson and Flynn 2020). With all this in mind, we focus our overview of Indigenous-municipal relationships on two key realities: municipalities are located on Indigenous lands, and most Indigenous Peoples reside in urban centres.

More Than Half of All Indigenous Peoples Are Located in Cities

Urban Indigenous identity is complex, with vast differences in the experiences of Indigenous Peoples who live, work, or have connections across municipal spaces (Heritz 2010). In Canada, cities are home to more than half of all Indigenous Peoples. Indigenous Peoples in municipalities may or may not have relationships with or be members of neighbouring First Nations. According to 2016 Census data, almost 52 per cent of Indigenous Peoples now live in urban areas in Canada (Statistics Canada 2017). Thirty per cent of urban Indigenous Peoples are second- or third-generation city residents (Andersen 2013). Based on the 2016 Census, the largest cities have the greatest numbers of Indigenous Peoples (Statistics Canada 2017).

The Canadian government defines who is Indigenous based on the provisions set out in the Constitution Act and the Indian Act. Indigenous nations may have different processes to determine who is a citizen or member of their community. Indigenous Peoples identify as Inuit, Métis, or as First Nations differently across cities. For example, in Winnipeg far more urban Indigenous residents identify as Métis than in other Canadian cities. It is critical to remember that Indigenous Peoples are not monolithic and, therefore, Indigenous Peoples residing in a particular municipality may not share the same cultures, laws, or traditions. So, while we tend to measure and discuss urban Indigenous populations as a bloc and conceptualize them as a population that shares similar challenges and concerns related to their urban experience, the reality is often much more complicated.

Municipalities Are Located on Indigenous Lands

Indigenous boundaries do not mirror municipal ones, and particular localities may hold political, spiritual, and economic meaning to Indigenous communities. By "Indigenous lands," we mean lands and resources that hold many kinds of interests for Indigenous people. These include reserves, as defined by the Indian Act, urban reserves, treaty lands, and traditional territories, each of which has its own legal frameworks. Indigenous nations have been located since time immemorial in lands that are now occupied by Canadian cities. Colonial powers came long after Indigenous nations, claiming rights to land and resources for European countries (Freeman 2010). When European powers came to Canada, they met Indigenous Peoples who had important trade routes and communities. These spaces served as bases for economic, political, and social activities, and they eventually became the sites of local governments. Over time, colonial powers removed Indigenous Peoples through disease, violence, treaties, and other means (Freeman 2010). Government officials specifically moved Indigenous Peoples from urbanizing areas (House of Commons Debate 1911).

This means that Canadian municipalities are located on Indigenous lands. The displacement of Indigenous communities in cities across Canada has historically been omitted from municipal websites or origin stories, but municipalities are increasingly including land acknowledgements. For example, the City of Toronto's statement reads, "The City of Toronto has been acknowledging the traditional territory since March 2014. Due to conversations with Indigenous leaders, including the Aboriginal Advisory Committee as part of the 2018 Toronto for All Campaign, the language the City of Toronto uses has evolved" (City of Toronto, n.d.). The City of Prince George includes information on the Lheidli T'enneh, as well as the agreements between the First Nation and the city (City of Prince George, n.d.).

In many (although not all) municipalities, there are treaty relationships and Indigenous claims within and adjacent to cities (Dorries 2012). Treaties are agreements entered into by First Nations and colonial governments and, later, the federal government, regarding the use of land and resources. For example, a treaty may recognize Indigenous rights to hunt, fish, and trap. Treaties are constitutionally protected. Local governments must be aware of and adhere to the treaty rights that apply. For example, municipalities must adhere to the Treaty Land Entitlement (TLE) process, which resolves obligations to First Nations in relation to lands to which they were entitled under Treaty. The TLE process has enabled First Nations to obtain lands within cities and to transfer these lands to reserve status. For example, the City of Saskatoon has worked with First Nations to sign agreements related to TLE lands (City of Saskatoon, n.d.).

In addition, some First Nations have reserves within or adjacent to municipalities, called urban reserves. These are not considered to be municipal lands. Instead, they are Indigenous lands. The Indian Act and other federal legislation set out what and how decisions can be made concerning them. There are now more than 120 urban reserves across Canada. They may have existed as reserve lands for decades, with an urban centre created around them – as with Calgary, for example. They may also have been acknowledged as a result of legal cases, as with Senakw in Vancouver. They may also have been established under the Additions to Reserve policy or TLE agreements (Indigenous Services Canada 2020, 2023). These latter policies provide lands to First Nations who did not receive the amount of land that was promised under treaties (Indigenous Services Canada 2020, 2023). Much of the process of creating urban reserves has taken place in Saskatchewan and Manitoba, though a number of others have been created in other provinces as well.

THE LEGAL FRAMEWORK FOR INDIGENOUS-MUNICIPAL RELATIONSHIPS

Despite the fact that close to half of all Indigenous People reside in urban areas, cities have fewer legal obligations under Canadian law with respect to Indigenous Peoples than any order of government; furthermore, like all Canadian orders of government, municipal authorities often have little awareness of distinct Indigenous laws and perspectives, meaning long-standing legal and governance frameworks held by Indigenous Peoples themselves.

Many different governments are involved in decision-making that affects Indigenous Peoples and communities. John Borrows writes that federal and provincial governments impose and apply laws that muddy their individual obligations as governments in relation to First Nations (Borrows 2017). The lack of clarity regarding the obligations of different levels of Canadian government has particular significance for urban Indigenous Peoples. As Joanne Heritz states, all levels of government in Canada are reluctant to accept responsibility in relation to urban Indigenous matters (Heritz 2017). This section explains s. 35(1), 91, and 92 of the Constitution Act, 1982, the duty to consult, and their relevance for Indigenous-municipal relationships. This section also sets out the other Canadian legal instruments that impact the legal and governance relationships between Indigenous Peoples, their representatives, and municipalities.

Constitutional Requirements

Canadian constitutional rights and protections of Indigenous Peoples are located in several documents and principles. Some of these provisions and principles impact Indigenous-municipal legal relationships, as explained in this section.

THE CONSTITUTION ACTS, 1867 AND 1982

Aboriginal and Treaty Rights of First Nations are recognized and affirmed under s. 35(1) of Canada's Constitution Act, 1982 and have been given additional context through Canadian courts. These courts have been forums for asserting and advancing Indigenous rights in relation to federal and provincial governments, including how and when governments must engage First Nations (Haida Nation v. British Columbia [Minister of Forests] 2004).

Although the Canadian Constitution recognizes and affirms Aboriginal Treaty Rights, barriers to meaningfully exercising those rights present one of the most pressing access-to-justice issues of our time. Despite Canada's purported nation-to-nation relationship, as outlined in treaties, our history is replete with examples of what then-chief justice Beverley McLachlin of the Supreme Court of Canada (SCC) would eventually call the national government's "cultural genocide" of Indigenous Peoples, whether through the creation of reserves and residential schools or the erosion of hunting and cultural rights (Howard-Hassmann 2015). The federal government has often refused to engage in discussions with Indigenous communities over treaty violations and Indigenous claims, such that legal actions have been required to bring the federal government to the negotiating table (Delgamuukw v. British Columbia 1997).

The Constitution Act, 1867 sets out the division of powers between federal and provincial governments. Under s. 92(8), municipal powers are within the exclusive jurisdiction of the provinces (R. v. Greenbaum 1993; 114957 Canada Ltée [Spraytech, Société d'arrosage]

v. Hudson [Town] 2001). As discussed in chapter 2, provinces set out municipal authority in legislation, often a general act that applies to all municipalities, but also other legislation, like planning acts. Large cities, such as Montreal and Toronto, have options for raising revenue and have oversight in such matters as social services and housing, which are also issues that matter greatly to urban Indigenous Peoples (Taylor and Dobson 2020). Since municipalities are creatures of the province and not named in the Constitution as governments, it is important to address gaps in understanding regarding their legal obligations to Indigenous Peoples (Makuch, Craik, and Leisk 2004).

THE DUTY TO CONSULT

One area of uncertainty is the scope and breadth of the duty to consult. Canadian courts have stated that the goal of the duty to consult and, where appropriate, to accommodate, is to achieve "reconciliation" (Chippewas of the Thames First Nation v. Enbridge Pipelines Inc. 2017). "Reconciliation" has not been given a definable legal meaning. As a result of cases brought by First Nations, the courts have decided that federal and provincial governments have a duty to consult, which arises when the Crown has knowledge of an Aboriginal right or title and is considering action that might adversely affect it. The duty to consult was recognized in a 2004 case, *Haida Nation v. British Columbia*, decided by the SCC. In this case, the Haida Nation sued the British Columbia government over transferring a logging licence from one company to another without consulting with the First Nation (Haida Nation v. British Columbia [Minister of Forests] 2004). The court in this case said that in a situation where there is no physical change to the land, notification of the change of licence holder and providing an opportunity to dialogue would have been considered sufficient consultation. If the government action was to begin logging land, there would be a physical change to the landscape and much more in-depth consultation would likely be required. The court stated that each situation requiring consultation would be different.

The duty to consult arises when a government considers an action that may affect First Nations, including matters like land development or the treatment of resources. In court cases to date, "the Crown" means federal and provincial governments, rather than municipal governments (Keewatin v. Ontario [Natural Resources] 2013). At its most basic level "consultation" consists of dialogue between government bodies and First Nations communities regarding government action with the intention of substantially addressing any First Nations concerns. There is no duty to agree, but consultation must be done in good faith. The Crown cannot give away the duty to consult, but it can delegate procedural aspects of consultation, like informing First Nations, to companies and other third parties (Haida Nation v. British Columbia [Minister of Forests] 2004).

This ruling on the duty to consult has led to significant changes in how federal and provincial governments engage with First Nations. As a result of court decisions, governments must pay attention to Indigenous interests by, among other measures, providing information to First Nations, translating material into the applicable Indigenous language, or accommodating the First Nation through financial settlements or jobs. There are no SCC cases that extend the duty to consult to municipalities. However, case law and provincial legislation suggest that municipalities should have a duty to consult. Examples of municipal decisions that could affect Indigenous people include decisions concerning reserves or the traditional territory of Indigenous Peoples, or treaty rights. For example, a proposed bike lane of the City of Toronto affected a Huron-Wendat burial site in 2010, ultimately requiring remediation efforts to ensure that Indigenous rights were protected (Sandburg 2021).

The leading appeal court decision, *Neskonlith Indian Band v. Salmon Arm (City)* (2012), states that municipalities have no independent constitutional duty to consult First Nations whose treaty and other interests may be affected by municipal decision-making (Imai and Stacey 2014). In this case, the Neskonlith were unsuccessful in challenging a decision made by the City of Salmon Arm that allowed a permit for development to be issued in a flood plain area located right beside their reserve. Even though Salmon Arm took steps to consult and accommodate the Neskonlith, the court held that the municipality did not owe a duty to consult, in part on the basis that small municipalities do not have the capacity to properly do so.

While the SCC has yet to consider the issue directly, a number of legal academics have analyzed whether or not municipalities ought to or do in fact hold that duty to consult. Kaitlin Ritchie (2013) worries that municipalities taking on that duty would water down the nation-to-nation relationship, thereby undermining the treaty and other relationships established between the Crown and Indigenous nations. In contrast, Felix Hoehn and Michael Stevens (2018) argue that, given the evolution of municipal autonomy, and given the fact that third parties have been put into positions where they are in effect an arm of the Crown, municipalities do in fact hold the duty to consult and accommodate. Angela D'Elia Decembrini and Shin Imai note that, practically speaking, local governments already consult with Indigenous Peoples impacted by planning and development decisions and, if they do not, provinces must step in. Regardless, municipalities must not proceed with projects until the duty to consult and accommodate has been fulfilled (Decembrini and Imai 2019, 945). Some scholars have argued that if a case similar to *Neskonlith* came to the courts now, the duty to consult would be extended to municipalities, based on other court decisions (Hoehn and Stevens 2018). If this were the case, cities would understand that they have a direct responsibility to First Nations governments on matters that affect them. However, the duty to consult is aimed at First Nations recognized under Canadian law only. Therefore, the duty to consult would not impact the relationship between municipalities and other Indigenous Peoples, such as those who do not have status under the Indian Act and those who are not affiliated with the First Nations on which the municipality is situated.

PROVINCIAL DIRECTION TO MUNICIPALITIES

We know from court decisions that provinces are a "Crown" and therefore have responsibilities in relation to First Nations, including a duty to consult. Through legislation, provinces have delegated responsibility and power to municipalities in areas like planning, social service delivery, and some aspects of housing, including the maintenance of social housing in some cities. But within the legislation that sets out municipal responsibility, provinces have mixed interpretations of how local governments are meant to consult with First Nations and Indigenous communities (Dorries 2012). Some provinces provide more straightforward direction to municipalities. For example, a Saskatchewan (2023) policy states that municipalities have a duty to consult whenever they independently exercise their legal authority in a way that might adversely impact the exercise of Treaty and Aboriginal rights or traditional uses on unoccupied Crown land or other lands to which First Nations and Métis have a right of access. Unlike Ontario, assistance and policy guidance are available to local governments in Saskatchewan in exercising this duty (Association of Municipalities of Ontario 2019).

In Ontario, the Planning Act (1990) sets out the specific rules that define the obligations of municipalities, the purposes of guiding documents such as official plans, and the requirements for public consultation. The website of the Province of Ontario's Ministry of Municipal Affairs and Housing (2018) states that "municipalities have a duty to consult in some circumstances," but little information is provided to these local governments regarding the scope of the duty, the roles of municipal, regional, and provincial bodies, and how local governments should engage with Indigenous communities.

In 2020, the Province of Ontario released an updated version of the Provincial Policy Statement (PPS), a document that addresses land-use planning policies and decision-making abilities. A PPS is a policy akin to a recommendation or guideline, with less weight than a law, but having considerable weight in local planning policies as well as particular decisions. Section 4.3 of the PPS states that it "shall be implemented in a manner that is consistent with the recognition and affirmation of existing Aboriginal and treaty rights in section 35 of the *Constitution Act, 1982*." In addition, PPS s. 1.2.2 states that "Planning authorities shall engage with Indigenous communities and coordinate on land use planning matters." Section 2.6.5 more specifically addresses heritage by stating: "Planning authorities shall engage with Indigenous communities and consider their interests when identifying, protecting and managing cultural heritage and archaeological resources." There is little guidance, nor a regulatory scheme to guide implementation. Since the PPS only includes vague generalities about planning with First Nations, it is not surprising that the province has provided limited guidance or training and few resources to instruct municipal planners on how to respectfully engage Indigenous governments and Peoples. Moreover, the PPS does not explicitly state that municipalities have a duty to consult and accommodate. There are no oversight mechanisms for ensuring that the PPS is used, appeal processes if it is not, nor information on how municipalities have interpreted provisions.

A provincial advocacy body called the Association of Municipalities of Ontario has released a report stating that municipalities do not have a legal duty to consult, and procedural requirements are imprecise (Association of Municipalities of Ontario 2019). Some municipalities in Ontario have decided that they do have a duty to consult (Town of Midland 2019). Indigenous communities and First Nations are therefore in the middle of a debate among provincial and municipal governments as to which party is responsible for exercising the duty to consult.

Agreements between First Nations and Municipalities

While municipalities do not have the right to make decisions regarding reserve lands, they may have legal relationships with First Nations, such as agreements to provide services, like water or sewage treatment (Alcantara and Nelles 2016). Even though reserve land is under the jurisdiction of a First Nation, provincial policies may require that First Nations negotiate agreements with urban municipalities (Western Economic Diversification Canada 2005). The agreements must cover tax loss compensation, bylaw compatibility, and a dispute resolution mechanism. The result is that most First Nations and cities end up with Municipal Services Agreements. A municipal servicing agreement provides for services such as water, garbage collection, police, and fire protection, at a cost that is generally equivalent to the amount the municipality would have collected through property taxes (Indigenous Services Canada 2020).

For example, a 2008 Fire Protection Agreement between Kamloops Indian Band and the City of Kamloops provides that the Kamloops Indian Band will pay the city for fire protection and rescue services on reserve while the Band agrees to enforce applicable and necessary fire prevention regulations and rules on the reserve lands (City of Kamloops and Kamloops Indian Band 2008). As another example, the Municipal Services Agreement between the City of Saskatoon and Muskeg Cree First Nation, created in 1993, outlines the relationship between the city and Muskeg Cree with regards to provision of services and payment for services (Western Economic Diversification Canada 2005). The city agrees to provide municipal services like garbage pickup, snow removal, police protection, and separated customer billing of water and electricity, and Muskeg Lake agrees to collect taxes on property and pay municipal service fees. Muskeg Lake also has the power to adopt its own bylaws. Under the terms of the agreement, Muskeg Lake must adopt a commercial municipal tax rate, applied to both First Nation and non-First Nation businesses on the First Nation's reserve lands, provide that land use and development will be the same as if the land were not reserve land, and that the businesses abide by city bylaws (Western Economic Diversification Canada 2005).

Many other municipalities and First Nations may have entered into agreements, including commitments to working together based on particular principles. For example, the Memorandum of Understanding between Regina and Cega'kin (Carry the Kettle) First Nation formalizes a commitment to a long-term relationship, mutual economic growth, and working toward a Municipal Services Agreement (Atter 2021). The Cultural Planning and Co-operation

Agreement between Tsleil-Waututh First Nation and Metro Vancouver Regional District, signed in 2020 regarding Belcarra Regional Park, "formalizes the ongoing collaboration between the two parties and seeks to identify common interests and share ideas on how they can work together to protect, preserve and enhance the regional park for the benefit of present and future generations" (Metro Vancouver 2020). The 2012 Municipality of Sioux Lookout Friendship Accord with Lac Seul First Nation and Slate Falls First Nation focuses on "relationship building, partnership dynamics, current challenges that the communities are facing and opportunities to work collaboratively" (Sioux Lookout Hub of the North 2013). These agreements offer a chance for First Nations and municipalities to set out the unique obligations that concern their respective governments.

Commission Reports

A government may initiate a commission in response to a policy or legal failure. Commissioners – who are arm's length from the government – research and report back, often with recommendations on how to move forward. The Royal Commission on Aboriginal Peoples, introduced next, was a crucial report in identifying gaps in relation to Indigenous-municipal relationships. It was especially important in noting that local governments, not just federal, have responsibilities toward Indigenous Peoples. Two decades later, the Truth and Reconciliation Commission report similarly spelled out the specific obligations of all Canadian governments, including municipalities, in ensuring that the country was on a path toward reconciliation.

REPORT OF THE ROYAL COMMISSION ON ABORIGINAL PEOPLES (RCAP)

While the Constitution states that responsibility for matters related to Indigenous Peoples rests with the federal government, municipalities are home to many Indigenous Peoples. However, there have historically been few representative opportunities for Indigenous Peoples within cities. In response to this governance gap, the 1996 Report of the Royal Commission on Aboriginal Peoples (RCAP) acknowledged the large number of Indigenous social services agencies in municipalities and the need for representation in local decision-making. RCAP stated definitively that all levels of government have constitutional responsibility to uphold Aboriginal and Treaty Rights in Canada, including those living in urban centres (RCAP 1996, 85). RCAP proposed two possible models of urban Indigenous governance. The "reform of urban government and public authorities" model called for greater Indigenous political participation through having Indigenous representation on municipal councils and related political bodies and the co-management of urban programs and services. In this model, RCAP advocated that municipalities ensure Indigenous representation on decision-making bodies, establish Aboriginal Affairs Committees, and co-manage urban initiatives with Aboriginal people (439). As will be explained in the next section, this model has received traction. Canadian courts in 2013 recognized that Indigenous Peoples living off-reserve are "self-organized, self-determining, and distinct communities" (Belanger 2013, 68). In addition, many municipalities have Indigenous affairs committees comprised of Indigenous representatives, all unique in their composition (Heritz 2016).

A "community of interest" model proposed greater Indigenous political autonomy through the voluntary association of a diversity of urban Indigenous organizations. In cities across Canada, there are examples of urban Indigenous agency co-operation and coordination for service delivery. RCAP reported that Indigenous agencies, not municipalities, are the main institutions that deliver social and housing services to Indigenous Peoples, but these agencies are often underfunded (Heritz 2010). In some cities, Indigenous-led organizations have statutory mandates in some areas, such as child welfare and education (Belanger 2013). These entities are delivering services and are not formal governments, although courts have recognized their importance in representing the interests of urban Indigenous Peoples (Belanger 2013). For example, the Toronto Aboriginal Research Project commissioned by the Toronto Aboriginal Support Services Council has developed a "community of interest" model of self-government that is representative of Indigenous social service agencies, their Boards of Directors and their membership (Heritz 2018).

RCAP identified the importance of urban organizations in providing much-needed services to and representation of Indigenous Peoples living in municipalities, but most operate under Canadian paradigms that bear little resemblance to Indigenous governance models. Over one hundred Friendship Centres across the country also serve as forums to bring together, represent, and advocate on behalf of Indigenous Peoples living in urban areas (Andersen 2013). Friendship Centres provide resources and services for families, youth, and elders regarding health and wellness support, housing support, education, employment and life skills training, legal services, support for ending violence, and referrals to other community organizations (National Association of Friendship Centres 2021). Friendship Centres are significant sites of service provision for Indigenous Peoples, as intermediaries between Indigenous Peoples and governments, and as sites for transformative relationships. Chapter 3 offers more detail on Indigenous resurgence in cities, which can include the important role of Friendship Centres.

TRUTH AND RECONCILIATION COMMISSION (TRC)

The Truth and Reconciliation Commission of Canada was a commission "like no other in Canada" (Truth and Reconciliation Commission of Canada 2015, iii). It was created as a result of the Indian Residential Schools Settlement Agreement, which settled the class actions brought against the federal government for the abuse of Indigenous children forcibly sent away from their families to residential schools. The TRC spoke to over six thousand witnesses in order to answer the question, "Now that we know about residential schools and their legacy, what do we do about it?" (iv). Although the Commission did not specifically address the role of cities in the context of residential schools specifically, the TRC Calls to Action include specific requests of municipal governments:

43 We call upon federal, provincial, territorial, and municipal governments to fully adopt and implement the *United Nations Declaration on the Rights of Indigenous Peoples* as the framework for reconciliation.

44 We call upon federal, provincial, territorial, and municipal governments to provide education to public servants on the history of Aboriginal peoples, including the history and legacy of residential schools, the *United Nations Declaration on the Rights of Indigenous Peoples*, Treaties and Aboriginal rights, Indigenous law, and Aboriginal–Crown relations. This will require skills-based training in intercultural competency, conflict resolution, human rights, and anti-racism.

As we will see in the following section, some municipal governments have implemented these TRC Calls to Action as a way to mobilize municipal policy change in respect of Indigenous Peoples.

INTERNATIONAL DECLARATIONS

The United Nations Declaration on the Rights of Indigenous Peoples (UNDRIP), adopted by the United Nations General Assembly in 2007, has like the TRC, has been an important catalyst for mobilizing municipal governance reforms across Canada. UNDRIP sets out the individual and collective rights of Indigenous Peoples around the world, not just Canada. It provides guidance on how states can develop cooperative relationships with Indigenous Peoples in areas such as culture, health, education, and community, and based on the principles of equality, partnership, good faith, and mutual respect. UNDRIP, which was created by Indigenous Peoples, makes room for a broader set of land and other interests of Indigenous Peoples. UNDRIP is meaningful in the municipal context because it acknowledges Indigenous laws and practices, and recognizes Indigenous land interests beyond those in the Indian Act. At the moment, the duty to consult applies to First Nations with land rights such as reserves, treaty lands, and traditional territories.

Many of UNDRIP's provisions relate to municipal actions. With regard to sustaining traditions while engaging with cities, for example, Article 5 states that "Indigenous Peoples have the right to maintain and strengthen their distinct political, legal, economic, social and cultural institutions, while retaining their right to participate fully, if they so choose, in the political, economic, social and cultural life of the State." Article 18 provides that Indigenous Peoples have the right to participate in decision-making in matters that would affect their rights, through representatives chosen by themselves and based on their own procedures, as well as to maintain and develop their own Indigenous decision-making institutions. Article 19 sets out the principle that states should consult and cooperate in good faith with Indigenous Peoples through their own representative institutions in order to obtain their free, prior, and informed consent before adopting and implementing legislative or administrative measures that may affect them.

In regard to social services, health, and housing and shelter matters, where some municipalities, like the City of Toronto, play a direct role, Article 21 of UNDRIP states that, "States shall take effective measures and, where appropriate, special measures to ensure continuing improvement of their economic and social conditions." Article 23 adds that Indigenous Peoples have the right to be actively involved in developing, determining and administering health, housing and other economic and social programs that affect them, ideally through their own institutions.

With respect to planning and use of lands, Article 25 sets out that Indigenous Peoples have the right to maintain and strengthen their distinctive spiritual relationships with traditionally owned or otherwise occupied or used lands, territories, and waters. Articles 26 and 27 state that Indigenous laws should apply to their land rights and that Indigenous Peoples must be involved in processes that relate to land that is "traditionally owned or otherwise occupied or used." Importantly, the references to lands, territories and resources are not limited to the lands set aside as "reserves" by Canada under the Indian Act. As former UN Special Rapporteur on the Rights of Indigenous Peoples James Anaya notes, given the vulnerable conditions of Indigenous Peoples, the duty to consult arises where particular interests are at stake, even if the interests do not correspond to a recognized land or other right under domestic law (Anaya 2009).

UNDRIP is not legally binding like a treaty or a covenant and is not signed or ratified by states. Declarations are instead political commitments from the states that vote in favour of adopting them. In 2016, Canada became a supporter of UNDRIP. Of all of the federal and provincial governments in Canada, British Columbia is the only one that has implemented UNDRIP (Gunn 2019). The province has committed to reviewing its laws to ensure consistency with UNDRIP, but at present it is unclear how UNDRIP will frame laws and relationships with First Nations and Indigenous Peoples, including the obligations of municipalities (British Columbia 2020).

In summary, the Canadian constitution does not clearly spell out the obligations of municipalities in relation to Indigenous Peoples, and each province may have a different view of how local governments should consult with Indigenous communities and First Nations. Since RCAP, there have been no national commission reports on Indigenous-municipal relationships, although the TRC and UNDRIP have provided helpful frameworks for Indigenous and municipal advocates in considering how to move forward. We turn next to how these legal constraints and policy initiatives are shaping Indigenous-municipal relationships in Canada.

EMERGING MODELS OF INDIGENOUS-MUNICIPAL RELATIONSHIPS

This section sets out the efforts taken by some Canadian municipal governments to improve Indigenous-municipal relationships. It explores measures such as Indigenous Affairs Offices, Indigenous Advisory Councils, the endorsement of UNDRIP, and co-management of urban park lands. This section also identifies urban reserves, explained earlier, as a key area of future legal development, with opportunities for infrastructure and service co-operation.

Indigenous-Municipal Governance Initiatives

Municipalities across Canada have introduced significant changes since around 2010. The following are some examples of developments in governance in various Canadian cities.

- *Indigenous advisory bodies*: A number of cities have introduced Indigenous advisory bodies, which provide advice on city policies and initiatives or nation-to-nation intergovernmental practices between city councils and First Nations leadership. Examples of where this has occurred include Vancouver, which created an advisory body in 2012, and Winnipeg, which introduced an advisory council in 2015. Indigenous leaders, sometimes from social service agencies, serve as members. They rarely have budgetary or decision-making power, but are staffed, with agendas and minutes available. Some cities also have intergovernmental working groups with First Nations, such as the City of Vancouver with the Squamish, Musequeam and Tsleil-Watuth Nations, introduced in 2015. The City of Edmonton established an Elders Circle through Native Counselling Services of Alberta to provide advice and guidance for the Edmonton Urban Aboriginal Dialogue in 2005.
- *Indigenous affairs offices within the municipality*: Some cities have established Indigenous affairs offices at a senior level within municipal bureaucracies. These offices often have staff members who identify as Indigenous and seek to build relationships with local First Nations and urban Indigenous Peoples. Staff may also provide input and advice to senior administrators and elected officials, and resolve disputes among Indigenous Peoples and municipal officials. For example, a dedicated Indigenous relations division within the City of Winnipeg was established in 2013.
- *Mandatory training for all municipal officials on Indigenous history and presence*: In 2018, the City of Edmonton committed to training each of its 10,000+ employees on the history of residential schools and their impact on Indigenous Peoples, and to open dialogue on reconciliation in the workplace. The City of Saskatoon introduced mandatory Indigenous awareness training to provide staff with knowledge of Indigenous cultures and languages in 2017.
- *Endorsement of the TRC and UNDRIP*: Long before federal and provincial governments were concerned with UNDRIP, some municipalities endorsed the Declaration and

Table 13.1. Municipal Initiatives in Relation to Indigenous-Municipal Relationships

City	Indigenous Affairs Office	Indigenous Advisory Committee(s)	Staff Training	Support for Adoption of UNDRIP	Addressing TRC Calls to Action
Toronto	Yes	Yes	Mandatory	Yes	Yes
Vancouver	Yes	Yes	Available	Yes	Yes
Edmonton	Yes	Yes	Available	Unclear	Yes
Calgary	Yes	Yes	Available	Yes	Yes
Saskatoon	Yes	Yes	Mandatory	No	Yes
Regina	No	Yes	Unclear	No	Yes
Winnipeg	Yes	Yes	Available	Yes	Yes
Montreal	Yes	Yes	Available	Yes	Yes
Halifax	No	Yes	In progress	No	Yes
Ottawa	No	Yes	Unclear	No	Yes

Source: Anderson and Flynn (2021, 15).

committed to the implementation of relevant TRC Calls to Action – including Vancouver in 2013, Toronto in 2014, and Edmonton in 2021. As of 2017, the City of Winnipeg uses UNDRIP as the framework for reconciliation and includes a role for Indigenous elders to provide traditional teachings.

Table 13.1 identifies which large municipalities have introduced these initiatives.

These developments are promising. Municipalities seem to be moving away from grouping Indigenous-related governance practices under equity approaches, which – while necessary and good – may not meaningfully incorporate the changes to governance imagined by RCAP, TRC, or UNDRIP. Adopting UNDRIP suggests a commitment to a model of Indigenous-municipal relationship that gives greater power and representation to Indigenous Peoples. However, adopting UNDRIP without meaningful action toward implementing it can strain relations with Indigenous partners. Particular attention should be paid toward Article 19 of UNDRIP, which states: "States shall consult and cooperate in good faith with the Indigenous Peoples concerned through their own representative institutions in order to obtain their free, prior and informed consent before adopting and implementing legislative or administrative measures that may affect them." This provision effectively means that consultation must take place with Indigenous groups, and that consent must be given in order to proceed with government action that will infringe on Indigenous interests.

As time goes on, it will become increasingly apparent whether municipalities are committed to different kinds of governance relationship with Indigenous Peoples and First Nations. Some municipalities seem to be ahead of federal and provincial governments – for example, by passing UNDRIP. However, it is too soon to tell whether these efforts are sincerely focused on creating new relationships with Indigenous Peoples and First Nations, through transfers of authority or lands outside of what is legally obligated, for example.

INTERNATIONAL EXAMPLES OF INDIGENOUS-MUNICIPAL RELATIONSHIPS

Indigenous-municipal relationships do not just matter in Canada. The following examples, drawn from New Zealand, Australia, and Mexico, showcase other ways in which local governments understand and are shifting their legal and governance obligations. While other countries have examples of Indigenous-municipal relationships, including the United States, we have selected the ones included in this section to show initiatives that move closer to nation-to-nation approaches. We caution against too strict of a comparison: every place has its own history and reality, and cookie-cutter approaches may ultimately undermine the process of Indigenous Peoples, First Nations, and municipal governments establishing governance practices that uphold the principles of respect and reciprocity. In addition, each country has legal frameworks that may enable or limit what municipalities can do. This section provides examples from New Zealand, Australia, and Mexico to offer a broader sense of how municipalities have developed Indigenous-municipal relationships within their legal frameworks.

New Zealand

New Zealand has a different framework than Canada as a result of the Treaty of Waitaingi, which is a written agreement between the British Crown and more than five hundred Māori rangatira (chiefs). After hundreds of years of grievances and differences in Treaty interpretations, the Treaty of Waitangi Act 1975 established a commission to consider treaty breaches and resolve grievances. Municipalities in New Zealand are governed by the Local Government Act (2002) (LGA), which incorporates the principles of the Treaty of Waitangi. In order to recognize and respect the Crown's responsibility to account for the Treaty's principles and maintain opportunities for Māori to contribute to local government decision-making, parts of the LGA provide principles and requirements for local authorities that are intended to facilitate Māori participation in such processes. Section 14 of the LGA sets out that in performing its role, a local authority should provide opportunities for Māori to contribute to its decision-making processes. Sections 81 and 82 of the LGA set out principles of consultation and require each local government to ensure it has processes in place for consulting Māori in accordance with those principles.

WELLINGTON

As part of its *Wellington Towards 2040: Smart Capital* vision and planning document, the city developed a framework, which sets out the city's strategies to implement its provisions for working together with Māori in a two-way partnership and emphasizes the importance of the city's partnership and relationship with Māori. The objectives of the framework are strong Māori communities, effective Māori participation, and the city's response to Māori needs and interests.

The city works with two Māori *mana whenua* organizations (collectives of people who have historic and territorial land rights) – the Port Nicholson Block Settlement Trust (*Taranaki Whānui ki te Upoko te Ika*) and *Te Rūnanga O Toa Rangatira* – in order to provide opportunities for Māori to participate in city decision-making processes, inform Māori contributions, and ensure that their contributions are represented. The city's responsibilities to these organizations are set out in two 2017 memorandums of understanding between the city and each organization, which provide a framework for strategic relationships between the groups and city council. The city also has a division called *Tira Poutama – Iwi Partnerships*, which manages the relationship between council and *mana whenua iwi* entities, and between council and Māori communities.

The city's key projects developed in consultation with local Māori groups have included the implementation of the *Te Reo* Māori Policy, which aims to revitalize the use of the Māori language in the city, and the *Te Taurapa* Māori Growth Strategy, which aims to improve Māori well-being and attract investment in local development projects. In implementing the *Te Reo* Māori Policy, Wellington City Council is working with *Te Taura Whiri i te Reo Māori* (the Māori Language Commission) to develop an action plan. The *Te Reo* Māori Policy is also supported by the *Te Māpihi Maurea* / Naming Policy, which sets out guidelines and principles to consider when deciding names of roads, spaces, facilities, localities and developments, as well as guidelines for engagement with *mana whenua*.

AUCKLAND

The City of Auckland (*Tāmaki Makaurau*) is located on the historic territory of nineteen tribes and subtribes of Māori people whose boundaries overlap. The city is advised by its *Ngā Mātārae* (Māori Outcomes Department) in determining and giving effect to its legislative responsibilities to local Māori (both *mana whenua* and *mataawaka*, Māori who live in Auckland but are not from a *mana whenua*). The Māori Outcomes Department has a central governance unit, and it also has Māori Outcomes Leads who sit in each of the city's People and Performance, Chief Planning Office, Community and Customer Services, Regulatory and Infrastructure, and Environmental Services divisions. The Māori Outcomes Department has articulated council's commitment to Māori through its Auckland Plan 2050, the Auckland Unitary Plan, a ten-year budget document, and local board plans. Māori Identity and Well-Being is one of the six outcomes outlined in the Auckland Plan 2050 and is focused on implementing Māori-centric models, involving Māori in decision-making, and giving effect to Treaty of Waitangi principles.

The city also has an Independent Māori Statutory Board with voting rights that puts forward issues to Auckland Council that are significant to Māori, provides advice, and makes sure council complies with legislation referring to the Treaty of Waitangi. The Independent Māori Statutory Board, along with other Māori-led organizations, support and contribute to implementing the Māori Identity and Well-Being outcome of the Auckland 2050 Plan.

The City of Auckland has co-governance authorities and boards established under Treaty of Waitaingi settlements, which involve the city working with *mana whenua* groups to co-govern various land and marine resources. These statutory bodies include the *Tūpuna Maunga o Tāmaki Makaurau* Authority, which governs the *Tūpuna Maunga* (ancestral mountains) that have importance to the spiritual and cultural identity of the *mana whenua* tribes of Auckland; the *Ngāti Whātua Ōrākei* Reserves Board, which is responsible for two spiritually and culturally important reserve lands in the region; and *Te Poari o Kaipātiki ki Kaipara*, which is responsible for reserve lands that provide access to a geothermal spring with healing qualities. In 2017, there were eight co-governance and co-management agreements and arrangements between Auckland Council and Māori groups.

The City of Auckland has also adopted *Te Aranga Māori* design principles, protocols, and guidelines to inform the design of public and private urban spaces, which recognize core Māori values, the status of Māori people, Māori names, the natural environment, environmental health, Māori narratives, significant sites and cultural landmarks, and the living and enduring presence of Māori and their relationships with place. The city has also adopted a Māori Language Policy and Māori Language Implementation Plan to foster the celebration, protection, revitalization, and integration of *te reo Māori* in Auckland council business, such that anyone accessing Auckland Council services and democratic services may do so in either *te reo Māori* or English. The Language Policy also provides a framework for use of language in naming and signage.

Australia

When Europeans arrived in what is now Australia in 1788, they determined that the land was terra nullius, or belonging to no one (Australia Human Rights Commission 2005). This view continued until the 1992 *Mabo* decision, which affirmed that Aboriginal and Torres Strait Islander Peoples were the first inhabitants of Australia and that there are numerous distinct Nations throughout Australia. Prior to 1901, each of the six colonies of Australia (New South Wales, Victoria, Queensland, South Australia, Western Australia, and Tasmania) was responsible for creating laws for its people. In 1869, the Victorian government became the first colony to pass laws relating to Aboriginal people (City of Darebin n.d.). In the state of Victoria, where Melbourne is located, the Aboriginal Protection Act 1869 allowed the Aboriginal Protectorate Board to regulate Aboriginal people's employment, marriage, social life, aspects of daily life, and where they lived, and it permitted the governor to remove any child from their family to a reformatory or industrial school. Such practices continued until approximately 1970. On January 1, 1901, Australia became an independent nation, and the Australian Constitution came into effect. The Constitution included s. 51 [xxvi], which allowed states to retain their power to make laws regarding Aboriginal people. Like Canada, Australia has introduced various policies to resolve land and other disputes, and the courts continue to play an important role in addressing Aboriginal rights and title. Australian states have more authority than Canadian provinces in relation to Indigenous issues and, like in Canada, states set out municipal authority.

MELBOURNE

The City of Melbourne is located on the traditional territory of the Boon Wurrung and Woi-wurrung (Wurundjeri) Peoples of the Kulin Nation. The city develops strategies, agreements, and protocols that celebrate and support Aboriginal cultures in collaboration with Aboriginal communities. The city has an Aboriginal Melbourne team that monitors and reports on the city's Aboriginal Heritage Action Plan and Reconciliation Action Plan, advises the city on Aboriginal interests and culture, and is the contact point for the Aboriginal community in raising awareness.

The 2015–18 Aboriginal Heritage Action Plan (AHAP) outlined Melbourne's approach to protecting, maintaining, and recognizing sites in and around Melbourne that are culturally important to Aboriginal communities. Through the AHAP, the City of Melbourne, together with the local Aboriginal and Torres Strait Islander community, advocates for reconciliation, eliminating racism and discrimination, the recognition and protection of Aboriginal sacred sites, and education of the larger community about Aboriginal and Torres Strait Islander heritage and culture. The AHAP outlines particular areas of collaboration with Traditional Owner groups and Aboriginal communities. Collaborative conservation measures include advising developers to undertake Cultural Heritage Management Plans for "high impact" building projects, recording different types of cultural heritage, managing and maintaining known heritage sites, and developing protocols and policies around heritage sites. Collaborative celebration measures include reviewing interpretive signage at Aboriginal heritage places, developing an Aboriginal Heritage Interpretation Policy, developing a culturally appropriate section of Melbourne's website, and establishing an "Aboriginal Melbourne" platform. Further collaboration is designated in the AHAP, specifically around working with Traditional Owner and Aboriginal community groups to determine the number of times relevant groups are consulted on heritage matters, ensuring that understandings that are reached with groups are protected and acknowledged, working with neighbouring municipal councils to ensure engagement is consistent across municipal boundaries, and developing a permanent arts installation to interpret the stories of important historic Aboriginal figures.

Melbourne's 2015–18 Reconciliation Action Plan (RAP) was developed through a six-week consultation period with the Aboriginal community, in addition to internal engagement with city departments and managers, to identify potential "action plan" initiatives and opportunities to integrate such initiatives as core municipal priorities. Two earlier RAPs had seen fourteen Aboriginal and Torres Strait Islander people placed in traineeships across the city and launched a biennial Indigenous Arts Festival. The RAP was driven by a Steering Committee made up of the city council's Executive Leadership Team, which meets twice per year. The RAP Steering Committee's discussions are informed by ongoing engagement with the Aboriginal community and Traditional Owner groups, as well as local organizations with RAPs, and other services and businesses. As part of the RAP, council created a procurement policy that ensures that equal opportunity is provided to Aboriginal and Torres Strait Islander businesses.

In 2012, Melbourne permanently raised the Aboriginal flag at Melbourne Town Hall. The city's protocol since 2008 includes Welcome to Country (a ceremony conducted by Traditional Owners on their land) and Acknowledgement of Traditional Owners (land acknowledgement conducted by settlers after the Welcome to Country) at appropriate events in the Australian parliament as a regular part of the Australian political process. The 2015–18 RAP outlined a commitment to including Welcome to Country at the first meeting of a newly elected city council and acknowledging Traditional Owners at all council events, events where councillors speak as representatives of the city, and at internal events.

SYDNEY

The City of Sydney is located on the traditional lands of the Gadigal of the Eora Nation, who are the Traditional Owners and Custodians of the land. City of Sydney official meetings, events, and special occasions begin with a Welcome to Country ceremony. The city has a number of Aboriginal protocols and cultural practice policies, in addition to a RAP. The city's Aboriginal and Torres Strait Islander Protocols document explains protocols around respecting and acknowledging Elders, gender protocols, Welcome to Country, naming the deceased, smoking ceremony, and fee for services. The document also includes protocols for respecting culture and heritage, including cultural ownership and intellectual property rights, and photographing and filming Aboriginal people. Another set of protocols outlines practices for Aboriginal and Torres Strait Islander community consultation, including information on why one should consult, whom to consult, how to obtain permission from a community, communication and language use, and cultural sensitivity and understanding. The final two sets of protocols centre around flag protocols for the use of the Australian Aboriginal flag and the Torres Strait Islander flag, and important dates for the Aboriginal and Torres Strait Islander community. Outside of the protocols document, the city also has a protocol recognizing the right of Aboriginal and Torres Strait Islander people to busk and practice their culture in public spaces without needing a permit.

The City of Sydney's Aboriginal and Torres Strait Islander Advisory Panel has a significant role in advising and guiding Sydney's policies and operations regarding matters of importance for the Aboriginal and Torres Strait Islander community. These include advising council on communities' needs, promoting knowledge and understanding of Aboriginal and Torres Strait Islander culture and society, advising council on the development of the city's Social Plan and Sustainable Sydney 2030 Strategy, advising council on programming, providing input on policy development where an area is likely to impact Aboriginal and Torres Strait Islander people, and promoting and facilitating reconciliation. The advisory panel also made many contributions to the Aboriginal and Torres Strait Islander Protocols document. The advisory panel meets six times per year and has increased engagement on projects such as the Eora Journey economic development plan, art, urban renewal projects, use of Aboriginal language, discussions of constitutional recognition, and social sustainability.

Through its RAP working group, City of Sydney staff meet throughout the year to support and monitor the RAP and assess whether its goals are being implemented and reported. In implementing the RAP, the city has sponsored a number of NAIDOC (National Aborigines and Islanders Day Observance Committee) events that celebrate Aboriginal and Torres Strait Islander culture, heritage, and achievements.

The City of Sydney has also developed the Eora Journey, a four-part project to celebrate the living culture of Aboriginal and Torres Strait Islanders in Sydney. One of the projects is an economic development plan, outlining how the city will work with Aboriginal and Torres Strait Islander communities and businesses over a ten-year period from 2016 to 2026. The plan was developed in consultation with the Aboriginal and Torres Strait Islander Advisory Panel and has action points related to building skills, providing access to resources, enabling connections, assisting job-seekers, improving opportunities in tertiary education, and developing opportunities in specific industries.

ADELAIDE

The City of Adelaide is located on the traditional lands of the Kaurna people of the Adelaide Plains. The city has had a protocol of acknowledging the traditional lands of the Kaurna people at council meetings since 2002. The city has a detailed protocol document outlining the difference between a "Welcome to Country" and an "Acknowledgement of Country" and providing information on how to engage in and prepare for either process, along with examples of how to deliver introductions for the people who have been invited to give the welcome. The city has a register of Kaurna people and groups that have been approved by the Kaurna Nation Cultural Heritage Committee to conduct a Welcome to Country.

The City of Adelaide Council signed a Reconciliation Statement in 1997 and has been developing and implementing RAPs since 2008. The current RAP for 2018–21 was created in collaboration with the city's Reconciliation Committee. The Reconciliation Committee is an advisory committee made up of the city mayor, three councillors, three Aboriginal and Torres Strait Islander representatives, one Kaurna Yerta Aboriginal Corporation representative, and three strategic agency representatives and two proxies who all identify as Aboriginal or Torres Strait Islander people. The Reconciliation Committee develops and monitors the city's RAP, provides input, and engages with government and non-government reconciliation groups to advance reconciliation and increase Aboriginal and Torres Strait Islander participation in council. Council also has a designated reconciliation officer who assists in jointly administering the Reconciliation Committee.

The current RAP is based on six guiding principles: participation, negotiation, communication and public awareness, service provision, cultural identity and heritage, and commemoration. The RAP outlines the city's commitment to entering a process of negotiation with local

Aboriginal communities, promoting cooperative approaches on issues, and minimizing the disadvantages experienced by Aboriginal and Torres Strait Islander people. In implementing the RAP, council works closely with cultural authorities, including the Kaurna National Cultural Heritage Committee and the Kaurna Yerta Aboriginal Corporation, as well as with other Aboriginal organizations. The current RAP stipulates a Reconciliation Action Plan Team (RAPT) that will meet quarterly to monitor RAP implementation and includes a number of actionable items relating to Aboriginal and Torres Strait Islander Cultural Awareness and Protocols.

The 1997 Reconciliation Statement resulted in the Kaurna Naming Project. In consultation with appropriate representatives and authorities, by 2012 Adelaide Council endorsed dual naming of Kaurna City parks and squares. Further, since 2015, there has been a *Mankurri-api Kuu* / Reconciliation Room located in Adelaide Town Hall, which is available for Aboriginal and Torres Strait Islander community groups to use free of charge.

Mexico

Mexico is home to sixty-eight Indigenous Nations representing over 15.1 per cent of the total population (Val et al. 2021). Mexico adopted the UN Declaration on the Rights of Indigenous Peoples in 2007, signed the International Labour Organization Convention 169 in 1990, and became a pluricultural nation by amending Article VI of the Constitution in 1992. Article 115 constitutionalizes municipalities, granting them far greater autonomy and status than Canadian cities. Article 2(B) of the Constitution also sets out obligations that all levels of government have toward Indigenous Peoples, including institutions to ensure Indigenous rights, guaranteed health and educational services, and consultation requirements.

Article 2 of the Mexico Constitution states: "The nation is multicultural, based originally on its indigenous peoples, described as descendants of those inhabiting the country before colonization and that preserve their own social, economic, cultural and political institutions, or some of them." The Constitution recognizes Indigenous self-governance, Indigenous law, and a right to representation at the municipal level. Article 2(a)(VII) states:

This Constitution recognizes and protects the indigenous peoples' right to self-determination and, consequently, the right to autonomy, so that they can:
Elect indigenous representatives for the town council in those municipalities with indigenous population.
The constitutions and laws of the States shall recognize and regulate these rights in the municipalities, with the purpose of strengthening indigenous peoples' participation and political representation, in accordance with their traditions and regulations.

Despite these constitutional innovations, in some state constitutions, Indigenous legal systems are not yet fully recognized, with Mexico City as an important counterpoint, as discussed next (Val et al. 2021).

MEXICO CITY

Mexico City is recognized as a state under Article 44 of the Mexico Constitution. The Indigenous population of Mexico City is diverse, with the greatest number coming from Nahuatl, Otomi, Mixtec, Zapotec, and Mazahua-speaking groups. Mexico City has a branch of the municipal public administration called the Secretariat of Peoples and Original Neighbourhoods and Resident Indigenous Communities (SEPI), which is responsible for matters related to designing, establishing, executing, guiding, coordinating, promoting, monitoring, and evaluating city policies, programs, projects, strategies, and actions related to Indigenous Peoples and their rights. Mexico City also has a Constitution, which includes an Article on the Rights of Indigenous Peoples in the city. Article 57 establishes that the implementation of UNDRIP is mandatory in Mexico City, and Article 59 sets out rights on self-determination and autonomy, the state's obligation to consult, rights to political participation, cultural rights, rights to self-development, communication, education, health, access to justice, and right to land, territory, and natural resources.

Within SEPI, there is a director of towns and original neighbourhoods who carries out actions to guarantee the exercise of collective rights of Indigenous towns and neighbourhoods in Mexico City. This Directorate has a Program for Strengthening and Supporting Native Peoples (FAPO) that provides financial aid for legal advice, collective rights projects, and community outreach and culture projects, as well as workshops on Indigenous rights. FAPO also distributes copies of the City Constitution and Chapter on the Rights of Indigenous Peoples.

Within SEPI there is also an executive director of Indigenous Rights, who protects the rights of Indigenous Peoples through the provision of free legal advice, facilitating a Network of Mutual Support of Indigenous Women to Prevent and Eradicate Violence and Discrimination, a Program for Strengthening the Autonomy and Economic Empowerment of Women from Indigenous Communities and Peoples of Mexico City, and co-operation with local, national, and international organizations. Further, SEPI has a Resident Indigenous Communities Directorate, which promotes community coordination. It also has a Program for Strengthening and Supporting Indigenous Communities (FACO), which promotes collective projects. The Directorate promotes the spread, use, and teaching of Indigenous languages, provides interpretation services, assists with visits to traditional doctors, facilitates links with Indigenous artisans and producers, and has departments dedicated to Indigenous education, and economic, social, and cultural rights.

In 2019, the city head of government entered an agreement creating the Inter-institutional Commission of Indigenous Peoples of Mexico City, in recognition of the city's constitutional responsibilities and Mexico's responsibilities as part of UNDRIP to respect, protect, promote, and guarantee the human rights of Indigenous Peoples. This commission is an inter-institutional coordination mechanism of the government to guarantee the rights of Indigenous Peoples, neighbourhoods, and communities. The commission is made up of the head of government, the SEPI, a number of other secretariats and ministries, and the sixteen mayors of Mexico City. Members have the right to speak and vote. The commission will coordinate with federal authorities and entities in the implementation of the rights of Indigenous Peoples, carry out research, and prepare an annual report on the status of the implementation of rights.

These international examples do not deeply examine the lived realities for Indigenous Peoples but do point to the interplay between legal rights for Indigenous Peoples and the development of Indigenous-municipal relationships. The case studies in New Zealand and Mexico illustrate the impact that constitutional and Treaty Rights at the national level can have for Indigenous Peoples located within cities. Specifically, where Indigenous rights are set out constitutionally at a national level, municipalities have greater accountability toward Indigenous Peoples, including participation in local government. New Zealand and Mexico also offer insights and examples as to how municipalities around the world are moving forward in recognizing Indigenous rights at the local scale, including recognition of Indigenous laws and languages. Canada has lessons to learn from the participatory and representative rights of Indigenous Peoples in these other countries, rights related to ceremony, procurement practices, and other areas.

CONCLUSION: NEXT STEPS IN INDIGENOUS-MUNICIPAL RELATIONSHIPS

Municipalities must acknowledge their obligations to Indigenous Peoples and First Nations, including that Aboriginal and Treaty Rights apply in relation to municipal spaces (Flynn 2021). Municipalities should create opportunities for members of Indigenous communities to play roles in decision-making. While the duty to consult can act as a bare minimum to remind municipalities of their requirement to engage with Indigenous communities, it is ultimately an incomplete framework to guide the work that needs to be done between Indigenous Peoples and local governments. We suggest instead some guidelines for Indigenous-municipal relationships moving forward.

Wael Hallaq uses the notion of "structural genocide" to explain the structural issues that circumvent meaningful change and provide the framework for the modern, homogenizing eradication of human and broader ecological diversity (Hallaq 2018). While Canadian leaders have acknowledged "cultural genocide," they have fallen short in acknowledging the many ongoing strategies and structures designed to eradicate Indigenous Peoples, remove any claims to lands, and bypass Indigenous laws and perspectives on treaties and covenants. Identifying structural genocide moves the conversation beyond "solutions" to "problems" that are part of the inherent legal and political structure. Hallaq asserts that the whole modern Western project is structurally genocidal to its very core. Municipalities are a part of this structural genocide. However, municipalities also have the potential to reimagine systems of government. They are closer to real peoples' control and to Indigenous lands, enabling people to engage with one another.

Provinces can obligate and enable local governments to move toward respectful, reciprocal relationships. For example, the Province of British Columbia has initiated a full review of planning processes across the province to modernize them in a manner that ensures collaboration with Indigenous governments in ways that are informed by UNDRIP and the TRC Calls to Action, and which involve local governments (British Columbia 2020). The goal is "to ensure consistency and co-ordination between local government and provincial–First Nations-led land use planning" (British Columbia 2020). The Government of British Columbia and the Union of British Columbia Municipalities (UBCM), which represents local governments in the province, signed a Memorandum of Understanding in 2018 that commits to "sincere and honest engagement" and notes that local governments are "key partners in achieving true, lasting reconciliation with Indigenous Peoples" (British Columbia and Business Council of British Columbia 2018). Further to this objective, UBCM provides support to local governments, First Nations, and Indigenous communities seeking sustained relationship building, including workshops that provide opportunities for local governments to respond to the Calls to Action delivered by the TRC's Report in 2015.

Unfortunately, there are few governmental resources aimed at the development of relationships between Indigenous and municipal communities, and municipalities are limited in how they can raise taxes. This includes funding for joint economic development planning and the inclusion of staff and advisory boards at the municipal level to develop and track relationship building. The foundational knowledge required to build such relationships must be fostered within local government frameworks and is needed to prevent continued colonization (Koch and Barry 2016).

Given the absence of government support, various non-profit organizations across Canada are engaging in proactive work to facilitate and support relationship building between municipalities and Indigenous communities. Since 2013, the Federation of Canadian Municipalities, in partnership with the Council for the Advancement of Native Development Officers, has run the Community Economic Development Initiative as well as the Community Infrastructure Partnership Project. Through multi-year partnerships, both programs enable formalized relationships between Indigenous communities, municipalities, and relevant stakeholders to be established and to flourish. In southern Ontario, a charitable organization called the Shared Path Consultation Initiative, which launched in 2015, creates opportunities for Indigenous and non-Indigenous communities to gather in order to examine, discuss, and deliberate about current policies around land use and relationships, as well as the changing legal landscape of consultation. These efforts move beyond the duty to consult and accommodate, striving toward a framework of relationship building.

While Canadian governmental funding and resources, as well as the non-profit relationship-building initiatives described above, are important for (and arguably incumbent on) Canada as well as Indigenous Peoples, this alone will not ensure the full development of Indigenous-municipal relationships. The active presence of Indigenous Peoples freely practising their cultures and responsibilities under their own Indigenous laws and cultural frameworks in urban centres, without interference under municipal bylaws or other forms of Canadian legislation, also needs to evolve in complex urban contexts. This re-emergence of Indigenous practices requires not so much resources as it requires that municipal officials stand aside and respect urban Indigenous cultural practices in urban sites as long as no harm is being done. To a significant extent, the possibility for just such an approach is showing some promise (Anderson and Flynn 2020).

This chapter brings us to a conclusion that needs further exploration: "relationship" implies mutually beneficial relationships and not merely a one-sided model that benefits local governments. Indigenous scholars urge a commitment to political change inspired by Indigenous worldviews, knowledges, and methodologies, including what we mean by the boundaries and definitions of urban spaces (Prusack, Walker, and Innes 2016). We suggest that relationships with Indigenous Peoples will make localities better. Municipalities are the Canadian political entities often closest to Indigenous Peoples, and as neighbours and (hopefully) friends sharing diverse community contexts, they are perhaps best positioned to exemplify and deepen what it means to uphold the honour of the Crown, in ways that more remote Canadian provincial and federal governments are challenged to realize.

REFERENCES

114957 Canada Ltée (Spraytech, Société d'arrosage) v. Hudson (Town), 2001 SCC 40.

Alcantara, Christopher, and Jen Nelles. 2016. *A Quiet Evolution: The Emergence of Indigenous-Local Intergovernmental Partnerships in Canada.* Toronto: University of Toronto Press.

Anaya, James. 2009. *Report of the Special Rapporteur on the Situation of Human Rights and Fundamental Freedoms of Indigenous People.* Geneva: United Nations.

Andersen, Chris. 2013. "Urban Aboriginality as a Distinctive Identity, in Twelve Parts." In *Indigenous in the City: Contemporary Identities and Cultural Innovation*, edited by Evelyn Peters and Chris Andersen, 46–68. Vancouver: UBC Press.

Anderson, Doug, and Alexandra Flynn. 2020. "Rethinking 'Duty': The City of Toronto, a Stretch of the Humber River and Indigenous-Municipal Relationships." *Alberta Law Review* 58, no. 1 (November): 107–32. https://doi.org/10.29173/alr2612.

———. 2021. "Indigenous-Municipal Legal and Governance Relationships." In *IMFG Papers on Municipal Finance and Governance*, no. 55. Toronto: Institute on Municipal Finance and Governance.

Association of Municipalities of Ontario. 2019. *Municipal Governments and the Crown's "Duty to Consult."* Toronto: Association of Municipalities of Ontario. https://www.amo.on.ca/policy/municipal-governance-indigenous-relations/municipal-governments-and-crowns-duty-consult.

Atter, Heidi. 2021. "Urban Reserve 'A Dream' of Past Cega'kin Leaders, Says Chief." *CBC News Saskatchewan*, February 8, 2021. https://www.cbc.ca/news/canada/saskatchewan/carry-the-kettle-first-nation-urban-reserve-1.5903528.

Australia Human Rights Commission. 2005. "Questions and Answers about Aboriginal & Torres Strait Islander Peoples." The Australian Human Rights Commission. Accessed February 6, 2022. Archived March 6, 2022, at the Wayback Machine. https://web.archive.org/web/20220306195231 /https://humanrights.gov.au/our-work/publications/questions-and-answers-about-aboriginal-torres -strait-islander-peoples.

Belanger, Yale D. 2013. "Breaching Reserve Boundaries: Canada v. Misquadis and the Legal Creation of the Urban Aboriginal Community." In *Indigenous in the City: Contemporary Identities and Cultural Innovation*, edited by Evelyn Peters and Chris Andersen, 69–87. Vancouver: UBC Press.

Borrows, John. 2017. "Canada's Colonial Constitution." In *The Right Relationship: Reimagining the Implementation of Historical Treaties*, edited by John Borrows and Michael Coyle, 17–38. Toronto: University of Toronto Press.

British Columbia. 2020. *Modernizing Land Use Planning in British Columbia: Working with Communities*. Victoria: Ministry of Forests, Lands, Natural Resource Operations and Rural Development. https://www2.gov.bc.ca/assets/gov/farming-natural-resources-and-industry/natural-resource-use /land-water-use/crown-land/land-use-plans-and-objectives/factsheets/mlup_working_with _communities_factsheet_mar2020.pdf.

British Columbia, and Business Council of British Columbia. 2018. *Memorandum of Understanding*. https://www2.gov.bc.ca/assets/gov/environment/climate-change/action/bcbc_mou_final.pdf.

Canada. 2017. *Evaluation of the Urban Aboriginal Strategy*. Ottawa: Indigenous and Northern Affairs Canada. https://www.rcaanc-cirnac.gc.ca/eng/1520261784524/1542202208787

Chippewas of the Thames First Nation v. Enbridge Pipelines Inc., 2017 SCC 41.

City of Darebin. n.d. "History of Aboriginal Victoria." City of Darebin. Accessed May 16, 2024. https://www.darebin.vic.gov.au/Community-and-pets/Aboriginal-Darebin/History-of-Aboriginal -Victoria.

City of Kamloops, and Kamloops Indian Band. 2008. *Fire Protection Agreement*. April 1, 2008. Archived June 12, 2014, at the Wayback Machine. https://web.archive.org/web/20140712103258/http:// www.civicinfo.bc.ca/Library/First_Nations_Service_Agreements/Fire_Protection_Agreement-- Kamloops_and_Kamloops_Indian_Band--2008.pdf.

City of Prince George. n.d. "About the Lheidli T'enneh First Nation." Accessed May 16, 2024. Archived October 4, 2022, at the Wayback Machine. https://web.archive.org/web/20221004123449 /https://www.princegeorge.ca/Things%20to%20Do/Pages/Learn%20about%20Prince%20George /LheidliTenneh.aspx.

City of Saskatoon. n.d. "Urban Reserves & Treaty Land Entitlement." Accessed February 6, 2022. https://www.saskatoon.ca/business-development/planning/regional-planning/urban-reserves -treaty-land-entitlement.

City of Toronto. n.d. "Land Acknowledgment." Accessed February 6, 2022. https://www.toronto.ca /city-government/accessibility-human-rights/indigenous-affairs-office/land-acknowledgement/.

Constitution Act, 1982, being Schedule B to the Canada Act 1982 (UK), c 11.

Coulthard, Glenn S. 2007. "Subjects of Empire: Indigenous Peoples and the 'Politics of Recognition' in Canada." *Contemporary Political Theory* 6, no. 4 (November): 437–60. https://doi.org/10.1057 /palgrave.cpt.9300307.

———. 2014. *Red Skin, White Masks: Rejecting the Colonial Politics of Recognition*. Minneapolis: University of Minnesota Press.

Decembrini, Angela D'Elia, and Shin Imai. 2019. "Supreme Court of Canada Cases Strengthen Argument for Municipal Obligation to Discharge Duty to Consult: Time to Put Neskonlith to Rest." *Alberta Law Review* 56, no. 3 (March): 935–49. https://doi.org/10.29173/alr2530.

Delgamuukw v. British Columbia, [1997] 3 SCR 1010, 153 DLR (4th) 193.

Dorries, Heather. 2012. "Rejecting the 'False Choice': Foregrounding Indigenous Sovereignty in Planning Theory and Practice." PhD diss., University of Toronto.

Flynn, Alexandra. 2021. "With Great(er) Power Comes Great(er) Responsibility: Indigenous Rights and Municipal Autonomy." *Journal of Law & Social Policy* 34: 111–27. https://doi.org/10.60082/0829-3929.1410.

Freeman, Victoria Jane. 2010. "'Toronto Has No History!' Indigeneity, Settler Colonialism and Historical Memory in Canada's Largest City." PhD diss., University of Toronto.Gunn, Brenda L. 2019. "Remedies for Violations of Indigenous Peoples' Human Rights." *University of Toronto Law Journal* 69, no. S1 (November): 150–70. https://doi.org/10.3138/utlj.69.s1.007.

Haida Nation v. British Columbia (Minister of Forests), 2004 SCC 73.

Hallaq, Wael B. 2018. *Restating Orientalism: A Critique of Modern Knowledge*. New York: Columbia University Press.

Heritz, Joanne. 2010. "Urban Aboriginal Peoples in Canada: Beyond Statistics." Paper presented at Canadian Political Science Association Annual Conference, Montreal, June 1–3, 2010.

———. 2016. "Municipal-Aboriginal Advisory Committees in Four Canadian Cities: 1999-2014." *Canadian Public Administration* 59, no. 1 (March): 134–52. https://doi.org/10.1111/capa.12158.

———. 2017. "The Multiplying Nodes of Indigenous Self-Government and Public Administration." *Canadian Public Administration* 60, no. 2 (June): 289–92. https://doi.org/10.1111/capa.12214.

———. 2018. "From Self-Determination to Service Delivery: Assessing Indigenous Inclusion in Municipal Governance in Canada." *Canadian Public Administration* 61, no. 4 (December): 596–615. https://doi.org/10.1111/capa.12277.

Hewitt, Jeffrey G. 2019. "Land Acknowledgment, Scripting and Julius Caesar." *The Supreme Court Law Review: Osgoode's Annual Constitutional Cases Conference* 88: 27–43. https://doi.org/10.60082/2563-8505.1359.

Hoehn, Felix, and Michael Stevens. 2018. "Local Governments and the Crown's Duty to Consult." *Alberta Law Review* 55, no. 4 (July): 971–1008. https://doi.org/10.29173/alr2483.

House of Commons Debates, 1911, 11th Parl, 3d sess, vol 3.

Howard-Hassmann, Rhoda E. 2015. "Introduction: The Human Right to Citizenship." In *The Human Right to Citizenship: A Slippery Concept*, edited by Rhoda E. Howard-Hassmann and Margaret Walton-Roberts, 1–18. Philadelphia: University of Pennsylvania Press.

Imai, Shin, and Ashley Stacey. 2014. "Municipalities and the Duty to Consult Aboriginal Peoples: A Case Comment on Neskonlith Indian Band v Salmon Arm (City)." *University of British Columbia Law Review* 47, no. 1 (January): 293–312. https://digitalcommons.osgoode.yorku.ca/cgi/viewcontent.cgi?article=1732&context=scholarly_works.

Indian Act, RSC, 1985, c I-5.

Indigenous Services Canada. 2020. "Approved Additions to Reserve Proposals." April to June 2020. https://www.sac-isc.gc.ca/eng/1466532960405/1611939046478.

———. 2023. "Additions to Reserve." Last modified March 17, 2023. https://www.sac-isc.gc.ca/eng/1332267668918/1611930372477.

Keewatin v. Ontario (Natural Resources), 2013 ONCA 158.

Koch, Madeleine, and Janice Barry. 2016. "Treaty Principles Are Planning Principles: Learning from the Experiences of Manitoban Planning Practitioners." *Plan Canada* 56, no. 4 (Winter): 22–4. https://doi.org/10.25316/IR-3028.

Makuch, Stanley, Neil Craik, and Signe Leisk. 2004. *Canadian Municipal and Planning Law*. 2nd ed. Toronto: Thomson Carswell.

Metro Vancouver. 2020. "Tsleil-Waututh Nation and Metro Vancouver Sign Co-operation Agreement for Belcarra Regional Park." February 18, 2020. https://metrovancouver.org/about-us /indigenous-relations.

Mexico. 1961. *Constitution of the United Mexican States, 1917 (as amended)*. Washington: Pan American Union.

National Association of Friendship Centres. n.d. "About the NAFC." Accessed May 16, 2024. https:// nafc.ca/about-the-nafc.

Nejad, Sarem, Ryan Walker, Brenda Macdougall, Yale Belanger, and David Newhouse. 2019. "'This is an Indigenous City; Why Don't We See it?': Indigenous Urbanism and Spatial Production in Winnipeg." *The Canadian Geographer* 63, no. 3 (Fall): 413–24. https://doi.org/10.1111 /cag.12520.

Neskonlith Indian Band v. Salmon Arm (City), 2012 BCCA 379.

Ontario Ministry of Municipal Affairs and Housing. 2018. *Municipal-Aboriginal Relationships: Case Studies*. https://iportal.usask.ca/record/66897.

Planning Act, Ontario, RSO 1990, c P.13.

Prusack, S. Yvonne, Ryan Walker, and Robert Innes. 2016. "Toward Indigenous Planning? First Nation Community Planning in Saskatchewan, Canada." *Journal of Planning Education and Research* 36, no. 4 (December): 440–50. https://doi.org/10.1177/0739456X15621147.

R. v. Greenbaum, [1993] 1 SCR 674, 100 DLR (4th) 183.

Ritchie, Kaitlin. 2013. "Issues Associated with the Implementation of the Duty to Consult and Accommodate Aboriginal Peoples: Threatening the Goals of Reconciliation and Meaningful Consultation." *University of British Columbia Law Review* 46, no. 2 (June): 397–438.

Royal Commission on Aboriginal Peoples. 1996. *Report of the Royal Commission on Aboriginal Peoples. Volume 2: Restructuring the Relationship*. Ottawa: Canada Communication Group. http://data2 .archives.ca/e/e448/e011188230-02.pdf.

Sandburg, L. Anders. 2021. *Looking for Huron-Wendat at York University*. Alternative Campus Tour, York University, August 12, 2021. https://alternativecampustour.info.yorku.ca/2021/08 /looking-for-the-huron-wendat-at-york-university-l-anders-sandberg/.

Saskatchewan. 2023. *First Nation and Métis Consultation Policy Framework*. Revised August 2023. Regina: Government of Saskatchewan. https://www.saskatchewan.ca/-/media/news-release -backgrounders/2023/aug/first-nation-and-metis-consultation-policy-framework.pdf.

Sioux Lookout Hub of the North. 2013. *Sioux Lookout Friendship Accord*. December 2, 2013. https://www.siouxlookout.ca/en/resources/pdfs/corpserv/Friendship-Accord-signed -Dec-2-2013.pdf.

Statistics Canada. 2017. "Aboriginal Peoples in Canada: Key Results from the 2016 Census." *The Daily*, released October 25, 2017. https://www150.statcan.gc.ca/n1/daily-quotidien/171025/dq171025a -eng.htm.

Taylor, Zack, and Alec Dobson. 2020. "Power and Purpose: Canadian Municipal Law in Transition." In *IMFG Papers on Municipal Finance and Governance*, no. 47. Toronto: Institute on Municipal Finance and Governance.

Town of Midland. 2019. *Official Plan for the Town of Midland*. Midland, ON: Planning and Building Services Department. https://www.midland.ca/en/business-development/resources/Planning /Official-Plan/Midland-Official-Plan.pdf.

Truth and Reconciliation Commission of Canada. 2015. *Canada's Residential Schools: Reconciliation: The Final Report of the Truth and Reconciliation Commission of Canada, Volume 6.* Montreal: McGill-Queen's University Press. https://nctr.ca/.

Val, José del, Juan Mario Pérez Martínez, Carolina Sánchez García, and María Teresa Romero Tovar. n.d. "Indigenous Peoples in México." International Working Group for Indigenous Affairs. Accessed February 6, 2022. https://www.iwgia.org/en/mexico.html.

Western Economic Diversification Canada. 2005. *Urban Reserves in Saskatchewan.* Saskatoon: Western Economic Diversification Canada, Saskatchewan Region. http://publications.gc.ca/collections /collection_2016/deo-wd/Iu92-4-36-2005-eng.pdf.

CHAPTER FOURTEEN

Confronting Anti-Black Racism in Cities

Tari Ajadi and Kristin R. Good

INTRODUCTION: CITIES AS RACIALIZED SPACES

The May 2020 murder of George Floyd at the hands of police officers in Minneapolis became a global flashpoint, causing millions of people to take to the streets in protest. These protests, emerging while the COVID-19 pandemic massively constrained social gatherings of any type in many nations, are said to be the largest in United States history (Buchanan, Bui, and Patel 2020).

The ramifications of Mr. Floyd's killing resonated far beyond the borders of the United States, prompting marches around the world. In cities across Canada, the United Kingdom, and in other parts of the world impacted by the history of the transatlantic slave trade and the artifice of white supremacy, these marches evolved into broader expressions of dissent against a political, social, economic, and environmental status quo. Protesters demanded a complete reconstitution of urban politics with calls to defund and abolish the police, while others fashioned mutual aid and community safety groups to replace social services that they perceived to be ill-equipped to support vulnerable residents during a tumultuous time.

Those unfamiliar with this subject might ask: why did George Floyd's death spur such upheaval, particularly in municipal contexts across Canada? What does the clarion call of "Black Lives Matter" have to do with urban politics?

The answer is that racialized citizens in Canada are also subject to mistreatment, violence, and social exclusion in cities across the country (Galabuzi 2012). Just two days after Mr. Floyd's death, Regis Korchinski-Paquet, an Afro-Indigenous woman living in Toronto, died after police officers conducted a "wellness check" in her apartment (Shoush, Bulle, and Boozary 2020). Her death, and the deaths of other Black, Indigenous, and people of colour in Canada at the hands of the police, are just some of the ways that racism is experienced across the Canadian federation.

Despite the urgent nature of these discussions, however, racism has been a neglected subject of academic inquiry in the Canadian urban politics literature. Urban political spaces are often the arenas within which invisible processes of structural racism become tangible for racialized citizens. City streets are the places of street checks and carding, of gentrification through "urban renewal" and environmental decay through infrastructural neglect. Nevertheless, those very same streets also facilitate racialized citizens' means of contesting racism and fostering solidarity through activism and coalition-building. How (and whether) municipalities grapple with the conflicts that emerge from racialized governance practices thus becomes a highly salient question.

This chapter aims to demonstrate how racial injustice is manifested in Canadian city politics and to explore the role of municipalities in both creating and potentially addressing processes of racialization in cities. It uses comparative methods, including sub-national, cross-national, and policy comparisons to probe the processes and impact of racialization as well as forms of activism to resist it. As we will discover, despite significant differences in national policy infrastructures, histories of racial oppression and colonization, and differences in the characteristics of the racialized populations themselves, similarities in the manifestation of racism and the racialization of space in these highly different national and sub-national contexts stand out.

This chapter begins with a few key definitions that will shape readers' understanding of the phenomena being discussed. It will then give readers a historical overview of the development of contemporary policing before discussing and comparing case studies of racial profiling in Canada, the United Kingdom, and the United States. Next, it discusses how planning and service decisions shape urban development, which is in turn shaped by environmental racism. The next part of the chapter engages with the Halifax case and the historic razing of Africville in its "urban renewal" period of urban development as well as more contemporary examples of environmental racism, specifically the Flint water crisis in the United States. The chapter will then conclude with a discussion of how municipalities across the country plan to address activist demands for transformation.

DEFINITIONS

Activist demands for municipalities to transform can be better understood with some conceptual clarity about racism. While racism can take many forms and can operate in multiple ways, we will be focusing specifically on structural and institutional racism in this chapter. Structural racism, according to Gee and Ford, is "the macrolevel systems, social forces, institutions, ideologies, and processes that interact with one another to generate and reinforce inequities among racial and ethnic groups" (2011, 116). Structural racism is historically rooted and often invisible, underpinning policies and processes that shape everyday life in urban contexts. In this chapter, we will be discussing structural racism within the context of policing as well as in the context of urban planning and environmental policies. We also focus primarily, though not exclusively, on how anti-Black racism unfolds in these urban contexts. Anti-Black racism refers to the policies and practices embedded in governing institutions that reflect and reinforce beliefs, attitudes, prejudice, stereotyping, or discrimination that is directed at people of African descent (City of Toronto 2017).

Structural racism also underpins how institutions are created and operate within municipalities, creating instances of institutional racism. Institutional racism operates in the meso-level and occurs when a person or people are discriminated against by public or private organizations as an outcome of established rules, laws, or customs because of their racial or ethnic origin (Cook et al. 1999). Unlike structural racism, institutional racism is often actively felt by the individuals and communities who bear the brunt of its effects. Institutional racism is not solely the intentional behaviours of discriminatory actors within an organization but also manifests itself in its everyday functions and procedures (Lea 2000).

Another key concept to clarify here is racialization. The designation and characterization of particular racial groups, while appearing like a neutral or natural process, is actually socially constructed and changes over time (Delgado, Stefancic, and Harris 2017). Racialization is the name given to that process. When applied to groups of people, racialization refers to the social process by which a particular group becomes "othered," "non-white," and perceived as inferior. In urban contexts, processes of racialization are often tied to particular spaces, affecting the way that particular neighbourhoods are perceived, as well as the services residents and communities are provided by municipal institutions (and other levels of government).

The term environmental racism is used to conceptualize how structural racism manifests in a pattern of decision-making that disproportionately locates noxious land uses close to racialized communities as well as normalizes the exposure of some groups to environmental risk. One might think of this term as a distinct manifestation of institutional racism as well as part of a process that racializes particular spaces. The term environmental racism is also relevant to patterns of mobilization around environmental issues that have historically failed to include racialized minorities and the environmental issues of importance to them (Waldron 2018b; Bennett 2004).

Crucial to discussions of racism at both the institutional and structural level is the concept of white supremacy, which is the presumed superiority of white racial identities that facilitates the political, economic, and cultural oppression and domination of non-white groups. White supremacy, therefore, functions as the defining logic that justifies racism and racialization in much of the world (Bonds and Inwood 2016).

Another key concept that shapes the ways that racism is expressed in municipalities is the carceral state, which refers to the infrastructure of punitive, surveillance, and punishment-based institutions and forms of governance that operate within municipal spaces (Weaver and Lerman 2010). The carceral state is often a significant way through which those that it targets – in particular racialized communities in cities – interact with government services of any kind.

Finally, the term settler colonialism (discussed further in chapter 13) is crucial to our understanding of how structural and institutional racism operate, particularly within North American territories. Settler colonialism is where the political and social orders of those who originate in a territory are displaced and upended by actors who move to that territory and establish relations of domination and control (Veracini 2013). In North America, this process has resulted in the genocide of First Peoples across the continent.

In addition to these definitions of extensive processes that typically occur and develop over extended periods of time, this chapter will discuss specific practices and procedures that have been associated with how racism is expressed by municipal institutions.

The first of these, racial profiling, occurs as a result of the stereotypes created in processes of racialization. It is an institutional practice and reflection of institutional racism. Racialized residents of municipalities are singled out (often by the police but also in private settings by security guards, for example) for individual scrutiny or differential treatment on the basis of their race, ethnicity, or place of origin as opposed to reasonable suspicion of being a threat to public safety (Bahdi 2003; Ontario Human Rights Commission, n.d.).

Carding is a subset of racial profiling. Carding interactions involve situations in which a police officer randomly asks an individual to provide identifying information when there is no objectively suspicious activity, the individual is not suspected of any offence, and there is no reason to believe that the individual has any information on any offence. That information is then recorded and stored in a police intelligence database (Tulloch 2018, xi).

Street checks are slightly different from carding and are an interaction or observation (without interaction) in which personal or identifying information is collected by an officer and entered into a database for future use (MacDonald and Taylor 2019).

POLICING

The often-strained relationship between police forces and racialized residents in urban spaces is, in many ways, the most tangible expression of racial tensions that residents may experience. This section outlines how practices of police surveillance such as street checks and carding have created hostile environments for racialized citizens in these communities. We begin by placing the institution of policing into historical context before comparing incidences of racial profiling in Toronto and Halifax to understand the similarities in the inequities faced by racialized citizens in both contexts despite the significant differences between the two municipalities. We then place these Canadian cities in international context by reviewing incidences of racial profiling in London and Bristol, England, as well as in New York City. We conclude this section by outlining the lessons that can be learned from comparisons across international municipalities with divergent histories, institutional structures, and approaches to municipal governance.

Policing in Historical Context

Formal police forces in what we now call Canada date back to the 1650s, when watchmen patrolled the streets of Quebec City. These officers scarcely resembled the modern, organized forces of today. Instead, the watchmen of seventeenth-century New France were appointed by justices of the peace (who themselves were not required to have any training), and their roles also included being tax collectors, sanitation inspectors, and cleaners (Hayes 2001, 149). Municipalities in what became Ontario (then named Upper Canada) followed a constabulary model that mirrored the rudimentary systems set up in England that allowed for freelancing and often corrupt constables to maintain the post-feudal social order (Dinnen and Braithwaite 2009, 162). Once the Seven Years' War led to British control over New France, the locally governed systems of policing in Quebec City and elsewhere switched to that of Upper Canada (Whetstone, n.d.). As municipalities like Toronto and Halifax began to incorporate in the middle of the nineteenth century, they set up local oversight of the police officers that did exist in their budding settlements and took inspiration from the colonial metropole, whose laws they followed.

The main innovation of the era as it relates to urban policing was the establishment of the Metropolitan Police Department in London, England, in 1829. The force, founded by Sir Robert Peel, was a highly organized and hierarchical organization that promoted from within but was crucially staffed by civilians. It differed from existing forces by focusing on "preventative policing" or the surveillance of communities via patrol as well as deterrence of crime via detective work (Styles 1987, 17). The Metropolitan Police model was to be conducted according to Peel's nine principles of policing (see Home Office 2012), which highlight a consensual, relationship-driven approach to policing. In Canada, municipally governed forces quickly sprouted following Peel's logic. The Toronto Police Service was founded in 1835 (Mukherjee 2013, 4), Quebec City and Montreal followed shortly thereafter (McCulloch 1990). Halifax and Vancouver's forces followed in 1864 and 1886, respectively (Vancouver Police Department, n.d.; Halifax Regional Police, n.d.).

These forces operated in contrast to the imperial paramilitary model of the Royal Irish Constabulary, which Peel also governed during his time as chief secretary for Ireland in the 1810s, and which was replicated in a Canadian context by the North West Mounted Force (later renamed the Royal Canadian Mounted Police) (Marquis 1997, 195). The imperial paramilitary model had far less room for community engagement, operating under the broad aegis of command and control. As Clive Emsley notes, these paramilitary forces operated as the "missionaries of European civilization" – the engines of settler colonialism whose primary role was to quell rebellions among the people whose lands and resources they stole, and whose culture they attempted to quash (Emsley 2014, 12).

In practice, however, the approaches to policing listed above often overlapped, and the idyllic, Peelian framing of the "police as the public, and the public as the police" stood far apart from the realities of the development of these institutions. After rebellions in Montreal and

Quebec City, for instance, municipal governance of police forces was temporarily suspended by the colonial government in favour of the paramilitary approach (Marquis 1997, 197). Police officers were well known during the era as the vanguard of class repression, suppressing labour strikes and generally operating as what historian Greg Marquis calls "glorified local bull[ies]" (Marquis 1990, 88). More often than not, in Canada as in other "White Dominions," colonial governments and municipalities alike blended approaches depending on the perceived needs – and racial/ethnic makeup – of the territory they intended to govern (Emsley 2014, 9).

The colonial context from which police forces emerge raises important areas to explore when we turn to modern-day analyses of police interactions with residents across Canada, in particular those interactions with racialized minorities. As municipalities transitioned from direct oversight of police forces to developing arms-length boards of police commissioners with oversight of the policy direction of forces, the issue of community consent for police operations became vital. Who gets to decide what consent means in an urban context, and in whose name consent is given, become the salient questions in urban policing as it relates to racialized communities.

Racial Profiling by Police Forces in Canada

The Peelian principles of preventive policing, in a vacuum, are enabled by well-established community relationships that mutually support public safety for all members of a community. In practice, racialized residents of urban municipalities across the country, and around much of the world, have been subject to racial bias in policing under the mandate of crime prevention and order maintenance. This bias has been particularly felt by Black and Indigenous residents of Canadian cities, who have long cited issues of racial profiling, disparities in the use of force, arrests, and surveillance as signs of institutional racism in police forces (Tator and Henry 2006, 55). Persistent racial profiling has also affected South Asian and Arab Canadian communities in the aftermath of 9/11 as police forces used the pretext of fighting terrorism to surveil Arab and Muslim communities (Bahdi 2003, 298). The mistrust that this bias fosters often undermines attempts by police forces to develop these community relationships, thus further undermining perceptions of public safety in these contexts. Racial profiling and the overpolicing of racialized communities have also prompted conflicts like the Yonge Street Uprising in 1992 in Toronto (Owusu-Bempah and Wortley 2014). This section will cover two case studies of communities affected by racial profiling to better understand why this practice has undermined trusting relationships between racialized communities and police forces in Canada.

RACIAL PROFILING IN TORONTO

The Toronto census metropolitan area (which includes much of what we might call the GTA) has 442,015 Black residents, or 36.9 per cent of Canada's total Black population (Statistics

Canada 2019). Black residents total 7.5 per cent of Toronto's total population, which is the highest proportion of Black residents in any CMA in Canada (Statistics Canada 2019). The racial profiling and disproportionately harsh treatment of African Canadians in the Greater Toronto Area by police forces has been a long-standing and deeply impactful issue in the region (Wortley and Owusu-Bempah 2011, 395). Paradoxically, however, the extent of racial profiling in the region also could not be quantified for many years because police forces like the Toronto Police Service were banned from analyzing data related to race by their police boards (Rankin, Quinn, and Shephard 2002). "Singled Out," a landmark 2002 study by the *Toronto Star*, used an access to information request to obtain arrest data going back to 1996 that demonstrated, among other findings, that Black residents were overrepresented in traffic stops that subsequently led to arrests (Rankin, Quinn, and Shephard 2002).

Investigations like "Singled Out" increased the scrutiny on forces like the Toronto Police Service, but a 2005 city-wide spike in gun violence prompted a doubling-down of police surveillance and presence in primarily Black neighbourhoods such as the Jane and Finch area under the auspices of a community policing strategy (Saberi 2017, 55). This strategy was named TAVIS, or the Toronto Anti-Violence Intervention Strategy, and was designed to empower and engage with community members, agencies, and organizations while using cutting-edge training and scientific methods to combat violence in "high-risk" areas (58). Instead, the TAVIS program was highly criticized for its use of militaristic raids akin to that used by military forces in warzones and also for its use of "carding" – a data collection technique used by the Toronto Police Service to stop and record the information of "persons of interest" (Friesen 2006; Ontario Human Rights Commission 2018, 128).

The dramatic increase in the use of carding under then-police chief Bill Blair, as well as a combination of studies and first-person experiential articles about the horrific effects of racial profiling, became the flashpoint that prompted the Toronto Police Services Board and the Government of Ontario to begin reconsidering the practice (Saberi 2017, 59; Cole 2015; Rankin 2015; 2010). Studies by the *Toronto Star* and scholars like Scot Wortley, Akwasi Owusu-Bempah, and others demonstrated that Black residents, especially men aged 15–24 were 2.5 times more likely to be stopped and carded by the police (Saberi 2017, 59; Rankin 2010; Wortley and Owusu-Bempah 2011).

Despite extensive pushback from the Toronto Police Service, the practice of carding was curtailed in stages by the city's Police Services Board and later by the province. The first intervention by the Police Services Board required police officers to produce a "receipt" for individuals they stopped, detailing the data they collected (Winsa and Rankin 2013). In 2015, Chief Blair moved to suspend the practice, citing what he framed as an impasse between community members and police leadership (Winsa and Rankin 2015). Finally, after an eleven-month province-wide consultation, Justice Michael Tulloch of the Ontario Court of Appeal issued a report reviewing the practice of carding and found that arbitrary stops of citizens should be banned and that any identifying information given to police in these contexts should be voluntary (Tulloch 2018, 223).

Restrictions levied by the provincial government severely curtailed the use of the practice, but the rules did not cover traffic stops or arrests (Draaisma 2017).

STREET CHECKS IN HALIFAX, NOVA SCOTIA

Halifax, Nova Scotia, has a markedly different demographic profile to that of Toronto. People of African descent, despite being the largest racialized group in Nova Scotia, make up 3.74 per cent of a census metropolitan area of approximately 400,000 people (Statistics Canada 2017). Unlike Toronto, the majority of African Nova Scotians were not only born in Canada but have roots in Nova Scotia extending back three generations or more (Statistics Canada 2019, 15). Many of those families are descended from the Black refugees who came to work and live in the province after the War of 1812, but some African Nova Scotians have roots that extend back to the times of slavery in the province (Saney 1998). Tensions between people of African descent and police forces in the municipality extend back for generations, with prominent figures like Burnley "Rocky" Jones leading protests in the 1960s against police overreach in the North End of the city (Jones and St. G. Walker 2016). The municipality is unique in Canada as it is policed by both the Halifax Regional Police (who patrol most of the urban core and the suburbs) and the Royal Canadian Mounted Police (who are contracted out to police mostly rural areas). The Board of Police Commissioners in the Halifax Regional Municipality (HRM), therefore, has a dual role in setting the policy direction for the Halifax Regional Police and for the RCMP detachment in the area.

Racial profiling in the municipality became a significant focus of activists after former heavyweight boxer Kirk Johnson testified to the Nova Scotia Human Rights Commission that he was stopped by a member of the Halifax Regional Police (HRP) because of his race, also noting that he had been stopped twenty-eight times over five years while driving in the area (Girard 2003). The commission found that the way the HRP treated Johnson was discriminatory and called for the HRP to develop a procedure to identify the role of race in traffic stops (Girard 2003). Such a procedure never came, and instead police forces in the area began to use street checks to record data about members of the public in 2005. An investigation by the CBC in 2017 found that Black Haligonians were three times more likely to undergo a street check compared to white residents (McGregor and MacIvor 2017). This investigation prompted the Nova Scotia Human Rights Commission to study the use of street checks in the municipality, and the resulting report written by Dr. Scot Wortley (2019) indicated that these numbers were actually under-reported. Initially, the Nova Scotia provincial government refused to intervene in the practice of street checks. After extensive advocacy by organizations including the African Nova Scotian Decade for People of African Descent Coalition (an umbrella advocacy group in Nova Scotia) and a legal opinion written by Michael MacDonald, retired justice of the Nova Scotia Court of Appeal, and Jennifer Taylor, a research lawyer, which stated that the practice was in fact illegal, the province decided to ban the use of street checks (Ray 2019).

Table 14.1. Comparing Racial Profiling in Toronto and Halifax

Municipality	Halifax, Nova Scotia	Toronto, Ontario
Census subdivision (2016)	403,131	2,731,571
% of Black Residents from Total Population	3%	8.9%
Police Forces Operating in Municipality	Halifax Regional Police, Royal Canadian Mounted Police	Toronto Police Service
Primarily First Generation/Primarily Third Generation or More?	Primarily third generation or more	Primarily first generation
Racial Profiling Targeting Black Residents?	Yes	Yes

Source: Data from Statistics Canada, 2016 Census of Population.

COMPARING CANADIAN CASES

The pernicious role that racial profiling via carding or street checks has played in shaping life for Black residents indicates the depth of racialized mythologies in both municipalities despite the significant differences between the size, histories, and present-day experiences of Black communities in both cities. Table 14.1 compares the two jurisdictions.

Table 14.1 demonstrates the durability of ideas of Black criminality in municipalities that are different in profound ways. Toronto is many times bigger than Halifax, has a far larger Black population that is densely concentrated in the urban centre as opposed to the rurally rooted Black population in Halifax, and this population is primarily first generation in Canada. The police forces that interact with Black residents in both jurisdictions, however, operate with similar levels of impunity and disregard through racial profiling. Comparing these jurisdictions in this manner, through a "most different systems design" (discussed in chapter 3), helps to illuminate the shared phenomena of racial profiling, as well as the ideological and discursive underpinnings of this practice.

Frances Henry and Carol Tator, authors of the text *Racial Profiling in Canada: Challenging the Myth of a "Few Bad Apples,"* note that this profiling of Black residents is formed from a social and political context where Black residents are "immediately perceived in terms of a particular body and colour image associated almost subliminally with a criminal disposition" (2006, 27). This perception, combined with mythologies and discourses that Black residents are "at variance with the White-defined norms that regulate modern societies," produces a social acceptance of strategies of racial profiling (Tator and Henry 2006, 33; Rose 2002).

Henry and Tator's hypothesis has been borne out in survey data collected by Scot Wortley and Akwasi Owusu-Bempah in Toronto in 2007. Their study shows that only 21 per cent of white residents and 14 per cent of Chinese residents perceived racial profiling as a big problem as compared to 60 per cent of Black residents (Wortley and Owusu-Bempah 2011, 397). While the practice of carding has been curtailed for three years, Black residents still report similar levels of police contact in the GTA (Wortley, Owusu-Bempah, and Lin 2021).

Wortley found a similar pattern in his research in Halifax. Of Black residents who answered his survey, 74 per cent believe that racial profiling is a major issue in the municipality compared to 36 per cent of white residents and 42 per cent of residents from other racial groups (Wortley 2019, 32). Moreover, despite the explicit ban on street checks in the municipality, advocates claim that police officers are using a reasonable suspicion "loophole" to continue to profile Black residents (Devet 2021).

The fight against racial profiling, therefore, is ongoing in both contexts despite formal legislation either banning or severely restricting its use as a practice in policing. A change in legislation in these municipalities is just one step in addressing a lineage of structural and institutional racism that manifests itself in the durability and widespread nature of the practice of racial profiling, as well as the logics and discourses that underpin that practice. As we will demonstrate below, cities across the United Kingdom and the United States reproduce markedly similar outcomes in terms of racial profiling despite different institutional arrangements, histories, and sizes.

COMPARING CITIES IN CANADA, THE UNITED KINGDOM, AND THE UNITED STATES

Social, historical, and political discourses that frame Black residents as predisposed to crime and criminality are not unique to Canadian contexts, and they are not mitigated by discourses of multiculturalism that emphasize surface-level explorations of cultural difference instead of a rigorous analysis of racialized power hierarchies that underpin governing institutions across the country (Ku et al. 2019). These ideas of Black criminality are part of the process of racialization that emerged from the enslavement of African peoples in the 1600s, deepened after the end of the transatlantic slave trade in the 1800s, and that has fundamentally shaped legislation, policy-making, and institutional behaviours across North America, Europe, Latin America, and the Caribbean. Though many understandings of nation-building in Canada ignore our involvement in the transatlantic slave trade and our complicity in these global paradigms, this section is going to use three examples of cities in the United States and the United Kingdom to illustrate that, despite differences in city size, composition, and institutional arrangements, policing in each of these contexts produces similar disparities in profiling that ultimately perpetuate anti–Black racism in each context. In so doing, this section argues that the fundamental ideologies that shape structural racism in each country are shared transnationally and are filtered through national and local institutions in a process that Debra Thompson (2016, 47) calls institutional translation.

Racial Profiling in the United Kingdom

The United Kingdom, as the former centre of the British Empire, has had a complicated relationship with discussions of race, racism, and policing. As noted above, both the "imperial paramilitary" model and the "community policing" models emerged from attempts by English governments in particular to control what they perceived as restive populations within and outside the metropole. Moreover, the legacy of British colonialism and the racial hierarchies these processes created and maintained live on not only in North America but also in the United Kingdom (Pemberton 2015, 321). The outcome of this history for Black British people across England and Wales in particular is a perceived link between race and criminality that provides a pretext for racial profiling. Statistics from across England and Wales show that Black people are nine times more likely to be stopped and searched than white people (Dodd 2020).

In London, home of Peel's "bobbies" and of the nine principles of community policing, Black people are four times more likely than white people to be subject to a stop and search. This figure rises to more than eleven times more likely in London and higher elsewhere since the requirement of "reasonable grounds" to stop a resident has been removed under section 60 legislation, despite crime rates decreasing in the city (Marsh 2020).[1] Given that London is the area of the United Kingdom with the most Black residents – 13 per cent of the total population of the city – this disproportionality in stop and search practices shapes the experiences of a significant portion of Black Britons and informs perceptions that the Metropolitan Police is institutionally racist (Lea 2000; Pearson and Rowe 2020). As Bernie Grant, the late MP for Tottenham (a borough of London) once noted:

> Nothing has been more damaging to the relationship between the police and the black community than the ill-judged use of stop and search powers. For young black men in particular, the humiliating experience of being repeatedly stopped and searched is a sad fact of life, in some parts of London at least. It is hardly surprising that those on the receiving end of this treatment should develop hostile attitudes towards the police. The right to walk the streets is a fundamental one, and one that is quite rightly jealously guarded. (Bowling and Phillips 2007, 936)

A discriminatory use of stop and search powers is not contained to the Metropolitan Police or to London. In smaller cities around the United Kingdom, similarly discriminatory policing practices have fostered long-standing tensions between Black residents and the police. One such example is Bristol, a city of around 460,000 people (6 per cent of whom identify as Black), where racial conflict between Black residents and police officers erupted in the form of the St. Pauls riots in 1980 (Mellen 2020). Since that time, Black residents have continued to experience the effects of discriminatory policing patterns. Bristol's mayor Martin Rees noted that Bristol is "one of the worst cities to be born Black in" due to the persistence of poverty and discrimination against Black residents within the criminal justice system (Mackinnon 2020). It is little wonder, then, that the Avon and Somerset Police (the force that covers the city of Bristol) stop Black residents at a rate 7.4 times higher than white residents (StopWatch 2021). The prevalence of discriminatory forms of policing in municipalities across the United Kingdom speaks to the durability of national racial hierarchies that are expressed within public institutions despite explicit attempts to demonstrate that these hierarchies are a thing of the past.

Racial Profiling in the United States

While a detailed history of racial profiling in the United States is beyond the scope of this textbook chapter, the practice is ubiquitous across the nation and stems from the origin of police forces as runaway slave patrols in the seventeenth and eighteenth centuries (Lepore 2020). The widespread use of racial profiling occurs despite being, in the words of the American Civil Liberties Union, "patently illegal, violating the U.S. Constitution's core promises of equal protection under the law to all and freedom from unreasonable searches and seizures" (American Civil Liberties Union 2021). New York City, the largest city in the country, has a particularly significant history with the development of racial profiling as a policing technique in the twentieth and twenty-first centuries. The New York Police Department (NYPD), and eventually the City of New York as a whole, embraced the "broken windows" theory of policing to address rising crime rates in the city. The "broken windows" theory, coined by James Wilson and George Kelling in the March 1982 issue of *The Atlantic*, emerges from an analogy that the authors make during the piece about community disorder:

> [At] the community level, disorder and crime are usually inextricably linked, in a kind of developmental sequence. Social psychologists and police officers tend to agree that if a window in a building is broken and is left unrepaired, all the rest of the windows will soon be broken. This is as true in nice neighborhoods as in rundown ones. Window-breaking does not necessarily occur on a large scale because some areas are inhabited by determined window-breakers whereas others are populated by window-lovers; rather, one unrepaired broken window is a signal that no one cares, and so breaking more windows costs nothing. (Wilson and Kelling 1982)

Wilson and Kelling's core thesis is that neighbourhood disorder, like broken windows on an abandoned building, and major crimes are connected. In this view, a neighbourhood with vandalism means that residents perceive the streets to be less safe, prompting disconnection and distrust, which then foster an environment that allows for violent crime to emerge. The role of the police in preventing such an environment to emerge is, therefore, to maintain order by enforcing statutes related to public disorder. This enforcement, coupled with a visible police presence, thus deters potential crime from emerging (Wilson and Kelling 1982).

The theory has been heavily critiqued by researchers, activists, and community members for its significant contribution to racial profiling in cities across North America, as well as for claiming that correlations between disorder and crime were in fact causal mechanisms. As Fagan et al. (2010, 331) note in their study of police stops in New York City between 1998 and 2006, stops of citizens during the era increased by 500 per cent, but their efficiency in terms of detecting crime declined by nearly 50 per cent over the same period. The process of intensified policing in mostly Black and Latino neighbourhoods in New York City reflects what Gruber calls "bluelining" or the maintenance of majority white middle- and upper-class spaces by police forces within urban environments (Gruber 2021).

The "broken windows" theory was massively influential in New York City. It reached its advent in the 1990s under the leadership of mayor Rudolph Guiliani and NYPD police commissioner William Bratton, who claimed that this approach (complete with arrests for turnstile-jumping, panhandling, graffiti, and more) was the cause behind falling violent crime rates in the city (Vedantam et al. 2016). The theory also allowed for the use of stop and frisk tactics, which go beyond street checks or carding to physically search individuals for weapons, drugs, or other illegal items (Matthews 2013). Black and Latinx residents of New York City were massively overrepresented in stop and frisk rates during the NYPD's extensive usage of the program: in 2011, Black residents were 53 per cent of all residents stopped, while Latinx residents were 34 per cent of stops despite both groups representing 26 per cent of the population in total (New York Civil Liberties Union 2012). Only 1.5 per cent of the stops resulted in police officers finding weapons, and of those stops, more of the suspects were white than were Latinx or Black. The significant correlation between race and ethnicity and police stops led to affected residents winning a class-action lawsuit against the NYPD in 2013, and the subsequent decline of stop and frisks in the city thereafter (Suero 2015).

Lessons from Comparison

The case studies above demonstrate that, despite divergent national, sub-national, and municipal contexts, policing in urban spaces has often produced discriminatory patterns of racial profiling that contravene legislative standards and institutional proclamations that state that racialized communities must be given equal treatment under the law. In each case, racial profiling has been used to confine, surveil, and criminalize Black residents in particular, creating urban environments that are exclusionary and harmful in nature. This is true in contexts in which Black populations have long histories in Canada (and pre-Canada) as well as in cities where the Black immigrant population is large and the city is highly multiracial and multicultural. The transnational and within-country comparisons that we have presented in this section demonstrate profound similarities in the ideologies and tactics that underpin racial profiling despite the unique histories and institutional arrangements that shape each police force in each municipality.

Moreover, advocates in each jurisdiction have had to use the judiciary to challenge these practices, with varying degrees of success. The similarities of these cases demonstrate that harmful ideas about race persist across international contexts and are translated through institutional and cultural norms and practices, informing the ways that municipalities conduct their business (Thompson 2016). As we will discuss later in the chapter, the ideological translation of ideas about race to different urban contexts also extends to activists, who have shared ideas, resources, and tactics to prompt policy change across borders.

URBAN PLANNING AND THE RACIALIZATION OF SPACE

Policing is not the only institution through which municipalities might sustain policies and practices that exclude racialized groups from fully participating in urban life. Just as police forces are agents of racialization within urban contexts, decisions around planning, zoning, and the environment in cities can reproduce or entrench racial discrimination in municipal contexts (Rutland 2018). In this section we discuss the role of planning in the racialization of space, focusing on the urban renewal period, a significant period for the study of urban politics and the politicization of urban space.

As described in chapter 3, a dominant focus of urban planning and development is growth, so much so that North American cities have been conceptualized as "growth machines" (Logan and Molotch 1987). Although relevant in a modified form today, this concept, originally developed by Molotch and Logan in the 1970s, describes American cities in the post–Second World War period in which the focus was on urban "renewal." A related theory, urban regime theory, which became the dominant theoretical paradigm in American urban politics literature, emerged in this period as well, conceptualizing an ongoing public-private form of collaboration from the 1940s until 1989 (Stone 1989). This period included the 1960s and 1970s, in which American cities had become increasingly politicized with the rise of the civil rights movement and other progressive social movements often based in cities.

Indeed, Clarence Stone's (1989) influential case study of Atlanta explored how collective action between Atlanta's white business community and its African American majority developed and was maintained to create and implement a downtown renewal agenda. He argues that the business community supported desegregation and provided middle-class African Americans jobs in exchange for the Black-led council's support for urban renewal. Atlanta became known as a progressive Southern city, whose motto was "The City Too Busy to Hate." Leaders in Atlanta's African American community were able to join the regime only because their numbers gave them control of city council. Whereas some concessions to progressive causes were made (including support for desegregation), one could just as easily characterize this alliance as co-optation of a more radical local civil rights agenda that would have benefited African Americans living in poverty and challenged forms of structural racism, including the carceral state, discussed above, and environmental racism. These leading American theories of urban politics offer important insights about the systemic biases of a capitalist economy in cities and the difficult question of creating the capacity to govern in a context of fragmented resources. However, as discussed in chapter 3, they fail to acknowledge the systemic nature of racism and the power of the state and municipal governments to oppress particular segments of the population in order to maintain the privilege of others, a point to which we return below.[2] Furthermore, the exchange relationship between the business community and middle-class African Americans described in *Regime Politics* (Stone 1989) did not lead to transformative change but rather only offered minor concessions to racial justice in exchange for support for the ongoing "value free development" (Logan and Molotch 1987) that was taking place in the city and benefiting the white population disproportionately, described more precisely as "racial capitalism" below. African American communities were removed from neighbourhoods around the University of Chicago, the city of Charlottesville, Virginia, and even in Atlanta, the so-called "City Too Busy to Hate." Indeed, the lasting coalition that became urban scholars' inspiration for urban regime theory led to the destruction of 55,000 Black homes (Newman 2002, 301–21).

Segregation and Divestment in the American Rust Belt – a Case Study

Racialization in American cities was not only shaped by discourses of renewal but also by discourses of denial and refusal. Northern cities in the United States, for instance, were shaped by the Great Migration of African Americans from the rural South in the early twentieth century who sought to avoid the punitive effects of Jim Crow-era segregation laws (Bennett 2004, 130). This migration was particularly significant in what we now call the Rust Belt: the areas of the Midwestern and Northeastern United States that were once manufacturing powerhouses but have since largely deindustrialized (Hackworth 2018, 54). African Americans who moved to the Rust Belt often ended up in neighbourhoods that were purposefully segregated with "redlining" policies that prevented Black residents from accessing financial services such as mortgages or home repair loans because of their race (Doan 2017, 182). These policies were called "redlining" because these specific neighbourhoods were marked by red lines on urban maps to denote areas that banks would refuse to invest in, and these maps were also used by the Federal Housing Administration during the New Deal to denote where to place new housing eventually purchased by affluent and predominately white borrowers, thus co-constructing the suburbs and areas of urban poverty (Doan 2017, 183; Greer 2014, 204).

In Rust Belt cities like Detroit, the presence of industrial powerhouses like General Motors further increased the migration of African Americans to the area seeking steady, well-paid employment in the factories that operated as the region's economic engine. The presence of more Black families, sometimes in formerly white neighbourhoods, prompted a phenomenon called "white flight" – where white families moved from inner cities to the suburbs to enforce a de facto municipal segregation akin to the de jure segregation maintained by redlining (Clotfelter 1976; Hammer 2018). Not only did white flight expand the "colour line" from particular neighbourhoods to entire municipalities, but it also facilitated what Hackworth calls extreme land abandonment in the areas that white families left behind as it added to perceptions that the presence of Black people would lead to increased crime and decreased property values (Hackworth 2018). The newly built suburbs that absorbed the white flight from the inner cities of the Rust Belt quickly incorporated, prompting municipal Balkanization. As Hammer (2018, 229) notes, southeastern Michigan is one of the most fragmented areas in the entire United

States, with over 150 municipalities covering a small region, all with strong laws governing the use of municipal finances.

The period in which growth machines and urban renewal-focused "regimes" reigned in the United States was also a period of intense activism. The civil rights movement, which strove to end segregation and achieve social, economic, and political equality for African Americans, gained steam in the 1960s. This movement (with others) would feed the environmental justice movement aimed at challenging environmental racism, a form of structural racism that locates environmentally undesirable land uses such as waste facilities near marginalized communities because they are "racialized" but that also contributes to entrenching racialization in turn. This form of structural racism spurred the development of the environmental justice movement in the United States (Cole and Foster 2001), a movement that has received little attention in Canada (but see Waldron 2018a, 2018b). In the United States, President Clinton's Executive Order on Environmental Justice, issued in 1994, brought "unprecedented recognition" to environmental racism in the United States (Cole and Foster 2001, 10). However, urban activism against environmental racism has a longer history in the United States. Some identify the beginning of the movement as 1982, when African American protests against a dump in Warren County, North Carolina, took place (Cole and Foster 2001, 19). Others have identified grassroots activism in earlier cases including in Houston in 1967 when an eight-year-old African American girl died by drowning in a garbage dump located in a residential area (19). Still others point out that, when he was assassinated, Rev. Dr. Martin Luther King Jr. was travelling to join and support striking garbage workers in Memphis (19). Cole and Foster (2001) also mention pesticide poisoning in the workplace as another early struggle in the 1960s. Although framed as a particular form of racism, these examples, which range from land-use decisions to workplace safety concerns, illustrate how society's willingness to put some groups at risk of harm due to exposure to toxic substances is a fundamental dimension of the violence inherent in racism.

The areas that were subject to redlining and white flight in cities like Detroit and Flint were also disproportionately chosen to be the sites of environmentally harmful infrastructure like oil refineries, leading to significant environmental and health effects (Benz 2019, 50). The salient factor in the placement of these toxic facilities is their racial composition – communities that are primarily Black or Latinx are more likely to bear the burdens of environmental degradation (Bennett 2004; Seamster and Purifoy 2021; Benz 2019). This environmental racism is not, as Seamster and Purifoy note, a simple product of the refusal of white Nimbyism, but is rather a process of creative extraction:

> Creative extraction describes how white towns catalyze their development with resources from beyond their borders. This occurs through three main mechanisms: theft of resources (land and public finance), gradual erosion (environmental degradation and denial of basic services), and political exclusion (denial of democratic participation or eroding the agency/

> effectiveness of representatives). Creative extraction is not an isolated strategy, but deeply
> connected to scarcity, competition, and colonial power relations created by racial capitalism –
> the system of accumulating material and social value through racial hierarchy. (Seamster and
> Purifoy 2021, 111)

The residents of white towns benefited from the de facto segregation caused by redlining and white flight by removing their financial contributions from majority-Black municipalities and investing in their own suburban enclaves. This process of divestment became cyclical and contributed to the economic collapse of what Benz calls "sacrifice zones" (2019, 51; Hammer 2018, 233).

Worse still, these white towns have also benefited from white flight by downloading the burdens of environmental and economic degradation onto the primarily Black areas they left behind, leading to cases like the Flint Water Crisis that began in 2014. The Flint Water Crisis was spurred by the economic collapse caused by decades of divestment from the city, which facilitated the suspension of municipal control over municipal affairs. Instead, the state of Michigan used legislation to appoint an emergency manager to save money on the municipality's behalf, and this emergency manager decided to switch the city's water supply from the Detroit water system to the Flint River in April 2014 despite studies from the Environmental Protection Agency (EPA) that showed lead levels exceeding the agency's standard for toxic waste (Stanley 2016; Benz 2019). Importantly, the surrounding suburban and primarily white area of Genesee County was spared the change of water systems (Stanley 2016, 34).

General Motors, a key employer in the area, ceased using the water in the area in October 2014, citing corrosion on its parts (Michigan Civil Rights Commission 2018, 115). Even the state of Michigan decided to provide water coolers and bottled water to their staff in Flint to protect them from the poor quality of the municipal drinking water (115). Despite outcry from Flint residents who identified the harmful change to their water, despite the EPA finding that lead levels in the water were 880 times acceptable federal limits, and despite studies from local researchers that found elevated lead levels in Flint children, the state continued to source its water from the Flint River until October 2015 (116). The state of Michigan subsequently switched the water source in Flint back to the Detroit water system before calling a state of emergency in January 2016 (116).

The Flint Water Crisis is an important example of what Hammer (2019, 2) calls strategic-structural racism:

> Strategic racism is the manipulation of intentional racism, structural racism and unconscious
> biases for economic or political gain, regardless of whether the actor has express racist intent,
> although the very act of engaging in strategic racism is itself a form of racist behavior. An
> intuitive way to understand this dynamic is that structural racism creates the vulnerability
> and strategic racism exploits it.

In this case, the Michigan state government exploited the vulnerability created by decades of white flight from the primarily Black urban core as a means to implement austerity measures to benefit state coffers and repay bondholders as opposed to protecting the health and well-being of all Flint residents. The state government chose, for instance, to cut funding to the City of Flint by US$60 million from 2003 to 2013 to balance its own budgets and subsequently installed an unelected and unaccountable "emergency manager" in the municipality who ultimately made the choice to switch water systems (Hammer 2019; Stanley 2016). The exploitation in the Flint case is compounded by the lack of responsiveness the state government showed to Flint residents, who had to mobilize in creative ways on social media to draw attention to their plight after being rebuffed by government officials and by the media for over a year (Moors 2019). Finally, in a manner that echoes the previous case study, technocratic means were used by a government that superseded the authority of a municipality as a means to achieve neo-liberal ends. These neo-liberal ends work, according to Benz, to silence "claims of systemic racism through reliance on the racially-coded narrative of individual choice and intent, while cutting funding to state regulatory agencies in the name of the free market" (2019, 58). By removing the capacity for Flint's municipal government to make policy decisions based on the well-being of its citizens, the Michigan state government exposed the harmful outcomes that can manifest from technocratic governance that purports to be value-neutral and financially efficient. As Stanley (2016, 41) notes, this form of governance is fundamentally contradictory:

> [Technocracy's] ideals – financial responsibility, efficiency, and value-neutrality – cannot be systematically combined. The notions of responsibility that these ideals invoke are deeply moralistic, and hence deeply value-laden. The people are financially irresponsible because they are spending too much money on themselves, money that is not theirs. Whose money are they spending? The money they are spending is the bondholders' money; they are spending capital they have borrowed from banks, and from other private, wealthy lenders. The paradigm of financial irresponsibility is to not pay back bondholders for their loans. The paradigm of financial responsibility is to refuse to honor pension promises or contracts with labor.

The values that Stanley discusses, when combined with a context of environmental and spatial racism, caused untold harm to Flint's citizens.

ENVIRONMENTAL RACISM IN CANADA

Although Canadians and urban political scientists in Canada have tended to view "race" as an American challenge, racialization of space has also been fundamental to Canadian urban development. Post–Second World War "growth machines" or what Lorimer calls the "new corporate city" (1978,77–9) also existed in some Canadian cities engaging in "urban renewal" initiatives in this period, funded by the federal government. Urban renewal led to bulldozing communities to "renew" them or to make way for expressways to accommodate more vehicles in urban centres. In some cases, entire Black communities, such as Hogan's Alley in Vancouver and Africville in the Halifax Regional Municipality (discussed further below), were demolished to make way for expressways (a bridge in the case of Africville) or in the name of what some decision-makers considered "urban renewal." The link between urban renewal and the racialization of space is so interconnected that one scholar asks: "But is urban renewal not itself about racism?" (Nelson 2008, 24). Indeed, the perceived need to "renew" neighbourhoods is often due to their racialization through ongoing neglect and environmental racism.

Although it has received little attention in the Canadian literature, environmental racism has also been at play in processes of racialization of minority communities in Canada and Canadian cities. In Nova Scotia, toxic facilities such as waste disposal, thermal facilities, and pulp and paper companies have been located close to African Nova Scotian and Mi'kmaq communities disproportionately (Waldron 2018b). Ingrid Waldron describes Africville, a historic settlement of African Nova Scotians in what is now North End Halifax, as a classic case of environmental racism in Nova Scotia (Waldron 2018b, 45). The Africville community was subject to a variety of environmentally toxic facilities: "a fertilizer plant, a slaughter house, a tar factory, a stone and coal crushing plant, a cotton factory, a prison, three systems of railway tracks and an open dump" (45). Furthermore, the city did not extend the basic services of paved roads and sewage systems to the community. The effects of environmental racism and the failure of the city to provide services were then used to justify the community's removal (Mackenzie 1991). Africville, though, is by no means the only African Nova Scotian community in what is now the Halifax Regional Municipality that suffered the effects of environmental racism. The former City of Dartmouth (amalgamated with the City of Halifax, Town of Bedford, and Halifax County in 1996 to form the current Halifax Regional Municipality) located its dump in a little-known Black community known by locals as "The Avenue" (Sehatzadeh 2008). The community of 132 residents as of the 1950s lacked municipal water until 1963 and a sewage line was not provided to the community until 1986 (Sehatzadeh 1998, 85). In 1991 (before amalgamation) the Metropolitan Authority chose to locate a dump in East Lake (in the North and East Preston Areas, historic African Nova Scotian areas in the city), which was resisted by East Lake and East Preston residents who filed a complaint against the authority with the provincial Human Rights Commission. Nevertheless, although the authority eventually reversed its decision, the dump was ultimately located near a community centre close to East Preston. An attempt to rezone additional land for that purpose (a municipal dump) was again resisted in 2015 (Waldron 2018b, 49–50).

Poor white residents have also been displaced by urban renewal projects in Halifax and elsewhere. Nevertheless, Ted Rutland argues that we can uncover the racism – anti-Blackness in the Halifax context – of these decisions in the normative conceptions of betterment that reflected the needs and experiences of white residents. More specifically, access to affordable rental housing was considered the "baseline" for improving lives in the HRM. However, most Black Haligonians owned their housing prior to urban renewal projects and, in the case of Africville, were moved from homes they owned into substandard rental housing, itself also slated for demolition (Mackenzie 1991). Indeed, as Waldron points out, residents in North and East Preston, which is home to long-standing Black communities in Halifax and subject to environmental racism in the form of multiple attempts to locate waste facilities there, had above average household incomes (Waldron 2018a). Class is not enough to explain marginalization in planning and through environmental racism. An intersectional lens that also considers "race" is necessary to understand urban planning decisions such as the ones discussed here.

The phenomenon of normative models of a particular type of resident informing planning decisions is widespread as we see in contemporary planning decisions in both Halifax and Toronto. In Halifax, a historical pattern of "displacing Blackness" is evident in planning practices in the Halifax Regional Municipality (Rutland 2018). After the 1960s, six non-urban Black communities in the HRM that had existed since the early nineteenth century were swallowed by the municipality: "In a process reminiscent of what occurred around Africville earlier in the century, each of these communities was increasingly engulfed by the expanding urban region and a newer, denser, and wealthier form of development" (Rutland 2018, 252). Two prominent examples are the communities of Beechville and Upper Hammonds Plains, both located in Greater Halifax. Peripheral land in the broader Halifax region where Black communities were established was inexpensive due to its racialization, making it attractive to developers. According to Rutland (2018), they bought up land in these places and then took steps to recast its image as "white." For instance, in Upper Hammonds Plains, a development on historically Black land was renamed "White Hill's Run" to recast its image. In a particularly blatant manifestation of this process of erasure, portions of historically Black East Preston were reclassified as belonging to the neighbouring and largely "white" community of Lake Echo. Although these communities are not defined by municipal boundaries, they are socially significant; they are marked by signage within HRM and subject to other governmental boundaries. In this case, the boundary change was an administrative one initiated by Canada Post (Rutland 2018, 253). Municipal planning staff and 150 white residents (who signed a petition) all pushed for the reclassification (253). Rutland notes that the HRM Planning Department "had reportedly issued deeds to white residents years earlier indicating their homes were located in Lake Echo" (253). As Rutland describes the politics of the situation:

> At stake in the name change, for white residents, was a major difference in property value. Homes built on undervalued Black-signified land would, in an instant, gain access to the higher market values typically associated with whiteness. For Black residents, the change meant losing a part of their community, created almost two centuries earlier, to newer white residents. The process struck some residents as a familiar one. Black East Preston resident

and activist Doug Sparks called it "a Christopher Columbus scenario," in which white groups move into an area and ignore, if not actively negate, its heritage. Black protests of the name change were ignored by city officials, all of whom ultimately backed the change. (254)

The case of the racialization and removal of Africville is not unique in the North American context during its "urban renewal period" during the 1950s and 1960s. In Canada, Black communities, Chinatowns, and Indigenous settlements such as a historic Métis settlement in Winnipeg called "Rooster Town" (1901–61) were subject to labelling and considered "other." Negative discourses, labels such as "slum," and policies and decisions of local governments (as well as those at other levels of government) were deployed to essentially make these places, as Nelson (2008) describes in her study of Africville, "appear, and eventually become, unsafe, unclean, and associated with disease, moral deficiency, and crime" (Nelson 2008, 41). For many racialized residents, despite the deficiencies of their communities due to neglect from the state, these essentially segregated areas served as places of community and place-making. For instance, Winnipeg's Rooster Town became a place where Indigenous Métis communities could survive in the city despite the lack of legal recognition of their Indigeneity by the federal government and therefore the right to have a home base on reserve lands (Peters, Stock, and Werner 2018, loc. 454).

Although demolishing entire communities was a common practice in the urban renewal era, such processes of racialization and cycles of the displacement of racialized minorities and their replacement with "whiteness" continue in more subtle forms through gentrification induced by neo-liberal policy-making. Consider the racialization of space in Toronto, Canada's "global city," touted as the most "multicultural" city in the world. The framing of "dangerous" areas of cities, and the attendant experiences of crime in some of these contexts is, in part, a product of urban planning decisions informed by macroeconomic policy decisions. As Saberi (2017, 52) notes, when discussing the concentration of non-white poverty in suburban areas of Toronto, neo-liberal economic policy on a national level has created profound economic inequality that shapes the housing markets in globally competitive cities like Toronto, prompting skyrocketing housing prices. These prices force those who cannot afford housing in wealthier areas – who are often both racialized and immigrants – into postwar rental accommodations that represent the only affordable housing in the region (Saberi 2017, 53). These areas were amalgamated into the rapidly gentrifying City of Toronto, and this process of amalgamation was paired with further cuts to affordable housing, income supplements, employment programs, and settlement services for new immigrants (Viswanathan 2010, 263). Without meaningful supports, these areas were quickly pathologized as hotbeds of criminality, as Saberi highlights:

> Repeatedly the image is invoked of (downtown) Toronto as a thriving "city of neighbour-hoods" and a competitive global city. The concentration of non-White poverty, on the other hand, is understood as an "immigrant" problem located in "immigrant neighbourhoods" in

the city's postwar suburbs, disconnected from the concentration of predominantly White wealth in gentrified downtown Toronto. (2017, 54)

This process of racialization pathologized neighbourhoods over time, and planners who make policy decisions about building codes, zoning, and even the complete destruction of long-standing communities thus have made choices that often result in further marginalization for racialized communities.

REGENT PARK – A CASE STUDY OF RACIALIZED "REVITALIZATION"

The revitalization of Regent Park in Toronto is a good example of this dynamic. Regent Park is an area near downtown Toronto designated for a significant public housing development in the 1940s to "eradicate slums" created by the mainly British and Irish working-class population (Kipfer and Petrunia 2009, 115). As Canada liberalized its immigration policy over the 1960s and 1970s, the residents of the neighbourhood increasingly became racialized immigrants, creating a neighbourhood of incredible linguistic and racial diversity (Kipfer and Petrunia 2009, 119). The neighbourhood increasingly became stigmatized in the eyes of the media and outsiders, echoing the discourses that prompted the creation of public housing in the area in the first place and leaving the name of the neighbourhood as a shorthand for racialized perceptions of crime (James 2010, 75). Responsibility for building and maintaining public housing was downloaded from the federal to provincial governments in 1993, which allowed the Ontario provincial government, led by Premier Harris, to cancel all new public housing commitments and cut support for 17,000 public housing units before downloading the responsibility for public housing onto municipalities who had neither the funding nor the capacity to effectively manage them (76). Residents of the community petitioned the Toronto Housing Authority (later the Toronto Community Housing Corporation, TCHC) to make improvements to address community safety concerns like changing the lighting in the area and opening up pathways to improve accessibility, as well as to provide social infrastructure like a school and other community-based amenities to reduce crime (Mele 2019, 32).

The devolution of public housing to the Toronto Community Housing Corporation prompted the housing authority to seek market-based means to ease fiscal pressure, and a study of redevelopment options for the area concluded that demolishing the entire public housing complex and replacing it would only cost 20 per cent more than repairing and updating the existing units (Mele 2019, 32). After a challenging consultation process, the housing authority created a three-stage revitalization plan that replaced all 2,087 public housing units in the area but also incorporated over five thousand market-based units, as well as a bank, a grocery store, and other amenities (James 2010, 78). Soon after this plan was launched, however, six hundred of the public housing units were planned to be reconstructed elsewhere in the city, leaving public housing residents in the minority in the area (Kipfer and Petrunia 2009, 123). While some residents were on board with the "revitalization" plan, many others disagreed with the process, deeming it to be "tokenism" that assists in manufacturing the consent necessary to force the housing project through. As August (2016, 29) articulates:

> Many observers have challenged the meaningfulness of these consultation efforts. While TCHC implies that tenants selected, directed, and shaped the plan, a planner hired to draft it in 2002 recalled that the key decisions had been made by TCHC in advance … Consultation may not have shaped revitalization, but the branding of revitalization as consultative and tenant-driven has likely worked to prevent opposition.

This tokenistic consultation process, combined with other factors August describes, including a fear of reprisal among residents for speaking out against the project and the co-optation of potential resistance by TCHC, meant that there was muted tenant resistance to the plan.

The Regent Park case study demonstrates the ways that urban spaces become racialized, leading to a market-driven "revitalization" that excludes and marginalizes residents who seek meaningful improvements in their quality of life. Race influences the justifications behind revitalization projects, which include perceptions that neighbourhoods are riddled with crime and "cut off" from other areas of the city (Mele 2019, 34). Race also vitally affects the ways that the new Regent Park will be understood and constructed. As Mele (2019, 35) notes, restrictions were placed by TCHC on the residents who are permitted to return after construction of the new units is complete to those who do not have a criminal record, meaning that tenants of the units are framed as the "redeemable" poor who are distinct from the "old," criminal, and racialized Regent Park. Moreover, units in the redeveloped Regent Park are smaller than before, meaning that multigenerational households are no longer an option in the area – which disproportionately affects racialized community members (37). The upshot of these choices is that the former Regent Park, with its challenges and profound strengths, is erased and replaced by a development that is technically "mixed" but that asks public housing residents to conform to a racialized norm of white, middle-class property owners and tenants (Kipfer and Petrunia 2009, 126; Mele 2019). Understanding the relationship between planning and the racialization of space requires interrogating the norms underlying planning priorities broadly as well as specific land uses through zoning.

This section demonstrates the significant impact that issues of urban planning and environmental justice can have on racialized communities across North America. Whether reflecting on the displacement of cohesive and long-standing communities in municipalities across Canada or discussing the racialization of urban spaces in the United States, the power of both municipal and sub-national governments to enact significant harms on racialized communities underwrites the history and present realities of urban politics across the continent. This section has highlighted several important lessons garnered from comparison across the divergent municipal and sub-national contexts we have covered.

First, the apolitical nature of discourses of urban renewal and revitalization obscures the disproportionate impact that policies in this vein have on racialized minorities who are more likely to be the targets of relocation and live in the communities that are perceived to be problematic. From Africville to Regent Park, the consistency of this approach demonstrates a form of colour-blind racism that underpins perceived rationality and neutral decision-making in urban planning and decision-making (Mele 2019; Rutland 2018; Loo 2010). The decisions that municipalities make – about land use, about environmental assessment, and even about the boundaries of the city itself – are intimately intertwined with taken-for-granted assumptions about for whom and for what municipal governance serves. These decisions are also profoundly important in shaping the policy outcomes for all communities within municipal limits.

Second, these cases illustrate the degree to which neo-liberalism has intertwined with racialized policy discourses to produce adverse policy outcomes for racialized minorities. In the Flint case and the Regent Park case, the challenges that racialized minorities face are founded in part upon the economic constraints placed upon municipalities by sub-national governments. The choices these sub-national governments made, which include municipal balkanization as well as the downloading of services onto municipal governments that were not equipped to handle them, allowed these sub-national governments to introduce market logic into municipal policy-making in ways that profoundly affected the lives of racialized communities.

Finally, these cases illustrate the significant impact of multilevel governance on municipal decision-making. As mentioned above, the ability of municipalities to make decisions about environmental assessments, infrastructure, and planning is affected by the choices of sub-national and national governments. In the Flint case, this dynamic meant that the Michigan state government entirely removed local control over budgeting and infrastructure under emergency management legislation. In the Regent Park case, the provincial government of Ontario downloaded the responsibility of managing public housing in Toronto to the municipal government without providing additional funding after the province itself was given the responsibility to manage housing by the federal government. Without the resources to adequately manage this housing responsibility, the municipal government was forced to find different forms of revenue to support this new responsibility, which meant introducing market housing into areas like Regent Park under the guise of revitalization. These limitations on municipal autonomy mean that municipal governments must innovate to fully address the concerns that racialized communities raise about urban policy-making.

Municipal Responses to Racism

Theoretical and popular conceptions of municipal governments in North America have stressed their jurisdictional limitations. For instance, American federalism and local government scholar

Paul Peterson's conception of the "limited city," discussed in chapter 3, suggested that because of their location in a competitive system of cities, municipalities must focus on developmental goals rather than redistributive ones. In Canada, due to their lack of independent constitutional status, municipalities have been dismissed as mere "creatures of the provinces," administrative extensions of provinces offering services to property with little political relevance.

Yet, as we see above, municipal decision-making has significant implications for racial and environmental justice. Through their planning decisions, bylaw-making, and governance, municipalities have shaped and continue to shape power relations in cities in significant ways. Furthermore, municipalities are not insignificant to grassroots movements and other forms of group politics; rather, such movements have challenged municipal decisions that marginalize and racialize particular communities, including attempts to locate waste facilities in racialized neighbourhoods.

However, as we saw in chapter 12, most Canadian and American municipalities that are active in the immigration policy field appear to be adopting policies that seek to include immigrants in local governance and services. There are strong incentives for municipalities to adopt immigrant-friendly measures, including a "business case," since immigrants are important sources of growth and human capital. For a variety of reasons, anti-immigrant measures are virtually absent in Canada and stand out as exceptional (though highly publicized) at the local level in the United States. In the United States, civil rights legislation creates legally enforceable standards for the translation of rights into the delivery of local services and governance, and it protects against the discriminatory application of housing codes to immigrants. In Canada, some credit official multiculturalism for creating diversity and immigrant-friendly cities and political culture. Although not official policy, some have used the discourse of multiculturalism to describe progressive initiatives taken in American cities such as New York City and Los Angeles (Qadeer 2016).

Nevertheless, in Canada, some also argue that official multiculturalism serves to perpetuate racism by failing to acknowledge deep forces of structural racism and by conceptualizing diversity as "cultural." In Canada, multiculturalism is not only an official policy but also a national narrative, one that erases the country's colonial history and reality as well as its related history of the enslavement of Black people and segregated schooling (Maynard 2017). As Canada's largest cities received large numbers of immigrants, the question of "race," where it was addressed at all, was addressed through "race relations" initiatives designed to "integrate" immigrants or "racial" minorities into local communities through what essentially amounted to intercultural relations initiatives. The problem was conceptualized as a question of individual attitudes, cultural misunderstanding, and integration rather than a deeper issue of "racism" that required an anti-racism lens (Henry et al. 1998, 37–42).

It is only very recently that deeper forms of structural oppression have been acknowledged by municipal governments. One such shift, discussed more fully in chapter 11, are municipal efforts to advance "reconciliation" with Canada's Indigenous Peoples. Indeed, in some cases, municipalities have included reconciliation and "decolonization" objectives as well as Indigenous representation in their local immigration policy-making to address the ways in which Canada continues to be "settled" without Indigenous consent and input into decision-making. In some cases, particular immigrant communities relate their history of structural racism to reconciliation efforts with Indigenous Peoples as in the case of the Chinese in Vancouver (and British Columbia). Such links challenge histories of white Europeans as the "pioneering" settlers of such cities in a unique way. They are examples of municipalities participating in conversations about Canada's deeply racialized history and what that means for reconciliation in the present.

Municipalities have been forced, in many ways, to engage in these conversations by significant activist movements that have emerged to challenge governments at all levels to address structural and institutional racism. The Black Lives Matter (BLM) movement is a transnational example of a movement that has upended traditional relationships between advocates and municipalities.

To counter a persistent cycle of violence against Black Americans with no accountability, and to respond to the acquittal of George Zimmerman in the death of Trayvon Martin in 2013, three African American queer women named Alicia Garza, Patrisse Cullors, and Opal Tometi coined the social media hashtag #BlackLivesMatter (Black Lives Matter 2017). The phrase, in the words of BLM founder Alicia Garza, is "an affirmation of Black folks' humanity, our contributions to this society, and our resilience in the face of deadly oppression" (Black Lives Matter 2017). While the phrase gained some currency in the aftermath of the Zimmerman verdict, it exploded onto mainstream media and political consciousness in the aftermath of the killing of unarmed eighteen-year-old Michael Brown at the hands of police officer Darren Wilson in Ferguson, Missouri, on August 9, 2014 (Mourão, Kilgo, and Sylvie 2021, 320).

When the Ferguson grand jury decided not to indict Wilson, protests erupted across North America with an intensity not seen for a generation (Taylor 2016, 157; Thompson 2017). Activists, both on the ground in Ferguson and across North America, connected the dots between incidences of police brutality in their cities and a broader structural critique of the role that structural racism plays in constraining the life choices and life chances of racialized residents (Taylor 2016, 156; Hesse 2017, 583).

The Ferguson uprising also prompted the creation of Black Lives Matter chapters from Vancouver to Los Angeles, New York City, and Toronto alongside affiliated local groups as part of a broader movement for Black lives (Thompson 2017, 244). Eventually, the movement became global, with forty chapters appearing in cities around the world. These connections were in part facilitated by the distinct intersectional and decentralized politics of the BLM movement, which allowed for organizers to adapt a shared ethic of solidarity and transformative justice to be responsive to local issues like the presence of police officers at Pride parades in Toronto after the killings of Jermaine Carby and Andrew Loku (Diverlus, Hudson, and Ware 2020). By centring the needs and amplifying the voices of groups that have been marginalized within previous civil rights movements, the Black Lives Matter movement shifted conversations around organizing and activism, opening a discursive and political space for alternative, non-hierarchical modes of political engagement in urban environments.

Municipal governments, confronted with urgent contests to their legitimacy, had to respond to movements like Black Lives Matter with policy proposals. A recent report identifies a variety of anti-racist initiatives at the municipal level, drawing mainly from American examples. The report was produced by University of Calgary researchers and supported by the university's Urban Alliance and the Faculty of Social Work. The report opens by noting that "the public killing of Mr. George Floyd has been a worldwide wake up call for racial justice" (King et al. 2021, 3). It builds upon consultations conducted in Calgary with members of Indigenous communities and racialized minorities in the summer of 2020 (King et al. 2021, 3). The report points out that although some action has taken place in Canadian municipalities to address racism, the formalization of municipal bylaws and policy initiatives in Canada has been uncommon (3). The report identifies corporate institutionalization, anti-racist participatory governance, and the application of a racial equity lens to all city policy-making as crucial (4). More specifically, the report discusses a variety of case studies of anti-racist initiatives, such as Seattle's Race and Social Justice Initiative, as an example of corporate institutionalization of capacity in anti-racist policy; King County's (the county in which the City of Seattle is situated) "equity impact review," which has been developed to measure the impact of county projects on low-income residents, racialized minorities, and residents with limited English language skills; participatory budgeting in New York City; and participatory planning in Boston (King et. al. 2021). The report's discussion of racism in property taxes illustrates how structural inequity can infuse all types of municipal decisions: in the United States, African Americans and Hispanics pay 10 to 13 per cent more in property taxes than whites for equivalent services because of the overvaluing of minority properties (44). King et al. (2021, 44–5) hypothesize that although this systemic practice may have been intentional in the past (assessors may have intentionally over-assessed minority properties), today, overassessments are likely due to assessors failing to acknowledge that properties in racialized communities appreciate at slower rates than in "white" neighbourhoods. Again, this example illustrates how norms based on whiteness can have a sometimes unintentional structural racist effect on racialized communities.

Recently, and largely as a result of Black activism, Toronto established the Confronting Anti-Black Racism Unit (CABR), a unique example in North America of municipal action on anti-Black racism being taken at the governmental (municipal) level. The Black Lives Matter movement, which had begun to receive increasing attention in the spring of 2016, provided a push for the city to address anti-Black racism, which had been previously documented in "41 years of reports, recommendations, and research which mainly said similar things about the effect of anti-Black racism on the lives of Black Torontonians" (City of Toronto 2019, 2). Those recommendations became the subject of extensive consultation with Toronto's diverse Black population, which informed the development of the Toronto Action Plan to Confront

Anti-Black Racism and its eighty actions (2). The CABR was established to support the implementation of this strategy, which was approved by council in December 2017 (1). The staff in the unit were activists from the community who are meant to drive change in Toronto's existing departments (City of Toronto 2019). In 2020, the City of Ottawa also established a more modest Anti-Racism Secretariat with an initial budget of C$100,000. The initiative was led by Ralston King, a Black councillor in Ottawa who has become the Council Liaison for Anti-Racism and Ethnocultural Relations initiatives. The city's website describes its role as such:

> The Secretariat will ensure the City collects and uses race-based data and applies an anti-racism lens when developing City policies. The Secretariat will work to actively remove barriers based on race and contribute to a society where resources are distributed and opportunities are created equitably for all, no matter the color of your skin. (City of Ottawa, n.d.)

Unlike Toronto's unit, this unit addresses all forms of racism rather than focusing on anti-Black racism. Regine King et al. raise the question of whether it is feasible for municipalities to dedicate a unit to a particular form of racism, noting practical challenges that would arise if multiple racialized groups insisted on having their own unit (King et al. 2021, 32).

Similarly, in Halifax, the African Nova Scotian Affairs Integration Office (ANSAIO) was created in 2010 as part of a settlement with the Africville Genealogy Society related to the removal of Africville (Halifax Regional Municipality, n.d.). The office's stated role is "to enable the municipality to better engage with the African Nova Scotian community" (Halifax Regional Municipality, n.d.). It is located in the municipality's Diversity and Inclusion Office. Although specific to African Nova Scotians, this office and its mandate still reflect an "intercultural relations" and community engagement function, which is no doubt sorely needed but that fails to name and commit to address more fundamental anti-Black racism. We see evidence of policy movement in other areas of the municipality including the Board of Police Commissioners, which, in response to grassroots Black activism, established a subcommittee to define "defunding" the police, which produced the report *Defunding the Police: Defining the Way Forward for HRM* (Jones et al. 2022). Although this policy change is potentially transformative, the extent to which it will result in transformative policy change remains to be seen.

CONCLUSION

Through sub-national comparisons of highly different cases (Halifax and Toronto) as well as international comparisons, this chapter shows that structural racism and, in particular, anti-Black racism are phenomena with global dimensions that are also shaped in contextually specific ways. In Canada, despite its international reputation as a leader in "multicultural" policy and the accommodation of "deep" diversity through state institutions and policies, we also see evidence of racism. This pattern holds in policing and planning despite differences in policing systems and the diversity of the Black population.

Similarly, there is evidence of environmental racism in cities in both Canada and the United States despite their very different histories of slavery and segregation. Although less research exists in Canada than the United States, Ingrid Waldron's work on environmental racism in Halifax and Nova Scotia highlights the tendency for the state (including the municipal state) to locate noxious land uses close to Indigenous populations and, in Nova Scotia, long-standing African Nova Scotian communities. Debates about the location of dumps have continued to reflect this pattern as late as 2015 (Waldron 2018a). Racism is also evident in the rebranding of historically racialized space in cities and in the cultural and other norms underpinning planning strategies and zoning.

Although municipal law and other decisions do not govern people directly, their decisions about land use affect who lives where and how the community is defined. It also contributes to racializing space. We saw these processes in the types of neighbourhoods that were slated for "urban renewal" and how "renewal" involved the demolition and displacement of communities rather than investment in the community for the community. In some instances, demolition and removal of entire communities were pursued; however, in others, the process of gentrification ensued. A racialized process of gentrification of neighbourhoods continues to this day, echoing the urban renewal initiatives of the 1960s and 1970s. In many ways, the patterns discussed here reflect the strategies of the colonial states, which suggests that "as Canadian cities grew, they employed three main strategies to address the issue of Indigenous peoples in cities: containment, expulsion, and erasure" (Peters, Stock, and Werner 2018, 341). Similar spatial management strategies have been used with respect to other racialized minorities who, unlike Indigenous Peoples, are settlers as well but who do not benefit from the white privilege afforded others. These processes and strategies have been called the "racialization of space" (Waldron 2018a), which takes multiple forms.

The strategy of containment involved expropriating Indigenous lands and creating a reserve system to keep Indigenous Peoples away from cities. The development of segregated neighbourhoods of poverty was another containment measure for urban Indigenous as well as other racialized minorities; paradoxically, although they developed due to structural racism of the majority society, these spaces fostered a strong sense of community among their members. This in turn explains why resistance to their destruction was strong. Racialized minorities and demands for racialized justice have also been "contained" by a discourse of multiculturalism that directs attention away from state violence and historically rooted oppression to a conceptualization of diversity that is more superficial.

Expulsion and erasure can be seen in the demolition of minority neighbourhoods such as Africville and others across Canada and the United States in the name of "urban renewal." More recently, the rebranding of historically Black land in the HRM reflects "erasure" in a particularly dramatic way.

The comparisons also reveal the fundamental role that municipalities play in racial justice in North American cities. Some recent developments at the municipal level are welcome, making important contributions to Canada's anti-racism policy infrastructure. The areas of policing and planning are crucial to addressing the extent to which racialized minorities experience state violence or safety as well as inclusion or displacement.

Municipalities' ability to create significant change is limited by their related constitutional, jurisdictional, and resource limitations. The small budgets invested in anti-racism units compared with the magnitude of structural racism – although a step in the right direction – cannot be expected to lead to transformational change alone. Fundamentally, the fact that provinces restrict Canadian municipalities mainly to the collection of property taxes implies a particular municipal role – providing services to property. This limits the political case for targeted policy interventions on social justice matters like racism, which can have a sense of urgency in cities. In some cases, such as with respect to the racialization of refugees and immigrants, many of whom are "racial" minorities, cities are limited in their jurisdictional capacity to include them in the democratic process or, in the case of undocumented migrants, to provide services to them or grant "sanctuary."

Nonetheless, there is much that can be done at the municipal level to address anti-Black racism. For instance, "mainstreaming" an anti-racism lens on all aspects of decision-making including planning could lead to fundamental changes in decision-making. We also see openness at the municipal level to fundamental debates on addressing violence against racialized minorities in areas such as policing due to ongoing advocacy at the local level. There is a great deal to learn about racism and the potential for transformative change by examining local struggles and engaging community knowledge in the process.

NOTES

1 As a recent Guardian article describes: "Orders under section 60 of the Criminal Justice and Public Order Act allow officers to stop and search people with no grounds for suspicion. Police are only supposed to authorise the use of section 60 when there has been serious violence or where there is a risk it may occur in a particular area."

2 See Thompson (2009) for a critique of leading theories of urban politics for their failure to accurately and adequately theorize the place of race in power relations in the American cities.

REFERENCES

American Civil Liberties Union. 2021. "Racial Profiling." Race and Criminal Justice. https://www.aclu.org/issues/racial-justice/race-and-criminal-justice/racial-profiling.

August, Martine. 2016. "'It's All about Power and You Have None:' The Marginalization of Tenant Resistance to Mixed-Income Social Housing Redevelopment in Toronto, Canada." *Cities* 57 (September): 25–32. https://doi.org/10.1016/j.cities.2015.12.004.

Bahdi, Reem. 2003. "No Exit: Racial Profiling and Canada's War against Terrorism." *Osgoode Hall Law Journal* 41, nos. 2–3 (Summer/Fall): 293–317. https://doi.org/10.60082/2817-5069.1413.

Bonds, Anne, and Joshua Inwood. 2016. "Beyond White Privilege: Geographies of White Supremacy and Settler Colonialism." *Progress in Human Geography* 40, no. 6 (December): 715–33. https://doi.org/10.1177/0309132515613166.

Bowling, Ben, and Coretta Phillips. 2007. "Disproportionate and Discriminatory: Reviewing the Evidence on Police Stop and Search." *The Modern Law Review* 70, no. 6 (November): 936–61. https://doi.org/10.1111/j.1468-2230.2007.00671.x.

Bennett, Michael. 2004. "Cities in the New Millennium: Environmental Justice, the Spatialization of Race, and Combating Anti-urbanism." *Journal of African American Studies* 8, nos. 1–2 (June): 126–41. https://doi.org/10.1007/s12111-004-1008-y.

Benz, Terressa A. 2019. "Toxic Cities: Neoliberalism and Environmental Racism in Flint and Detroit Michigan." *Critical Sociology* 45, no. 1 (January): 49–62. https://doi.org/10.1177/0896920517708339.

Black Lives Matter. 2017. "Editorial: HerStory." July 7, 2017. https://blacklivesmatter.com/herstory/.

Buchanan, Larry, Quoctrung Bui, and Jugal K. Patel. 2020. "Black Lives Matter May Be the Largest Movement in U.S. History." *The New York Times*, July 3, 2020, sec. U.S. https://www.nytimes.com/interactive/2020/07/03/us/george-floyd-protests-crowd-size.html.

City of Ottawa. n.d. "Anti-racism and Ethnocultural Relations Initiatives." Accessed June 17, 2024. https://engage.ottawa.ca/anti-racism-and-ethnocultural-relations-initiatives.

City of Toronto. 2019. *1st Annual Report Confronting Anti-Black Racism Unit: 2018-2019*. Toronto: Confronting Anti-Black Racism Unit. https://www.toronto.ca/wp-content/uploads/2019/11/97ab-cabr-annual-report-2018-2019.pdf.

Clotfelter, Charles T. 1976. "The Detroit Decision and 'White Flight.'" *The Journal of Legal Studies* 5, no. 1 (January): 99–112. https://www.jstor.org/stable/724076.

Cole, Desmond. 2015. "The Skin I'm In: I've Been Interrogated by Police More than 50 Times – All Because I'm Black." *Toronto Life* (blog), April 21, 2015. https://torontolife.com/city/life/skin-im-ive-interrogated-police-50-times-im-black/.

Cole, Luke W., and Sheila R. Foster. 2001. *From the Ground Up: Environmental Racism and the Rise of the Environmental Justice Movement*. New York: New York University Press.

Cook, Tom, Richard Stone, John Sentamu, and Sir William Macpherson. 1999. *The Stephen Lawrence Inquiry*. London: Home Office, Government of the United Kingdom. https://assets.publishing.service.gov.uk/government/uploads/system/uploads/attachment_data/file/277111/4262.pdf.

Doan, Michael D. 2017. "Epistemic Injustice and Epistemic Redlining." *Ethics and Social Welfare* 11, no. 2: 177–90. https://doi.org/10.1080/17496535.2017.1293120.

Delgado, Richard, Jean Stefancic, and Angela Harris. 2017. *Critical Race Theory: An Introduction*. 3rd ed. New York: NYU Press. https://doi.org/10.2307/j.ctt1ggjjn3.

Devet, Robert. 2021. "Loophole Allows Illegal Street Checking Practice to Continue in Nova Scotia." *Nova Scotia Advocate* (blog), March 25, 2021. https://nsadvocate.org/2021/03/25/loophole-allows-illegal-street-checking-practice-to-continue-in-nova-scotia/.

Dinnen, Sinclair, and John Braithwaite. 2009. "Reinventing Policing through the Prism of the Colonial Kiap." *Policing and Society* 19, no. 2 (June): 161–73. https://doi.org/10.1080/10439460802187571.

Diverlus, Rodney, Sandy Hudson, and Syrus Marcus Ware, eds. 2020. *Until We Are Free: Reflections on Black Lives Matter in Canada*. Regina: University of Regina Press.

Dodd, Vikram. 2020. "Black People Nine Times More Likely to Face Stop and Search than White People." *The Guardian*, October 27, 2020, sec. Police. http://www.theguardian.com/uk-news/2020/oct/27/black-people-nine-times-more-likely-to-face-stop-and-search-than-white-people.

Draaisma, Muriel. 2017. "New Ontario Rule Banning Carding by Police Takes Effect." *CBC News*, January 1, 2017. https://www.cbc.ca/news/canada/toronto/carding-ontario-police-government-ban-1.3918134.

Emsley, Clive. 2014. "Policing the Empire / Policing the Metropole: Some Thoughts on Models and Types." *Crime, Histoire & Sociétés / Crime, History & Societies* 18, no. 2: 5–25. https://doi.org/10.4000/chs.1483.

Fagan, Jeffrey A., Amanda Geller, Garth Davies, and Valerie West. 2010. "Street Stops and Broken Windows Revisited: The Demography and Logic of Proactive Policing in a Safe and Changing City." In *Race, Ethnicity, and Policing: New and Essential Readings*, edited by Stephen K. Rice and Michael D. White, 309–48. New York: NYU Press. https://doi.org/10.18574/nyu/9780814776155.003.0013.

Friesen, Joe. 2006. "A Show of Community, Not Force." *Globe and Mail*, May 15, 2006. https://www.theglobeandmail.com/news/national/a-show-of-community-not-force/article18162648/.

Galabuzi, Grace-Edward. 2012. "Social Exclusion as a Determinant of Health." In *Oppression: A Social Determinant of Health*, edited by Elizabeth Anne McGibbon, 97–112. Halifax: Fernwood Publishing.

Gee, Gilbert C., and Chandra L. Ford. 2011. "Structural Racism and Health Inequities: Old Issues, New Directions." *Du Bois Review: Social Science Research on Race* 8, no. 1 (Spring): 115–32. https://doi.org/10.1017/S1742058X11000130.

Girard, Philip, and Kirk Johnson. 2003. *Nova Scotia Human Rights Commission*. December 2003. https://humanrights.novascotia.ca/sites/default/files/2003-Johnson.pdf.

Greer, James, L. 2014. "Historic Home Mortgage Redlining in Chicago." *Journal of the Illinois State Historical Society* 107, no. 2 (Summer): 204–33. https://doi.org/10.5406/jillistathistsoc.107.2.0204.

Gruber, Aya. 2021. "Policing and 'Bluelining.'" *Houston Law Review* 58, no. 4 (Symposium): 867–936. https://papers.ssrn.com/abstract=3746717.

Hackworth, Jason. 2018. "Race and the Production of Extreme Land Abandonment in the American Rust Belt." *International Journal of Urban and Regional Research* 42, no. 1 (January): 51–73. https://doi.org/10.1111/1468-2427.12588.

Halifax Regional Municipality. n.d. "Diversity and Inclusion: ANSAIO: A Result of the Africville Agreement." African Nova Scotian Affairs Integration Office. Accessed June 17, 2024. https://www.halifax.ca/about-halifax/diversity-inclusion/african-nova-scotian-affairs/ansaio.

Halifax Regional Police. n.d. "The History of Halifax Regional Police." About Halifax Regional Police. Accessed April 14, 2021. https://www.halifax.ca/fire-police/police/about-halifax-regional-police/history.

Hammer, Peter J. 2018. "Detroit 1967 and Today: Spatial Racism and Ongoing Cycles of Oppression Part II: Why Detroit Rebelled: The Intersection of Racism and Social Control in the City: Section III: Detroit Today: The Reproduction of Systems of Control." *Journal of Law in Society* 18, no. 2 (Fall): xvii–235.

———. 2019. "The Flint Water Crisis, the Karegnondi Water Authority and Strategic–Structural Racism." *Critical Sociology* 45, no. 1 (January): 103–19. https://doi.org/10.1177/0896920517729193.

Hayes, Colin. 2001. "The Relationship between Police Boards and Chiefs of Police in Canada." *The Police Journal* 74, no. 2 (April): 149–54. https://doi.org/10.1177/0032258X0107400206.

Henry, Frances, Carol Tator, Winston Mattis, and Tim Rees. 1998. *The Colour of Democracy: Racism in Canadian Society*. 2nd ed. Scarborough, ON: Nelson.

Hesse, Barnor. 2017. "White Sovereignty (...), Black Life Politics: 'The N★★★★r They Couldn't Kill.'" *South Atlantic Quarterly* 116, no. 3 (July): 581–604. https://doi.org/10.1215/00382876-3961494.

Home Office. 2012. "Definition of Policing by Consent." Government of the United Kingdom. December 10, 2012. https://www.gov.uk/government/publications/policing-by-consent/definition -of-policing-by-consent.

James, Ryan K. 2010. "From 'Slum Clearance' to 'Revitalisation': Planning, Expertise and Moral Regulation in Toronto's Regent Park." *Planning Perspectives* 25, no. 1 (January): 69–86. https://doi .org/10.1080/02665430903421742.

Jones, Burnley, and James W. St. G. Walker. 2016. *Burnley "Rocky" Jones: Revolutionary: An Autobiography.* Halifax: Roseway Publishing, an imprint of Fernwood Publishing.

Jones, El, Tari Ajadi, Harry Critchley, and Julia Rodgers. 2022. *Defunding the Police: Defining the Way Forward for HRM.* Halifax: Halifax Board of Police Commissioners. https://www.halifax .ca/sites/default/files/documents/city-hall/boards-committees-commissions/220117bopc1021.pdf.

King, Regine U., Melissa Fundira, Kaylee Ramage, Carieta Thomas, Omer Jamal, and Barry Phipps. 2021. *Scoping Review: Municipal Anti-racist Practices That Might Work.* Calgary: City of Calgary and the Urban Alliance of the University of Calgary and the Faculty of Social Work. https://www.calgary. ca/content/dam/www/csps/cns/documents/anti-racism/King-2021-Scoping-Review-City-of -Calgary.pdf.

Kipfer, Stefan, and Jason Petrunia. 2009. "'Recolonization' and Public Housing: A Toronto Case Study." *Studies in Political Economy* 83, no. 1 (March): 111–39. https://doi.org/10.1080/19187033 .2009.11675058.

Ku, Jane, Rupaleem Bhuyan, Izumi Sakamoto, Daphne Jeyapal, and Lin Fang. 2019. "'Canadian Experience' Discourse and Anti-Racialism in a 'Post-Racial' Society." *Ethnic and Racial Studies* 42, no. 2 (January): 291–310. https://doi.org/10.1080/01419870.2018.1432872.

Lea, John. 2000. "The Macpherson Report and the Question of Institutional Racism." *The Howard Journal of Criminal Justice* 39, no. 3 (August): 219–33. https://doi.org/10.1111/1468-2311.00165.

Lepore, Jill. 2020. "The Invention of the Police." *The New Yorker,* July 13, 2020. https://www.newyorker .com/magazine/2020/07/20/the-invention-of-the-police.

Logan, John R., and Harvey L. Molotch. 1987. *Urban Fortunes: The Political Economy of Place.* Berkeley: University of California Press.

Loo, Tina. 2010. "Africville and the Dynamics of State Power in Postwar Canada." *Acadiensis* 39, no. 2 (Summer/Autumn): 23–47. https://id.erudit.org/iderudit/acad39_2art02.

Lorimer, James. 1978. *The Developers.* Toronto: James Lorimer.

MacDonald, J. Michael, and Jennifer Taylor. 2019. "NS Human Rights Commission – Independent Legal Opinion on Street Checks." Nova Scotia Human Rights Commission. October 15, 2019. https://humanrights.novascotia.ca/sites/default/files/editor-uploads/independent_legal_opinion _on_street_checks.pdf.

Mackenzie, Shelagh, dir. 1991. *Remember Africville.* Montreal: National Film Board. 35 min. https:// www.nfb.ca/film/remember-africville/.

Mackinnon, Mark. 2020. "Statues and Symbols Are Just the Start of Bristol's Struggle with Racism, City's Black Mayor Says." *Globe and Mail,* July 12, 2020. https://www.theglobeandmail.com /world/article-statues-and-symbols-are-just-the-start-of-bristols-struggle-with/.

Marquis, Greg. 1990. "The History of Policing in the Maritime Provinces: Themes and Prospects." *Urban History Review / Revue d'histoire Urbaine* 19, no. 2 (January): 84–99. https://doi.org /10.7202/1017677ar.

———. 1997. "The 'Irish Model' and Nineteenth-Century Canadian Policing." *The Journal of Imperial and Commonwealth History* 25, no. 2 (May): 193–218. https://doi.org/10.1080/03086539708582998.

Marsh, Sarah. 2020. "Met Police Increased Use of Section 60 Stop and Search during Lockdown." *The Guardian*, July 27, 2020, sec. Metropolitan Police. http://www.theguardian.com/uk-news/2020/jul/27/met-police-increased-use-of-section-60-stop-and-search-during-lockdown.

Matthews, Dylan. 2013. "Here's What You Need to Know about Stop and Frisk – and Why the Courts Shut It Down." *Washington Post*, August 13, 2013, sec. Economic Policy. https://www.washingtonpost.com/news/wonk/wp/2013/08/13/heres-what-you-need-to-know-about-stop-and-frisk-and-why-the-courts-shut-it-down/.

Maynard, Robyn. 2017. *Policing Black Lives: State Violence in Canada from Slavery to the Present*. Halifax: Fernwood Publishing.

McCulloch, Michael. 1990. "Most Assuredly Perpetual Motion: Police and Policing in Quebec City, 1838–58." *Urban History Review* 19, no. 2 (January): 100–12. https://doi.org/10.7202/1017678ar.

McGregor, Phlis, and Angela MacIvor. 2017. "Black People 3 Times More Likely to Be Street Checked in Halifax, Police Say." *CBC News*, January 9, 2017. https://www.cbc.ca/news/canada/nova-scotia/halifax-black-street-checks-police-race-profiling-1.3925251.

Mele, Christopher. 2019. "The Strategic Uses of Race to Legitimize 'Social Mix' Urban Redevelopment." *Social Identities* 25, no. 1 (January): 27–40. https://doi.org/10.1080/13504630.2017.1418603.

Mellen, Steve. 2020. "St Pauls Riots in Bristol Remembered 40 Years On." *BBC News*, April 2, 2020, sec. Bristol. https://www.bbc.com/news/uk-england-bristol-52105853.

Moors, M. Rae. 2019. "What Is Flint? Place, Storytelling, and Social Media Narrative Reclamation during the Flint Water Crisis." *Information, Communication & Society* 22, no. 6: 808–22. https://doi.org/10.1080/1369118X.2019.1577477.

Mourão, Rachel R., Danielle K. Kilgo, and George Sylvie. 2021. "Framing Ferguson: The Interplay of Advocacy and Journalistic Frames in Local and National Newspaper Coverage of Michael Brown." *Journalism* 22, no. 2 (February): 320–40. https://doi.org/10.1177/1464884918778722.

Mukherjee, Alok. 2013. *A Civilian Perspective on the Evolution of Policing and Police Governance*. National Summit on the Economics of Policing. Ottawa: Department of Public Safety, Canada. https://www.publicsafety.gc.ca/lbrr/archives/cnmcs-plcng/cn33021-eng.pdf.

Nelson, Jennifer J. 2008. *Razing Africville: A Geography of Racism*. Toronto: University of Toronto Press. https://doi.org/10.3138/9781442686274.

Newman, Harvey K. 2002. "Race and the Tourist Bubble in Downtown Atlanta." *Urban Affairs Review* 37, no. 3 (January): 301–21. https://doi.org/10.1177/10780870222185351.

New York Civil Liberties Union. 2012. "Stop-and-Frisk Data." New York Civil Liberties Union, January 2, 2012. https://www.nyclu.org/en/stop-and-frisk-data.

Ontario Human Rights Commission. 2018. *A Collective Impact: Interim Report on the Inquiry into Racial Profiling and Racial Discrimination of Black Persons by the Toronto Police Service*. Toronto: Ontario Human Rights Commission. https://www.ohrc.on.ca/en/public-interest-inquiry-racial-profiling-and-discrimination-toronto-police-service/collective-impact-interim-report-inquiry-racial-profiling-and-racial-discrimination-black.

Owusu-Bempah, Akwasi, and Scot Wortley. 2014. "Race, Crime, and Criminal Justice in Canada." In *The Oxford Handbook of Ethnicity, Crime, and Immigration*, edited by Sandra M. Bucerius and Michael Tonry, 281–320. Oxford: Oxford University Press. https://doi.org/10.1093/oxfordhb/9780199859016.013.020.

Pearson, Geoff, and Mike Rowe. 2020. "We Spent Seven Years Observing English Police Stop and Search – Here's What We Found." *The Conversation* (blog), November 16, 2020. http://theconversation.com/we-spent-seven-years-observing-english-police-stop-and-search-heres-what-we-found-149563.

Pemberton, Sarah X. 2015. "Criminal Justice as State Racism: Race-Making, State Violence, and Imprisonment in the USA, and England and Wales." *New Political Science* 37, no. 3 (July): 321–45. https://doi.org/10.1080/07393148.2015.1056429.

Peters, Evelyn, Matthew Stock, and Adrian Werner. 2018. *Rooster Town: The History of an Urban Métis Community, 1901–1961*. Winnipeg: University of Manitoba Press. Kindle. https://doi.org /10.1515/9780887555688.

Qadeer, Mohammad Abdul. 2016. *Multicultural Cities: Toronto, New York, and Los Angeles*. Toronto: University of Toronto Press.

Rankin, Jim. 2010. "Police Stop Blacks More Often than Whites, Data Shows." *Toronto Star*, February 5, 2010, sec. GTA. https://www.thestar.com/news/gta/police-stop-blacks-more-often -than-whites-data-shows/article_77fbbe53-0dba-5444-9016-b3ecdac2e2fd.html.

———. 2015. "How the Cards Have Played Out since 1957." *Toronto Star*, May 26, 2015, sec. GTA. https://www.thestar.com/news/gta/how-the-cards-have-played-out-since-1957/article_ec145745 -e14d-571b-a20b-86e95740be2b.html.

Rankin, Jim, Jennifer Quinn, and Michelle Shephard. 2002. "Singled Out." *Toronto Star*, October 19, 2002, sec. Known to Police. https://www.thestar.com/news/gta/known-to-police/singled-out /article_abe5f144-b412-5692-8290-683a291a2a37.html.

Ray, Carolyn. 2019. "Street Checks Permanently Banned in N.S. after Review Calls Them Illegal." *CBC News*, October 18, 2019. https://www.cbc.ca/news/canada/nova-scotia/halifax-street -checks-illegal-1.5326217.

Rose, William. 2002. "Crimes of Color: Risk, Profiling, and the Contemporary Racialization of Social Control." *International Journal of Politics, Culture, and Society* 16, no. 2 (December): 179–205. https:// doi.org/10.1023/A:1020572912884.

Rutland, Ted. 2018. *Displacing Blackness: Planning, Power, and Race in Twentieth-Century Halifax*. Toronto: University of Toronto Press.

Saberi, Parastou. 2017. "Toronto and the 'Paris Problem': Community Policing in 'Immigrant Neighbourhoods.'" *Race & Class* 59, no. 2 (December): 49–69. https://doi.org/10.1177 /0306396817717892.

Saney, Isaac. 1998. "Canada: The Black Nova Scotian Odyssey: A Chronology." *Race & Class* 40, no. 1 (July): 78–91. https://doi.org/10.1177/030639689804000107.

Seamster, Louise, and Danielle Purifoy. 2021. "What Is Environmental Racism For? Place-Based Harm and Relational Development." *Environmental Sociology* 7, no. 2: 110–21. https://doi.org/10.1080 /23251042.2020.1790331.

Sehatzadeh, Adrienne Lucas. 1998. "Survival of An African Nova Scotian Community: Up the Avenue, Revisited." Master's thesis, Dalhousie University, Halifax Nova Scotia, September 1998.

———. 2008. "A Retrospective on the Strengths of African Nova Scotian Communities." *Journal of Black Studies* 38, no. 3 (January): 407–12. https://www.jstor.org/stable/40034388.

Shoush, Suzanne, Semir Bulle, and Andrew Boozary. 2020. "Policing Is a Public Health Crisis." *Toronto Star*, June 26, 2020, sec. Contributors. https://www.thestar.com/opinion/contributors/policing-is -a-public-health-crisis/article_066cd5ff-59f4-5608-b768-c3b188bf7930.html.

Stanley, Jason. 2016. "The Emergency Manager: Strategic Racism, Technocracy, and the Poisoning of Flint's Children." *The Good Society* 25, no. 1 (May): 1–45. https://doi.org/10.5325/goodsociety.25.1.0001.

Statistics Canada. 2017. "Census Profile, 2016 Census – Halifax [Census Metropolitan Area], Nova Scotia and Nova Scotia [Province]." Released November 29, 2017. https://www12 .statcan.gc.ca/census-recensement/2016/dp-pd/prof/details/page.cfm?Lang=E&Geo1 =CMACA&Code1=205&Geo2=PR&Code2=12&SearchText=halifax&SearchType =Begins&SearchPR=01&B1=All&TABID=1&type=0.

———. 2019. *Diversity of the Black Population in Canada: An Overview*. Ethnicity, Language and Immigration Thematic Series. Ottawa: Statistics Canada. http://publications.gc.ca/collections /collection_2019/statcan/89-657-x/89-657-x2019002-eng.pdf.

Stone, Clarence N. 1989. *Regime Politics: Governing Atlanta, 1946-1988*. Lawrence, KS: University of Kansas Press.

StopWatch. 2021. "Avon & Somerset Police Stop and Search Statistics." https://www.stop-watch.org /dashboard/.

Styles, John. 1987. "The Emergence of the Police – Explaining Police Reform in Eighteenth and Nineteenth Century England." *British Journal of Criminology* 27, no. 1 (Winter): 15–22. https://doi .org/10.1093/oxfordjournals.bjc.a047647.

Suero, Waleska. 2015. "Lessons from Floyd v. City of New York: Designing Race-Based Remedies for Equal Protection Violations in Stop & Frisk Cases Notes." *Georgetown Journal of Law & Modern Critical Race Perspectives* 7, no. 1 (Spring): 139–48.

Tator, Carol, and Frances Henry. 2006. *Racial Profiling in Canada: Challenging the Myth of "a Few Bad Apples."* Toronto: University of Toronto Press.

Taylor, Keeanga-Yamahtta. 2016. *From #BlackLivesMatter to Black Liberation*. Chicago: Haymarket Books.

Thompson, Debra. 2016. *The Schematic State: Race, Transnationalism, and the Politics of the Census*. 1st ed. Cambridge: Cambridge University Press. https://doi.org/10.1017/CBO9781316442951.

———. 2017. "An Exoneration of Black Rage." *South Atlantic Quarterly* 116, no. 3 (July): 457–81. https://doi.org/10.1215/00382876-3961439.

Thompson, J. Phillip. 2009. "Race and Urban Political Theory." In *Theories of Urban Politics*, edited by Jonathan S. Davies and David L. Imbroscio, 2nd ed., 188–203. London: Sage.

Tulloch, Michael H. 2018. *Report of the Independent Street Checks Review*. Toronto: Government of Ontario. https://www.ontario.ca/page/report-independent-street-checks-review.

Vancouver Police Department. n.d. "History." About the VPD. Accessed April 14, 2021. https://vpd .ca/police/about/history/index.html.

Vedantam, Shankar, Chris Benderev, Tara Boyle, Renee Klahr, Maggie Penman, and Jennifer Schmidt. 2016. "How A Theory of Crime and Policing Was Born, and Went Terribly Wrong." *WBUR News*, November 1, 2016. https://www.wbur.org/npr/500104506/broken-windows -policing-and-the-origins-of-stop-and-frisk-and-how-it-went-wrong.

Veracini, Lorenzo. 2013. "'Settler Colonialism': Career of a Concept." *The Journal of Imperial and Commonwealth History* 41, no. 2 (June): 313–33. https://doi.org/10.1080/03086534.2013.768099.

Viswanathan, Leela. 2010. "Contesting Racialization in a Neoliberal City: Cross-Cultural Collective Formation as a Strategy among Alternative Social Planning Organizations in Toronto." *GeoJournal* 75, no. 3 (June): 261–72. https://doi.org/10.1007/s10708-009-9305-6.

Waldron, Ingrid. 2018a. "Re-thinking Waste: Mapping Racial Geographies of Violence on the Colonial Landscape." *Environmental Sociology* 4, no. 1 (January): 36–53. https://doi.org/10.1080 /23251042.2018.1429178.

———. 2018b. *There's Something in the Water: Environmental Racism in Indigenous and Black Communities*. Halifax: Fernwood Publishing.

Weaver, Vesla M., and Amy E. Lerman. 2010. "Political Consequences of the Carceral State." *American Political Science Review* 104, no. 4 (November): 817–33. https://doi.org/10.1017/S0003055410000456.

Whetstone, Thomas. n.d. "Police – The Development of Police in Canada." In *Encyclopedia Britannica*, sec. Law, Crime & Punishment. Last updated May 17, 2024. https://www.britannica.com/topic /police.

Wilson, James Q., and George L. Kelling. 1982. "Broken Windows." *The Atlantic*, March 1, 1982. https://www.theatlantic.com/magazine/archive/1982/03/broken-windows/304465/.

Winsa, Patty, and Jim Rankin. 2013. "Carding by Toronto Police Drops Sharply." *Toronto Star*, November 18, 2013, sec. GTA. https://www.thestar.com/news/gta/carding-by-toronto-police -drops-sharply/article_81debde1-1a10-5f15-9b6b-2d170ab1b6e8.html.

———. 2015. "Toronto Police Chief Bill Blair Suspends Controversial Practice of Carding." *Toronto Star*, January 6, 2015, sec. Crime. https://www.thestar.com/news/crime/toronto-police-chief-bill -blair-suspends-controversial-practice-of-carding/article_e8a3eb09-2744-529f-b205-90b9637f50b6 .html.

Wortley, Scot. 2019. *Halifax, Nova Scotia: Street Checks Report*. Halifax: Nova Scotia Human Rights Commission. https://humanrights.novascotia.ca/sites/default/files/editor-uploads/halifax_street _checks_report_march_2019_0.pdf.

Wortley, Scot, and Akwasi Owusu-Bempah. 2011. "The Usual Suspects: Police Stop and Search Practices in Canada." *Policing and Society* 21, no. 4 (December): 395–407. https://doi.org/10.1080 /10439463.2011.610198.

Wortley, Scot, Akwasi Owusu-Bempah, and Huibin Lin. 2021. *Race and Criminal Injustice: An Examination of Public Perceptions of, and Experiences with, the Criminal Justice System among Residents of the Greater Toronto Area*. Toronto: Canadian Association of Black Lawyers. https://cabl.ca/wp -content/uploads/2021/02/CABL-Report-Race-and-Criminal-Injustice-Feb-10-2021.pdf.

CHAPTER FIFTEEN

Addressing Poverty and Social Polarization

Mara Sidney and Adam Straub

In New York City, the average janitor earns roughly US$27,000 per year, while the average accountant earns about US$108,000 per year, according to the popular salary aggregator, Glassdoor. In Toronto, the average janitor earns C$34,000 per year, while the average accountant earns C$69,000 per year. In New York City, most low-income households now live far outside of Manhattan in the surrounding boroughs of the Bronx and Queens as previously affordable neighbourhoods in and near Manhattan and in Brooklyn have rapidly gentrified. In Toronto, poverty has shifted to the city's northwest and northeast corners since 1970, and the proportion of low-income neighbourhoods has increased from 19 per cent to 53 per cent over the span of thirty-five years (Hulchanski 2007). More than one in four children live in poverty in Toronto, including one in three minority children, and upward of three out of four Indigenous children (Wilson et al. 2018). In New York City, nearly one in four children live in poverty and Black and Latinx children are about twice as likely to live in poverty (CCC NY 2019).

This data offers a glimpse of the nature of poverty and polarization in cities. Cities, especially "global cities," are places of extremes – bringing together great wealth and deep poverty within their boundaries. The growth of poverty and polarization in cities threatens individual life chances and the well-being of society. Because these conditions depress the political voice of the most vulnerable groups, their growth also threatens democracy and the achievement of social justice. Impoverished people tend to have a harder time influencing government and attaining public office. Poverty and polarization intersect with systems of racial hierarchy and other axes of oppression. In many cities with diverse racial and ethnic populations, Black, Latinx, Indigenous, and other groups of colour are persistently more likely than white people to experience poverty and less likely to be represented among a city's most wealthy residents.

In this chapter, we compare levels of poverty and social polarization in Canadian cities, and then across countries and cities worldwide. To understand how city leaders can reduce poverty and polarization, we take an in-depth look at housing and education policies. Many cities do not have enough affordable housing to meet their residents' needs; families without affordable housing often experience poverty or homelessness. That's why increasing access to affordable housing can pull families out of poverty. The location of housing matters too because where families live shapes their prospects for finding good jobs and good schools. When kids attend high-quality schools, their prospects for the future are better. As more students obtain the skills and opportunities for higher-wage jobs, a city's poverty rate may decline. For these various reasons, when cities invest in affordable housing and ensure that their schools offer high-quality education to all children, they may see declines in poverty and polarization.

As we examine some ways that urban leaders around the world have tried to address inequalities in education and housing, we also show their challenges. Sometimes local leaders do not have a lot of control over their housing and education systems because provincial or federal governments hold authority. In other cases, they face powerful stakeholders such as real estate developers and financial institutions that profit from high-cost housing and resist government intervention in housing markets. When it comes to schools, leaders may face resistance from wealthy residents who want to reserve the best schools for their children or who resist higher taxes that could provide more resources to the school district. Systemic racism and discrimination against minority racial and ethnic families and students also pose challenges to reform efforts that would expand housing and education opportunities. Each of these elements plays out somewhat differently from city to city and country to country. In many cities, advocacy groups develop reform ideas, rally, and pressure elected officials to take action on behalf of poor and marginalized communities.

We highlight core tensions that mark the politics of housing and education. For example, we discuss how housing's "use value" and "exchange value" often exist in tension with one another. When housing's property values are maximized, its accessibility to low-income households is constrained. Relatedly, we compare market-based and progressive approaches to housing and education reform. In general, the problems of poverty and polarization are complex, with multiple and varied drivers from country to country. Cities can alleviate these conditions or their negative impacts, and we discuss many such efforts here. These efforts do make a difference in the lives of city residents. However, interventions at higher levels of government are generally also needed to have a significant impact on levels of poverty and polarization.

Cities in Canada compare favourably in some ways to cities in other world regions. In general, levels of inequality are lower than those in the United States and Latin America, but that does not imply that problems of poverty and polarization are less urgent. When compared with the United States and some other countries, Canadian cities show somewhat less embrace of neo-liberal policy models especially in education policy, although they are more evident in the housing arena. Grassroots mobilization in cities around housing and education seems more common in the United States and Brazil than in Canada and Europe. Drivers of change in Canadian cities more often, though not always, emerge from within government more so than from outside it. As well, provincial and national government initiatives drive change more often than those originating at the municipal level.

HOW TO DEFINE AND MEASURE POVERTY AND POLARIZATION

How can we tell if a household is poor? What are the signs that a city is socially polarized? There are different ways to measure both poverty and polarization, and each method reveals different dimensions of the problems, including how they might be lessened through housing and education policies.

We can think about and measure poverty in absolute, relative, or multi-dimensional terms. Absolute measures set thresholds of income below which people cannot obtain the basic necessities of life. For example, the World Bank developed three poverty lines to show gradations of poverty worldwide. Their data indicates that one-tenth of the world's population lives in extreme poverty at US$1.90 per day or less, whereas about a quarter of the population lives on up to US$3.30 and almost half live on up to US$5.50 per day (World Bank Group 2020). Relative measures assess poverty by examining a household's income in relation to the income distribution and standard of living in a particular city or country. That is, the definition of poverty will differ depending on where one lives; whether a household is considered poor depends on how far its income is from what households typically earn in that city.

But poverty goes beyond income. Poverty can include dimensions such as access to education, water, electricity, and the like; that is, poverty reflects inadequate availability of infrastructure and opportunities. According to a World Bank study, "When poor people are asked … what makes them feel poor, they indicate … not having enough to eat, having inadequate housing material, being sick, having limited or no formal education, having no work, and living in unsafe neighborhoods" (World Bank Group 2020, 43).

Canada uses the Market Basket Measure to measure poverty, a relative and multi-dimensional measure based on local thresholds for the cost of basic goods, including housing, food, clothing, transportation, and other expenses that vary across cities. In 2020, the poverty line was set at about C$50,000 in Toronto and Calgary, about C$51,000 in Vancouver, and about C$45,000 in Winnipeg. Further, Canada's Dimensions of Poverty Hub tracks poverty across twelve indicators, including access to basic needs such as housing, food, health care, and education, as well as measures related to resiliency, opportunity, and polarization. One of these twelve indicators, unmet housing needs, has grown in recent years, even while Canada's overall poverty rate has fallen, demonstrating the multi-directional nature of trends related to poverty.

Social polarization refers to gaps in the distribution of income, wealth, opportunity, and general well-being. Income inequality is the most common measure of polarization. UN-Habitat

(2016, 74) reports that income inequality is growing across most world regions and that "two thirds of the world's population live in cities that are more unequal today than 20 years ago." For example, in Toronto, the top 1 per cent earned 17 per cent of total income in 2019, whereas in New York City, the top 1 per cent earned about 35 per cent of total income in 2018 (Statistics Canada 2019a; NYC IBO 2020). Studies show that the United States has larger gaps between rich and poor than many countries in Western Europe and in countries with "emerging" economies, such as India, China, South Africa, Argentina, and Colombia (UN-Habitat 2016, 18).

Another way to measure polarization is in terms of shared prosperity. Shared prosperity measures "the extent to which economic growth is inclusive" (World Bank Group 2020, 81). Measures track the well-being of the share of the population in the bottom 40 per cent of a country's income distribution. For example, we can ask whether the average annual income growth of households in the bottom 40 per cent matches the overall average annual income growth in the entire country's households. If lower-income people's wages are growing more slowly than those of higher earners, then low-income households are not sharing in a country's overall economic growth (World Bank Group 2020). In Canada, the bottom 40 per cent income share was about 21 per cent in 2019 (Statistics Canada 2019b).

Like measures of poverty, some measures of inequality assess dimensions beyond income. For example, because education can enhance future earnings, it is important to examine levels of inequality in access to education. Researchers have measured educational inequality by analyzing gaps in achievement on international test scores across socioeconomic groups of students, finding that gaps emerge at different ages – they develop early in some countries, grow substantially in adolescence in others, or explode in adulthood (OECD 2018).

Polarization also can refer to the physical spaces of a city. Do people at different income levels share space, or do they occupy separate zones of the city? The degree of spatial segregation shapes urban residents' opportunities to obtain basic infrastructure, jobs, schooling, and housing. In cities with more segregation, economic mobility is lower (Chetty et al. 2014). Some policies therefore aim to disperse affordable housing and quality schools throughout a city.

TRACKING POVERTY AND POLARIZATION IN CITIES

Poverty and polarization do not necessarily rise and fall together. Poverty rates worldwide have declined since 1990 as the middle class grew, but at the same time, levels of income inequality have risen (UN-Habitat 2016, 74). Poverty globally reduced from 43 per cent in 1990 to 21 per cent in 2010, but the Gini coefficient measuring inequality increased from 0.65 in 1980 to 0.70 in 2010 (74), meaning that not all households shared in the growing wealth worldwide because the income distribution actually became more unequal. The Gini

Table 15.1. Poverty and Inequality in Selected Cities

Country/City	Poverty Rate	Gini Coefficient
Australia	12.4%	0.33
Sydney	12.6%	0.50
Austria	10%	0.27
Vienna	N/A	0.27
Brazil	21.5%	0.48
Rio de Janeiro	N/A	0.52
São Paulo	N/A	0.53
Canada	11.6% / 6.4%[*]	0.30
Calgary	6.8%[*]	0.45
Edmonton	5.2%[*]	0.39
Montreal	5.4%[*]	0.35
Quebec City	3.2%[*]	0.38
Toronto	8.6%[*]	0.4[*]
Vancouver	7.8%[*]	0.4[*]
Winnipeg	6.6%[*]	0.36
Denmark	6.4%	0.26
Sweden	8.5%	0.28
Stockholm	6.8%	0.30
Switzerland	10.5%	0.31
Basel	6.1%[†]	0.51
Zurich	4.5%[†]	0.49
United Kingdom	12.4%	0.37
London	28%	0.43
United States	18%	0.40
Chicago	18.4%[†]	0.41
New York City	17.9%[†]	0.42

[*] Multi-dimensional measure

[†] Absolute measure based on national poverty line

Notes: Poverty rate defined as relative poverty (% of population with less than 50% of median income), unless otherwise noted. All country-level data sourced from the OECD Income Distribution Database (OECD, n.d.); city Gini coefficients sourced from OECD (2020) when available; remaining city-level Gini coefficients and poverty rates from national/local sources listed below. Data varies by the date of most recent available data (2013–20). "N/A" means data not available.

Sources: OECD (n.d.); OECD (2020); Vidyattama, Tanton, and NCOSS (2019) (Australia); CEIC (2017) (Brazil); Statistics Canada (2022); Statistics Sweden (2024); FSO (n.d.) and FTA (2015) (Switzerland); UK DWP (2024); US Census (2022).

coefficient ranges from 0 to 1, with 0 being perfect equality and 1 being complete inequality. The coefficient summarizes information on how a city or country's total earned income is distributed across the population of earners (UN-Habitat 2014, 28). The UN reported that the "gap between the rich and the poor in most countries is at its highest level [in] 30 years," noting that this growing gap "stigmatizes and even removes large groups of the urban population from a socially and economically productive life; and it excludes by preventing them and their children from benefiting from opportunities to advance in the society at large" (UN-Habitat 2016, 17).

Dissonance between rates of poverty and polarization is most common in developing countries that are rapidly urbanizing, where dramatic declines in rural poverty occur alongside expanding urban inequality. This trend can be seen in Sub-Saharan Africa, much of Latin America, and some of Asia. In China, both rural and urban poverty have dramatically reduced over the past four decades due to rapid development; however, inequality has grown recently and is now at a level similar to the United States. Nations in the Global North are generally less unequal, as seen throughout Europe and in Canada, but the United States is a significant exception, with its high levels of inequality.

Table 15.1 compares the levels of poverty and social polarization in some of the countries and cities whose housing and education policies we examine. We track national and local poverty rates (which sometimes vary in terms of definition and measurement, as noted below) as well as Gini coefficients, the most common measure of income inequality. In general, although the average income level of urban areas tends to be higher than in rural areas, urban places have higher levels of inequality (Boulant, Brezzi, and Veneri 2016). While cities within countries vary in terms of inequality, larger, more global cities show higher levels than smaller cities (Boulant, Brezzi, and Veneri 2016). Across Canadian metro areas, inequality was highest in Calgary, Vancouver, and Toronto, and lowest in Montreal, Winnipeg, and Quebec City (Boulant, Brezzi, and Veneri 2016, 17). European metro areas show recent increases in inequality, including in Denmark, Norway, Sweden, and France (15). The same is true for cities in the United States. Despite rising inequality, Western Europe remains the most egalitarian region in the world (UN-Habitat 2016, 18), with the exception of London, where rapidly increasing housing costs have contributed to high poverty rates and growing wealth disparities (Travers, Sims, and Bosetti 2016). We also see that Canada's low Gini coefficient is comparable to those in Europe while the United States and Brazil have relatively higher figures. In the 1980s, Brazil was one of the most unequal countries, but these trends reversed in the 1990s due to growing social assistance programs (Barrientos 2013). Recent reductions in spending for these programs have coincided with rising inequality. Relatedly, recent poverty data from the United States and Canada reflects a temporary reduction in poverty due to enhanced unemployment and stay-at-home benefits during the COVID-19 pandemic.

THE ROLE OF CITIES IN ADDRESSING POVERTY AND SOCIAL POLARIZATION

Since poverty affects a significant portion of urban residents, and polarization rises in many cities, it's important to consider what city leaders can do to reverse course and create inclusive places to live. Governmental systems vary in the degree to which cities can independently develop, implement, and finance public policies, including policies related to poverty and social polarization such as housing and education. Political arrangements also vary in how much funding cities receive from national governments, which shapes the ability of mayors and city councils to address poverty and polarization.

One important difference across cities is whether they are part of centralized or decentralized government systems. In centralized systems, the national government determines and funds most policies, with provinces and cities carrying them out. In such systems, cities are primarily policy implementers, with less opportunity for leaders to create policies that address their cities' specific needs and constituencies. In decentralized systems, cities have more authority to design public policies but may also need to raise revenue through taxes and fees to pay for them. City leaders thus may be at odds with wealthy corporations or individuals who resist paying higher property or income taxes, or they may generate conflict by raising taxes that everyone pays – on utilities, consumer goods, parking, or public institutions like arenas or skating rinks. In general, Western European political systems are more centralized, and North and South American systems are more decentralized. The different levels of freedom cities have to develop housing and education policies shape politics since activists will focus on the government officials with the most authority to enact policy change, whether at city, provincial, or national levels.

Cities in Canada have traditionally had little formal autonomy because they depend, constitutionally, on provinces for their scope of authority, and often for significant parts of their revenues (Eidelman and Taylor 2010; Taylor and Bradford 2020). Provincial officials therefore are key players in cities, especially as social policy has devolved from national to provincial governments, such as in the area of social housing. However, during the past two decades, provinces have enlarged the scope of cities' authority (Taylor and Bradford 2020), with many Canadian cities now able to impose taxes and fees. National and provincial government transfers nonetheless still represent key parts of local budgets (Taylor and Bradford 2020, 45). As national and provincial leaders develop more collaborative governance, some cities have gained greater voice and independence (45). For example, under Prime Minister Trudeau, significant funding has been available to cities for projects that create "inclusive growth," including developing affordable housing and strategies to reduce homelessness (43). This funding was made available through the National Housing Strategy Act of 2019, which established a right to housing and provides funding to provinces and municipalities to produce more affordable housing and address housing problems like homelessness. The act also established the position of federal housing advocate, and its first appointee, Marie-Josée Houle, has been critical concerning the need for greater attention in the areas of homelessness, financialization, and vulnerable communities (Houle 2022). When it comes to policies that address poverty and social polarization, cities in Canada can become designers as well as implementers. In some provinces, cities deliver provincial social assistance programs (Taylor and Bradford 2020). Cities are also responsible for land-use regulation, which can influence spatial polarization. In the United States, decentralization is more firmly rooted over a longer period of time. Although cities' powers are determined by state governments, states generally leave cities much room to establish policies in critical areas, such as education, land use, economic development, health and safety, environmental sustainability, and more. US cities have some state-imposed restrictions on how they may raise revenue, but they are generally able to impose sales and property taxes, licensing and user fees, and to borrow money through private financial markets and with municipal bonds. Some cities may also impose income taxes.

In Europe, while data shows a general growth in local autonomy since 1990, levels vary significantly. For example, Germany and Scandinavian countries have higher levels of local autonomy, in contrast to lower levels in the United Kingdom, France, and Italy (Ladner, Keuffer, and Baldersheim 2016; Savitch and Kantor 2002). In Scandinavian countries, which have the most egalitarian welfare states, local governments have strong fiscal, political, and administrative capacities, are tightly integrated into national systems, and are supported by the national government as key elements in delivering welfare-state programs that address poverty and polarization (Sellers and Lidström 2007). In the United Kingdom, France, and Italy, the national government plays a key role in formulating urban policy.

In Latin America, national governments have decentralized authority since the 1980s, often granting taxation power to states and cities (Stren 2012; Van Lindert 2016). Cities have developed and experimented with participatory governance and citizen consultation (Van Lindert 2016). Brazil, with a federal structure organized into states, offers an example of these trends. The 1988 Constitution decentralized resources and authority over provision of social services and facilitated local participation in these processes (Stren 2012, 582). Cities are considered equal to states as members of the national federation and have substantial discretion over land and housing policies (85). Large cities have a strong revenue base. Brazilian cities can raise funds through taxes and can develop their own housing policies. They have track records as policy innovators: activists and officials have developed policies that were adopted at the national level. For example, the country's primary anti-poverty program, Bolsa Familia, emerged from municipal experimentation in the 1980s. Once adopted and expanded by the federal government, cities were responsible for implementation and outreach (Barrientos 2013). As municipal institutions become more empowered, the local state has partnered with the private sector to pursue major development projects. Cities partner with development banks to fund major housing projects, alongside other levels of government (Barrientos 2013, 86).

HOW HOUSING AND EDUCATION POLICY ADDRESS POVERTY AND POLARIZATION

Countries, then, start from different places when it comes to addressing poverty and polarization. Each has these problems in their cities to different degrees; each has different governance systems that shape how and where actions might be taken to mitigate them. In some, the structures allow for city officials and residents to independently develop and experiment with local solutions, whereas in others, it is the province or the national government where policies are developed. Nonetheless, we can understand a city's housing and education systems and policies as key entry points to reducing a city's levels of poverty and polarization.

Housing affordability is a growing problem across most of the world (Marquardt and Glaser 2023). Lack of affordable housing can push families into poverty. When families must choose between paying for their home or purchasing food, medical care, and other necessities of life, they may sink into poverty and ill health. When families cannot make monthly housing payments, they may lose their homes to eviction or foreclosure and become homeless. Thus, when cities increase the supply and the quality of affordable housing, poverty may decline. The location of affordable housing also matters. In some countries, cities are more segregated by race and class, often as a result of racial discrimination in housing markets and exclusionary zoning policies that limit where multi-family or subsidized housing can be built. Many cities have made efforts to reduce concentrations of poverty and to improve infrastructures in lower-income neighbourhoods so that residents have access to transit, jobs, and schools. This is one way that housing may reduce the negative impacts of social polarization.

Education is another policy area where cities may play a role in addressing poverty and social polarization. Schools teach basic skills and develop the critical thinking necessary for students to develop and pursue their goals. They support the local economy by preparing students for the labour market. They also may foster community and cohesion and prepare citizens to participate in the political process (Sadovnik et al. 2017). Decades of education reform, especially in Global North cities, have focused on improving school quality and increasing access to quality schools. Cities in the Global South have made significant progress toward universal access to basic education. Ensuring that children from marginalized groups receive a high-quality education remains a key issue globally (OECD 2018). When poor or racial and ethnic minority children systematically do not receive high-quality education compared to wealthier majority-group children, social polarization persists over generations.

In each of these policy areas, we can see struggles in cities among officials and stakeholders over the best way to bring about change. One key element in the conflict is often between neo-liberal approaches and more egalitarian or community-centred approaches. Neo-liberalism is a philosophy that arose in the 1970s, now espoused by many local officials, domestic policy institutes, and global institutions. Neo-liberal policy approaches embrace an individualistic, market-based logic and are defined by a dramatic reduction in spending from the federal government (Weaver 2022).

Table 15.2. Examples of Market-Based and Progressive Policies by Country

| Country | Market-Based Policies | | Progressive Policies | |
	Housing	Education	Housing	Education
Canada	Mixed-income public housing redevelopment (Toronto) Inclusionary zoning (Montreal, Quebec, Vancouver)	School choice (Toronto, Vancouver, Calgary, Edmonton) Charter schools (Calgary, Edmonton)	Mixed-income public housing redevelopment[*] (Toronto)	Afrocentric education (Toronto) Indigenous education (Winnipeg)
United States	Mixed-income public housing redevelopment (Chicago, federal urban policy) Inclusionary zoning (New York City)	Charter schools	Community land trusts	Local school councils (Chicago)
Brazil	Inclusionary zoning (São Paulo)	School choice (Rio de Janeiro)	Social housing and homeownership development (São Paulo, federal urban policy) Informal housing and infrastructure upgrading (Rio de Janeiro)	Charter schools (Rio de Janeiro) Citizen school project (Porto Alegre)
Europe		Independent (Charter) schools (Stockholm, Sweden) Performance and testing-based school reforms (Zurich, Switzerland)	Social housing development (Vienna, Austria)	Migrant inclusion (Basel, Switzerland)

[*] In Toronto, public housing redevelopment replaced all units of demolished affordable housing and added market-rate housing. In the United States, this replacement did not occur.

Under this political economic theory, state power should support free trade, open markets, and private property (Weaver 2022, 14). In other words, this theory values competition to produce best outcomes. For example, in the field of education, school choice embraces these principles by encouraging competition among schools and removing regulatory barriers to it. With voucher and charter policies, the theory predicts that families will operate as consumers seeking to advance their individual interests, selecting the best schools for their children, and avoiding schools with poor outcomes. Leaders of those "failing" schools would need to find innovative ways to improve their schools so as to attract "consumers" in the form of students. The theory predicts that all schools in a system will improve and diversify as a result of market competition.

Egalitarian approaches, on the other hand, defend liberal advancements in civil rights while promoting new policies to empower marginalized groups (Weaver 2022). This perspective values equality, social justice, and social citizenship instead of the business interests and market logic served by neo-liberalization. In the context of education, the egalitarian perspective privileges public neighbourhood schools and seeks to identify root causes of educational disparities beyond a lack of competition, including poverty, polarization, and systemic racism. This approach emphasizes solutions such as equalizing funding across school districts to help under-resourced schools and districts provide the quality and services that are needed.

Table 15.2 summarizes the policy initiatives discussed in this chapter. In general, the United States stands out with a predominance of market-based policies whereas other countries and regions have a mix of approaches, including significant examples of progressive policies.

Housing Policies

Housing policy's political dynamics centre on the tension between use and exchange value. That is, housing is a basic need, necessary for life, and it is also an important sector of the economy. Besides involving many industries and livelihoods (real estate, finance, development, construction, building materials, and consumer goods), housing is a source of profit and wealth-building for individual homeowners. Housing's exchange value matters to the private sector, but also to the public sector, because provincial and local governments often rely on revenue from taxes on property and real estate transactions. Furthermore, real estate development in tandem with publicly provided infrastructure importantly shape a city's built environment, creating (or detracting from) public value and quality of life, alongside private profits (or losses). The housing industries employ many people, which is also important to local officials who want their cities to have healthy economies. On the other hand, housing's use value has led the United Nations and some countries to declare housing to be a human right, with the implication that governments should ensure that everyone has shelter. In Brazil, the Constitution asserts "the social function of property," that is, "the obligation for land uses that contribute to the common good" (Friendly and Stiphany 2019, 273).

These different purposes (using housing for basic survival and using housing for purposes of income or wealth) create the potential for alliances and conflicts among different groups of city residents, corporations, and local officials. The core questions surrounding housing policy involve how the government should intervene in the housing market, for whose benefit, and at whose cost. Political struggles over housing policy also centre on groups' various visions for the city and its neighbourhoods. Consistent data across cities, world regions, and over time shows continuing need for affordable housing with adequate sanitation, safe construction, and other measures of habitability. This data suggests that private markets are not capable on their own of producing housing to meet the needs of the lowest earners. Usually, governments – whether national, state, or local – step into that gap.

There are several ways to measure the gap between need and availability of affordable housing, including foreclosure and eviction rates, trends in homelessness, and gaps between income levels and rent levels. The most common measure of unmet housing need is whether families can secure housing for less than 30 per cent of their income. One study found that a majority of New York City tenants paid more than 30 per cent of their incomes for rent, and 70 per cent of extremely low-income households paid more than 50 per cent (Stein 2018, 773). Canada combines this 30 per cent threshold with a measure of access to housing quality, including in "housing need" the share of families who spend less than 30 per cent of their incomes on housing but live in homes either in poor condition or too small, given family size. Data shows that nearly 13 per cent of families had unmet housing needs in 2016 (Statistics Canada 2017, table 1). Toronto has the highest rate of unmet housing need, at nearly 19 per cent of households, while Quebec City has the lowest at about 7 per cent (Statistics Canada 2017, figure 1).

Housing policies that aim to reduce social polarization and poverty focus on increasing the affordability of housing and decreasing the concentration of affordable housing and low-income households in certain parts of cities. But there are many strategies to work toward those goals. We see two broad types of public policies. On the one hand, some policies remove housing units from the private market. These policies are called decommodification strategies because once removed from the market, housing is no longer a commodity to be exchanged for profit. When housing is built or operated by non-profit groups or government, the purpose is to provide shelter, not to make a profit. Another broad category of policies regulates the private market. The idea is that with the right rules and incentives, private developers and landlords will provide affordable housing. Neo-liberal housing policies leverage the private market to provide affordable housing by attempting to inject market incentives into the field. As we discuss below, with inclusionary zoning, these have mixed results, often benefiting private companies and market-rate renters and owners more than low-income households. Finally, housing policies vary in the degree of influence that community members have on the strategy selection and implementation. Within each category of housing policies, there are examples of cities where residents and community members have been able to exert more control over the priorities and design of housing policies. Cities also vary in the degree to which local governments defer to the private sector or impose requirements and restrictions on them.

HOUSING DECOMMODIFICATION: SOCIAL HOUSING

Programs that take housing out of the private market ensure long-term affordability. The primary form of decommodified housing is social or public housing. Many European and North American governments began to build social housing (government- or non-profit-owned and operated subsidized housing) in cities after the Second World War in the context of housing shortages. More recently, the stock of social housing has declined, especially since the 1990s. Access to this housing is means-tested, usually targeting households at the lowest or near-lowest income levels. Households typically pay a designated portion of their incomes (often 30 per cent) in rent. Many countries began to cut funding for maintaining these affordable multi-family rental complexes, switching to providing subsidies for households living in private housing. In some cases, social housing units were sold to tenants (Gurstein, Patten, and Rao 2015).

One result of declining funding has been the deterioration of the physical condition of social housing complexes, alongside growing concerns that concentrated poverty contributes to inequality, inhibits opportunities for families, and results in social polarization. In response, many cities have worked to redevelop social housing apartment complexes into mixed-income neighbourhoods by partnering with private sector developers to build market-rate housing alongside existing or new social housing. On the one hand, this strategy may raise funds for social housing from the sale of land and taxes on private housing. But mixed-income redevelopment can displace low-income residents, exclude them from planning processes, and contribute to gentrification by raising property values and housing costs in the neighbourhood. Examples of these processes in Toronto and Chicago are discussed below. On the other hand, some cities have invested in expanding the stock of social housing. Vienna and São Paulo offer some examples.

REDEVELOPING PUBLIC HOUSING

In Canada, the federal government funded and built public or social housing until the 1990s, when much of federal housing policy was devolved to the provinces, leading to reductions in financial contributions; in some provinces, city governments became responsible for its funding and administration (Gurstein, Patten, and Rao 2015; Rosa 2018). Many cities began to partner with non-profit organizations and the private sector to manage social housing, and they coped with the withdrawal of funding by engaging in redevelopment projects that transformed social housing communities into mixtures of social and market-rate housing. Alongside this decline in public funding for social housing was a change in the resident population. Although initial residents of many social housing projects were white Euro-Canadians, by the 1970s, the majority of residents were immigrants from Latin America, Asia, and South Asia. With immigration, then, combined with unequal opportunities for social mobility and for access to private-market housing, public housing became a racialized space (Rosa 2018).

Regent Park and Don Mount Court are two examples of Toronto's redevelopment of social housing into mixed-income neighbourhoods. Proponents of this strategy believe that mixed-income housing counteracts the social isolation of traditional social housing through the transmission of "social norms about workforce participation" (August 2008). The idea is that "behavioural patterns of lower-income tenants will be altered by interaction with higher-income neighbours" (August 2008, 94). The strategy also meets the reality of decreased public funding for social housing in Canada and other countries. It seeks to leverage funds for subsidized housing with profits from market-rate housing development. Both cases show some of the trade-offs and pitfalls of mixed-income redevelopment for meeting the housing needs of a city's lowest-income residents.

Regent Park and Don Mount Court were originally built with funds from the 1944 National Housing Act to clear neighbourhoods identified as slums, replacing them with social housing; Regent Park was built in the late 1940s and Don Mount in the late 1960s. By 2000, both developments had experienced serious physical deterioration and were deemed failures for isolating residents within the city (August 2016; Rosa 2018). In both cases, the Toronto Community Housing Corporation (TCHC), the non-profit organization responsible for public housing in Toronto, decided on redevelopment instead of repair, and on the creation of a new community that would include both social housing and market-rate units.

Don Mount Court, now called Rivertowne, was the first redevelopment of public housing in Canada to adopt the mixed-income approach and was soon followed by the larger redevelopment of Regent Park. Over ten years, Don Mount's structures were demolished, its modernist design replaced by New Urbanist-style housing and community design, emphasizing traditional street grids, front porches, and open, rather than enclosed, public spaces intended to promote "eyes on the street" (August 2016). All 232 units of public housing were replaced, and nearly 200 market-rate units were added. But years after the new project took shape, studies showed that tenants were less satisfied with the new units and experienced community tension with the new residents (August 2016). They disliked the reduced privacy, the absence of individual yards, the shared front stoops, the open-concept designs of the new units, and the shoddy soundproofing of shared walls between units. These design changes subjected them to surveillance from neighbours to the extent that they expressed a diminished sense of security and community.

In Regent Park, the TCHC laid out a plan in 2005 to sell the land to private developers and public-private partnerships to produce a mixed-use, mixed-income community, also designed according to New Urbanist principles (Rosa 2018). Increasing the density of the sites and opening them to market development was intended to generate income to produce and maintain the subsidized units. Officials planned to build the same number of subsidized units as were demolished although some of these would be off-site, resulting in a majority market-rate community in place of what had been a fully subsidized development. As long as the market is strong, this strategy can generate revenue, but downturns in the housing market would threaten its ability to produce sufficient income to develop the subsidized units (Moore and Wright 2017). Additionally, the redevelopment may have "[opened] up east downtown Toronto to gentrification, a process that has been held off in the area largely due to the presence of Regent Park" (August 2008, 95).

The United States has arguably been the leader in the scale and the breadth of redeveloping public housing into mixed-income neighbourhoods. The federal government's Housing Opportunities for People Everywhere (HOPE) programs have, since the 1990s, significantly dismantled and downsized the nation's public housing stock through demolition, redevelopment, and sale of housing units (Goetz 2011a). While originally intended to address "severely distressed" public housing, the program's reach went well beyond the estimated 6 per cent of the public housing stock that might have qualified as such (Goetz 2011a, 270).

The Chicago Housing Authority (CHA) implemented the largest public housing reform program in the country with its Plan for Transformation, which includes the broadest mixed-income redevelopment strategy in the United States (Chaskin, Khare, and Joseph 2012). The plan emerged when the city regained control of the public housing authority after three years of federal emergency management. The CHA's record of mismanagement of the city's racially segregated, isolated, crime-ridden public housing eventually spurred the takeover. In the wake of regained local control, Chicago mayor Richard M. Daley asserted the intention to completely transform public housing's physical and social landscape (Chaskin, Khare, and Joseph 2012, 871). As part of the plan, ten new mixed-income developments with sixteen thousand housing units would stand on the footprints of some of the city's public housing projects. These developments were partnerships between private and non-profit developers, with for-sale and rental units, often in townhouse styles. Social services were present on-site, as well as mechanisms for resident engagement. In a study of three developments where measures were taken to promote social mixing of residents, researchers found that public housing residents felt safer and more secure, compared to their previous public housing units. But interviews with residents in the new communities showed significant social tensions surrounding differing expectations and evaluations of behaviours, including gathering on sidewalks or common areas. The market-rate owners expressed their orientation toward the exchange value of their housing, and they worried about the property values affected by things like repairing cars on the street or hanging laundry on balconies (Chaskin and Joseph 2013, 492). The public housing residents considered their homes from a use-value perspective, complaining about feeling monitored. Furthermore, moral judgments about low-income residents as being inferior to higher-income residents are at the root of the theory of social mix and were evident in the study's findings.

Such judgments propelled the redevelopment in the first place. Local officials and development advocates used narratives of isolated, even deviant, criminal residents to justify redevelopment but overlooked the strong communities that residents forged under adverse circumstances, communities lost as residents dispersed during redevelopment (Goetz 2011a). In addition, studies showed that Black residents bore the brunt of the HOPE programs' demolition and dispersal, but in general their housing conditions did not uniformly improve as a result. Rather, they tended to move to other segregated high-poverty neighbourhoods while new residents who could pay market-rate rents moved into transformed neighbourhoods poised to gentrify (Goetz 2011a, 2011b). In chapter 14, we see that the systemic racism evident in processes of gentrification in the United States are also evident in Canadian cities.

INCREASING SOCIAL HOUSING STOCK AND IMPROVING INFRASTRUCTURE

Many cities have adopted different variations of the mixed-income model to redevelop public housing projects while others instead chose to expand social housing. Although the size of the social housing stock has declined in most countries and cities and represents a small percentage of the total housing stock, there are some exceptions. In Sweden, Denmark, the Netherlands, and Austria, social housing represents from 23 to 40 per cent of the housing stock. In France, the size of the social housing stock has grown since the 1990s (Gurstein, Patten, and Rao 2015).

Vienna offers a particularly robust example of a long-term, multi-faceted commitment to maintaining and increasing the social housing sector. First, governments, from federal to province to city, state that housing policy should advance social policy goals rather than correct temporary market imbalances (Marquardt and Glaser 2023, 15). A broad segment of Vienna households has access to social housing, which makes up 43 per cent of the city's housing stock. It is not designated exclusively for those with the lowest incomes, as is the case in most other places. Units are permanently affordable, meaning tenants have long-term housing security. Broad access to affordable housing translates into a broad base of political support for social housing to remain robust in the city (13). The city's policy framework also produces new units steadily and at lower cost when compared to other countries, enabling Vienna to more effectively meet the housing challenges of a rapidly growing city (11). Most of the city's social housing is built and managed by limited-profit housing associations (LPHAs) or by the city itself, with a smaller share held by private builders (6). LPHAs receive corporate tax exemption and must reinvest profits into "new housing, refurbishment, or land purchase," providing continuous production regardless of economic cycles (6). Tenants contribute to the construction cost or can receive a public loan to cover this requirement. Recently the city designed "SMART" flats with lower square footage and simpler amenities to become one-third of all social housing projects, thus aiming to incorporate the lowest-income households fully into all new developments (7).

Brazil also has invested in new construction of affordable housing, focused on owner-occupancy, with the Mi Casa Mi Vida (My House My Life, MCMV) program, which began in 2009. About 3.5 million homes in social housing estates have been built through the program (Stiphany and Ward 2019). Families become owners after ten years. Local governments' role was to register and organize beneficiaries, as well as provide land and additional infrastructure for the projects (Klink and Denaldi 2014, 224). Many homes were sited in peripheral locations, serving to consolidate the social segregation of poor families, while nevertheless increasing access to affordable housing. Program evaluation also found that it had difficulty reaching the lowest-income families: 40 per cent of the new housing was designated for them, but they represent 90 per cent of the housing deficit. The program also may have allowed landowners to sell parcels of land otherwise undesirable for their peripheral locations and environmental degradation; local groups acquiring them incurred higher development costs because of some of these problems (Stiphany and Ward 2019, 316).

The program mandated a participatory process at the city level, engaging stakeholders and prospective residents to plan the projects. This process unfolded unevenly across cities. Where there was strong local government capacity in housing and commitment to working together with progressive housing and advocacy movements, MCMV did generate a significant amount of housing for the neediest residents. Participants were attracted by the opportunity to become homeowners. Stiphany and Ward (2019) examined two São Paulo communities that are developing MCMV sites, each located on the periphery of the informal, self-built neighbourhood. Residents who buy into the new housing estate will move from a more central location within the neighbourhood to a more peripheral one, which, depending on the community, may be less well connected via public transit and may initially have fewer resources such as access to health care and schools. The study found that architects and officials present information to the community and to prospective buyers without necessarily explaining some of the deficits of the sites. This renders the participatory process superficial.

In the Global South, public investment in upgrading the infrastructure in informal settlements (in Brazil, these are called favelas) can reduce social polarization by connecting these communities to the wider city, potentially improving the quality of life for residents. Infrastructure improvements might include paved roads, public transit, electrification, sanitation systems, water systems, social services, and government offices situated in the favelas. In Brazil, favela dwellers are a major voting bloc, so elected officials have incentives to invest in these communities. The country's Constitution includes a right to adverse possession, recognizing squatters' ownership of land after five years of occupation. Although Brazil's policy is considered more progressive than those in other countries, initiatives tend to be threatened by increasing land values as a result of upgrading. Increasing interest in attracting mega-events such as the World Cup or the Olympics entices officials to clear and redevelop favelas for other purposes, along the lines seen in North America's public housing redevelopments. These become sources of contestation between advocates for the poor and for housing justice and the mayor and private developers.

In Rio de Janeiro, where nearly a quarter of the city's population lives in favelas, several mayors have undertaken infrastructure upgrading, often in negotiation with powerful local NGOs active in movements for housing justice (Ren 2018). The city funds these programs alongside federal and state governments and international lending agencies. Its Master Plan recognized favelas as part of the city in 1992 and recommended working to preserve their local character. This signalled for a time a re-orientation away from favela demolition that had regularly occurred under the country's military dictatorship. Commitment to recognition and preservation meant the state had an obligation to provide infrastructure and services in a context-sensitive manner. Two programs offer examples: Favela-Bairro (1998–2008) and Morar Carioca (2008–present). Newly elected mayor Cesar Maia initiated Favela-Bairro to upgrade public spaces in favelas, including streets, street lighting, water and sewerage, and recreation space. He established a new city department to coordinate the program and appointed an architect to oversee it. The next version of favela upgrading was Morar Carioca. This one emphasized community participation, contracting with NGOs to solicit feedback from local residents who would guide projects. Architectural competitions were held to select specific community projects. These programs became highly contested during mayoral elections as rival candidates sought to point out deficiencies and incumbents were pressured to increase and improve them. By 2012 however, with the 2016 Olympics on the horizon, mayors and other officials scaled back these programs in favour of port improvements and rapid transit bus projects to support Olympic activity. Removals and evictions from favelas with locational interest in Olympic planning became commonplace but triggered a new wave of housing rights activism. With well-organized, experienced NGOs, such actions, though they occur in cities worldwide, will be challenged in Brazil.

HOUSING DECOMMODIFICATION: COMMUNITY LAND TRUSTS

Besides social housing, another form of housing decommodification that is less widespread is the community land trust (CLT). Land trusts are non-profit organizations with membership-based governance structures that own land for purposes determined by members (Bunce and Aslam 2016). In cities, land trusts have been used to remove land from the private market to provide permanently affordable housing. Because profit is not the mission of CLT members, housing on CLT land can be rented or sold at below-market rates. To purchase homes on CLT land, buyers agree to resale price restrictions intended to maintain affordability while allowing some equity to be captured. Community control is central to the original concept, but actual community control varies in the implementation of the land trust model (DeFilippis, Stromberg, and Williams 2018). A small number of CLTs have been established in Canadian cities, including Toronto and Montreal.

MARKET-BASED HOUSING POLICY: INCLUSIONARY ZONING

As funding for social housing declines, market-based approaches to affordable housing have become prevalent (Gurstein, Patten, and Rao 2015). Local officials develop rules, programs, and subsidies to mandate or incentivize the private sector to build or fund affordable housing. Tools that local governments use to promote affordable housing include inclusionary zoning, rent control regulations, tax subsidies or exemptions, and the formation of public-private partnerships. Cities have increasingly turned to these methods as national governments have withdrawn or decreased public funding for affordable housing, making the private sector even more necessary to expand supply. However, working with the private sector entails accommodating its logic and motivation for operating – to increase the exchange value of housing and to make a profit. For this reason, housing scholars see the turn to market-based housing policies as part of the neo-liberalization of urban policy. The empowerment and participation of low-income community members and their advocates become even more important.

Inclusionary housing regulations either mandate or encourage developers to include affordable housing units in new housing developments. Because local government almost always regulates land use, enforces building codes, and grants occupancy and building permits, in addition to building and maintaining infrastructure, city officials can use these processes to increase affordable housing supply. Some inclusionary regulations mandate that a certain percentage of units in new multi-family buildings be affordable; others allow for zoning variances to be granted for increased housing density in exchange for developers building affordable units on other sites, hiring a non-profit developer to do so, or contributing to an affordable housing fund (Stein 2018). This is called a "density bonus": developers receive permission to build more housing units on a site than the zoning code would allow in exchange for building or funding affordable housing.

In Canada, cities' inclusionary zoning policies vary by province. For example, Quebec's cities, with the recent exception of Montreal, are not permitted to impose mandatory inclusionary zoning, whereas in British Columbia, the Vancouver Charter gives the city authority to do so. Ontario allows cities to grant density bonuses in exchange for community benefits. Montreal had a voluntary program until 2021, in which city officials and housing advocates had to persuade real estate developers to participate, and they have developed the skills and track record to do so in many cases. More recently the province authorized Montreal to adopt a mandatory measure. In Toronto, officials negotiate with developers to provide a set of community benefits in exchange for a density bonus; research shows that these agreements rarely require developers to build affordable housing, but that developers provide the city with funds or land that the city can use to develop such housing (Mah and Hackworth 2011). In Vancouver, 20 per cent of units must be designated for social housing, a rule that worked as long as federal and provincial social housing programs existed. In their absence, local officials find it harder to mandate, and agreements tend to be worked out case by case. Mah and Hackworth (2011) conclude that the process of implementing inclusionary zoning is complex and that the presence of housing and neighbourhood activists is critical in the cases where developers have actually delivered affordable housing or land and funds.

The case of New York City also shows the pitfalls of inclusionary zoning as an affordable housing policy. Mayor Bill de Blasio developed a Mandatory Inclusionary Housing program in 2014, requiring affordable housing to be built where the city allows the construction of luxury housing (Stein 2018). De Blasio responded to decades of inclusionary zoning programs in the city, which were criticized for not producing much affordable housing, and for price points that were too high for low-income households (Stein 2018). Therefore, his policy was mandatory, not voluntary, and included a menu of options for developers, with fewer units mandated if the price points were accessible to low-income families, and more units designated for the higher-income groups within the "low-income" category (Stein 2018). That said, critics noted limits which together tend to exacerbate gentrification. Providing affordable units only within the context of luxury housing and in neighbourhoods rezoned for higher density means that land values increase, putting additional pressure on housing prices, even as some affordable housing is built. In neighbourhoods undergoing rezoning, the existing privately owned units become subject to higher market value too, and landlords may displace tenants before new construction begins. "Rather than putting housing in the public domain, it enshrines private landlords as the primary and rightful providers of shelter" (Angotti and Morse 2016, cited in Stein 2018, 776). "Meanwhile, it raises land values and encourages speculation, further moving housing away from the realm of 'use values' or shelter – and toward 'exchange values' or accumulation vehicles" (Logan and Molotch 1987, cited in Stein 2018, 776).

Similar approaches are used in Latin America. In Brazil, local officials have used zoning to identify areas where affordable housing is needed. For example, São Paulo requires that, in exchange for density bonuses, real estate developers contribute to a fund that is used for a range of projects, including affordable housing. But similar dynamics to the New York City case occur, such that land values in these zones appreciate as a result of the private development. In São Paulo, affordable housing built using these funds is often sited in outlying areas, contributing to displacement and marginalization of lower-income groups (Santoro 2019). In other words, when the values of the private real estate sector are leveraged to generate affordable housing funds, as in designating for redevelopment zones that will be attractive to the private sector, then affordable housing remains a marginal by-product of private development instead of a central public purpose that truly harnesses the private sector to public needs (Santoro 2019; Stein 2018).

Education Policy and Politics

Education outcomes are both a product and driver of social and economic inequality; policies might contribute to or reduce social mobility and polarization. While education is a priority across countries and political spectrums, perspectives on inequality and institutional dynamics vary. We discuss two types of education reform seen across cities: (1) market-based reforms focused on improving schools through privatization and competition between schools, and (2) progressive reforms focused on improving schools by increasing local control and providing opportunities for disadvantaged groups of students. Market-based reforms can be compatible with conservative, moderate, or liberal political perspectives, and are therefore generally common, while progressive reforms generally find support from liberal or leftist groups. Local politics is often a key element of education policy-making, as discussed by both Canadian and American scholars of education and urban politics (Stone et al. 2001; Gaskell and Levin 2011). But reforms may also target the degree of centralization in an education system. Systems vary across countries and over time and whether local, provincial, or national officials make key decisions.

EDUCATION AND INEQUALITY

Inequality in education is characterized by the relatively poor educational attainment of a variety of marginalized groups of students compared with those students who are more advantaged.

Despite these inequalities, schools are widely considered an instrumental factor in reducing poverty and increasing social mobility. This paradox is evident in many countries where education is touted as the way out of poverty, but students from disadvantaged backgrounds consistently lag behind. In immigrant communities, where schooling is seen as the path toward assimilation, it may also lead to further marginalization. In part depending on policy choices, education can reduce poverty and promote social cohesion. Other policy choices may maintain or deepen inequalities and exacerbate polarization. Further, poor educational attainment in the aggregate can drag down the social capital and economic competitiveness of nations, localities, and groups of people.

The extent to which education promotes social and economic mobility varies widely across and within countries (OECD 2018). Analyses find that disparities in performance for socioeconomically disadvantaged groups generally develop early, but that there is significant variation, especially in trends at different life stages in different countries (OECD 2012, 2018). For example, in the United Kingdom and the United States, disparities are comparatively large for children under the age of ten, but below average in Australia and relatively small in Canada. However, disparities explode during adolescence in Canada and Australia and continue to expand in the United States, while remaining more stable in the United Kingdom (OECD 2018). Countries like Brazil, where free universal education was attained more recently, generally have the largest socioeconomic disparities as more marginalized groups catch up to the progress of those who have had longer access to good schools. Canada, on the other hand, has had compulsory education since the nineteenth century and is generally a high-performing nation in international comparisons, but it has relatively poor outcomes in terms of inequality and social mobility. In other words, inequality in some countries can be understood in terms of the recent expansion of education access while in others, the causes of inequality are less easily explained. This unevenness signals important differences in the nature of education and pathways for reform across and within nations.

Social polarization in education is also considered in terms of distinct racial, ethnic, and gender disparities that mutually reinforce socioeconomic inequality (Zajda and Freeman 2009). These factors are closely tied to historical and cultural context. For example, the effects of racial stratification are prominent in the American context due to long histories of racial oppression that include racial and ethnic segregation in housing and education as well as contemporary racialized tracking or streaming systems in schools that group students by perceived abilities (Clotfelter 2011; Tyson 2011). In Canada, a similar system of streaming has also led to racialized dynamics, particularly for Black students. Racialization is also a key factor in nations with many ethnic groups and those with significant Indigenous populations, such as Australia, New Zealand, and Canada, as well as those with higher levels of immigration, such as Sweden, Germany, and the United Kingdom. Gender inequality also persists in education despite improvements in access and achievement in many developed countries, as evidenced by significant gender disparities in literacy and school attendance rates globally. Some regions with high gender gaps, like North Africa and South Asia, have made progress, while others, like Sub-Saharan Africa and the Middle East, have remained stagnant (Zajda and Freeman 2009).

Educational mobility is measured by the share of students who attain a higher level of education than their parents. An OECD (2018) report uses this metric to analyze four ten-year cohorts beginning with those who started school in the 1950s to measure changing educational mobility over time. Declining upward educational mobility is observed in twenty-one of the thirty-three countries sampled, and of those, eleven saw declining educational mobility for each subsequent cohort, including Canada, Denmark, Sweden, and the United States. On the other hand, Italy, Spain, Singapore, and Turkey were the only countries with gains in educational mobility across cohorts, while Greece, Iceland, and Korea have seen overall gains in educational mobility despite slight declines for some cohorts. These measures signal uneven but generally declining progress in education globally.

NATIONAL CONTEXTS FOR URBAN EDUCATIONAL POLICY

Although the nature of educational inequality varies across nations and regions, the overall tendency toward local control of schools makes cities important sites for policy-making. In most countries, local or municipal school boards control the day-to-day functioning of schools. Which level of government primarily funds education varies, as does the degree to which local school boards control the delivery and content of education. Indeed, even countries with a strong national role in education, like the United Kingdom, or a strong provincial role, like Canada, generally rely on cities and local school boards to generate and implement reforms.

Despite the common significance of local politics, Canadian and American approaches to urban education policy diverge dramatically (Gaskell 2010; Eidelman and Taylor 2010). In the 1960s, both countries focused on civil rights and anti-poverty programs as a means toward greater equality in education, and there was strong support for community involvement and teachers' unions. In the United States, the federal government took a stronger role in education, with major anti-poverty legislation, federally mandated racial integration of schools, and the creation of a Cabinet-level Education Department in the federal government. State involvement has generally been limited to oversight and regulating instruction as most responsibilities are transferred down to local school boards, though states sometimes engage in broader reform efforts. Funding local schools falls primarily to state governments and local school boards, with a strong reliance on property taxes. The federal government relies on local districts to implement federal reforms like President Bush's No Child Left Behind, which encouraged high-stakes testing, and President Obama's Race to the Top, which focused on advancing charter schools, merit pay, and further high-stakes accountability measures for schools and teachers. Indeed, in the United States, a bipartisan consensus supports neo-liberal reforms, including charter schools, vouchers, school closures, and the weakening of teachers' unions, despite consistent community opposition (Gaskell 2010; Ferman 2020).

Large urban school boards in the United States have struggled, with school funding reliant on local property taxes leading to highly unequal funding of schools across the country, exacerbating inequality (Kozol 1991). State takeovers of failing urban school districts have also become more common but are generally opposed by community groups and have not led to better or more equal outcomes (Morel 2018). Scholars have also noted the difficulty of achieving sustained reform and the deep political conflicts that urban educational policy brings to the surface, many related to the long history of racism in American cities and their suburbs (Stone et al. 2001).

In Canada, the federal government has consistently maintained a limited role in education. Provinces largely control education governance and funding, resulting in a greater equality of funding across provinces compared to federal systems that rely on local funding for education (Eidelman and Taylor 2010). The administrative power of local school boards has generally been centralized in many provinces, with provinces like Nova Scotia and Quebec greatly reducing the number of school boards and even eliminating them entirely, while Toronto maintains a strong district-level school board (Ungerleider and Levin 2007). Provincial ministries of education are solely responsible for funding schools, except in Manitoba and Nova Scotia, where funds are also raised by local property taxes. Another exception is Toronto, where the school board has raised additional funds for reforms, despite full funding at the provincial level. In the case of Ontario, nearby suburban districts underperform Toronto, an inverse of American trends (Gaskell 2010). Indeed, in addition to more equal funding across schools and regions, urban education reform in Canada has diverged from the American context on many other key dimensions: Canadian teacher unions remain strong; charter schools are virtually non-existent; accountability measures are meant to evaluate reforms and governance rather than individual students and teachers; and there is an overall tendency to help underperforming schools rather than further disrupt them (Gaskell 2010). Despite generally high performance in international comparisons of education systems, inequality is still a major concern in Canadian schools, especially in Toronto, where income inequality outpaces that of any other city, growing at double the national rate (McDonough et al. 2015). There have also been calls for greater federal intervention in urban education, which provinces generally resist, but fiscal constraints make provinces unlikely to reject increased support for urban school districts (Gaskell 2010; Stoney and Graham 2009).

The differences between the American and Canadian contexts demonstrate the variation between local, municipal, regional, and federal roles in education reform. In particular, financing education at the regional or national level leads to more equal funding across cities, as seen in Canada, the United Kingdom, Australia, and Norway. In contrast to the Canadian provincial system and the highly localized US system, the UK system is highly centralized, with funding from the national government and few responsibilities for local authorities outside of day-to-day operations (Fullan and Boyle 2014). Despite the diminished role of local governance, recent national reforms have focused on the municipal level, and London in particular.

In Brazil, there has been widespread decentralization in education governance following the country's transition from military dictatorship to democracy in 1985 (OECD 2015). At the same time, the Brazilian government has maintained a strong federal role in education funding and policy-making. Further, education was a key component of the country's municipally run anti-poverty programs, and states have also been mandated to contribute funds for education. Conversely, while Sweden also had a highly centralized system, it has been extensively decentralized following school choice reforms in the 1990s and is now becoming more unequal in terms of access and achievement. Few other countries mirror the emphasis on local funding and accountability that exists in the United States and Sweden, though Sweden emphasizes school choice as a mechanism of accountability of schools, whereas high-stakes testing is prevalent in the United States.

MARKET-BASED URBAN EDUCATION POLICY

Market-based education policies described here have become increasingly common in Canada and around the world. School choice generally refers to policies that expand families' options for education beyond their local public school. Using market logic, the idea is that if individual "consumers" can choose the best school for their children, rather than being required to attend their local school, school quality will increase overall in a district as schools compete to attract students. Some policies make school choice available to targeted groups of students; others make choice available to all students. Choices sometimes include only nearby public schools, but others also include quasi-private options like charter schools and traditional private schools. Charter schools emerged in the United States in the early 1990s and have spread to most states, as well as some other countries, including Sweden and the United Kingdom. These privately operated institutions rely on public funding but are not restricted by many of the practices and regulations that govern most public schools. While there are some notable exceptions, results in terms of student achievement are mixed. Scandals regarding unfair practices, discrimination, and excessive discipline have become increasingly common in the United States, especially in "no-nonsense" or "no-excuses" approaches. Practitioners, policy-makers, and researchers also criticize charter schools' tendency to pursue profits and point to their undemocratic nature since local school boards do not have authority over their operations (Ferman 2020). They argue that the spread of charter schools weakens the public system by opening it up to private corporate participants (Ferman 2020; Lipman 2015).

While school choice has a longer history in some countries with a tradition of religious boarding and private schools like Canada, Belgium, and the Netherlands, many other countries began exploring school choice strategies in the 1980s. In Chile and Sweden, school choice policies have been implemented using voucher systems, in which the government transfers funds to private schools. Colombia, India, and Argentina have developed more targeted programs aimed at providing vouchers to poor and urban populations to attend private schools. Other countries, like England and New Zealand, have developed voucher programs that are limited to government-funded schools. In the United States, a series of federal, state, and local school choice policies operate concurrently but vary in terms of where vouchers can be used, and which groups have access to them. In Canada, market-based reforms are much less pervasive but equally uneven, with Toronto, Vancouver, Calgary, and Edmonton experiencing the bulk of efforts toward these kinds of policies.

In Toronto and Vancouver, school choice is based on concerns for social justice and ensuring access to religious, ethnic, and other alternative schools. In the 1970s and '80s, Canada's provincial education ministries began absorbing some private religious, francophone, anglophone, and other alternative schools in their education systems, in part to comply with constitutional rights to French schooling outside of Quebec and anglophone schooling within Quebec; Ontario started its French Immersion system in this period as well (Gaskell 2016). In Toronto, as well as in most other Canadian cities, school choice systems are limited to public alternative schools, including Indigenous and Afrocentric schools. Still, scholars have found that students in specialized schools tend to come from more advantaged neighbourhoods while students in disadvantaged neighbourhoods are more likely to attend their neighbourhood schools (Yoon, Marmureanu, and Brown 2020).

While most provinces use a school choice approach similar to that of Toronto and Ontario, with select private schools fully integrated into their public education systems, some have taken a different approach. British Columbia has funded a greater number and wider variety of private schools, though only at rates of up to 50 per cent of public school funding per pupil, depending on compliance with provincial regulations (Yoon and Lubienski 2017). Indeed, in Vancouver, expanded school choice has led to more spatial and socioeconomic polarization because, as with Toronto, low-income and marginalized groups are significantly more likely to stay in their local neighbourhood schools due to high transportation costs, lack of social support, and unfamiliarity with other schools and how to access them (Parekh, Flessa, and Smaller 2016; Yoon and Lubienski 2017).

Alberta has pursued school choice to a greater extent than any other province, even incorporating American-style charter schools, where publicly funded schools can operate independently, bypassing local school board oversight as well as some provincial regulations. Alberta passed charter school legislation in 1994, shortly after Minnesota adopted the first charter school law in the United States. Alberta capped the number of charter schools at fifteen but some operate multiple campuses for different cohorts; most of these are in the province's two largest cities, Edmonton and Calgary. However, these charter schools are much more strictly regulated than those in the United States, and the province has not committed to expanding charter schools, in part due to public sentiment against the commodification associated with them (Bosetti and Butterfield 2016). Alberta's Ministry of Education also developed a rigorous approval process that promotes accountability. The province's experiment with charter schools, therefore, is not a sustained and systemic reform and is not meant to encourage the market competition sought by charter-dominant approaches to school choice seen in much of the United States. Indeed, in Edmonton, tight regulation has had direct impacts on the types of schools granted charters, which populations they serve, and how the province and school board view them (Taylor and Mackay 2008).

Charter schools have been adopted in most US states. American cities have incorporated charter schools into their school systems to varying degrees, reflecting various levels of restrictions on the number of schools and the types of schools approved. In some cities, charters enrol most students in the district, such as New Orleans, where 93 per cent of students attend charter schools, and Detroit, where 53 per cent of students attend charter schools. In others, the enrolment levels are lower, as in New York City, where only 8 per cent of students attend these schools (NAPCS 2015). In many cities with high levels of charter enrolment, achievement has not improved and segregation has increased (Adamson and Galloway 2019). Many states and school boards also have open enrolment policies, in which certain students can transfer to nearby schools. The federal government has played a large role in expanding choice and charter schools. Recent Presidents Clinton, Bush, Obama, and Trump have differing political perspectives but have all pursued market-based education reform by incentivizing states and school boards to advance neo-liberal education policies, with particularly deep impacts on urban school districts, where underperforming schools are concentrated (Lipman 2015).

Sweden combines Canada's more widespread system of school choice with universal vouchers and the expansion of charter schools. The Swedish equivalent of charter schools – independent schools – are run by partnerships with ethnic organizations, religious institutions, business and other private interests, and civil society groups, and they are fully funded from the same streams as local public schools (Bunar 2010). In Stockholm, independent schools grew in the 1990s, overtaking the number of municipal schools in 2005. In 1997, 80 per cent of children in Stockholm still attended their neighbourhood school; by 2014, less than 40 per cent did (Dahlstedt and Fejes 2019). Sweden has arguably become the most market-oriented education system in the world and continues to pursue market reforms and deregulation, but it has recently fallen in international rankings as disadvantaged students are more likely to remain in their local schools, leading to rising inequality in education outcomes (Dahlstedt and Fejes 2019; Bunar 2010).

Brazil generally has not adopted market-oriented education reforms. One exception is Rio de Janeiro, which established an open enrolment system shortly after democratization in the 1980s and provides free transportation for students who choose schools further from their neighbourhoods (Alves et al. 2015). Rio has also experimented with charter schools with its Schools of Tomorrow program. These schools receive additional supports, services, and infrastructural improvements (Elwick 2018). The approach is notably different from the more punitive charter school policies in other countries, namely the United States.

INCLUSIONARY AND EQUITY-BASED URBAN EDUCATION POLICY

In many cities, the market-based or neo-liberal reforms described above are shaping education systems. But some cities have adopted progressive, equity-focused reforms. These progressive policies generally require significant grassroots mobilization at the local level, unique political opportunities or sustained resources, and restructuring from multiple levels of government. We discuss below examples of cities where activists and officials have restructured education systems to reach marginalized communities or to ensure equal funding across schools.

The Path toward Progressive Reform in Toronto and Winnipeg. Following a slew of neo-liberal and neo-conservative reforms in the 1980s and '90s, Canadian provinces were decreasing their role in education, with reductions in funding for schools and their diversity programs (Dei 2006; Thompson and Wallner 2011).

In Ontario, the centre-right Mike Harris government (1995–2003) and its Common Sense Revolution reduced funding, cancelled anti-racism protocols for school boards, and pursued punitive disciplinary measures (Thompson and Wallner 2011). Prior to the Harris administration, Indigenous-centred education had gained steam in Toronto, securing recognition for the city's first Indigenous school in 1983. At the same time, grassroots mobilization for Afrocentric education intensified following a 1987 Toronto District School Board (TDSB) report that revealed alarming trends for Black students in the city. After years of contentious debates about Afrocentric schools and assimilation, the 1992 Yonge Street Uprising took place in response to the killing of a young Black man in Toronto and once again returned the spotlight to the proposal for Afrocentric schools. But Harris's election quashed hopes for the reform (Thompson and Wallner 2011).

Debates re-emerged in 2006, in response to continued inequity as well as advocacy from George Dei, an anti-racist education researcher at the University of Toronto (Joshee 2009; Thompson and Wallner 2011). While the political context of this period presented similar obstacles to the early 1990s, the 2007 school shooting of a fifteen-year-old Black student proved instrumental in building the political pressure that finally led to the opening of Toronto's first Afrocentric school in 2009.

In Winnipeg, now home to the country's largest Indigenous population, the fight for ethnic schools played out differently. Manitoba is the only province where schools raise substantial funding at the local level, making grassroots mobilization more effective than in Toronto. Despite a conservative provincial government through the 1990s, community groups, including local Indigenous activists as well as a national movement for Indigenous education, were able to pressure Winnipeg's school board to fund two new Indigenous schools and develop an Indigenous policy for the district's other schools (Gaskell and Levin 2011). Hard-fought victories for ethnic schools in Toronto and Winnipeg have become models for Canada and are no longer contentious within the local school districts.

Toronto's 2009 victory for Afrocentric education occurred alongside provincial reforms, referred to collectively as the Ontario Strategy, initiated by the centre-left McGuinty government in 2003. TDSB played a crucial role in provincial educational reform as the largest and most independent school board in Ontario, covering all of Toronto's English language public-secular schools. Provincial-local collaboration was key to the implementation of various reforms focused on capacity building, leadership development, literacy, and other areas. This collaboration did not come easy, however, because of prior distrust between Ontario and Toronto stemming from the contentious Common Sense Revolution reforms that reduced the power of local school boards. TDSB also pursued its own reforms: an expanded version of the province's leadership development program for teachers and administrators and a slew of reforms focused on equity and inclusion such as Focus on Youth Toronto, which encouraged non-profit partnerships with schools to hire youth workers for after-school activities, and the Model Schools for Inner Cities program, which provided vital resources and supports to schools with the highest concentration of poverty to focus on closing opportunity and achievement gaps (Fullan and Boyle 2014). TDSB also remained on the forefront of alternative and ethnic schools, with new programs to support Indigenous education like the Urban Indigenous Education Centre.

Other cities and countries have had different experiences with similar reforms. In London, the United Kingdom's centralized system leaves little room for effective grassroots mobilization for alternative schools (Johnson 2013). In Sydney, local opposition to Islamic schools is extensive. In Brazil, a long struggle for recognition of far-reaching disparities for Black and Indigenous people led to national curricular policies for Afro-Brazilian education in 2003 and Indigenous education in 2008, although these have lacked institutional and financial support, leaving teachers to discover and implement curriculum changes on their own (Gonçalves e Silva and Araújo-Olivera 2009; Scott et al. 2019).

Progressive Reforms in Cities around the World. Progressive policies heavily rely on grassroots mobilization and are generally limited to individual schools or curricular changes, but in some cases cities have transcended these limits. Some Swiss cities have seen sustained progressive reforms. In Basel, civil society actors and educators connected a variety of school-based and other programs meant to facilitate the integration of migrant students and families (Koch 2013). Although these were not legislated reforms, they have become embedded in a cross-sectoral network of organizations and actors that relies on some public funds but generally operates outside of the formal political process. In Zurich on the other hand, school-based reforms for the inclusion of migrants were eventually scaled up to the canton (state), which is much larger than that of Basel and includes over a hundred smaller cities and towns. But contentious relations between Zurich and its canton led to coalitions with a much different frame than the social integration reforms in Basel. Zurich's school-based reforms shifted drastically away from a focus on social cohesion and toward an approach focused on performance and testing, as the right-wing politics of the canton controlled resources and the policy-making process (Koch 2013).

Two other cases show sustained progressive reforms in the United States and Brazil. In the late 1980s, Chicago and Porto Alegre both implemented significant reforms toward the democratization of education governance. In Chicago, local school councils (LSCs) were established, where elected community members had the authority to fire and hire principals, allocate discretionary spending, and develop school improvement plans. However, less than a decade later, the state of Illinois recentralized Chicago's school system by granting control to the mayor, Richard Daley, who would then pursue far-reaching neo-liberal reforms. In Porto Alegre, on the other hand, the democratization of the school system under the Citizen School Project was even more extensive, but it was also part of a sustained nationwide wave of decentralization under the ruling Workers' Party, ensuring that the city's reforms were unobstructed and ultimately successful (Fischman and Gandin 2016; Edwards 2010). These two cases further emphasize the impact of broader political environments. Specifically, the fate of Chicago's LSCs makes clear the political challenges of enacting progressive reforms in neo-liberal or conservative political environments.

CONCLUSION: THE IMPACTS OF THE COVID-19 PANDEMIC ON URBAN HOUSING AND EDUCATION POLICY

In this chapter, we have described variations in the problems of poverty and social polarization in cities globally, and examined how local governments, often in conjunction with national and provincial governments, have addressed these problems in recent years. We show that neo-liberal, market-based policies are frequently employed, but that there are some places where local advocates and government officials have instituted progressive alternatives. We close with some discussion of how the COVID-19 pandemic has revealed anew the cracks in cities' social safety nets, especially in the arenas of housing and education. We note how some governments and local organizations have worked to address these new challenges, with particular focus on Canada's emerging national childcare strategy.

Helping families to keep their homes has become an important part of housing policy. Governments have intervened in the foreclosure and eviction processes to stop or slow financial institutions and landlords from dispossessing tenants and homeowners. Programs and resources include expanding access to housing attorneys, imposing moratoriums on evictions, and requiring or subsidizing financial institutions to renegotiate mortgage loans that are in default.

Eviction bans and their enforcement varied greatly by city, region, and country. In the United States, for example, eviction courts in Arizona, Florida, Georgia, Tennessee, Texas, and Missouri were regularly reported to allow lenient use of regulatory loopholes or altogether ignore eviction bans (Morgenson 2020; Rice 2020). On the other hand, in New York, eviction moratoriums were strengthened and extended beyond federal guidelines. New York State developed its own rent relief fund for residents who were not able to pay rent due to the pandemic. Cities also developed additional measures to address homelessness. For example, city officials in San Francisco, Los Angeles, New York City, and Newark began to use hotels and other buildings left empty due to the pandemic to house homeless people.

In Canada, temporary eviction bans and rent freezes were implemented at the provincial level. In many cases, these measures were tied to lockdown measures and local states of emergency, which were often short-term and periodic. This has been the case in both Ontario and British Columbia. In addition to these, other tenant protections were put into place in various provinces. For instance, the governments of Yukon and British Columbia offered rental supplements of up to 50 per cent of rent for tenants impacted by the pandemic (Béland et al. 2020; Yukon 2020). At the federal level, Canada also approved the use of federal funds to insure the mortgages of Canadian homeowners affected by the pandemic. Still, the pandemic has illustrated gaps in policy regarding homelessness as Canadian cities have struggled in their response to growing homeless encampments across the country. An absence of intergovernmental coordination on this issue led to widespread and highly publicized punitive responses including "ticketing, arrests, forced eviction, and the destruction of tents and personal property," which violate the National Housing Strategy Act (Flynn et al. 2022, 4).

Global responses varied widely (Open Society Foundations 2020). Germany instituted a rent payment deferral for two years, a lease flexibility scheme, and a national law banning evictions during the pandemic. Brazil, on the other hand, did not implement any measures, federal or local, to alleviate the burden of rent on tenants (Peet 2021). Evictions have increased throughout the country leading civil society to demand the implementation of a moratorium. This has resulted in a surge in the construction of informal urban settlements and an increase in homelessness.

The exact impacts of COVID-19 on education are still unclear, but decades of research suggest that time away from the classroom during lockdowns will have significant impacts, especially on poor and marginalized youth. Notably, many countries and localities have cancelled or delayed standardized tests that track educational outcomes, increasing the difficulty of assessing the issue. The pandemic also revealed deep inequalities as many schools lack the infrastructure and resources needed to maintain proper ventilation and social distancing, as well as to develop their use of remote instruction.

In the United States, local school boards have faced tensions regarding the reopening of schools and mandates for masking and vaccination. In Canada too, schools have been subject to intermittent periods of reopening and closure. A major inequality highlighted by the pandemic has been the "digital divide," in which many students lacked access to technology and were forced to attend virtual classrooms from their phones or in public places with internet. Some cities and states, such as New Jersey, saw significant yet contested pushes to close this divide by directly supplying students with laptops and internet access. In Canada, the majority of schools offered online learning while some opted for homeschool curricula. Further, Ontario offered asynchronous lessons sent to students via email or through e-learning platforms like TVO, the province's public educational television and media network (Aurini and Davies 2021). In the Brazilian states of Amazonas and Paras, school curriculum was consistently broadcast on television and YouTube due to a history of reliance on educational media in the Amazon region (World Bank 2020). Similar broadcasts were made available to countries ranging from Austria to Argentina and Mexico, and they were especially vital in countries with varied access to the internet and technology.

In its 2021 federal budget, the Canadian government enacted a national childcare strategy in partnership with its provinces; while these partnerships faced political challenges, agreements have been reached with all thirteen provinces and territories (ESDC 2024). Although the program is universal and does not specifically target those in poverty, a similar long-running childcare benefit in Quebec suggests that universal childcare reduces poverty and promotes gender equality in the labour market (Béland et al. 2022). Programs such as these illustrate a multi-dimensional approach to addressing poverty that works hand in hand with social policy in the arenas of housing and education.

In coming years, we expect to see pandemic-related inequalities and impacts shaping the policy responses of local governments in the arenas of housing and education.

ACKNOWLEDGEMENTS

We thank Tamara Velasquez Leiferman for research assistance in preparing this chapter.

REFERENCES

Adamson, Frank, and Meredith Galloway. 2019. "Education Privatization in the United States: Increasing Saturation and Segregation." *Education Policy Analysis Archives* 27, no. 129 (October): 1–48. https://doi.org/10.14507/epaa.27.4857.

Alves, Fatima, Gregory Elacqua, Mariane Koslinki, Matias Martinez, Humberto Santos, and Daniela Urbina. 2015. "Winners and Losers of School Choice: Evidence from Rio de Janeiro, Brazil and Santiago, Chile." *International Journal of Educational Development* 41 (March): 25–34. https://doi.org/10.1016/j.ijedudev.2014.12.004.

Angotti, Tom, and Sylvia Morse, eds. 2023. *Zoned Out! Race, Displacement, and City Planning*. New York City: New Village Press.

August, Martine. 2008. "Social Mix and Canadian Public Housing Redevelopment: Experiences in Toronto." *Canadian Journal of Urban Research* 17, no. S1: 82–100.

———. 2016. "Revitalisation Gone Wrong: Mixed-Income Public Housing Redevelopment in Toronto's Don Mount Court." *Urban Studies* 53, no. 16 (December): 3405–22. https://doi.org/10.1177/0042098015613207.

Aurini, Janice, and Scott Davies. 2021. "COVID-19 School Closures and Educational Achievement Gaps in Canada: Lessons from Ontario Summer Learning Research." *Canadian Sociological Association* 58, no. 2 (May): 165–85. https://doi.org/10.1111/cars.12334.

Barrientos, Armando. 2013. "The Rise of Social Assistance in Brazil." *Development and Change* 44, no. 4 (July): 887–910. https://doi.org/10.1111/dech.12043.

Béland, Daniel, Shannon Dinan, Philip Rocco, and Alex Waddan. 2020. "Social Policy Responses to COVID-19 in Canada and the United States: Explaining Policy Variations between Two Liberal Welfare State Regimes." *Social Policy & Administration* 55, no. 2 (March): 280–94. https://doi .org/10.1111/spol.12656.

———. 2022. "COVID-19, Poverty Reduction, and Partisanship in Canada and the United States." *Policy and Society* 41, no. 2 (June): 291–305. https://doi.org/10.1093/polsoc/puac002.

Bosetti, Lynn, and Philip Butterfield. 2016. "The Politics of Educational Reform: The Alberta Charter School Experiment 20 Years Later." *Global Education Review* 3, no. 2 (April): 103–19. https://ger .mercy.edu/index.php/ger/article/view/199/199.

Boulant, Justine, Monica Brezzi, and Paolo Veneri. 2016. "Income Levels and Inequality in Metropolitan Areas: A Comparative Approach in OECD Countries." *OECD Regional Development Working Papers*, no. 2016/06, OECD Publishing, Paris. https://doi.org/10.1787/5jlwj02zz4mr-en.

Bunar, Nihad. 2010. "Choosing for Quality or Inequality: Current Perspectives on the Implementation of School Choice Policy in Sweden." *Journal of Education Policy* 25, no. 1 (January): 1–18. https:// doi.org/10.1080/02680930903377415.

Bunce, Susannah, and Farrah Chanda Aslam. 2016. "Land Trusts and the Protection and Stewardship of Land in Canada: Exploring Non-governmental Land Trust Practices and the Role of Urban Community Land Trusts." *Canadian Journal of Urban Research* 25, no. 2 (Winter): 23–34.

CEIC. 2017. "Brazil Gini Coefficient." Brazilian Institute of Geography and Statistics. https://www .ceicdata.com/en/brazil/gini-coefficient-household-income-by-region/gini-coefficient -household-income-per-capita-southeast-rio-de-janeiro.

Chaskin, Robert J., and Mark L. Joseph. 2013. "'Positive' Gentrification, Social Control and the 'Right to the City' in Mixed-Income Communities: Uses and Expectations of Space and Place." *International Journal of Urban and Regional Research* 37, no. 2 (March): 480–502. https://doi .org/10.1111/j.1468-2427.2012.01158.x.

Chaskin, Robert, Amy Khare, and Mark Joseph. 2012. "Participation, Deliberation, and Decision Making: The Dynamics of Inclusion and Exclusion in Mixed-Income Developments." *Urban Affairs Review* 48, no. 6 (November): 863–906. https://doi.org/10.1177/1078087412450151.

Chetty, Raj, Nathaniel Hendren, Patrick Kline, and Emmanuel Saez. 2014. "Where Is the Land of Opportunity? The Geography of Intergenerational Mobility in the United States." *The Quarterly Journal of Economics* 129, no. 4 (November): 1553–623. https://doi.org/10.1093/qje/qju022.

Citizens' Committee for Children of New York (CCC NY). 2019. "Keeping Track Online Database: Child Poverty, 2019." Economic Conditions. https://data.cccnewyork.org/data/map/96/child -poverty#96/a/3/146/62/a/a.

Clotfelter, Charles T. 2011. *After Brown: The Rise and Retreat of School Desegregation*. Princeton, NJ: Princeton University Press.

Dahlstedt, Magnus, and Andreas Fejes, eds. 2019. *Neoliberalism and Market Forces in Education: Lessons from Sweden*. London: Routledge. https://doi.org/10.4324/9780429470530.

DeFilippis, James, Brian Stromberg, and Olivia R. Williams. 2018. "W(h)ither the *Community* in Community Land Trusts?" *Journal of Urban Affairs* 40, no. 6 (August): 755–69. https://doi.org /10.1080/07352166.2017.1361302.

Dei, George J. Sefa. 2006. "Black-Focused Schools: A Call for Re-visioning." *Education Canada* 46, no. 3 (Summer): 27–31. https://eric.ed.gov/?id=EJ740504.

Edwards, D. Brent, Jr. 2010 "A Comparison of Local Empowerment in Education: Porto Alegre, Brazil and Chicago, USA." *Research in Comparative and International Education* 5, no. 2 (June): 176–84. https://doi.org/10.2304/rcie.2010.5.2.176.

Eidelman, Gabriel, and Zack Taylor. 2010. "Canadian Urban Politics: Another 'Black Hole'?" *Journal of Urban Affairs* 32, no. 3 (August): 305–20. https://doi.org/10.1111/j.1467-9906.2010.00507.x.

Elwick, Alex. 2018. "New Forms of Government School Provision – an International Comparison." *Journal of Education Policy* 33, no. 2 (March): 206–25. https://doi.org/10.1080/02680939.2017.1329551.

Employment and Social Development Canada (ESDC). 2024. "Towards \$10-a-Day: Early Learning and Child Care." ESDC Campaigns and Promotions. Last modified May 17, 2024. https://www.canada.ca/en/employment-social-development/campaigns/child-care.html.

Federal Statistics Office (FSO) Switzerland. n.d. "Social Assistance Rate in Selected Swiss Cities and Agglomerations, 2020." Accessed May 26, 2022. https://www.bfs.admin.ch/asset/en/30166541.

Federal Tax Administration (FTA) Switzerland. 2015. "Kartographische Darstellung der Einkommensverteilung 2015." http://www.estv2.admin.ch/d/dokumentation/zahlen_fakten/karten/dbst/2015/grafiken_2015.php.

Ferman, Barbara. 2020. "Preserving Education as a Public Good: Lessons from the Grassroots." *Urban Affairs Review* 56, no. 3 (May): 921–9. https://doi.org/10.1177/1078087419867160.

Fischman, Gustavo E., and Luis Armando Gandin. 2016. "The Pedagogical and Ethical Legacy of a 'Successful' Educational Reform: The *Citizen School Project*." *International Review of Education* 62, no. 1 (February): 63–89. https://doi.org/10.1007/s11159-016-9542-0.

Flynn, Alexandra, Joe Hermer, Caroline Leblanc, Sue-Ann MacDonald, Kaitlin Schwan, and Estair Van Wagner. 2022. *Overview of Encampments across Canada: A Right to Housing Approach*. Ottawa: Office of the Federal Housing Advocate, Canadian Human Rights Commission. https://publications.gc.ca/site/eng/9.919503/publication.html.

Friendly, Abigail, and Kristine Stiphany. 2019. "Paradigm or Paradox? The 'Cumbersome Impasse' of the Participatory Turn in Brazilian Urban Planning." *Urban Studies* 56, no. 2 (February): 271–87. https://doi.org/10.1177/0042098018768748.

Fullan, Michael, and Alan Boyle. 2014. *Big-City School Reforms: Lessons from New York, Toronto, and London*. New York: Teachers College Press.

Gaskell, Jane. 2010. "Urban Education Policy in Canada and the United States." *LEARNing Landscapes* 3, no. 2 (July): 29–35. https://doi.org/10.36510/learnland.v3i2.333.

———. 2016. "The Expansion of School Choice in Toronto." *Education Canada* 56, no. 2 (Summer): 16–18. https://www.edcan.ca/articles/the-expansion-of-school-choice-in-toronto/.

Gaskell, Jane, and Ben Levin. 2011. "The Challenges of Poverty and Urban Education in Canada: Lessons from 2 School Boards." In *Education and Poverty in Affluent Countries*, edited by Carlo Raffo, Alan Dyson, Helen Gunter, Dave Hall, Lisa Jones, and Afroditi Kalambouka, 148–60. New York: Routledge.

Goetz, Edward G. 2011a. "Where Have All the Towers Gone? The Dismantling of Public Housing in US Cities." *Journal of Urban Affairs* 33, no. 3 (August): 267–87. https://doi.org/10.1111/j.1467-9906.2011.00550.x.

———. 2011b. "Gentrification in Black and White: The Racial Impact of Public Housing Demolition in American Cities." *Urban Studies* 48, no. 8 (June): 1581–604. https://doi.org/10.1177/0042098010375323.

Gonçalves e Silva, Petronilha Beatriz, and Sonia Stella Araújo-Olivera. 2009. "Achieving Quality Education for Indigenous Peoples and Blacks in Brazil." In *The Routledge International Companion to Multicultural Education*, edited by James A. Banks, 526–39. New York: Routledge.

Gurstein, Penelope, Kristin Patten, and Prajna Rao. 2015. *The Future of Public Housing: Trends in Public Housing Internationally*. Vancouver: School of Community and Regional Planning, University of British Columbia. https://scarp-futureofpublichousing.sites.olt.ubc.ca/files/2016/07/The-Future -of-Public-Housing-Report-05-11-15.pdf.

Houle, Marie-Josée. 2022. *Housing Is a Human Right: The Office of the Federal Housing Advocate's 2021–2022 Annual Report to the Minister*. Ottawa: Canadian Human Rights Commission. https:// www.housingchrc.ca/en/housing-is-a-human-right-the-office-of-the-federal-housing-advocates -2021-2022-annual-report-to-the-minister.

Hulchanski, J. David. 2007. *The Three Cities within Toronto: Income Polarization among Toronto's Neighbourhoods, 1970–2005*. Research Bulletin 41. Toronto: Cities Centre, University of Toronto.

Johnson, Lauri. 2013. "Segregation or 'Thinking Black'? Community Activism and the Development of Black-Focused Schools in Toronto and London, 1968–2008." *Teachers College Record* 115, no. 11 (November): 1–25. https://doi.org/10.1177/016146811311501106.

Joshee, Reva. 2009. "Multicultural Education Policy in Canada: Competing Ideologies, Interconnected Discourses." In *The Routledge International Companion to Multicultural Education*, edited by James A. Banks, 116–28. New York: Routledge.

Klink, Jeroen, and Rosana Denaldi. 2014. "On Financialization and State Spatial Fixes in Brazil. A Geographical and Historical Interpretation of the Housing Program My House My Life." *Habitat International* 44 (October): 220–6. https://doi.org/10.1016/j.habitatint.2014.06.001.

Koch, Philippe. 2013. "Progressive and Sustained School Reforms: Framing and Coalition Building in Swiss Cities." *Journal of Urban Affairs* 35, no. 1 (February): 43–57. https://doi.org/10.1111 /juaf.12000.

Kozol, Jonathan. 1991. *Savage Inequalities: Children in America's Schools*. New York: Crown Publishers.

Ladner, Andreas, Nicolas Keuffer, and Harald Baldersheim. 2016. "Measuring Local Autonomy in 39 Countries (1990–2014)." *Regional and Federal Studies* 26, no. 3 (May): 321–57. https://doi.org/10.1080 /13597566.2016.1214911.

Lipman, Pauline. 2015. "Urban Education Policy under Obama." *Journal of Urban Affairs* 37, no. 1 (February): 57–61. https://doi.org/10.1111/juaf.12163.

Logan, John Richard, and Harvey Luskin Molotch. 1987. *Urban Fortunes: The Political Economy of Place*. Berkeley: University of California Press.

Mah, Julie, and Jason Hackworth. 2011. "Local Politics and Inclusionary Housing in Three Large Canadian Cities." *Canadian Journal of Urban Research* 20, no. 1 (Summer): 57–80. https://www.jstor .org/stable/26193840.

Marquardt, Susanne, and Daniel Glaser. 2023. "How Much State and How Much Market? Comparing Social Housing in Berlin and Vienna." *German Politics* 32, no. 2 (April): 361–80. https://doi.org/10 .1080/09644008.2020.1771696.

McDonough, Laura, Mihaela Dinca-Panaitescu, Stephanie Procyk, Charlene Cook, Julia Drydyk, Michelynn Laflèche, and James McKee. 2015. *The Opportunity Equation: Building Opportunity in the Face of Growing Income Inequality*. Toronto: United Way Toronto.

Moore, Aaron A., and Jordana Wright. 2017. "Toronto's Market-Oriented Subsidised Housing PPPs: A Risk Worth the Reward." *Cities* 69 (September): 64–72. https://doi.org/10.1016/j .cities.2017.05.010.

Morel, Domingo. 2018. *Takeover: Race, Education, and American Democracy*. New York: Oxford University Press. https://doi.org/10.1093/oso/9780190678975.001.0001.

Morgenson, Gretchen. 2020. "Large Corporate Landlords Have Filed 10,000 Eviction Actions in Five States since September." *MSNBC*, October 20, 2020. https://www.nbcnews.com/business/personal-finance/large-corporate-landlords-have-filed-10-000-eviction-actions-five-n1244711.

National Alliance for Public Charter Schools (NAPCS). 2015. *A Growing Movement: America's Largest Charter School Communities*. 10th ed. Washington, DC: NAPCS. https://publiccharters.org/news/a-growing-movement-americas-largest-charter-school-communities-tenth-edition/.

New York City Independent Budget Office (NYC IBO). 2020. "New York City Residents' Income and Tax Liability." https://ibo.nyc.ny.us/iboreports/highlights-from-ibos-updated-tables-on-new-york-city-residents-income-and-income-tax-liability-in-2020-nycbtn-2022.pdf.

OECD (Organisation for Economic Co-operation and Development). 2012. *Equity and Quality in Education: Supporting Disadvantaged Students and Schools*. Paris: Organisation for Economic Co-operation and Development.

———. 2015. *Education Outlook: Brazil*. Paris: Organisation for Economic Co-operation and Development. https://web-archive.oecd.org/2021-01-22/379199-Brazil-country-profile.pdf.

———. 2018. *Equity in Education: Breaking Down Barriers to Social Mobility*. Paris: Organisation for Economic Co-operation and Development. https://www.oecd.org/education/equity-in-education-9789264073234-en.htm.

———. n.d. "Income Distribution Database." Accessed April 19, 2021. https://www.oecd.org/social/income-distribution-database.htm.

———. 2020. "Metropolitan Areas: Income Distribution." Last updated April 19, 2021. https://stats.oecd.org/Index.aspx?DataSetCode=CITIES.

Open Society Foundations. 2020. "Protecting the Right to Housing during the COVID-19 Crisis." Justice Initiative Briefing Paper. https://www.justiceinitiative.org/publications/protecting-the-right-to-housing-during-the-covid-19-crisis.

Parekh, Gillian, Joseph Flessa, and Harry Smaller. 2016. "The Toronto District School Board: A Global City School System's Structures, Processes, and Student Outcomes." *London Review of Education* 14, no. 3 (November): 65–84. https://doi.org/10.18546/LRE.14.3.06.

Peet, Charlotte. 2021. "Nowhere to Go: Brazil's COVID 'Refugees' Struggle after Eviction." *Al Jazeera*, July 8, 2021. https://www.aljazeera.com/economy/2021/7/8/nowhere-to-go-brazils-covid-refugees-struggle-after-eviction.

Ren, Xuefei. 2018. "Governing the Informal: Housing Policies over Informal Settlements in China, India, and Brazil." *Housing Policy Debate* 28, no. 1 (January): 79–93. https://doi.org/10.1080/10511482.2016.1247105.

Rice, Glenn. 2020. "Federal Judge Denies KC Tenants Lawsuit Urging Evictions Stop during COVID-19 Pandemic." *The Kansas City Star*, November 25, 2020. https://www.kansascity.com/news/local/article247414780.html.

Rosa, Vanessa. 2018. "Social Citizenship and Urban Revitalization in Canada." *Canadian Journal of Urban Research* 27, no. 2 (Summer): 25–36.

Sadovnik, Alan R., Peter W. Cookson, Jr., Susan F. Semel, and Ryan W. Coughlan. 2017. *Exploring Education: An Introduction to the Foundations of Education*. 5th ed. New York: Routledge. https://doi.org/10.4324/9781315408545.

Santoro, Paula Freire. 2019. "Inclusionary Housing Policies in Latin America: São Paulo, Brazil in Dialogue with Bogotá, Colombia." *International Journal of Housing Policy* 19, no. 3 (July): 385–410. https://doi.org/10.1080/19491247.2019.1613870.

Savitch, Harold V., and Paul Kantor. 2002. *Cities in the International Marketplace: The Political Economy of Urban Development in North America and Western Europe.* Princeton, NJ: Princeton University Press. https://doi.org/10.1515/9780691186504.

Scott, David M., Colleen Kawalilak, Roswita Dressler, and Wilson Alves de Paiva. 2019. "Investigating Educational Responses to Diversity in Brazil during a Time of Curriculum Change." *Comparative Education Review* 63, no. 3 (August): 377–97. https://doi.org/10.1086/703982.

Sellers, Jefferey M., and Anders Lidström. 2007. "Decentralization, Local Government, and the Welfare State." *Governance* 20, no. 4 (October) 609–32. https://doi.org/10.1111/j.1468-0491.2007.00374.x.

Statistics Canada. 2017. "Core Housing Need, 2016 Census." Released November 15, 2017. https://www12.statcan.gc.ca/census-recensement/2016/dp-pd/chn-biml/index-eng.cfm.

———. 2019a. "Table 11-10-0055-01: High Income Tax Filers in Canada." https://doi.org/10.25318/1110005501-eng.

———. 2019b. "Table 11-10-0193-01: Upper Income Limit, Income Share and Average of Adjusted Market, Total and After-Tax Income by Income Decile." https://doi.org/10.25318/1110019301-eng.

———. 2022. "Table 11-10-0135-01: Low Income Statistics by Age, Sex and Economic Family Type." https://doi.org/10.25318/1110013501-eng.

Statistics Sweden. 2024. Persistent At-Risk-of-Poverty Rate by Municipality. Year 2020 figures. https://www.scb.se/en/finding-statistics/statistics-by-subject-area/household-finances/income -and-income-distribution/income-and-tax-statistics/pong/tables-and-graphs/income---equivalised -disposable-income-and-income-standard-counties-and-municipalities/persistent-at-risk-of -poverty-rate-by-county-and-municipality-2014-2022/.

Stein, Samuel. 2018. "Progress for Whom, toward What? Progressive Politics and New York City's Mandatory Inclusionary Housing." *Journal of Urban Affairs* 40, no. 6 (August): 770–81. https://doi.org/10.1080/07352166.2017.1403854.

Stiphany, Kristine M., and Peter M. Ward. 2019. "*Autogestão* in an Era of Mass Social Housing: The Case of Brazil's *Minha Casa Minha Vida-Entidades* Programme." *International Journal of Housing Policy* 19, no. 3 (July): 311–36. https://doi.org/10.1080/19491247.2018.1540739.

Stone, Clarence N., Jeffrey R. Henig, Bryan D. Jones, and Carol Pierannunzi. 2001. *Building Civic Capacity: The Politics of Reforming Urban Schools. Studies in Government and Public Policy.* Lawrence, KS: University Press of Kansas.

Stoney, Christopher, and Katherine A.H. Graham. 2009. "Federal-Municipal Relations in Canada: The Changing Organizational Landscape." *Canadian Public Administration* 52, no. 3 (September): 371–94. https://doi.org/10.1111/j.1754-7121.2009.00088.x.

Stren, Richard. 2012. "Cities and Politics in the Developing World: Why Decentralization Matters." In *The Oxford Handbook of Urban Politics,* edited by Peter John, Karen Mossberger, Susan E. Clarke, 567–89. New York: Oxford University Press. https://doi.org/10.1093/oxfordhb /9780195367867.013.0028.

Taylor, Alison, and Jesse Mackay. 2008. "Three Decades of Choice in Edmonton Schools." *Journal of Education Policy* 23, no. 5 (September): 549–66. https://doi.org/10.1080/02680930802192774.

Taylor, Zack, and Neil Bradford. 2020. "Governing Canadian Cities." In *Canadian Cities in Transition,* edited by Markus Moos, Tara Vinodrai, and Ryan Walker, 33–50. Oxford University Press.

Thompson, Debra, and Jennifer Wallner. 2011. "A Focusing Tragedy: Public Policy and the Establishment of Afrocentric Education in Toronto." *Canadian Journal of Political Science/Revue canadienne de science politique* 44, no. 4 (December): 807–28. https://doi.org/10.1017/S000842391100076X.

Travers, Tony, Sam Sims, and Nicolas Bosetti. 2016. *Housing and Inequality in London.* London: Centre for London.

Tyson, Karolyn. 2011. *Integration Interrupted: Tracking, Black Students, and Acting White after Brown.* New York: Oxford University Press. https://doi.org/10.1093/acprof:oso/9780199736447.001.0001.

UK Department for Work and Pensions (DWP). 2024. "Households below Average Income (HBAI) Statistics." Published June 14, 2013; last updated March 21, 2024. https://www.gov.uk/government/collections/households-below-average-income-hbai--2.

Ungerleider, Charles, and Ben Levin. 2007. "Accountability, Funding and School Improvement in Canada." In *International Handbook of School Effectiveness and Improvement*, edited by Tony Townsend, 411–24. Dordrecht, NL: Springer. https://doi.org/10.1007/978-1-4020-5747-2_23.

UN-Habitat. 2014. *Construction of More Equitable Cities: Public Policy for Inclusion in Latin America.* Nairobi, Kenya: UN Human Settlements Program. https://unhabitat.org/sites/default/files/download-manager-files/Constructionmoreequitablecitiessmall.pdf.

———. 2016. *Urbanization and Development: Emerging Futures World Cities Report 2016.* Nairobi, Kenya: UN Human Settlements Program (UN-Habitat).

US Census Bureau. 2022. "Current Population Survey Quick Facts." https://www.census.gov/quickfacts/.

Van Lindert, Paul. 2016. "Rethinking Urban Development in Latin America: A Review of Changing Paradigms and Policies." *Habitat International* 54, pt. 3 (May): 253–64. https://doi.org/10.1016/j.habitatint.2015.11.017.

Vidyattama, Yogi, Robert Tanton, and NSW Council of Social Service (NCOSS). 2019. *Mapping Economic Disadvantage in New South Wales.* Canberra, ACT: Institute for Governance and Policy Analysis, University of Canberra. https://www.ncoss.org.au/wp-content/uploads/2019/10/Web-Version-Mapping-Economic-Disadvantage-in-New-South-Wales-report1.pdf.

Weaver, Timothy P.R. 2022. "Charting Change in the City: Urban Political Orders and Urban Political Development." *Urban Affairs Review* 58, no. 2 (March): 319–55. https://doi.org/10.1177/1078087420988608.

Wilson, Beth, Raglan Maddox, Michael Polanyi, michael kerr, Manolli Ekra, and Anita Khanna. 2018. *2018 Toronto Child & Family Poverty Report: Municipal Election Edition.* Toronto: Social Planning Toronto.

World Bank. 2020. "How Countries Are Using Edtech (Including Online Learning, Radio, Television, Texting) to Support Access to Remote Learning during the COVID-19 Pandemic." News release, April 2, 2020. https://reliefweb.int/report/austria/how-countries-are-using-edtech-including-online-learning-radio-television-texting.

World Bank Group. 2020. *Poverty and Shared Prosperity 2020: Reversals of Fortune.* Washington, DC: The World Bank. https://doi.org/10.1596/978-1-4648-1602-4.

Yoon, Ee-Seul, and Christopher Lubienski. 2017. "How Do Marginalized Families Engage in School Choice in Inequitable Urban Landscapes? A Critical Geographic Approach." *Education Policy Analysis Archives* 25, no. 42 (April): 1–22. https://doi.org/10.14507/epaa.25.2655.

Yoon, Ee-Seul, Cosmin Marmureanu, and Robert S. Brown. 2020. "School Choice and the Polarization of Public Schools in a Global City: A Bourdieusian GIS Approach." *Peabody Journal of Education* 95, no. 3 (May): 229–47. https://doi.org/10.1080/0161956X.2020.1776071.

Yukon. 2020. "New Support Will Help Tenants Pay Rent during COVID-19." Yukon Housing Corporation, news release no. 20-129, November 5, 2020. https://yukon.ca/en/news/new-support-will-help-tenants-pay-rent-during-covid-19.

Zajda, Joseph, and Kassie Freeman, eds. 2009. *Race, Ethnicity and Gender in Education: Cross-Cultural Understandings.* Heidelberg, Germany: Springer. https://doi.org/10.1007/978-1-4020-9739-3.

Conclusion: Exploring the Tensions

The Possibilities and Limitations of Local Politics and Comparative Urban Research

Jen Nelles and Kristin R. Good

THE EVOLUTION OF CANADIAN URBANISM

The chapters compiled in this volume speak to the range of challenges that face urban areas in Canada and around the world. While many of these are not new, recent decades have seen an intensification of urban issues and the addition of new, complex, and pervasive problems that are both straining the capacity of local governments to respond while also challenging them to find innovative solutions. The ongoing impact of climate change, which has the potential to affect our access to and quality of resources, overwhelm our infrastructure, and require significant adaptation efforts to contain, is just one of the most poignant of these challenges. Public health is once again on the local radar at an unprecedented scale as the globe continues to adjust to life in a pandemic (COVID-19). However, urban areas around the world are also grappling with other health issues as a wave of opioid crises is also cresting in many cities. The impact of an aging population, predominantly based in urban areas, is also a looming question. New social movements are arising in urban areas as well, speaking with increasing outrage against the injustices bred there. Both Black Lives Matter and the Freedom Convoy exercised their rights to protest in major cities, illustrating the diversity of viewpoints that (ideally) compete for political space in local politics and (less ideally) clash in the streets. As the places we live in become more diverse and often less affordable, local governments are being called on to navigate through increasingly complex waters.

In such circumstances, there are major questions about the appropriate role for municipal governments and the opportunities and limits that they face in grappling with emerging issues. These turbulent times also provoke us, as students of Canadian urbanism, to contribute to shaping the evolution of our urban politics and places. While there are many questions to ask, it is striking that some of the most fundamental are still a matter of debate. Namely:

What should cities do?
What resources should they have to tackle the issues they face?
What relationships should exist to support urban challenges?
How should they deliver on their responsibilities?
For whom should they be governing?

The fact that these are not settled questions should not be cause for alarm but rather an indication that Canadian urban politics is alive and well. That the answers to these questions have shifted over time is a sign of evolution, flexibility, and openness. That is not to say that our path has been "right" or uncontested. Far from it. It speaks to how the status and suitability of our most local forms of governance are subject to critical analysis, debate, and even conflict, providing opportunities for both consolidation and change.

In this volume, we reflect on these questions by assessing the Canadian urban system, and the major issues that play out within it, in a comparative perspective. We do this by looking at the lessons of the past, by exploring different approaches across provinces, and by looking to cities around the world to develop theories about the evolution of Canadian urbanism and to appreciate the tradeoffs inherent in pursuing different paths. This chapter highlights some of the major trends and tensions in urban politics and policy. And while we do not definitively answer the questions posed here (nor would we presume that is possible), we have compiled the perspectives presented in this book to sketch the boundaries of the political playing field and issue a challenge to you, current students of Canadian urbanism and future generations, to engage critically with urban spaces and politics.

GLOBAL THEMES/LOCAL PERSPECTIVES

If one strand stands out clearly from the contributions assembled here it is that Canadian cities are not alone in feeling a wide range of pressures from sources largely beyond their control. Globalization and the intensification of urbanization, while proceeding at different paces and degrees, have generated a set of common challenges that have intensified the effects of phenomena such as the pandemic, as well as creating conditions that magnify other crises, such as climate change, urban affordability, and social unrest. A convergence – albeit also at different paces and degrees – toward neo-liberal responses, which privilege the market and recast citizens as consumers of public services, has also shifted the governance of urban areas in meaningful ways.

Cities themselves are increasingly required to compete with peers globally. In this, they are incentivized to seek out local *and* international competitive advantages by shaping policies and urban environments to be attractive to certain types of residents, businesses, and non-profit organizations that are more prized than others because they possess certain strategic resources, such as jobs, property value, income, education, skills, civic virtues, or family support (Deas and Giordano 2002; Kresl 2002; Begg 2002; Asheim and Isaksen 1997; Wolfe and Bramwell 2008; Graham 2002; Florida 2012). Spicer (chapter 10) argues that the threat of competition begets a degree of urban policy convergence, which tends to privilege wealthy taxpayers and businesses who can take their investments elsewhere (Einstein and Kogan 2016). This involves both a form of urban entrepreneurialism, where urban policy and service provision are seen primarily as vehicles to facilitate new markets and investment, and the retreat of the public sector in providing many services that is justified by a view of citizens as human capital responsible for seeing to their own needs through the marketplace (Joy and Vogel 2021). Peterson (1981) theorized that since cities cannot effectively regulate labour and capital flows, the only lever remaining to them is land, leaving local leaders with little choice but to advance developmental policies and use land to attract resources. Although this remains largely true today in North American cities, municipalities are now pushing the boundaries of their roles to attract human capital as illustrated clearly in the chapter on local immigration policy-making. A focus on growth politics continues but the tools that municipalities use have changed, and both "immigrant control" measures as well as diversity policies have become key policy instruments in their toolboxes. Still, municipalities in North America and farther afield are limited in the extent to which they have the resources to address the challenges of immigrant integration and have been pushed to act following a "logic of emergency." Cities' limits continue to have important political and social consequences for both urban policy and their physical development.

Municipalities are being asked to do more with less as the neo-liberal agenda has broadly entailed policy decentralization from central to local governments without a commensurate increase in their revenues or capacities. The intergovernmental dimension of this is discussed in more depth below, but this offloading has resulted in chronic service and infrastructure underfunding that creates gaps that need to be filled by private business or non-profit responses (Peck 2012). While the consequences of this trend are too vast to be described here, one area in which the infiltration of private interests has become more visible, and captured the attention of critical scholars, is in the increasing financialization of infrastructure development. Cities, and agencies within them, are expected to raise resources for their infrastructure projects through financial markets, opening what are typically local projects up to the influence of global(ized) interests with significant consequences for the types of projects that are feasible, the urban built environment, and the socioeconomic relationships that rely on them (Grafe and Mieg 2019; O'Brien and Pike 2017).

Sutcliffe and Cipkar (chapter 9) note that there is some disagreement about how powerful these pressures are, what their impacts are, and the latitude that local governments have to resist the imperatives of a neo-liberal agenda. They note that while all governments experience these pressures, their responses are often quite different (Hackworth 2007; Massey 2007). Chapters in this volume note various ways in which municipalities are pushing back against these forces – such as the cancellation of Sidewalk Labs' experimental neighbourhood on the Toronto waterfront and opposition to Amazon's decision to locate one of its new headquarters in New York City. However, the scope for local resistance or, probably more accurately, management of neo-liberal pressures remains an open question that directly influences the "for whom?" local authorities are engaged in governing. We will return to this theme later in the chapter.

Another significant implication of the neo-liberal turn across all political scales is the impetus to rethink which levels of government deliver services and the resources they have to do so. Municipal governments in many countries have been affected by senior governments who are also pushing an agenda that seeks lower government regulation of the marketplace, a business-friendly municipal environment, and services aimed at attracting mobile capital and workers rather than spending on social services that help the most vulnerable members of society (Moskowitz 2018; Harvey 2005, 2013; Sassen 2001), with significant effects on local resources and capacities. This ideational environment has contributed to a significant reduction of transfers to sub-national levels of government, including municipalities, in what has been described in Canada as tri-level "downloading" (Graham, Phillips, and Maslove 1998, 174). This involved increased municipal financial responsibility for service delivery to address the impacts of cutbacks in services offered by other levels of government, which were overwhelmingly felt in cities.

Both Good and Horak (chapters 2 and 4) observe that these processes have necessarily entailed a somewhat complex and gradual recalibration of intergovernmental relationships and urban responsibilities. This has happened across at least two dimensions: vertically, where responsibilities are shifted between levels of government in a process that is broadly characterized as rescaling;[1] and horizontally, as policy spaces at all scales have opened up to new actors (for better or worse, as in the case of financialization) in a turn from government to *governance* (see chapter 4). Good (chapter 2) notes that urban municipalities across Canada emerged from the 1990s with more responsibilities – in areas such as services to immigrants and new approaches to waste management – and fewer resources than before in a context of declining intergovernmental support. This can, however, be situated in the context of a longer historical arc of intergovernmental relations in which responsibilities have been both superseded (such as when the provincial government took on the responsibility for social services after the Second World War that had previously been municipally provided) *and* devolved. Even more recently, the shift of responsibilities has not always been downward, and far more proposals to upload service delivery to the provinces have been tabled than achieved (see ongoing discussions around uploading the Toronto Transit Commission to the province of Ontario).

In the context of this neo-liberal turn, and the institutional and regulatory responses of senior levels of government, it is tempting to perceive municipalities as entities being buffeted by forces beyond their control. And to a certain extent that is right. However, in Canada, as elsewhere, they are not totally powerless to negotiate their relationships between senior levels of government, to explore strategic alternatives, or to empower themselves to chart a different course. It is undeniable that in Canada municipalities have been cast as weak, particularly within the institutional structures that shape urban affairs. They are weak – but not powerless. While this section reflects on changes to what urban governments *do*, the following section digs deeper into institutional and intergovernmental relationships that shape and constrain their scope for action to bring together insights across this collection about whether municipalities have the resources, capacity, and networks to meet these complex challenges.

WEAK, NOT POWERLESS? RESOURCES, CAPACITY, AND INTERGOVERNMENTAL COMPLEXITY IN CANADIAN URBAN POLITICS

The previous section raises questions about how much capacity cities have in the Canadian context to navigate and respond to the forces that are affecting both their political calculus and those of other levels of government. Institutional structures and division of authority have typically put Canadian cities in a weak position. While this is largely true, relative to other levels of government, institutional disadvantages are not cut and dried. Rather than enumerating the institutional contexts so adeptly described in the introductory chapters of this book (and echoed throughout), this section reiterates the argument that … it's complicated. It is true that while formal institutions are instrumental in shaping the profile of possibilities open to Canadian municipal governments, they have been interpreted differently over time, have acquired different weights at different points, and are regularly superseded by the unanticipated consequences of political realities and practices. This muddies the waters considerably regarding municipalities' scope for action and should encourage scholars of Canadian urbanism to move beyond simple dichotomies of weak and strong enshrined in political language about who policy-makers and policy-takers actually are.

One example of the fuzziness of our institutional traditions is evident in Good's discussion (in chapter 2 of this volume) of one of the most fundamental tenets of Canadian urban politics. She argues that standard accounts place all Canadian municipalities in the category of Dillon's Rule, but there is also evidence of movement toward home rule as many provinces have introduced empowering legal concepts into municipal legislation. Among these are the introduction of permissive legal concepts such as spheres of jurisdiction and natural persons powers. A popular local government textbook describes this as moving our understanding of urban legal status into a "mushy middle" between the two poles of Dillon's Rule and home rule (Tindal et al. 2017). Although control over boundary changes and political institutions remain firmly situated at the Dillon's Rule end of the spectrum, British Columbia's Community Charter stands as an interesting exception that may ultimately position it as the vanguard in a new wave of political change.

Horak (chapter 4) dives deeper into the nuances of how senior levels of government can exert influence beyond constitutional relationships. He outlines how, unlike downloading, many of the forces that constrain urban governance are passive. For instance, national policies can have local implications (e.g., immigration, see chapter 12). Provincial rules and regulations also limit scope to manoeuvre. Horak points to local planning and development activities as examples of factors shaped by provincial laws that "prescribe everything from minimum road widths and building standards, to the right of citizens to participate in local decision processes about development." In Ontario, more than 280 provincial statutes and other provincial regulations, policy frameworks, and service standards shape how urban governments deliver services (Wilson 2019). Fenn and Côté (2014) describe this as a "tangled web" of overlapping obligations complicated even further with the addition of federal funding.

These regulatory and financial arrangements are not always conceptualized as mechanisms of control but are often constructed with strings attached. Slack (chapter 6) points to government transfers as mechanisms that limit urban autonomy. Municipalities are often required to spend the funds they receive according to the guidelines of senior governments and not their own interests (Slack 2011, 2016). These funds are sometimes also accompanied by requirements to match contributions, which constrains and burdens local governments but also limits accountability and skews incentives in spending activities. The cumulative effect of these policy, regulatory, and financial constraints is incredibly difficult to apprehend in any given urban context, much less to understand over time. The broad consensus is that this burden is increasing, but the consequences for local autonomy are difficult to firmly establish.

But, of course, even as senior levels exert their influence in a variety of passive and active ways, it is vital to recognize that senior levels of government need local governments too. Central governments are increasingly recognizing a need to communicate and coordinate with sub-national and local governments to achieve their policy objectives. Horak (chapter 4) highlights that the federal government's commitment to invest in green infrastructure (such as public transit) cannot be delivered without support from local governments, which are directly responsible for both transit and land-use planning. He reiterates that there are numerous policy fields in which the relevant powers and resources are distributed among different levels of government, so coming up with effective policy responses requires coordinated action across spatial scales. In other cases, policy initiatives such as federal funding of local immigration partnerships among organizations in civil society, often with municipal involvement or leadership (discussed in chapter 12), reflect a desire to bring local knowledge to bear on "national" policy-making. The literature on multilevel governance (see Horak, chapter 4) effectively documents a sort of symbiosis that creates opportunities for actors at all scales to negotiate their interests. While these relationships will likely not fundamentally alter constitutionally imposed hierarchies, they do open up a fuzzier space of political engagement in which those hierarchies exert less power. Mévellec, Bolduc, Chiasson, and Donatien (chapter 8) add further nuance to this perspective by noting that the presence of multiple types of intergovernmental and multilevel arrangements means that the sphere of urban autonomy expands and contracts over time and differently in different policy arenas. Taylor and Dobson (2020, 8) echo this when they point out that "in certain domains, municipalities are policy takers, functioning as the field offices of provincial ministries; in others, they are policy-makers, devising innovative solutions to local problems."

All of this suggests that intergovernmental relationships and municipal functions probably do not have an "ideal" form or equilibrium. They have shifted (however imperfectly) over time, but the fact that they can shift is possibly an advantage of less strongly institutionalized intergovernmental relations. The extent to which one agrees with this statement depends in part on your view of what local governments should be (e.g., their purpose and potential). The reality is, however, that Canadian municipalities are limited in their authority, resources, and scope. And, local governments – even large, institutionally powerful ones – "will always only be part of a multi-level system of government for cities" (Sancton 2008, 32) and not the sole masters of urban affairs. This is true not only in Canada, but around the world. The upshot is that although these relationships are evolving, cities and their municipalities cannot rely on intergovernmental or multilevel engagement (even where it does result in a degree of de facto autonomy). This leaves Canadian cities grappling with the challenge of how to govern effectively in a sometimes fuzzy and evolving institutional context and mercurial multilevel engagement.

UNLEASHING CANADIAN CITIES OR LEARNING TO DANCE?

Given this context, what can cities do? Clearly, the script of weak cities at the mercy of national and provincial governments and global forces is not totally accurate. However, it is also the case that urban governments in Canada, and students of them, do not feel as though they are adequately positioned to take on the challenges arrayed against them. This has led to ongoing discussions about how to manage urban affairs. This debate is often cast as one in which senior levels should consider institutional reforms to empower local governments (a process that Good notes in chapter 2 is underway, particularly for larger cities, to a limited degree in Canadian provinces) or where local governments should recognize and exercise their power to act unilaterally outside of existing institutional arrangements. What emerges will likely combine aspects of both. However, what is certain is that as challenges intensify, Canadian urban affairs will continue to evolve. This section explores these options with a focus on discussing some of the tradeoffs inherent in these paths.

Unleashing ... ?

The conversation about transforming the potential of Canadian cities often begins and ends with institutional change. And in some senses, rightly so. Despite the shifting practices described in the previous section, the institutions that govern Canadian urban politics have been remarkably durable or, less charitably, "stagnant" (Hirschl 2020a). Hirschl argues that constitutions enacted between the late eighteenth century and the 1970s accord little to no status to cities and that efforts at reform have not been particularly transformative (Hirschl 2020a, 2020b). Indeed, Hirschl (2020a) paints the constitutions of the Western world as behind in their adaptation to the global urban reality, arguing that it is the newer constitutions in countries of the Global South including, for instance, South Africa, that are the most innovative.

Although municipalities could be recognized in a variety of ways in Canada's federal Constitution, including as an order of government with clearly delineated areas of jurisdiction (as in the South African Constitution, for instance), as students of Canadian politics know well, it would be very difficult to reach an agreement for constitutional reform that would satisfy Canada's requirements for a constitutional amendment following the general amending formula which, in addition to federal Parliament, would require the consent of at least seven provinces representing at least 50 per cent of the population. As previous sections (and chapters) have pointed out, large "C" constitutional change is not the only option on the menu. In Canada, the provinces have considerable scope to expand the powers of their municipalities. Good (chapter 2) notes that since 2000 all provinces, except for Nova Scotia and Newfoundland, have enacted municipal legislation to give local governments broader spheres of authority (see also Taylor and Dobson 2020) while many large cities that had previously been governed by general-purpose legislation got their own special governing legislation. Although such changes are often characterized as merely "legislative" rather than "constitutional," when one considers municipalities' significance as democratic governments and the flexible nature of provincial constitutions, one could interpret this as a form of small "c" constitutional change *to provincial constitutions* (Good 2019). Municipalities could be granted a "soft" form of entrenchment in provincial constitutions in at least two ways: (1) through manner and form limitations on provincial action in municipal affairs in acts establishing municipal systems (general municipal acts and city charters), with British Columbia's Community Charter (2003) constituting a leading example (as discussed in chapter 2); (2) through a broader process of clarifying and consolidating provincial constitutions (Good 2024). Still, while changes to municipal legislation have moved the needle slightly, provinces remain wary of ceding too much power (Taylor and Bradford 2020, 46), in the same way as they are reluctant to change other aspects of their democratic institutions (and provincial constitutions) through electoral reform. First ministers, including the prime minister but also provincial premiers, have become increasingly powerful in recent decades with power shifting from cabinet to central agencies and the PMO or premier's office. In such an environment, local institutions and democracy are subject to the shifting policy and reform ideas of Canadian premiers. Indeed, as many have pointed out in past chapters, the City of Toronto has been subject to provincially imposed reforms to its political institutions, including a controversial amalgamation in the 1990s, a reduction in the size of its city council, and a bestowal of "strong-mayor" powers. Although provinces' flexibility to change municipal systems could be seen as a virtue of Canada's institutional system, "liberty," a central regime principle in Canada, is arguably undermined by top-down interference in local democracy (particularly in a context in which provincial legislatures are limited in their ability to hold the government to account). As a result, scholars and city advocates continue to argue that the Canadian system must evolve further and that this will require granting more resources, legal autonomy, and protection against provincial intervention to local governments (Good 2021).

Although increasing municipal autonomy has definite advantages for urban governance, it is not without notable drawbacks. As local autonomy increases, tensions can potentially (though do not necessarily) increase with efficiency, equity, and collaboration. For instance, Good (chapter 2) cites Magnusson's (1986) argument that the logic of efficiency that underpins the Anglo model and has shaped the Canadian model of democracy devalues local government as a fundamental form of democratic practice. In principle, this means that while autonomy supports efficiency at the local scale in some policy areas, that may not be the case in others. This returns us to our fundamental question of what local governments should be doing and what resources they should have through the question of autonomy *in what* and *for what*. While certain values can be designed into the institutions, provincial reluctance to release control of some of their key policy levers and create potential rivals that may reduce their own policy effectiveness and efficiency is understandable.

There is also a danger that ceding too much autonomy can create problems of interlocal equity that, over time, become path dependent and difficult to resolve. Taylor (2021) warns that the combined effects of high dependence on local revenues (from fiscal independence), a hands-off approach with respect to urban issues at senior levels of government, combined with (and partially responsible for) relatively inflexible local boundaries, can create conditions where there are have and have-not municipalities, both within and across metropolitan areas. Under such circumstances, richer municipalities can provide good services to their populations and offer residents real policy choices while poorer municipalities often have difficulty attracting (or retaining) residents and businesses, maintaining property values, and consequently providing basic services. Taylor (2021, 7) describes this autonomy as "illusory," and one does not have to employ too much imagination to conjure scenarios where the independent pursuit of local interests widens the gulf between winners and losers (both between governments and households).

The American context teaches us that increasing autonomy tends to make local boundaries more rigid as communities seek to control what is "theirs," and this reduces potential for boundary changes (such as annexations and amalgamations) that may create urban spaces at scales more aligned with contemporary realities and economies of scale. Such rigidity is certainly a goal of measures that seek to increase municipal protections against provincial meddling in urban structures. However, this also raises the likelihood of municipal fragmentation, which both increases the necessity for interlocal collaboration and the complexity of achieving it (Nelles 2012).

While these tensions are, for the most part, not serious enough to argue against increasing local autonomy, they are a useful reminder that institutional change is fraught with (sometimes unintended) consequences. Arguments to enhance local autonomy would do well to weigh these and other considerations and incorporate them into proposed designs. Comparative research has an important role to play in understanding the potential consequences of institutional meddling.

Autonomy movements in Canada are likely to make only incremental headway and face important provincial barriers. However, it is useful to reflect on the influence of gains so far. Most scholars suggest that the impact of these changes has been limited partly because *local governments have been reluctant to test the limits of their enhanced authority* (Good 2019). That is, municipalities may not use the policy tools or the space that they are given.

The question, then, is whether or not autonomy is *required* to move city agendas forward, and, if so, what that means (e.g., what kinds of autonomy, for what?).

Dancing…?

There is a charming phrase used in complexity theory and systems thinking that holds that you cannot solve complex problems, but you can manage your way through by "learning to dance" with them. In many ways, approaches that focus on constitutional or institutional change conceptualize the challenges of urban governance as merely complicated but not complex. These formal changes are seen as solutions or fixes that, even if they were feasible or successful, may not impact problems that are much more complex – as much as their architects would hope. This does not mean that there is no place for institutional reform, but that these should probably not be considered ends unto themselves. Rather, as Horak concludes his chapter (chapter 4): "More responsive, effective urban governance will require, above all, an understanding that governing cities is an inherently multilevel enterprise," one in which the division of power among the various actors and institutions involved is crucial. How we build a multilevel political system in which the many moving parts work together, rather than at cross purposes, is also important. Horak is, in essence, advocating that we learn to dance a bit better within our system of urban governance.

Multilevel governance arrangements offer one framework for this and one of the most powerful ways to translate a "seat at the table" with senior levels of government into genuine local empowerment. Intergovernmental relations in which municipalities are consulted, but not partners, are a distant second to more embedded solutions where local governments are involved in policy co-production, not as subordinates, but as equals. However, that is easier said than done, and as Horak demonstrates in his chapter, it is fraught with political pitfalls. He specifically points to problems associated with accountability, where actors that have a shared political goal but are held to account by constituencies at different scales can see unity fail in the face of changing political priorities, a change of administration, or a turning of public opinion of one or more constituencies. Other accountability issues can arise from the fact that collaboration makes it difficult to know whom to hold responsible when things go wrong. Furthermore, it is impractical to partner on everything, returning us to the perennial question of what local governments should be doing, but this time adding the qualifier "independently" or "in partnership."

Within the intergovernmental and multilevel context there is potentially some scope to expand the role of the federal government. Good (chapter 2) observes that a sustained and institutionalized federal role in urban affairs has been lacking in Canada. Other chapters list some of the areas of urban affairs that federal policy has touched, including housing (through the National Housing Strategy), local economic development (through the Innovation Superclusters program), and relief funding to municipalities affected by COVID-19 (through the Safe Restart Agreement). While Bradford (2018) has described the accumulation of federal policy initiatives as an implicit federal urban agenda, the country has never engaged in a sustained effort (as others have) to craft a national strategy for its cities. Doing so would almost certainly open a dialogue about "who does what" even if it would be a relatively contentious process and could precipitate conversations about how to delegate resources or direct federal spending to support local governments in achieving their goals.

At the other end of the spectrum of options is for cities to empower themselves. Mévellec, Bolduc, Chiasson, and Donatien (chapter 8) argue that:

> Cities are acting more and more on a widened policy agenda that they themselves are creating …. poverty, homelessness, housing, integration, and Indigenous presence are cross-cutting issues on which they have no choice but to act. Canadian cities are also confronted with issues such as security threats, immigration, and climate change. These transnational challenges have pushed many cities to voluntarily adopt action plans and innovative policy measures in order to respond to these issues, thus becoming "policy-makers."

In this collection, we have presented no shortage of examples of municipal governments and their leaders using what tools they have to make impacts on policy areas that are typically beyond their purviews. Whether it is adopting local measures to reduce greenhouse gas emissions through tactical urbanism (Cleveland and Schwartz in chapter 11), defying directives from their provinces on mask mandates, creating programs to welcome Syrian (and now Ukrainian) refugees, setting up task forces to address drug addiction and overdose or mental health (Good, Graham, and Helmer in chapter 7), or making efforts to build new relationships with Indigenous Peoples (Anderson and Flynn in chapter 13), each demonstrates that local governments can use meagre tools and a significant platform to great effect. Perhaps ironically, the process of senior levels of government downloading and offloading responsibilities, inattention, or formal retrenchment from issue areas affecting Canadian urban places has encouraged local governments to develop their own problem-solving capacity. This policy learning, capacity, and expertise may be indispensable to senior governments' policy efforts in the future, effectively changing the nature of traditional hierarchical relationships across a variety of policy spaces. Where this imbalance between formal authority and capacity in government will lead is an interesting question for Canadian politics and political science.

In this volume, and elsewhere, Nelles (2012) has argued that regionalism offers another way for municipalities to amplify their voices and increase their political relevance relative to other levels of government. Coming together in regional partnerships and forums can create critical mass at the metropolitan scale, generating political momentum behind shared issues to get them onto national and provincial agendas. The power of partnership was demonstrated recently during the COVID-19 pandemic, when an informal group of mayors in the Greater Toronto and Hamilton Area came together to collectively influence emerging federal and provincial public health policy and recovery packages. Nelles's work, and that of numerous other regionalists in Canada, demonstrates that horizontal partnerships and collective action can also be instrumental for local governments looking to solve their own problems. Research on Indigenous-municipal co-operation (Alcantara and Nelles 2016) shows how interlocal partnerships not only helped communities govern more effectively but also how these innovations created a (generally) productive and collaborative space for dialogue in the context of a relatively contentious intergovernmental policy environment. There are, of course, drawbacks to relying on horizontal arrangements, but these exist as yet another one of the "moves" that municipalities can use in their dance with the complexities of intergovernmental urbanism.

CITIES FOR WHOM?

To this point, this chapter has focused specifically on the first set of the core fundamental questions of urban politics. Understanding the contours of what cities do (or could or should do) with what powers, resources, and networks (existing or potential) is a function of the institutional environment and intergovernmental system. How they deliver those responsibilities and for whose benefit are questions that pertain primarily to the internal structures and processes of urban governance. These questions are more fundamentally about how governance is organized, who has a voice in governing, how interests are synthesized, and how decisions are made. Interestingly, the "for whom" piece of the puzzle flows in large part from the design of local government structures and processes, with each alternative shifting balances (slightly or significantly) to favour specific groups and outcomes.

For instance, Mévellec, Bolduc, Chiasson, and Donatien (chapter 8) identify the traits of the Canadian municipal democratic model as "a property-owner democracy, low turnouts in elections, representation dominated by white, middle-aged males following the gifted amateur" and suggest that these have deep roots in Canadian urban experience. In other words, these are a product of institutional designs that have tended to privilege a certain set of interests, to which there are certainly alternatives.

The first aspect – the "property-owner democracy" – is both a product of the time in which (Anglo settler colonial) political cultures were coalescing and of path dependence associated with institutions that arose to support local service delivery. Indeed, Canada is one of few liberal democracies where property continues to influence voting rights because non-resident voting, a type of property franchise, exists at the local (municipal) level in five provincial jurisdictions: British Columbia, Saskatchewan, Manitoba, Ontario, and Quebec. Moreover, although Britain has eliminated non-resident voting except for in the City of London (Sawer 2007), local government systems in other Westminster countries including Australia and New Zealand continue to extend rights to vote based on property. An American economist, William Fischel (2001, 2005) coined the phrase "homevoter" based on his observations that concern about uninsurable risks to the value of homes, stemming in large part from local policies, motivates homeowners to become more active in local politics. Zoning, which is a responsibility of Canadian municipalities, controls what gets built where, whether that is residential, commercial, industrial, infrastructural, or public. Homeowners who believe that rezoning proposals or other policies or projects will negatively impact the value of their properties have a strong incentive to engage in local politics, not just by voting at higher rates than tenants do (DiPasquale and Glaeser 1999; Dietz and Haurin 2003; McCabe 2013; McGregor and Spicer 2016) but also by engaging in other forms of political participation such as contacting a representative or attending a public meeting about a rezoning at city hall. This configuration leads to an electorate that tends to be "owner, older, richer and more educated" than the average (Breux and Lavalette 2020).

Adding to this propensity is the fact that property taxes are the most significant own-source revenue for Canadian municipalities, further engaging the interests of homeowners (who have visibility into how much they are paying) in the process of deciding how those public resources should be spent.

These institutions are not necessarily barriers to broader participation, but they do create a tendency for property owners to vote and engage with their representatives in greater numbers than people who do not own property, making them the core constituencies to which politicians pitch their campaigns (and their activities while in office). And while property owners as a group do not have homogeneous politics or policy interests, their tendency to want to protect their property values makes their interests relatively predictable (even if their perceptions about what will negatively impact these values do not always align with reality). Unsurprisingly, this balance of power of interests tends to benefit property owners with the general effect of making policies that benefit disadvantaged groups or that are redistributive in nature more difficult to propose and enact.

Slack (chapter 6) adds that while the property tax is appropriate for funding many city services, it may not be for all. For example, because the property tax is not as suitable a source of funding for services of a redistributive nature, there have been calls to increase the types of taxes available to Canadian municipalities (Kitchen and Slack 2016). She argues that it might be more appropriate for municipalities to fund redistributive services from more progressive taxes such as the income tax or a value-added tax that includes mitigation for low-income households in the design. Without more progressive and appropriate funding sources, local governments find it difficult to enact policies with broader social benefits as this constrains their ability to engage in redistributive programs. Again, the "how" piece of the puzzle here has significant influence on the "for whom" piece, as institutions favour the voices of specific groups.

Of course, representatives, once elected, are free to interpret their policy mandates more broadly. However, they are ultimately held accountable by their constituencies, so how local governments determine representation – both ideologically and geographically – also influences which voices are heard loudest (and which are less evident).

As Good, Graham, and Helmer (chapter 7) discuss in their chapter, electoral institutions that delineate spaces of representation affect the configuration of interests that underpin debates in council. They note that each system – at large or ward based – has advantages and disadvantages. For instance, at-large systems using first-past-the-post tend to privilege numerically dominant groups (e.g., suburban homeowners) over smaller groups with different interests (e.g., city renters). While at-large elections tend to encourage elected officials to consider city-wide issues, in practice they are aware of the geographical concentrations and core interests of their voters (Koop and Kraemer 2016). Ward-based elections are thought to enable councils with a greater diversity of (geographically anchored) interests but are not always a panacea. How the boundaries of wards are drawn and how many of them there are can also have a strong influence on who is elected, on what platform, and for whom. Mévellec, Bolduc, Chiasson, and Donatien (chapter 8) note that critics of the ward system also point to the fact that geographical representation can favour parochialism, making it difficult to address city-wide concerns.

The geography of representation in electoral systems is only partially responsible for the diversity deficit we observe on Canadian municipal councils. Research cited in the chapters in this volume (most notably Mévellec, Bolduc, Chiasson, and Donatien [chapter 8]) applaud the progress that has been made in electing more women, Indigenous people, and people from diverse ethnic backgrounds. However, on average, men are more likely to be elected and to occupy key offices such as that of mayor. The chapters in this collection detail institutional barriers to greater diversity linked to electoral institutions such as campaign finance, costs, fundraising, and other rules. While it is reasonable to ask what importance such diversity has on municipal politics if elected officials are primarily tasked to represent the interests of their constituents rather than their own, descriptive representation and equity in electoral contests are perhaps both outcomes worth pursuing. This is particularly worth debating in the context of changing demographic patterns (chapter 12), the importance of reconciling Indigenous and non-Indigenous governing practices (chapter 13), and rising inequality (chapter 15). As in intergovernmental relations, who has a seat at the table and how their voices are integrated through processes of governing matters.

Of course, Mévellec, Bolduc, Chiasson, and Donatien (chapter 8), Sutcliffe and Cipkar (chapter 9), and others reiterate that voter turnout in municipal elections in Canada tends to be low. This has consequences for who is elected and for the voices they represent as Latinx,

Asian, and Black populations tend to vote at significantly lower rates than white voters in local elections. Young people, those newly arrived, and other demographic groups have lower turnout rates. While hypotheses abound as to reasons for disconnection from local elections – such as perceptions that local politics is not important to lack of information – Mévellec, Donatien, and Chiasson (2020) again point to the tendency for voters and elected officials to be older and white (and male, in the case of politicians) as a result of the connection between local politics and property. In their view, Canadian municipal democracy is struggling to reach and include constituents who hold different interests, something which may create a negative feedback loop that actively alienates a more diverse set of voters who could drive change. Exploring these causes and effects and their consequences for both the substance of local politics and for the alignment of Canadian values with democratic practices presents a crucial challenge for Canadian urban research.

Sutcliffe and Cipkar (chapter 9) discuss alternatives to electoral engagement, noting that the ballot box is not the only way to influence local decision-making. They cite participatory processes and social movements, which can directly or indirectly shape local outcomes. However, while they present important examples of how emerging forms of participation can produce concrete results, they express doubt that these mechanisms provide adequate alternatives. For one, marginalized groups face similar barriers to participation in social movements and participatory processes as they do to electoral ones. Second, these avenues of influence are typically limited to specific facets of local decision-making (as in participatory budgeting) or have relatively uncertain pathways to translation and impact (social movements). There is also some debate about the areas in which public input should be considered and adopted over expert opinion. Furthermore, countless local decisions are taken in departments, agencies, boards, and commissions over which council may have oversight but does not control the minutia of decisions. Citizens are largely unaware of the millions of choices that make up local public policies and are often powerless to amend them without considerable effort and organization.

Indeed, as Ajadi and Good discuss in chapter 14, a discussion of "for whom" cities govern is incomplete without acknowledging the structural racism that influences local decision-making. Racialized minorities and Indigenous residents are subject to a disproportionate level of police surveillance and violence by municipal police forces and others that operate within municipal and city boundaries (including the RCMP in some local jurisdictions). This chapter demonstrates that the issue of disproportionate street checks and carding of Black residents as well as the police violence that we have witnessed in Canadian cities is a transatlantic phenomenon. Environmental racism is another common challenge faced by racialized communities that have been subject disproportionately to the negative consequences of noxious land uses located near their communities. These and other examples demonstrate that although municipalities are presented as weak in the intergovernmental system, the services they offer and the decisions they make with respect to urban development and land use have the potential to constitute a form of state violence against some communities.

As Anderson and Flynn in chapter 13 discusses, cities are also places of erasure of Indigenous histories and cultural practices, which are currently being revived through acts of resurgence in Canadian cities and beyond. Acknowledging that much work remains to be done, they identify a series of initiatives that municipalities are developing to engage and develop new relationships with Indigenous Peoples both in Canadian cities and globally. The challenge of decolonizing cities is a global one that must be contextualized locally given the diversity of Indigenous communities, laws, and histories that have shaped urban places as well as the different legacies and ongoing forms of colonization that shape contemporary cities.

Taken together, chapters 13 and 14 demonstrate that cities are not only places of oppression of racialized minorities and Indigenous Peoples, they are also spaces of resistance and resurgence, tied to global movements for racial justice and Indigenous rights. The Black Lives Matter movement present in Canadian cities but also across the globe is but one example. As Canadian municipalities grapple with how to address racism and pursue relationships inspired by transformative reconciliation with Indigenous Peoples, they might look to examples in jurisdictions across the globe for inspiration.

Another more forward-looking debate about "for whom" municipalities govern that is raised in this volume is the question of the impacts of climate change on future generations of residents. This challenge will vary by city, but as Cleveland and Schwartz show in chapter 11, municipalities play crucial roles in contributing to solutions for future generations. As governments with significant jurisdiction over planning and infrastructure decisions that lock cities into particular paths in terms of transportation options, municipalities across the globe are shaping our climate's future.

This section summarizes some of the many factors that influence which voices are represented and have influence in local politics. As in the sections where we discussed institutional and intergovernmental contexts and the limits they impose and opportunities they present for local governments, the Canadian urban system is not resolved or ideal, nor has it stopped evolving. This is where the work begins for students of Canadian urbanism and where comparative research can contribute to enriching the debates that continue to shape this evolution.

A final point about representation is in order: comparative urban research in political science would benefit enormously from engagement with a *greater diversity of scholarship* in Canada and globally as well as a *broader range of cases*. Although Enright (2020) warned against the potentially imperial consequences of comparisons seeking to generalize about urban governance across unique contexts, with Turgeon, Good, and Triadafilopoulos (2014), we see great value in pursuing cross-national comparisons across geographic regions in the globe and, more generally, in employing most different systems designs in urban comparisons. For instance, with Hugill (2019), we see huge potential in tracing similarities among very different cases as a way to highlight and centre both processes of marginalization and dispossession like colonialism and structural racism and the resistance to them. In comparative politics, most similar systems designs tend to predominate, which privileges Western knowledge and cases. Ran Hirschl's global examination of how constitutions have responded to urbanization is an excellent example of the innovation in urban governance that can be revealed by engaging with very different cases, such as those in the Global South. In yet another example of bringing a greater diversity of perspectives to understanding municipalities' place in Canada, Magnusson (2005, 2) argues that many Canadian Indigenous legal scholars have developed pragmatic and "non-absolutist" concepts of sovereignty that allow for the complex coexistence of multiple orders of government. Such ideas could help students of urban politics to imagine a broader range of organizing political authority and more democratic forms of coexistence among levels of government. From a practical perspective, Anderson and Flynn (chapter 13) also see similarities between, and potential of cross-fertilization across, Indigenous and municipal orders of government, the latter of which are paradoxically both part of what they call the structural genocide of current state structures that have been imposed on Indigenous communities and uniquely positioned to contribute to building more honourable relations. As they put it:

> Municipalities are the Canadian political entities closest to Indigenous Peoples, and as neighbours and (hopefully) friends sharing diverse community contexts, they are perhaps best positioned to exemplify and deepen what it means to uphold the honour of the Crown, in ways that more remote Canadian provincial and federal governments are challenged to realize.

CONCLUSION: A FINAL CHALLENGE

This book aimed to better understand both the broader forces that are generating contemporary urban challenges and the scope within which Canadian urban governments can respond, grow, and increase resilience. With these contributions, presented with a comparative lens, we hoped to enable a deeper appreciation of the place of Canadian cities in the federation and the world, and how other cities' experiences can shed light on how our institutions and contexts have influenced the evolution of our municipal system – lessons and inspiration we can use to chart Canada's urban future.

The comparative approach demonstrates that our cities are not alone. Municipalities globally are grappling with similar issues, albeit in their own institutional contexts. This work also shows that the municipal experiment is far from complete. Cities and their citizens everywhere continue to debate and contest their own urban evolutions. In some cases, it may appear that municipalities elsewhere have institutional advantages – more power, greater resources, lower complexity, greater support. However, in each case, the institutions themselves are only part of the story. How they are interpreted, used, and navigated in practice; how they interact with each other in ways unique to each institutional context; how norms moderate or modify their intended outcomes; and what disadvantages these also entail are very important to consider.

While the authors in this volume have pointed out exemplary cases and, in some cases, best practices, they are also careful to consider their suitability to the Canadian context and the barriers to their adoption here.

Institutions may be fixed – in the double sense of the word – but there is always some scope to manoeuvre and space for innovation. That is, they may be fixed in the sense that they can be altered through concerted action or gradual change in practice. Or they can be fixed in that they are unchanging (or difficult to change). In all likelihood, what we will see is a combination of both change and continuity as Canadians grapple with politics at the local level. The vital point here is that institutional rigidity is not permanent, nor is it debilitating to political movements and moments. Canadian cities are already rising to the challenges in creative ways even if in other ambitions they still face barriers. Institutions are not everything, but more importantly, they will not change on their own. Engaging actively in urban futures can and will make a difference.

These are tasks that the authors in this volume and the scores of researchers cited attack with relish. The answers that emerge, and indeed even the debates that they spawn, will fundamentally shape the urban experience. And now it is also up to you, as a reader and student of Canadian urban governance, to join the conversation. A new generation of students of urban politics and citizens will have to decide whether they want to take hold of local government and use it as a tool for democratic empowerment or accept the current trajectory of urban evolution. Understanding where we have been, and what constrains (or enables) the path ahead, is increasingly important as we enter into a period of urban crisis that may precipitate, or require, a redefinition of Canadian urban politics and the potential of local government in the broader political system.

NOTE

1 Rescaling itself is a contested term and ideally refers to a specific form of power/responsibility shift between levels of government and/or the creation of new political scales accompanied by the resources and capabilities to meet demands. Offloading or downloading are terms that denote a change of scale without necessarily accompanying these with associated levers.

REFERENCES

Alcantara, Christopher, and Jen Nelles. 2016. *A Quiet Evolution: The Emergence of Indigenous-Local Intergovernmental Partnerships in Canada*. Toronto: University of Toronto Press. https://doi.org/10.3138/9781442625884.

Asheim, Bjørn T., and Arne Isaksen. 1997. "Location, Agglomeration and Innovation: Towards Regional Innovation Systems in Norway?" *European Planning Studies* 5, no. 3 (June): 299–330. https://doi.org/10.1080/09654319708720402.

Begg, Ian. 2002. *Urban Competitiveness: Policies for Dynamic Cities*. Bristol: The Policy Press. https://doi.org/10.46692/9781847425423.

Bradford, Neil. 2018. *A National Urban Policy for Canada? The Implicit Federal Agenda.* IRPP Insight 24. Montreal: Institute for Research on Public Policy. https://irpp.org/research-studies /national-urban-policy-canada-implicit-federal-agenda/.

Breux, Sandra, and Salomé Lavalette. 2020. "Voter à l'échelle municipale au Québec : significations et portée chez certains jeunes électeurs." *Revue Jeunes et Sociétés* 5, no. 1: 50–70. https://doi .org/10.7202/1070525ar.

Deas, Iain, and Benito Giordano. 2002. "Locating the Competitive City in England." In *Urban Competitiveness: Policies for Dynamic Cities*, edited by Iain Begg, 191–210. Bristol: The Policy Press. https://doi.org/10.46692/9781847425423.010.

Dietz, Robert D., and Donald R. Haurin. 2003. "The Social and Private Micro-level Consequences of Homeownership." *Journal of Urban Economics* 54, no. 3 (November): 401–50. https://doi .org/10.1016/S0094-1190(03)00080-9.

DiPasquale, Denise, and Edward L Glaeser. 1999. "Incentives and Social Capital: Are Homeowners Better Citizens?" *Journal of Urban Economics* 45, no. 2 (March): 354–84. https://doi.org/10.1006 /juec.1998.2098.

Einstein, Katherine Levin, and Vladimir Kogan. 2016. "Pushing the City Limits: Policy Responsiveness in Municipal Government." *Urban Affairs Review* 52, no. 1 (January): 3–32. https://doi.org/10.1177 /1078087414568027.

Enright, Theresa. 2020. "Beyond Comparison in Urban Politics and Policy Analysis." In "Symposium, Toward an Urban Policy Analysis," special issue, *PS: Political Science & Politics* 53, no. 1 (January): 29–32. https://doi.org/10.1017/S1049096519001367.

Fenn, Michael, and André Côté. 2014. "Provincial-Municipal Relations in Ontario: Approaching an Inflection Point." In *IMFG Papers on Municipal Finance and Governance*, no. 17. Toronto: Institute on Municipal Finance and Governance. https://imfg.munkschool.utoronto.ca/research /doc/?doc_id=275.

Fischel, William A. 2001. "Homevoters, Municipal Corporate Governance, and the Benefit View of the Property Tax." *National Tax Journal* 54, no. 1 (March): 157–73. https://doi.org/10.17310 /ntj.2001.1.08.

———. 2005. *The Homevoter Hypothesis: How Home Values Influence Local Government Taxation, School Finance, and Land-Use Policies.* Cambridge: Harvard University Press.

Florida, Richard. 2012. *The Rise of the Creative Class – Revisited and Expanded.* New York: Basic Books.

Good, Kristin R. 2019. "The Fallacy of the 'Creatures of the Provinces' Doctrine: Recognizing and Protecting Municipalities' Constitutional Status." In *IMFG Papers on Municipal Finance and Governance*, no. 46. Toronto: Institute on Municipal Finance and Governance.

———. 2021. *Reconsidering the Constitutional Status of Municipalities: From Creatures of the Provinces to Provincial Constitutionalism.* Montreal: Institute for Research on Public Policy.

———. 2024. "Moving Beyond the 'Creatures of the Provinces' Doctrine: Exploring Pathways to Municipal Empowerment in Provincial Constitutions." In *Cities and the Constitution: Giving Local Governments in Canada the Power They Need*, edited by Alexandra Flynn, Richard Albert, and Nathalie Des Rosiers, 243–71. Montreal: McGill-Queen's University Press.

Grafe, Fritz-Julius, and Harald A. Mieg. 2019. "Connecting Financialization and Urbanization: The Changing Financial Ecology of Urban Infrastructure in the UK." *Regional Studies, Regional Science* 6, no. 1 (January): 496–511. https://doi.org/10.1080/21681376.2019.1668291.

Graham, Katherine A., Susan D. Phillips, and Allan M. Maslove. 1998. *Urban Governance in Canada: Representation, Resources, and Restructuring.* Toronto: Harcourt Brace Canada.

Graham, Stephen. 2002. "Bridging Urban Digital Divides? Urban Polarisation and Information and Communication Technologies (ICTs)." *Urban Studies* 39, no. 1 (January): 33–56. https://doi.org/10.1080/00420980220099050.

Hackworth, Jason. 2007. *The Neoliberal City: Governance, Ideology, and Development in American Urbanism.* Ithaca: Cornell University Press.

Harvey, David. 2005. *A Brief History of Neoliberalism.* Oxford: Oxford University Press. https://doi.org/10.1093/oso/9780199283262.001.0001.

———. 2013. *Rebel Cities: From the Right to the City to the Urban Revolution.* London: Verso.

Hirschl, Ran. 2020a. *City, State: Constitutionalism and the Megacity.* New York: Oxford University Press. https://doi.org/10.1093/oso/9780190922771.001.0001.

———. 2020b. "Cities in National Constitutions: Northern Stagnation, Southern Innovation." In *IMFG Papers on Municipal Finance and Governance*, no. 51. Toronto: Institute on Municipal Finance and Governance.

Hugill, David. 2019. "Comparative Settler Colonial Urbanisms: Racism and the Making of Inner-City Winnipeg and Minneapolis, 1940–1975." In *Settler City Limits: Indigenous Resurgence and Colonial Violence in the Urban Prairie West*, edited by Heather Dorries, Robert Henry, David Hugill, Tyler McCreary, and Julie Tomiak, loc. 1682–2200. Winnipeg: University of Manitoba Press. Kindle. https://doi.org/10.1515/9780887555893-005.

Joy, Meghan, and Ronald K. Vogel. 2021. "Beyond Neoliberalism: A Policy Agenda for a Progressive City." *Urban Affairs Review* 57, no. 5 (September): 1372–409. https://doi.org/10.1177/1078087420984241.

Kitchen, Harry, and Enid Slack. 2016. "More Tax Sources for Canada's Largest Cities: Why, What, and How?" In *IMFG Papers on Municipal Finance and Governance*, no. 27. Toronto: Institute on Municipal Finance and Governance.

Koop, Royce, and John Kraemer. 2016. "Wards, At-Large Systems and the Focus of Representation in Canadian Cities." *Canadian Journal of Political Science/Revue canadienne de science politique* 49, no. 3 (September): 433–48. https://doi.org/10.1017/S0008423916000512.

Kresl, Peter. 2002. "The Enhancement of Urban Economic Competitiveness: The Case of Montreal." In *Urban Competitiveness: Policies for Dynamic Cities*, edited by Iain Begg, 211–32. Bristol: The Policy Press. https://doi.org/10.46692/9781847425423.011.

Magnusson, Warren. 1986. "Bourgeois theories of local government." *Political Studies* 34, no. 1 (March): 1–18. https://doi.org/10.1111/j.1467-9248.1986.tb01869.x.

———. 2005. "Are Municipalities Creatures of the Provinces?" *Journal of Canadian Studies* 39, no. 2 (Spring): 5–30. https://doi.org/10.1353/jcs.2006.0019.

Massey, Doreen. 2007. *World City.* Cambridge: Polity Press.

McCabe, Brian J. 2013. "Are Homeowners Better Citizens? Homeownership and Community Participation in the United States." *Social Forces* 91, no. 3 (March): 929–54. https://doi.org/10.1093/sf/sos185.

McGregor, Michael, and Zachary Spicer. 2016. "The Canadian Homevoter: Property Values and Municipal Politics in Canada." *Journal of Urban Affairs* 38, no. 1 (February): 123–39. https://doi.org/10.1111/juaf.12178.

Mévellec, Anne, Veika Donatien, and Guy Chiasson. 2020. "Municipal/Local Politics: The False Pretences of the Municipal Level in Canada." In *The Palgrave Handbook of Gender, Sexuality, and Canadian Politics*, edited by Manon Tremblay and Joanna Everitt, 249–71. Cham: Palgrave Macmillan. https://doi.org/10.1007/978-3-030-49240-3_13.

Moskowitz, Peter. 2018. *How to Kill a City: Gentrification, Inequality, and the Fight for the Neighborhood.* New York: Nation Books.

Nelles, Jen. 2012. *Comparative Metropolitan Policy: Governing beyond the Local Boundaries in the Imagined Metropolis.* Oxon, UK: Routledge.

O'Brien, Peter, and Andy Pike. 2017. "The Financialization and Governance of Infrastructure." In *Handbook on the Geographies of Money and Finance,* edited by Ron Martin and Jane Pollard, 223–52. Cheltenham, UK: Edward Elgar Publishing. https://doi.org/10.4337/9781784719005.00017.

Peck, Jamie. 2012. "Austerity Urbanism: American Cities under Extreme Economy." *City* 16, no. 6 (December): 625–55. https://doi.org/10.1080/13604813.2012.734071.

Peterson, P.E. 1981. *City Limits.* Chicago: University of Chicago Press.

Sancton, A. 2008. The Limits of Boundaries: Why City-Regions Cannot Be Self-Governing. Montreal: McGill-Queen's Press. https://doi.org/10.1515/9780773574977.

Sassen, Saskia. 2001. *The Global City: New York, London, Tokyo.* 2nd ed. Princeton, NJ: Princeton University Press. https://doi.org/10.1515/9781400847488.

Sawer, Marian. 2007. "Property Voting in Local Government: A Relic of a Pre-democratic Era?" *Representation* 43, no. 1 (April): 45–52. https://doi.org/10.1080/00344890601177123.

Slack, Enid. 2011. "Financing Large Cities and Metropolitan Areas." In *IMFG Papers on Municipal Finance and Governance,* no. 3. Toronto: Institute on Municipal Finance and Governance.

———. 2016. "Local Finances and Fiscal Equalization Schemes in Comparative Perspective." In *Das Teilen beherrschen, Analysen zur Reform des Finanzausgleichs 2019,* edited by René Geißler, Felix Knupling, Sabine Kropp, and Joachim Weiland, 283–312. Berlin: Nomos. https://doi .org/10.5771/9783845259284-283.

Taylor, Zack. 2021. "From Local Autonomy to the Metagovernance of Place." Paper presented at Canadian Political Science Association Annual Meeting, June 2021.

Taylor, Zack, and Alec Dobson. 2020. "Power and Purpose: Canadian Municipal Law in Transition." In *IMFG Papers on Municipal Finance and Governance,* no. 47. Toronto: Institute on Municipal Finance and Governance. https://tspace.library.utoronto.ca/bitstream/1807/99780/1/IMFG _Paper_No47_Power_and_Purpose_Taylor_Dobson.pdf.

Taylor, Zack, and Neil Bradford. 2020. "Governing Canadian Cities." In *Canadian Cities in Transition,* edited by Markus Moos, Ryan Walker, and Tara Vinodrai, 6th ed., 33–50. Toronto: Oxford University Press.

Tindal, C. Richard, Susan Tindal, Kennedy Stewart, and Patrick Smith. 2017. *Local Government in Canada.* 9th ed. Toronto: Nelson Education.

Turgeon, Luc, Kristin R. Good, and Triadafilos Triadafilopoulos. 2014. "Conclusion: Cities as Dynamic Sites of Integration and Segmentation." In *Segmented Cities? How Urban Contexts Shape Ethnic and Nationalist Politics,* edited by Kristin R. Good, Luc Turgeon, and Triadafilos Triadafilopoulos, 277–92. Vancouver: UBC Press. https://doi.org/10.59962/9780774825856-015.

Wilson, Matthew. 2019. "Municipal Money Matters: Our Fiscal Future." Presentation to AMO Annual Conference, August 19, 2019. https://web.archive.org/web/20191106153400/https://www.amo. on.ca/AMO-PDFs/Events/19/Monday/MoneyMatters-Conference-fiscal-issues-session.aspx.

Wolfe, David A., and Allison Bramwell. 2008. "Innovation, Creativity and Governance: Social Dynamics of Economic Performance in City-Regions." *Innovation: Organization & Management* 10, nos. 2–3 (October): 170–82. https://doi.org/10.5172/impp.453.10.2-3.170.

Contributors

Tari Ajadi is an assistant professor of political science at McGill University. His research compares how Black activists in municipalities across Canada strategize to build durable coalitions toward justice. As a British-Nigerian immigrant to Canada, Professor Ajadi's goal is to produce research that supports and engages with the heterogeneous experiences of Black communities across the country. He is a co-author of the *Defunding the Police: Defining the Way Forward for HRM* report released in January 2022. In addition, he is a frequent contributor and commentator on issues facing Black communities across Canada in both local and national media outlets. He holds a PhD and an MA from Dalhousie University in Canadian politics.

Doug Anderson is Bungee Métis (Kinosota/Reedy Creek, Manitoba) and lives in Toronto, where he works as an educator and author. He is committed to helping preserve Indigenous knowledge within Indigenous communities and to ethically facing this knowledge on its own terms into diverse contexts. He plays a vital role in land-based learning in Toronto, and in the establishment of large medicine and food gardens under regional Indigenous principles. Doug teaches at the University of Toronto and with elementary schools in the land. He is a founder and creative director at Invert Media, where he has helped to ethically bring diverse Indigenous perspectives into various education systems and media.

Brandon Bolduc holds a master's degree in public administration from the University of Ottawa. His research has focused on paradiplomacy in the City of Montreal.

Guy Chiasson teaches political science and regional studies at the Université du Québec en Outaouais. His main research interests are local governance in midsized Canadian cities as well as politics related to natural resources. His most recent research projects relate to municipal participation in forest governance. He recently co-authored *La gouvernance forestière entre secteur et territoires* (*Forest Governance between Sectors and Territories*). He is a member of the *Centre de recherche sur le développement territorial,* a network of researchers on regional development and the director of the *Observatoire du développement de l'Outaouais.*

Sarah Cipkar is a PhD candidate at the University of Toronto in the Department of Geography & Planning. Her research interests include citizen participation, critical urban theory, missing middle housing, and Canadian urban governance. In addition to her academic contributions, Sarah is passionate about translating that knowledge into practical, on-the-ground action to create more equitable communities. As the founder and CEO of Resimate Inc. and ADUSearch, a CMHC-funded research project through the Housing Supply Challenge, Sarah led a team to develop an online tool that helps Canadians discover the potential for additional dwelling units in their own backyards in thirty cities across Canada. In 2020, Sarah built her own detached additional dwelling unit (ADU) in Windsor, ON, which has informed all her work in helping homeowners, researchers, and policy-makers alike.

Tristan Cleveland is an urban planner and researcher with Happy Cities, a consulting firm that uses the science of well-being to create healthier, happier, and more inclusive communities. He has a PhD in political science from Dalhousie University, in which he researched how to overcome political and institutional barriers to transform suburban areas into healthy, walkable communities. He has also helped design sustainable suburban developments in Nova Scotia and British Columbia. Tristan's writing has appeared in the *Toronto Star, National Post,* Strong Towns, and elsewhere, and he is a regular co-host on CBC radio on call-in shows about urban issues. Tristan has also given keynotes on urban design in cities across North America.

Veika Donatien is a PhD candidate in public administration at the University of Ottawa's School of Political Studies. She earned a master's degree from the Graduate School of Public and International Affairs at the University of Ottawa. Her main research interests include municipal politics, territorial governance, local development in developing countries, and issues relating to gender and public policies. Prior to her graduate studies, she was the head of the gender unit of a Haitian human rights organization. She also worked as a project officer in the field of gender-based violence and gender-mainstreaming at the United Nations Entity for Gender Equality and the Empowerment of Women.

Alexandra Flynn is an associate professor of law at the University of British Columbia's Allard School of Law. Her research focuses on municipal law and governance, including municipal-Indigenous legal relationships and the constitutional status of cities. Her research, which has been referenced by the Supreme Court of Canada, has been published in a variety of journals, including the *Osgoode Hall Law Journal,* the *McGill Law Journal,* and the *Canadian Bar Review.*

She has a long history of volunteer work in the areas of homelessness and access to justice and is a frequent media commentator.

Kristin R. Good is an associate professor in the Department of Political Science at Dalhousie University. Her research focuses on local (municipal) immigration policy-making – with a current interest in the potential of such processes to contribute to decolonization and reconciliation with Indigenous Peoples – and critically interrogates municipalities' constitutional significance and status in Canada. Among her most significant works are two books: *Municipalities and Multiculturalism: The Politics of Immigration in Toronto and Vancouver* (2009), which won the Canadian Political Science Association's 2010 Donald Smiley Prize for the best English-language book published on Canadian politics in 2009 and has been quoted by the Supreme Court of Canada (in 2021); and her co-edited (with Luc Turgeon and Triadafilos Triadafilopolis) *Segmented Cities? How Urban Contexts Shape Ethnic and Nationalist Politics* (UBC Press, 2014). Some of her more recent work has appeared in a variety of more public-facing venues such as the Institute on Municipal Finance and Governance (Munk School of Global Affairs & Public Policy, University of Toronto) and the Institute for Research on Public Policy (Montreal). She is a founding co-editor (with Martin Horak) of the McGill-Queen's Studies in Urban Governance book series.

Kate Graham researches, writes, teaches, and speaks about politics in Canadian communities. She is an assistant professor in the Governance, Leadership, and Ethics program at Huron University, in addition to teaching in the local government program at Western University. In 2021, Kate was awarded the MacNaughton Prize for Excellence in Teaching together with Neil Bradford. Before completing her PhD (local government) at Western University, Kate spent a decade working in local government, most recently as the Director, Community and Economic Innovation at the City of London. Kate is a senior advisor with Colliers Project Leaders, supporting local government clients across Canada on issues related to strategy, governance and public policy. Kate is the creator and host of *No Second Chances*, a popular podcast about the rise and fall of women in Canada's top political roles. She has since published two books on the project, *No Second Chances* (Second Story Press, 2022) and *Govern Like a Girl* (Second Story Press, 2021).

Jesse Helmer is a senior research associate at the Smart Prosperity Institute, where he focuses on climate-friendly housing policy and the real costs of urban sprawl. Based in London, Ontario, where he has served two terms as a city councillor, including six years on the planning and environment committee, two years as deputy mayor (2018–20) and eight years on the transit commission. He is particularly interested in the intersection of housing, mobility, and climate policy and actionable strategies to build cleaner, greener, and more affordable cities and communities. He was named one of London's Top 20 Under 40 in 2019. Jesse is a graduate of the

University of Waterloo (BA) and Queen's University (MPA) and is a PhD candidate in political science at Western University, where his research focuses on the political participation gap between homeowners and tenants (https://www.greatsuppression.ca/). He teaches part-time at Western in the local government program and at Huron University College.

Martin Horak is an associate professor of political science at Western University. His teaching and research interests include Canadian and comparative urban politics and the multi-level governance of cities. His current research includes work on the distribution of intergovernmental infrastructure grants in Canada, local election dynamics, and the politics and governance of big transit infrastructure projects, among others. His books include *Governing the Post-Communist City* (University of Toronto Press, 2007), *Sites of Governance: Multilevel Governance and Policy Making in Canada's Big Cities* (McGill-Queen's University Press, co-edited with Robert Young, 2012), and *Urban Neighborhoods in a New Era* (University of Chicago Press, co-authored with Clarence Stone et al., 2015). His work has also appeared in journals such as *Urban Affairs Review*, *City & Community*, and *Urban Research & Practice*.

Anne Mévellec is a full professor at the University of Ottawa's School of Political Studies. Her research focuses on the political sociology of elected municipal officials and on territorial policies. She is particularly interested in the dynamics of the professionalization of elected municipal officials as well as gender issues; she is also working on land-use planning policies in the Ottawa-Gatineau region. She recently published on municipal election campaigning and on forest governance (with Guy Chiasson). She has also recently published two books: *La Gouvernance forestière entre secteur et territoires* (Presses de l'Université de Laval, co-authored with Guy Chiasson, Jacques L. Boucher, and Luc Bouthiller, 2023) and *Dictionnaire politique de la scène municipale québécoise* (Presses de l'Université de Laval, co-edited with Sandra Breux, 2024).

Jen Nelles is a professor and senior research fellow with the Innovation Caucus and co-director of the Oxford Regions, Innovation, and Enterprise Lab (ORIEL) at Oxford Brookes Business School. She also has a visiting professor position at the Network and Governance Lab at the University of Illinois and Chicago. Jen specializes in the areas of innovation and productivity policy, urban and metropolitan governance, regional economic development, infrastructure, and system dynamics with a specific interest in regional governance organizations and their abilities to coordinate policy across jurisdictional boundaries. She is the author of *Comparative Metropolitan Policy: Governing across Boundaries in the Imagined Metropolis* (Routledge, 2012); and co-author of *A Quiet Evolution: The Emergence of Indigenous-Local Intergovernmental Partnerships in Canada* (University of Toronto Press, 2016); *Discovering American Regionalism: An Introduction to Regional Intergovernmental Organizations* (Routledge, 2018); and *Mobilizing the Metropolis: How the Port Authority Built New York* (University of Michigan Press, 2023).

Elizabeth Schwartz is an assistant professor of political science at Memorial University, and director of the Hub for the Study of Local Governance in Newfoundland and Labrador (SLG Hub). Her research interests include municipal climate change policy, sustainable transportation, and local governance. She has published in a variety of peer-reviewed journals, including the *Canadian Journal of Political Science*, *Review of Policy Research*, and *Canadian Public Policy*. Through the SLG Hub, she partners with governments and community organizations to conduct and facilitate applied policy research that responds to local needs and builds local policy capacity.

Mara Sidney is professor of political science at Rutgers University-Newark (USA) and co-directs the Global Urban Studies doctoral program. She co-edits the *Urban Affairs Review*. Her research examines intersections of urban politics, race/ethnicity, immigration, and public policy. Current projects include a study of two New York City neighbourhoods entitled "The Everyday City: How People and Policies Create Neighborhoods Day-to-Day," and collaborative work on frameworks of urban policy analysis (with David Kaufmann, ETH-Zurich) including the forthcoming edited volume *Global Urban Policy: A Framework for Analysis* from the University of Michigan Press.

Enid Slack is the director of the Institute on Municipal Finance and Governance (IMFG) at the School of Cities at the University of Toronto. IMFG focuses on the fiscal health and governance challenges facing cities and city-regions in Canada and around the world. Enid has published several books and numerous articles on property taxes, intergovernmental transfers, municipal restructuring, and municipal infrastructure finance. Two co-edited books are *Funding the Canadian City* and *Is Your City Healthy? Measuring Urban Fiscal Health*. Enid consults with governments and international agencies such as the World Bank, UN Habitat, Inter-American Development Bank, and the International Growth Centre in countries that include Brazil, Chile, Colombia, India, Mexico, Mongolia, South Africa, Tanzania, and Uganda. In 2012, Enid was awarded the Queen's Diamond Jubilee Medal for her work on cities.

Zachary Spicer is an associate professor in the School of Public Policy and Administration at York University, where he also serves as the head of New College and as a faculty affiliate with both the CITY Institute and the Robarts Centre for Canadian Studies. He previously served as an assistant professor in the Department of Political Science at Brock University, the director of Research and Outreach with the Institute of Public Administration of Canada and as a senior policy advisor to Ontario's Ministry of Municipal Affairs and Housing. He received his PhD from the Department of Political Science at the University of Western Ontario and completed post-doctoral fellowships at Wilfrid Laurier University and the University of Toronto.

Adam Straub is a PhD candidate in the Global Urban Studies program at Rutgers University-Newark. His research interests include housing policy, gentrification, displacement, public policy, and urban governance. Recent projects include collaborative work on stalled gentrification in Newark, NJ, as well as his ongoing dissertation research, which explores affordable housing policy feedback and housing justice activism in the New York/New Jersey region.

John B. Sutcliffe is a professor in the Department of Political Science at the University of Windsor. His research interests include the study of public participation in municipal decision-making as well as the role of municipal governments in multi-level policy-making. His work also includes study of the United States-Canada border. He is the co-author of *The Canada-US Border in the 21st Century: Trade, Immigration and Security in the Age of Trump* (Routledge, 2019). His research has been published in the *Local Government Studies*, *Regional and Federal Studies*, *Canadian Journal of Urban Research*, and *American Review of Canadian Studies*.

Index

Note: The letter *f* following an italicized page number denotes a figure; the letter *t*, a table.